# Lecture Notes in Computer Science

*Commenced Publication in 1973*
Founding and Former Series Editors:
Gerhard Goos, Juris Hartmanis, and Jan van Leeuwen

Sabrina De Capitani di Vimercati
Paul Syverson   Dieter Gollmann (Eds.)

# Computer Security – ESORICS 2005

10th European Symposium on Research in Computer Security
Milan, Italy, September 12-14, 2005
Proceedings

 Springer

Volume Editors

Sabrina De Capitani di Vimercati
Universitá degli Studi di Milano
Dipartimento di Tenologie dell'Informazione
Via Bramante 65, 26013 Crema (CR), Italy
E-mail: decapita@dti.unimi.it

Paul Syverson
Naval Research Laboratory Washington
Center for High Assurance Computer Systems
Washington DC 20375, USA
E-mail: syverson@itd.nrl.navy.mil

Dieter Gollmann
TU Hamburg-Harburg, 21071 Hamburg, Germany
E-mail: diego@tu-harburg.de

Library of Congress Control Number: Applied for

CR Subject Classification (1998): E.3, D.4.5, C.2.0, H.2.0, K.6.5, K.4.4

ISSN      0302-9743
ISBN-10   3-540-28963-1 Springer Berlin Heidelberg New York
ISBN-13   978-3-540-28963-0 Springer Berlin Heidelberg New York

Springer is a part of Springer Science+Business Media

springeronline.com

© Springer-Verlag Berlin Heidelberg 2005
Printed in Germany

Typesetting: Camera-ready by author, data conversion by Scientific Publishing Services, Chennai, India
Printed on acid-free paper      SPIN: 11555827      06/3142      5 4 3 2 1 0

# Preface

## Foreword from the Program Chairs

These proceedings contain the papers selected for presentation at the 10th European Symposium on Research in Computer Security (ESORICS), held September 12-14, 2005 in Milan, Italy.

In response to the call for papers 159 papers were submitted to the conference. These papers were evaluated on the basis of their significance, novelty, and technical quality. Each paper was reviewed by at least three members of the program committee. The program committee meeting was held electronically, holding intensive discussion over a period of two weeks. Of the papers submitted, 27 were selected for presentation at the conference, giving an acceptance rate of about 16%. The conference program also includes an invited talk by Barbara Simons.

There is a long list of people who volunteered their time and energy to put together the symposiom and who deserve acknowledgment. Thanks to all the members of the program committee, and the external reviewers, for all their hard work in evaluating and discussing papers. We are also very grateful to all those people whose work ensured a smooth organizational process: Pierangela Samarati, who served as General Chair, Claudio Ardagna, who served as Publicity Chair, Dieter Gollmann who served as Publication Chair and collated this volume, and Emilia Rosti and Olga Scotti for helping with local arrangements.

Last, but certainly not least, our thanks go to all the authors who submitted papers and all the attendees. We hope you find the program stimulating.

Sabrina De Capitani di Vimercati and Paul Syverson
ESORICS 2005 Program Chairs

## Foreword from the General Chair

It is my pleasure to welcome you to the 10th European Symposium On Research In Computer Security in Milan. Initially established as the European conference in research on computer security, ESORICS has reached the status of a main international event gathering researchers from all over the world. The conference, hosted for the first time in Milan, offers an outstanding technical program, including one invited talk and twenty seven papers selected.

An event like this just does not happen; it depends on the volunteer efforts of a host of individuals. I wish to express my sincere appreciation to all the people who volunteered their time and energy to put together the conference and made it possible. First and foremost, thanks are due to Sabrina De Capitani di Vimercati and Paul Syverson and the members of the program committee for selecting the technical papers for presentation and to Barbara Simons for agreeing to deliver the keynote speech. I am also grateful to all those people who ensured a smooth organization process: Dieter Gollmann, for collating the proceedings volume and ensuring that these proceedings be ready for distribution at the conference; Claudio Ardagna for serving as Publicity Chair; Emilia Rosti for helping with the organization and taking care of local arrangements; and Olga Scotti for her helping with local arrangements.

Special thanks are due to: the University of Milan, for granting us the conference location and service; the Department of Information Technologies of the University for its support; the Italian Association for Information Processing (AICA) for its financial support and for providing help in the secretarial and registration process; and the sponsors for their support.

Last but certainly not least thanks to all you for attending the conference. I hope you find the program stimulating and enjoy your time in Milan!

Pierangela Samarati
ESORICS 2005 General Chair

# Organization

## Program Committee

| | |
|---|---|
| Rakesh Agrawal | IBM Almaden Research Center, USA |
| Gerard Allwein | Naval Research Laboratory, USA |
| Ross Anderson | University of Cambridge, UK |
| Vijay Atluri | Rutgers University, USA |
| Michael Backes | IBM Zurich Research Laboratory, Switzerland |
| Giampaolo Bella | University of Catania, Italy |
| Jan Camenisch | IBM Zurich Research Laboratory, Switzerland |
| David Chadwick | University of Kent, UK |
| LiWu Chang | Naval Research Laboratory, USA |
| Marc Dacier | Institut Eurécom, France |
| Ernesto Damiani | Università degli Studi di Milano, Italy |
| George Danezis | University of Cambridge, UK |
| Sabrina De Capitani di Vimercati (Co-chair) | Università degli Studi di Milano, Italy |
| Simon Foley | University College Cork, Ireland |
| Philippe Golle | Palo Alto Research Center, USA |
| Marit Hansen | ICPP Schleswig-Holstein, Germany |
| Philippa Hopcroft | Oxford University, UK |
| Sushil Jajodia | George Mason University, USA |
| Dogan Kesdogan | RWTH Aachen, Informatik IV, Germany |
| Peng Liu | Pennsylvania State University, USA |
| Javier Lopez | University of Malaga, Spain |
| Patrick McDaniel | Pennsylvania State University, USA |
| Heiko Mantel | ETH-Zentrum, Switzerland |
| Nick Mathewson | The Free Haven Project, USA |
| Richard E. Newman | University of Florida, USA |
| Peng Ning | NC State University, USA |
| Bart Preneel | Katholieke Universiteit Leuven, Belgium |
| Emilia Rosti | Università degli Studi di Milano, Italy |
| Peter Ryan | University of Newcastle upon Tyne, UK |
| Kazue Sako | NEC Corporation, Japan |
| Pierangela Samarati | Università degli Studi di Milano, Italy |
| Paul Syverson (co-chair) | Naval Research Laboratory, USA |
| Vanessa Teague | University of Melbourne, Australia |
| Brent Waters | Stanford University, USA |
| Mariemma I. Yagüe | University of Malaga, Spain |
| Alec Yasinsac | Florida State University, USA |
| Sheng Zhong | State University of New York at Buffalo, USA |

# Additional Reviewers

Todd Andel
Ben Aziz
Walid Bagga
Sebastiano Battiato
Birgit Baum-Waidner
Meletis Belsis
Peter Berlich
Mike Bond
Kevin Butler
Achim Brucker
Jeremy Bryans
Christian Cachin
Shiping Chen
Shu-Ching Chen
Yannick Chevalier
Richard Clayton
Andrew Conway
Amy Corman
Lavinia Egidi
Will Enck
Jun Furukawa
Michael Goldsmith
Steven Greenwald
Qijun Gu
Huiping Guo
Markus Hansen
Shan He
Boniface Patrick Hicks
Martin Hirt
Dennis Hofheinz
Susan Hohenberger
Toshinori Araki
Toshiyuki Isshiki
Tobias Kölsch
Kameswari Kotapati
Fengjun Li
Huiyun Li
Lunquan Li
Jay Ligatti
Anyi Liu
Donggang Liu
Wesam Lootah
Gavin Lowe
Ashwin Machanavajjhala

Todd McDonald
Martin Meints
Jose A. Montenegro
Kengo Mori
Barry Mulcahy
Gregory Neven
Tom Newcomb
Satoshi Obana
Jose A. Onieva
Joseph Pamula
Chi-Chun Pan
Udaya Parampalli
Thea Peacock
Alexis Pimenidis
Fabien Pouget
Thomas Probst
Ahmad-Reza Sadeghi
Ralf Rantzau
Arnon Rosenthal
Sankardas Roy
Patrizia Scandurra
Tim Seipold
Christos Siaterlis
Barbara Sprick
Rainer Steinwandt
Isamu Teranishi
Patrick Traynor
Ingrid Verbauwhede
Frederik Vercauteren
Ulrich Waldmann
Hai Wang
Lingyu Wang
Xinyuan Wang
Bogdan Warinschi
Ralf Wienzek
Duminda Wijesekera
Min Wu
Dingbang Xu
Jun Xu
Meng Yu
Stefano Zanero
Justin Zhan
Lei Zhang
Hongbin Zhou

# Table of Contents

# Computerized Voting Machines: A View from the Trenches

Barbara Simons

simons@acm.org

As a result of Florida 2000, some Americans concluded that paper ballots simply couldn't be counted, even though businesses, banks, racetracks, lottery systems, and others count and deal with paper all the time. Instead, paperless computerized voting systems (Direct Recording Electronic or DREs) were touted as the solution to "the Florida problem".

Election officials in the U.S. were told that DREs in the long run would be cheaper than alternative voting systems. They also were told that DREs had been extensively tested and that the certification process guaranteed that the machines were reliable and secure. No mention was made of the costs ballot design, of pre-election testing, and of secure storage of DREs; nothing was said about the threat of hidden malicious code; no mention was made of the inadequacy of the testing and certification processes, to say nothing of the difficulty of creating bug-free software.

Why were independent computer security experts not consulted about such a major and fundamental change in how elections are held? Why were some election officials and policy makers hostile when computer security experts warned of the risks of computerized voting to the point of accusing computer scientists of being "fear mongers" and Luddites? How could Harris Miller, the President of the Information Technology Association of America, a lobbying organization that has received compensation from voting machine vendors, claim on Election Day 2004 that, "Electronic voting machine issues that have been cited are related to human error, process missteps or unsubstantiated reports"? How would he know? Why would anyone listen to him?

Why do many election officials and politicians believe that internet voting would increase voter turnout in the U.S., even though no rigorous testing has occurred? And, even if internet voting would increase turnout, how can these same people who have been reading about internet viruses for years not understand that internet voting is a very very risky proposition?

In short, why have DRE vendors and many election officials succeeded at challenging the expertise of computer scientists and computer security experts?

The refusal of policy makers to listen to the computing community hardly began with the introduction of poorly engineered and insecure voting machines. Many computer scientists and computer security experts became involved with policy debates over crypto policy, copyright, patents, and computerized surveillance – to name some of the major issues.

The disconnect between the computing community and policy makers is perhaps best illustrated by the Digital Millennium Copyright Act (DMCA),

S. De Capitani di Vimercati et al. (Eds.): ESORICS 2005, LNCS 3679, pp. 1–2, 2005.

which became part of US law in 1998. It was only by chance that I learned why implementation of the most controversial aspects of the DMCA, the anti-circumvention and anti-dissemination provisions, was postponed until 2000. The delay was written into the DMCA because lawmakers knew, or someone they trusted told them, that aspects of the DMCA might criminalize work on securing software against Y2K problems. Yet, the fact that Y2K was hardly the only software security issue that would require the kinds of reverse engineering that was done to fix Y2K bugs was either unknown to the lawmakers or a matter of indifference to them.

A discussion of the DMCA brings us full circle back to the issue of computerized voting systems. In the U.S. the software that is deployed in these systems is secret, as is the testing – paid for by the software vendors – and the test results. Because of the anti-circumvention provisions of the DMCA, computer security experts risk violating U.S. Federal law if they wish to reverse engineer voting machine software to search for bugs or malicious code. Consequently, a law that was crafted by the movie and record industries to prevent unauthorized copying is assisting voting machine vendors with concealing their software from meaningful independent review.

Clearly, we computing professionals have been failing at explaining the risks of inappropriate, careless, or poorly designed software to the general public and especially to policy makers, at least in the U.S. (At this conference I hope to learn more about what is happening in Europe). While perhaps not enough of us have become involved with efforts to educate policy makers, there are some fundamental reasons why our expertise is frequently ignored:

1. People who have never done much programming do not understand how difficult it is to find bugs in software.
2. Because people don't understand point 1, they certainly don't understand that last minute software patches are very dangerous.
3. Consequently, most people have a hard time believing computer security experts when they say that it's possible to write malicious code and conceal it in a large program. They just don't understand why it can be very difficult to determine that malware is present, let alone locate it in a large body of code.

In addition, we are a relatively young profession, and many of us have an independent streak and a casual mode of dress that, taken together, make some politicians view us as potential trouble makers, rather than as people whose views the politicians should take seriously.

Yet, we must make our voices heard. The issues are too critical to allow us to be shut out of the debate.

I'll give an overview of some of the technological and policy issues relating to computerized voting machines, and perhaps touch on how we might do a better job of getting our message across. I also look forward to hearing ideas that others might have of how we might better explain software-related risks to non-technical decision makers.

# XML Access Control with Policy Matching Tree

Naizhen Qi (Naishin Seki) and Michiharu Kudo

IBM Research, Tokyo Research Laboratory,
1623-14, Shimo-tsuruma, Yamato-shi,
Kanagawa 242-8502, Japan
{naishin, kudo}@jp.ibm.com

**Abstract.** XML documents are frequently used in applications such as
business transactions and medical records involving sensitive information. Access control on the basis of data location or value in an XML
document is therefore essential. However, current approaches to efficient
access control over XML documents have suffered from scalability problems because they tend to work on individual documents. To resolve this
problem, we proposed a table-based approach in [28]. However, [28] also
imposed limitations on the expressiveness, and real-time access control
updates were not supported. In this paper, we propose a novel approach
to XML access control through a policy matching tree (PMT) which
performs accessibility checks with an efficient matching algorithm, and
is shared by all documents of the same document type. The expressiveness can be expanded and real-time updates are supported because of
the PTM's flexible structure. Using synthetic and real data, we evaluate the performance and scalability to show it is efficient for checking
accessibility for XML databases.

## 1 Introduction

XML [7] data is becoming more prevalent as more businesses and systems become integrated over the Web. In applications such as business transactions and
medical records, sensitive data may be scattered throughout an XML document
and access control at the node level (element or attribute) is required to ensure
that sensitive data can only be accessed by authorized users. Access control must
be expressive and be able to support rules that select data based on the location
and value(s) of the data. In practice, the number of access control rules can be
on the order of millions, which is a product of the number of document types
(in 1,000's) and the number of user roles (in 100's). Therefore, the solution also
requires high scalability and performance.

Several XML access control models [4,11,17,23] provide expressive access control over XML documents. These approaches usually support grant or denial
access control specifications, a propagation mechanism whereby descendant elements inherit rules from their parents, and conflict resolution in case the data is
covered by multiple access control rules. Since these models perform access control by traversing XML documents at runtime, the enforcement imposes heavy

S. De Capitani di Vimercati et al. (Eds.): ESORICS 2005, LNCS 3679, pp. 3–23, 2005.

computational costs especially for deeply layered XML documents with large and expressive access control rules.

Ideas to efficiently provide expressive access control have been proposed in [3,9,12,28,30]. These approaches are effective in efficiently searching for access controlled nodes [3,12,30], or in eliminating unnecessary accessibility checks at runtime [9]. These research efforts have managed to improve the efficiency of expressive access control. However, since they generally focus on document-based optimizations, XML databases with frequent updates of either the documents or access control rules may incur unacceptable costs. In our previous research [28], we proposed an efficient table-driven access control model that takes into account XML document updates. It provides runtime efficiency but has limitations on access control expressiveness and the real-time update of access control rules was not supported.

In this paper, we develop an effifffcient and expressive access control model applicable to existing access control models [4,11,23] for XML documents. The novelties of this access control model are a data-independent optimization so that XML data updates will not trigger any recomputations, and that real-time policy update is supported. The key idea is to build a policy matching tree, a PMT, on the basis of the access control rules. The accessibility check is performed by matching the access request against the PMT and deciding on the basis of the matching results. Since all of the rules in the PMT are isolated from each other, the PMT is capable of handling real-time PMT updates. An accessibility cache improves runtime performance by skipping duplicated accessibility evaluations on the same paths. Through experiments, we show the PMT is capable of supporting millions of access control rules efficiently.

The rest of this paper is organized as follows. After reviewing the concerned access control model in Section 2, we present our solution, the PMT model in Section 3. In Section 4 we describe how to match an access request against the PMT for an accessibility decision. Section 5 describes the access control system on the basis of the PMT. Experimental results are reported in Section 6 and in Section 7 we summarize our conclusions and consider future work.

## 1.1  Related Work

Many approaches for enforcing XML access control have been proposed. Some of them [17,23] support full [10] expressions to provide expressiveness with straightforward implementations by creating the projection of the access control policy on a DOM [19] tree. However, these approaches incur massive runtime costs when handling a large access control policy or a deeply layered XML document. The mechanisms proposed in [2,4,11,12] perform more efficiently but also encounter the same problem at runtime since node-level access control on a DOM-based view can be expensive when processing large numbers of XML documents.

To overcome this problem, several efficient access control models have been proposed [25,28]. Qi et al. [28], our previous research, presents a method that performs in near-constant time regardless of the number of access control rules. This is achieved by using an access condition table generated from the access control rules independently of the XML data. However, this approach places limitations on the XPath expressions, and does not provide an efficient runtime evaluation mechanism for value-based conditions. Murata et al. [25] optimized the pre-processing steps by minimizing the number of runtime checks for determining the accessibility of nodes in a query with automata. However, the mechanism was limited to XPath-based languages such as XQuery [6], and cannot handle other query languages or primitive APIs such as DOM. XPath-based document filtering systems [1,8,14] also provide value-based access control enforcement and independence of the XML data through a precomputed data structure. However, these filtering systems focus more on data filtering rather than data selection. For example, they cannot specify denial access on document fragments in a grant subtree. Therefore, they are unable to completely satisfy the needs of real XML database access control applications.

A different approach with document-level optimizations was proposed by Yu et al. [30]. Their scheme enforces efficient access control with an accessibility map that is generated by compressing neighboring accessibility rules to improve the efficiency. However, since the maps are generated on the basis of the documents, document updates or policy updates may trigger expensive computations espe-cially for a large XML ndatabase. In addition, the above efficient enforcement algorithms cannot support real-time updates on the access control rules.

Optimizations were also the focuse in a number of research efforts on XML query languages (e.g., XPath and XQuery). The methods include query optimiza-tion based on (i) the tree pattern of queries [9,13,27] (ii) XML data and XML schema [16,21,22,24]; and (iii) the consistency between integrity constraints and schemas [15]. However, these approaches usually perform efficient data selec-tion at the level of documents and require indices. Therefore, in a large XML database, such as a database with 10,000 document collections and 10,000 doc-uments for each document collection, such optimization mechanisms may con-sume a prohibitive amount of space. Moreover, these technologies are designed for XPath-based languages and they cannot handle other query languages and primitive APIs such as DOM.

## 2  Abstract of Access Control Policy

Various access control policy models have been proposed. We used the one pro-posed by Murata et al. [25] in which an access control policy contains a set of 3-tuple rules with the syntax[1] $(Subject, +/- Action, Object)$. The subject has a prefix indicating the type such as $userID$, $role$, or $group$. A user with a unique $userID$ may be in multiple groups, and the accessibility is decided on the basis of the accessibility results of the rules for the $userID$ and each for each $group$. A '+' stands for positive authorization (granted), while a '−' is for negative autho-rization (denied). Action can be $read$, $update$, $create$, and $delete$. A capitalized rule with $+Read$ or $−Read$ means that propagation is permitted and that the

---

[1] The syntax of the policy can be represented in XACML [26]. We use this form for simplicity.

access can be propagated downward to the entire subtree, while +*read* has an effect only on the selected node. As an example, (*role* : *Doctor*, +*Read*, /*record*) specifies a doctor's access to /*record* is allowed and implicitly extended to the descendants. In addition, according to *denial downward consistency* as defined in [25] the descendants of an inaccessible node are also inaccessible, since there is an accessibility dependency between the ancestors and the descendants. Therefore, it is obvious that −*read* and −*Read* are equivalent to each other, and therefore we specify denial rules using only −*Read* in this paper. We call the action permission ('+' or '−') together with the propagation permission the access effect. The object is the expression of the subset of XPath.

In addition, in order to maximize data security, we (i) resolve access conflicts with the *denial-takes-precedence* [25] rule and (ii) apply the default denial permission on the paths if no explicit or implicit access control is specified.

## 3  Policy Matching Tree (PMT) Model

The PMT model provides a fast matching mechanism to resolve the access control matching problem. The PMT searches for matched rules by matching the request against a tree that is the internal data structure of the access control policy. The PMT outputs matched target(s) upon which the accessibility, *grant* or *deny*, can be decided.

In this section, we first introduce the access control matching problem and then present the PMT model to represent the access control policy. Then, we present the matching algorithm.

### 3.1  The Access Control Matching Problem

A request defines the requestors' access requests to an XML data object or an XML instance by specifying property values. In the case of an XML instance, each path is individually checked against the access control rules. A matching element *ele* is a condition evaluation for requests. We say a request *req* matches a matching element *ele* if and only if *match*(*req*, *ele*) = *true*. In the access control matching problem, we are given an access request *req* and a finite rule set *Policy* which is translated into a set of matching elements. Subsequently, the goal is to determine all those rules in *Policy* that match *req*.

In our model, each request contains at least five properties: a *userID*, *role*, *group*, *action*, and *path*. The *group* is a list containing all of the groups the requester belonging to. The *path* is the simple path expression requested by the user. Besides these five properties, other properties such as current time and date may also be included. The rule set *Policy* is represented as an internal tree *Policy Matching Tree*.

### 3.2  PMT Components

The PMT model consists of four components: a node, edge, match target, and link. The node represents a property name of the access request. The edge represents a matching condition on the property name. The matching condition

| Element | Symbol | Assignment | Example |
|---|---|---|---|
| Node | ◯ | Property name | action |
| Edge | → | Matching condition  linking two nodes, or a node to a match target | = 'update' |
| Match target | ▢ | Matching result, and additional data | GRANT_ON_NODE |
| Link | - - - -▸ | Linking a match target to a node for further matching | - |

**Fig. 1.** PMT model components

**Table 1.** Matching result of access effects for *read* action

| Access effect | Matching result |
|---|---|
| +r | GRANT_ON_NODE |
| +R | GRANT_ON_SUBTREE |
| -R | DENY |
| Nothing | UNDECIDED |

consists of an operator and the associated value. The edge ends at another node for further refinement or at a match target which is the leaf node representing the matching result. As occasion demands, the match target may also contain a property list, and a link for further matching. Fig. 1 depicts the PMT model components. The matching result in a match target is prepared in accordance with the access effect of the concerned rule. Table 1 shows the access effect for a *read* action with the corresponding matching results.

### 3.3 Property Matches of PMT

A PMT represents a set of access control rules. Each access control rule is a conjunction of property matches, where each property match represents a condition evaluation on the property name. Suppose an access control rule $rule : (Sub, +/ - Act, Obj)$, in which if value-based predicate(s) is imposed, the predicate(s) are represented as *Pred*, and the object after removing *Pred* is represented as *Obj*. To match a request *req* against *rule*, $match(req, rule)$ can be done as follows:

$match(req, rule) := match(req, Sub) \land match(req, Act) \land match(req, Obj) \land match(data\ value, Pred)$

Only when all of the property matches result in *true* is the rule matched and a matching result output. Each property match is represented by nodes and edges. The PMT is therefore constructed by adding or sharing nodes, edges, and match targets for the property matches of each rule. As a consequence, the policy is converted to a PMT consisting of four matching parts which match the request against *Act*, *Sub*, *Obj*, and *Pred*, respectively, as shown in Fig. 2. Since the access control rules are often imposed on the same object, in order to minimize the duplicated parts in the PMT, the *Pred* matching is shared. For the same reason, the match target of the *Pred* matching does not hold a matching result

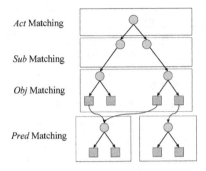

**Fig. 2.** A Sample PMT

specified for the rules. However, the *Pred* matching consumes extra computation owing to the data retrievals from the XML database. Therefore, to reduce the extra data retrievals, the *Pred* matching is started only when a match target is reached during the *Obj* matching no matter where the location where the predicates are imposed.

The matching result is only held by the match target of the *Obj* matching. If predicates are involved, then the match target of the *Obj* matching also provides a link for the *Pred* matching.

### 3.4   PMT Construction

Each access control rule is individually converted into three property matchings, or four in the case a predicate(s) is involved, with corresponding match targets.

***Act* Matching and *Sub* Matching Construction.** *Act* matching and *Sub* matching generation is simple in that "Act" and "Sub" are the nodes, and the values of *Act* and *Sub* specified by the rule are on the edges. As an example, we have an access control policy P1 as:

$R1 : (role : employee, +read, /Record)$
$R2 : (role : employee, +Read, /Record/Item[Key = \$userID])$
$R3 : (group : manager, +Read, /Record)$
$R4 : (group : manager, -Read, /Record//Info)$ In P1, $\$userID$ represents

a unique employee identifier. The corresponding *Act* matching and the *Sub* matching of $P1$ are generated as in Fig. 3. In the figure, two edges are coming from the *action* node, and the one to the role node is shared by $R1$ and $R2$. The other edge to the group node is for $R3$ and $R4$. Note the matching conditions on the edges from the action node are both $=' read'$ in which the propagation permission is not included. In our PMT model, the propagation permission is carried by the *Matching Result* in the *Obj* matching.

***Obj* Matching Construction.** Here we consider the XPath expressions as compositions of five basic elements: $/x, /*, //x, //*$, and an $[x\ operator\ value]$

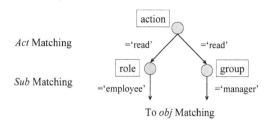

**Fig. 3.** *Act* matching and *Sub* matching of *P*1

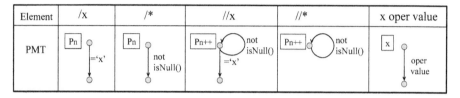

**Fig. 4.** Five basic elements to represent XPath expressions

where the last one represents a predicate and the operator can be any mathematical operator. Though other axes are not included as they would be in a general access control model, these elements are sufficient to select the concerned nodes.

The *Obj* matching is represented by the first four basic elements, while the *Pred* matching uses the last one. Fig. 4 shows how the five basic elements are represented.

$P_n$ represents the node name of *Obj* at depth $n$. However, $P_{n++}$ appearing in $//x$ and $//*$ automatically increases the depth counter variable for each loop. The corresponding *Obj* matching for *P*1 is shown in Fig. 5.

All of the match targets hold a matching result, which not only represents the access permission, but also represents the propagation permission to the descendants. For $r$, the positive authorization is not permitted to propagate downward, so a test on whether the requested path is the descendant of the object is performed by $isNull()$ as *R*1 shows. Beyond the normal matching result, the match target of *R*2 also contains a property list and a link to further refinement on */Record/Item* through a predicate.

The property list contains pairs of the property name and the data name appearing in the predicate where the property name is used in the *Pred* matching in place of the data name. The data name is more than a single element node name or attribute name, since the relative path from the object to the node being appended with the predicate is also included. For example, when it is */Record/Item[Key = $empID]/Priority*, the property list is $pred0 = "../Key"$, since to traverse from *Priority* to *Key*, we must go up to *Item* first, which is represented by '../'. To retrieve XML data from the database for predicate evaluation, the data name is passed to the data retrieval processor at runtime. Since the runtime has knowledge of the accessed node location with both the matched

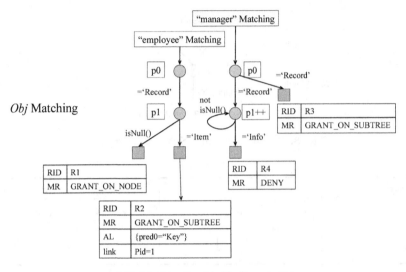

MR: Matching Result    AL: Property List

Fig. 5. Obj matching of P1

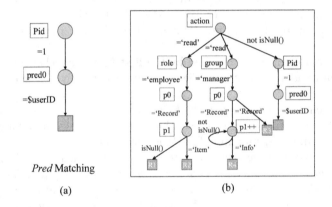

Fig. 6. Pred matching and the entire PMT

node location and the relative path from the matched node, the location of the required data can be found.

**Pred Matching Construction.** A predicate is a condition for comparison to the XML data or a conjunction of such conditions. The condition is directly converted to the *Pred* matching. By separating the Pred matching from the *Obj* matching, the predicate evaluation is optimized in the way: 1) unless the match on the *Obj* matching reaches a match target, the match for the *Pred* matching is not started; 2) multiple predicates imposed on the same object are processed in a single *Pred* matching operation; and 3) the *Pred* matching is shared by the set of access control rules.

The *Pred* matching of $P1$ is shown in Fig. 6(a) and Fig. 6(b) gives the entire PMT for $P1$. Beyond the condition matching for $[pred0 = \$userID]$, the link which connects the *Obj* matching with the *Pred* matching is also shown in the figure. Owing to the link ID *Pid*, the *Pred* matching can be shared by multiple rules, if the same predicate is involved.

However, when a predicate *Pred* appears after with //, since multiple requested paths match the object owing to //, the property list for *Pred* cannot be specified in the match target during PMT generation without knowledge of the requested path. Therefore, in the current PMT model, a limitation is placed on the expressions that predicates never come after //. As a consequence, XPath expressions such as $/Record//Info[@type =' classified']$, and $// * [@type =' classified']$ are not supported.

### 3.5   Complexity Analysis

**PMT Generation Time Complexity.** For each access control rule that we need to add to the PMT, we spend generation time proportional to the number $A$ of properties, where the properties are the action, the subject, the node tests appearing in the object, or the nodes involved if there is a predicate(s). Therefore, if there are $N$ access control rules, the total time spent on PMT generation is $O(AN)$. If the maximum depth of the object is $D$, and the maximum number of conditions in a predicate is $P$, $A$ is no bigger than $(3+D+P+2)$, where that 3 is from the *Act* matching, the *Sub* matching, and a link from the *Obj* matching to the *Pred* matching, and the 2 is for the match targets of the *Obj* and *Pred* matchings. Therefore, $A$ is no larger than $(5+D+P)$, which are integers, and hence the PMT generation time is linear with respect to the number of access control rules.

**PMT Space Complexity.** For the space complexity, note that each rule can add at most $(5+D+P)$ nodes to the PMT. Thus, the largest space required for the PMT is $O((5 + D + P)N)$, that is, linear in the number of access control rules.

## 4   PMT Matching

Our approach resolves the access control matching problem by matching the request against the PMT to determine the access effects of the rules that match the request. In this section, we present the matching algorithm, and then analyze the complexity.

### 4.1   PMT Matching Algorithm

The input of the PMT is an access request that contains at least five properties: a userID, role, group, action, and path. However, the path cannot be input directly into the PMT, since the PMT cannot match the path against the nodes and edges. Therefore, preprocessing is required to convert the path into a set of node tests. The output of the PMT is the set of matching results as shown in Table 1. By combining the matching results and resolving any access conflicts, the accessibility decision, *grant* or *deny*, is decided. The PMT matching algorithm is given in Fig. 7. The idea is to walk the PMT from the root node by performing the matching prescribed by each node and following the edge that satisfies the condition for that node. The set of matching results are the match targets that are visited. This algorithm is independent of the traversal ordering on the PMT. We can traverse the tree in a depth-first order, but it is clear that other orderings, such as breadth-first, would also work.

As an example matching $M1$, we demonstrate how to decide the accessibility using the PMT in Fig. 6(b). Suppose the access request *req* is {*userID:'T29595'*, *group:'manager'*, *action:'read'*, *path:'/Record/Item/Address'*}. Path is further processed to a property list {*p0:'Record'*, *p1:'Item'*, *p2:'Address'*}. As a result, the pairs of name and value input into the PMT eventually becomes {*userID:'T29595'*, *group:'manager'*, *action:'read'*, *p0:'Record'*, *p1:'Item'*, *p2:'Address'*}.

The input data traces two routes in the PMT. One is stopped halfway before reaching a match target, and the other one reaches the match target of $R3$ as:

$$action(=' read') \rightarrow group(=' manager') \rightarrow p0(=' Record') \rightarrow$$
$$p1(=' Item') \rightarrow p2(=' Address') \rightarrow p3$$
$$action(=' read') \rightarrow group(=' manager') \rightarrow p0(=' Record') \rightarrow$$
$$R3's\ match\ target$$

Since the matching result of $R3$ is *GRANT_ON_SUBTREE*, the accessibility is therefore decided as *grant*, and the manager's access to /*Record/Item/Address* is permitted. Suppose one more PMT input is {*userID:'T29595'*, *role:'employee'*, *group:null*, *action:'read'*, *p0:'Record'*, *p1:'Item'*, *p2:'Address'*}. The match target of $R2$ is reached by the route:

---

**Input** The pair of property name $n$ and value $v$ of the access request

**Step 1** If $v$ of $n$ satisfies the condition on the edge from $n$, then follow the edge.
    If no matched $n$, then return *UNDECIDED*.

**Step 2** If the node below the edge is node $n$, then repeat Step 1.

**Step 3** If the node below the edge is a match target, then
    - if it contains a link, then retrieve the value, repeat Step 1 with the data value and the access request.
    - if it contains *GRANT_ON_NODE* or *GRANT_ON_SUBTREE*, return *GRANT*.
    - else it is the match target of *Pred* matching, returns *true* to *Obj* matching.
    If the matching result of *Obj* matching is *GRANT_ON_NODE* or *GRANT_ON_SUBTREE*,
    then return *GRANT*. Otherwise, return *UNDECIDED*.

**Output** The set of returned matching results.
    - if *DENY* exists, the decision is *DENY*.
    - else if all of the matching results are *UNDECIDED*, the decision is *DENY*.
    - otherwise, the decision is *GRANT*.

---

**Fig. 7.** PMT Matching Algorithm

$action(=' read') \rightarrow role(=' employee') \rightarrow p0(=' Record') \rightarrow p1(=' Item') \rightarrow$
$R2's$ match target

In this case, beyond the matching result, a property list $pid0 =' Key'$ and a link $Pid = 1$ are also included. Therefore, the value of the required data 'Key' is retrieved and the *Pred* matching is performed. The PMT input is updated to {*userID:'T29595', role:'employee', group:null, action:'read', Pid:1, pred0:'T29590'*}. The *Pred* matching becomes:

$action(\neq isNull()) \rightarrow Pid(= 1) \rightarrow pred0(\neq \$userID)$

The match target is not reachable in the *Pred* matching, and hence *false* is returned. With the matching results in *GRANT_ON_SUBTREE* from the *Obj* matching and *false* from the Pred matching, the accessibility decision results in *deny*, and the access to */Record/Item/Address* is denied.

## 4.2   Matching Time Complexity

We measured the access request matching times by counting the number of PMT nodes that are visited during the match. In any reasonable implementation of the matching algorithm, this number is proportional to the actual time necessary to match the access request, since the algorithm performs a simple matching for each node, which is assumed to take constant time.

The matching time is a function of the access request being matched, since different access requests cause different sets of nodes to be visited during matching even if the set of access control rules is constant.

In the rest of this section, we compute the expected time to match an access request, and show the expected time is sub-linear with respect to the number of access control rules. We assume that all properties range over the same set of values for simplicity. Henceforth, let $K$ be the number of properties of a rule; $V$ be the number of possible values for a property; $P$ be an arbitrary set of rules; $PMT(P)$ be the PMT generated for $P$; and $T(P)$ the expected time to match a request.

**Theorem 1.** *Given that all access requests are equally likely, then the expected time $T(P)$ to match a random access request is bounded by*

$$T(P) \leq 2(K+1)|P|^{1-\lambda}(lnV + ln(K+1)) \text{ where } \lambda := \frac{lnV}{lnV + ln(K+1)}.$$

For each node $n$ in $PMT(P)$, we define $cost(n)$ to be the number of times that this node is visited when we run the matching algorithm with all the possible $VK$ requests. The probability that a node $n$ is visited when matching a random request is therefore equal to $V^{-K}cost(n)$. Thus, the expected number $T(P)$ of nodes of $PMT(P)$ visited is:

$$T(P) = V^{-K} \sum_{n \in nodes(PMT(P))} cost(n) \tag{1}$$

where $nodes(PMT(P))$ is the set of nodes of $PMT(P)$.

**Lemma 2.** *For* $0 \leq j \leq K$, *PMT(P) contains at most* $(K+1)((K+1)V)^j$ *nodes with cost* $V^{K-j}$.

*Proof.* A node $n$ has cost $V^{K-j}$ if and only if the route from the root to the node has exactly $j$ non-* edges. The number of edges $i$ is between $j$ and $K$; the positions of the non-* edges are $j$ distinct numbers between the root and $n$, and so there are $\sum_{i=j...K} \binom{i}{j} = \binom{K+1}{j+1}$ ways of choosing routes without involving *-edges. Moreover, we can assign $V$ distinct values for each non-* edge. Therefore, the number of paths in PMT(P) with exactly $j$ non-* edges is at most $V^j \binom{K+1}{j+1}$. Moreover,

$$V^j \binom{K+1}{j+1} \leq V^j \frac{(K+1)^{j+1}}{(j+1)!} \leq (K+1)((K+1)V)^j. \tag{2}$$

**Lemma 3.** *PMT(P) has at most* $(K+1)|P|$ *nodes.*

*Proof.* An access control rule is associated with subject, action, and object, leading to $K$ edges and $K+1$ nodes including the match target. Thus, if the policy has $|P|$ rules, it has at most $(K+1)|P|$ nodes.

Let $f(i)$ be cost of the $i$-th node in order, by using Equation (1) and Lemma 3, we have that $T(P) = V^{-K} \sum_{i=1}^{(K+1)|P|} f(i)$.
  Let $g(x) := (Ax + B)^{-\lambda}$ where $A := V^{-(K+1)/\lambda}(V - 1/(K+1))$, $B := V^{-(K+1)/\lambda}$, and $\lambda := \frac{lnV}{lnV + ln(K+1)} < 1$.

**Lemma 4.** $f(x) \leq g(x)$.

*Proof.* By Equation (2) and the definition of $f(x)$, we have that for each $i$ such that $0 \leq i \leq K$ and for each $j$ such that $\sum_{p=0...i-1}(K+1)((K+1)V)^p < j \leq \sum_{p=0...i}(K+1)((K+1)V)^p$, the following holds: $f(j) \leq V^{K-i}$.
  Now, $g\left(\sum_{p=0...i}(K+1)((K+1)V)^P\right) = g\left(K\frac{((K+1)V)^{i+1}-1}{(K+1)V-1}\right)$. By using the definition of $g(x)$, we conclude $g\left(\sum_{p=0...i}(K+1)((K+1)V)^P\right) = V^{K-i}$.

*Proof (Proof of Theorem 1).* We have that $T(P) = V^{-K}\sum_{x=1}^{K|P|} f(x) \leq V^{-K}\sum_{x=1}^{K|P|} g(x) \leq V^{-K}\int_0^{K|P|} g(x)dx = V^{-K}\frac{(AK|P|+B)^{1-\lambda}-B^{1-\lambda}}{A(1-\lambda)}$. By replacing the values of $A$ and $B$ and simplifying, we obtain

$$T(P) \leq \frac{V(K+1)((V(K+1)|P| - |P| + 1)^{1-\lambda} - 1)}{(V(K+1)-1)(1-\lambda)}.$$ After using $V(K+1)|P| - |P| + 1 \leq V(K+1)|P|$ and $(V(K+1))^{1-\lambda} = K+1$, and after replacing the value of $\lambda$, we obtain

$$T(P) \leq \frac{V(K+1)((K+1)|P|^{1-\lambda} - 1)(lnV + ln(K+1))}{(V(K+1)-1)ln(K+1)}. \tag{3}$$

  Since $V \geq 2$ and $K+1 \geq 2$, we have $V(K+1)/(V(K+1)-1) \leq 4/3$ and $1/ln(K+1) < 3/2$. By introducing thees values in (3), we obtain $T(P) \leq 2(K+1)|P|^{1-\lambda}(lnV + ln(K+1))$.

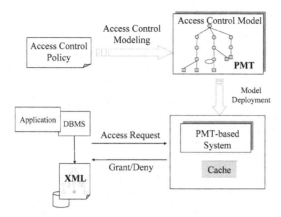

**Fig. 8.** PMT-based Access Control System

# 5    PMT Access Control System

In this section, we present the construction of the access control system. Then
we show a cache optimization to improve performance by skipping the PMT
matching and accessibility evaluation. Lastly, we describe the runtime policy
update mechanism.

## 5.1    Access Control System

The proposed access control system is constructed through Access Control Modeling and Model Deployment shown in Fig. 8. In Access Control Modeling, the
access control policy is converted to an internal data structure, a PMT, so that
each rule is represented by a set of nodes and by edges with one or two match
targets. In Model Deployment, an empty cache table is prepared.

At runtime, given an access request from an application or a DBMS, the
access control system runs an evaluation for the accessibility decision. The system may add a new entry to the cache, as long as the corresponding entry is
not found in the cache and the accessibility decision is uniquely decided owing
to independency of the data values. Otherwise, the previously cached value is
returned directly without PMT matching.

This system structure separates the access control system from the database
engine so that security-related support is not required from the underlying database. In addition, it enables any DBMS to offer access control even if it is an
off-the-shelf product.

## 5.2    Optimization with an Accessibility Cache

Since the accessibility status of a path remains unchanged even if the XML data
changes as long as the access control does not involve any value-based evaluations, the result of an accessibility evaluation can be cached, thereby improving
runtime performance. This is particularly beneficial if a path appears multiple

times in an XML document(s), or in a document type, because obtaining the accessibility result by looking at the accessibility cache allows the system to avoid repeating accessibility evaluations.

The accessibility cache, generated individually for each action type, is a table of 3-tuples: *subject*, *path*, and *accessibility decision*. During an evaluation with no predicate, an entry will be added to the accessibility cache table. Otherwise, when the accessibility depends on the data values in the XML document, the accessibility results may be different with different subtrees and different documents, and therefore, the accessibility evaluation involving predicates must be performed at every access.

We show an example using the access control policy $P1$. The initial accessibility cache table is empty. When $M1$ as presented in Sect. 4.1 finishes, we obtain an accessibility cache table for *read* action which contains 1 entry:

{*group:'manager', /Record/Item/Address, grant*}.

There is only one entry in the cache table since the second access request was evaluated on the basis of an XML data value. Meanwhile, though the first access request contains both userID and group data, the subject of the corresponding cache entry only holds the group. This is because for PMT matching, the userID does not affect the accessibility decision that a manager's access to */Record/Item/Address* is always granted without regard to the userID. If any manager accesses the same path, */Record/Item/Address*, in another XML document, the *grant* is looked up and directly returned as the accessibility decision.

When a user is bound to multiple groups such that the accessibility is decided by multiple matching results, rather than generate a single cache entry, it is efficient to generate one entry for each group. The cache entries can easily be reused by other requesters in the same group(s). However, for rules involving a userID or a role, the number of entries inserted into the accessibility cache table is limited to one.

To generate a proper accessibility cache entry, the *subject* information that decides the accessibility is required. Howevner, without recording each visited path in the PMT, there is no way to know the corresponding matched subject. This calls for extra computation to obtain the matched object information with the current PMT structure, especially when multiple match targets for userID and groups are visited. To resolve this problem, we enhance the match target of the *Obj* matching by retaining the subject of the access control rule. Because each access control rule is bound to an individual match target, carrying the subject along with the match target can meet the requirements for accessibility cache generation.

## 5.3   Access Control Policy Update

In some real applications, the access control policy may be updated at runtime. For instance, if a new role is introduced into the running system, then the corresponding access control rules should be added to the system as well. In our previous work Qi et al.[28], real time policy update was not supported, since multiple access control conditions were combined into an access condition expression. In the PMT model, it is possible to perform real time updates on the PMT when the policy is updated during runtime, since each rule has a corresponding match target which is distinguished by a unique rule ID $RID$.

The $RID$ in the match target plays a crucial role in runtime rule removal. The match target, nodes and edges are removed bottom-up if the components are not shared by other rules. When a rule is updated, the PMT reacts by removing and adding the corresponding components without changing the $PID$ in the match target. It costs $O(m(2+D+1))$ time to add, remove, or update the rules, where $m$ is the number of new rules, 2 is from the $Act$ matching, and the $Sub$ matching, $D$ is the maximum depth of the objects, and 1 is for the match target.

# 6   Experiments

In this section, we describe our experiments to evaluate the performance of our PMT-based access control mechanism for XML documents. All of the experiments were conducted on a machine with a 1.8GHz Pentium 4 CPU, 1.5GB of main memory, and IBM JDK1.4.2. We discuss the experimental data in Sect. 6.1 and present the results in Sect. 6.2.

## 6.1   Experimental Data

To demonstrate the scalability of the system, we examined the memory requirements when a large access control policy is loaded into main memory, and the access control processing times when a large XML document is processed. To show the expressiveness of the access control specification, we ran experiments involving predicates and we collected the update performance. In addition, we show the performance gains achieved with the accessibility cache and evaluation-skipping mechanisms.

We use two XML document types in our experiments. The first one, *Orders*, is a real data set describing business transactions, and we prepared two different documents of that type, with sizes of 100 KB and 4 MB. The other type is the XMark benchmark data, where we used a 111MB *standard.xml* file. Both document types contain subtrees with similar structures occurring repeatedly at the same level.

## 6.2   Results

**Scalability for Large Access Control Policies.** In practice, the number of access control rules is on the order of millions, which is a product of the number of document types (in 1000's) and the number of user roles (in 100's). The main purpose of this experiment is to see whether or not the PMT model can support large access control policies. For simplicity, we specified 760,000 access control rules for 30,400 users for the *Orders* document type. Each user was associated with a set of 25 access control rules specified with simple path expressions and $+r$. Fig. 9(a) shows the rule set for User1, and Fig. 9(b) shows

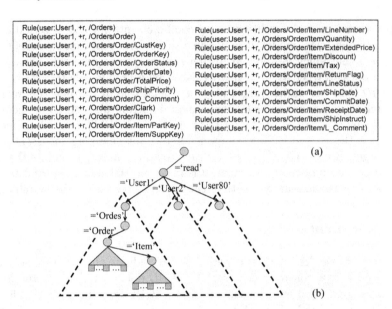

Rule(user:User1, +r, /Orders)
Rule(user:User1, +r, /Orders/Order)
Rule(user:User1, +r, /Orders/Order/CustKey)
Rule(user:User1, +r, /Orders/Order/OrderKey)
Rule(user:User1, +r, /Orders/Order/OrderStatus)
Rule(user:User1, +r, /Orders/Order/OrderDate)
Rule(user:User1, +r, /Orders/Order/TotalPrice)
Rule(user:User1, +r, /Orders/Order/ShipPriority)
Rule(user:User1, +r, /Orders/Order/O_Comment)
Rule(user:User1, +r, /Orders/Order/Clark)
Rule(user:User1, +r, /Orders/Order/Item)
Rule(user:User1, +r, /Orders/Order/Item/PartKey)
Rule(user:User1, +r, /Orders/Order/Item/SuppKey)

Rule(user:User1, +r, /Orders/Order/Item/LineNumber)
Rule(user:User1, +r, /Orders/Order/Item/Quantity)
Rule(user:User1, +r, /Orders/Order/Item/ExtendedPrice)
Rule(user:User1, +r, /Orders/Order/Item/Discount)
Rule(user:User1, +r, /Orders/Order/Item/Tax)
Rule(user:User1, +r, /Orders/Order/Item/ReturnFlag)
Rule(user:User1, +r, /Orders/Order/Item/LineStatus)
Rule(user:User1, +r, /Orders/Order/Item/ShipDate)
Rule(user:User1, +r, /Orders/Order/Item/CommitDate)
Rule(user:User1, +r, /Orders/Order/Item/ReceiptDate)
Rule(user:User1, +r, /Orders/Order/Item/ShipInstruct)
Rule(user:User1, +r, /Orders/Order/Item/L_Comment)

(a)

(b)

**Fig. 9.** Sample Access control rules and the corresponding PMT

the corresponding PTM image, showing that the subtree structure for the *Sub* matching is actually identical. The experiment shows that 760,000 access control rules use almost 640 MB implying each rule takes about 0.84KB on average.

**Scalability for Large XML Documents.** In many access control systems, it is necessary to support access control for large XML documents. For example, XML-formatted documents for record retention may be several megabytes in size. In this experiment, we show the performance of the system by examining the total processing time when the XML documents are 100 KB and 4 MB.

For each subject, we specified 25 access control rules such as shown in Fig. 9(a) for *Orders.xml*. All rules specified a +r permission. Both documents contain repeated sub-structures under */Orders/Order* and so most parts of the access control are duplicated at multiple locations. We used the SAX API of the XML parser to parse the entire document, and checked the accessibility when encountering either an element or an attribute. The processing time includes the XML parsing time, the access control time, and the garbage collection time if it occured. In this experiment, we defined the total time excluding the parsing time as the AC Time. We also measured the performance improvements achieved with caching. In Fig. 10, the processing times of the full documents are shown.

From the bars, it is clear that the accessibility cache makes a significant improvement in processing times. For the 100 KB document, the accessibility cache reduces the AC time by almost 51%. For the 4 MB document, the AC time is reduced to 21%. Since 4MB document contains more duplicated *Order* subtrees, it derives more benefit from the accessibility cache.

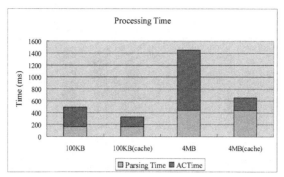

**Fig. 10.** Processing time for entire documents

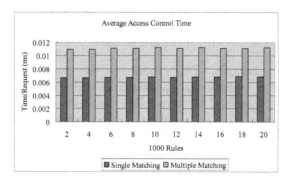

**Fig. 11.** Access control times vs. #s of Rules

**Effect of Policy Size.** In this experiment, we see the relationships between the access control performance, mostly decided by the matching time, and the policy size. The accessibility cache was disabled in this experiment. We specified various policy sizes from 2,000 to 20,000 rules, in which $80 \sim 800$ users are bound to the kind of access control rules presented in Fig. 9(a). For comparison, we also prepared a group of rules that led to multiple matched targets by specifying parts of the rules in Fig. 9(a) with $+R$.

By processing the paths of an entire XML instance *record.xml*, we calculated the average access control times on random paths. The results are shown in Fig. 11, from which the XML parsing time has been eliminated.

To match an access request against the PMT, on average it costs close to 6.6 microseconds when a single target is matched (S), and 11 microseconds when multiple targets are matched (M). The results show that the access control time is affected by the number of matched targets, but little affected by the policy size for our access control model.

In Sect. 4.2, we showed why the expected matching times and the number of visited nodes during the matching should be sub-linear with regards to the policy size. The experimental results are different from our analysis in that to the same access control request each matching on the corresponding PMT of

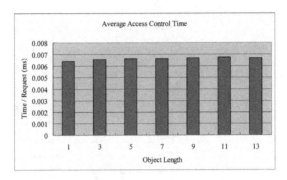

**Fig. 12.** Access control times vs. Object Length

both $S$ and $M$ results in static outgoing edge(s) in the *Act* matching, the *Sub* matching, and the *Obj* matching. As a consequence, the number of visited nodes for a specific user is static without regard to the policy size.

**Effect of Object Length.** This experiment was run to examine the relationship between the access control performance and the depths of the targets of the access control rules. The accessibility cache was disabled in the experiment. We specified policies with different object paths varying from $1 \sim 13$ for *standard.xml*. The experimental results are shown in Fig. 12. As the figure shows, the average access control time varies from $6.4 \sim 6.8$ microseconds, showing that it increases only slightly as the object length increases.

As above two experiments show, for the current implementation, the number of matched targets has more effect on the access control performance. The reason is that when multiple match targets are visited during the match, the accessibility can be decided by combing the matching results, during which access conflicts should be resolved.

**Performance on Predicates.** As presented in the section on the *Pred* matching construction in Sect. 3.4, regardless of the number of the predicates involved, the predicate evaluation is performed only once during the *Pred* matching. Since the performance of data retrieval from the XML database depends on the performance of database itself, we eliminated the time spent on data retrievals in the experiment. The accessibility cache was disabled in this experiment.

Since the match on the PMT is performed twice, once for the *Obj* matching and again for the *Pred* matching, the results show that the access control time is almost twice the time without predicate evaluation: $11 \sim 17$ microseconds per path. The cost was independent of the number of predicates.

**Performance on Policy Updating.** Real-time update is supported by the PMT, as shown in Sect. 5.3, and both adding and removing access control rules costs $O(m(3 + D))$ time, where $m$ is the number of access control rules, $D$ is the maximum depth of he objects. We tested the update performance by measuring the times for adding 20,000 rules and removing 20,000 rules. From the experiments, the results show that the average time to add an access control rule to an existing PMT is 33 microseconds, and that the average time to remove an access control rule from the PMT is almost 17 microseconds. Therefore, to update a rule, it takes almost 50 microseconds, since we first remove the original rule and then add the new one. This time is considered to be reasonable for a real access control system.

## 7    Conclusions and Future Work

In this paper, we have proposed a policy matching tree (PMT) model for providing expressive and scalable access control for XML databases. We first present the PMT generated on the basis of the access control rules. We then described the accessibility evaluation mechanism that matches each access request against the PMT, and decides the accessibility on the basis of the matched results. The PMT also supports // and predicates involved access control, and the expected matching times are shown to be sub-linear relative to the policy size. To improve the performance, we enhanced the access control system with a cache mechanism that eliminates the need for matching when the same subject accesses the same path repeatedly. Comparing with our previous work, the limitations on the expressiveness are expanded, and the runtime PMT updates are supported for policy updates.

To demonstrate the scalability and efficiency of the proposed model, we performed experiments using synthetic and real XML documents. Experimental results show that the PMT model supports 760,000 access control rules and can perform accessibility checks in $6.4 \sim 11$ microseconds per path. This model also supports access control involving predicates at a cost of $11 \sim 17$ microseconds. An accessibility cache further improves performance by a factor of 2 to 5, depending on the XML data structures.

Through these experiments, we also found that when multiple match targets are matched, the performance is twice as slow as the case for a single matched target. In future work, we plan to improve the PMT implementation to achieve better performance for multiple matched targets. We also plan to build the PMT with less memory.

## References

1. M. Altinel and M. Franklin: Efficient filtering of XML documents for selective dissemination of information. VLDB (2000) pp.53-64.
2. E. Bertino, S. Castano, E. Ferrari, and M. Mesiti: Controlled access and dissemination of XML documents. ACM WIDM (1999) pp.22-27.
3. E. Bertino, S. Castano, E. Ferrari, and M. Mesiti: Specifying and Enforcing Access Con-trol Policies for XML document Sources. World Wide Web Journal (2000), Vol. 3, No. 3, pp. 139-151.
4. E. Bertino and E. Ferrari: Secure and selective dissemination of XML documents. ACM TISSEC (2002) pp.290-331.
5. M. Bishop, L. Snyder. The transfer of information and authority in a protection system. Proc. 17th ACM Symposium on Operating Systems Principles, 1979.

6. S. Boag, D. Chamberlin, M. F. Fernandez, D. Florescu, J. Robie, and J. Simeon: XQuery 1.0: An XML query language, W3C Working Draft 12 November 2003. http://www.w3.org/TR/xquery/.
7. T. Bray, J. Paoli, and C. M. Sperberg-McQueen: Extensible Markup Language (XML) 1.0. W3C Recommendation. Available at http://www.w3g.org/TR/REC-xml (Feb. 1998).
8. C. -Y. Chan, P. Felber, M. Garofalakis, and R. Rastogi: Efficient filtering of XML documents with XPath expressions. ICDE (2002) pp.235-244.
9. S. Cho, S. Amer-Yahia, L. V. S. Lakshmanan, and D. Srivastava: Optimizing the secure evaluation of twig queries. VLDB (2000) pp.490-501.
10. J. Clark and S. DeRose: XML Path Language (XPath) version 1.0. W3C Recommendation. Available at http://www.w3g.org/TR/xpath (1999).
11. E. Damiani, S. De Capitani di Vimercati, S. Paraboschi, and P. Samarati: Design and Implementation of an Access Control Processor for XML documents. WWW9 (2000).
12. E. Damiani, S. De Capitani di Vimercati, S. Paraboschi, and P. Samarati: A Fine-Grained Access Control System for XML Documents. ACM TISSEC (2002) pp.169-202.
13. A. Deutsch and V. Tannen: Containment of regular path expressions under integrity constraints. KRDB (2001).
14. Y. Diao, P. Fischer, M. Franklin, and R. To.: YFilter: Efficient and scalable filtering of XML documents. Demo at ICDE (2002) pp.341.
15. W. Fan and L. Libkin: On XML integrity constraints in the presence of DTDs. Symposium on Principles of Database Systems (2001) pp.114-125.
16. M. F. Fernandez and D. Suciu: Optimizing regular path expressions using graph schemas. ICDE (1998) pp.14-23.
17. A. Gabillon and E. Bruno: Regulating Access to XML Documents. Working Conference on Database and Application Security (2001) pp.219-314.
18. L. Gong: A Secure Identity-Based Capability System. Proc. IEEE Symposium on Security and Privacy, pp.56-65, 1989.
19. A. L. Hors, P. L. Hegaret, L. Wood, G. Nicol, J. Robie, M. Champion, and S. Byrne: Document Object Model (DOM) Level 3 Core Specification. Available at http://www.w3.org/TR/2004/PR-DOM-Level-3-Core-20040205 (2004).
20. A. K. Jones, R. J. Lipton, and L. Snyder. A Linear Time Algorithm for Deciding Security. Proc. 17th Symposium on Foundations of Computer Science, pp. 33-41, 1976.
21. R. Kaushik, P. Bohannon, J. F. Naughton, and H. F. Korth: Covering indexes for branching path queries. ACM SIGMOD (2002) pp.133-144.
22. D. D. Kha, M. Yoshikawa, and S. Uemura: An XML Indexing Structure with Relative Region Coordinate. ICDE (2001) pp.313-320.
23. M. Kudo and S. Hada: XML Document Security based on Provisional Authorization. ACM CCS (2000) pp.87-96.
24. Q. Li and B. Moon: Indexing and Querying XML Data for Regular Path Expressions. VLDB (2001) pp.361-370.
25. M. Murata, A. Tozawa, M. Kudo and S. Hada: XML Access Control Using Static Analysis. ACM CCS (2003 ) pp.73-84.
26. OASIS. OASIS Extensible Access Control Markup Language (XACML), Feb. 2003. http://www.oasis-open.org/committees/xacml/docs.
27. F. Neven and T. Schwentick: XPath containment in the presence of disjunction, DTDs, and variables. ICDT (2003) pp.315-329.

28. N. Qi and M. Kudo: Access-condition-table-driven access control for XML data-bases. ESORICS (2004) pp.17-23.
29. R. S. Sandhu, E. J. Coyne, H. L. Feinstein, C. E. Youman. Role-Based Access Control Models. IEEE Computer, Volume 29, No 2, pp.38-47, February 1996.
30. T. Yu, D. Srivastava, L. V. S. Lakshmanan, and H. V. Jagadish: Compressed Accessibility Map: Efficient Access Control for XML. VLDB (2002) pp.478-489.

# Semantic Access Control Model: A Formal Specification*

Mariemma I. Yagüe, María-del-Mar Gallardo, and Antonio Maña

Dpto. de Lenguajes y Ciencias de la Computación,
University of Málaga, 29071 Málaga, Spain

**Abstract.** The Semantic Access Control Model (SAC), built on the basis of separation of the authorization and access control management responsibilities, provides adequate solutions to the problems of access control in distributed and dynamic systems with heterogeneous security requirements. SAC is characterized by its flexibility for accommodating dissimilar security policies, but also by the ease of management and control over a large number of distributed elements and the support for interoperability of authorization mechanisms. In this paper, we present the semantic validation algorithms developed in SAC to detect semantically incomplete or incorrect access control policies. Additionally, the formal model of SAC along with some proofs of its soundness is introduced. This formalization is the basis for additional model checking of the semantic validation algorithms developed.

**Keywords:** Access Control, Authorization, Distributed Systems Security, Formal Methods in security.

## 1 Introduction

When security requirements for distributed applications are considered, *authorization* often emerges as a central element in the design of the whole security system. Many other security requirements depend on the flexibility, trustworthiness and expressiveness of the authorization scheme. On the other hand, *access control* is the mechanism that allows resource owners to define, manage and enforce the access conditions for each resource [16]. These two concepts are very closely related because authorizations are usually the basis for the access decision in access control systems.

The notions upon which an access control model is defined determine its flexibility to be applied in different environments and systems. Traditional access control models have been designed to provide access control in some specific scenarios. However, the mechanisms provided by these models are not expressive enough to deal with very dynamic environments with a high volume of heterogeneous data, where new resources are incorporated to the system continuously,

---

* Work partially supported by the Spanish Ministry of Science and Technology under the Research Projects PRIVILEGE (TIC2003-08184-C02-01) and SELF (TIN2004-7943-C04-01).

S. De Capitani di Vimercati et al. (Eds.): ESORICS 2005, LNCS 3679, pp. 24–43, 2005.

each resource possibly needing a different access control policy, and where policies may change frequently. Furthermore, traditional access control schemes are not suitable for scenarios where the local registration and authorization of users is not appropriate or with a very large number of heterogeneous registered users. In these systems, for scalability reasons, it is not practical to keep access and authorization information for each user.

In this paper, we present the formalization of a more general access control model developed for these new environments. The *Semantic Access Control* (SAC) model [20] was especially designed for handling the access control in heterogeneous, distributed and large environments. This model solves the above mentioned scalability problems, facilitates access control management, and provides a means to express access conditions in a natural and flexible way.

SAC considers the operation of several independent access control systems and authorization entities. The access control to resources is independent of their location. Additionally, the identification of the user or client is not mandatory. On one hand, the client possesses a set of attributes and, on the other hand, the access control to resources is based on the specification of a set of attributes that the client has to present to gain access to them. For interoperability and security reasons, client attributes must be digitally signed (in the form of an attribute certificate) by a trusted certification entity, external to the access control management system. The independence of the certification of attributes is the key to the interoperability achieved because it allows attributes to be safely communicated avoiding the necessity of being locally recorded by the system administrator. Additionally, this approach avoids the registration phase of the client, and the recording of a client attribute for each access control system. For this approach to be secure, a mechanism to establish the trust between these access control systems and the authorization entities was required. We addressed this problem using semantic information about the certifications issued by each authorization entity. One of the main characteristics of the SAC model is that, as opposed to traditional schemes, the attributes required to access a resource may depend on the semantic properties of the resources. The allocation of the policy corresponding to a resource is not based on the storage structure of resources but on their semantic properties. Of course, it is also possible to consider the structure of storage.

An orthogonal problem when defining an access control model is to assure that it is semantically sound. In this context, soundness means that users not fulfilling the access policy cannot access resources. SAC enables the semantic validation of the access control policies. Additionally, in order to prove soundness, we have formalized the SAC model using inference rules. The construction of the formal model makes use of the semantic information handled through the different SAC metadata models [23]. In this formalisation, we have defined two different entailment relations: the first one is able to infer whether a target satisfies an attribute; the second relation deals with the access policies. In this last case, we have introduced some useful operators that combine different access rules. It is worth noting that the formal model presented has inherited the flexibility of SAC in the sense that, if necessary, we may add new operators transparently.

In summary, SAC was developed to facilitate the management of complex access control systems, while guaranteeing the simplicity, correction and safety of the system. To deal with this, SAC provides a set of algorithms for the automatic validation of the access control policies defined by the system administrator. This work presents the formal basis to prove its correctness.

This paper is organized as follows. Section 1 presents some related works. Afterwards and before introducing the formal model of SAC, Section 2 shows some background on SAC which helps its formalisation. Section 3 introduces the formal model of SAC with the formalization of the Source of Authorizations of a PMI and the derivation rules to deduce information from certificate classes. We finalize with some conclusions and projected work for the near future. Lastly but not least, an example and proofs of theorems are illustrated in the appendices.

## 2   Related Works

Traditional access control models such as Discretionary (DAC) [1], Mandatory (MAC) [15] and Role-Based (RBAC) [17] Access Control were developed for closed environments. Consequently, they are built on the basis of modelling the environments that motivated their development [23]. Among these models, RBAC is commonly accepted as the most appropriate paradigm for the implementation of access control in complex scenarios. RBAC can be considered a mature and flexible technology. In RBAC, the structure of groups is defined by the security administrator and it is usually static. Although grouping users can suffice in many different situations, it is not flexible enough to cope with the requirements of more dynamic systems where the structure of groups can not be anticipated by the administrators of the access control system. In these scenarios, the structure of the system may be increased dynamically with new resources which may possibly need a different group structure and access control policy. Additionally, the policy for a given resource may change frequently.

We believe that a more general approach, such as the one presented by the Semantic Access Control model, is needed in order to properly deal with these new environments. For example, in the referred situations, groups are artificial substitutes of a more general tool: the attribute. In fact, groups are usually defined on the basis of the values of some specific attributes (employer, position, $\cdots$). Some attributes are even built into most of the current access control models. This is the case of the user element; the identity is just one of the most useful attributes, but it is not necessary in all scenarios and, therefore, it should not be a built-in component of a general model. Recent literature in the area of access control for distributed heterogeneous resources from multiple sources shows the use of attribute certificates and PMIs. Firstly, we highlight two research projects, Akenti [7] and Permis [5]. Akenti Project proposes an access control system to restrict access to distributed resources controlled by multiple stakeholders. The requirement for the stakeholders to trust the rest of the servers in the network, as well as some security vulnerabilities related to the existence of positive and negative use-conditions, are the main drawbacks of Akenti. The PERMIS Project [13] objective is to set up an integrated infrastructure to solve identification and authorization problems. A specific goal is to specify the authorization policy in a language that can be both easily parsed by computers and read by the security administrators with or without software tools. The PERMIS group concluded that XML is the most appropriate candidate for a policy specification language. However, because PERMIS system is based on the RBAC model, it shares its limitations. Moreover, the requirement of supporting a PKI is hard to fulfil and it is not necessary in many authorization scenarios.

Regarding the different XML-based languages proposed for access control, digital rights management, authentication and authorization, many similarities and interesting features can be found among them. Some other features, such as policy parameterisation and composition are not supported. Moreover, some features provided by those languages are not appropriate in heterogeneous and dynamic scenarios. Two relevant proposals for access control to XML documents are the Author-X system [2] and the FASTER project [6]. They differ from SAC in that both systems have been specifically developed for XML documents, unlike the general definition of resource in this work. Author-X is based on credentials that are issued by the access control administrator. Therefore, in practice, each credential will be useful only for a single source, limiting interoperability. A direct consequence of this approach is that users must subscribe to sources before they can access their contents. In the Semantic Access Control Model (SAC) however we have semantically integrated a Privilege Management Infrastructure that will be responsible for issuing digitally signed attribute certificates. Another relevant proposal is XACML [14], an OASIS standard that proposes two XML-based languages to describe access control policies and access decision requests and responses. Although XACML and SAC share some similarities, there are important differences [21].

Other access control languages have been developed in the security community to support different access control approaches. Jajodia et al. present in [9] a logical language which allows users to specify the policy according to what access control decisions are to be made as well as the authorizations. SAC is focused in this direction, but in the SAC case we are interested in access control for highly dynamic systems with an important volume of heterogeneous data and multiple independent data sources. We use XML and XML Schema to enable the definition of policies expressed by means of rules and the representation of derivation rules for the attribute classes used in the policies semantic validation.

Some works have used formal semantics for policy representation and evaluation such as [19] but this work differs from ours in that they address issues such as positive and negative authorizations. Another interesting work is the Policy Maker system [3,4], which focuses on construction of a practical algorithm for determining trust decisions. The main drawback of this proposal is the use of a policy language with a low abstraction level and it is very cumbersome, unlike the SPL policy language defined in SAC.

Finally, we must highlight an innovative feature presented by SAC which is semantic and contextual validation of policies. In SAC we have taken into account that the creation and maintenance of access control policies is a difficult and error prone activity. Therefore, in the design of SAC we have considered that this access control model must facilitate and guarantee the correct administration of the system. To reach this objective, a set of algorithms have been defined to detect incorrect access control policies. The semantic algorithms carry out inference processes using the rules defined in the Source Of Authorization Description (SOAD) documents and have been implemented as part of the Semantic Policy Validator (SPV) tool.

## 3  Fundamentals of the Semantic Access Control Model (SAC)

Most of current access control schemes base their authorization approaches on locally-issued credentials that are based on user identities. This type of credential presents many drawbacks. Among them we highlight:

(a) they are not interoperable;
(b) the same credentials are issued many times for each user, which introduces management and inconsistency problems;
(c) credentials are issued by the site administrator, however, in most cases, the administrator does not have enough information or resources to establish trustworthy credentials; and
(d) they depend on user identity. However, in practice, frequently the identity of the user is not relevant for the access decision. Sometimes, it is even desirable that the identity is not considered or revealed. Furthermore, in systems based on identity, the lack of a global authentication infrastructure (a global Public Key Infrastructure, PKI) forces the use of local authentication schemes. In these cases, subscription is required and users have to authenticate themselves to every accessed source.

To solve the aforementioned problems, single-sign-on mechanisms are becoming popular [18]. Although these mechanisms represent an improvement, they do not enable interoperability while maintaining the diversity. The reason is they are based on federation of sources and all federated sources must agree on a homogeneous access control scheme. Additionally, credentials remain local, not to a site, but to a set of them.

On the other hand, digital certificates [8] can securely convey authorizations or credentials. Attribute certificates bind attributes to keys and make authorizations interoperable and mobile, since attribute certificates can securely transport authorization information. This mobility provides the foundation for a better alternative to actual Single Sign-On schemes.

Another important advantage of attribute certificates is that they can be used for various purposes. They may contain group membership, role, clearance, or any other form of authorization. As a consequence, digital certificates provide means for the deployment of scalable and flexible access control schemes, since access conditions are expressed in terms of sets of attributes instead of users or groups. Users must possess attribute certificates attesting that they meet the requirements. As opposed to traditional access control schemes, a high number of users and attributes do not degrade performance and manageability of this solution.

On the other hand, when discussing how to establish the access conditions applicable to a particular resource, two main approaches must be considered: (i) conditions are established on the basis of the location of the resources or, (ii) conditions are based on the properties of the resources. The fact is that conditions and restrictions of access naturally depend on the semantic properties of the target resource that are neglected in structure-based approaches. Therefore, an approach based on semantic descriptions of the contents is much more flexible and natural. Moreover, it is easy to incorporate structure-based requirements in the semantic model. Additionally, the structure is much more volatile than the semantics. The incompatibility between the structure required for the application domain and the ones that match the security requirements confirms that structure-based approaches are not able to represent these situations in a natural way.

Another drawback of structure-based approaches is that the number of policies becomes very large. In fact, these approaches usually imply the definition of several policies for each resource. Positive and negative authorizations are used in these cases to facilitate the definition of simple policies and to reduce the number of policies. The price to pay is the presence of ambiguities, which in turn requires the definition of conflict resolution rules. Consequently, the administration of the system becomes complex and difficult to understand, increasing the chance of incorrect policies being produced.

The Semantic Access Control model (SAC) [20] was developed following a different approach. It was called this because semantics are the basis of the access conditions and its design follows a semantic approach. The SAC model is based on the semantic properties of the resources to be controlled, properties of the clients that request access to them, semantics about the context and finally, semantics about the attribute certificates trusted by the access control system. The semantic-based and modular approach adopted in SAC, facilitates the definition and management of policies avoiding the use of positive and negative authorizations. Tools provided to support the policy specification, composition and validation also serve this objective. The Semantic Access Control model has been implemented on the basis of the Semantic Policy Language (SPL) to specify the access control criteria and the semantic integration of an external authorization entity.

## 3.1   Semantic Policy Language (SPL)

SPL XML-Schema based policy definition language [24] was designed to specify policies in a simple way, enabling high level expressiveness and efficient evaluation. Usual components of access policies include the target resource, the conditions under which access is granted/denied and, sometimes, access restrictions. As opposed to other languages, specifications in SPL do not include references to the target object. Instead, a separate specification called *Policy Applicability Specification* (PAS) is used to relate policies to objects dynamically when a request is received. Both SPL Policies and PAS use semantic information about resources, included in *Secured Resource Representations* (SRRs), and other contextual information documents.

SPL Policies and PAS can be parameterised allowing the definition of flexible and general policies, thus reducing the number of different policies to be managed. Parameters, which can refer to complex XML elements, are instantiated dynamically from semantic and contextual information. Additionally, policies can be composed, importing components from other policies without ambiguity. This compositional approach allows us to define the abstract meaning of the elements of the policies, providing a mechanism to achieve abstraction, which also helps in reducing the complexity of management.

The schema for SPL specifications is represented as a set of XML-Schema templates that facilitate the creation of these specifications, allowing their automatic syntactic validation [24]. SPL policies can include components defined locally as well as imported elements. The ability to import elements enables the modular composition of policies based on the XPath standard. An SPL Policy is composed of a set of *access_Rule* elements. Every *access_Rule* defines a particular combination of attribute certificates required to gain access, associated with an optional set of actions (such as *Notify_To*, *Payment* and *Online_Permission*) to be performed before access is granted. In this way, provisional authorization or PBAC [10] is enabled in SPL.

### 3.2  Semantic Description of the Sources of Authorization (SOAD)

As we have already mentioned, one of the basis of SAC is the separation of the certification of attributes and access control management responsibilities, in order to build a scalable and flexible solution.

A *Privilege Management Infrastructure* (PMI) [8] provides attribute certification services. It is then reasonable to expect that the PMI includes different certification authorities (SOAs), each one with a well-defined certification domain. That is, each SOA should be authoritative for a limited set of attributes and users. Ideally, each attribute would be certified only by one SOA. This raises the issue of the interoperability of the attribute certificates.

For example, suppose that `Peter Smith` is an authorized broker at the Chicago Board of Trade. Then `Peter` will have two separate certificates: an identity certificate attesting to his identity information and an attribute certificate attesting to his being an authorized broker at the Chicago Board of Trade. Both certificates can be related, for instance, by including the serial number and/or a hash value of the identity certificate in the attribute certificate. Suppose now that our friend `Peter Smith` is also member of the `Chicago Siesta Club` (CSC), a `public library`, `Greenpeace`, etc. If centralized access control schemes are used in these institutions, each one will have to locally register the different attributes of `Peter Smith` that are applicable to their access control policies. For instance, if the `CSC` has a discount for `Greenpeace` members then it is necessary to record `Peter` 's `Greenpeace` membership in the local database of users of `CSC`. However, how can `CSC` be sure that `Peter` is member of `Greenpeace`? What if `Peter` leaves `Greenpeace`? How does `CSC` know about this?

On the contrary, if the attribute certification function is separated then access control systems responsibilities are limited to establishing the local access control policies, making the system simpler, more dynamic and flexible, and more secure. Obviously, this approach requires that the access control system is complemented by an external component providing certification functions. The PMI is precisely that component. A consequence of the separation of access control and authorization functions (now provided by the PMI) is that the access control administrators do not have control over some factors that are used in their access control systems. Consequently, a mechanism to establish the trust between these administrators and the PMI is required.

In SAC, we addressed this problem using semantic information about the certifications issued by each SOA. This assists the security administrators in the creation and semantic validation of access control policies. In SAC, every SOA produces and digitally signs a set of Source Of Authorization Descriptions (SOADs) that express the semantics of the attribute certificates it issues [22]. These metadata documents describe the different attributes certified by a SOA, including names, descriptions and relations of attributes. SOADs are used to establish the trust between the PMI and the access control systems. They convey the information needed by the access control system to understand the semantics of the attribute certificates, which is essential in order to take appropriate access decisions.

## 3.3  Semantic Validation of Policies

The information contained in SOADs is also essential for the semantic validation of the policies, enabling the detection of semantically incomplete (or incorrect) policies through a Semantic Policy Validator (SPV) tool developed with this objective [20]. The SPV makes inference processes using the rules defined in the SOAD documents. The semantic validation ensures that the policies written by the security administrator produce the desired effects. An interesting feature of the SPV is that it allows policies to be validated in the context where they will be applied. The use of semantic information about the context allows the administrator to include relevant contextual considerations in a transparent manner. The SPV can perform three types of validations:

1. Test Case Validation: Given a request to access a resource and a set of attribute certificates, this algorithm outputs the sets of attribute certificates needed for accessing that resource. Most of the time, this feature will be used to check that a set of attribute certificates is incompatible with the access criteria for that resource. For instance, the administrator of our university can use this validation to guarantee that it is not possible for a student

to access a given resource (i.e., documents containing marks). During the validation process, the SPV generates the sets of attribute certificates that are not excluded by the input set, and checks the generated ones against all possible combinations of attribute certificates that grant access to the resource.

2. Access Validation: Given a request to access a resource, this algorithm outputs the sets of certificates that grant access to that resource. For this validation process, the SPV generates the policy for the resource and all sets of attribute certificates equivalent to those required by the policy.

3. Full Validation: The goal of this process is to check which resources can be accessed given a set of attribute certificates. Therefore, SPV generates the policy for each resource and, afterwards, all attribute certificates that can be derived from the input set of attribute certificates. Finally, it informs of every resource that can be accessed using the input attribute certificate set.

## 4   Formal Model of the Semantic Access Control

In this section, we formalize the deductive approach followed by the SAC model in order to grant/deny a request to access a given resource.

A *target* is any entity that may hold properties. In the SAC model, targets may be clients or resources. Properties of the targets are called *attributes*. Let $T$ and $\mathcal{A}$ be, respectively, the sets of all possible targets and (atomic) attributes in a given application domain. We assume that each attribute $a \in \mathcal{A}$ has a negative counterpart $\neg a \in \mathcal{A}$ denoting the opposite attribute. For instance, attribute "non-student" is the negative counterpart of "student". In addition, we suppose that $\neg\neg a = a$. The first step to formalize SAC is to associate each target $t$ with the set of attributes it holds at every instant in time. To this end, we define the set $\mathcal{A}^* = \mathcal{A} \cup \{!a | a \in \mathcal{A}\}$.

Function $K : \mathbb{N} \to (T \to \wp(\mathcal{A}^*))$[1] defines the true attributes held by targets in each time instant as follows:

- $a \in K(m)(t)$ means that target $t$ holds attribute $a$ at time instant $m$.
- Targets cannot hold simultaneously an attribute $a$ and its negation $\neg a$ in an specific time instant $m$. Thus, $a \in K(m)(t) \Rightarrow \neg a \notin K(m)(t)$. On the other hand, it is possible that some attributes cannot be associated to certain targets. Thus, it may be that both $a \notin K(m)(t)$ and $\neg a \notin K(m)(t)$ hold. For instance, it makes no sense to apply attributes "divorced"/"non-divorced" to a "printer".
- Operator ! is a weak version of $\neg$ whose meaning is given as

$$!a \in K(m)(t) \text{ iff } a \notin K(m)(t) \tag{4.1}$$

That is, $!a \in K(m)(t)$ means that $t$ does not hold attribute $a$ at time instant $m$. But it says nothing about $\neg a$. However, when $\neg a \in K(m)(t)$, following the previous discussion, we have that

$$\neg a \in K(m)(t) \Rightarrow !a \in K(m)(t) \tag{4.2}$$

---

[1] $\wp(\mathcal{A}^*)$ denotes the powerset of set $\mathcal{A}^*$.

It is worth noting that time is introduced in the formal model because attributes held by targets may vary with time. Thus, it is possible for a target to hold an attribute $a$ in a given instant $m$ and to hold $\neg a$ in some future instant $f > m$. For example, target María may currently have the attribute "student", but it is very probable that, in the future, when she finishes her studies, María holds attribute "non-student". In order to properly deal with time, we assume that function $ctime :\to \mathbb{N}$ returns the current time instant.

In contrast to the *true facts* represented by function $K$, the SAC model makes use of SOAs to certify such facts. In other words, SOAs are the formal artefact devoted to providing certificates about targets that must be consistent with the reality represented by function $K$. In the rest of this section, we formally define how SOAs infer information about targets when required.

### 4.1   Formalizing SOAs

As mentioned above, a Source of Authorization k.a. SOA is a certification entity responsible for issuing *attribute certificates* attesting to a set of properties about targets. Each SOA has a *certification domain*, i.e. a set of targets and properties that can be certified by this SOA. For instance, the SOA of a university may issue certificates related to the enrollment of its students in courses, but not about their marital status. Likewise, it can not issue certificates related to the enrollment of students from other universities. Let $S$ be the set of all SOAs in a given domain. In the sequel, we will use symbols $\sigma$, $\tau$, etc. as elements of $S$.

Given a SOA $\sigma \in S$, an attribute certificate signed by $\sigma$ is an expression of the form $\sigma\langle\langle a,t\rangle\rangle_d$, where $d$ represents the temporal limit of the validity of the sentence. Thus, $\sigma\langle\langle a,t\rangle\rangle_d$ means that $\sigma$ certifies that target $t$ holds attribute $a$ from the current time instant until the validity of the certificate expires in time $d$. We assume, without loss of generality, that the holder $t$ of this attribute certificate will be identified by its public key[2]. Let $T_\sigma \subseteq T$ be the set of all targets in the certification domain of $\sigma$.

Besides attribute certificates, in our model, SOAs also provide rules (represented in SOAD metadata documents) defining semantic relations among attributes using the so-called *certificate classes*. Given an attribute $a \in \mathcal{A}^*$, the certificate class $\sigma\langle\langle a\rangle\rangle$ is used by the rules to express that SOA $\sigma$ is responsible for checking attribute $a$. Thus, the notation of *certificate classes* allows us to easily represent the *trust relationship* among SOAs.

Formally, each SOA $\sigma \in S$ is constituted by a 3-uple $\langle \mathcal{D}_\sigma, \Sigma_\sigma, SOAD_\sigma \rangle$ where

1. $\mathcal{D}_\sigma \subseteq S$ is the set of SOAs in which $\sigma$ trust to delegate the task of issuing attribute certificates. We assume that $\sigma \in \mathcal{D}_\sigma$.
2. $\Sigma_\sigma \subseteq \mathcal{A}^* \times T_\sigma \times \mathbb{N}$ is the set of all attribute certificates attested by $\sigma$ with the corresponding deadline. As on commented above, elements of $\Sigma_\sigma$ are

---

[2] In asymmetric encryption schemes each user has a pair of related keys. One of these keys, the Public Key, is publicly distributed while the other one, the Private Key, must be kept secret. Public Key's are included in digital certificates, so that other users can verify their authenticity.

denoted as $\sigma\langle\langle a,t\rangle\rangle_d$. Sometimes, we will write them as $\langle\langle a,t\rangle\rangle_d$ for the sake of simplicity. We assume that SOAs only sign true certificates, that is, the following assertion holds:

$$\langle\langle a,t\rangle\rangle_d \in \Sigma_\sigma \Rightarrow \forall m \in \mathbb{N}.(ctime \leq m \leq d \Rightarrow a \in K(m)(t)) \qquad (4.3)$$

3. Let $\mathcal{C}_\sigma = \mathcal{D}_\sigma \times \mathcal{A}$ be the set of certificate classes regarding SOA $\sigma$. Then, $SOAD_\sigma \subseteq \wp(\mathcal{C}_\sigma) \times OpSet \times \mathcal{A}^*$ is the SOA description constituted by a set of rules, each one representing a relation between a set of certificate classes and a given certificate class. The set of relational operators considered is $OpSet = \{\rightarrow, \Phi\}$, where $\rightarrow$ is the usual implication, and operator $\Phi$ is used to denote *inconsistency* and it will be formally defined below. For example, assuming that $\tau \in \mathcal{D}_\sigma$, rule $\tau\langle\langle b\rangle\rangle, \sigma\langle\langle c\rangle\rangle \rightarrow \sigma\langle\langle a\rangle\rangle$ could be an element of $SOAD_\sigma$, indicating that any target holding attributes $b$ and $c$ also holds $a$. In addition, the rule also expresses that $\sigma$ delegates the task of checking $b$ to SOA $\tau$. It is worth noting that certificate classes appearing at the right side of rules always refer to the SOA defining the rule, this is why no SOA identifier is needed and it will be omitted for the sake of simplicity. As before, we assume that SOAD rules only establish true relations among attributes, that is, the following assertion holds

$$\sigma_1\langle\langle a_1\rangle\rangle, \cdots, \sigma_n\langle\langle a_n\rangle\rangle \rightarrow \langle\langle a\rangle\rangle \in SOAD_\sigma \Rightarrow$$
$$\forall m \in \mathbb{N}, \forall t \in T_\sigma.(\{a_1, \cdots, a_n\} \subseteq K(m)(t) \Rightarrow a \in K(m)(t)) \qquad (4.4)$$

The Semantic Access Control (SAC) makes use of SOAD rules to derive information about properties. We have developed two derivation relations, $\vdash_r^\sigma$ (Figure 1) deduces information from certificate classes, and $\vdash_{at}^\sigma$ (Figure 2) deals with attribute certificates. In order to avoid confusion, from now on, we call d-rules the rules appearing in these two figures.

In the d-rules appearing in the figures, we are assuming that $\sigma$ is the SOA from which new rules or attribute certificates are being inferred. The rest of the SOAs are supposed to belong to $\mathcal{D}_\sigma$.

Next, we give short explanations about the meaning of each d-rule of Figure 1.

$$\textbf{R1} \quad \frac{\sigma_1\langle\langle a_1\rangle\rangle, \cdots, \sigma_n\langle\langle a_n\rangle\rangle \rightarrow \langle\langle b\rangle\rangle \in SOAD_\sigma}{\vdash_r^\sigma \sigma_1\langle\langle a_1\rangle\rangle, \cdots, \sigma_n\langle\langle a_n\rangle\rangle \rightarrow \langle\langle b\rangle\rangle} \qquad (SOAD_\sigma \text{ rules})$$

$$\textbf{R2} \quad \frac{\vdash_r^\sigma \sigma_1\langle\langle a_1\rangle\rangle, \cdots, \sigma_n\langle\langle a_n\rangle\rangle \rightarrow \langle\langle a\rangle\rangle, \vdash_r^\sigma \sigma\langle\langle a\rangle\rangle \rightarrow \langle\langle b\rangle\rangle}{\vdash_r^\sigma \sigma_1\langle\langle a_1\rangle\rangle, \cdots, \sigma_n\langle\langle a_n\rangle\rangle \rightarrow \langle\langle b\rangle\rangle} \quad \text{(Transitivity)}$$

$$\textbf{R3} \quad \frac{\vdash_r^\sigma \sigma_1\langle\langle a_1\rangle\rangle, \cdots, \sigma_n\langle\langle a_n\rangle\rangle \rightarrow \langle\langle !b\rangle\rangle}{\vdash_r^\sigma \sigma_1\langle\langle a_1\rangle\rangle, \cdots, \sigma_n\langle\langle a_n\rangle\rangle \Phi\langle\langle b\rangle\rangle} \qquad \text{(Inconsistency)}$$

$$\textbf{R4} \quad \frac{\vdash_r^\tau \sigma\langle\langle b\rangle\rangle \rightarrow \langle\langle !a\rangle\rangle}{\vdash_r^\sigma \tau\langle\langle a\rangle\rangle \rightarrow \langle\langle !b\rangle\rangle} \qquad \text{(Exclusion)}$$

**Fig. 1.** d-rules for certificate classes

**R1** Every $SOAD_\sigma$ rule is directly derived by $\vdash_r^\sigma$. Note that the left part of each rule may contain references to other SOAs meaning delegation for checking the corresponding attribute. Since $\sigma \in \mathcal{D}_\sigma$, **R1** also deals with rules of the form $\sigma\langle\langle a\rangle\rangle \rightarrow \langle\langle b\rangle\rangle$.

**R2** This d-rule defines transitivity. It may be directly inferred using the d-rules for $\vdash_{at}^\sigma$ described below. However, we define it explicitly in order to simplify the algorithms implementing the SAC deductive system.

**R3** This d-rule defines the inconsistency between a given certificate class issued by $\sigma$ and a set of them. If we can deduce $\sigma_1\langle\langle a_1\rangle\rangle, \cdots, \sigma_n\langle\langle a_n\rangle\rangle \rightarrow \langle\langle !b\rangle\rangle$ then we conclude that attributes $\sigma_1\langle\langle a_1\rangle\rangle, \cdots, \sigma_n\langle\langle a_n\rangle\rangle$ and $\langle\langle b\rangle\rangle$ are inconsistent, that is, they cannot be held simultaneously. We use symbol $\Phi$ to denote inconsistency.

**R4** The exclusion d-rule says that both $\tau\langle\langle b\rangle\rangle \rightarrow \langle\langle !a\rangle\rangle$ in $SOAD_\sigma$ and $\sigma\langle\langle a\rangle\rangle \rightarrow \langle\langle !b\rangle\rangle$ in $SOAD_\tau$ may be used to prove that attributes $a$ and $b$ are inconsistent. Note that although these two assertions are logically equivalent, it is possible that we can prove only one of them, depending on the rules appearing in the corresponding SOADs. This d-rule also includes the case where SOAs $\sigma$ and $\tau$ coincide.

The following proposition proves that $\vdash_r^\sigma$ only produces true relations among certificate classes. See appendix for proofs of this section.

**Proposition 1.** *If* $\vdash_r^\sigma \sigma_1\langle\langle a_1\rangle\rangle, \cdots, \sigma_n\langle\langle a_n\rangle\rangle \rightarrow \langle\langle c\rangle\rangle$ *then* $\forall m \in \mathbb{N}, t \in T_\sigma$, *if* $\{a_1, \cdots, a_n\} \subseteq K(m)(t) \Rightarrow c \in K(m)(t)$.

Note that the previous proposition does not consider operator $\Phi$ because it only provides a specific notation for the rules having on their right side attributes of the form $!b$.

**Definition 1 (Consistency).** *We say that certificate class* $\sigma\langle\langle a\rangle\rangle \in \mathcal{C}_\sigma$ *is consistent with the certificate classes* $\sigma_1\langle\langle a_1\rangle\rangle, \cdots, \sigma\langle\langle a_n\rangle\rangle \in \mathcal{C}_\sigma$, *and denote it as* $\sigma_1\langle\langle a_1\rangle\rangle, \cdots, \sigma\langle\langle a_n\rangle\rangle \copyright \sigma\langle\langle a\rangle\rangle$, *iff* $\nvdash_r^\sigma \sigma_1\langle\langle a_1\rangle\rangle, \cdots, \sigma_n\langle\langle a_n\rangle\rangle \Phi\langle\langle a\rangle\rangle$.

It is worth noting that Proposition 1 implies that if SOA $\sigma$ proves inconsistency then we have assured that the corresponding attributes cannot hold simultaneously. On the other hand, the fact that SOA $\sigma$ cannot prove inconsistency does not necessarily imply that attributes are consistent. That is, the notion of *consistency* is weaker than that of *inconsistency*.

Figure 2 shows the system derivation used by a given SOA $\sigma$ to infer certificate classes. We have denoted this relation with $\vdash_{at}^\sigma$.

In the following, we briefly explain the derivation rules given in the figure.

**A1** Non expired attribute certificates in $\Sigma_\sigma$ are directly inferred by $\vdash_{at}^\sigma$.

**A2** Given a rule deduced using $\vdash_r^\sigma$, if each SOA $\sigma_i$ asserts that target $t$ holds attribute $a_i$, and the corresponding deadline $d_i$ has not been reached, then $\sigma$ derives the attribute certificate $\langle\langle a, t\rangle\rangle_d$, $d$ being the minimum of the deadlines $d_i$.

**A3** This d-rule simply applies the d-rule for inconsistency **R3**.

$$\mathbf{A1} \frac{\langle\langle a,t\rangle\rangle_d \in \varSigma_\sigma, ctime \leq d}{\vdash^\sigma_{at} \langle\langle a,t\rangle\rangle_d} \qquad\qquad \text{(SOA At. Certif.)}$$

$$\mathbf{A2} \frac{\begin{array}{l} \vdash^\sigma_r \sigma_1\langle\langle a_1\rangle\rangle, \cdots, \sigma_n\langle\langle a_n\rangle\rangle \rightarrow \langle\langle a\rangle\rangle, \\ \forall 1 \leq i \leq n.(\vdash^{\sigma_i}_{at} \langle\langle a_i,t\rangle\rangle_{d_i}, ctime \leq d_i), d = min(d_1, \cdots, d_n) \end{array}}{\vdash^\sigma_{at} \langle\langle a,t\rangle\rangle_d} \quad \text{(Rule Application)}$$

$$\mathbf{A3} \frac{\begin{array}{l} \vdash^\sigma_r \sigma_1\langle\langle a_1\rangle\rangle, \cdots, \sigma_n\langle\langle a_n\rangle\rangle \varPhi\langle\langle a\rangle\rangle, \\ \forall 1 \leq i \leq n, (\vdash^{\sigma_i}_{at} \langle\langle a_i,t\rangle\rangle_{d_i}, ctime \leq d_i), d = min(d_1, \cdots, d_n) \end{array}}{\vdash^\sigma_{at} \langle\langle !a,t\rangle\rangle_d} \quad \text{(Inconsistency)}$$

**Fig. 2.** d-rules for attribute certificates

The following theorem proves the correctness of the information provided by SOAs. In summary, it establishes that each certificate issued is true.

**Theorem 1 (Soundness).** *For each attribute $a \in \mathcal{A}^*$ and target $t \in T_\sigma$, if a SOA $\sigma$ exists such that $\vdash^\sigma_{at} \langle\langle a,t\rangle\rangle_d$ then $\forall m.ctime \leq m \leq d$, $a \in K(m)(t)$, that is, SOAs only certify true attribute certificates.*

## 4.2 Dealing with Negation

In the previous section we have managed three types of negation: "$\neg$", "!" and "$\nvdash^\sigma_{at}$". In this section, we clarify the relations among them, and their effect when a particular SOA $\sigma$ must issue certificates.

**Definition 2.** *We say that $\sigma \in S$ does not issue an attribute certificate $\langle\langle a,t\rangle\rangle_d$ and denote it as $\vdash^\sigma_{at} \neg\langle\langle a,t\rangle\rangle_d$ iff $\nvdash^\sigma_{at} \langle\langle a,t\rangle\rangle_d$.*

Observe that $\vdash^\sigma_{at} \neg\langle\langle a,t\rangle\rangle_d$ has the effect of denying target $t$ the access to resources if attribute $a$ is necessary. However, this refutation may be produced due to very different motives, as commented on below.

Expression $\vdash^\sigma_{at} \neg\langle\langle a,t\rangle\rangle_d$ means that SOA $\sigma$ cannot assert $\langle\langle a,t\rangle\rangle_d$. This may occur when $\langle\langle a,t\rangle\rangle_d$ cannot be deduced because there is no sufficient information in SOAs to assure it. However this situation may also take place if $\sigma$ may deduce the opposite attribute, i. e., if $\vdash^\sigma_{at} \langle\langle \neg a,t\rangle\rangle_d$. That is, $\vdash^\sigma_{at} \neg\langle\langle a,t\rangle\rangle_d$ is weaker than $\vdash^\sigma_{at} \langle\langle \neg a,t\rangle\rangle_d$. It may be that $\sigma$ cannot derive $\langle\langle a,t\rangle\rangle_d$, even although the assertion is true, that is, $\forall m.ctime \leq m \leq d, a \in K(m)(t)$, or equivalently, target $t$ does hold $a$ until time instant $d$.

On the other hand, note that $\langle\langle !a,t\rangle\rangle_d$ is different from $\langle\langle \neg a,t\rangle\rangle_d$. The first expression assures that target $t$ does not hold $a$ until time $d$, while the second one says that $t$ holds $\neg a$ until time $d$.

From the user point of view, as commented on above, the three negations imply that $t$ is not allowed to access a given resource, if attribute $a$ is necessary.

We now formalize the relations among these three types of negations.

Using condition (4.2), it is sound to add the d-rules of Figure 1 to Figure 3.

$$\mathbf{R0} \quad \frac{\forall \tau \langle\langle \neg a \rangle\rangle \in \mathcal{C}_\sigma}{\vdash_r^\sigma \tau \langle\langle \neg a \rangle\rangle \to \langle\langle !a \rangle\rangle} \quad \text{(Negation)}$$

**Fig. 3.** New d-rules for certificate classes

The following proposition shows how "$\neg$", "$!$" and "$\not\vdash_{at}^\sigma$" are related.

**Proposition 2.** $\forall \sigma \in \mathcal{S}, t \in T_\sigma, m \in \mathbb{N}$,

$$\vdash_{at}^\sigma \langle\langle \neg a, t \rangle\rangle_m \Rightarrow \vdash_{at}^\sigma \langle\langle !a, t \rangle\rangle_m \Rightarrow \vdash_{at}^\sigma \neg\langle\langle a, t \rangle\rangle_m. \tag{4.5}$$

## 5   Conclusions and Further Work

The SAC model has proven to be scalable and applicable to different environments with heterogeneous and complex access criteria. Moreover, other access control models can be represented within SAC. An infrastructure implementing this access control model called XSCD (XML-based Secure Content Distribution), complemented by autonomous enforcement mechanisms, has been developed and successfully applied to information commerce [12], digital rights management [13] and secure content distribution in digital libraries [22]. Another interesting application scenario for SAC is Web Services, where SAC achieved the desired semantic interoperability [21], and CORBA architecture [11].

The ability to perform a semantic validation of access control policies was an essential design goal of the SAC model. Both the Semantic Policy Language (SPL) defined in SAC and the semantic descriptions of the certificates issued by each SOA (conveyed by SOAD documents) were designed to serve this objective. The semantic validation ensures that the policies written by the security administrator produce the desired effects. In this paper, we have presented the semantic validation algorithms for access control policies developed as part of SAC. Additionally, the SAC model has been formalized and some important features have been formally proved. More specifically, the inference rules for deducting new information have been presented as part of this formal model, providing proofs of the correctness of SAC inference rules.

Regarding future work, model checking of the semantic validation algorithms will be developed in the near future. On the other hand, we are now working on the extension of the Semantic Policy Language with additional digital rights specification, along with semantic models for its management.

## References

1. A. Baraani, J. Pieprzyk, and R. Safavi-Naini. Security In Databases: A Survey Study, 1996.
2. E. Bertino, S. Castano, and E. Ferrari. Securing XML documents with Author-X. *IEEE Internet Computing*, 5(3):21–31, May/June 2001.

3. M. Blaze, J. Feigenbaum, J. Ioannidis, and A.D. Keromytis. The role of trust management in distributed systems security. *Secure Internet Programming: Issues in Distributed and Mobile Object Systems*, pages 185–210, 1993.
4. M. Blaze, J. Feigenbaum, and J. Lacy. Decentralized Trust Management. In *Proc. of the IEEE Symposium on Security and Privacy*, pages 164–173, 1996.
5. D. W. Chadwick and A. Otenko. The PERMIS X.509 role based privilege management infrastructure. *Future Generation Computer Systems*, 19(2):277–289, 2003.
6. E. Damiani, S. de Capitani di Vimercati, S. Paraboschi, and P. Samarati. A Fine-Grained Access Control System for XML Documents. *In ACM Transactions on Information and System Security (TISSEC)*, 5(2):169–202, May 2002.
7. M. Thompson et al. Certificate-based Access Control for Widely Distributed Resources. In *Proc. of the 8th USENIX Security Symposium*, pages 215–227, 1999.
8. ITU-T. Recommendation X.509: Information Technology - Open Systems Interconnection - The Directory: Public-key and attribute certificate frameworks. http://www.itu.int/rec/recommendation.asp?type=folders&lang=e&parent=t-rec-x.509, 2000.
9. S. Jajodia, P. Samarati, and V.S. Subrahmanian. A Logical Language for Expressing Authorizations. In *Proc. of the IEEE Symposium on Security and Privacy*, pages 31–42, 1997.
10. M. Kudo and S. Hada. XML Document Security based on Provisional Authorisation. In *Proc. of the 7th ACM Conference on Computer and Communications Security*, pages 87–96, 2000.
11. J. López, A. Maña, J.J.Ortega, J.M. Troya, and M.I. Yagüe. Integrating PMI services in CORBA Applications. *Computer Standards and Interfaces Journal*, 25(4):391–409, 2003.
12. A. Maña, M.I. Yagüe, and V. Benjumea. Ec-gate: Electronic commerce based on e-gate technology, Golden Award of EGATE Open Contest 2002, paris, november 2002.
13. A. Maña, M.I. Yagüe, and V. Benjumea. EC-GATE: An Infrastructure for DRM. In *Proc. of the IASTED Intl. Conference on Communication, Network, and Information Security*, pages 283–288, 2003.
14. OASIS. XACML 1.1 Specification Set, 2003.
15. X. Qian and T.F. Lunt. A MAC Policy Framework for Multilevel Relational Databases. *IEEE Transactions on Knowledge and Data Engineering*, 8(1):1–14, February 1996.
16. P. Samarati and S. de Capitani di Vimercati. Access Control: Policies, Models, and Mechanisms. In *FOSAD 2000*, volume 2171 of *Lecture Notes in Computer Science*, pages 137–196. Springer, 2001.
17. R.S. Sandhu, E.J. Coyne, H.L. Feinstein, and C.E. Youman. Role-Based Access control Models. *IEEE Computer*, 29(2):38–47, 1996.
18. T. Sundsted. With Liberty and single sign-on for all. The Liberty Alliance Project seeks to solve the current online identity crisis, 2002.
19. T.Y.C. Woo and S.S. Lam. Authorizations in distributed systems: A new approach. *Journal of Computer Security*, 2(2):107–136, 1993.
20. M.I. Yagüe. *Modelo basado en Metadatos para la Integración Semántica en Entornos Distribuidos. Aplicación al Escenario de Control de Accesos*. Ph.D. dissertation, Computer Science Department. University of Málaga, 2003.
21. M.I. Yagüe, A. Maña, and J. López. A Metadata-based Access Control Model for Web Services. *Internet Research Journal: Electronic Networking Applications and Policy*, 25(1):99–116, 2005.

22. M.I. Yagüe, A. Maña, J. López, J. Pimentel, and J.M. Troya. A Secure Solution for Commercial Digital Libraries. *Online Information Review Journal*, 27(3):147–159, 2003.
23. M.I. Yagüe, A. Maña, J. López, and J.M. Troya. Applying the Semantic Web Layers to Access Control. In *Proc. of the Int. Workshop on Web Semantics*, pages 47–63. IEEE Computer Society Press, September 2003.
24. M.I. Yagüe and J.M. Troya. A Semantic Approach for Access Control in Web Services. In *Proc. of the W3C Euroweb 2002 International Conference*, 2002.

# A   Example

To illustrate the inference rules stated on SOAD documents as the basis for the semantic validation of policies, let us consider an editorial and its digital library composed of books, magazines, bulletin news and other relevant publications. The editorial has some special discounts for some customers; and also privileged customers who can freely access some types of resources. For example, the University of Málaga has a particular membership with this editorial which grants some privileges to their staff.

The access control system is based on the Semantic Access Control model, and hence we have the separated specifications of PAS, SRR, and Policy to describe access control criteria. Figure 4 is the XML representation of the semantic properties relevant to access to the Computer News magazine. Figure 5.a shows a simple policy (FreeDownload.xml) that defines as access criteria to be holder of an attribute certificate signed by the SOA of the editorial attesting the subscription to the editorial Portal. Figure 5.b represents the Policy Allocation Specification document which allocates the FreeDownload.xml policy to magazine items accessible in the digital library through the portal.

When a user tries to access the Computer News magazine through the Mc-Grow portal, thanks to the semantic information represented in the Secured Resource Representation for this object (Figure 4), dynamic allocation is made on the basis of PAS of Figure 5.b. Therefore, the policy of Figure 5.a is used to control the access to this object, based on its semantic property of being a magazine.

As in any access control scheme based on attribute certificates, the semantics of policies in the SAC model heavily depend on the semantics of attribute

```
<?xml version="1.0" encoding="UTF-8"?>
<SRR xmlns="http://www.lcc.uma.es/~yague"
xmlns:xsi="http://www.w3.org/2001/XMLSchema-instance"
xsi:schemaLocation="http://www.lcc.uma.es/ yague SRR.xsd"
Resource="http://www.mcgrow.com/" >
        <Property>
            <PropertyName>PublicationName</PropertyName>
            <PropertyValue>Computer_News</PropertyValue>
        </Property>
        <Property>
            <PropertyName>PublicationType</PropertyName>
            <PropertyValue>magazine</PropertyValue>
        </Property>
</SRR>
```

Fig. 4. SRR for the Computer_News magazine

```
<?xml version="1.0" encoding="UTF-8"?>
<Policy xmlns="http://www.lcc.uma.es/~yague"
xmlns:xsi=
"http://www.w3.org/2001/XMLSchema-instance"
xsi:schemaLocation=
"http://www.lcc.uma.es/~yague Policy.xsd" >
<AccessRules>
    <AccessRule>
        <AttributeSet>
            <Attribute>
                <AttributeName>Subscription
                </AttributeName>
                <AttributeValue>Portal
                </AttributeValue>
                <SOA_ID>McGrow_SOA</SOA_ID>
            </Attribute>
        </AttributeSet>
    </AccessRule>
</AccessRules>
</Policy>
```

```
<?xml version="1.0" encoding="UTF-8"?>
<PAS xmlns=
"http://www.lcc.uma.es/~yague"
xmlns:xsi="http://www.w3.org/2001/XMLSchema-instance"
xsi:schemaLocation=
"http://www.lcc.uma.es/~yague pas.xsd" >
<Policy>FreeDownload.xml</Policy>
<Object>
  <ObjectLocation>http://www.mcgrow.com/portal/
  </ObjectLocation>
  <Conditions>
    <Condition>
        <PropertyName>PublicationType
        </PropertyName>
        <PropertyValue>magazine
        </PropertyValue>
    </Condition>
  </Conditions>
</Object>
</PAS>
```

**Fig. 5.** (a) FreeDownload.xml policy (b) PAS for magazines

```
<?xml version="1.0" encoding="UTF-8"?>
<SOAD xmlns:xsi="http://www.w3.org/2001/XMLSchema-instance"
xsi:noNamespaceSchemaLocation="SOAD.xsd" >
    <SOA_ID>UMA_SOA</SOA_ID>
    <ACDeclarations>
        <SOAAttribute>
            <AttributeName>Member</AttributeName>
            <AttributeValue>UMA</AttributeValue>
        </SOAAttribute>
    </ACDeclarations>
    <ACRelations>
        <SOARule>
            <AttributeSet>
            <SOAAttribute>
                <AttributeName>Member</AttributeName>
                <AttributeValue>CSDepartment</AttributeValue>
                <SOA_ID>CSDpt_SOA<SOA_ID>
            </SOAAttribute>
            </AttributeSet>
            <Relation>Implies</Relation>
            <AttributeSet>
            <SOAAttribute>
                <AttributeName>Member</AttributeName>
                <AttributeValue>UMA</AttributeValue>
            </SOAAttribute>
            </AttributeSet>
        </SOARule>
    </ACRelations>
</SOAD>
```

**Fig. 6.** SOAD of the University of Málaga SOA

certificates which we have modelled in SOAD (Source of Authorization Description) documents. Figure 6 shows the descriptions of the source of authorization that certifies the membership to the University of Malaga (UMA). The rule of this SOAD states that the Source Of Authorization (SOA) of UMA trusts in the SOA of the Computer Science Department for attesting to membership to the department. That is, in order to prove UMA membership, to present an attribute certificate signed by the CS department SOA attesting to being a member of this department will be equivalent to presenting an attribute certificate signed by the UMA attesting to membership of the UMA. Figure 7 shows the descriptions of the source of authorization corresponding to the McGrow editorial. Relations among attributes certified by each SOA are also described in these documents.

The SOAD corresponding to the McGrow editorial has two rules. The first rule states that to be a member of UMA with a trusted certificate from UMA_SOA implies being a McGrow special customer and, additionally, being

```
<?xml version="1.0" encoding="UTF-8"?>
<SOAD xmlns:xsi=
"http://www.w3.org/2001/XMLSchema-instance"
xsi:noNamespaceSchemaLocation="SOAD.xsd">
<SOA_ID>McGrow_SOA</SOA_ID>
<ACDeclarations>
    <SOAAttribute>
        <AttributeName>Suscription
        </AttributeName>
        <AttributeValue>McGrow_Portal
        </AttributeValue>
    </SOAAttribute>
    <SOAAttribute>
        <AttributeName>Subscription
        </AttributeName>
        <AttributeValue>Computer_News
        </AttributeValue>
    </SOAAttribute>
    <SOAAttribute>
        <AttributeName>Subscription
        </AttributeName>
        <AttributeValue>Math_News
        </AttributeValue>
    </SOAAttribute>
    <SOAAttribute>
        <AttributeName>Customer
        </AttributeName>
        <AttributeValue>Privileged
        </AttributeValue>
    </SOAAttribute>
</ACDeclarations>
```

```
/* being member of UMA implies to be a customer with
some privileges and subscription to the editorial portal */
<ACRelations>
<SOARule>
    <AttributeSet>
        <SOAAttribute>
        <AttributeName>Member</AttributeName>
        <AttributeValue>UMA</AttributeValue>
        <SOA_ID>UMA_SOA</SOA_ID>
        </SOAAttribute>
    </AttributeSet>
    <Relation>Implies</Relation>
    <AttributeSet>
        <SOAAttribute>
        <AttributeName>Customer</AttributeName>
        <AttributeValue>Privileged</AttributeValue>
        <SOA_ID>MacGrow_SOA</SOA_ID>
        </SOAAttribute>
        <SOAAttribute>
        <AttributeName>Subscription</AttributeName>
        <AttributeValue>McGrow_Portal </AttributeValue>
        <SOA_ID>MacGrow_SOA</SOA_ID>
        </SOAAttribute>
    </AttributeSet>
</SOARule>
</ACRelations>

<ACRelations>
<SOARule>
    <AttributeSet>
        <SOAAttribute>
        <AttributeName>Suscription</AttributeName>
        <AttributeValue>McGrow_Portal</AttributeValue>
        </SOAAttribute>
    </AttributeSet>
    <Relation>Implies</Relation>
    <AttributeSet>
        <SOAAttribute>
        <AttributeName>Subscription</AttributeName>
        <AttributeValue>Computer_News</AttributeValue>
        </SOAAttribute>
    <AttributeSet>
        <SOAAttribute>
        <AttributeName>Subscription</AttributeName>
        <AttributeValue>Math_News</AttributeValue>
        </SOAAttribute>
    </AttributeSet>
</SOARule>
</ACRelations>
</SOAD>
```

**Fig. 7.** SOAD of the McGrow Editorial SOA

| $\sigma_{uma}\langle\langle\text{MemUma}\rangle\rangle \rightarrow \langle\langle\text{CPriv}\rangle\rangle$ | $\sigma_{cs}\langle\langle\text{MemCS}\rangle\rangle \rightarrow \langle\langle\text{MemUma}\rangle\rangle$ |
|---|---|
| $\sigma_{uma}\langle\langle\text{MemUma}\rangle\rangle \rightarrow \langle\langle\text{S\_MGPortal}\rangle\rangle$ | |
| $\sigma_{mg}\langle\langle\text{S\_MGPortal}\rangle\rangle \rightarrow \langle\langle\text{S\_CNews}\rangle\rangle$ | |
| $\sigma_{mg}\langle\langle\text{S\_MGPortal}\rangle\rangle \rightarrow \langle\langle\text{S\_MNews}\rangle\rangle$ | |

**Fig. 8.** Rules in $\text{SOAD}_{\sigma_{mg}}$ and $\text{SOAD}_{\sigma_{uma}}$

subscribed to its portal. The second rule states that a certificate of being subscribed to the portal implies a certificate of subscription to the Computer_News
and Math_News magazines.

To see the important role of the inference mechanisms developed, we consider a professor of UMA who wants to access one of the CS_News magazines.
If this professor presents an attribute certificate signed by the Computer Science department SOA stating he/she is a professor of this University then this
certificate will be equivalent to an attribute certificate signed by the McGrow
Editorial of being subscribed to the portal. Therefore, the policy requisites stated

on the access control policy will be satisfied and he/she will get free access to
this document.

Finally, let us consider derivation rules stated in SOAD documents and how
information from certificate classes is deduced. Let $\sigma_{mg}$, $\sigma_{uma}$ and $\sigma_{cs}$ be the
SOAs for the McGrow Editorial, the University of Málaga and the Computer
Science Department. Figure 8 shows the rules included in the Source Of Authorization Description (SOAD) documents of MacGrow and UMA. In SOAD$_{\sigma_{mg}}$,
the first rule states that to be member of UMA implies to be a Privileged Customer of MacGrow. Second rule states that to be a member of UMA implies
being subscribed to the MacGrow Portal. Last two rules state that to be subscribed to this portal implies being subscribed to the Computer News and Math
News magazines, respectively. The only rule of SOAD $_{\sigma_{uma}}$ states that to be a
member of the Computer Science Department implies being a member of the
University of Malaga. Now, suppose that $\vdash_{at}^{\sigma_{cs}} \sigma_{cs}\langle\langle \text{MemCS}, \text{MYagüe}\rangle\rangle$, that is, the
Computer Science Department is able to certify that MYagüe is a member of the
Department.

The following derivation shows how SOA $\sigma_{mg}$ infers she can access the Computer News magazine, using the d-rules described above. For the sake of simplicity, we have dropped the time parameter, assuming that attribute certificates are
always valid. We have divided the derivation into three parts. The last derivation
makes use of the results previously obtained to reach the conclusion. Note that
the rule applied appears at the left side of each derivation.

$$\textbf{(A2)} \quad \textbf{(R1)} \; \frac{\sigma_{cs}\langle\langle \text{MemCS}\rangle\rangle \rightarrow \langle\langle \text{MemUma}\rangle\rangle \in SOAD_{\sigma_{uma}}}{\vdash_r^{\sigma_{uma}} \sigma_{cs}\langle\langle \text{MemCS}\rangle\rangle \rightarrow \langle\langle \text{MemUma}\rangle\rangle}$$
$$\frac{\vdash_{at}^{\sigma_{cs}} \langle\langle \text{MemCS}, \text{MYagüe}\rangle\rangle}{\vdash_{at}^{\sigma_{uma}} \langle\langle \text{MemUma}, \text{MYagüe}\rangle\rangle}$$

$$\textbf{(R1)} \; \frac{\sigma_{uma}\langle\langle \text{MemUma}\rangle\rangle \rightarrow \langle\langle \text{S\_MGPortal}\rangle\rangle \in SOAD_{\sigma_{mg}}}{\vdash_r^{\sigma_{mg}} \sigma_{uma}\langle\langle \text{MemUma}\rangle\rangle \rightarrow \langle\langle \text{S\_MGPortal}\rangle\rangle}$$

$$\textbf{(R1)} \; \frac{\sigma_{mg}\langle\langle \text{S\_MGPortal}\rangle\rangle \rightarrow \langle\langle \text{S\_CNews}\rangle\rangle \in SOAD_{\sigma_{mg}}}{\vdash_r^{\sigma_{mg}} \sigma_{mg}\langle\langle \text{S\_MGPortal}\rangle\rangle \rightarrow \langle\langle \text{S\_CNews}\rangle\rangle}$$

$$\textbf{(R2)} \; \frac{\vdash_r^{\sigma_{mg}} \sigma_{uma}\langle\langle \text{MemUma}\rangle\rangle \rightarrow \langle\langle \text{S\_MGPortal}\rangle\rangle \; \vdash_r^{\sigma_{mg}} \sigma_{mg}\langle\langle \text{S\_MGPortal}\rangle\rangle \rightarrow \langle\langle \text{S\_CNews}\rangle\rangle}{\vdash_r^{\sigma_{mg}} \sigma_{uma}\langle\langle \text{MemUma}\rangle\rangle \rightarrow \langle\langle \text{S\_CNews}\rangle\rangle}$$

$$\textbf{(A2)} \; \frac{\vdash_{at}^{\sigma_{uma}} \langle\langle \text{MemUma}, \text{MYagüe}\rangle\rangle \; \vdash_r^{\sigma_{mg}} \sigma_{uma}\langle\langle \text{MemUma}\rangle\rangle \rightarrow \langle\langle \text{S\_CNews}\rangle\rangle}{\vdash_{at}^{\sigma_{mg}} \langle\langle \text{S\_CNews}, \text{MYagüe}\rangle\rangle}$$

# B   Proofs

**Proposition 1.** If $\vdash_r^{\sigma} \sigma_1\langle\langle a_1\rangle\rangle, \cdots, \sigma_n\langle\langle a_n\rangle\rangle \rightarrow \langle\langle c\rangle\rangle$ then $\forall m \in \mathbb{N}, t \in T_{\sigma}$, if
$\{a_1, \cdots, a_n\} \subseteq K(m)(t) \Rightarrow c \in K(m)(t)$.

*Proof.* Denote $R \equiv \; \vdash_r^{\sigma} \sigma_1\langle\langle a_1\rangle\rangle, \cdots, \sigma_n\langle\langle a_n\rangle\rangle \rightarrow \langle\langle c\rangle\rangle$, and consider $t \in T_{\sigma}$
and $m \in \mathbb{N}$ such that $\{a_1, \cdots, a_n\} \subseteq K(m)(t)$. Now, we reason by induction on
the depth of the derivation tree to produce $R$.

- Base case. If $\sigma_1\langle\langle a_1\rangle\rangle, \cdots, \sigma_n\langle\langle a_n\rangle\rangle \rightarrow \langle\langle c\rangle\rangle \in SOAD_{\sigma}$, the proof is directly
  derived from condition (4.4).
- Inductive case. We have two possible cases:

1.  If $R$ has been obtained applying rule **R2**, there exists $d \in \mathcal{A}$ and two rules such that $\vdash_r^\sigma \sigma_1\langle\langle a_1\rangle\rangle, \cdots, \sigma_n\langle\langle a_n\rangle\rangle \rightarrow \langle\langle d\rangle\rangle$, and $\vdash_r^\sigma \sigma\langle\langle d\rangle\rangle \rightarrow \langle\langle c\rangle\rangle$. Applying successively the induction hypothesis to these rules, firstly we deduce $d \in K(m)(t)$, and then $c \in K(m)(t)$.

2.  If $R$ has been obtained applying rule **R4**, then $\exists b \in \mathcal{A}.c =!b$ and $R \equiv \vdash_r^\sigma \tau\langle\langle a\rangle\rangle \rightarrow \langle\langle !b\rangle\rangle$. Applying the induction hypothesis to $\vdash_r^\tau \sigma\langle\langle b\rangle\rangle \rightarrow \langle\langle !a\rangle\rangle$, we have that if $b \in K(m)(t)$ then $a \notin K(m)(t)$. Thus, assuming that $a \in K(m)(t)$, we deduce that $b \notin K(m)(t)$, or equivalently by definition (condition (4.1)) that $c =!b \in K(m)(t)$.

**Theorem 1.** For each attribute $a \in \mathcal{A}^*$ and target $t \in T_\sigma$, if a SOA $\sigma$ exists such that $\vdash_{at}^\sigma \langle\langle a, t\rangle\rangle_d$ then $\forall m.ctime \leq m \leq d, a \in K(m)(t)$, that is, SOAs only certify true attribute certificates.

*Proof.* By induction on the depth of the derivation tree to assert $\langle\langle a, t\rangle\rangle_d$.

–  If $\langle\langle a, t\rangle\rangle_d \in \Sigma_\sigma$ then, by condition (4.3), we have that $\forall m.ctime \leq m \leq d, a \in K(m)(t)$.

–  Let us assume that we have applied rule **A2** to deduce $\langle\langle a, t\rangle\rangle_d$. Consider an index $i(1 \leq i \leq n)$. By induction hypothesis, if $\vdash_{at}^{\sigma_i} \langle\langle a_i, t\rangle\rangle_{d_i}, ctime \leq d_i$ then $\forall m_i.ctime \leq m_i \leq d_i, a_i \in K(m_i)(t)$. Thus, defining $d = min(d_1, \cdots, d_n)$, we deduce that $\forall m.ctime \leq m \leq d, \{a_1, \cdots, a_n\} \subseteq K(m)(t)$. Finally, applying Proposition 1 to $\vdash_r^\sigma \sigma_1\langle\langle a_1\rangle\rangle, \cdots, \sigma_n\langle\langle a_n\rangle\rangle \rightarrow \langle\langle a\rangle\rangle$, it is derived $\forall m.ctime \leq m \leq d, a \in K(m)(t)$.

–  The proof corresponding to applying **A3** in the derivation is similar to the previous one.

# A Generic XACML Based Declarative Authorization Scheme for Java
## Architecture and Implementation

Rajeev Gupta and Manish Bhide

IBM India Research Lab, Block 1, IIT Delhi, India, +91-11-26861100
{grajeev, abmanish}@in.ibm.com

**Abstract.** Security and authorization play a very important role in the development, deployment and functioning of software systems. Java being the most popular platform for component-based software and systems, Java security is playing a key role in enterprise systems. The major drawback in the security support provided by J2EE and J2SE is the absence of a standard way to support instance level access control. JAAS does provide some help, but it is not without its share of problems. The newest standard related to security - XACML, provides a standard simple way to represent security policies. In the paper we propose a unique way to extend JAAS technology so that it can support class-instance level access control in a declarative manner. We then showcase how this extension can be molded in the XACML architecture, thereby providing an end-to-end standard based access control specification and implementation for J2SE and J2EE applications. The major advantage of our technique is that, being declarative it does not require any change to the security code when - either the security policies are changed or the security infrastructure is deployed in a new environment.

## 1 Introduction

The exponential growth of e-commerce in the recent past has lead to a proportional increase in the complexity of software systems. This complexity has also lead to an increase in security and authorization needs of enterprise applications. In order to deal with this complexity, various proprietary and application specific languages [1, 2, 3] that help in specifying access control policies of enterprise systems have been proposed. XACML is one such general-purpose access control policy language, which in addition to being a standard, is generic, distributed and powerful [4]. It provides an XML based access control policy language as well as an access control decision request/response language, which can be used by applications and systems to fulfill their access control needs. The XACML specification deals with the framework and the exact implementation details of the access control engine are left for the implementers.

Java is the most popular platform for component based software and has played a key role in the popularity of e-commerce applications. Java has its own

S. De Capitani di Vimercati et al. (Eds.): ESORICS 2005, LNCS 3679, pp. 44–63, 2005.

standardized mechanism to provide user-based security and access control called, Java Authentication and Authorization service (JAAS). JAAS has played a key role in securing these enterprise applications. The advancements in enterprise applications have lead to rapid changes in the requirements and needs of the software developer. The Java language has tried to keep pace with these needs by adding new features such as Data Access Objects [6], remote monitoring and management of JVM [5], class data sharing, generic types etc. But fulfilling the security needs of Java applications is still closely tied with application code [13], leading to an ad-hoc, application specific development of security and access control implementations.

In the J2EE architecture, providing authentication and access control is delegated to the application server. A declarative XML based mechanism is used to specify the access control needs of the J2EE applications. But such an access control can be provided only at a method-level granularity. The state or logic of the software object/component does not factor into the access control decision. This is very restrictive and policies such as: *"Employees can only view their own salaries from the salary database";* are implemented programmatically.

This paper tries to bridge the gap between XACML based specification of access control needs and standard security implementation for Java and outlines an XACML implementation for Java applications. The XACML implementation proposed in this paper provides a generic and declarative mechanism for providing access control in Java applications. Our technique uses an innovative extension of JAAS to attain our objectives. Thus, the contributions of this paper include:

- We propose a standard based implementation of XACML for Java using an innovative extension of JAAS. In other words, we show how XACML and JAAS can co-exist thereby providing end-to-end standards based access control specification and implementation for Java language.
- Our technique provides a mechanism for supporting instance level authorization in Java applications using declarative specifications.
- We provide a method of writing declarative security policies for Java applications

The rest of the paper is organized as follows: A brief introduction to XACML architecture is given in section 2. Section 3 gives an overview of Java security and JAAS, explaining their deficiencies in providing fine-grained access control. Section 4 outlines how JAAS can be extended so as to provide declarative authorization support in Java while using XACML standards. Related work is discussed in Section 5 and Section 6 concludes the paper.

## 2   XACML

One of the basic reasoning for the development of XACML was the need to have a standard, generic and powerful access control specification language. Existence of various proprietary languages provided piecemeal solutions to security issues

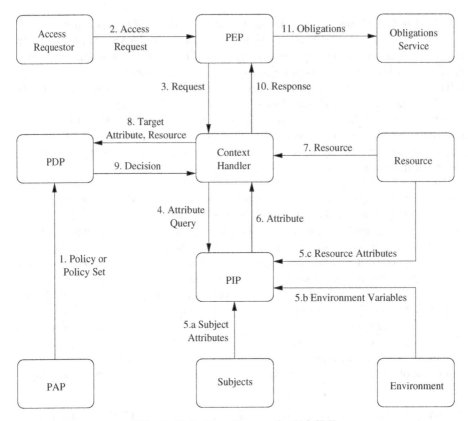

**Fig. 1.** Data flow diagram for XACML

of the enterprise. XACML tries to bridge this gap and provides a common language for expressing security policy across the enterprise. It allows the enterprise to manage the enforcement of all the elements of its security policy in all the components of its information systems. XACML is generic thus it can be used in various environments. As XACML is used across various components of the enterprise application, management of the access control policy becomes easier.

The data flow diagram of Figure 1 shows the major actors in the XACML domain, which are important for our approach. Main components of this architecture are:

1. **PEP:** The Policy Enforcement Point is the system entity that performs access control by making decision request and enforcing authorization decisions. This is the entry point for access control infrastructure. Consider an example of an e-commerce application, which supports auctions. In this application, each request (to bid, to create an auction etc.) made by the user will be routed through a software component, which will send it out to an entity responsible for making the access decision (allow/deny). Such an entity, which makes a callout to the access control component, is the PEP of the application.

2. **PDP:** This is the core of the framework and is responsible for evaluating the applicable access control policies and to render the authorization decision as one of four values: *permit, deny, indeterminate or not applicable*. In the above example, the entity which makes the decision to allow or deny the request is the PDP. The PDP will evaluate the access control rules, which could include policies like *"Only a user who has created the auction should be able to modify it"*.

3. **PIP:** This component acts as a source of attribute values. The responsibility of this component is to provide all the information that might be required by the PDP to make the access decision. Attributes are characteristics of the resource being managed (e.g. *who is the owner of auction bid*), the user making the request, action (*read or modify*) or environment (*office hours*).

4. **Context Handler:** This is a system entity that converts decision requests in the native request format to the XACML canonical form and converts authorization decisions in the XACML canonical form to the native response format. The context handler allows the use of XACML in a variety of application environments. This component is one of the key components of our solution, as it allows the JAAS specific data to be converted into decision requests, which are understood by the PDP.

The context handler forms the access control request based on the attributes of the requester, action, resource and environment. This information is provided to the PDP to find the access control policy applicable for the request. The access control policy is defined in terms of the attributes of the requester, action, environment and resource. The policy can also include functions defined on these attributes. The PDP performs the following two operations to arrive at a decision: (1) It first tries to find all the policies applicable for the request and (2) then it evaluates these policies and returns the decision back to the PEP (via the context handler). PAP is the policy administrative point, responsible for managing access control policies. The curious reader is requested to refer to [4] for further details about XACML. We now explain why standard JAAS based access control is not sufficient for enterprise applications, and how JAAS can be extended to overcome its drawbacks.

# 3   Java Security and JAAS

## 3.1   Java 2 Security

Java 2 uses policy based security architecture. The security policy (Figure 2) is defined by a set of permissions for code in various locations (*codeBase*) and by various signers. These permissions allow certain actions on a certain resource. Resource names and their associated actions are enumerated in a policy file. In Java 2, *AccessController* is used as the security enforcer. The example policy file in Figure 2 gives all permissions to the jar files present in the *${java.home}/lib/ext* directory, whereas read permissions on some system properties, are given to all the other code bases.

```
grant codeBase "file:${java.home}/lib/ext/*" {
   permission java.security.AllPermission;
};

grant {
   permission java.util.PropertyPermission "os.name", "read";
   permission java.util.PropertyPermission "os.version", "read";
   permission java.util.PropertyPermission "os.arch", "read";
};
```

**Fig. 2.** Policy file in Java

```
SafeFileWriter() {
   Permission perm = new java.io.FilePermission("foo.txt", "write");
   AccessController.checkPermission(perm);
   // Write to foo.txt
}
```

**Fig. 3.** Protecting a method using AccessController

The example method in Figure 3 shows the typical way in which a protected resource is accessed using Java methods. Before performing the operation, the method calls the *AccessController* with the permissions required to perform operations on the resource being accessed. The *AccessController* checks the requested permission with the application's current authorization policy. If any permission defined in the policy file implies the requested permission, the method *checkPermission* simply returns; otherwise an *AccessControlException* is thrown. The *SafeFileWriter* is used for writing in the file *foo.txt*. Thus before writing, the *AccessController* is called to check whether writing to the file is allowed. The major drawback of Java 2 security is that it does not have user, role or object based permissions. The user based access control is added in Java 2 using JAAS, which is explained next.

### 3.2   Java Authentication and Authorization Service

The Java Authentication and Authorization Service (JAAS) is a set of APIs that enable Java applications to authenticate and enforce access controls upon users. JAAS reliably and securely determines who is currently executing the Java code and whether the user is allowed to do so. JAAS adds subject-based policies to the Java 2 security model. For this the user is first authenticated and the *javax.security.auth.Subject* class is used to encapsulate the credentials of the authenticated user. A *Subject* can have multiple identities called *Principals*. In a JAAS policy file, each grant statement is associated with a *Principal*. For each *Principal* associated with the *Subject*, the *AccessController* gets permissions

```
grant codebase "file:./MyAction.jar",
      Principal sample.principal.ExamplePrincipal "Bob" {
           permission java.io.FilePermission "max.txt", "read";
      };
```

**Fig. 4.** Principal based authorization in JAAS

from the policy file and checks whether any permission implies the requested permission. Otherwise, it throws an *AccessControlException*. Figure 4 shows a typical authorization policy file in JAAS. It allows Java classes in *MyAction.jar* to read *max.txt* if the particular class is accessed by *Bob*. All other users are not allowed to access the resource.

The standard policy file format of JAAS does not support security policies that are based on the properties of the application object on which the policy is defined. This precludes the definition of policies such as *"A manager is allowed to edit the salary information only of his direct reports"*. Using JAAS, if a user (manager) is allowed to call method *editSalary* then the user is allowed to edit salaries of all the employees irrespective of whether the employee is his/her direct report or not. Such policies are very common in any application and custom code is required to enforce such policies. However, JAAS does recognize such needs and it provides mechanisms to extend its standard interfaces to suite the client needs. Possible extensions to JAAS are explained next.

### 3.3   JAAS Extensions

JAAS is build on top of the pre-existing security model of Java, which depends on the *codeBase* accessing the resource and uses the plaintext format policy file implementation. JAAS makes authorization decision based on the *Subject* who is performing the action, the action being performed and the resource being accessed. Thanks to pluggable-features of JAAS, writing custom authentication and authorization sub-modules can change its default behavior. In this section we explain possible extensions which can be used for XACML implementation using JAAS. In order to support instance level access control in JAAS the following JAAS artifacts can be changed:

o *java.security.Principal*: The *Principal* interface represents the abstract notion used to represent an entity such as an individual, an organization, a group or a login id. By extending the *Principal* one can add custom properties which can be used for authorization.

o *java.security.Permission*: The *Permission* class is used in two places namely, (1) The policy file where it represents the permissions given to a user on a *codeBase* and (2) the permission object which is constructed in the code before accessing a resource. In the code the object represents the permission required by the code for accessing a resource. If the policy file grants the requested permission to the *codeBase*, then the action is allowed by JAAS.

As explained in Figure 3, the *AccessController* calls *checkPermission* to know whether the caller has authority to perform the requested action. By default the *Permission* object can specify things like name of the permission (which may indicate the resource on which access is required), action for which the resource is accessed, etc. The *Permission* class implements the *implies* method, which takes as input another *Permission* object. This method is called by the *AccessController* to know whether the requested permission (present in the code) is implied by any permission present in the policy file.

o *java.security.PermissionCollection*: This abstract class is used for representing a collection of *Permission* objects. This class can be implemented to have the desired way of storing the granted *Permission's* and comparing them with the requested *Permission*.

o *java.security.Policy*: It is an abstract class for storing security policies in Java application environment. The *AccessController* contacts the *Policy* implementation to get the set of permissions defined in the policy file for an authenticated *Subject* on a *codeBase*. By-default the *Policy* class is extended by the *PolicyFile* class to read the policy file as depicted in Figure 4. The *Policy* class has *getPermissions* method, which parses the policy file and returns an appropriate *PermissionCollection* object enumerating the permissions of the *codeBase* for the calling *Subject*.

From the above discussion it is fairly clear that JAAS can be extended in a variety of ways to attain various authentication and authorization objectives. But for these extensions one needs to write code to implement or extend various JAAS interfaces and classes respectively. Writing new code, whenever there is change in security requirements, is cumbersome and makes the code difficult to maintain. Further, it precludes the possibility of changing the security settings at deployment time thereby preventing the reuse of code across different domains.

Hence there is clearly a need for a security approach, which is flexible, standard based and which gracefully handles the extension or changes in the security policy without requiring changes to the security code. The key points to be considered while addressing these problems are:

1. JAAS being a Java security standard, the solution should adhere to JAAS security framework
2. The solution should provide fine grained (instance based) access control
3. The solution should enable the modification of the security policy without requiring any change to the security code.

XACML provides a representation of fine-grained security policies across the enterprise. This motivates us to explore whether the marriage of these two technologies/standards can be a solution to our problems? As it turns out, this indeed is the case. The next section outlines our proposed extension to JAAS, which allows XACML to be used with Java applications while having standard based implementation.

# 4    Extending JAAS for XACML Implementation

In the last section we listed the requirements which JAAS based implementation of XACML should meet. In this section we present our XACML implementation for Java, which is generic and declarative. It enables changes in security settings without writing any new code. It is assumed here that the resource being protected is accessed through various Java methods with different methods performing different actions on the resource. In Section 4.1 we present our extensions to JAAS which are required to support generic authorization. Section 4.2 explains the code-flow between a user making an access request and the *AccessController* returning a response. Section 4.3 deals with the mapping between XACML and our unique JAAS extension.

## 4.1    Generic Authorization Using JAAS

To attain the objectives of providing generic and declarative authorization we propose a technique that modifies JAAS in a unique way so that its extension can be written in a declarative manner rather than the conventional programmatic way. Following are the extensions that we have implemented to the standard JAAS classes/interfaces described in the previous section:

1. *GenericPermission*: It extends the standard *Permission* class of JAAS. For implementing attribute level authorization, as mandated by XACML, the class instance (object) representing the resource on which access is requested, needs to be passed to the *Permission* object. The *GenericPermission* has a constructor that takes the object (on which access is requested) as input. The *implies* method of *GenericPermission* is written in such a way that it takes into consideration the attributes of the action, the attributes of the object and the environment variables for deciding whether the granted permission implies the requested permission. The attributes of the resource object required for XACML implementation can be obtained by calling the getter methods on the object instance using Java reflection. This unique extension of the implies method acts as PDP component of the XACML architecture.

2. *GenericPolicy*: The core of our technique lies in the representation of the authorization framework in an XACML policy file. Our *GenericPolicy*, which is an extension of *java.security.Policy* class of JAAS, interprets the authorization policies, written in XACML language. The *getPermissions* method of *GenericPolicy* parses the XACML based policy file and retrieves all the *GenericPermission*'s granted to the specified *Subject* and *codeBase* in the policy file. The permissions are returned in the form of a *GenericPermissionCollection* which is explained next.

3. *GenericPermissionCollection*: This class is used to represent a collection of *GenericPermission* objects.

The access control policy is represented in terms of getter methods (for getting attributes of the resource object) defined on the application objects. The policy allows the use of expressions, which operate on the values returned by the getter methods. If the getter method(s) used in XACML policy are not implemented, the context handler (which is responsible for invoking the getter methods and calling the PDP) throws an exception. For example consider the policy – "*Only a user who has created the auction should be able to modify it*". In this policy, access control is based on *whether the caller is the owner of the auction object.* Thus, we pass the *auction* object to the *GenericPermission* constructor so that the *owner* of the auction can be obtained using *getOwner* method of the auction object.

## 4.2  Code Flow

Here we explain the steps required to protect a resource as well as the steps followed when a user wants to perform some action on the protected resource. Our technique assumes that all resource actions are implemented as methods, and hence whenever a user wants to perform some action on a resource, the corresponding method is accessed. Thus protecting a resource is equivalent to protecting methods performing some action on a Java object representing the resource. Each method, which is required to be protected, needs to start with the construction of *GenericPermission* object having three parameters:

1. The class to which the method belongs,
2. The action which the method wants to perform and
3. The resource object on which the method is called.

This *GenericPermission* object represents the permissions necessary to execute the method. At run-time, if the policy file grants this permission to the code and the user invoking the method, then the access will be allowed by JAAS. Figure 5 shows a method, which updates an auction object, creating the *GenericPermission* object. Then a call is made to the *AccessController* provided by Java. The *GenericPermission* object is passed as a parameter to the *checkPermission* call of the *AccessController*. This ensures that any user who does not have the permissions as indicated by the *GenericPermission* object will be thrown an *AccessControlException*. What follows next are the steps through which the *AccessController* determines permissions for an authenticated user.

```
updateAction() {
     Permission perm = new GenericPermission(String auction,
                              String update, Object auction1);
     AccessController.checkPermission(perm);
     // perform action
}
```

**Fig. 5.** Method protection using by GenericPermission

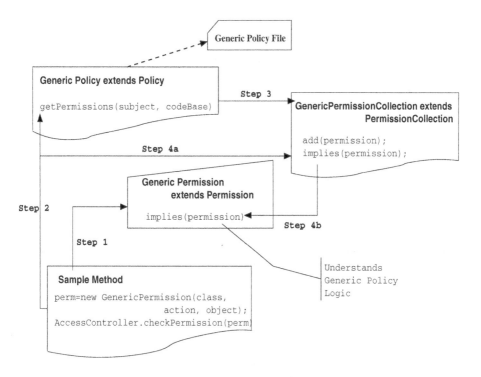

**Fig. 6.** Code Flow for Generic Authorization

Figure 6 shows the code flow of an authorization decision using our generic authorization scheme. In Step 1, a *GenericPermission* object is created. As mentioned earlier, this *GenericPermission* object represents the permission that is necessary to execute the method i.e., to perform the action on the resource. This permission object is then passed as a parameter to the *checkPermission* call of the *AccessController*. The *AccessController* uses the Policy implementation of JAAS to make the authorization decision. The standard Policy implementation of JAAS (*PolicyFile*) cannot understand the XACML policy file. We have extended the *Policy* implementation (called *GenericPolicy*) and our implementation is equipped to handle the XACML format. The Policy implementation to be used by the *AccessController* is specified using the *auth.policy.provider* parameter in the *java.security* file. Changing this parameter setting ensures that the JVM uses the *GenericPolicy* for evaluating the authorization decision instead of the normal PolicyFile provided by JAAS.

The *GenericPolicy* class finds the granted permissions for the given *Subject* and *codeBase* by parsing the XACML file in the *getPermission* method (Step 2). In other words, if a user authenticated as *"Foo"* is accessing some code (in *"abc.jar"*), which is trying to perform an action on an object (resource), then the *getPermissions* method will try to find all the permissions that are given to *"Foo"* for *codeBase* *"abc.jar"* in the XACML policy file. The *getPermission* method returns *GenericPermissionCollection* which is a set of *GenericPermis-*

*sion* objects given to the *Subject* ("Foo") for the given *codeBase* ("abc.jar") in
the XACML policy file (Step 3).

After getting the *GenericPermissionCollection* corresponding to the calling *Subject* and *codeBase*, the *AccessController* calls the implies method of the
*GenericPermissionCollection* (Step 4a). This method has one parameter which
is the *GenericPermission* Object constructed in Step 1. The logical meaning
of this is to find if any one of the permissions in the *GenericPermissionCollection* implies the requested permission (which is constructed in Step 1). In
order to do this, the *implies* method of the *GenericPermissionCollection* iterates through each of the constituent *GenericPermission*'s in the collection. For
each of these *GenericPermission*'s it calls the *implies* method of the *GenericPermission* class (Step 4b). The *implies* method of *GenericPermission* understands
the semantics of the declarative authorization policy specified in the XACML
policy file. Based on the authorization policy specified in the XACML file, it
checks if the requested permission (constructed in Step 1) can be implied from
the granted permission (which is represented by the *GenericPermission* object
itself on which the implies is called). If the *AccessController* finds that any one
of the *GenericPermission.implies* returns true, then it simply returns. If the requested permission is not granted by any policy present in the XACML file or if
is not implied by any of the policies, then an *AccessControlException* is thrown.

The *implies* method of *GenericPermission* uses the resource object instance
to get the values of attributes by calling the getter method using Java reflection
technology. These values are used in the expressions defined on the object attributes as well as environment variables to decide on the imply relationships.
For e.g., consider an authorization policy *"Only a gold user is allowed to access
critical data between 10AM and 4 PM"*. In this policy, the application object, say
an entity bean, will have a getter method that returns the criticality (high/low
etc.) of the data and the policy will be expressed in terms of the return value
of this getter method. If this policy is later changed to *"Only gold and silver
customers are allowed to access stock history data"*, then such a change will
only require a minor change in the XACML policy and no change in the code.

```
grant codebase "file:./MyAction.jar",

    Principal sample.principal.GenericPrincipal "GoldCustomer" {

        permission com.ibm.jaas.GenericPermission
                            Object="StockInfo" action="read";

        CompoundCondition operator="AND" name="C1" name="C2";

        Condition name="C1" type="method" mName="getType"
                        operator="equals" value="confidential";

        Condition name="C2" type="environmentValue"
            mName="getTime" operator="between" lower="10AM"
                                            upper="4PM";

    };
```

**Fig. 7.** XACML based sample JAAS extension policy file

However, using conventional JAAS implementation, even this minor change will require a change in the security code of the application. Thus a clever use of Java reflection and the unique representation of the XACML based authorization policy file, allow us to support fine-grained access control, which can be changed without warranting any change to the authorization code. A sample XACML based JAAS policy is given in the appendix. In order to highlight the difference between the normal JAAS and our extended JAAS implementation, Figure 7 shows the JAAS generic policy represented in non-XACML format. It should be noted that we use an XACML based JAAS policy file (given in appendix), but the non-XACML format (Figure 7) is given for illustrating the differences between the normal and extended version of JAAS.

### 4.3   JAAS and XACML

In this section we explain how our implementation fits into XACML architecture. The policy in XACML can either deny or permit an action on a resource. The parallel of a policy in JAAS is a *permission*, which as the name suggests, only provides closed policy authorizations [16]. Hence our framework consists of permit policies only. Extending the architecture for other response alternatives of XACML (open authorization policy) needs a different implementation of *Policy* which is part of our future work. In Java, the *AccessController* handles access requests, thus it acts as the PEP for Java applications. When the PEP makes an evaluation request to the PDP of the XACML architecture, the PDP first tries to find out the policies that apply for the given target. Then it evaluates the applicable policies for making access decisions. The *getPermissions* method of *GenericPolicy* is similar to the initial work done by the PDP. The implies method of the *GenericPermission* class consists of an engine that can do evaluation of logic expressions. It uses the values of the various (resource object, environment etc.) attributes provided by the context handler (using Java reflection) to evaluate the authorization decisions. Thus it does the second function of PDP. The context handler is responsible for converting application specific objects to an XML format which is understood by the PDP. In our extension of JAAS, the context handler does the reflection on the application object. Figure 8 summarizes how our extension fits into XACML architecture. The major steps of the flow are:

- When an access request is made, the PEP calls the *GenericPolicy. getPermissions* method. As mentioned earlier, one of the functionality of the PDP is to find all the policies relevant to the given decision request. In the standard XACML framework, this functionality is not independently accessible from outside of PDP. In JAAS, the *GenericPolicy.getPermissions* does a similar work (of finding the relevant policies). Hence in our framework the *GenericPolicy.getPermissions* is part of the PDP and the *AccessController* (which is part of the PEP) calls this method. Thus we have externalized some of the functionality of the PDP. This is one of the extensions, which is required to the XACML framework to support our JAAS extension.

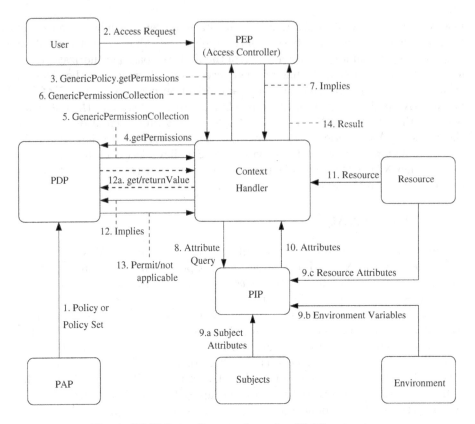

**Fig. 8.** XACML implementation using JAAS extensions

- Once the *GenericPermissionCollection* is received by the PEP, it calls the *implies* method on the *GenericPermissionCollection*. This is implemented in the PEP and it iterates over the *GenericPermssion*'s and calls the *implies* method of each of the constituent *GenericPermission* objects (Step 7).
- The context handler uses reflection to find out the values returned by the getter methods. It then constructs the decision request (which is an XML document) and sends it to the PDP (Step 12). The *GenericPermission.implies* method is the core of the PDP. It evaluates the policy/rule and returns its decision to the PEP.
- The XACML policy is represented in terms of expressions on the values returned by the getter methods of the resource object. Hence we need to represent the resource (Java) object in terms of an XML document. There are known techniques such as XStream [15] and SYS-CON [14] for converting Java objects as XML documents. Using these techniques, each property of the resource object can be easily represented in terms of an XPATH expression on an XML document. The values of the getter methods defined on the resource are obtained by the context handler (using Java reflection)

and sent out as part of the decision request. Invoking all the getter methods can have a lot of overhead. Hence the other option is for the PDP to call back the context handler (Step 12a) to obtain the value of the necessary getter methods. The information about the getter methods will be present in the policy file. The PDP will send this information to the context handler in Step 12a. E.g. the method to obtain the value of *owner-id* will be represented as *auctionEntry/auctionInfo/owner-id* in the policy file. This will be used by the context handler which will call the getter methods in a sequence (i.e. call *getAuctionInfo().getOwnerID()* ) and will return the results to the PDP. For more information, please refer to the appendix.

It is to be noted that we can afford some flexibility in the XACML framework, but doing so in JAAS is not possible as the architecture and its data flow is coded inside the JVM. Our framework requires a minor change of externalizing the *getPermissions* API present in the PDP but it does not jeopardize the XACML architecture. Although we have given examples of resources being protected by Java methods, our scheme can be easily extended to J2EE environment. The various J2EE methods can be classified as actions on a resource (in which case the action name can be replaced by the method name). Whenever those methods are called on a Java object, the J2EE application server would have to create the *GenericPermission* object corresponding to the intended action on the intended Java object. The container would then invoke the *AccessController* before the actual method call. Thus our technique can fit seamlessly into a J2EE as well as J2SE environment.

## 5   Related Works

There are various attempts to represent the access control policies in XML format and for providing granular authorization. [1] deals with XML based access control specification for dynamic web services using role based access control (X-RBAC). [3] deals with a security mechanism that can support a wide range of security models and policies in an efficient and unified manner. These models include ACLs, lattice based access control models, etc. But their implementation is ad-hoc without focusing on any particular language. [7] provides a naive mechanism for management of security policies using XML in a distributed environment. It proposes a schema, which represents the Role based access control (RBAC) policies in XML. This XML policy file is interpreted using a standard API. The paper is very general and does not provide instance level access control, nor does it provide authorization using any standard such as JAAS. [12] proposes *dynFAF*, a constraint logic programming based approach for expressing and enforcing constraints. These constraints are evaluated at run-time. Our instance based access control also fits in that definition. We give the implementation of such a framework using Java. [8] explains how meta-programming can help in expressing and implementing security policies. It presents three different types of meta-object protocols (MOP). Compile time

MOP's reflect language constructs available at compile time. Load-time MOP's reflect on the byte-code using a modified class loader. Run-time MOP's use a modified version of JVM. Out of these three, the first two cannot support instance level access control, which is the central theme of our paper. Run time MOP's can provide instance level access control, but it requires changing the JVM, which is not required in our approach. In [9], a Java secure execution framework (JSEF) is presented which introduces higher-level abstraction for defining security policies. Using JSEF one can define permit as well as deny policies. It also provides support for security negotiation in the case of insufficient permissions at runtime. This paper is related to Java security but it does not give mechanism a to express conditional authorization based on object instance. It does not follow any standard as we do using JAAS and XACML. A UML based modeling language for specifying security requirement of an application is presented in [10]. The model is used to automatically generate access control infrastructure. Authorization constraints are represented using Object Constrained Language (OCL). Besides this, there are various other Java security implementations, which cater to some particular kinds of applications or platforms. [11] describes Java based security model used in IBM's WebSphere Commerce Suite (WCS). This paper deals with policy based access control by modeling relationship between business objects and users. But, the authorization code is embedded in the application and the implementation is not JAAS based. Our work is unique in the sense that using our standards based extensions, Java applications can get flexibility of programmatic authorization using declarative specification.

## 6    Conclusions

Java is one of the most popular languages for developing e-commerce and web applications. Java has evolved over time, but the surprising fact of the day is that Java security still leaves a lot to be desired. Even the basic class instance level access control cannot be supported in a standard way using Java. This has lead to the use of custom security code which is difficult to maintain and is prone to security errors. In this paper we have proposed an innovative technique that: (1) provides a declarative access control support for Java applications using an extension of JAAS, and (2) shows how the XACML framework can be used to cater to the needs of JAAS security policies. Our innovative extension of JAAS enables the declarative specification of the Java security, which can complement the security provided in J2EE as well as J2SE applications. This mechanism has the potential to reduce the re-engineering work, which is in the order of months to the order of hours and will also allow the specification of Java security policies using the XACML representation, thereby providing a consistent and standard way of representing security policies across the enterprise.

*Acknowledgments.* We would like to thank Neeran Karnik and Vishal Batra for their helpful comments and discussions.

# References

[1] R. Bhatti, J. B. Joshi, E. Bertino, and, A. Ghafoor: "Access Control in Dynamic XML-based Web-Services with X-RBAC". First International Conference on Web Services, Las Vegas, June-2003.

[2] T. Fink, M. Koch, and C. Oancea: "Specification and Enforcement of Access Control in Heterogeneous Distributed Applications". International Conference on Web Services (ICWS), Germany, Sept-2003.

[3] Ungureanu, V. and N. H. Misnky: "Unified Support for Heterogeneous Security Polices in Distributed Systems". $7^{th}$ USENIX Security Symposium, Texas, Jan-1998.

[4] OASIS extensible Access Control Markup language (XACML). http://www.oasis-open.org/committees

[5] J2SE 5.0 in a nutshell. http://java.sun.com/developer/technicalArticles/releases/j2se15

[6] Core J2EE patterns, Data Access Object. http://java.sun.com/blueprints/corej2eepatterns/Patterns/DataAccessObject.html

[7] N. Vuong, G. Smith, and Y. Deng: "Managing security policies in a distributed environment using eXtensible markup language". The 2001 ACM Symposium on Applied Computing, Las Vegas, March-2001.

[8] J. Vayssiere: "Security and Meta Programming in Java". European Conference Object Oriented Programming - Workshop on Reflection and Meta-Level Architectures, France, May-2000.

[9] M. Hauswirth, C. Kerer, and R. Kurmanowytsch: "A Secure Exceution Framework for Java". $7^{th}$ ACM Conference on Computer and Communications Security, Greece, Nov-2000.

[10] T. Lodderstedt, D. Basin, and J. Doser: "SecureUML: A UML based Modeling Language for Model-Driven Security". Proceedings of UML'2002 - Unified Modelling Language, $5^{th}$ International Conference, Germany, Sept-2002.

[11] R. Goodwin, S.F. Goh, and F.Y. Wu: "Instance-level access control for business-to-business electronic commerce". IBM Systems Journal. Vol. 41, Number 2, 2002.

[12] S. Chen, D. Wijesekera and Sushil Jajodia: "Incorporating Dynamic Constraints in the Flexible Authorization Framework". $9^{th}$ European Symposium on Research in Computer Security (ESORICS'2004), France, Sept-2004.

[13] D. Wallach, D. Balfanz, D. Dean and E. Felten: "Extensible Security Architectures for Java". $16^{th}$ Symposium on Operating Systems Principles, France, Oct-1997.

[14] XML Serialization of Java Objects (SYS-CON). http://www.sys-con.com/story/?storyid=37550\&DE=1

[15] XStream: Java to XML Serialization and back again. http://joe.truemesh.com/blog/000261.html

[16] S. De Capitani di Vimercati, P. Samarati, and S. Jajodia: "Policies, Models, and Languages for Access Control". Workshop on Databases in Networked Information Systems, Japan, March-2005.

# A   Appendix

In this section we provide a sample security policy of JAAS represented in XACML format. The policy is for an e-auction site and is to ensure the following rule: "*Only the owner of an auction is allowed to modify the closing-date of an auction*". This is mapped to executing a method "*updateClosingDate*" on the Auction object. We first present the policy stated in XACML format. It consists of the following parts:

- The Policy
- The Rule

The policy can consist of multiple rules, which apply to the e-commerce site. In our case the policy consists of only a single rule, which is of "Permit" type. This means that if the rule fires then the subject is permitted to do the requested operation. The "Target" part of the policy decides the conditions under which this policy (and the rules in this policy) will be applicable.

The target of the rule decides the conditions under which the rule will be applicable. In this case the rule target states that it will apply to any subject who is trying to execute the *updateClosingDate* method of the Auction object. The condition part of the rule states the conditions that should hold true for the action to be permitted. In this rule, it is stated that the customer-id given in the request context should be equal to the owner-id of the auction that the user is trying to update.

```
<?xml version="1.0" encoding=''UTF-8"?>
<Policy xmlns="urn:ibm:names:tc:xacml:1.0:policy"
 xmlns:xsi="http://www.w3.org/2001/XMLSchema-instance"
 xsi:schemaLocation="urn:ibm:names:tc:xacml:1.0:policy
 http://www.ibm.com/irl/xacml/1.0/cs-xacml-schema-policy-01.xsd"
 PolicyId="identifier:example:JaasPolicy1"
 RuleCombiningAlgId="identifier:rule-combining-algorithm:permit-overrides">
<Description>
   JAAS based Access Control policies for an e-Auction Site.
</Description>
<Target>
   <Subjects>
       <AnySubject/>
   </Subjects>
   <Resources>
      <Resource>
         <!-- match document target namespace -->
         <ResourceMatch MatchId=
            "urn:ibm:names:tc:xacml:1.0:function:string-equal">
              <AttributeValue
                 DataType="http://www.w3.org/2001/XMLSchema#string">
                 file:./Auction.jar
              </AttributeValue>
              <ResourceAttributeDesignator AttributeId=
                 "urn:ibm:names:tc:xacml:1.0:resource:target-namespace"
                 DataType="http://www.w3.org/2001/XMLSchema#string"/>
         </ResourceMatch>
      </Resource>
   </Resources>
   <Actions>
```

```
        <AnyAction/>
    </Actions>
</Target>
<Rule RuleId="urn:ibm:names:tc:xacml:examples:ruleid:1" Effect="Permit">
<Description>
    Only the owner of an auction is allowed to modify the
    closing date of an auction.
</Description>
<Target>
    <Subjects>
        <AnySubject/>
    </Subjects>
    <Resources>
        <Resource>
            <ResourceMatch MatchId=
                "urn:ibm:names:tc:xacml:1.0:function:xpath-node-match">
                    <AttributeValue
                      DataType="http://www.w3.org/2001/XMLSchema#string">
                        Auction
                    </AttributeValue>
                    <ResourceAttributeDesignator
                      AttributeId="urn:ibm:names:tc:xacml:1.0:resource:xpath"
                      DataType="http://www.w3.org/2001/XMLSchema#string"/>
            </ResourceMatch>
        </Resource>
    </Resources>
    <Actions>
        <Action>
            <!-- Match ``updateClosingDate" action -->
            <ActionMatch MatchId=
                "urn:ibm:names:tc:xacml:1.0:function:string-equal">
                <AttributeValue
                  DataType="http://www.w3.org/2001/XMLSchema#string">
                    updateClosingDate
                </AttributeValue>
                <ActionAttributeDesignator AttributeId=
                    "urn:ibm:names:tc:xacml:1.0:action:action-id"
                  DataType="http://www.w3.org/2001/XMLSchema#string"/>
            </ActionMatch>
        </Action>
    </Actions>
</Target>
<Condition FunctionId="urn:ibm:names:tc:xacml:1.0:function:and">
    <!-- compare customer-id subject attribute with the
                                owner-id value in the document -->
    <Apply FunctionId="urn:ibm:names:tc:xacml:1.0:function:string-equal">
        <Apply FunctionId=
            "urn:ibm:names:tc:xacml:1.0:function:string-one-and-only">
            <!-- customer-id subject attribute -->
            <SubjectAttributeDesignator AttributeId=
```

```
            "urn:ibm:names:tc:xacml:1.0:examples:attribute:customer-id"
            DataType="http://www.w3.org/2001/XMLSchema#string"/>
        </Apply>
        <Apply FunctionId=
          "urn:ibm:names:tc:xacml:1.0:function:string-one-and-only">
          <!-- owner-id element in the document -->
            <AttributeSelector RequestContextPath=
              "//ac:auctionEntry/ac:ownerInfo/ac:owner-id/text()"
              DataType="http://www.w3.org/2001/XMLSchema#string">
            </AttributeSelector>
        </Apply>
      </Apply>
   </Condition>
 </Rule>
</Policy>
```

**Request Context**

What follows next is an example of the request context that is constructed by
the Context handler. This is created when a user makes a request to update
the closing-date of an auction. The context handler creates this document by
using Java reflection on the auction object which is passed by the PEP to the
context handler. This request context states that a subject with the name "Joe"
and with customer-id *jh1234* is trying to update the closing date of an auction
whose owner-id is *jh1234*.

```
<?xml version="1.0" encoding="UTF-8"?>
<Request xmlns="urn:ibm:names:tc:xacml:1.0:context"
  Xmlns:xsi="http://www.w3.org/2001/XMLSchema-instance"
  xsi:schemaLocation="urn:ibm:names:tc:xacml:1.0:context
  http://www.ibm.com/irl/xacml/1.0/cs-xacml-schema-context-01.xsd">
    <Subject>
      <Attribute AttributeId=
          "urn:ibm:names:tc:xacml:1.0:subject:subjectid"
          DataType="urn:ibm:names:tc:xacml:1.0:data-type:rfc822Name">
          <AttributeValue>Joe</AttributeValue>
      </Attribute>
      <Attribute AttributeId=
          "urn:ibm:names:tc:xacml:1.0:example:attribute:customer-id"
          DataType="http://www.w3.org/2001/XMLSchema#string">
          <AttributeValue>jh1234</AttributeValue>
      </Attribute>
    </Subject>
    <Resource>
      <Attribute AttributeId=
          "urn:ibm:names:tc:xacml:1.0:resource:ufspath"
          DataType="http://www.w3.org/2001/XMLSchema#anyURI">
          <AttributeValue>
              Auction
          </AttributeValue>
```

```
      </Attribute>
      <Attribute AttributeId=
         "urn:ibm:names:tc:xacml:1.0:example:attribute:owner-id"
         DataType="http://www.w3.org/2001/XMLSchema#string">
          <AttributeValue>jh1234</AttributeValue>
      </Attribute>
   </Resource>
   <Action>
      <Attribute AttributeId=
         "urn:ibm:names:tc:xacml:1.0:action:action-id"
         DataType="http://www.w3.org/2001/XMLSchema#string">
          <AttributeValue>updateClosingDate</AttributeValue>
      </Attribute>
   </Action>
</Request>
```

## Response Context

The PDP evaluates the rule applicable for the decision request and constructs a response context. In this example, the user "Joe" is also the owner of the auction and hence is permitted to update the closing-date of the auction as per the access control rule. Hence the PDP returns a result of "Permit". The syntax of the response context is given below.

```
<?xml version="1.0" encoding="UTF-8"?>
<Response xmlns="urn:ibm:names:tc:xacml:1.0:context"
 xsi:schemaLocation="urn:ibm:names:tc:xacml:1.0:context
 http://www.ibm.com/irl/xacml/1.0/cs-xacml-schema-context-01.xsd">
   <Result>
        <Decision>Permit</Decision>
   </Result>
</Response>
```

# Specification and Validation of Authorisation Constraints Using UML and OCL

Karsten Sohr[1], Gail-Joon Ahn[2,*], Martin Gogolla[1], and Lars Migge[1]

[1] Department of Mathematics and Computer Science,
Universität Bremen, Bibliothekstr. 1,
28359 Bremen, Germany
[2] Department of Software and Information Systems,
University of North Carolina at Charlotte
Charlotte, NC 28223, USA

**Abstract.** *Authorisation constraints* can help the policy architect design and express higher-level security policies for organisations such as financial institutes or governmental agencies. Although the importance of constraints has been addressed in the literature, there does not exist a systematic way to validate and test authorisation constraints. In this paper, we attempt to specify non-temporal constraints and history-based constraints in Object Constraint Language (OCL) which is a constraint specification language of Unified Modeling Language (UML) and describe how we can facilitate the USE tool to validate and test such policies. We also discuss the issues of identification of conflicting constraints and missing constraints.

## 1 Introduction

Today information technology pervades more and more our daily life. This applies to very different domains such as healthcare, e-government, banking. On the other hand, new technologies go along with new risks, which must be systematically dealt with, such as preventing unauthorised access. Hence it is mandatory to establish adequate mechanisms that enforce the security and protection requirements demanded by the rules and laws relevant to the organisation in question. For example, in Europe there do exist strong data protection requirements as those formulated in the Directive 95/46/EC [7]. This directive among other areas applies to clinical information systems where in particular the principle of patient consent must be enforced [4]. In contrast, in the banking domain other security requirements such as data integrity are more important such that often separation of duty policies (SoD) [17,5] must be enforced.

Implementing such higher-level organisational security policies in computer systems can be cumbersome and inefficient. However, it has turned out that

---

* This work of Gail-J. Ahn was partially supported at the Laboratory of Information of Integration, Security and Privacy at the University of North Carolina at Charlotte by the grants from National Science Foundation (NSF-IIS-0242393) and Department of Energy Early Career Principal Investigator Award (DE-FG02-03ER25565).

S. De Capitani di Vimercati et al. (Eds.): ESORICS 2005, LNCS 3679, pp. 64–79, 2005.

one of the great advantages of role-based access control (RBAC) is that SoD rules can be implemented in a natural way [9]. Generally speaking, role-based authorisation constraints are an important means for laying out higher-level security policies [1,13]. Although there are several works on the specification of role-based authorisation constraints, e.g., [1,13], there is a lack of appropriate tool support for the validation, enforcement, and testing of role-based access control policies. Specifically, tools are needed which can be applied quite easily by a policy designer without too much deeper training.

As demonstrated in [2,18], the Unified Modeling Language (UML) and the Object Constraint Language (OCL) can be conveniently used to specify several classes of role-based authorisation constraints. Moreover, owing to the fact that OCL has proved its applicability in several industrial applications[1], OCL is a good means for such a practically relevant process like the design of security policies.

However, as mentioned above, tool support is needed in order to have a broader practical use. Hence, we demonstrate in this paper how to employ the USE system (UML Specification Environment) [19,20] to validate and test access control policies formulated in UML and OCL. In particular, USE is a validation tool for UML models and OCL constraints, which has been reportedly applied in industry and research [19]. With the help of this tool, a policy designer can detect conflicting and missing authorisation constraints.

The paper is now organised as follows: Section 2 gives a short overview of RBAC, UML/OCL, and introduces the USE system. In Section 3 typical and partly more complex authorisation constraints are specified in OCL and in a temporal OCL extension. Section 4 then demonstrates how USE can be employed to validate and enforce RBAC security policies and test RBAC configurations while Section 5 sketches related work. Section 6 summarises and gives an outlook on future work.

## 2  Related Technologies

We first give a short overview of RBAC, then we briefly describe UML and OCL, and finally introduce the USE tool, which can be employed to validate OCL constraints.

### 2.1  RBAC and Authorisation Constraints

RBAC has received considerable attention as an alternative to traditional discretionary and mandatory access control. One reason for this increasing interest is that in practice permissions are assigned to users according to their roles/functions in the organisation (governmental or commercial) [8]. In addition, the explicit representation of roles greatly simplifies the security management and allows one to use well-known security principles like separation of duty and least privilege.

---

[1] OCL is UML's constraint specification language and UML has been widely adopted in software engineering discipline.

In the sequel, we briefly describe RBAC96, a family of RBAC models introduced by Sandhu et al. [22]. RBAC96 has the following components:

- Users, Roles, P, S (sets of users, roles, permissions, activated sessions)
- $UA \subseteq Users \times Roles$ (user assignment)
- $PA \subseteq Roles \times P$ (permission assignment)
- $RH \subseteq Roles \times Roles$ is a partial order also called the role hierarchy or role dominance relation written as $\leq$.

Users may activate a subset of the roles they are assigned to in a *session*. $P$ is the set of ordered pairs of operations and objects. In the context of security and access control all resources accessible in an IT-system (e.g., files, database tables) are referred to by the notion *object*. An *operation* is an active process applicable to objects (e.g., read, write, append). The relation $PA$ assigns to each role a subset of $P$. So $PA$ determines for each role the operation(s) it may execute and the object(s) to which the operation in question is applicable for the given role. Thus any user having assumed this role can apply an operation to an object if the corresponding ordered pair is an element of the subset assigned to the role by $PA$.

An important advanced aspect of RBAC are *authorisation constraints*. Authorisation constraints are sometimes argued to be the principal motivation behind the introduction of RBAC [22]. They allow a policy designer to express higher-level organisational security policies. Depending on the organisation, different kinds of authorisation constraints are required such as SoD in the banking field [5] or constraints on delegation and context constraints in the healthcare domain [24]. Later in this paper, different kinds of authorisation constraints are specified and discussed.

## 2.2 Overview of UML and OCL

**Unified Modeling Language.** The Unified Modeling Language (UML) [21] is a general-purpose visual modeling language in which we can specify, visualize, and document the components of software systems. It captures decisions and understanding about systems that must be constructed. UML has become a standard modeling language in the field of software engineering.

UML permits the description of static, functional, and dynamic models. In this paper, we concentrate on the static aspects of UML. A static model provides a structural view of information in a system. Classes are defined in terms of their attributes and relationships. The relationships include specifically associations between classes. In Figure 1, the conceptual static model for RBAC is depicted.

**Object Constraint Language.** The Object Constraint Language (OCL) [25] is a declarative language that describes constraints on object-oriented models. A constraint is a restriction on one or more values of an object-oriented model. OCL is an industrial standard for object-oriented analysis and design.

Each OCL expression is written in the context of a specific class. In an OCL expression, the reserved word `self` is used to refer to a contextual instance.

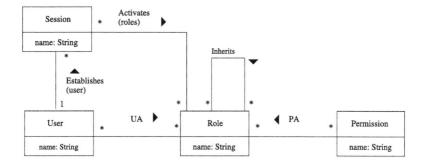

**Fig. 1.** Conceptual Class Model for RBAC-Entity Classes

The type of the context instance of an OCL expression is written with the `context` keyword, followed by the name of the type. The label `inv:` declares the constraint to be an invariant. Consider the RBAC model from Figure 1: If the context is `Role`, then `self` refers to an instance of `Role`. The following line shows an example of an OCL constraint expression describing a role with at most two users:

```
context Role inv: self.user->size()<2
```

`self.user` is a set of `User` objects that is selected by navigating from objects of class `Role` to `User` objects through an association. The ''`.`'' stands for a navigation. A property of a set is accessed by an arrow ''`->`'' followed by the name of the property. A property of the set of users is expressed using the `size` operation in this example.

The following shows another example describing that a user can be assigned to a role `r2` only if she is already member of `r1`:

```
context User inv:
self.role_->includes('r2') implies self.role_->includes('r1')
```

The expression `self.role_->includes('r2')` means that `r2` is a member of the set of roles the user is assigned to. The `implies` connector is similar to logical implication.

Furthermore, OCL has several built-in operations that can iterate over the members of a collection (set, bag, ...) such as forAll, exists, iterate, any and select (cf. [25]).

## 2.3   The USE Tool

This section explains the functionality of the UML Specification Environment (USE) which allows the validation of UML and OCL descriptions. USE is the only OCL tool allowing interactive monitoring of OCL invariants and pre- and postconditions, and the automatic generation of non-trivial system states. These system states or snapshots consist of the current objects and links between those objects adhering to the UML model in question.

The central idea of the USE tool is to check for software quality criteria like correct functionality of UML descriptions already in the design level in an implementation-independent manner. This approach takes advantage of descriptive design level specifications by expressing properties more concisely and in a more abstract way. Such properties are given by invariants and pre- and post-conditions, and these are checked by the USE system against the test scenarios, i.e., object diagrams and operation calls given by sequence diagrams, which the developer provides. These abstract design level tests are expected to be also used later in the implementation phase.

The USE tool expects as an input a textual description of a model and its OCL constraints (for an example of such a description refer to Figure 3). Then syntax checks of this description are carried out, which verify a specification against the grammar of the specification language, basically a superset of OCL extended with language constructs for defining the structure of the model. Having passed all these checks, the model can be displayed by the GUI provided by the USE system. In particular, USE makes available a project browser which displays all the classes, associations, invariants, and pre- and post-conditions of the current model.

Figure 2 shows a USE screenshot with an example. On the left we see the project browser displaying the classes, associations, invariants, and operation pre- and post-conditions. In a detail window below, the selected class is pictured with all details. On the right, we identify a sequence diagram presenting the operations which lead to the current system state given in the object diagram window below. The evaluation of the invariants in this system state is pictured in the class invariant window to the right of the object diagram window. The

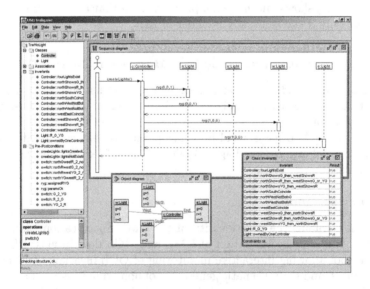

**Fig. 2.** USE screenshot

developer gets feedback from USE about the validity of the invariants in the invariant window and the validity of the pre- and post-conditions in the sequence diagram window. Further information about the validity of invariants can be requested by a dialog window for evaluating arbitrary OCL expressions. This dialog allows ad-hoc queries useful for navigating and exploring a system state at any time. Hence, USE helps the developer in analysing situations when an invariant or a pre- or post-condition fails. This query window will be used several times in Section 4.

# 3    Constraints Specification

In this section, different types of authorisation constraints are specified in OCL. In the first subsection, non-temporal authorisation constraints are formulated in OCL, whereas in the second subsection history-based authorisation constraints are formalised in a temporal extension of OCL.

## 3.1    Non-temporal Authorisation Constraints

Subsequently we give three examples that demonstrate how to use OCL to specify authorisation constraints.

*Example 1: Simple Static Separation of Duty (SSOD)*
The first example concerns a separation of duty constraint. Consider two (or more) conflicting roles such as accounts payable manager and purchasing manager. Mutual exclusion in terms of the user assignment UA specifies that one individual cannot have both roles. This constraint on UA can be specified using the OCL expression as follows [2]:

```
context User inv SSOD:
let
    CR:Set={{AccountsPayableManager, PurchasingManager}, ...}
in
    CR->forAll(cr|cr->intersection(self.role_)->size()<=1)
```

This formulation of SSOD is based upon the SSOD specification given in [1]. Specifically, CR denotes a set which consists of conflicting role sets.

*Example 2: Prerequisite Roles*
The second example is based upon the concept of prerequisite constraints as introduced in [22]. In this example, we consider a prerequisite constraint stating that a user can be assigned to the engineer role only if the user is already assigned to the employee role.

---

[2] For the sake of simplicity, we have left out here the part for the creation of the instances AccountsPayableManager and PurchasingManager. Similar remarks hold for the subsequent OCL specifications.

```
context User inv Prerequisite Role:
self.role_ ->includes(engineer) implies self.role_->includes(employee)
```

*Example 3: Static Separation of Duty - Conflict Users (SSOD-CU)*

By means of OCL even more complex authorisation constraints can be formulated. One example of such a constraint is SSOD-CU identified by Ahn in [1]. SSOD-CU means that two or more colluding users cannot be assigned to conflicting roles. For example, it might be the company policy that members of the same family cannot be assigned to the roles accounts payable manager and purchasing manager. SSOD-CU can now be expressed in OCL in the following way:

```
context User inv SSOD-CU:
let
    CU:Set(Set(User))=Set{Set{Michael,Frank,Susan},Set{Lars,Maria}},
    CR:Set(Set(Role))=Set{Set{AccountsPayableManager, BillingClerk},
    Set{Cashier, CashierSupervisor}, ...}
in
    CR->forAll(cr|cr->intersection(self.role_)->size()<=1)
and
    CU->forAll(cu|
        CR->forAll(cr|cr->iterate(r:Roles; result:Set(User)=Set{}|
        result->union(r.user))->intersection(cu)->size()<=1))
```

SSOD-CU is a composite constraint consisting of two parts, *an SSOD part* and *an additional part concerning the conflicting users*. The SSOD part is required because otherwise obviously the whole constraint would not be useful. The `iterate` operation iterates over all roles `r` belonging to a set of conflicting roles and collects all users of these roles. `CR` has the same meaning as in example 1 whereas `CU` is a set consisting of all conflicting user sets.

## 3.2 History-Based Constraints

OCL is quite similar to first-order predicate logic. As expressions of the predicate calculus, OCL expressions used in invariants are evaluated in a system state. However, due to the fact that we consider here only one snapshot of the system, we have no notion of time. Hence, authorisation constraints that consider the execution history such as history-based or object-based dynamic SoD [10] cannot be adequately expressed.

In the following, we sketch how history-based authorisation constraints can be specified in TOCL (Temporal OCL) [26], an extension of OCL with temporal elements. In particular, temporal operators like **always** (in the future), **sometime** (in the future), and **next** are available. To demonstrate how history-based authorisation constraints can be formulated in TOCL, we take dynamic object-based SoD as an example, which has been introduced informally by Nash and Poland [17]. Dynamic object-based SoD roughly speaking means that a user must not act upon an object that the same user has previously acted upon. Other dynamic SoD constraints enumerated in [10] can clearly be expressed in TOCL, too.

```
model RBAC                        association PA  between
-- classes                            Permission[*]  role permission
                                      Role[*]  role role.
class Role                        end
attributes                        association establishes  between
   name:String                        Users[1]  role user
end                                    Session[*]  role session
                                  end
class User
attributes                        association  activates  between
   name:String                        Session[*]  role session
end                                    Role[*]  role role.
                                  end
class Permission
attributes                        association inherits between
   name:String                        Role[*]  role senior
   op:Operation                       Role[*]  role junior
   o:Object                       end
end
                                  constraints
class Object                      context Users  inv PrerequisiteRole:
attributes                            self.role.->includes(r2)
   name:String                        implies self.role.->includes(r1)
end
                                  --constraint: user part of SSOD-CU
class Operation                   context Role  inv SSOD-CU:
attributes                        let
   name:String                        CU:Set(Set(User))=Set{{u1,u2,u3},{u4,u5}}
end                               in
                                  let
class Session                         CR:Set(Set(Role))=Set{Set{r1,r2},...}
attributes                        in
   name:String                        CU->forAll(cu|
end                                     CR->forAll(cr|cr->iterate(r:Role;
                                        result:Set(User)=oclEmpty(Set(User))|
-- associations                         result->union(r.user))->intersection(cu)->size()<=1))
association UA  between
   User[*]  role user
   Role[*]  role role.
end
```

**Fig. 3.** USE specification of an RBAC security policy

In order to specify dynamic object-based SoD in TOCL, we use two predicates introduced in [16], namely $auth(u, op, obj)$ and $exec(u, op, obj)$. The former
predicate means that a user $u$ is authorised to execute operation $op$ on object
$obj$ while the latter means that user $u$ executes operation $op$ on object $obj$ in the
present state. For the sake of simplicity, the full details of those predicates are
left out here. The interested reader is referred to [16] to obtain more information
on that topic.

Due to the fact that **exec** and **auth** are ternary predicates and OCL supports
only binary associations we extend OCL with additional predicates **Exec** and
**Auth** to express ternary associations, as proposed in [12].

With this extension, we obtain the following TOCL specification for object-
based dynamic SoD (using the **always** operator):

```
context Object inv ObjDSoD:
Operation.allInstances->forAll(op,op1|
    User.allInstances->forAll(u|
(Exec(u,op,self) and op1<>op) implies always not Auth(u,op1,self))))
```

This corresponds to the specification of dynamic object-based SoD in first-
order linear temporal logic as given in [16]:
$\forall u : Users; op, op1 : OpSet; obj : Object.op \neq op1 \wedge exec(u, op, obj)$
$\Rightarrow \Box\neg auth(u, op1, obj).$

# 4   Validation and Testing of RBAC Security Policies

With OCL we have a light-weight formalism at hand, which can help specifying RBAC security policies. What is however missing is a tool which helps a
policy designer in validating her RBAC policy. Hence, in the sequel it will be
demonstrated how the USE tool, which is a general-purpose validation tool for
OCL constraints, can be employed for this purpose (cf. Section 4.1). Specifically, authorisation constraints such as those categorised in [1] can be handled.
Additionally, USE can also be applied to test concrete RBAC configurations
against certain conditions (cf. Section 4.2). The last section sketches how the
USE functionality can be used to build an RBAC authorisation editor.

## 4.1   Validation of RBAC Security Policies

As mentioned in section 2.3, the main application of the USE tool is the validation of UML/OCL models. The same can be carried out with an RBAC security
policy. The USE specification of a security policy is given in Figure 3 with the
authorisation constraints expressed by OCL constraints. This policy will serve
as an example within this section.

Through the validation of RBAC policies conflicting constraints can be detected and missing constraints identified. The validation can be done *before the
deployment* of the RBAC policy, i.e., during the design phase. As indicated above,
the USE approach for validation is to generate system states (snapshots) and
check these states against the specified constraints. In our case, the system states
are certain RBAC configurations (consisting of users, roles, the relations between
these entities). The RBAC configurations could be created automatically by running a script with the state manipulation commands, which are supported by
the USE tool, or as an alternative with a GUI provided by the USE system. This
animation-based approach for the validation of security policies can be regarded
as a complement to a rigorous formal verification, which often requires deeper
training in formal methods.

The result of the validation can lead to different consequences. Firstly, we
may have reasonable system states that do not satisfy one or more authorisation
constraints of the policy. This may indicate that the constraints are too strong
or the model is not adequate. Secondly, the security policy may allow undesired
system states, i.e., the constraints are too weak. In the following both situations
are discussed more thoroughly.

**Conflicting Constraints.** USE may help the policy designer find conflicting
constraints. This will be subsequently demonstrated by an example, considering
the RBAC policy presented in Figure 3. Clearly, this example policy is rather
simple, but in reality we often have to deal with considerably more complex
policies. Now, let us further assume that the policy designer has forgotten that
he had once defined a prerequisite role constraint between $r1$ and $r2$. Later, the
policy designer decided to define $r1$ and $r2$ mutually exclusive due to a change
of organisational rules/policies. Obviously, both constraints could not be satisfied at the same time and hence the composite constraint is too strong. The

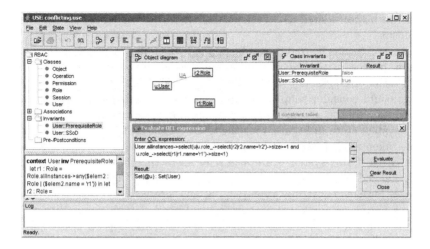

**Fig. 4.** USE screenshot: two conflicting constraints

USE screenshot in Figure 4 displays the situation after user $u$ has been assigned to $r2$. Clearly, the policy designer cannot have assigned $u$ to role $r1$; otherwise the new SSOD constraint would be violated. However, now the constraint **User::PrerequisiteRole** is evaluated to false (cf. "Class invariants" view in Figure 4), and hence the current RBAC configuration is not a correct system state according to the given policy specification.

Admittedly, the mere information that a constraint is false might often not help to find the real reason for the problem and to resolve the conflict. Additional information is required which objects and links of the current state violate the constraint. For such a purpose, the policy designer can debug the constraints that are not satisfied by the current system state with the "Evaluate OCL expression" dialog. For example, in Figure 4 the result of the query "all users who are assigned to $r2$ but not to $r1$" applied to the given RBAC configuration is shown. Here, one can learn that $u$ is not assigned to $r1$, although this is required by the prerequisite role constraint. If the policy designer now conversely tries to assign $u$ to $r1$, the SSOD constraint fails, and one can conclude that both constraints are contradictory. A policy designer could employ USE in a similar way for other constraint types such as cardinality constraints or other SoD properties. In particular, this approach is helpful if a new constraint is added to the policy, in order to check if it is in conflict with the composition of the already defined constraints.

Nevertheless, USE may find conflicts only in certain cases, and there is no guarantee that all conflicts can be detected. Had $u$ not been assigned to $r2$, the conflict would have remained undetected. In order to eliminate contradictory constraints in general, a more formal approach such as model checking is required. On the other hand, the USE approach is only meant to improve the design of a security policy, and does not aim at a formally proven design. Given the condition that there is often a lack of tools for policy analysis, the USE approach can be considered as a first pratical step towards more reliable security mechanisms.

However, various heuristics can be applied which may streamline the conflict detection process with USE. For example, system states (snapshots) could be created which are *specially tailored* towards certain constraint types. In particular, we could consider snapshots which satisfy the constraint in question and which contain all the parameters (objects and links) occurring in this constraint (cf. the system state in Figure 4 for the SSOD constraint). Such a snapshot can then be taken as a *starting point* for the conflict detection process. Specifically, we can check if this system state also adheres to the composition of the other already defined constraints. As a further improvement, we could store snapshot templates for each constraint type (e.g., SSOD, prerequisite roles) and instantiate these templates for a certain constraint if needed. This way, a library with snapshot templates is available, which can be reused and appropriately combined with other snapshots to obtain test cases for conflict detection.

**Detection of Missing Constraints.** The second consequence of constraint validation may be that the policy permits undesirable system states, i.e., the authorisation constraints are too weak. Once again suppose that the policy designer has defined a complex security policy. Let us further assume that she has forgotten to define the SSOD part of the SSOD-CU constraint mentioned above (cf. Figure 3) and that an undesirable system state has been created by USE in which $u$ is assigned to both the roles $r1$ and $r2$. Now, USE can help in detecting the missing constraint in this scenario: all constraints (in our case specifically the conflict user part of the SSOD-CU constraint) defined so far are evaluated to true and hence the policy seems supposedly to be correct. On the other hand, the policy permits a user to be assigned to the mutually exclusive roles $r1$ and $r2$. Therefore, a further SSOD constraint must be added to the policy in order to exclude the undesirable state.

But how can we create a system state which reveals the missing constraint? One possible solution is to create an RBAC configuration tailored towards the missing constraint as described in the previous section, but with the difference that now snapshots must be considered that violate the missing constraint. Another possibility is to use the test generator provided by USE [11]. By means of this generator we can create system states at random and then check if the created system state violates certain conditions with the help of the "Evaluate OCL expression" dialog.

## 4.2   Testing a Given RBAC Configuration with USE

Beyond the validation of constraints, USE can be employed for testing an RBAC configuration *after* the constraints have been deployed. However, observe that we consider here a *predefined* RBAC configuration of users, roles, etc. which corresponds to a real-world RBAC configuration of an organisation.

Testing an RBAC configuration may be mandatory in several situations. For example, in some domains (e.g., healthcare) strict data protection laws must be fulfilled such as the European Directive 95/46/EC [7]. In order to assess the current RBAC configuration defined for security-relevant applications, often some external review is required, e.g., from an government agency responsible for data protection as established in Germany. What is often missing is a tool that supports an external reviewer in checking a concrete RBAC configuration of an organisation against certain properties such as data protection rules. In addition, the ability to test RBAC configurations may also be helpful for administrators in order to check if a security policy has been implemented correctly.

USE can now be employed as an ad hoc query tool to check certain properties of the current RBAC configuration such as:

- there is no common user of mutually exclusive roles
- only clinicians of a patient's current ward may have access to the patient's electronic patient record[3]

For this purpose, the "Evaluate OCL expression" dialog is helpful again. For example, a reviewer can check the current RBAC configuration if and which users are assigned to the roles $r1$ and $r2$, which ought to be mutually exclusive. Due to the fact that an administrator or external reviewer usually is not an expert in specification formalisms like OCL an authorisation editor should be made available which hides the formalism behind a GUI. This is discussed in the following.

## 4.3   Authorisation Editor

We have implemented an RBAC authorisation editor built upon the Java API made available by the USE system. This way, the USE system is hidden from the administrator and hence she need not be familar with UML/OCL and USE. The authorisation editor can enforce several types of authorisation constraints like those listed in [1]. More explicitly speaking, the authorisation editor can be used in principle to specify and enforce all authorisation constraints expressible in OCL. As a consequence, types of authorisation constraints beyond those enumerated in [1] can also be formulated and enforced such as context constraints.

In the following, the functionality of the authorisation editor will be presented in more detail. First, the prototype of the authorisation editor currently supports most of the functionality demanded by the ANSI standard for RBAC [3]. This means that we have implemented administrative functions, system functions, and review functions. According to [3] *administrative functions* allow the creation and maintenance of the element sets (e.g., User, Role, Permission) and the RBAC relations (e.g., UA, PA). For example, AddUser, DeleteUser, and AssignUser belong to this class of functions. *System functions* are required by the authorisation editor for session management and making access control decisions. Thus, examples are CreateSession, and AddActiveRole. *Review functions* allow for reviewing the results of the actions created by administrative functions. Typical examples of review functions are AssignedUsers, and UserPermissions.

---

[3] We assume here that there is a further attribute "ward" for certain roles and for users.

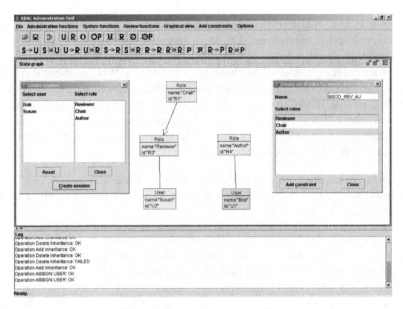

**Fig. 5.** The authorisation editor

Administrative and system functions can be implemented by the state manipulation commands provided by the USE system. Due to the aforementioned query facilities of USE, RBAC review functions can also be easily implemented.

Beyond this basic functionality, the RBAC authorisation editor provides mechanisms for defining and enforcing authorisation constraints (e.g., simple static SoD, object-based static SoD, cardinality constraints). The basic idea of the constraint checking mechanism is now as follows: The authorisation editor, or to put it in another way, the USE system checks if the relevant authorisation constraints are still satisfied *after* an administrative function has been carried out. If any constraint is violated, the last function is automatically revoked. As a consequence, the tool can only produce states that are consistent with the specified constraints.

The authorisation editor can also deal with role hierarchies, which are not restricted to inheritance trees, but can also in general form directed acyclic graphs. Moreover, the tool can detect and then prevent inconsistencies such as a senior role which inherits two mutually exclusive junior roles. For example, assume we have a role *Chair* and two junior roles *Reviewer* and *Author*. Further assume both junior roles are mutually exclusive. Then the role *Chair* is strictly speaking useless because no user can ever be assigned to this role. To give a better overview, a screenshot of the current prototype of the authorisation editor is shown in Figure 5. In the upper part of the window, there are several buttons, each button stands for a special administrative function. The large window in the middle of the tool visualises the current system state (RBAC configuration). The visualisation of the system state will be immediately renewed when the system state has been changed by an administrative function. At the bottom of the window there is a log window, which displays the result of the last applied administrative function. There are currently two windows open: On the right-hand side there is a small window to create a set of roles for a simple static SoD constraint; on the left-hand side there is a window to create a session for a user with active roles.

## 5   Related Work

There are several works concerning the specification of RBAC authorisation constraints, e.g., a graphical language [13] and the RCL 2000 language based upon restricted first-order logic [1]. As demonstrated in [1], various classes of authorisation constraints can be expressed with RCL 2000. Although the classification and the case studies are insightful, no tool support for constraint validation, enforcement, and testing has been implemented so far. In [18] and [2], constraints are formulated in UML/OCL, but once again no tool support for the validation is available. In this respect, the USE approach fills this gap.

In [14,15], another approach for the verification of RBAC policies is presented, based upon graph transformations. However, this approach does not tackle the problem of conflicting constraints, but the problem of graph rules conflicting with constraints. Due to the fact that some constraints can only be expressed clumsily (e.g., SSOD-CU, operational SoD) a formulation of those constraints in OCL is often more intuitive.

In [6], an authorisation editor is presented which is similar to the one described in Section 4.3. However, with the approach from [6], for example, the SSOD-CU constraint cannot be specified and enforced. On the other hand, with USE no history-based SoD constraints can be enforced because TOCL is currently not supported.

## 6   Conclusion and Future Work

In this paper we demonstrated that with the help of OCL several classes of authorisation constraints and even complex composite constraints can be specified. Due to the fact that the UML/OCL is quite familiar in industrial environments there is hope that OCL can be used by policy designers in many organisations. In addition, we demonstrated how the USE tool, a validation tool for OCL constraints, can be employed to fulfill several practical needs such as constraint validation, testing of RBAC configurations and building an authorisation editor.

Owing to the fact that USE can only check the current snapshot of an RBAC configuration, history-based authorisation constraints [23] cannot be dealt with. For this purpose a temporal extension of OCL like that sketched in this paper is needed. Hence, it remains future work to extend USE in order to deal with temporal constraints. Another goal is to integrate the authorisation editor into middleware. Specifically, Web services could be an interesting target to enforce authorisation constraints due to the high access control requirements of this technology.

# References

1. G.-J. Ahn, *The RCL 2000 language for specifying role-based authorization constraints*, Ph.D. thesis, George Mason University, Fairfax, Virginia, 1999.
2. G.-J. Ahn and M.E. Shin, *Role-Based Authorization Constraints Specification Using Object Constraint Language*, Proc. of the 10th IEEE International Workshops on Enabling Technologies: Infrastructure for Collaborative Enterprise, IEEE, 2001, pp. 157–162.
3. American National Standards Institute Inc., *Role Based Access Control*, 2004, ANSI-INCITS 359-2004.
4. R. Anderson, *A security policy model for clinical information systems*, Proceedings of the IEEE Symposium on Research in Security and Privacy (Oakland, CA), IEEE Computer Society Press, May 1996, pp. 30–43.
5. D. D. Clark and D. R. Wilson, *A comparison of commercial and military computer security policies*, Proceedings of the 1987 IEEE Symposium on Security and Privacy (1987), 184–194.
6. J. Crampton, *Specifying and enforcing constraints in role-based access control*, Proc. of the 8th ACM Symposium on Access Control Models and Technologies (New York), ACM Press, June 2–3 2003, pp. 43–50.
7. EU, *Directive on the protection of individuals with regard to the processing of personal data and on the free movement of such data. Directive 95/46/EC. http://www.privacy.org/pi/intl_orgs/ec/eudp.html*, 1995.
8. D. Ferraiolo, D. Gilbert, and N. Lynch, *An examination of federal and commercial access control policy needs*, Proc. of the NIST-NCSC Nat. (U.S.) Comp. Security Conference, 1993, pp. 107–116.
9. D.F. Ferraiolo, D.R. Kuhn, and R. Chandramouli, *Role-based access control*, Artec House, Boston, 2003.
10. V. D. Gligor, S. I. Gavrila, and D. Ferraiolo, *On the formal definition of separation-of-duty policies and their composition*, 1998 IEEE Symposium on Security and Privacy (SSP '98), IEEE, May 1998, pp. 172–185.
11. M. Gogolla, J. Bohling, and M. Richters, *Validation of UML and OCL Models by Automatic Snapshot Generation*, Proc. 6th Int. Conf. Unified Modeling Language (UML'2003), Springer, Berlin, LNCS 2863, 2003, pp. 265–279.
12. Martin Gogolla and Mark Richters, *Transformation Rules for UML Class Diagrams*, Proc. 1st Int. Workshop Unified Modeling Language (UML'98), Springer, Berlin, LNCS 1618, 1999, pp. 92–106.
13. T. Jaeger and J.E. Tidswell, *Practical safety in flexible access control models*, ACM TISSEC **4** (2001), no. 2, 158–190.
14. M. Koch, L. V. Mancini, and F. Parisi-Presicce, *A Graph Based Formalism for RBAC*, ACM Transactions on Information and System Security (TISSEC) **5** (2002), no. 3, 332–365.
15. M. Koch and F. Parisi-Presicce, *Visual Specification of Policies and their Verification*, Proc. of Fundamental Approaches to Software Engineering (FASE) 2003, LNCS, no. 2621, Springer, 2003, pp. 278–293.
16. T. Mossakowski, M. Drouineaud, and K. Sohr, *A temporal-logic extension of role-based access control covering dynamic separation of duties*, Proc. of TIME-ICTL 2003, Cairns, Queensland, Australia, July 8–10 2003.
17. M. J. Nash and K. R. Poland, *Some conundrums concerning separation of duty*, Proc. IEEE Symposium on Research in Security and Privacy, 1990, pp. 201–207.

18. I. Ray, N. Li, R. France, and D.-K. Kim, *Using UML to visualize role-based access control constraints*, Proc. of the 9th ACM symposium on Access control models and technologies, ACM Press New York, USA, 2004, pp. 115–124.

19. M. Richters, *A Precise Approach to Validating UML Models and OCL Constraints*, Ph.D. thesis, Universität Bremen, Fachbereich Mathematik und Informatik, Logos Verlag, Berlin, BISS Monographs, No. 14, 2002.

20. M. Richters and M. Gogolla, *Validating UML Models and OCL Constraints*, Proc. 3rd Int. Conf. Unified Modeling Language (UML'2000), Springer, Berlin, LNCS 1939, 2000, pp. 265–277.

21. J. Rumbaugh, I. Jacobson, and G. Booch, *The Unified Modeling Language Reference Manual, Second Edition*, Object Technology Series, Addison Wesley Longman, Reading, Mass., 2004.

22. R.S. Sandhu, E.J. Coyne, H.L. Feinstein, and C.E. Youman, *Role-based access control models*, Computer **29** (1996), no. 2, 38–47.

23. R. Simon and M. Zurko, *Separation of duty in role-based environments*, 10th IEEE Computer Security Foundations Workshop (CSFW '97), June 1997, pp. 183–194.

24. K. Sohr, M. Drouineaud, and G.-J. Ahn, *Formal Specification of Role-based Security Policies for Clinical Information Systems, Santa Fe, New Mexico*, Proc. of the 20th ACM Symposium on Applied Computing, 2005, To appear.

25. J. Warmer and A. Kleppe, *The Object Constraint Language: Getting your models ready for MDA*, Addison-Wesley, Reading/MA, 2003.

26. P. Ziemann and M. Gogolla, *An OCL Extension for Formulating Temporal Constraints*, Research Report 1/03, Universität Bremen, 2003.

# Unified Index for Mobile Object Data and Authorizations*

Vijayalakshmi Atluri and Qi Guo

Rutgers University, Newark NJ 07012, USA
{atluri, qiguo}@cimic.rutgers.edu

**Abstract.** Often, enforcing security incurs overhead, and as a result may degrade the performance of a system. In this paper, we attempt to address this problem in the context of enforcing access control policies in a mobile data object environment. There are a number of applications that call for fine-grained specification of security policies in guaranteeing the confidentiality of data or privacy of individuals in a mobile environment. In particular, the security policies state the rules for providing controlled access to the mobile user profiles, to their current location and movement trajectories, to mobile resources, and stationary resources based on the mobile user location. Either a subject or an object in an authorization specification can be a moving object. The access requests in such an environment can typically be based on *past, present* and *future* status of the moving objects. To effectively serve such access requests, one must efficiently organize the mobile objects as well as authorizations.

Although implementation of authorizations as access control list, capability list or access matrix is suitable for traditional data, it is not suitable to search mobile object authorizations as they are based on spatial and temporal attributes of subjects and objects, rather than subject and object identifiers. When a subject issues an access request, the system must first retrieve the relevant objects from the moving object database, and then verify whether there exists an authorization that allows the subject to access these objects. Since both the moving objects and authorizations are spatiotemporal in nature, for efficient processing of access requests, it is essential that they both be organized using some index structures. As a result, processing an access request requires searching two indexes - one, the moving object index, and the other, the authorization index. To improve the response time of access requests, in this paper, we propose a unified index structure, called $^S$TPR-tree to index both moving objects and authorizations that govern access to them. As a result of the unified index, access requests can be processed in one pass, thereby improving the response time. Note that current access control systems do not use any index for authorizations; our work is a step in this direction. We show how the $^S$TPR-tree can be constructed and maintained, and provide algorithms to process access requests.

## 1 Introduction

Recent advances to mobile communication, Global Positioning System (GPS) and Radio Frequency Identification (RFID) technologies have propelled the growth of a number of mobile services. Among them, *location-based service* (LBS) is becoming the

---

* This work is supported in part by the National Science Foundation under grant IIS-0242415.

S. De Capitani di Vimercati et al. (Eds.): ESORICS 2005, LNCS 3679, pp. 80–97, 2005.

most widely used services. LBS presents a major new market for the mobile industry, which includes (i) navigation services, (ii) providing business descriptions in a given geographical radius, real-time alerts on traffic conditions and information about highway services, (iii) personalized point-of-need information delivery, such as travel reservations, new or interesting products and services, and (iv) mobile advertising, which includes personalized, location-aware, and context-sensitive advertising, based on mobile customer profiles and preferences, as mobile devices are ideal for marketing channels for impulse buying [19]. For example, a wireless shopping site can be designed to present users with targeted content such as clothing items on sale, based on prior knowledge of their preferences and/or knowledge of their current location, such as proximity to a shopping mall [25]. LBS can be also be used in emergency situations to transmit messages via a reverse 911 service to individuals. To deliver LBS, service providers require access to customers' preference profiles either through a proprietary database or through an arrangement with an LBS provider, who matches customer profiles to vendor offerings. In order to implement such services, customization and personalization based on the location information, customer needs, and vendor offerings are required. Industrial and corporate applications, including tracking of material through the supply chain and inventory, and tracking physicians, patients, and equipment in a hospital. This relies on the deployment of RFID technologies, which is becoming inexpensive and will likely be used by a number of retail businesses.

In all the above applications, the mobile objects may include mobile phones, wireless PDAs, GPS equipped units such as boats, trucks, automobiles, airplanes, and soldiers, objects with RFID tags, a variety of moving sensors and other wireless computing devices.

In delivering mobile services, one encounters a number of security and privacy concerns, which are discussed below.

- **Location privacy:** Privacy of mobile users can be compromised by disclosing the location and movement. Note that it is essential to identify the location of the mobile object due to the following two reasons. First, to effectively function, location-based services require information about the location of the communication device. Second, in countries like U.S., the European Union and Japan, laws require that mobile telephones be able to provide location data with a fairly detailed accuracy for the purposes of emergency situations.

  Although identifying (and sometimes tracking) of the location of a mobile object is essential in delivering a mobile service, it could pose a threat to privacy of the person carrying the mobile device.

  Unlike the internet, location information has the potential to allow an adversary to physically locate a person, and therefore wireless subscribers carrying mobile devices have legitimate concerns about their personal safety, if such information should fall into the wrong hands. Laws and rules of varying clarity, offering different degrees of protection, have been or are in the process of being enacted in the U.S., the European Union and Japan [2].

- **User Information Privacy:** Privacy of mobile users can be compromised by revealing the sensitive profile information of the mobile users to unintended users. The needs of mobile commerce applications go beyond tracking users' locations, for example, they may additionally need to track user profiles and preferences in order to achieve mass personalization. This is because, to be effective, targeted advertising should not overwhelm the mobile consumers and must push information only to a certain segment of mobile consumers based on their preferences and profiles, and based on certain marketing criteria. Obviously, these consumers should be targeted only if they are in the location where the advertisement is applicable at the time of the offer. It is important to note here that user profile information may include both sensitive and non-sensitive attributes such as name, address, linguistic preference, age group, income level, marital status, education level, etc.

While mobile consumers like to benefit from personalization, they usually are not willing to share their sensitive profile information to all the merchants. To ensure the privacy of mobile users, it is important that the sensitive profile information is revealed to the respective merchants only on the need-to-know basis.

- **Security:** In addition to the privacy concerns mentioned above, there are a number of applications that call for securing resources based on the criteria of mobile objects. These include context (location)-sensitive access control, and ubiquitous computing environment, where access is permitted based on the location of the subjects/objects during a specific time.

In particular, the security policies provide controlled access to the mobile user profiles, to their current location and movement trajectories, to mobile resources, stationary resources based on the mobile user location. Therefore, an appropriate access control mechanism must be in place to enforce the authorization specifications reflecting the above security and privacy needs.

Access policies are specified as a set of authorizations, where each authorization states if a given subject possesses privileges to access an object. In the mobile environment, both subjects and objects can either be mobile or non-mobile. As a result either a subject or an object in an authorization specification can be a moving object. The access requests in such an environment can typically be on *past, present* and *future* status of the moving objects [26,13]. To effectively serve such access requests, one must efficiently organize the mobile objects as well as authorizations.

Although implementation of authorizations as access control list, capability list or access matrix is suitable for traditional data, it is not suitable to search authorizations in a mobile object environment, as they are based on spatial and temporal attributes of subjects and objects, rather than subject and object identifiers. Therefore, when a subject issues an access request, be it a past, future or current, the system must first retrieve the relevant object(s) from the moving object database, and then verify whether there exists an authorization that allows the subject to access these objects. Since both the moving objects and authorizations are spatiotemporal in nature, for efficient processing of access requests, it is essential that they both be organized using some index structures. As a result, processing an access request requires searching two indexes - one, the moving object index, and the other, the authorization index. To improve the response time of access requests, in this paper, we propose a unified index structure to index both moving objects and authorizations that govern access to them. Essentially, our index is created by carefully overlaying authorizations on top a moving object index, based on their spatiotemporal parameters.

Recently, a number of moving object index structures have been proposed. Unlike traditional spatiotemporal objects, moving objects are characterized by the moving spatial location that changes with time. In other words, a moving object can be specified as $\langle \bar{x}, \bar{v} \rangle$, where $\bar{x}$ represents its initial position vector and $\bar{v}$ its velocity vector. Current moving object index structures can be categorized primarily into three types: The first type stores the moving objects as transformed points in 2-dimensional dual $\langle \bar{x}, \bar{v} \rangle$ space [12,14], where dual transformation [15] is adopted. The second type stores them as lines in (d+1)-dimensional $\langle \bar{x}, t \rangle$ space (TB-tree and STR-tree [18,17]) by adding time $t$ as an addition dimension. The third type stores them as points in native, d-dimensional $\langle \bar{x} \rangle$ space (TPR-tree [20]). Our proposed unified index structure, $^S$TPR-tree, is constructed by carefully overlaying authorizations on top the TPR-tree, based on their spatiotemporal parameters. As a result of the unified index, access requests can be processed in one pass, thereby improving the response time. Note that current access control systems do not use any index for authorizations; our work is a step in this direction. We show how the $^S$TPR-tree can be constructed and maintained, and provide algorithms to process access requests.

This paper is organized as follows. We first present the preliminaries of the TPR-tree in section 2. In section 3, we propose our moving object authorization model. In section 4, we present our proposed novel unified index structure, the $^S$TPR-tree and illustrate our approach and strategy to overlay authorizations on top of the TPR-tree. In section 5, we describe how to process an access request that involves both searching for a moving object and evaluation of an authorization can be performed simultaneously. In section 6, we discuss the properties and limitations of our $^S$TPR-tree. Related work is presented in section 7. We conclude the paper by providing some insight into our future research in this area in section 8.

## 2    Preliminaries of the TPR-Tree

In this section, we present the details of the TPR-tree[20] since our $^S$TPR-tree is based on this. In particular, we present how a moving object is represented in the tree and how the tree is constructed to index these objects for efficient retrieval.

### 2.1    Representation of Moving Objects

Moving objects are data with attributes that change with time. Generally speaking, these objects may move in a d-dimensional embedding space. In this paper, for ease of visualization and explanation, we consider the space to be 2-dimensional. However, the formalism can be easily extended to higher dimensional spaces.

Let the set of moving objects be $MO = (mo_1, mo_2, \ldots mo_k)$. In the d-dimensional space, objects are specified as points which move with constant velocity $\bar{v} = \{v_1, v_2, \ldots v_d\}$ and initial location $\bar{x} = \{x_1, x_2, \ldots x_d\}$. The position $\bar{x}(t)$ of an object at future time $t(t \geq t_c)$ can be computed through the linear function of time, $\bar{x}(t) = \bar{x}(t_0) + \bar{v}(t - t_0)$ where $t_0$ is the initial time, $t_c$ the current time and $\bar{x}(t_0)$ the initial position. Considering a two-dimensional space, a moving object $mo_i$ moving in $\langle x, y \rangle$ space can be represented as follows: $mo_i = ((x_i, v_{i_x}), (y_i, v_{i_y}))$.

## 2.2   Time Parameterized Rectangle ($tpr$)

Given the trajectories of a set of moving objects $MO$ in the time interval $[t_0, t_0 + \delta t]$ in $\langle x, y, t \rangle$ space, we define the $tpr$ of $MO$ as a 3-dimensional bounding trapezoid which bounds all the moving objects in $MO$ during the entire time interval $[t_0, t_0 + \delta t]$. The $tpr$ of $MO$ can be defined as $(x^\vdash, x^\dashv, v_x^\vdash, v_x^\dashv, y^\vdash, y^\dashv, v_y^\vdash, v_y^\dashv)$ and its projection on $\langle x, t \rangle$ space is a time-parameterized bounding interval $[x^\vdash(t), x^\dashv(t)] = [x^\vdash(t_0) + v_x^\vdash(t - t_0), x^\dashv(t_0) + v_x^\dashv(t - t_0)]$ and the projection on $\langle y, t \rangle$ space is another time-parameterized bounding interval $[y^\vdash(t), y^\dashv(t)] = [y^\vdash(t_0) + v_y^\vdash(t - t_0), y^\dashv(t_0) + v_y^\dashv(t - t_0)]$, where $\forall i \in \{1, 2, \ldots, k\}$

$$
\begin{aligned}
x^\vdash &= x^\vdash(t_0) = min_i\{x_i(t_0)\} & v_x^\vdash &= min_i\{v_{i_x}\} \\
x^\dashv &= x^\dashv(t_0) = max_i\{x_i(t_0)\} & v_x^\dashv &= max_i\{v_{i_x}\} \\
y^\vdash &= y^\vdash(t_0) = min_i\{y_i(t_0)\} & v_y^\vdash &= min_i\{v_{i_y}\} \\
y^\dashv &= y^\dashv(t_0) = max_i\{y_i(t_0)\} & v_y^\dashv &= max_i\{v_{i_y}\}
\end{aligned}
$$

For example, figures 1 and 2 show a time parameterized rectangle and the trajectory of three moving objects a,b and c in $[t_0, t_0 + H]$ time interval, together with their projections on both $x-$ and $y-$ dimensions, respectively. We explain how this $tpr$ can be constructed using figure 3, which depicts 3 moving objects, a,b and c in $\langle x, y, t \rangle$ space. Based on their respective velocities, the lines represented by $a_x$ and $c_x$ form the lower and upper bound in the x-dimension, and $a_y$ and $c_y$ in y-dimension, respectively. As a result, the $tpr$ shown in the shaded region in figure 4 is formed. Note that the axes in figures 3 and 4 have been changed from those of figures 1 and 2 to improve readability. As shown in figure 1, at each time point, say $t_0$, $t_i$ and $t_0 + H$ the the slice of the $tpr$ is a rectangle with area $A_0$, $A_i$, and $A_H$, respectively.

**The $tpr$ hierarchy:** Given a set of $tpr$s, they can be organized in a hierarchical structure. As can be seen in figure 5, $tpr$ C encloses $tpr$s A and B. These three can be organized as a hierarchical structure with A and B being the children of C, as shown in figure 6. Essentially, at the bottom most level of the hierarchy, a set of moving objects could be grouped to form $tpr$s. Each $tpr$ of the next higher level is the bounding $tpr$ of the set of $tpr$s of all of its children. The root of the hierarchy is thus the bounding $tpr$ covering all its lower level $tpr$s in a recursive manner. Each $tpr$ has exactly the same attributes as its children $tpr$s except being larger in terms of its *spatial* magnitude while temporal span remains the same.

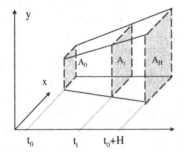

**Fig. 1.** TPR

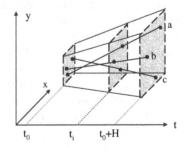

**Fig. 2.** The Trajectory of Moving Objects in TPR

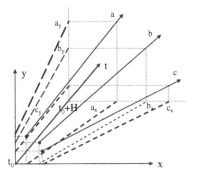

**Fig. 3.** The three moving objects a,b,c

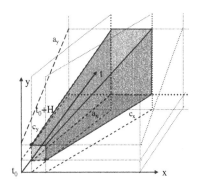

**Fig. 4.** The resultant *tpr* of figure 3

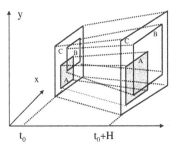

**Fig. 5.** The *tpr* Hierarchy

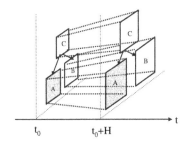

**Fig. 6.** The *tpr* hierarchy forming a tree

## 2.3  The TPR-Tree

In this section, we first introduce some essential parameters related to the TPR-tree.

**Time Horizon** ($H$): Recall that each moving object is represented by its initial position and velocity. However, given a moving object, it is unrealistic to assume that its velocity remains constant. Therefore, the predicted future location of a object specified as a linear function of time becomes less and less accurate as time elapses [20]. To address this issue, the TPR-tree defines a *time horizon*, $H$, representing the time interval during which the velocities of the moving objects hold good. It assumes that the tree is constructed by bulkloading the moving objects at some point in time (say $t_0$) and reconstructs the tree after $H$. In essence, the tree is good during $[t_0, t_0 + H]$ interval and all predictions made within this interval are acceptable in terms of the degree of accuracy. However, the tree deteriorates beyond its time horizon.

**Construction of the TPR-Tree:** TPR-tree is a time parameterized variant of R*-tree [10]. Each node in the TPR-tree represents a *tpr* of a set of moving objects. The way objects and in turn *tprs* are grouped and therefore be placed in a specific node is based on an *objective function* that can be specified using any of the following strategies, including the smallest sum of volumes of *tprs*, the smallest sum of the overlapping regions among *tpr*s, etc. One may adopt an appropriate strategy based on the application under consideration. So each node stores the bounding rectangle that grows with time to cover the enclosing moving objects. Thus, the bounding rectangle forms the 3-dimensional bounding trapezoid. While objects are stored only at the leaf nodes, the purpose of the upper level nodes is to direct the search via a specific path(s) to efficiently retrieve the objects that satisfy a user request.

The tree is constructed via the consecutive insertion operation into an initially empty *tpr* root. The candidate node to insert an object should either spatiotemporally enclose the new object being inserted, or needs the least volume enlargement to enclose this new object in time interval $[t_0, t_0 + H]$. The *tpr* of its ancestor node should be expanded to cover its children *tpr*s, if necessary. The detailed steps for insertion are similar to that of R*-tree. We use $N^\square$ to denote the *tpr* of node $N$.

## 3   Moving Object Authorization Model

In this section, we propose an authorization model suitable for moving object data. An authorization, in general, is specified on the basis of three parameters, $\langle s, o, p \rangle$. This triple specifies that subject $s$ is authorized to exercise privilege $p$ on object $o$. Note that both subjects and objects can be a moving object. To avoid confusion, from now on, we denote the objects as *auth-objects* (stands for authorization objects) and *mov-objects* (stands for moving objects). Let $S = \{s_1, s_2 \ldots\}$ denote a set of subjects, and $O = \{o_1, o_2 \ldots\}$ a set of auth-objects, and $MO$ a set of mov-objects. Note that in a moving object environment, authorization specifications should be capable of specifying access control policies based on spatiotemporal attributes of both subjects and auth-objects.

*Example 1. Examples of policies include:*

- **Policy 1:** *A mobile (phone/service) customer is willing to reveal his personal profile information to certain merchants only during the evening hours, and when he is close to the shopping mall. Note that, in this case, only the auth-object is a mov-object and this policy is based on object's spatiotemporal attributes.*
- **Policy 2:** *An employee may use print services only between "9am and 5pm" and while he is "in the office." Note that in this case, while the subject is a mov-object, the auth-object is not. Also note that the policy is based on the subject's spatiotemporal attributes.*

In the following, we discuss the auth-objects, subjects, privilege modes, and define authorization specifications. We have defined the mov-objects in section 2.

**Definition 1.** [Authorization] A *authorization* $\alpha$ is a 4 tuple $\langle ce, ge, p, \tau \rangle$, where $ce$ is a *credential expression* denoting a group of subjects, $ge$ is a *object expression* denoting a set of auth-objects, $p$ is a set of privilege modes, and $\tau$ is a temporal term.  $\square$

In this paper, we assume the formalism developed in [6] to specify $ce$, $ge$ and $\tau$. Due to space limitations, we do not review the details. Essentially, $ce$ can simply be a subject identifier(s) or an expression specified over the spatiotemporal attributes of subject credentials. Similarly, $ge$ can be an auth-object identifier or spatiotemporal attributes of the auth-object. $\tau$ can be a time point, a time interval or a set of time intervals.

As mentioned earlier, subjects can either be moving or static. For example, while the subject is static in policy 1, it is mobile in policy 2. In other words, the credential expression may involve attributes of the subject that are mobile in nature. for database access purpose. As an example, a police officer may exercise her privileges and issue a traffic violation ticket only if she is in her jurisdiction.

Auth-objects to be protected may include the traditional objects that are not mobile in nature, as well as attributes of the mov-objects. Again, some of the attributes of the moving objects are time dependent (rather mobile) such as the location or trajectory information of the mov-object, whereas certain other attributes are time-independent (e.g., the profile information of the person carrying a mov-object.)

The privilege modes include the traditional modes such as `read`, `write` and `update` as well as those specific to moving objects such as `locate` and `track`.

*Example 2. Examples of policies include:*
- $\alpha_1 = \langle merchant(i), \{profile(i) \wedge rectangle(j)=(50,60,10,10) \wedge [5pm, 9pm]\}, read \rangle$
- $\alpha_2 = \langle \{Tom(i) \wedge rectangle(j)=(50,60,10,10) \wedge [9pm, 5pm]\}, \{printer\}, execute \rangle$

Given an authorization $\alpha = \langle ce, ge, p, \tau \rangle$, we use $S^\alpha$ to denote the set of subjects that satisfy $ce$, $x_b^\alpha$, $x_e^\alpha$, $y_b^\alpha$ and $y_e^\alpha$ to denote the spatial extent specified by $ge$ represented by the lower and upper bounds in the $x$ and $y$ dimensions, respectively, and $[\tau_b^\alpha, \tau_e^\alpha]$ to denote the time interval during which $\alpha$ is valid. We use $\alpha^\square$ to denote the spatiotemporal region specified by the authorization $\alpha$. Essentially, $\alpha^\square$ is nothing but the region specified by $x_b^\alpha, x_e^\alpha, y_b^\alpha, y_e^\alpha, \tau_b^\alpha$, and $\tau_e^\alpha$.

## 4   The $^S$TPR-Tree

In this section, we present the $^S$TPR-tree, which is a secure extension of the TPR-tree in which authorizations are carefully overlaid on the nodes of the TPR-tree based to allow efficient evaluation of access requests. Recall that the TPR-tree is valid only for a fixed duration of the time, $H$, since the location of the objects is constantly changing. In other words, the tree accurately represents the data values during $H$, but there are no guarantees on its accuracy that may deteriorate beyond $H$ as the velocity of the mov-object recorded in the tree may no longer hold. While $H$ is typically of a relatively of short duration, the time interval ($[\tau_b, \tau_e]$) associated with the authorizations that specifies the validity period of the authorizations, is much longer. Therefore, in order to overlay authorizations on the short-lived TPR-tree, we must slice each authorization based on $H$. Recall that $\alpha_\tau$ can a timestamp or a single interval or multiple intervals. For the sake of simplicity, in the following, our discussion and formalism primarily focuses on a single time interval$[\tau_b, \tau_e]$. Our formalism can be easily extended to multiple intervals. Note that a timestamp can be represented as an interval $[\tau_b, \tau_b + 1]$.

Whenever $[\tau_b^\alpha, \tau_e^\alpha] > H$, we partition that $\alpha$ such that the time intervals of the partitions are mutually disjoint fragments whose interval does not exceed $H$.

**Definition 2. [Authorization Partition]** Given an authorization $\alpha$ and the time horizon $H$, the set of partitions of $\alpha$, $\mathcal{P}^\alpha = \{\alpha_1, \alpha_2 \ldots \alpha_s\}$ such that $\forall \alpha_r \in \mathcal{P}^\alpha$, the following properties are satisfied:

1. $\tau^{\alpha_i} \cap \tau^{\alpha_j} = \emptyset, i \neq j$;
2. $[\tau_b^{\alpha_r}, \tau_e^{\alpha_r}] \leq H$;
3. $\cup_{r=1}^{s} [\tau_b^{\alpha_r}, \tau_e^{\alpha_r}] = H$; and
4. $\forall i, j \in \{1 \ldots s\}, i \neq j, x_b^{\alpha_i} = x_b^{\alpha_j}, x_e^{\alpha_i} = x_e^{\alpha_j}, y_b^{\alpha_i} = y_b^{\alpha_j}$ and $y_e^{\alpha_i} = y_e^{\alpha_j}$.   □

Essentially, the above definition states that the time interval of each authorization is partitioned into intervals no greater than $H$ and the union of the intervals of all partitions should be same as $H$. Moreover, authorization partitioning does not change the spatial extent of the authorization. From now on, we denote an authorization partition as an authorization since their structures are the same except for the difference in their time interval. Without loss of generality, from now on in this paper, we use authorizations to refer to their partitions since we are concerned about a single time horizon $H$ at any given time.

### 4.1 Categorization of Authorizations

Given the spatiotemporal extent of the authorization $(\alpha^\square)$ and the *tpr* of a node $N$ in the tree $(N^\square)$, we are interested in the following three possible cases: (i) the former fully contains the latter, (ii) the former overlaps with the latter and (iii) the former is disjoint with the latter. Based on these three cases, we determine whether to overlay an authorization on a specific node in the tree. Accordingly, we label the authorizations (or rather their partitions), as one of the four types: *enclosing authorization, overlapping authorization, disjoint authorization* and *pending authorization*.

Let the binary operators $\supset_{\{x,y,t\}}, \cap_{\{x,y,t\}}$ and $\otimes_{\{x,y,t\}}$ denote *enclose, overlap* and *disjoint*, respectively, in all $x$, $y$ and $t$ dimensions.

**Definition 3.** Given a tree $T$, node $N$ in $T$, and an authorization $\alpha$, we define,

- *Enclosing Authorizations,* $\alpha_E(N) = \{\alpha | \alpha^\square \supset_{\{x,y,t\}} N^\square = True\}$;
- *Overlapping Authorizations,* $\alpha_O(N) = \{\alpha | \alpha^\square \cap_{\{x,y,t\}} N^\square = True\}$;
- *Disjoint Authorizations,* $\alpha_P(N) = \{\alpha | \alpha^\square \otimes_{\{x,y,t\}} N^\square = True\}$; and
- *Pending Authorizations,* $\alpha_P(T) = \{\alpha | \forall N \in T \, (\alpha \in \alpha_P(N))\}$.   □

For example, in figure 7, the TPR-tree consists of 3 nodes A, B and C with A and B being the children of C. Let there be 4 authorizations $\alpha_1, \alpha_2, \alpha_3$ and $\alpha_4$. Each shaded area represents the intersecting region between an authorization and a tree node. As we can be seen, $\alpha_1 \in \alpha_O(C)$ and $\alpha_2 \in \alpha_O(B)$. Note that at the same time it could be possible that $\alpha_1 \in \alpha_P(A)$, if $\alpha_1^\square$ is disjoint with $A^\square$. Since $\alpha_4$ is disjoint with $A^\square, B^\square$ and $C^\square$, $\alpha_4 \in \alpha_P(T)$.

### 4.2 Authorization Overlaying

In this section, we present our approach and strategy to overlay authorizations on top of the TPR-tree. The resultant tree is the $^S$TPR-tree. Algorithm 1 presents the details of our spatiotemporal overlaying approach. An authorization is overlaid on a node if it is an enclosing authorization, that is, if it both spatially *and* temporally encloses the node's *tpr*. Essentially, it enforces the following two rules.

**Authorization Overlaying Rules:** Given a TPR-tree $T$, for *each* path from root node to a leaf node, it enforces the following two overlaying rules, Rule 1 and Rule 2. These rules are applied in a specific order, first Rule 1 and then Rule 2.

- **Rule 1:**
  - **a:** If the authorization $\alpha \in \alpha_E(N)$, that is, if its spatiotemporal extent completely encloses that of node $N$, overlay $\alpha$ on $N$ and add it to the list of enclosed authorizations, $Auth_E(N)$. Halt the overlaying process of this authorization on this path.
  - **b:** If the authorization $\alpha \in \alpha_P(N)$, that is, if its spatiotemporal extent is disjoint with that of $N$, halt the overlaying process of this authorization on this path.
- **Rule 2:** If $N$ is the leaf node, overlay $\alpha$ on $N$ and add it to the list of enclosed authorizations, $Auth_O(N)$.

In the following, we provide the details of the various steps of our spatio-temporal overlaying algorithm. Essentially, algorithm 1 traverses the tree recursively in a top down manner starting from the root node. At each node $N$, $\alpha^{\square}$ is compared with $N^{\square}$. Several cases could occur based on the result of this comparison.

**Case 1:** If the authorization fully encloses the node, we will stop traversing the subtree of $N$ and overlay $\alpha$ on that node, specifically in $Auth_E(N)$. This is because, it is reasonable to assume that, if a subject is allowed to access objects within a certain spatiotemporal region, it is always allowed to access objects in the *subregion* of that. Therefore, after overlaying an authorization on a node, there is no need to overlay the same authorization on any of its descendents. However, we still need to check if the authorization's spatiotemporal extent overlaps with that of any of its sibling nodes. Since the enclosing relation between $\alpha$ and $N$ has no implication on the spatiotemporal relations between $\alpha$ and $N$'s siblings, this step is essential.

**Case 2:** If the authorization's extent overlaps with that of the node, then we handle it differently depending on the level of the node in the tree.

- If the node is at the leaf level, then we overlay $\alpha$ and store it in $Auth_O(N)$ associated with that leaf node. This is because, when the authorization only overlaps with a leaf node, it means that it cannot fully enclose any node from root to that leaf in that path. However, to ensure that no relevant authorizations are discarded, this must be overlaid on the leaf node only.
- If the node is at the non-leaf level, then we traverse to the level below, and compare $\alpha^{\square}$ with *each* of the children nodes of $N$. This is because, the authorization may have different spatiotemporal relationships with each of its children nodes.

**Case 3:** If the spatiotemporal extent of the authorization is disjoint with the node, then we stop traversing the subtree and store $\alpha$ in $Auth_P(N)$ to be included in the pending authorizations of the tree. After each $H$ interval, when a new TPR-tree is constructed based on the new position and velocity information of each moving object, the previously non-applicable authorizations may become relevant.

Based on this overlaying strategy, we can make the following observations:

- It is possible that an authorization may be overlaid on more than one node, resulting in a number of copies of the same authorization being stored in the tree. However, given a specific path from the root to a leaf, there may exist at most one copy of an authorization, regardless of its location or whether it is stored in $Auth_E(N)$ or $Auth_O(N)$.

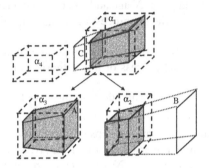

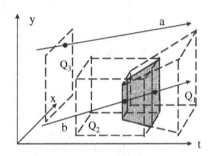

**Fig. 7.** Four categories of authorizations          **Fig. 8.** The different query types

- Although the spatiotemporal extent of an authorization at node $N$ may not completely enclose the spatiotemporal extents of the authorizations at the descendents of $N$, it may *cover* them. By cover we mean that, it is not necessary to further traverse the subtree if an authorization is found at that node. For example, if an authorization is overlaid on node C in the $^S$TPR-tree in figure 7, it covers C's children nodes A and B for the same subject(s) in the overlaid authorization.
- The enclosing authorizations are overlaid on a node as high as possible in the tree. In other words, an authorization $\alpha$ will be overlaid on a node $N$ if there exists no other node $M$ at higher level than $N$ in the tree such that $\alpha \in \alpha_E(M)$.
- Leaf nodes may be associated with two sets of authorizations, $Auth_E(N)$ and $Auth_O(N)$, whereas, non-leaf node have only one set of authorizations, $Auth_E(N)$, associated with them.

## 5   Access Request Evaluation

In this section, we present our approach to processing the access requests for different types of queries posed in the mobile object environment.

### 5.1   Query Types

The user request can fall into one of the following query types.

**Definition 4. [Generalized Query]** We define a generalized query, denoted as a quadruple $Q = \langle R_b, R_e, \tau_b, \tau_e \rangle$, which is a 3-dimensional trapezoid in the spatiotemporal space that has two parallel rectangular bases $R_b$ and $R_e$ projected to point $\tau_b$ and $\tau_e$ on the temporal dimension respectively.

There are two special cases of the generalized query, which are as follows:

- **Time Point Query:** is the generalized query such that $R_b = R_e = R$, $\tau_b = \tau_e = \tau$.
- **Time Interval Query:** is the generalized query such that $R_b = R_e = R$.

For example, figure 8 depicts the above three types of queries. Evidently, $Q_1$ is a generalized query, $Q_2$ is a time interval query and $Q_3$ is a time slice query. Note that, while the moving object $a$ satisfies $Q_3$, the moving object $b$ satisfies both $Q_1$ and $Q_2$.

### 5.2    User Request Evaluation

This section presents the user request evaluation, presented in algorithm 2, to retrieve the moving objects that satisfy the request. Formally, a user request is a tuple, $U = \langle s, Q \rangle$. We use $U^{\square}$ and $s^{U}$ to denote the spatiotemporal extent and the subject of the access request $U$.

The spatiotemporal query evaluation presented in algorithm 2 is based on our spatiotemporal overlaying strategy. In the following, we explain the various steps of algorithm 2. It traverses the tree from the root down to each node on the leaf level. During this traversal, it compares the spatiotemporal extent of $U$ with that of each node $N$.

1. If the spatiotemporal extent of user request either overlaps or fully contains that of the node, the authorizations in either $Auth_E(N)$ or $Auth_O(N)$ are evaluated. Essentially, it checks if there exists any relevant authorization for the subject issuing the access request. If the node is at the leaf level, $Auth_E(N)$ is first checked for relevant authorizations. If none is found, then $Auth_O(N)$ is checked. If the node is a non-leaf node, $Auth_E(N)$ is checked for relevant authorizations. If none is found, the traversal continues. If a relevant authorization is found, there is no need to check any authorization associated with $N$'s descendents. Since we do not consider negative authorizations, the subject under consideration is allowed access to the spatiotemporal extent of the descendents of $N$.
2. If the spatiotemporal extent of user's access request is disjoint with that of the node $N$, we simply stop the search since we already know that no relevant authorizations can be found in $N$'s subtree to satisfy the user request. However, the spatiotemporal extent of user's access request may still overlap or enclose with other nodes on the same level of the tree, thus we still need to check $N$'s siblings.

Note that, in algorithm 2, we use HEIGHT$_{leaf}$ to denote the height of the tree, i.e. the length of the path from the root to a leaf. The operation $\cup_{\{x,y,t\}}$ is *not* a boolean operator; it produces the union of the spatiotemporal extents. Also, we assume the default value of the boolean variable *authorized* is FALSE, which means that by default subjects are *not* entitled access unless an explicitly specified relevant authorization is found. The operation EVALUATE( ) computes and returns the intersecting region among its parameters, it returns $\emptyset$ if the intersection among the parameters is empty EVALUATE() is a *overloading* function in that it can take different number of parameters. RETRIEVE( ) takes the spatiotemporal extents as the parameter and retrieves all moving objects falling into those spatiotemporal extents.

## 6    Discussion

In this section, we discuss the properties of our proposed $^{S}$TPR-tree with respect to completeness and efficiency, as well as its limitations which are planned to be addressed as part of our future work.

### 6.1    Properties of $^{S}$TPR-Tree

In this section, we demonstrate that our overlaying strategy and evaluation strategies are both *complete* and *efficient*.

**Theorem 1.** Given a set of authorizations $A$, Algorithm 1 overlays authorizations on the $^S$TPR-tree in such a way that the evaluation of access request $U$ by algorithm 2 is *complete*.

**Proof sketch:** By complete, we mean, given a user access request $U$ by subject $s$, we evaluate every authorization relevant to $s$. Let this set of relevant authorizations be $\alpha(s^U)$. This can be proved in three steps. First, we can prove that our overlaying procedure (algorithm 1) overlays every authorization in $\alpha(s^U)$ on the *search path* of $U$. Second, we can prove that our evaluation procedure (algorithm 2) traverses every search path and therefore it evaluates all $\alpha(s^U)$. Third, we can prove that our halting strategies of traversal in both the algorithms do not violate the completeness principle.
□

In addition to being complete our overlaying strategy is efficient in the sense it does not do any additional traversal than necessary. This is achieved as a result of the two of the following strategies we adopt during the overlay process: We overlay the authorizations on the first node encountered on the search path that totally encloses the region covered by the node.As a result, authorizations are overlaid as high up as possible in the tree. Since the search path is from root to the leaf, we will encounter the relevant authorizations as early as possible during the traversal. Our traversal essentially avoids evaluating (1) non-relevant authorizations as much as possible, and 2) relevant but redundant authorizations as much as possible.

## 6.2   Limitations of Our $^S$TPR-Tree

Our proposed index structure is not capable of layering authorizations with privilege mode `track`. This is because, in order to entertain such privilege mode, it requires persistent storage of the moving object location information. As such it requires the index that maintains historical information (in addition to the current and future). We defer this to our future work.

Moreover, our index structure is capable of overlaying authorizations where either subjects or auth-objects are moving objects. However, it is not capable of overlaying authorizations where both subjects and auth-objects are moving objects. For example, it is not capable of supporting authorization policies similar to the one specified in the example below. This is because, subjects and auth-objects are represented by different nodes of the moving object index tree. As a result, supporting such authorization overlaying may require splitting the subject and auth-object components. We defer this to our future work.

- **Policy 3:** A manager can access the location of his employee (John) information between "9am and 5pm" and while the manager is "in the office." Note that both the subject (manager in this case) and auth-object (his employee) are mov-objects. This policy is based on the subject's as well as auth-object's spatiotemporal attributes.

## 7   Related Work

Recently, there has been a flurry of activity in developing indexing structures for moving object databases to effectively serve queries of *past, present* and *future* types [26,13] on moving objects. Sistla et al. [23] propose a Moving Objects Spatio-temporal Model (MOST) to model object location as a linear function of time. A modification to R-trees to represent past trajectories of moving points as polylines has been proposed by Pfoser et al. [18]. Other work on indexing future trajectories include the PMR-Quadtrees [21,24] by Tayeb et al. that index the future linear trajectories of one-dimensional moving point objects as line segments. These methods do not seem to apply to more than one dimension. Kollios et al. [12] provide theoretical lower bounds for this indexing problem. Basch et al. [9] propose main-memory data structure (kinetic) for mobile objects, whose ideas are applied by Agarwal et al. [3] to external range trees [4]. The Time Parameterized R-trees (TPR-trees) [20], which is an extension of R*-trees, proposed by Saltenis et al., rather than attempt to continuously update moving object locations [26], represent objects as functions of time. Saltenis et al. claim that, similar to regular R-trees, the TPR-trees are capable of indexing points in any number of dimensions and are easily extended to accommodate objects that are not points. In [16], Palanis et al. extend the TPR-tree to accommodate past queries.

Atluri and Mazzoleni have proposed a unified index, called RMX-Quadtree [8], for geo-spatial data and authorizations that govern access to them. In [7], Atluri and Guo have proposed a unified index called STAR-Tree that can uniformly index both spatiotemporal objects and the authorizations. STAR-Tree relaxes several restrictive assumptions of RMX-Quadtree and therefore is more general. While the above two contributions are relevant but are limited to index data as well as authorizations specified on spatiotemporal data that is static in nature. The focus of this paper is to provide uniform indexing scheme for mobile data and the respective authorizations.

An index scheme for moving object data and user profiles has been proposed by Atluri et al. [5]. However, this does not consider authorizations. Beresford et al. [11,22] have proposed techniques that let users benefit from location-based applications, while preserving their location privacy. Mobile users, in general, do not permit the information shared among different location based services. Primarily, the approach relies on hiding the true identity of a customer from the applications receiving the user's location, by frequently changing pseudonyms so that users avoid being identified by the locations they visit. A system for delivering permission-based location-aware mobile advertisements to mobile phones using Bluetooth positioning and Wireless WAP Push has been developed [1]. An index structure has been proposed to index authorizations ensuring that the customer profile information be disclosed to the merchants based on the choice of the customers [27]. However, this provides separate index structures for data and authorizations, and therefore is not a unified index.

# 8   Conclusions and Future Work

Often, enforcing security incurs overhead, and as a result, may degrade the performance of a system. In this paper, we address this problem in the context of enforcing access control policies in a mobile data object environment. Although implementation of authorizations as access control list, capability list or access matrix is suitable for traditional data, it is not suitable to search authorizations as they are based on spatial and temporal attributes of subjects and objects, rather than subject and object identifiers.

Therefore, when a subject issues an access request, the system must first retrieve the relevant object(s) from the moving object database, and then verify whether there exists an authorization that allows the subject to access these objects. Since both the moving objects and authorizations are spatiotemporal in nature, for efficient processing of access requests, it is essential that they both be organized using some index structures. As a result, processing an access request requires searching two indexes - one, the moving object index, and the other, the authorization index. To improve the response time of access requests, in this paper, we have proposed a unified index structure, called $^S$TPR-tree to index both moving objects and authorizations that govern access to them. Essentially, our index has been created by carefully overlaying authorizations on top a moving object index, specifically the TPR-tree. As a result of the unified index, access requests can be processed in one pass, thereby improving the response time. We have shown how the $^S$TPR-tree can be constructed and maintained, and provided algorithms to process access requests.

Currently, we are conducting a performance evaluation to demonstrate that our uniform indexing scheme indeed has significant impact on the response time. Note that current access control systems do not use any index for authorizations. Our work is a step in this direction of improving the response time of access requests.

Our proposed unified indexing scheme is not capable of historical queries, which requires persistent storage of moving objects [16]. As a result, our $^S$TPR-tree cannot overlay and evaluate authorizations with the privilege mode *track*. In addition, our overlaying strategy we have adopted in the $^S$TPR-tree is not capable of overlaying authorizations in which both subject and authorization objects happen to be moving objects. We will enhance our $^S$TPR-tree to address these issues. Support for negative authorizations require significant changes to the overlaying of authorizations as well as evaluating access requests. In this paper, we do not consider negative authorizations; we will extend our work to support negative authorizations.

# References

1. L. Aalto, N. Gthlin, J. Korhonen, and T. Ojala. Bluetooth and wap push based location-aware mobile advertising system. In *Proceedings of the international conference on Mobile systems, applications, and services*, pages 49–58, 2004.
2. L. Ackerman, J. Kempf, and T. Miki. Wireless location privacy: A report on law and policy in the United States, the Eureprean Union, and Japan. *DoCoMo USA Labs Technical Report DCL-TR2003-001*, 2003.
3. P. Agarwal, L. Arge, and J. Erickson. Indexing moving points. In *Proceedings of the ACM Symposium on Principles of Database Systems*, pages 175–186, 2000.
4. L. Arge, V. Samoladas, and J. Vitter. On two-dimensional indexability and optimal range search indexing. In *Proceedings of the ACM Symposium on Principles of Database Systems*, pages 346–357,1999.
5. V. Atluri, N. Adam, and M. Youssef. Towards a unified index scheme for mobile data and customer profiles in a location-based service environment. In *Workshop on Next Generation Geospatial Information (NG2I'03)*, 2003.
6. V. Atluri and S. Chun. An authorization model for geospatial data. *IEEE Trans. Dependable Sec. Comput.*, 1(4):238–254, 2004.

7. V. Atluri and Q. Guo. STAR-Tree: An index structure for efficient evaluation of spatiotemporal authorizations. In *IFIP TC11/WG 11.3 Eighteenth Annual Conference on Data and Applications Security*, pages 31–47, 2004.

8. V. Atluri and P. Mazzoleni. Uniform indexing for geospatial data and authorizations. In *DBSec*, pages 207–218, 2002.

9. J. Basch, L. Guibas, C. Silverstein, and L. Zhang. A practical evaluation of kinetic data structures. In *Proceedings of the annual symposium on Computational geometry*, pages 388–390, 1997.

10. N. Beckmann, H. Kriegel, R. Schneider, and B. Seeger. The R*-Tree: an efficient and robust access method for points and rectangles. In *SIGMOD Conference*, pages 322–331, 1990.

11. A. Beresford and F. Stajano. Mix zones: User privacy in location-aware services. In *PerCom Workshops*, pages 127–131, 2004.

12. G. Kollios, D. Gunopulos, and V. Tsotras. On indexing mobile objects. In *Proceedings of the ACM Symposium on Principles of Database Systems*, pages 261–272, 1999.

13. J. Moreira, C. Ribeiro, and T. Abdessalem. Query operations for moving objects database systems. In *Proceedings of the eighth ACM international symposium on Advances in geographic information systems*, pages 108–114. ACM Press, 2000.

14. D. Papadopoulos, G. Kollios, D. Gunopulos, and V. Tsotras. Indexing mobile objects on the plane. In *DEXA Workshops*, pages 693–697, 2002.

15. D. Papadopoulos, G. Kollios, D. Gunopulos, and V. Tsotras. Indexing mobile objects using duality transforms. *IEEE Data Eng. Bull.*, 25(2):18–24, 2002.

16. M. Pelanis, S. Saltenis, and C. Jensen. Indexing the past, present and anticipated future positions of moving objects. *A TIMECENTER Technical Report TR-78*, 2004.

17. D. Pfoser. Indexing the trajectories of moving objects. *IEEE Data Eng. Bull.*, 25(2):3–9, 2002.

18. D. Pfoser, C. Jensen, and Y. Theodoridis. Novel approaches in query processing for moving object trajectories. In *Proceedings of 26th International Conference on Very Large Data Bases*, pages 395–406, 2000.

19. A. Rao, C. Papadimitriou, S. Shenker, and I. Stoica. Geographic routing without location information. In *MOBICOM*, pages 96–108, 2003.

20. S. Saltenis, C. Jensen, S. Leutenegger, and M. Lopez. Indexing the positions of continuously moving objects. In *Proceedings of the 2000 ACM SIGMOD International Conference on Management of Data*, volume 29, pages 331–342, 2000.

21. H. Samet and M. Tamminen. Approximating csg trees of moving objects. *The Visual Computer*, 6(4):182–209, 1990.

22. D. Scott, A. Beresford, and A. Mycroft. Spatial security policies for mobile agents in a sentient computing environment. In *FASE*, pages 102–117, 2003.

23. P. Sistla, O. Wolfson, S. Chamberlain, and S. Dao. Modeling and querying moving objects. In *Proceedings of the Thirteenth International Conference on Data Engineering, April 7-11, 1997 Birmingham U.K*, pages 422–432, 1997.

24. J. Tayeb, O. Ulusoy, and O. Wolfson. A Quadtree-Based Dynamic Attribute Indexing Method. *The Computer Journal*, 41(3):185–200, 1988.

25. V. Venkatesh, V. Ramesh, and A. Massey. Understanding usability in mobile commerce. *Commun. ACM*, 46(12):53–56, 2003.

26. O. Wolfson, B. Xu, S. Chamberlain, and L. Jiang. Moving objects databases: Issues and solutions. In *10th International Conference on Scientific and Statistical Database Management, Proceedings, Capri, Italy, July 1-3, 1998*, pages 111–122, 1998.

27. M. Youssef, N. Adam, and V. Atluri, Preserving Mobile Customer Privacy: An Access Control System for Moving Objects and Customer Information, *International Conference on Mobile Data Management*, Lecture Notes in Computer Science, 2005.

# A   Algorithms

---

**Algorithm 1.** Spatiotemporal Overlay

---

1: **Input:** tree root $N$, authorization to be overlaid $\alpha$, tree height $h$
2: **Output:** none
3: **Assumption:** the height of the root is 0
4: **Constant Variable:** HEIGHT$_{leaf}$
5: **Initialization:**$h = 0$
6: **Procedure** ST-Overlay $(N, \alpha, h)$
7: **if** $(h = \text{HEIGHT}_{leaf})$ **then**
8:     **if** $(\alpha^\square \supset_{\{x,y,t\}} N^\square)$ =TRUE **then**
9:         $Auth_E(N) \leftarrow \alpha$
10:     **else if** $(\alpha^\square \cap_{\{x,y,t\}} N^\square)$ =TRUE **then**
11:         $Auth_O(N) \leftarrow \alpha$
12:     **else**
13:         $Auth_P \leftarrow \alpha$
14:     **end if**
15:     **return**
16: **end if**
17: **if** $(\alpha^\square \supset_{\{x,y,t\}} N^\square)$ =TRUE **then**
18:     $Auth_E(N) \leftarrow \alpha$
19:     **return**
20: **end if**
21: **for** each child $C_i$ of $N$ **do**
22:     ST-Overlay$(C_i, \alpha, h + 1)$
23: **end for**

---

---

**Algorithm 2.** Spatiotemporal Query Evaluation

---

1: **Input:** tree root $N$, user query $U$, tree height $h$
2: **Output:** the identifiers of targeted objects
3: **Assumption:** the height of the root is 0
4: **Constant Variable:** HEIGHT$_{leaf}$
5: **Initialization:** $h = 0, authorized =$ FALSE
6: **Procedure** ST-QueryEval($N, U, h, authorized$)
7: **if** $(U^\square \otimes_{\{x,y,t\}} N^\square) =$ TRUE **then**
8:     **return** $\emptyset$
9: **end if**
10: $overlap \leftarrow \emptyset$
11: **if** $authorized =$ FALSE **then**
12:     **if** $\exists \alpha \in Auth_E(N)((s^U \in S^\alpha) \wedge ((U^\square \cap_{\{x,y,t\}} \alpha^\square) =$TRUE $))$ **then**
13:         $authorized \leftarrow$ TRUE
14:     **end if**
15:     **if** $(authorized =$ FALSE $) \wedge (h =$HEIGHT$_{leaf})$ **then**
16:         **for** each $\alpha \in Auth_O(N)$ **do**
17:             **if** $s^U \in S^\alpha$ **then**
18:                 $overlap \leftarrow overlap \cup_{\{x,y,t\}}$ EVALUATE $(U^\square, N^\square, \alpha^\square)$
19:             **end if**
20:         **end for**
21:         **return** RETRIEVE $(overlap)$
22:     **else if** $h =$HEIGHT$_{leaf}$ **then**
23:         $overlap \leftarrow$ EVALUATE($U^\square, N^\square$)
24:         **return** RETRIEVE($overlap$)
25:     **end if**
26: **else if** $h =$HEIGHT$_{leaf}$ **then**
27:     $overlap \leftarrow$ EVALUATE($U^\square, N^\square$)
28:     **return** RETRIEVE($overlap$)
29: **end if**
30: **for** each child $C_i$ of $N$ **do**
31:     ST-QueryEval($C_i, U, h + 1, authorized$)
32: **end for**

---

# On Obligations*

Manuel Hilty, David Basin, and Alexander Pretschner

Information Security, ETH Zürich, Switzerland
{hiltym, basin, pretscha}@inf.ethz.ch

**Abstract.** Access control is concerned with granting access to sensitive data based on conditions that relate to the past or present, so-called provisions. Expressing requirements from the domain of data protection necessitates extending this notion with conditions that relate to the future. Obligations, in this sense, are concerned with commitments of the involved parties. At the moment of granting access, adherence to these commitments cannot be guaranteed. An example is the requirement "do not re-distribute data", where the actions of the involved parties may not even be observable. We provide a formal framework that allows us to precisely specify data protection policies. A syntactic classification of formulas gives rise to natural and intuitive formal definitions of provisions and obligations. Based on this classification, we present different mechanisms for checking adherence to agreed upon commitments.

## 1 Introduction

With the ever increasing use of modern communication technologies in the commercial and public sectors, the adequate handling of personal data is a growing concern. Such data is often distributed across many public and commercial databases, and processed by many applications. This opens the door to illegitimate access and misuse of data. To prevent misuse, many countries have passed data protection laws and privacy regulations, but these are often not adequately reflected in the distributed information systems that store and process sensitive data. When building such systems, one needs firstly to be able to precisely define and specify the underlying requirements, and secondly a means of ensuring that personal data is handled in accordance with applicable laws and regulations. To date, neither problem is solved in a fully satisfactory manner.

By controlling who may access which data, traditional access control mechanisms solve one part of the problem. However, they are unable to make decisions based on *how* the data will be used once accessed, and this is an essential aspect of many data protection regulations. For instance, it should be possible to grant read access to personal data under the stipulation that the data be used exclusively for certain predefined purposes. An example is a database maintained by one government agency that must not disclose citizen data to other administrations unless the data is used solely for statistical purposes. Retention, protection,

---

* This work was partially supported by the SBF Project 03.0468-1, "GUIDE: Creating a European Identity Management Architecture for eGovernment".

S. De Capitani di Vimercati et al. (Eds.): ESORICS 2005, LNCS 3679, pp. 98–117, 2005.

or redistribution of data are further examples of relevant issues in the context of data protection. This paper discusses the handling of *data protection requirements*: statements that, in addition to specifying who may access which data, also impose constraints on how the data may be used. Our formal framework makes it possible to precisely define and specify a large subset of data protection requirements, and, upon implementation, also to control adherence to commitments related to data protection. This makes the framework attractive as a stepping stone to future, practical, data protection specification languages. Naturally, it also gives rise to the possibility of formally analyzing data protection requirements, e.g. to determine their consistency.

Our system model consists of agents that own or request access to data. Access is granted or denied by a reference monitor based on conditions that are expressed in (formalized) data protection requirements. In the form of *provisions*, these conditions can relate to the past or present, e.g. "explicit owner consent must be presented when access to data is granted". In the form of *obligations*, the conditions can also relate to the future, e.g. "data must be deleted within a month", or "the further distribution of the data must be logged". We consider obligations from two perspectives: time and observability, i.e. the possibility of checking adherence to a commitment. Our formalization of obligations leads to a natural classification along these two dimensions.

*1. Time:* Obligations are either concerned with fixed time intervals, or are defined as eternally valid conditional statements—invariants. We will argue that unbounded eventuality—roughly, liveness—is not relevant in the context of data protection.

*2. Observability:* We address the problem exemplified by the obligation to delete data some time after it has been obtained from the reference monitor. From the monitor's perspective, this is usually impossible to enforce and because it is not directly observable, difficult to check. We show how to transform non-observable events into observable ones, which then can be checked by the reference monitor. Upon violation of an obligation, the reference monitor can take necessary actions.

Existing generalizations of traditional access control models cannot capture the entirety of the above data protection issues. Some omit certain classes of data protection requirements and thus leave room for generalization; others do not provide a precise semantics for their frameworks (Section 5).

To summarize, the *problem* that we tackle is the lack of precise definitions of data protection requirements (that necessarily precede a practically useful specification language for data protection policies) and, in particular, the lack of a precise understanding of how adherence to obligations can be checked. Our *solution* consists of a conceptual and a methodological part. Conceptually, to precisely define and understand the cornerstones of data protection requirements, we show how to specify them in a logic that adds the dimension of distribution to classical temporal logics. This allows for the intuitive distinction between provisions and obligations on the one hand, and between observability and non-observability on the other. Methodologically, we show how to specify mechanisms that rely on the transformation of non-observable parts of an obligation into observable ones. Overall, we see our *contribution* as (a) the extension of access control models in the context of data protection with precisely defined concepts, (b) a classification of data protection requirements along the dimensions of time and observability, and (c) the description of generic mechanisms to cope with non-observable parts of obligations.

The remainder of this paper is organized as follows. We take an informal look at data protection and set the scene at the beginning of Section 2. Then we introduce Distributed Temporal Logic (DTL) [5,6], which we use to define our formal framework and to classify data protection requirements. In Section 3 we show how non-observable requirements can be transformed into requirements that can be checked by a central reference monitor. We use Section 4 to illustrate the ideas of this paper with an example. In Sections 5 and 6 we describe related work and our conclusions. Formal details on DTL can be found in the appendices.

## 2   Data Protection Requirements

In this section, we examine data protection requirements. First we introduce the kinds of problems we are concerned with from an informal point of view. Then we present our formalism and show how it can be used to formalize data protection policies. We also present a classification of data protection requirements based on their temporal structure and the kinds of observations that different principals in a distributed system can make.

### 2.1   An Informal View on Data Protection

Privacy is concerned with anonymity and data protection. Our work focuses on data protection, i.e. controlling the access to and the usage of sensitive personal data. By personal data, we denote any data that is, or can be, associated with a person. We consider systems consisting of two kinds of agents: a server reference monitor $r$ and a set of subjects $Sub$. $Dat$ is a set of personal data objects. The reference monitor[1] controls access to the data items in $Dat$. We consider scenarios where a subject $s_i \in Sub$ attempts to access a data object $d_k \in Dat$. In this case, we also refer to $s_i$ as the *requester*.

We examine policies that define how to control the flow of sensitive data in a distributed environment (this involves access control decisions made by $r$ as well as controlling the further distribution of data between the subjects), and how the data must be used by the subjects. Sources for the different kinds of requirements were existing privacy policy description languages like P3P [19], scientific papers such as [11], and data protection regulations from different countries.

Data protection requirements include (1) access control requirements, which should be as flexible as possible, i.e. able to express different access control

---

[1] We will use the term reference monitor rather liberally to describe control programs that can not only monitor and prohibit actions, but can also trigger corrective actions such as the application of penalties.

paradigms; (2) actions that must be performed prior to the access, e.g. presenting a certificate or gathering the consent of the data owner; (3) actions that must be performed within a certain time period or on a recurring basis, e.g. informing the data owner about the access or about any usage of the data; (4) restrictions on the further distribution of the data; (5) restrictions on the possible purposes for which the data may be used; (6) limitations on the retention time; (7) mandatory uses of protection mechanisms; and (8) duties of keeping the data up-to-date.

## 2.2  Gentle Introduction to DTL

We use Distributed Temporal Logic (DTL) to formally express privacy requirements. In this section, we give a brief, high-level overview of DTL, relegating
the formal presentation to Appendix A.

DTL [5,6] can be seen as a generalization of Linear Temporal Logic (LTL)
[13] and our explanation here will focus on the differences. DTL contains temporal operators for reasoning about the past and the future. In addition, it
provides a distributed view of systems. Whereas LTL formulas express a global
view of a distributed system in terms of temporal properties of its traces, DTL
formulas formalize system properties from the local view of the system's agents.
Statements $\varphi$ refer to an agent $a$'s local data space; this is expressed as $@_a[\varphi]$.
$@.[\cdot]$ formulas cannot be nested. Intuitively, $\varphi$ includes *state propositions* such
as "$a$ possesses a certificate", and *actions* such as "$a$ deletes a file". $\varphi$ may also
express temporal behavior relative to the agent's past or future. Action symbols and state propositions are domain dependent and must be defined for each
concrete scenario. Examples are given later in this section and in Section 4.

Agents $a$ and $b$ can communicate messages time-synchronously and reliably
via *snd/rcv* pairs, which are parts of their respective set of local actions: the
action $snd(b, m)$ denotes the sending of message $m$ to agent $b$ and $rcv(b, m)$
denotes the simultaneous reception of message $m$ from agent $b$.

DTL future-time operators are the unary operators $X$ (*next*) and $G$ (*always*),
and the binary $U$ operator (*weak until*). DTL past-time operators are the unary
operators $Y$ (*previous*), $P$ (*sometime in the past*), and $H$ (*always in the past*), and
the binary operator $S$ (*since*). $X^n$ is shorthand for $n$ repeated applications of $X$.
As further syntactic sugar, we define $F^{\leq n}\varphi \equiv \bigvee_{i=0}^{n} X^i \varphi$ for any $n \in \mathbb{N}$. We will
employ a similar shorthand with $G$ (replacing $\vee$ by $\wedge$ in the above). Analogously,
by substituting $X$ with $Y$ in the definition $F^{\leq n}\varphi$ (respectively $G^{\leq n} \varphi$), we get the
definition of $P^{\leq n} \varphi$ ($H^{\leq n} \varphi$).

Grossly simplifying matters, the semantics of DTL—formally defined in Appendix A—is similar to LTL and it takes into account that (a) propositions can
be true only for specific agents and (b) there is communication (synchronization)
between agents.

## 2.3  Formal Representation of Data Protection Policies

We now show how the kinds of systems introduced in Section 2.1 can be described
using DTL, and how privacy policies can be formally expressed. To simplify

notation, we assume discrete time, e.g. one time step per day for the examples given later.

We define two subsets of DTL formulas: *provisional formulas* and *obligational formulas*. Provisional formulas are formulas $@_a[\varphi]$ for an agent $a$ that contain no future-time temporal operators. Obligational formulas are formulas of the same form that do contain future-time temporal operators, but no past-time temporal operators. Further, obligational formulas must not contain temporal operators that are under the scope of a negation, respectively on the left-hand side of an implication.[2]

We also divide DTL formulas into observable formulas and non-observable formulas. These are defined from the reference monitor $r$'s point of view. Intuitively, observable formulas are only concerned with $r$'s local state or actions that $r$ can observe. Actions that $r$ can observe are either local actions of $r$ or communication involving $r$. More formally, *observable formulas* are of the form $@_r[\varphi]$ or $@_{s_i}[snd(r, msg)]$, for a subject $s_i$ and a message $msg$. *Non-observable formulas* are all other formulas.

The policies we consider are conjunctions of *decision rules*, which are formulas of the form

$$@_r[authorize(s_i, d_k)] \Rightarrow (p_1 \wedge \dots \wedge p_m \wedge o_1 \wedge \dots \wedge o_n),$$

where $p_1, \dots, p_m$ are observable provisional formulas, $o_1, \dots, o_n$ are obligational formulas, and $m, n \geq 0$. The action $authorize(s_i, d_k)$ stands for authorizing subject $s_i$ to access data $d_k$. Such decision rules may exist for each possible subject/object pair. Of course, access policies are often expressed in a simpler and more compact way by introducing hierarchies or roles, thereby eliminating the necessity of having an entry for each subject/object pair. Without loss of generality, we assume that decision rules of the form presented above may be derived from a more compact representation.

Note that the right-hand side of the implication is only a necessary precondition for the access to be authorized. One reason is that we do not reflect the fact that an access is only authorized after it has been requested by the subject. The acceptance of obligations (explained in Section 2.5) is not reflected in our representation of a decision rule either. Thus, we formulate an implication rather than an equivalence.

## 2.4   Provisions

A provisional formula that appears in a decision rule is called a *provision*. Intuitively, provisions cover traditional access control requirements. This is because the information stored in $r$'s local state (cf. Section 2.3) can contain attributes about the other subjects and about the data objects, which enables us to express rules in different access control paradigms. Many practical examples can

---

[2] By restricting this, we cannot express liveness properties in our formalism. This is intentional and it is not a restriction in our context since liveness does not appear to be of practical relevance for formulating privacy requirements. In practice, one generally sets a time limit for carrying out an action.

therefore be found in the access control area, e.g. "$s_i$ has the role *manager*". This could be formalized as $@_r[role(s_i, manager)]$, where $role(s_i, manager)$ is a local state proposition that holds whenever $s_i$ has the role *manager*.

Provisions may also concern actions that must have occurred before the authorization. This is referred to as provisional authorization in the literature [8]. For brevity, we focus only on the results of such provisional authorizations (e.g. that the owner's consent must be present before allowing access), and not on how this result is achieved (e.g. how and when the owner's consent is gathered). Therefore, we assume that all aspects of $r$'s past that are relevant for the current access decision are reflected in $r$'s current local state, and we restrict ourselves to expressing provisions without using past-time temporal operators. This can be done without loss of generality. For example, instead of stating that a certificate must be submitted *before* access is authorized, we demand that the certificate be present *at the time* of the access decision.

As the reference monitor needs to be able to evaluate provisions before authorizing access, we restrict the allowed provisional formulas to observable ones. In other words, we allow only provisions that $r$ is able to check. Addressing non-observable provisions is an area for future work.

## 2.5   Obligations

*Obligations* impose conditions on the future (i.e. the time after an access is authorized) that an agent is bound to fulfill. An obligational formula becomes an obligation when a binding is established. Such a binding may be created in many ways, for example by the subject explicitly committing himself to an obligation, or by a law that applies to all agents of a system. For simplicity's sake, we assume that the reference monitor ensures that for all obligational formulas in a decision rule, the bindings are established before the access is authorized and, consequently, we do not explicitly state this in the decision rules. In the remainder of this paper, we hence drop the conceptually important distinction between obligations and obligational formulas, and we will use the term obligation for all obligational formulas in the context of a data protection policy.

We now explain what it means for an obligation to be *violated*. We give an intuitive description here, and refer to Appendix B for a formal definition of this notion. Consider a decision rule of the form $@_r[authorize(s_i, d_k)] \Rightarrow (... \wedge o_l \wedge ...)$, where $o_l$ is an obligation. We assume that each action $authorize(s_i, d_k)$ occurs at most once,[3] which allows us to uniquely relate an obligation to a specific access decision. The obligation $o_l$ is *violated* at a time point $t_k$ if the action $@_r[authorize(s_i, d_k)]$ occurred at a previous time point $t_j$, and the formula $@_r[authorize(s_i, d_k)] \wedge \neg o_l$ holds at $t_j$ for all possible futures after $t_k$.

Consider the example $@_r[authorize(s, d)] \Rightarrow @_s[\mathsf{F}^{\leq 3} send(r, m)]$ for a subject $s$, data item $d$, and message $m$. This decision rule states that $s$ must send $m$ to $r$ within three time steps after the authorization. Let $t_0$ be the time point where $authorize(s, d)$ occurs, and $t_l$ be $l$ time steps later. If $send(r, m)$ does not

---

[3] This is without loss of generality. From a theoretical perspective, one may safely assume arbitrarily many copies of each rule, each copy uniquely indexed.

occur in the time span between $t_0$ and $t_3$, then the obligation $@_s[F^{\leq 3} send(r, m)]$ is violated at $t_4$ and at every subsequent time step. If $send(r, m)$ does not occur at times $t_0$, $t_1$, or $t_2$, then the obligation is not violated at any of these time points: $send(r, m)$ could still occur at $t_3$, and thereby satisfy the decision rule.

We have classified data protection requirements in terms of provisions and obligations. As provisions have been thoroughly analyzed in the literature (see Section 5 for references), we henceforth focus on the part of the landscape that is not yet as well-understood: obligations.

## 2.6 Classification of Obligations

We classify obligations along two dimensions: temporal structure and distribution. This categorization provides a useful mapping from requirements to enforcement mechanisms, as we will see in Section 3. In the temporal dimension, we have the categories of *bounded future* and *invariance* properties.

We call an until statement $\varphi \cup \psi$ *temporally bounded* if there is an upper time limit for the occurrence of $\psi$, i.e., there is a constant $n \in \mathbb{N}$ such that $\varphi \cup \psi$ can be rewritten as $\bigvee_{j=1}^{n} (X^j \psi \wedge \bigwedge_{i=0}^{j-1} X^i \varphi)$ without changing the semantics of the formula that contains the until statement. We require that temporally bounded until statements be transformed into the equivalent statement that contains only X operators. With this transformation, we can syntactically distinguish between bounded future (in particular, no U) and invariance properties.[4]

| | |
|---|---|
| *Bounded Future* | Only X as the temporal operator |
| *Invariance Properties* | At least one G or U, and any number of X operators |

In the distribution dimension, we distinguish between observable and non-observable formulas as defined in Section 2.3. This classification results in four categories of obligations named $\mathcal{C}_I$ through $\mathcal{C}_{IV}$.

| Time/Distribution | Observable | Non-Observable |
|---|---|---|
| Bounded Future | $\mathcal{C}_I$ | $\mathcal{C}_{II}$ |
| Invariance Properties | $\mathcal{C}_{III}$ | $\mathcal{C}_{IV}$ |

For each category of obligations, we describe their intuitive nature, present practical examples, and show how some of these examples can be formalized. We continue the convention of calling the reference monitor $r$ and the requester $s_i$.

*Category I—Bounded future, observable:* Intuitively, $\mathcal{C}_I$-obligations make statements about properties and events that are observable for $r$ and cover a limited time frame. A classical example comes from the domain of e-commerce: the obligation to pay a fee within a fixed number of days. Data protection examples for $\mathcal{C}_I$-obligations include "Data item $d_k$ may not be accessed for $x$ days" or "$r$ must notify the data owner about the access within $x$ days". The latter could be formalized as $@_r[F^{\leq x} snd(Owner, released(d_k, s_i))]$, where $Owner$ is the data owner, and $released(d_k, s_i)$ is a message indicating that $d_k$ was given to $s_i$.

---

[4] The transformation of temporally bounded until statements into sequences of X is decidable because we are concerned with propositional statements only.

*Category II—Bounded Future, Non-observable:* This category is similar to $\mathcal{C}_I$, with the difference that we are dealing with non-observable formulas. Privacy-relevant examples include "$d_k$ must be deleted within $x$ days" or "must not be redistributed in the next $x$ days". The former obligation could be formalized as $@_{s_i}[\mathsf{F}^{\leq x}(del(d_k))]$, where the action $del(d_k)$ corresponds to deleting $d_k$.

*Category III—Invariance Properties, Observable:* A practical example for a $\mathcal{C}_{III}$-obligation is "Re-access the data at least every $x$ days", which can be formalized as $@_{s_i}[\mathsf{G}(\mathsf{F}^{\leq x}snd(r, request(d_k)))]$, where $request(d_k)$ is a message used to request $d_k$. This obligation is relevant to data protection since the freshness of data is sometimes demanded by existing data protection regulations.

*Category IV—Invariance Properties, Non-observable:* $\mathcal{C}_{IV}$-obligations occur often in practice. Examples include "Only for statistical analysis", "Do not distribute further", "Each usage of the data must be reported immediately", or "Must be protected with protection level $L$ until it is declassified by the owner". We formalize the latter obligation as $@_{s_i}[protect(d_k, L) \cup rcv(Owner, declassify(d_k))]$. Here $protect(d_k, L)$ reflects that $d_k$ is protected according to protection level $L$, *Owner* is the data owner, and $declassify(d_k)$ is a message that indicates the declassification of $d_k$.

# 3    Coping with the Non-observable

In this section we address the question of how a central reference monitor can ensure that data protection requirements are adhered to. In some sense, this is an impossible task, because it is difficult to imagine how a reference monitor can *enforce* something that it cannot even observe. We use a generalized notion of enforcement here. It covers not only the strict sense of enforcement defined in [14] (the prevention of unwanted executions of a system through system monitoring and denying actions that would violate the policy), but also execution monitoring combined with compensating actions (e.g. penalties) in case the execution violates the policy. More specifically, such a penalty can be applied once an obligation is violated (as defined in Section 2.5 and in the Appendix).

Therefore, a crucial point for achieving enforceability is to be able to monitor the relevant parts of the system. We show how a reference monitor can use non-technical mechanisms, such as audits or legal means, to support the task of making non-observable actions observable, and how the use of such mechanisms can be reflected in the policy of the reference monitor.

As in the previous section, our focus is on obligations. Enforcing provisions is something that has been studied in many variations (see Section 5) and is well understood. We first show how observable obligations can be enforced, and then we show how we can use those enforcement mechanisms also for enforcing non-observable obligations.

## 3.1    Enforcing Observable Obligations

For observable obligations, suitable enforcement mechanisms have already been described by other authors, e.g. [3]. We give a short overview here, as these mechanisms will play a role in enforcing the non-observable obligations as well. Among the observable obligations in $\mathcal{C}_I$ and $\mathcal{C}_{III}$, we have three cases, which require different means of enforcement.

First, obligations that are requirements on $r$'s local actions or $r$'s local state are called *r-obligations*. An example is that $r$ must notify the owner of a data item after it has been accessed, or that $r$ must gather evidence about the usage of a data item after some predefined time. Such obligations are of the form $@_r[\varphi]$, and they are enforced by specifying and implementing $r$ such that it always respects them. In other words, we consider $r$ to be a "trusted system". Thus no additional mechanisms are needed.

Second, those obligations that are enforceable by preventing unwanted executions (EM enforceable in the sense of [14]) form a strict subset of the $\mathcal{C}_I$ and $\mathcal{C}_{III}$-obligations. This is, for example, the case for an obligation that prohibits a subject from accessing a certain data object in the future. Here, $r$ can just deny the respective access requests in order to enforce the obligation.

Third, an approach for enforcing all other $\mathcal{C}_I$-obligations is presented in [3]. A reference monitor can check if the obligation is violated at the end of the bounded time period. If this is the case, the reference monitor can penalize the subject, e.g by reducing its service level, lowering some trust or credibility rating of the subject, or taking legal action. This approach can also be applied to $\mathcal{C}_{III}$-obligations. In this case, the obligation must be continuously monitored, not only for a predefined amount of time.

## 3.2 Enforcing Non-observable Obligations

How can we enforce non-observable obligations? We show how, in some cases, it is possible to reuse existing mechanisms for provisions and observable obligations. Namely, we present three strategies for transforming a non-observable obligation into a set of provisions and observable obligations that specify a similar goal. It is likely that the transformed policy will not specify exactly the goals the original policy expresses. This is the cost of observability. To what extent the original goals are weakened by such a transformation depends on the mechanisms that are used and is explored in the remainder of this section as well as in the next section. The first two strategies we present below aim at making the non-observable parts of an obligation observable, thereby enabling $r$ to monitor their fulfillment. The third strategy limits possible executions to prevent violations of the obligations.

*(1) Reserving the right to pull evidence:* In this strategy, the reference monitor reserves the right to obtain evidence in the future, for example through an audit. This right could be executed after some deadline (in $\mathcal{C}_{II}$) or whenever $r$ suspects that the obligation has been violated (in $\mathcal{C}_{IV}$). Conceptually, the aim of such an audit is to make certain local events and parts of the local state of the subject visible to the reference monitor. To obtain the above mentioned right, $r$ demands a legal binding (e.g. in the form of a digitally signed statement from the requester) that allows it to trigger an investigation in the future. Demanding a legal binding is now a requirement that can be evaluated in the present, and

therefore a provision. As we illustrate in the next section, this provision is accompanied by a set of $r$-obligations that define when and under which conditions $r$ must perform an investigation, and how it should react to the result.

(2) *Imposing the duty to push evidence:* Another strategy is that the requester must commit himself to delivering evidence. The evidence could be delivered by presenting the results of an audit performed by a trusted third party. Delivery of such evidence can occur just once (as a prerequisite for gaining access, which can be expressed by a provision), or on a recurring basis (which constitutes a $\mathcal{C}_{III}$-obligation). As in strategy (1), this requirement needs to be accompanied by a set of $r$-obligations.

(3) *Limiting possible executions:* The third possibility for the reference monitor is to limit of possible executions of the agents to those that do not violate the obligation. In order to achieve this, $r$ may put the data into an environment that imposes restrictions on how the data can be used. Basically, this is the idea of digital rights management (DRM) [16,17,18]. It remains to be seen how suitable DRM is for enforcing data protection policies, since any data which is output outside the DRM environment can be re-recorded. At the very least, DRM can act as a support mechanism to the two strategies listed above and thereby increase the likelihood that the obligations are fulfilled, or at least prevent unintended violations resulting from carelessness.

These three strategies are not necessarily applicable to all non-observable obligations. In the case of further distribution, for example, implementing one of the first two strategies might be difficult as $r$ might not be able to audit every subject that could possibly have received the data. The three strategies can at least be applied to some non-observable obligations, however, and the question of which enforcement mechanisms can enforce a given set of requirements is the subject of future work. In the following example, we examine the application of the pull-evidence strategy (1) to enforce $\mathcal{C}_{II}$-obligations.

## 4    Example

We now show how a simple data protection policy containing provisions, observable obligations, and non-observable obligations can be formalized and enforced. We sketch the semantics of the different requirements and use the pull-evidence strategy to transform the non-observable obligations into observable ones. We also discuss the results of this transformation, and how they relate to the original policy.

Our system consists of two government agencies $A$ and $B$, a citizen *Owner*, and a trusted auditor $T$. $A$ acts as the reference monitor and maintains a database of citizen information, where data items $d_1$ and $d_2$, belonging to *Owner*, are stored. These data items are sensitive, e.g. medical records, criminal records, or tax statements. $B$ is the only subject in the sense introduced in Section 2, whereas $T$ and *Owner* are additional agents introduced for different purposes.

Recall that our policies contain decision rules for each subject/object pair. To keep things simple, we just present the entries for the pairs $(B, d_1)$ and $(B, d_2)$.

$A$'s policy requires the following for authorizing $B$ to access $d_1$: (**R1**) $B$ must have role *statistician*; (**R2**) $A$ must notify *Owner* immediately after the access; and (**R3**) $B$ must delete $d_1$ after at most 90 days. For the pair $(B, d_2)$, the policy requires that (**R4**) $B$ must have trust level *high*; (**R5**) $B$ must notify *Owner* immediately after the access; and (**R6**) $B$ must ensure that its copy of $d_2$ is never older than 30 days.

R1 and R4 are provisions because the roles and trust levels of the different agents can be reflected in state propositions of $A$. R2 is a $C_I$-obligation for $A$ (recall the notion of $r$-obligations introduced in Section 2). R3 is a $C_{II}$-obligation because it is non-observable and belongs to the bounded future category. R5 looks similar to R2, but is also a $C_{II}$-obligation because the action of $B$ notifying *Owner* is not observable to $A$ in our definition. To formalize R6, we must define more precisely what it means for $B$ to ensure that the data is kept fresh. In order to get a new copy of the data, $B$ must request it again, $A$ must grant the request and send the data to $B$, and $B$ must update its local record of the data with the new version received. $B$ cannot be responsible for the request being granted and the data being sent. Therefore we only demand the following two things in our policy: that $B$ regularly (at least every 30 days) requests $d_2$, and that $B$ updates its local record every time it receives the new version. This corresponds to a $C_{III}$-obligation for the regular requests and a $C_{IV}$-obligation for the updating. Therefore, we will formalize this as two separate requirements in our policy.

### 4.1   Formalization

We need to define appropriate actions and state propositions for our agents, as well as the messages that are exchanged. We also introduce the actions and state propositions that will be used when transforming the policy later. In these definitions, we use the convention that $s_i$ is an arbitrary subject, $d_k$ is a data item, *obl* is the textual representation of an obligation, and *penalty* $\in$ *Penalties*, where *Penalties* is a set of applicable penalties in case a requirement is violated. This could be the lowering of a trust or credibility rating, or a legal action.

For the agency $A$, acting as the reference monitor, we define *authorize*$(s_i, d_k)$, the action of allowing $s_i$ to access $d_k$ (this includes delivering the data item, i.e. sending $d_k$ to $s_i$), and *penalize*$(s_i, penalty)$, the action of penalizing $s_i$ by applying *penalty*. The state propositions include: *role*$(s_i, statistician)$, for reflecting that $s_i$ is a *statistician*, *trustlvl*$(s_i, high)$, for reflecting that $s_i$ has trust level *high*, and *investigate*, which reflects the value of a function that outputs *true* or *false* (we will use this later for implementing the pull-evidence approach).

For the agency $B$, we define *del*$(d_k)$, the action of deleting $d_k$ (i.e. no copies of $d_k$'s value are retained), *update*$(d_k)$, the action of updating the previously stored value of $d_k$, and no state propositions.

The *snd* and *rcv* actions are defined for all agents as explained in Section 2.2. In addition, the following messages may be exchanged, where *procedure* is an element of a set of procedures like *push* or *pull*:

- *request*$(d_k)$ — message that a subject uses to request $d_k$ from $A$;
- *released*$(s_i, d_k)$ — message that $A$ uses to indicate the release of $d_k$ to $s_i$;

- $accessed(d_k)$ — message that $B$ uses to indicate that it accessed $d_k$;
- $doc(d_k)$ — document containing data item $d_k$;
- $accept(obl, procedure, penalty)$ — message that a subject sends to accept that $A$ may use the indicated procedure for checking the obligation, and to accept the penalty in case the obligation is violated;
- $reqAudit(obl)$ — message that $A$ uses to request an audit regarding $obl$; and
- $viol(obl)$ — message sent as the result of an audit, indicating that the obligation represented by $obl$ is violated.

Now we are in a position to write down the two policy entries for $(B, d_1)$ and $(B, d_2)$. We again assume discrete time with one day per time step. We formalize the policy entries regarding $B$ accessing $d_1$ and $d_2$ as

$$@_A[authorize(B, d_1)] \Rightarrow (@_A[role(B, statistician)]$$
$$\wedge @_A[\mathsf{X}\, snd(Owner, released(d_1, B))] \wedge @_B[\mathsf{F}^{\leq 90} del(d_1)])$$

and

$$@_A[authorize(B, d_2)] \Rightarrow (@_A[trustlvl(B, high)] \wedge @_B[\mathsf{X}\, snd(Owner, accessed(d_2))]$$
$$\wedge @_B[\mathsf{G}\,\mathsf{F}^{\leq 30} snd(A, request(d_2))] \wedge @_B[\mathsf{G}(rcv(A, d_2) \Rightarrow \mathsf{X}\, update(d_2))]).$$

## 4.2   Transformation

We have three non-observable obligations in this policy as discussed above: one $\mathcal{C}_{II}$-obligation deriving from R3, one $\mathcal{C}_{II}$-obligation deriving from R5, and one $\mathcal{C}_{IV}$-obligation that defines a part of R6. We now transform the obligation $@_B[\mathsf{F}^{\leq 90} del(d_1)]$ into a set of provisions and observable obligations. We do this in two steps. In the first step, we follow our notion of enforcement introduced in Section 3 and require that if $B$ does not delete $d_1$ within 90 days, then it will be penalized within a certain time period, say an additional 30 days. This goal can be formalized as

**(G1)**  $@_B[\mathsf{G}^{\leq 90}(\neg del(d_1))] \Rightarrow @_A[\mathsf{X}^{90}\,\mathsf{F}^{\leq 30} penalize(B, pen)],$

where $pen \in Penalties$.

In the second step, we define how this goal should be achieved using the pull-evidence approach. Roughly, the strategy is as follows. $A$ must obtain $B$'s permission to perform audits that check whether the obligation is violated (recall that this is in addition to accepting the obligation itself, which is done implicitly as stated in Section 2). 90 days after the access, $A$ can ask the auditor to check whether $d_1$ was really deleted by $B$. For this to work, we must address the following issues.

First, we must specify under which conditions $A$ requests such an audit. The reason for employing the pull-evidence strategy instead of the push-evidence strategy is that such an audit is not necessary in all cases. This reduces the auditing overhead. Generally, there are two options for triggering audits. One option is that audits are performed randomly as control samples, and the other option is to perform an audit only when suspicion arises. For both options, the state proposition *investigate* indicates whether an audit should be performed.

Second, we assume that the auditor is able to determine if the data was actually deleted, given that $B$ allows the audit to be performed. $B$ must agree to this audit beforehand. Furthermore, we assume that upon request from $A$, the auditor $T$ always performs an audit and returns the result within a given time period, say one day. This assumption can be formalized as follows (where $o_1$ is the textual representation of the obligation $@_B[\mathsf{F}^{\leq 90}del(d_1)]$):

**(A1)** $(@_A[snd(T, reqAudit(o_1))] \land \neg @_B[\mathsf{P}^{\leq 90}\, del(d_1)]) \Rightarrow @_T[\mathsf{X}(snd(A, viol(o_1)))]$

Note that this assumption also expresses that the auditor is able to decide a violation at run-time: we know that the audit request will (if ever) be sent 90 days after the access decision, and therefore the obligation is violated at that point if the data has not been deleted within the last 90 days.

Applying the pull-evidence strategy yields an new set of requirements:

**(P1)** $@_B[snd(A, accept(o_1, pull, pen))]$
**(P2)** $@_A[\mathsf{X}^{90}\, (investigate \iff snd(T, reqAudit(o_1)))]$
**(P3)** $@_A[\mathsf{X}^{91}\, (rcv(T, viol(o_1)) \Rightarrow \mathsf{X}\, penalize(B, pen))]$

Requirement P1, which is a provision, expresses the fact that $B$ must accept the procedures and penalties used for enforcing the original obligation. P2 is in $\mathcal{C}_I$ and states that, after 90 days, if an audit should be performed then $A$ sends an audit request to $T$. Requirement P3 is in $\mathcal{C}_{III}$ and defines when a penalty must be applied.

## 4.3   Comments

G1 is a consequence of A1 and P1–P3 under the semantics of DTL, provided that *investigate* is always true when the obligation is violated. This means that if the audit is always performed, our goal can be achieved. If audits are only performed at random, then this is not always the case and the success of the enforcement strategy depends on whether the possibility of being penalized acts as a deterrent or not. This depends on the agents of a particular system, and is not within the scope of this paper. But the example shows how the application of such a strategy works, and the kinds of assumptions it requires. These assumptions derive from the fact that the result of such a transformation is usually only an approximation of the original policy, as mentioned in Section 3.

We have also shown that to give a formal semantics to data protection requirements, we need to define the actions and state propositions for a concrete system. In this example, we have kept these definitions at a relatively abstract level, but for a practical application this needs to be done in more detail.

The representation of the policy we introduced in Section 2 has its focus on the semantics of the requirements. It does not define when the reference monitor has to authorize an access. There are two reasons for this. First, we only have an implication in a decision rule, not an equivalence (cf. Section 2.3). Second, if obligations are involved, the reference monitor will not be able to decide whether to authorize the access or not, because it does not yet know if the obligations will be violated. This can only be determined from a global point of view where we know the full, potentially infinite executions. In a concrete realization of such a reference monitor, one would authorize the access exactly when all the provisions are satisfied and the obligations are accepted by the subject.

Finally, note that our formalism is rich enough to allow formulas that do not make sense from a practical point of view. For example, it is possible to express the requirement $@_A[\mathsf{X}\, rcv(B, msg)]$, which is equivalent to $@_B[\mathsf{X}\, snd(A, msg)]$. However, it does not make sense from a practical point of view to make $A$ responsible for receiving a message that may never be sent. Addressing this problem is the subject of future work.

## 5  Related Work

Many extensions and generalizations of access control have been proposed. Jajodia et al. [9] present a framework for combining multiple access control policies within a single system. Temporal criteria may also be used for access decisions whereby access to data is only allowed at certain time points or intervals [2,15] or based on temporal attributes of data, such as the creation date [7]. In our model, these are all provisions, given that the current time is reflected in the reference monitor's state. Policies of the same expressiveness are considered in [10], which introduces the concept of policy automata. Policy automata combine defeasible logic with state machines and represent complex policies as combinations of simpler policies. A variant of access control called provisional authorization is discussed in [8]. Provisional authorization stipulates that access be only authorized if the requester or the system takes certain actions prior to authorizing the request. In our model, this corresponds to provisions that contain action symbols.

The UCON model [12,21] extends access control by introducing decision continuity and attribute mutability. In terms of our model, UCON covers both provisions (including temporal criteria and provisional authorization) and $\mathcal{C}_I$-obligations (provided they do not contain negations). The latter are also discussed in [3], where the authors present a logical framework for monitoring these obligations, and for taking compensating actions when obligations are violated. EPAL [1] is a description language for privacy policies (data protection policies in our terminology) that can express all categories presented in this paper, but does not specify a semantics for obligations. An XML-based syntax for describing privacy statements for web sites is defined in the P3P standard [19].

A collection of obligations encountered in practice is given in [11]. The authors have a more operational view of obligations, and differentiate between short-term obligations, long-term obligations and ongoing obligations. Formal definitions of the corresponding predicates are not given, but practical examples are provided for each category.

The terms *obligation* and *provision* are often but not consistently used in the literature to describe different types of data protection requirements. Some authors (e.g. [12]) use obligations to refer to actions that principals must perform, or must have performed *before* an access is authorized. For other authors (e.g. [3]), obligations concern actions that must be performed in the future, *after* the access is authorized. We adopt and generalize the latter definition: obligations are agreed-upon conditions that not only concern actions that are to be performed in the future, but also more general propositions about the future, for example the mandatory presence of certain protection mechanisms. From [3], we also adopt and generalize the notion of provisions. In our model, provisions are conditions that must hold before an access is authorized, whereas in [3], they are specific actions that must be taken before an access is authorized.

## 6   Conclusions and Future Work

In this paper, we showed how different aspects of data protection can be handled by an extension of access control models. This extended model allows us to precisely specify a broad range of data protection requirements—provisions and obligations—that take into account observable and non-observable elements. We showed how existing approaches to enforcing non-observable obligations fit into our conceptual and formal framework.

We are aware that our syntactic classification imposes a restriction on the presentation of requirements. For example, a provisional formula may have a semantic equivalent that does not fit the syntactic criterion for a provisional formula. This restriction does not seem too strong when the criterion is used a-priori rather than a-posteriori, e.g. by describing policies in a dedicated policy editor that simply forbids certain constructs. Whether or not our syntactic separation into provisions and obligations leaves out some important semantic constructs remains to be investigated.

One promising direction for future work is to use the framework as a basis for a practically useful policy language that caters for both provisions and obligations. It is likely that "policy patterns" in such a language can address many recurring data protection needs. Since our framework language (DTL) has a formal semantics, it is amenable to formal reasoning about policies and their composition (interesting aspects include consistency and subsumption). Another direction to explore, by case studies, is the practical applicability of the mechanisms presented in this paper. This is important in identifying the boundary between those requirements that can be technically enforced and those that require non-technical mechanisms, such as legal ones. It will also shed light on how much non-observable requirements must be weakened when transforming them into observable ones. Our long-term goal here is to design a server-side reference monitor controlling access to sensitive personal data. Finally, the use of DRM mechanisms for handling obligations, as mentioned in Section 3, also requires further investigation. In particular, we currently do not know how much can be achieved by using client-side reference monitors. A related question concerns honest subjects, where we need only to prevent careless, but not malicious, behavior. In this case, the mechanisms are likely to be weaker than in the case of potentially malicious subjects.

*Acknowledgments.* P. Hankes Drielsma, F. Klaedtke, P. E. Sevinç, C. Sprenger and L. Viganò provided useful comments on earlier versions of the paper.

# References

1. M. Backes, B. Pfitzmann, and M. Schunter. A toolkit for managing enterprise privacy policies. In *Proc. ESORICS'03*, Springer LNCS 2808, pages 162–180. 2003.
2. E. Bertino, C. Bettini, E. Ferrari, and P. Samarati. An access control model supporting periodicity constraints and temporal reasoning. *ACM Transactions on Database Systems*, 23(3):231–285, 1998.
3. C. Bettini, S. Jajodia, X. S. Wang, and D. Wijesekera. Provisions and obligations in policy rule management. *J. Network and System Mgmt.*, 11(3):351–372, 2003.
4. C. Caleiro, L. Viganò, and D. Basin. Metareasoning about security protocols using distributed temporal logic. In *Proc. IJCAR'04 Workshop on Automated Reasoning for Security Protocol Analysis (ARSPA'04)*. ENTCS 125(1), 2005.
5. H.-D. Ehrich and C. Caleiro. Specifying communication in distributed information systems. *Acta Informatica*, 36:591–616, 2000.
6. H.-D. Ehrich, C. Caleiro, A. Sernadas, and G. Denker. Logics for specifying concurrent information systems. In *Logic for Databases and Information Systems*, pages 167–198. Kluwer Academic Publishers, 1998.
7. A. Gal and V. Atluri. An authorization model for temporal data. In *Proc. 7th ACM Conference on Computer Communications Security*, pages 144–153. ACM Press, 2000.
8. S. Jajodia, M. Kudo, and V. Subrahmanian. Provisional authorizations. In A. Gosh, editor, *E-Commerce Security and Privacy*, pages 133–159. Kluwer, 2001.
9. S. Jajodia, P. Samarati, M. L. Sapino, and V. S. Subrahmanian. Flexible support for multiple access control policies. *ACM Transactions on Database Systems*, 26(2):214–260, 2001.
10. M. McDougall, R. Alur, and C. A. Gunter. A model-based approach to integrating security policies for embedded devices. In *Proc. 4th ACM international conference on Embedded software*, pages 211–219. ACM Press, 2004.
11. M. C. Mont. Dealing with privacy obligations in enterprises. Technical report, HP Laboratories Bristol, Jun 2004.
12. J. Park and R. Sandhu. The UCON ABC Usage Control Model. *ACM Transactions on Information and Systems Security*, 7:128–174, 2004.
13. A. Pnueli. The temporal semantics of concurrent programs. In *Proc. Intl. Symp. on Semantics of Concurrent Computation*, pages 1–20. Springer-Verlag, 1979.
14. F. B. Schneider. Enforceable security policies. *ACM Transactions on Information and System Security*, 3(1):30–50, 2000.
15. F. Siewe, A. Cau, and H. Zedan. A compositional framework for access control policies enforcement. In *Proc. 2003 ACM workshop on Formal methods in security engineering*, pages 32–42. ACM Press, 2003.
16. S. W. Smith. *Trusted Computing*. Springer-Verlag, 2005.
17. P. van Oorschot. Revisiting software protection. *Information Security, LNCS*, 2851:1–13, 2003.
18. P. van Oorschot. Software protection and application security: understanding the battleground. In *State of the art and evolution of computer security and industrial cryptography*, 2003.
19. W3C. The Platform for Privacy Preferences 1.0 (P3P1.0) Specification, April 2002. Available at `http://www.w3.org/TR/P3P/`.
20. G. Winskel. Event structures. In *Petri Nets: Applications and Relationships to Other Models of Concurrency*, Springer LNCS 255, pages 325–392. 1987.
21. X. Zhang, J. Park, F. Parisi-Presicce, and R. Sandhu. A logical specification for usage control. In *Proc. 9th ACM symp. on Access control models and technologies*, pages 1–10. ACM Press, 2004.

# A   Distributed Temporal Logic

In this appendix, which is adopted from [4], we explain the basics of DTL.

The syntax of DTL is defined over a *distributed signature*

$$\Sigma = \langle Id, \{Act_i\}_{i \in Id}, \{Prop_i\}_{i \in Id} \rangle$$

of a system, where $Id$ is a finite set of *agent identifiers* and, for each $i \in Id$, $Act_i$ is a set of *local action symbols* and $Prop_i$ is a set of *local state propositions*. The *global language* $\mathcal{L}$ is defined by the grammar $\mathcal{L} ::= @_i[\mathcal{L}_i] \mid \perp \mid \mathcal{L} \Rightarrow \mathcal{L}$, for $i \in Id$, where the *local languages* $\mathcal{L}_i$ are defined by

$$\mathcal{L}_i ::= Act_i \mid Prop_i \mid \perp \mid \mathcal{L}_i \Rightarrow \mathcal{L}_i \mid \mathcal{L}_i \cup \mathcal{L}_i \mid \mathcal{L}_i \, \mathsf{S} \, \mathcal{L}_i \mid j{:}\mathcal{L}_j$$

with $j \in Id$. Locally for an agent, $\mathsf{U}$ and $\mathsf{S}$ are respectively the *weak until*[5] and *since* temporal operators. Actions correspond to true statements about an agent when they have just occurred, whereas state propositions characterize the current local states of the agents. Note that the global formula $@_i[\varphi]$ means that $\varphi$ holds at the current local state of agent $i$. A local formula $j{:}\varphi$ appearing inside a formula in $\mathcal{L}_i$ is called a *communication formula* and it means that agent $i$ has just communicated with agent $j$ for whom $\varphi$ held. The interpretation structures of $\mathcal{L}$ are suitably labelled distributed life-cycles, built upon a simplified form of Winskel's *event structures* [20]. A *local life-cycle* of an agent $i \in Id$ is a pair $\lambda_i = \langle Ev_i, \rightarrow_i \rangle$, where $Ev_i$ is the set of *local events* and $\rightarrow_i \subseteq Ev_i \times Ev_i$ is the *local successor relation*, such that the transitive closure $\rightarrow_i^*$ defines a well-founded total order on $Ev_i$, called *local causality*. A *distributed life-cycle* is a family $\lambda = \{\lambda_i\}_{i \in Id}$ of local life-cycles such that the transitive closure $\rightarrow^*$ of $\rightarrow = \bigcup_{i \in Id} \rightarrow_i$ defines a partial order on the set $Ev = \bigcup_{i \in Id} Ev_i$ of all events, called *global causality*. This last condition is essential since events can be shared by several agents at communication points.

We can check the progress of an agent by collecting all the local events that have occurred up to a certain point. This yields the notion of the *local configuration* of an agent $i$: a finite set $\xi_i \subseteq Ev_i$ closed under local causality, i.e. if $e \rightarrow_i^* e'$ and $e' \in \xi_i$ then also $e \in \xi_i$. The set $\Xi_i$ of all local configurations of an agent $i$ is clearly totally ordered by inclusion and has $\emptyset$ as the minimal element. In general, each non-empty local configuration $\xi_i$ is reached, by the occurrence of an event that we call $last(\xi_i)$, from the local configuration $\xi_i \setminus \{last(\xi_i)\}$. We can also define the notion of a *global configuration*: a finite set $\xi \subseteq Ev$ closed for global causality, i.e. if $e \rightarrow^* e'$ and $e' \in \xi$ then also $e \in \xi$. The set $\Xi$ of all global configurations constitutes a lattice, under inclusion, and has $\emptyset$ as the minimal element. Clearly, every global configuration $\xi$ includes the local configuration $\xi|_i = \xi \cap Ev_i$ of each agent $i$. Given $e \in Ev$, note that $e{\downarrow} = \{e' \in Ev \mid e' \rightarrow^* e\}$ is always a global configuration.

An *interpretation structure* $\mu = \langle \lambda, \alpha, \pi \rangle$ consists of a distributed life-cycle $\lambda$ plus families $\alpha = \{\alpha_i\}_{i \in Id}$ and $\pi = \{\pi_i\}_{i \in Id}$ of local labelling functions. For

---

[5] In contrast to the strong until operator, the weak until operator does not require $\gamma$ to eventually happen in the formula $\varphi \, \mathsf{U} \, \gamma$.

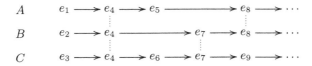

**Fig. 1.** A distributed life-cycle for agents $A$, $B$ and $C$

$$\pi_A(\emptyset) \xrightarrow{\alpha_A(e_1)} \pi_A(\{e_1\}) \xrightarrow{\alpha_A(e_4)} \pi_A(\{e_1, e_4\}) \xrightarrow{\alpha_A(e_5)} \pi_A(\{e_1, e_4, e_5\}) \xrightarrow{\alpha_A(e_8)} \cdots$$

**Fig. 2.** The progress of agent $A$

each $i \in Id$, $\alpha_i : Ev_i \to Act_i$ associates a local action to each local event, and $\pi_i : \Xi_i \to \wp(Prop_i)$ associates a set of local state propositions to each local configuration.

Fig. 1 illustrates the notion of a distributed life-cycle, where each row comprises the local life-cycle of one agent. In particular, $Ev_A = \{e_1, e_4, e_5, e_8, \dots\}$ and $\to_A$ corresponds to the arrows in $A$'s row. We can think of the occurrence of the event $e_1$ as leading agent $A$ from its initial configuration $\emptyset$ to the configuration $\{e_1\}$, and then of the occurrence of the event $e_4$ as leading to configuration $\{e_1, e_4\}$, and so on; the state-transition sequence of agent $A$ is displayed in Fig. 2. Shared events at communication points are highlighted by the dotted vertical lines. Note that the numbers annotating the events are there only for convenience since no global total order on events is in general imposed. Fig. 3 shows the corresponding lattice of global configurations.

We can then define the *global satisfaction relation* at a global configuration $\xi$ of $\mu$, where $\Xi_i$ is the set of all local configurations of agent $i$ in $\mu$, as

- $\mu, \xi \Vdash @_i[\varphi]$ if $\mu, \xi|_i \Vdash_i \varphi$;
- $\mu, \xi \nVdash \bot$;
- $\mu, \xi \Vdash \gamma \Rightarrow \delta$ if $\mu, \xi \nVdash \gamma$ or $\mu, \xi \Vdash \delta$,

where the *local satisfaction relations* at local configurations are defined by

- $\mu, \xi_i \Vdash_i act$ if $\xi_i \neq \emptyset$ and $\alpha_i(last(\xi_i)) = act$;
- $\mu, \xi_i \Vdash_i p$ if $p \in \pi_i(\xi_i)$;
- $\mu, \xi_i \nVdash_i \bot$;
- $\mu, \xi_i \Vdash_i \varphi \Rightarrow \psi$ if $\mu, \xi_i \nVdash_i \varphi$ or $\mu, \xi_i \Vdash_i \psi$;
- $\mu, \xi_i \Vdash_i \varphi \mathsf{U} \psi$ if the following holds: if there exists $\xi_i'' \in \Xi_i$ with $\xi_i \subsetneq \xi_i''$ such that $\mu, \xi_i'' \Vdash_i \psi$, then $\mu, \xi_i' \Vdash_i \varphi$ for every $\xi_i' \in \Xi_i$ with $\xi_i \subsetneq \xi_i' \subsetneq \xi_i''$; otherwise, $\mu, \xi_i' \Vdash_i \varphi$ for every $\xi_i' \in \Xi_i$ with $\xi_i \subsetneq \xi_i'$;
- $\mu, \xi_i \Vdash_i \varphi \mathsf{S} \psi$ if there exists $\xi_i'' \in \Xi_i$ with $\xi_i'' \subsetneq \xi_i$ such that $\mu, \xi_i'' \Vdash_i \psi$, and $\mu, \xi_i' \Vdash_i \varphi$ for every $\xi_i' \in \Xi_i$ with $\xi_i'' \subsetneq \xi_i' \subsetneq \xi_i$;
- $\mu, \xi_i \Vdash_i j{:}\varphi$ if $\xi_i \neq \emptyset$, $last(\xi_i) \in Ev_j$ and $\mu, (last(\xi_i) \downarrow)|_j \Vdash_j \varphi$.

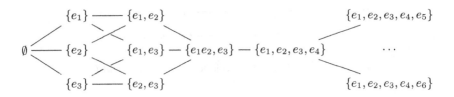

**Fig. 3.** The lattice of global configurations

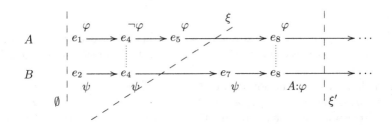

**Fig. 4.** Satisfaction of formulas

We say that $\mu$ is a model of $\Gamma \subseteq \mathcal{L}$ if $\mu, \xi \Vdash \gamma$ for every global configuration $\xi$ of $\mu$ and every $\gamma \in \Gamma$. Fig. 4 illustrates the satisfaction relation with respect to communication formulas of our running example. Clearly $\mu, \emptyset \Vdash @_B[\psi \cup A:\varphi]$, because $\mu, \xi' \Vdash @_B[A:\varphi]$. Note however that $\mu, \xi \not\Vdash @_B[A:\varphi]$, although $\mu, \xi \Vdash @_A[\varphi]$.

Other usual logical operators are defined as abbreviations, e.g. $\neg$, $\top$, $\vee$, and $\wedge$. We also define the following temporal operators:

$X\varphi \equiv \bot \cup \varphi$ (weak next)
$Y\varphi \equiv \bot S\varphi$ (previous)
$P\varphi \equiv \top S\varphi$ (sometime in the past)

$G\varphi \equiv \varphi \cup \bot$ (always in the future)
$H\varphi \equiv \neg P\neg\varphi$ (always in the past)

Let *Msg* be a (not necessarily finite) set of messages. For each agent $a \in Id$, the set of actions $Act_a$ includes $snd(b, m)$ (send message $m$ to agent $b$) and $rcv(b, m)$ (receive message $m$ from agent $b$), where $b \in Id$ is another agent, and $m \in Msg$. Now we introduce the following axiom.

$$\forall \, a, b \in Id, m \in Msg : @_a[snd(b, m) \iff b:rcv(a, m)]$$

This axiom defines a reliable and synchronous communication channel for each pair of agents. In this paper, we do not make other use of the $j:\varphi$ operator, i.e. the *local languages* $\mathcal{L}_i$ are only defined by

$$\mathcal{L}_i ::= Act_i \mid Prop_i \mid \bot \mid \mathcal{L}_i \Rightarrow \mathcal{L}_i \mid \mathcal{L}_i \cup \mathcal{L}_i \mid \mathcal{L}_i S \mathcal{L}_i,$$

in the body of this paper. The reason is that we do not need this operator for our policy language, but only to define the semantics *snd* and *rcv*. Moreover, omitting this simplifies the syntactical classification between observable formulas and non-observable formulas that we introduce in Section 2.

# B    Violation of Obligations

Let $\mu = \langle \lambda, \alpha, \pi \rangle$ be an interpretation structure with $\lambda = \{\langle Ev_i, \rightarrow_i \rangle\}_{i \in Id}$ and $\xi = \bigcup_{i \in Id} Ev_i$ a global configuration of $\mu$. We consider a formula of the form $@_j[a] \Rightarrow \varphi$, where $a$ is a local action symbol that is only defined for agent $j$ and has exactly one pre-image under $\alpha_j$, and $\varphi \in \mathcal{L}_i$ for some $i \in Id$. The subformula $\varphi$ is *violated* with respect to $\mu$ iff there exists $\xi' \in \Xi$ with $\xi' \subseteq \xi$ such that $\mu, \xi' \Vdash a \wedge \neg \varphi$.

The reason why $a$ must only be related to one single event is that otherwise, there could be $\xi'', \xi''' \in \Xi$ with $\xi'' \subseteq \xi; \xi''' \subseteq \xi; \mu, \xi'' \Vdash a \wedge \neg \varphi$ and $\mu, \xi''' \not\Vdash a \wedge \neg \varphi$. In our context of obligations and authorization actions, this would mean that the actions that follow two different authorizations could interfere.

Note that this formal definition of violation cannot be used by a reference monitor *at runtime*. This is because our characterization is with respect to a *fixed* interpretation structure of the logical formulas that make up our models of a system. Because this interpretation is fixed, and, in this sense, encompasses everything that has happened, it does not leave any room for decisions of the agents. Without formalizing it here, we hence assume an "operational" definition that allows the auditor to decide violation at runtime.

# A Practical Voter-Verifiable Election Scheme*

David Chaum[1], Peter Y.A. Ryan[2], and Steve Schneider[3]

[1] Votegrity
[2] School of Computing Science, University of Newcastle
[3] Department of Computing, University of Surrey

**Abstract.** We present an election scheme designed to allow voters to verify that their vote is accurately included in the count. The scheme provides a high degree of transparency whilst ensuring the secrecy of votes. Assurance is derived from close auditing of all the steps of the vote recording and counting process with minimal dependence on the system components. Thus, assurance arises from verification of the election rather than having to place trust in the correct behaviour of components of the voting system. The scheme also seeks to make the voter interface as familiar as possible.

## 1 Introduction

Since the dawn of democracy, it has been recognised that the process of recording and counting votes could be the target of attempts at corruption. The Ancient Greeks investigated the use of (primitive) technological devices to provide trustworthy voting systems and avoid the need to trust voting officials [1]. The challenge is to provide voters with complete confidence that their vote will be accurately recorded and counted whilst at the same time guaranteeing the secrecy of their vote.

Most traditional approaches to this problem involve placing significant trust in the technology, mechanisms or processes used to process votes. Thus, for the traditional paper ballot, the handling of the ballot boxes and counting process must be trusted, i.e., the boxes must not be lost or manipulated and that the counting process is accurate. Various observers are introduced to the process which helps to spread the dependence on the technology but does not eliminate it.

With many of the touch screen devices widely used in the recent US presidential elections, the voter at best gets some form of acknowledgement of the way she casts her vote. After that, she can only trust in the assurances of the manufacturers and certifiers that her vote will be accurately included in the final tally.

By contrast, in [3], Chaum presents a digital voting scheme that enables voter verification, i.e., provides each voter with a means to assure themselves that her vote has been accurately included in the vote tally. This scheme combines a number of cryptographic techniques and primitives to provide a high degree of transparency whilst at the same time preserving ballot secrecy. Rather than

* This work was partially funded by the EPSRC DIRC project, www.dirc.org.uk.

S. De Capitani di Vimercati et al. (Eds.): ESORICS 2005, LNCS 3679, pp. 118–139, 2005.

having to place trust in the components to perform correctly, steps of the vote recording and tallying process are closely monitored to detect any malfunction or corruption.

The key elements in voter-verification are:

– when a voter casts her vote in a booth, she gets a receipt showing her vote in encrypted form.
– a voter confirms in the booth that her intended vote is correctly encoded in the receipt. The vote cannot be read subsequently outside the booth.
– a number of tellers perform anonymising mixes and decryption on the batch of encrypted ballot receipts. The decrypted votes emerge at the end of this process, with all links between the original receipts and the final decrypted values lost in the multiple mixes. Intermediate steps of the tellers processing are posted to a bulletin board, which might be published via the web for example.
– random checks are performed on all steps of the process to ensure that, with high probability, any attempt to corrupt vote capture and counting will be detected.

The point of the encrypted receipt is to provide the voter with a means to check that her ballot is entered into the tallying process and, if her receipt has not been included, to prove this to a third party. The fact that her vote is in encrypted form ensures that there is no way for a third party to know which way she voted. A voter can visit the bulletin board and check that her (encrypted) ballot receipt has been correctly posted. The tellers process these posted receipts and there are mechanisms in place to ensure that all posted receipts are entered into the tallying process.

The anonymising mixes performed by the tellers ensure that there is no link between the encrypted ballot receipt and the decrypted version that is finally output by the tallying process.

The design philosophy is to minimise trust in components. The approach is to strive for maximal transparency of the whole vote casting, recording and counting process, consistent with maintaining ballot secrecy. Thus, the integrity of the ballot forms and the correctness of the tellers' transformations are closely audited. The encryption of the voter's choice on the receipt is performed in the booth, is transparent, and does not depend on the intercession of any hardware or software devices that might be susceptible to failure or corruption.

## 2   Prêt à Voter

The original scheme of [3] uses visual cryptography to encrypt the receipts and perform the decryption in the booth. The scheme presented here uses a more conventional representation of the vote, i.e., ballot forms with the candidates or voting options listed in one column, and the voter choices entered in an adjacent column. As a result, the scheme is easier to understand and implement.

An earlier paper, [7], introduced the idea of encoding the vote in terms of two aligned columns, one carrying the candidate or option list in randomised order (independent for each ballot form) whilst the other strip carries the voter choice. In this version, the voter was invited to choose which of the left and right columns to retain as the receipt. This introduced a certain asymmetry with both cryptographic and psychological implications.

In this paper we introduce some further innovations: we use ballot forms that are generated and printed in advance. As before, these have two columns, one of which shows the candidate list in scrambled order. Now however, rather than choosing between columns as previously, the voter will always discard the left hand column containing the candidate list, and submit the right hand column containing the marked vote. This avoids the asymmetry in the choice between left and right columns of the previous scheme.

A further innovation is to use the tellers in an oracle mode to enable the checks on the well-formedness of the ballot forms. This is in addition to the previous use of the tellers to perform the anonymising mix during the tallying phase. Besides allowing independent auditing authorities to perform random checks, this also opens up the possibility of novel checking modes, including enabling the voters to cast a dummy vote and have the tellers return the decryption to them as a check on the construction of the ballot forms.

The scheme presented here provides a number of appealing innovations, notably:

- Voters should find the vote casting process entirely familiar.
- Cryptographic commitments are generated before voter choices are known.
- Voter checks on the correct construction of the ballot forms are supplemented by random audits. Thus, voters are able to contribute to the verification of the vote capture process but the assurance of the scheme is not dependent on the voters being sufficiently diligent.
- Checks on the correct construction of the ballot forms are performed before votes are cast, thus simplifying the recovery strategies.
- The vote recording devices in the voting booths do not learn the voters' choices. This neatly avoids any threats of such devices leaking the voters' choices.
- The scheme is conceptually much simpler than others that have been proposed, thus easing its implementation and increasing the chances of voter acceptance.
- The current scheme shows considerable flexibility, suggesting that it could readily be adapted to different electoral requirements.

## 3   The Election Setup

A number of tellers are appointed. Each is assigned or creates *two* secret/public key pairs. The use of two keys per teller is a technical convenience arising from the audit process that will become clear later. These public keys are publicised and certified.

An authority creates a large number of ballot forms, significantly more than required for the electorate. These will have a familiar appearance: a left hand column listing the candidates or options and a right hand column into which the voter can insert her selection. This might just be an X in one cell for a single choice election or a ranking for a Single Transferable Vote (STV) system. Thus, for a four candidate race, a typical ballot form might look like:

| Nihilist | |
|----------|------------|
| Buddhist | |
| Anarchist | |
| Alchemist | |
| | $7rJ94K$ |

However, the order in which the candidates are listed will be randomised for each ballot form, that is, for any given ballot, the candidate order shown should be unpredictable. The random looking value at the bottom of the right hand column (which we call an 'onion' for reasons that will become apparent in Section 5) contains the information from which the candidate ordering can be reconstructed, buried cryptographically under the public keys of the tellers. The precise construction of the onions will be described in Section 5.2.

The exact details of the voting procedure can be varied according to the nature of the election and according to the perceived nature of threats to which the system is exposed. For simplicity of presentation we outline one simple procedure. Other procedures are possible and indeed one of the advantages of this scheme is that it appears to be significantly more flexible than previous variants.

## 4 An Example

The scheme is best introduced by way of a simple example. We will give a more formal and general description later. Suppose for simplicity that we are dealing with a simple election system in which each voter selects exactly one candidate and the winner will be the candidate who garners the most votes. This allows us to present the example using simple cyclic shifts of the candidate ordering. Generalisations to deal with options to select more than one candidate or to rank them, etc. are straightforward and discussed later. Clearly, a "none of the above" option could also be included.

### 4.1 Processing Votes

Suppose that there are four candidates and these are given a base ordering:

Anarchist
Alchemist
Nihilist
Buddhist

Since we are considering only cyclic shifts in this example, there are four possible candidate lists, corresponding to the four possible offsets, 0 to 3, from the base candidate list. The generation of the random offsets and cryptographic values will be described in detail later.

For convenience of the mathematical manipulations, we also adopt a canonical numbering convention for the candidates from 0 to 3 as indicated. Thus a vote for Anarchist will be represented as 0, for Alchemist as 1 etc. This numerical representation is purely for the machine manipulations and need not trouble the voter.

Consider the following ballot form:

| Buddhist | |
| Anarchist | |
| Alchemist | |
| Nihilist | |
| | $Qqkr3c$ |

This has an offset of 1. Thus the onion—$Qqkr3c$—encodes the value 1. Suppose the system is to process a vote for Nihilist. This would be represented by a mark in the Nihilist box:

| Buddhist | |
| Anarchist | |
| Alchemist | |
| Nihilist | X |
| | $Qqkr3c$ |

Once the voter has marked her choice, the left hand column that shows the candidate ordering is detached and destroyed, to leave a ballot receipt of the form:

Such right hand strips showing the position of an $X$ and an onion value constitute the ballot receipts.

This is now fed into the voting device, presumably an optical reader, which transmits the information on the strip, the position of the $X$ (as a numerical value 0, 1, 2 or 3) and the value of the onion, to the tellers. The tellers use their secret keys to perform the decryption of the onion (see later), and generate the decrypted vote value corresponding to the vote in the base ordering. In this case the decryption process yields the offset 1, so the vote value is the position of the vote (3) with the appropriate offset removed, yielding candidate $3 - 1 = 2$:

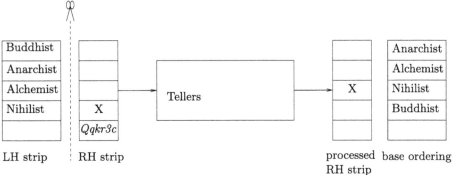

| Buddhist |
| Anarchist |
| Alchemist |
| Nihilist |
| |

LH strip

| |
| |
| |
| X |
| *Qqkr3c* |

RH strip

Tellers

| |
| |
| X |
| |
| |

processed
RH strip

| Anarchist |
| Alchemist |
| Nihilist |
| Buddhist |
| |

base ordering

**Fig. 1.** Processing a vote

Nihilist. This process is illustrated in Figure 1. A more detailed description will be provided later.

## 4.2 Casting the Vote

Our voter, Anne, first authenticates herself and registers at the polling station. She is invited to select, at random, a ballot form. She now enters a booth with her ballot form and marks her $X$ in the usual way. Suppose that she decides to vote for the "Buddhist" candidate:

| Nihilist | |
| Buddhist | X |
| Anarchist | |
| Alchemist | |
| | *e1rg38* |

She now removes the left hand strip (for shredding), and feeds the right hand strip into the voting device. This checks that the ballot strip is unused and reads the position of Anne's $X$, and the value of the onion. The device marks the strip as having been used to cast a vote and returns it to Anne for her to retain as the ballot receipt.

Note that the vote recording device does not learn which way Anne voted. Its role is merely to read the information on Anne's receipt and relay it to the the tellers via the bulletin board. This is a significant advantage of this scheme over many other schemes where the voting device necessarily learns the voter's choice, raising the possibility that the device could somehow leak this information.

The device transmits its digital record of the receipt to a central server for subsequent posting to the bulletin board once the election has closed. Anne will later be able to visit the bulletin board and confirm that her receipt is correctly posted and hence that it is correctly entered into the tallying process. The tallying process is deliberately constructed to hide the link between specific ballot receipts and the resulting decrypted votes, in order to provide voter anonymity. Thus Anne cannot directly link her input vote strip to any specific resulting vote, and so she cannot directly verify that her vote has been correctly decrypted. However, the fact that the votes are all correctly processed can be checked to a high degree of confidence, which provides Anne with the assurance that her vote will be decrypted correctly.

Observe that Anne's receipt alone does not reveal which way she voted. Unless the tellers are involved, this can only be determined if the left hand strip (now destroyed), that carries the candidate ordering, is aligned against it. Only the totality of the tellers, acting in consort, using their collection of secret keys are able to extract the seed information and so reconstruct the candidate ordering for that ballot form.

# 5    Construction of the Ballot Forms

The above description should have provided the reader with the key intuitions. We now give some of the mathematical details.

## 5.1    Construction of the Cryptographic Seeds and Offsets

For each ballot form, the authority will generate a unique, random seed. Suppose that there are $k$ tellers (numbered 0 to $k-1$), then this seed will be made up of a sequence of $2k$ values that we will call the germs:

$$seed := g_0, g_1, g_2 \cdots g_{2k-1}$$

Each of these germs should be drawn from some modest size field, perhaps $2^{32}$. Thus, for $k = 3$ say, the seed values will then range over $2^{192}$. These numbers can be adjusted to achieve whatever cryptographic strength is required.

The offset for the candidate list is now calculated from these germ values as follows. First a publicly known cryptographic hash function is applied to each of the germs and the result taken modulo $v$, where $v$ is the size of the candidate list:

$$d_i := hash(g_i) \pmod{v} \quad i = 0, 1, 2, \ldots, 2k - 1$$

The cyclic offset $\theta$ that will be applied to the candidate list on this form is now computed as the $(mod\ v)$ sum of these values:

$$\theta := (\textstyle\sum_{i=0}^{2k-1} d_i) mod\ v.$$

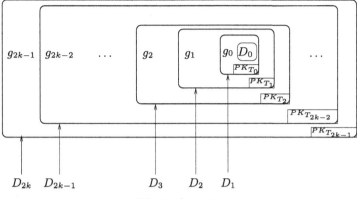

**Fig. 2.** An onion

## 5.2 Construction of the Onions

In order to facilitate auditing of the tellers whilst preserving anonymity of the voters (see [3] or [2] for more details), each teller performs two Chaum mixes and, accordingly, has two independent secret/public key pairs assigned to it. Teller $i$ will have public keys $PK_{T_{2i}}$ and $PK_{T_{2i+1}}$, and corresponding secret keys. The onion is formed by nested encryption of the germs under these public keys, and is given by:

$$\{g_{2k-1}, \{g_{2k-2}, \{\ldots, \{g_1, \{g_0, D_0\}_{PK_{T_0}}\}_{PK_{T_1}} \cdots\}_{PK_{T_{2k-3}}}\}_{PK_{T_{2k-2}}}\}_{PK_{T_{2k-1}}}$$

We introduce a little more notation to denote the intermediate layers of the onions. $D_0$ is a random, nonce-like value, unique to each onion. The subsequent layers are defined as follows:

$$D_{i+1} := \{g_i, D_i\}_{PK_{T_i}}$$

$$Onion := D_{2k}$$

Where $i$ ranges over $\{0, 1, \ldots, 2k - 1\}$. The construction of an onion is pictured in Figure 2.

## 6 The Role of the Tellers

The primary role of the tellers is to perform an anonymising mix and decryption on the batch of encrypted ballot receipts posted to the bulletin board. This ensures that the decrypted votes that emerge at the end of mix cannot be linked back to the encrypted receipts that are input to the process. Aside from some minor differences, the role of the tellers and the auditors are essentially as in the Chaum original. For completeness we give a brief overview here. More detailed descriptions can be found in [3] or [2].

The first, left hand column, of the bulletin board shows the receipts in exactly the same form as the printed receipts held by the voters. A voter can check this column to verify that her receipt has been accurately posted. An easy way to do this would be to search on the string representing the onion value and check that the $X$ appears in the correct box, i.e., as shown on the voter's receipt.

The information in the first, left hand column of the bulletin board is then passed to the first teller, $Teller_{k-1}$, for processing. There is no shuffling of the information when it is passed to the teller. The position of the $X$ on the voting slip is encoded as an integer $r$, and the correctness of this encoding can be simply and publicly verified.

The tellers will subsequently manipulate the numerical representations of the receipts, i.e., pairs of the form $(r_i, D_i)$, where $r_i$ is between 0 nd $v - 1$, and $D_i$ is an $i$th level onion. The initial value of $r_{2k}$ is the encoding of the position of the $X$ as originally placed by Anne on her receipt.

Each column (apart from the first, which contains the actual receipts) shows only the simplified, digital representation: a pair $(r_{2k}, D_{2k})$ consisting of a value $r$ from $Z_v$ and the value $D$ of the onion layer.

Each teller accepts an input column of votes $(r, D)$ from the previous teller, and then carries out two manipulations, to produce a middle column of votes and an output column of votes. The output column produced by the teller is then passed to the next teller in the chain.

Thus for each of the $(r_{2i}, D_{2i})$ pairs in the batch in the input column, $Teller_{i-1}$ will:

- apply its first secret key, $SK_{T_{2i-1}}$ to strip off the outer layer of the onion $D_{2i}$ to reveal the enclosed germ $g_{2i-1}$ and the enclosed onion $D_{2i-1}$.

$$g_{2i-1}, D_{2i-1} = \{D_{2i}\}_{SK_{T_{2i-1}}}$$

- apply the hash function to the germ value and take the result (mod $v$) to recover $d_{2i-1}$:

$$d_{2i-1} = hash(g_{2i-1}) \pmod{v}$$

- subtract $d_{2i-1}$ from $r_{2i}$ (mod $v$) to obtain a new $r$ value $r_{2i-1}$:

$$r_{2i-1} = r_{2i} - d_{2i-1} \pmod{v}$$

- form the new pair $(r_{2i-1}, D_{2i-1})$

Having completed these transformations on all the pairs in the initial batch as posted in its input column, the teller applies a secret shuffle to the resulting, transformed pairs and posts the resulting (transformed and shuffled) pairs to its middle column on the bulletin board.

$Teller_{i-1}$ now repeats this process on the contents of the middle column using its second secret key, $SK_{T_{2i-2}}$ to obtain a new set of $(r_{2i-2}, D_{2i-2})$ pairs. It will apply a second secret shuffle, independent of the previous one, to this batch of new pairs. The resulting transformed and shuffled $(r_{2i-2}, D_{2i-2})$ pairs are now posted to the output column on the bulletin board, and passed on to the next teller, $Teller_{i-2}$. This process is illustrated in Figure 3.

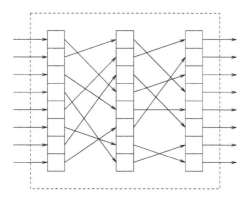

**Fig. 3.** A teller

*ballots*                                                                                                    *votes*

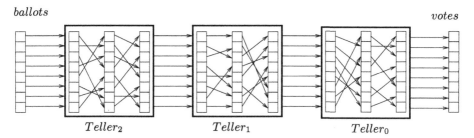

$Teller_2$              $Teller_1$              $Teller_0$

**Fig. 4.** Three tellers anonymising mix

This process is repeated by all the tellers in sequence, as illustrated in Figure 4 for a sequence of three tellers. The value of any of the intermediate $r$ values is thus given by:

$$r_{2k-i} = r_{2k} - \Sigma_{j=1}^{i} d_{2k-i} \ \ (mod \ v)$$

When the last teller performs the final transformation it outputs a batch of pairs which comprise a final $r$ value, $r_0$, and the inner onion value $D_0$. The final $r_0$ values are the values of the original votes in the canonical, base ordering. Figure 5 illustrates the effect of the process on a single vote.

To see this, observe that the candidate list on each form is shifted by the $(mod \ v)$ sum of the $d$ values, i.e., $\theta$. Thus the initial $r$ value is the candidate value plus $\theta$ modulo $v$. For each ballot pair, the tellers will have subtracted out the $d$ values from the initial $r$ value, thus cancelling the original shift of the candidate list and so recovering the original candidate value. Thus:

$$r_0 = r_{2k} - \Sigma_{j=1}^{2k} d_{2k-i} \ \ (mod \ v) = r_{2k} - \theta \ \ (mod \ v)$$

Consider the example of Anne's vote again (illustrated in Figure 5). The form she used to cast her vote had an offset of 2 and her $X$ was in the second box, value 1. Hence the initial value of $r_{2k}$ was 1 in her case. The tellers will in effect compute:

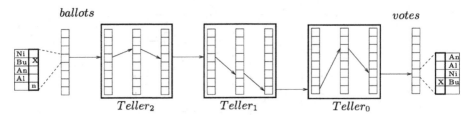

**Fig. 5.** A vote processed by three tellers

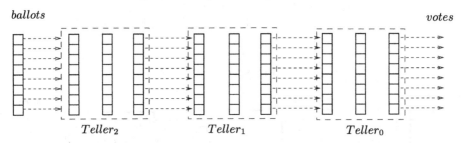

**Fig. 6.** Information posted by the sequence of three tellers

$$r_0 = r_{2k} - \sum_{j=1}^{2k} d_i (mod\ 4) = 1 - 2(mod\ 4) = 3$$

Thus the final $r$ value $r_0 = 3$ does indeed translate to a vote for "Buddhist" in the base ordering. The encryption of the vote can thus be thought of as a (co-variant) transformation of the frame of reference, decryption to the corresponding (contra-variant) transformation.

The overall effect then, is to have posted on the bulletin board, in the left hand column, the batch of initial receipts as posted by the voting devices. In the right hand column we will have the fully decrypted votes. In between there will be a set of columns with the intermediate, partially decrypted $(r, D)$ pairs. Each column will be some secret permutation and decryption of the previous one, and the permutation will not be published. This is illustrated in Figure 6. Note that the decryptions at each mix stage prevent the permutation being reconstructed by simple matching of onions or $r$ values.

The purpose of using the hash of the germ values buried in the onion layers to transform the $r$ values is to foil guessing attacks on the mixes. Without these hashes it would be possible to guess links through the mixes and check the guess by performing the appropriate computations (with the knowledge of the tellers' public keys). With the hash functions, these checks would require the computation of pre-images of the hashes, thus rendering such attacks intractable. We will see later that, for audited links the tellers are required to reveal not only the link but also the associated germ. The computations performed by the auditors are thus perfectly tractable.

Assuming that all the tellers perform their transformations correctly, there will be a one-to-one correspondence between the elements of each column and the next. The exact correspondence, namely which $(r, D)$ pair in one column corresponds to which pair in the next column, will be hidden and known only to the teller who performed the transformation between those columns. Thus, the receipts will have undergone multiple, secret shuffles between the first column as posted by the voting devices and the final decrypted column. This ensures that no voter can be linked to her vote, so ensuring ballot secrecy.

The fact that several tellers are used gives several layers of defence with respect to voter privacy: even if several of the tellers, but not all, are compromised, the linkage of a voter with her vote will remain secret.

The decrypted votes are posted in the final column so the overall count can be verified by anyone.

# 7   Auditing the Process

The description so far has assumed that all the steps of the vote casting, recording and counting are performed correctly, to specification. In fact, we want to avoid having to place such trust in the components of the scheme: the authority that generates the ballot forms, the device that records and transmits the receipt values and the tellers that perform the mixes and decryptions. In this section we identify the failure modes and corresponding counter-measures.

We assume for the purposes of this paper that measures are taken to prevent failures of the surrounding system, for example, in the maintenance of the electoral role, voter authentication etc. Here we concentrate on the failure modes of the cryptographic core of the scheme. With respect to the accuracy requirement there are three failure modes of the technical core of the scheme:

- Incorrectly constructed ballot forms, i.e., forms for which the cryptographic seed information buried in the onion does not correspond to the candidate order printed on the form.
- Incorrect recording of the values on the receipts and/or transmission to the Bulletin Board for tabulation.
- Errors or corruption in the transformations by the tellers on the ballot pairs.

Any of the failure modes could lead to vote values being incorrectly decrypted, i.e., resulting in decrypted vote values different from those intended by the voters. We now detail the checking processes that are employed to detect, with high probability, any such failures. We start with role of the authority tasked with generating the ballot forms.

## 7.1   Checking on the Authority

Suppose that a suitable authority has generated and distributed a large number of printed ballot forms to the polling stations. Independent auditors will be appointed whose task is to subject a random sampling of these ballots to well-formedness checks. These checks are designed to establish that the seeds buried cryptographically in the onions correctly correspond to the candidate list that appears on the form, given the declared public keys of the tellers. The auditors might also be tasked with checking the quality of the entropy used in the creation of the ballot forms.

Further random audits could also be performed during the election. Indeed, once the election has closed, left-over forms could also be routinely audited as well.

In addition to the checks performed by the auditors, mechanisms can also be provided to enable the voters to perform checks on the integrity of the ballot forms of their own, as detailed shortly. Thus, the voters are empowered to contribute to the verification of the election. First we describe the auditor checks, then we describe those that could be made available to the voters.

**Auditing the Ballot Forms.** A set of independent auditing authorities are appointed. These should be chosen in such a way as to minimise the chance of collusion. They might, for example, be drawn from civil liberties groups, the political parties etc. Each would be invited to make a random sampling of, say, 5% of the ballot forms generated by the authority.

To check the construction of the forms, some access to the cryptographic seeds is required. This could be achieved by requiring the authority to store the seeds along with their association with the onion values on the forms. However, the storing and selective release of such crypto material is potentially rather delicate and fragile. A novel and more elegant and robust approach is to use the tellers to strip off the layers of encryption for forms selected for audit and reveal the seed material.

Once the seed material for a ballot form selected for audit has been revealed, the form's integrity can be verified by recomputing the offset and onion value. If these match those printed on the form then it is safe to conclude that the form was indeed correctly constructed. Note that these calculations can be performed and verified by anyone, since the public keys of the tellers and the crypto hash functions are all public knowledge, More precisely, to check a ballot form, the following actions are performed:

- the auditor sends a digital copy of the onion on the form to the tellers.
- the tellers strip off the layers of encryption using their private keys to reveal the germs.
- the sequence of germ values are returned to the auditor.
- given the germ values, and knowing the public keys of the tellers, the auditors are able to reconstruct the value of the onion and can check that this agrees with the value printed on the form.
- they now recompute the offset value as the $(mod\ v)$ sum of the hashes of the germs.
- they can now check that the offset applied to the candidate list shown on the form agrees with the value obtained above.

If these checks are successful, it is safe to conclude that the ballot form in question was correctly constructed. Checked ballot forms, for which the seed has been revealed, are then discarded. If a random sampling of a significant proportion of forms all pass the checks, then it is safe to conclude that all the forms are correctly formed. The statistical calculations of the levels of confidence afforded by such random sampling are straightforward and, of course, the sampling rates can be adjusted to achieve whatever confidence levels are required.

Note further, that the algorithms for these checks are publicly known, so in principle, anyone could construct such a checker and make it freely available. Similarly anyone could examine such a checker to establish that it was performing correctly. Note also that any interested party could volunteer to perform some of the auditing. Thus, for example, the Electoral Reform Society could act as auditors. Representatives of the political parties could act as auditors. Furthermore, any results produced by an auditor can be double checked by independent parties.

**Voter Checks on Ballot Form Integrity.** In addition to the integrity checks performed by the auditors described above, the scheme also allows for checks on ballot form integrity to be performed by the voters themselves. This empowers the voters to contribute to the dependability of the election outcome, a sort of dependability for the people, by the people!.

The technique of using the tellers as an oracle during the voting phase suggests a number of alternative modes for checking the integrity of the ballot forms. These do not involve the revealing of the seed information.

1. Single dummy vote.
2. Multiple or ranked dummy vote.
3. Given the onion value, the tellers return the candidate ordering.

In the first, the voter would cast a dummy vote in exactly the same way that she will later cast her real vote in the booth, except that in this case the dummy vote would probably be cast in the presence of voting officials. Thus, she could put a cross against a random selection and send the receipt off to the tellers. They would decrypt the onion and return what they believe was the vote cast. If the onion was correctly constructed, this should of course agree with the dummy vote selected.

This has interesting psychological implications: assuming that the check succeeds, it should provide the voter with some assurance that when she comes to cast her real vote, it will also be correctly counted. On the other hand it might undermine her confidence that the secrecy of her vote will be assured.

Such a single dummy vote provides a rather weak check on the ballot form construction, probing only part of the construction. The second mode seeks to rectify this: by allowing the voter to cast several dummy votes, either in series or in parallel by making a ranking selection. In the latter case, given the receipt, the tellers should return what they believe to be the candidate ranking chosen by the voter. This provides a more complete check on the construction of the ballot form. Both of these suffer the drawback that the voter is expected to make random choices in the presence of officials.

The third mode is perhaps the most satisfactory. It provides a complete check on the ballot form but does not require the voter to make any random selections. Here, given only the onion value, the tellers should return what they believe to be the candidate ordering as shown on the ballot form.

We note that, in contrast to the auditor checking mode, these three modes are vulnerable to collusion attacks. If the authority that generated the forms is in collusion with one of the tellers there is the possibility of corrupting forms without detection by these modes. For example, the authority could flip a pair of candidates on the ballot forms. The colluding teller performs the corresponding flip during the checking phase, but not during the tallying phase.

The auditor checking mode is not vulnerable to such collusions and so is more rigorous. It therefore appears to be more suitable for the auditing authorities. It could also be made available to voters, but it seems less intuitive and so perhaps less reassuring to the voters. The psychological aspects of these checking modes from a voter perspective will be investigated in future work.

Thus, a possible voting procedure might be to allow a voter when she registers at the polling station to select a pair of ballot forms at random and nominate one for checking. This could then be checked in the presence of officials using, say, the third mode described above. Assuming that the check goes through okay, the checked form is discarded and the voter can proceed to the booth with her "real" ballot form. If any check fails, she should notify an official who should then investigate and diagnose the source of the error. We will discuss the error handling and recovery strategies later.

As noted earlier, care has to be taken in assessing the assurance provided by the voter checks as these are vulnerable to collusion attacks. Various counter-measures could be adopted to limit the likelihood of such collusions going un-detected. One possibility is to use an $l$ out of $k$ threshold scheme for the onion encryptions. The $l$ cardinality subsets of the $k$ tellers could then be chosen ran-domly for each dummy voting request. If the colluding tellers were omitted when a corrupted dummy vote was decrypted, an error would be flagged. In any case, the random checks by the auditors would catch such manipulated ballot forms as these are not vulnerable to such collusion attacks.

The tellers might return incorrect germ values but this will of course throw up a mismatch between the recomputed onion value and the value on the form. It might be that a teller malfunctions, or is loaded with the wrong keys. In this case the checks serve a useful role in debugging such configuration errors.

Note that the encryptions are all bijective, hence the germ values are uniquely determined by the onion value. The tellers cannot therefore find alternative germ values that would give the same onion value but a different offset.

Together, these checks ensure that if a malicious or corrupted authority tried to corrupt votes by providing a candidate ordering that does not correspond to the seed information buried in the onion, they stand a high chance of being detected. The chance of corruption going undetected falls off exponentially with the number of ballots they try to corrupt.

We stress that all the checks detailed here serve purely to probe the well-formedness of the ballot forms, i.e., serve to detect any failure of the candidate orderings on the forms to correspond to the information buried in the onions. These checks do not provide any detection of corruption during the tallying phase. A form that is correctly constructed in this sense will correctly capture the voter's intention. Of course, this does not of itself ensure that the vote will ultimately be correctly decrypted. For this we need additional mechanisms to ensure that all ballot receipts will be correctly recorded, transmitted and decrypted. These we address next.

## 8    Checking on the Vote Recording Devices

We need to ensure that ballot receipts are faithfully recorded, transmitted and entered into the tallying process. This is where the bulletin board comes into play. Once voting has closed, all ballot receipts are posted to the bulletin board. The material posted to the bulletin board will be publicly available in read-only mode. Thus any voter can visit the board and confirm that her receipt appears correctly in the input column.

If her receipt does not appear, or appears in corrupted form (in particular, if the position of the $X$ is incorrect), this should be reported. The voter has her receipt to prove to an official that her receipt does not appear correctly. In practice all ballot forms would be printed with anti-counterfeiting measures and would have been stamped and digitally signed by the device in the booth when the vote was cast to prevent attempts to fake receipts.

Assuming that voters are reasonably diligent in performing these checks, any failures to faithfully post receipts to the bulletin board, and hence to enter them into the tallying, should be detected. Precautions would also be needed to prevent anyone inserting additional, invalid receipts. One simple precaution would be to ensure that the number of posted receipts matched the number of cast ballots. The digital signatures applied by the voting devices could also be used to help prevent fake ballots being introduced.

A further possible enhancement is for the device in the booth to produce a paper copy of the ballot receipt. This copy is posted into a locked and sealed audit box (perhaps after being viewed under glass and confirmed by the voter in the manner of the 'Mercuri method' [5]). Now, independent auditors can perform checks of the correspondence between published receipts and the paper audit trails stored in the audit boxes. This serves to supplement the checks performed by a voter on the appearance of her receipt in the published list. This last enhancement has similarities to the Voter Verifiable Paper Audit Trail (VVPAT [5]) and has the advantage that the checks on ballot receipts on the bulletin board performed by the voters are supplemented by auditor checks. The assurance of the scheme is thus less dependent on the diligence of the voters in checking the appearance of their receipts in the published list.

## 9    Checking on the Tellers

The checks described above should ensure that voters' intentions are correctly encrypted in the ballot receipts and that all receipts are correctly entered in the tabulation process. Now we must ensure that all the receipts are accurately decrypted. For this, we must ensure that all the transformations performed on the receipts by the tellers during the anonymising mixes are correct.

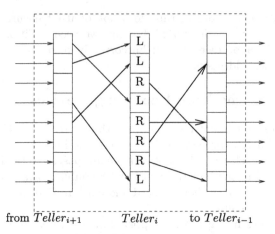

from $Teller_{i+1}$          $Teller_i$        to $Teller_{i-1}$

**Fig. 7.** Auditing $Teller_i$

As in the original Chaum scheme, the auditing of the tellers is based on the notion of partial random checking proposed in [4]. This takes place after the teller processing has finished, and is applied to the information committed to by the tellers on the bulletin board.

For each teller an auditing authority goes down the middle column and randomly assigns $R$ or $L$ to each $(r, D)$ pair. For pairs assigned an $R$, the auditor requires the teller to reveal the outgoing link (to the right) to the corresponding pair in the next column along with the corresponding germ value. For all pairs assigned an $L$, the auditor requires the teller to reveal the incoming link (from the left) along with the germ value.

This way of selecting links ensures that, for any given teller, no complete route across the two shuffles performed by that teller are revealed by the audit process. Hence no ballot receipt can be traced across the two mixes performed by any given teller. Each ballot transformation has a 50/50 chance of being audited.

This is illustrated in Figure 7, with the selected links included. The remaining links are not revealed.

For each teller the auditor performs such a random audit. Given the property that there are no full links revealed across any teller's mixes, the L/R selection can be made quite independently for each teller. This is the rationale for making each teller perform two mixes.

Suppose that, for a revealed link, the pair has been transformed thus:

$$r_i, D_i \longrightarrow r_{i-1}, D_{i-1}$$

Knowing this and the corresponding germ value $g_{i-1}$ (which the teller is required to provide for each revealed link), it can be checked that the following hold:

$$D_i = \{g_{i-1}, D_{i-1}\}_{PK_{T_{i-1}}}$$

and

$$r_{i-1} = r_i - hash(g_{i-1}) (mod \ v)$$

*ballots*                                                                                    *votes*

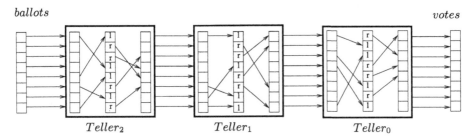

$Teller_2$                          $Teller_1$                          $Teller_0$

**Fig. 8.** Auditing the three tellers

If these equalities hold on a link we can conclude that the teller executed the correct transformation on this ballot pair. Some additional reasoning is required to show that it is not possible for a teller to perform a corrupted mix and be able to reveal false links in such a way as to pass any audit.

Figure 8 illustrates the audit across the sequence of three tellers.

## 10   Error Handling and Recovery Strategies

So far we have only described the checks that can be performed. A full description of the scheme requires detailing error handling and recovery modes. Due to lack of space we will not attempt to give an exhaustive description here.

Let us just consider the error handling strategy for a failed voter check. The first step for the official is to confirm that there is a real disagreement. Anne will have both parts of the dummy ballot form so she can prove which way she cast her dummy vote and she has the printout for the tellers. The official can thus establish that the problem is genuine and not just a case of voter error.

If the problem is real, the official should now run a further, auditor check: use the tellers as an oracle to extract the seed value and use this value to reconstruct the onion value and candidate list offset. If these values agree with those shown on the ballot, then it is fair to conclude that the form was correctly constructed by the authority. The error must then lie with the decryption of the vote performed by the tellers.

If this check fails, it can mean one of two things: the form was incorrectly constructed by the authority, or the form was perhaps actually correctly formed but the seed value returned by the tellers is incorrect.

Clearly, errors have to be diagnosed and collated. Strategies for dealing with patterns of errors must be specified. Thus, if a significant number of ballot forms were found to be malformed, doubt would be cast on the integrity of the authority charged with generating the forms. Note another pleasing feature of the scheme: any significant corruption on the part of the authority generating the ballot forms would almost certainly be detected by random audits before the election opens. Hence, this authority could be replaced before the election even starts.

A full description of error handling and recovery strategies is the topic of current research.

## 11    Generalising Ballots

This paper has so far considered ballots that allow a vote against a single candidate. More generally, elections may allow votes or preferences to be cast against a number of candidates. In this case a right hand strip may contain a number of $X$'s, or perhaps a list of numbers against candidates.

In this case, in order to avoid leaking information about votes, it is necessary to allow any permutation of the candidate list on the left hand strip, rather than just a cyclic permutation.

In order to achieve this, the germs could be used as keys for a cryptographic permutation function. The overall permutation applied to the candidate list as shown on the ballot form would then be a composition of the $2k$ separate permutations obtained from the $2k$ germs.

We use a publicly known hash function $h$ that maps germs to permutations, so that $p_i = h(g_i)$ is a permutation of names on ballots. The overall permutation is given by the composition of the permutations for all the germs:

$$\pi = p_{2k-1} \circ p_{2k-1} \circ \ldots \circ p_0$$

(where $f \circ g(x) = f(g(x))$). If the base candidate ordering is $base$, then the candidate list on the ballot is given by $\pi(base)$. Thus a corresponding vote $r$ on the right hand strip corresponds to a vote of $\pi^{-1}(r)$ against the base ordering.

The steps in the tellers take $(r_{i+1}, D_{i+1})$ to $(r_i, D_i)$, where each step reverses one permutation comprising $\pi$. Here, the $r$ values will encode either a ranking or an element of the power set of candidates as appropriate. The onion is unpeeled as previously to extract the associated seed $g_i$ and the inner onion $D_i$. In this case the computation of $r_i$ is given by:

$$r_i := (h(g_i))^{-1}(r_{i+1}) \qquad = \qquad p_i^{-1}(r_{i+1})$$

Given that the initial vote $r$ provided to the tellers is $r_{2k}$, we obtain that

$$r_i = (p_i^{-1} \circ p_{i+1}^{-1} \circ \ldots \circ p_{2k-1}^{-1})(r_{2k})$$

and thus the final vote $r_0$ posted by $Teller_0$ is $\pi^{-1}(r)$, which is indeed the vote cast.

## 12    Related Work and Conclusions

A large number of cryptographic voting schemes have been proposed over the past 20 years or so. These use a variety of cryptographic techniques, ranging from blind signatures to cryptographic homomorphisms etc. The idea of providing the voter with an encrypted receipt goes back to the original scheme proposed by Chaum. Another scheme, that also uses encrypted receipts and has similar goals, is the VoteHere scheme of Adler and Neff, [6]. The cryptographic primitives used there are quite different from those of this paper and appear to be significantly more complex.

We have presented a new voter-verifiable election scheme based on the original Chaum scheme. This variant preserves the essential features of the original whilst sidestepping the complexity of the visual cryptography of the original. The presentation of the encoding on the vote is quite intuitive and familiar. A pleasing spin-off is that the randomisation of the candidate order counters any tendency to bias the voter choice that might arise from a fixed order.

The new scheme provides some interesting advantages over previous variants:

- The format of the ballot forms and the process of casting a vote is quite familiar.
- The cryptographic commitments are generated before the voter choices are revealed, even before the election period starts.
- The vote recording devices do not learn the voter choices. This avoids the possibility of such devices leaking this information.
- Voters get to perform their own checks on the correct construction of their dummy ballot forms. This should help instil confidence that their real votes will ultimately be correctly decrypted during the tallying process.
- The checking performed by the voters is supplemented by audits performed by various auditing agencies.
- The problem of storing and selectively revealing seed information is solved by the novel use of the tellers during the voting period as oracles to reveal the seeds for ballot forms used for auditing.
- Voters get to run their checks before casting their vote. This avoids some of the messiness in the recovery mechanisms of earlier variants when a voter discovers a mal-formed receipt after casting their vote.
- The initial auditing phase performed on the ballot forms forms should serve to weed out any corrupt authority even before the election opens.

Precautions need to be taken to prevent double voting. In particular, care needs to be taken to ensure that ballot forms used for checking cannot be reused to cast real votes. These details of such mechanisms will be discussed in a future paper.

Similarly, precautions are need to clearly separate the two functions of the tellers: the on-demand ballot form integrity checking function and the anonymising mix function. In particular it is essential to ensure that no ballot form that has been used to cast a "real" vote can be subsequently used in a checking mode. Various procedures can be envisaged to prevent this: appropriately marking a receipt that has been used to cast a vote and ensuring that it cannot be reused for either dummy or real voting. It would be satisfying to develop cryptographic mechanisms to enforce this.

For the purposes of illustration we have described how the scheme can be used for a single vote system, i.e., in which voters get to choose just one of a set of options or candidates. Where a voter can rank the candidates in order of preference (or indeed where she can vote for more than one candidate), full permutations in place of the simple cyclic shifts presented here. In practice, full permutations would probably be used even for single selection elections.

## 13  Future Directions

The destruction of the left hand strips of the ballot forms is essential to prevent both coercion and vote buying. An issue that requires careful consideration then is how to best enforce the destruction and ensure that it is not possible for the voter to exit the booth with both parts of the ballot form. Mechanical devices that enforce the destruction when the vote is cast are a possibility. Another interesting possibility is to ensure that plenty of dummy left hand strips are available in the booth, rather than trying to enforce destruction of this strip. If a voter is threatened with coercion she can simply select an appropriate strip that will keep the coercer happy.

Another issue is that, as presented, the scheme entails the authority knowing the association of all onions and candidate lists. Thus, if the authority were compromised, it could jeopardise the secrecy of the election. Various measures can be envisaged to counter or at least minimise this risk. Ballot forms could be generated in some distributed fashion using various sources of entropy. Alternatively, ballot forms could be generated and printed on demand. An intriguing possibility is to use entropy derived from the paper used to print the forms, for example using optical fibres stirred into the paper during manufacture. Ballot forms could be supplied in sealed envelopes to prevent the information being garnered in transit. The problem remains that there is still a point at which the onion and candidate list must be presented to the voter.

For the three voter checking modes, the germ values do not have to be revealed. This suggests the possibility of reusing a "dummy" ballot form to cast a real vote. This has the advantage that the form used for the real vote will itself have been tested. Ballot forms could come equipped with two onion values, both of which should yield the candidate ordering shown. One could be used for checking, the other to cast the real vote. This possibility may however open up vulnerabilities and would need to be subjected to careful analysis. This is the subject of current research.

This scheme would appear to be readily adapted to remote voting. The simplest adaption is to distribute ballot forms by post. Votes could then be cast by providing the onion value along with suitable indicators of the voter selection in the right hand column. Alternatively, protocols could be used for on-line, authenticated distribution of the crypto material. Of course, the threat of coercion that plagues remote voting systems rears its head again, but there may be ways to offset this.

These avenues are the subject of current research.

## Acknowledgements

The authors would like to thank Ben Adida, Jeremy Bryans, Roberto Delicata, Jeroen van der Graaf, Michael Jackson, Cliff Jones, Steve Kremer, Aad van Moorsel, Thea Peacock, Rene Peralta, Brian Randell, Ron Rivest, Mark Ryan, Fred Schneider, Robert Stroud, and Poorvi Vora for many helpful discussions.

# References

1. Robert S. Brumbaugh. *Ancient Greek Gadgets and Machines*. Thomas Y. Crowell, 1966.
2. Jeremy W. Bryans and Peter Y. A. Ryan. A Dependability Analysis of the Chaum Voting Scheme. Technical Report CS-TR-809, University of Newcastle, 2003.
3. David Chaum. Secret-Ballot Receipts: True Voter-Verifiable Elections. *IEEE Security and Privacy*, 2(1):38–47, Jan/Feb 2004.
4. M. Jakobsson, M. Juels, and R. Rivest. Making Mix Nets Robust for Electronic Voting by Randomised Partial Checking. In *USENIX'02*, 2002.
5. R. Mercuri. A better ballot box? *IEEE Spectrum*, 39(10), 2002.
6. C. Andrew Neff. A verifiable secret shuffle and its application to e-voting. In *ACM-CCS*, 2001.
7. Peter Y. A. Ryan. A Variant of the Chaum Voter-Verifiable Scheme. Technical Report CS-TR 864, University of Newcastle, 2004. Also in WITS 2005: Workshop on Issues in the Theory of Security.

# Machine-Checked Security Proofs of Cryptographic Signature Schemes

Sabrina Tarento

INRIA Sophia-Antipolis, France
Sabrina.Tarento@sophia.inria.fr

**Abstract.** Formal methods have been extensively applied to the certification of cryptographic protocols. However, most of these works make
the perfect cryptography assumption, i.e. the hypothesis that there is no
way to obtain knowledge about the plaintext pertaining to a ciphertext
without knowing the key. A model that does not require the perfect cryptography assumption is the generic model and the random oracle model.
These models provide non-standard computational models in which one
may reason about the computational cost of breaking a cryptographic
scheme. Using the machine-checked account of the Generic Model and
the Random Oracle Model formalized in Coq, we prove the safety of
cryptosystems that depend on a cyclic group (like ElGamal cryptosystem), against interactive generic attacks and we prove the security of
blind signatures against interactive attacks. To prove the last step, we
use a generic parallel attack to create a forgery signature.

## 1  Introduction

Cryptographic protocols are designed to provide certain security guarantees
between agents communicating in a hostile environment. Numerous application domains including distributed systems and web services used cryptographic
schemes. However, designing secure cryptographic mechanisms is extremely difficult to achieve [1], the literature abounds of attacks against cryptosystems
that were previously proven correct. Recently, a significant research effort has
been directed at linking the formal and computational approaches. One of the
first result is presented by Abadi and Rogaway [2]: they prove the computational soundness of formal encryption in the case of a passive attacker. Since
then, many results [3,15,19,14] have been obtained. Efforts are also under way
to formulate syntactic calculi for dealing with probabilism and polynomial-time
considerations, in particular [16,12,17] and a second step, to encode them into
proof tolls. Therefore, there has lastly been an increasing interest in provable
security. A system is said to have provable security if its security requirements
are stated formally in an adversarial model and there is a proof that these security requirements can be met provided that some well studied cryptographic
primitives (such as RSA) are secure. While provable cryptography has become
an important tool in the validation of cryptographic schemes, there are regular
attacks against cryptographic schemes that were deemed sound using methods

S. De Capitani di Vimercati et al. (Eds.): ESORICS 2005, LNCS 3679, pp. 140–158, 2005.
© Springer-Verlag Berlin Heidelberg 2005

from provable security. Formal proofs enable to detail assumptions so by using a proof assistant like Coq, we do not have implicit requirements.

The objective of our work, initiated in [5], is to use proof assistants for formalizing provable cryptography. There are two motivations for our work. From the point of view of cryptography, proof assistants provide an excellent tool to highlight hidden assumptions that permeate proofs in cryptography. Furthermore, proof assistants solve another (milder) shortcoming of cryptographic proofs, namely the imprecision on bounds for the attacker's advantage. From the point of view of formal mathematics, provable cryptography covers a range of concepts including algebraic structures, polynomials, matrices and probabilities.

*Contribution.* In earlier work [5], we established the security of cryptographic schemes against non-interactive attacks, using the Generic Model (or GM for short), which provides non-standard computational models for reasoning about the probability and computational cost of breaking a cryptographic scheme. In such a scenario, the attacker tries to launch an attack without any external help. However in most practical scenarios the attacker is able to interact with oracles that provide useful information for launching an attack. Different forms of oracles include:

- a hash oracle: an interaction with the hash oracle is a query to a random hash function $H : G \times M \to \mathbb{Z}_q$ where $G$ is an arbitrary group of prime order $q$ and $M$ is the set of all cyphertexts.
- a signature oracle (signer for short): an interaction with the signer provides to the attacker the signature of a message.

The main contribution of this paper is to extend our security proofs to such interactive attacks, building on a combination of the GM and of the Random Oracle Model (or ROM for short) that assuming the hash function to be collision resistant (collisions of random functions have negligibly small probability).

We consider scenario in which we focus on signature forgery attacks, where the attacker aims at forging a message that will appear as having been signed by another party. In order to prove the security of a cryptographic signature scheme, one must at least establish that it is resistant to signature forgery attacks, since schemes that are subject to forgery attacks cannot guarantee the identity of signers nor can they enforce non-repudiation. In order to establish the security of signature schemes against forgery attacks, we are led to consider the ROS problem:

Find an overdetermined, solvable system of linear equations modulo $q$ with random inhomogeneities. Specifically, given a random function $F : \mathbb{Z}_q^l \to \mathbb{Z}_q$ and coefficients $a_{k,l} \in \mathbb{Z}_q$, find a solvable system of $l+1$ distinct equations (1) in the unknowns $c_1, \ldots, c_l$ over $\mathbb{Z}_q$:

$$a_{k,1}c_1 + \ldots + a_{k,l}c_l = F(a_{k,1}, \ldots, a_{k,l}) \quad \text{for } k = 1, \ldots, t. \tag{1}$$

As in our earlier work, we improve on pen-and-paper proofs in two aspects:

- pen-and-paper proofs about GM and ROM are carried out on examples, rather than in the general case. In contrast, our results deal with arbitrary interactive generic algorithms;
- pen-and-paper proofs about GM and ROM often ignore events that occur with a negligible probability, i.e. events whose probability tends to 0 when the size of the group tends to ∞. In contrast, we take all events into account and we provide accurate bounds on the attacker's advantage.

*Contents of the paper.* The remainder of the paper is organised as follows. Section 2 provides a brief account of the Coq proof assistant, and presents our formalization of probabilities and polynomials, which are required to prove our main results. Section 3 provides a brief review of our formalization of GM. Section 4 describes parallel attacks and Section 5 provides the formalization of ROM in which the attacker makes interactions with the signer. We conclude in Section 6.

## 2    Preliminaries in Coq

This section provides a brief overview of the proof assistant Coq, and discusses some of issues with the formalization of algebra. Further, it describes our formalization of probabilities and of multivariate polynomials.

### 2.1    Coq

Coq [8] is a general purpose proof assistant based on the Calculus of Inductive Constructions, which extends the Calculus of Constructions with a hierarchy of universes and mechanisms for (co)inductive definitions.

Further, logical statements can be used in specifications, e.g. in order to form the "subset" of prime numbers as the type of pairs $\langle n, \phi \rangle$ where $n$ is a natural number and $\phi$ is a proof that $n$ is prime. There are, however, some limitations to the interaction between specifications and propositions. In particular, dependent type theories such as the Calculus of Inductive Constructions lack intensional constructs that allow the formation of subsets or quotients. In order to circumvent this problem, formalizations rely on *setoids* [4], that is mathematical structures packaging a carrier, the "set"; its equality, the "book equality"; and a proof component ensuring that the book equality is well-behaved. For the sake of readability, we avoid in as much as possible mentioning setoids in our presentation, although they are pervasive in our formalizations. The declaration mechanism allows the user to specify his own basic objects. Declared objects play the role of axioms or parameters in mathematics. To define simple inductive type, we use the command **Inductive** and to define recursive functions, we use the command **Fixpoint** that allows to define inductive objects using a fixed point construction.

### 2.2    Probabilities

As there is no appropriate library for probabilities in the reference libraries and contributions in Coq, we have developed a collection of basic definitions and results for discrete probabilities i.e, probabilities over finite sets [11]. Due to lack of space, we only provide the definition of probabilities and conditional probabilities, and the statement of one illustrative result.

Before delving into details, let us point out that there are several possible approaches for defining discrete probabilities i.e, probabilities over finite setoids. One possibility is to assume that the setoid is finite, i.e. isomorphic to some initial segment of $\mathbb{N}$, for a suitable notion of isomorphism of setoids. We have found slightly more convenient to define probabilities w.r.t. an arbitrary type V and a finite subset E of V, given as a (non-repeating) V-list. The probability space is the finite set E where every base element has the same probability.

Given a fixed type V and a fixed enumeration E:list V, we define an event to be a predicate over V, i.e. Event : **Type** := V →Prop. Then, we define the probability of an event A being true as the ratio between the number of elements in E for which A is true and the total number of elements in E, i.e.

**Definition.** $Pr_E$(L:Event):=length (filter E L)/(length E).

where length and filter are the usual functions on lists, i.e. (length l) computes the length of the list l, and (filter l P) removes from the list l all its elements that do not satisfy the predicate P.

Then, one can check that $Pr_E$ satisfies the properties of a probability measure, e.g.:

- for every event A, $0 \leq Pr_E$(A)$\leq 1$;
- if True is the trivial proposition, which always holds, then $Pr_E$($\lambda$a.True)=1;
- for any sequence $A_i$ of disjoint events $Pr_E$($\bigcup_{1\leq i\leq n}A_i$)=$\sum_{1\leq i\leq n}Pr_E$($A_i$), where $\bigcup_{1\leq i\leq n}A_i=\lambda$a.$A_1(a) \vee \cdots \vee A_n(a)$.

Conditional probabilities are defined in the usual way, i.e.

**Definition.** Pr_cond(L M:Event):=$Pr_E$(L $\wedge$ M)/$Pr_E$(M).

In the sequel, we denote Pr_cond(L M) by $Pr_E$(L|M).
Then, one can check that $Pr_E$ satisfies properties such as
$Pr_E$(A) =$Pr_E$(A|B) $Pr_E$(B) + $Pr_E$(A|¬B) (1−$Pr_E$(B))
In the sequel, E will often be omitted to adopt the notation Pr(A).

## 2.3 Polynomials

For our work, we need to have a formalization of polynomials in which we can compute easily the degree of a polynomial in several variables; and in particular for proving Schwartz lemma, we need to have a formalization that allows us to view a polynomial in $n+1$ variables as a polynomial in n or 1 variables. We have extended the formalization of polynomial on one variable.

Pol1 is the type of all polynomials in one variable in C.

**Inductive** Pol1:**Type**:=
|Pc : C→ Pol1
|PX : Pol1 → C → Pol1.

We define the equality of polynomials with inference rules.

```
Inductive ≡:Poll → Poll → Prop :=
  |Eq1_Pc_Pc : ∀ p q: C, p=q→(Pc p)≡(Pc q)
  |Eq1_Pc_PX :∀ p q: C, ∀ Q1:Poll,
        p=q→Q1≡0→(Pc p)≡(PX Q1 q)
  |Eq1_PX_Pc :∀ p q: C, ∀ P1:Poll,
        p=q→P1≡0→(PX P1 p)≡(Pc q)
  |Eq1_PX_PX :∀ p q:C, ∀ P1 Q1 :Poll,
        p=q→P1≡Q1→(PX P1 p)≡(PX Q1 q).
```

where Pc is the constructor for constant polynomials and PX P c=P*X+c.

We formalize the set of coefficients as a ring with usual operations and properties; with this formalization of polynomials on one variable, we can recover the operations and properties of a ring for C[X]. By induction we extend it for several variables so a polynomial in n variables in C is of the type $(C[X_1]...[X_{n-1}])[X_n]$.

Having this formalization of polynomials, we can formalize and prove an useful lemma for our proofs on security.

**Lemma** Schwartz:
$$\forall \ (p \ : \mathbb{Z}_q[X_1,\ldots,X_n}, \ q \neq 0 \ \rightarrow \ p \not\equiv 0 \ \rightarrow$$
$$Pr_{x_1,\ldots,x_n\in\mathbb{Z}_q^n}(p(x_1,\ldots,x_n)\equiv 0) \ \leq \ (\text{degree p})/q.$$

The probability that an element $x \in \mathbb{Z}_q^n$ is a zero of a polynomial p is smaller than the degree of the polynomial divided by q. Here, the ring is the set $\mathbb{Z}_q$ and we have n variables $X_1,\ldots,X_n$.

## 2.4    Remarks on Formalization of Group

In our work, we consider a cyclic group $G$ of prime order $q$; as we have an isomorphism between the group $G$ and the ring $\mathbb{Z}_q$ [13], assuming that $g$ is the generator of the group, each element of the group are an exponentiation of the generator and the function:

$$G \rightarrow \mathbb{Z}_q$$
$$g^a \mapsto a$$

is a one-to-one correspondance (more precisely an isomorphism).

Thus, instead of considering an element $g^a$ of the group, we will always consider the exponent $a$.

For example, for the multivariate exponentiation, we do not use the function

$$mex : \mathbb{Z}_q^d \times G^d \rightarrow G$$

$$(a_1,\ldots,a_d,g_1,\ldots,g_d) \mapsto \prod_{i=1}^{d} g_i^{a_i}$$

but by assuming $g_i = g^{s_i}$, we define the function

$$mex : \mathbb{Z}_q^d \to \mathbb{Z}_q^d \to \mathbb{Z}_q$$

$$(a_1, \ldots, a_d), (s_1, \ldots, s_d) \mapsto \sum_{j=1}^{d} a_j s_j.$$

## 3   A Review of the Generic Model

The generic model, GM for short, was introduced by Shoup [22] and Nechaev [18], and can be used to provide an overall guarantee that a cryptographic scheme is not flawed [20,21,24]. For example, the GM is useful for establishing the complexity of the discrete logarithm or the decisional Diffie-Hellman problem, which we describe below.

### 3.1   Informal Account

The GM focuses on generic attacks, i.e. attacks that do not exploit any specific weakness in the underlying mathematical structures, which in the case of GM is a cyclic group $G$ of prime order $q$. More concretely, the GM focuses on attacks that work for all cyclic groups, and that are independent of the encoding of group elements; in practice, this is achieved by leaving the group $G$ unspecified. Furthermore, the GM constrains the behavior of the attacker so that he cannot access oracles, and can only gain information about the secret through testing group equalities (a.k.a. collisions). In order to test group equalities, the attacker performs repeatedly modular exponentiations of the program inputs, using coefficients that are chosen randomly and with uniform distribution over the probability space $\mathbb{Z}_q$.

   More precisely, a generic attacker $\mathcal{A}$ over $G$ is given by its list of secrets, say $s_1, \ldots, s_n \in \mathbb{Z}_q$, its list of inputs, say $l_1, \ldots, l_{t'} \in \mathbb{Z}_q$, which depends upon secrets, and a generic algorithm, which is a sequence of multivariate exponentiation (mex) steps. For the latter, the attacker selects arbitrarily, and independently of the secrets the coefficients $a_{i,1}, \ldots, a_{i,t'} \in \mathbb{Z}_q$ and computes for $t' < i \leq t$ the group elements $f_i = \prod_{j=1}^{t'} f_j^{a_{i,j}}$, where $f_j = g^{l_j}$ for $1 \leq j \leq t'$. The output of the generic algorithm is the list $f_1, \ldots, f_t$, from which the attacker will test for collisions, i.e. equalities $f_j = f_{j'}$ with $1 \leq j < j' \leq t$.

   The objective of the GM model is to establish upper bounds for the probability of a generic attacker to be successful. To this end, the GM model assumes that a generic attacker $\mathcal{A}$ is successful if it finds a non-trivial collision, i.e. a collision that reveals information about secrets (those collisions which do not reveal information are called trivial, and are defined as collisions that hold with probability 1, i.e. for all choices of secret data). The assumption incurs a loss of precision in the bounds one gives (since finding a non-trivial collision may not be sufficient to reveal all secrets); however, it allows to show that the probability is negligible for a sufficiently large order $q$ of the group $G$ and a reasonable number of steps $t$ of the generic algorithm.

## 3.2    Formalization

The main difficulty in formalizing generic algorithms is to pinpoint the notion
of secret. The formal definition of a generic algorithm is given in the figure 1. In
order to model the notion of secrets, we introduce a type $Sec$ of formal secret
parameters (see line 1) and model inputs as a list of non-repeating polynomial
expressions over secrets (see line 2). If the set $Sec$ has $n$ secrets $s_1, \ldots, s_n$,
$\mathbb{Z}_q[Sec] = \mathbb{Z}_q[s_1, \ldots, s_n]$. Then, we consider symbolic algorithms (see line 4) in
which the attacker selects arbitrarily and independently of the secrets a list of
coefficients $a_{i,1}, \ldots, a_{i,t'} \in \mathbb{Z}_q$. The function $mex$ (see line 8) takes the exponents instead of the group elements and returns the logarithm of the results of
the function $concretemex$. Symbolic outputs (see line 16) are polynomials constructed as linear combinations of inputs, i.e. of the form $a_{i,1}l_1 + \cdots + a_{i,t'}l_{t'}$
(which correspond to the logarithm of the mex-steps) and concrete outputs (see
line 21) are obtained from the symbolic outputs by using the extension of an
interpretation function $\sigma$ from polynomial expressions to elements in $\mathbb{Z}_q$, more
precisely, $[| \ |]_\sigma : \mathbb{Z}_q[Sec] \rightarrow \mathbb{Z}_q$ returns the evaluation of a polynomial in $\mathbb{Z}_q[Sec]$
by using an interpretation function $\sigma$. An interpretation function $\sigma : Sec \rightarrow \mathbb{Z}_q$
maps formal secret parameters to actual secrets in $\mathbb{Z}_q$. We can define the set
of non-trivial collision (see line 24), we can find a non-trivial collision if we can
find two polynomials e e' $\in$ (SymbOutput r) non identically equal such that
the interpretation of the polynomial e-e' under $\sigma$ is 0. By considering only
polynomials non identically equal, we eliminate trivial collisions.

The advantage of the attacker is the probability of finding non-trivial collisions. Such an over-approximation is quite coarse since we consider the attacker
to be successful whenever he gains some informations about the interpretation
function $\sigma$. In principle, one could try to be more precise and estimate the probability of the attacker to find the function $\sigma$ (i.e. its value for all inputs).

In order to give an upper bound for the probability of finding non-trivial
collisions, one can then rely on Schwartz Lemma (see the section 2), as usual
with the generic model.
In the sequel, we write $\mathcal{CO}(\mathcal{A})$ if the attacker $\mathcal{A}$ finds non-trivial collisions. Furthermore, we let $d$ be the maximal degree of the inputs i.e, the polynomials $l_j$
for $1 \leq j \leq t'$, let $t$ be the number of steps $\mathcal{A}$ performs.

**Proposition 1.** $\forall \mathcal{A} : $ GA, $Advantage(\mathcal{A}) = Pr(\mathcal{CO}(\mathcal{A})) \leq \dfrac{\binom{t}{2}d}{q - \binom{t}{2}d}$

*Proof.* All outputs are of the form $p_i = \sum_{1 \leq j \leq t'} a_{i,j}\, l_j(s_1, \ldots, s_k)$, where $p_i$ is
a polynomial of degree $d$. Hence there exists a collision $f_i = f_{i'}$ iff $(s_1, \ldots, s_k)$
is a root of $p_i - p_{i'}$. There are $\binom{t}{2}$ equalities of the form $f_i = f_{i'}$ to test, hence
$\binom{t}{2}$ polynomials of the form $p_i - p_{i'}$, each of which is not identical to 0 (as there
are non-trivial collisions), and has degree $\leq d$. So we can apply an extension of
Schwartz Lemma to deduce the expected result.

We can instantiate the proposition to specific cryptographic schemes.

```
1 Parameter Sec:Set.
2 Parameter input:list Z_q[Sec].
3
4 Inductive GA:Type:=
5    nostep:GA
6   |step:GA→ (list Z_q) →GA.
7
8 Fixpoint mex(a:list Z_q) (e:list Z_q[Sec]) :Z_q[Sec]:=
9    match a with nil⇒ 0
10                |b::bs ⇒
11      match e with nil ⇒ 0
12                  |x::xs ⇒ x*b + (mex xs bs)
13      end
14   end.
15
16 Fixpoint SymbOutput( A :GA): (list Z_q[Sec]) :=
17    match A with nostep ⇒ nil
18        | (step A' e) ⇒(mex e input)::(SymbOutput A')
19   end.
20
21 Definition ConcrOutput( A :GA) (σ:Sec→Z_q) :list Z_q:=
22 map λx:Z_q[Sec].[|x|]_σ   (SymbOuput A).
23
24 Definition CO ( A :GA) (σ:Sec →Z_q) :=
25 ∀ e e':Z_q[Sec], e ∈ (SymbOutput A) ∧
26        e' ∈ (SymbOutput A) ∧ e-e'≠0 ∧ [|e − e|]_σ=0.
```

**Fig. 1.** Formalization of the GM

*Example 1 (Discrete logarithm).* The algorithm is given as input the group generator $g \in G$ and the public key $h = g^r \in G$, and outputs a guess $y$ for $\log_g h = r$. Observe that any non-trivial collision reveals the value of $r$: indeed, every $f_i$ will be of the form $g^{a_i}(g^r)^{a'_i} = g^{(a_i + ra'_i)}$. Hence for any collision $f_i = f_j$, we have $g^{(a_i + ra'_i)} = g^{(a_j + ra'_j)}$, and so $r(a'_i - a'_j) \equiv a_j - a_i \ [q]$. If the collision is non-trivial, then $a'_i - a'_j \neq 0$ and we can deduce the value of $r$.

In this example, there is a single secret $r$ and the formal inputs are the polynomials $1 := \log_g g$ and $r := \log_g g^r$ as we take the exposant instead of the exponentiation, thus the maximal degree of an input is $d = 1$ so the probability of finding the secret is $\mu + \frac{1}{q(1-\mu)}$, where $\mu = \frac{\binom{t}{2}}{q-\binom{t}{2}}$.

Note that Proposition 1 only holds for a secret $x : Sec$ ranging uniformly over $\mathbb{Z}_q$. For some problems however, such as the Decisional Diffie-Hellman problem below, $x$ ranges uniformly over a subset of $\mathbb{Z}_q$. In this case, the probability of finding a secret is $\mu + \frac{1}{q'(1-\mu)}$, where $\mu = \frac{\binom{t}{2}d}{q-\binom{t}{2}d}$ and $q'$ is the cardinal of the set of possible values for $x : Sec$.

*Example 2 (Decisional Diffie-Hellman Problem [9]).* The algorithm is given as input the group generator $g \in G$, the group elements $g^x$ and $g^y$, and the group elements $g^{xy}$ and $g^z$ in random order, where $x, y, z$ are random in $\mathbb{Z}_q$, and outputs a guess for $g^{xy}$ (or equivalently, for the order of $g^{xy}$ and $g^z$). In this example, there are three secrets $x$, $y$ and $z$, and the formal inputs are the polynomials $1 := log_g g$, $x := log_g g^x$, $y := log_g g^y$, $xy := log_g g^{xy}$ and $z := log_g g^z$, thus the maximal degree of an input is $d = 2$. Here $q' = 2$ so the probability of finding the secret is $\mu + \frac{1}{2(1-\mu)}$, where $\mu = \frac{2\binom{t}{2}}{q-2\binom{t}{2}}$.

## 4   The Random Oracle Model

Interactive generic algorithms are extension of generic algorithms in which the attacker is able to interact with oracles through interactive steps. Such interactive algorithms can be modeled using the Random Oracle Model, or ROM for short, that was introduced by Bellare and Rogaway [6] but its idea originates from earlier work by Fiat and Shamir [10].

For the purpose of our work, we do not need to develop a general framework for interactions; instead we focus on two typical oracles with whom the attacker can interact: queries to hash functions and signers.

The ROM assumes a random hash function and is a stronger assumption that assuming the hash function to be collision resistant; the fundamental assumption of ROM is that the hash function $H : G \rightarrow M \rightarrow \mathbb{Z}_q$ is chosen at random with uniform probability distribution over all functions of that type. Let $G$ be a cyclic group of prime order $q$ with generator $g$ and $H$ be an hash function, modelled as an oracle, that given an input (query) outputs a random number in the range of $H$. An interactive generic algorithm $\mathcal{A}$ can read an input, or take a mex-step, or perform an interaction. We consider two common forms of interactions in cryptographic algorithms: queries to hash functions and signers. These forms of interaction are used in particular in the signed ElGamal encryption protocol. A $\mathcal{A}$ over $G$ is given by:

- its input $l_1, \ldots, l_{t'} \in \mathbb{Z}_q$, which depends upon a set of secrets, typically secret keys, say $s_1, \ldots, s_n \in \mathbb{Z}_q$. In the sequel, we define the group input $f_1, \ldots, f_{t'} \in G$ of the algorithm by $f_k = g^{l_k}$;
- a run, i.e. a sequence of $t$ steps including $t''$ mex-steps, $\tau$ query to the hash oracle and $l$ interactions with the signer. A step can either be an input step, a multivariate exponentiation (mex) step, a query to the hash function or a interaction with the signer. An input step reads some input from the group input. For $1 \leq i \leq t''$, we assume that the algorithm at step $i$ takes a mex step, i.e. selects arbitrarily $a_{i,1}, \ldots, a_{i,t'} \in \mathbb{Z}_q$ and computes $f_i = \prod_{1 \leq j \leq t'} g^{l_j a_{i,j}}$.
- For a query to the hash oracle, we apply to $H$ a group element $f_j$ and a claimed ciphertext $m_j$ to compute $c = H(f_j, m_j)$
- A interaction with the signer is a three rounds deterministic protocol.

Each interaction with the signer provides an element $r_i$ and increases the length of the input by one, so after the ith interaction, the input becomes:

$$l_1, \ldots, l_{t'}, r_1, \ldots, r_i.$$

**Schnorr Signatures.** Blind signatures are generated by an interaction with the signer who controls the secret signature key. Schnorr signatures refer to an arbitrary group $G$ of prime order $q$ and a arbitrary message space $M$. A signer interaction is an interactive protocol that enables a user to generate Schnorr signatures of message of its choice. Signatures will be based on a ideal hash function $H : G \times M \to \mathbb{Z}_q$, where $M$ is the set of messages.

The private key $x$ of the signer is random in $\mathbb{Z}_q$ and the corresponding public key $h = g^x$ is a random group element.

A Schnorr signature on a message $m$ is a triple $(m, c, z) \in M \times \mathbb{Z}_q^2$ such that $H(g^z h^{-c}, m) = c$. The standard signature $(m, c, z)$ on a message $m$ is constructed as follow: we pick random $r, s \in \mathbb{Z}_q$, compute $g^r$, $c = H(g^r, m)$ and $z := r + cx$. The result is valid since we have $g^z h^{-c} = g^{r+cx} g^{-cx} = g^r$, and thus $H(g^z h^{-c}, m) = c$.

A signer interaction is a three rounds interactive protocol between the signer and a user. The user can generate from this protocol the standard signature $(m, c, z)$ by selecting $c = H(g^r, m)$ but he has more options than that (he can generate a transformation $(m, c', z')$ of this signature). The signer picks a random $r \in \mathbb{Z}_q$ and sends the commitment $g^r$ to the user. The user selects a challenge $c \in \mathbb{Z}_q$ and sends $c$. The signer responds by sending $z := r + cx \in \mathbb{Z}_q$.

### 4.1   Signature Forgery Attack

We study security against the one-more signature forgery, security means that an attacker can not obtain $l + 1$ valid signatures from $l$ interactions with the signer (signature oracle).

**Parallel attack.** This is the generic parallel attack for Schnorr signatures. We assume that the attacker makes $\tau$ queries to the hash oracle, $l$ interactions with a signer and we construct a $l + 1$ valid signature. For the attack to succeed, we do not use the generator $g$ and the public key $h$.

The signer picks $r_1, \ldots r_l$ and sends commitments $g_1 := g^{r_1}, \ldots, g_l := g^{r_l}$. The attacker computes the group elements $f_i := \prod_{j=1}^{l} g_j^{a_{i,j}}$ and $H(f_i, m_i)$ for $i = 1, \ldots, \tau$. Then the attacker takes a subsystem of $l+1$ equations among these $\tau$ equations (2) in the unknowns $c_1, \ldots, c_l$ over $\mathbb{Z}_q$.

$$H(f_i, m_i) = \sum_{j=1}^{l} a_{i,j} c_j \quad for \ i = 1, \ldots, \tau \tag{2}$$

If the attacker solves this subsystem, it obtains a solution $c_1, \ldots, c_l$ and it sends the obtained solution to the signer that responds by $z_j := r_j + c_j x \in \mathbb{Z}_q$ for $j = 1, \ldots, l$. The attacker gets a valid signature $(m_i, c, z)$ by setting

$$c := \sum_{j=1}^{l} a_{i,j} c_j = H(f_i, m_i) \quad and \; z := \sum_{j=1}^{l} a_{i,j} z_j$$

In the ROM, the coefficients $a_{i,j}$ selected by the attacker are arbitrary values and the values $H(f_i, m_i)$ are random. The generic parallel attack uses a solution of the ROS-problem (see (1)).

The objective of this interactive model is to etablish upper bounds for the probability of a generic attacker to construct a one more signature forgery.

Let us explain the ways to make a valid signature. We assume that the algorithm outputs a signature $sig := (m_i, c'_i, z'_i)$; a signature $(m, c, z)$ is valid if $c = H(g^z h^{-c}, m)$; so sig is valid if $c'_i = H(g^{z'_i} h^{-c'_i}, m_i)$ and the group element $g^{z'_i} h^{-c'_i}$ must be among the computed elements $f_1, \ldots, f_{t'}$ (because $c'_i$ is taken among the results of the hash queries, so there exists $k \in \{1, \ldots, \tau\}$ such that $c'_i = H(f_k, m_i)$); we let $f_k = g^{z'_i} h^{-c'_i}$. By the equations $g^{z'_i} h^{-c'_i} = f_k = g^{a_{k,-1} + a_{k,0} x + \sum_{j=1}^{l} a_{k,j} r_j}$ and $r_j = z_j - c_j x$, we have:

$$z'_i = log_g \, g^{z'_i} h^{-c'_i} + c'_i x$$

$$z'_i = a_{k,-1} + \sum_{j=1}^{l} a_{k,j} z_j + (a_{k,0} - \sum_{j=1}^{l} a_{k,j} c_j + c'_i) x \tag{3}$$

$z'_i$ is valid one of the following two cases occur:

- if $c'_i = -a_{k,0} + \sum_{j=1}^{l} a_{k,j} c_j$ (4.1) then the equation (3) does not depend on the secret key $x$ and $z'_i = a_{k,-1} + \sum_{j=1}^{l} a_{k,j} z_j$ where the coefficients $a_{k,-1}, \ldots, a_{k,l}$ and the signer responses are known to $\mathcal{A}$.
- $c'_i \neq -a_{k,0} + \sum_{j=1}^{l} a_{k,j} c_j$ and so we solve the equation (3) in $x$.

A one-more signature forgery can only succeed in either of four cases:

1. $\mathcal{A}$ find among the $\tau$ equations $H(f_k, m_i) = -a_{k,0} + \sum_{j=1}^{l} a_{k,j} c_j$ (4.1) a solvable subsystem of $l + 1$ equations. We must apply the ROS-problem to find a bound of the probability of finding a solvable subsystem of $l + 1$ equations. This corresponds to the first case to obtain a valid signature $z'_i$. This is the generic parallel attack. We let $Par\_Attack(\mathcal{A})$ be this condition for an attacker $\mathcal{A}$.
2. For some $i$, $1 \leq i \leq l+1$ equation (4.1) does not hold but equation (3) holds. Each interaction with the signer provides a polynomial $log_g g^{z'_i} h^{-c'i} + c'_i * x - z'_i$ (2), thus after $l$ interactions with the signer, we obtain a list of $l$ polynomials (2). We obtain information on the secret if we can find a zero of a polynomial that belongs to this list. This corresponds to the second case to obtain a valid signature $z'_i$. We let $Sign(\mathcal{A})$ be this condition for an attacker $\mathcal{A}$.
3. There is a collision of group elements. We let $\mathcal{CO}(\mathcal{A}))$ be this condition for an attacker $\mathcal{A}$.
4. There is a collision of hash values $H(f_i, m_i) = H(f_j, m_j)$, where $m_i = m_j$, $f_i \neq f_j$ and $a_{i,k} = a_{j,k}$ for $k = 0, \ldots, l$. We let $\mathcal{CO}_H(\mathcal{A}))$ be this condition for an attacker $\mathcal{A}$.

By having a collision (of group elements or hash values), we get a bound of the probability of finding the secret $x$; if we have the secret $x$, we can generate a valid signature $z = c + rx$ where $c$ and $r$ are knowned by the algorithm and $x$ is found by the algorithm.

In an interactive generic algorithm, the attacker might obtain a one more signature forgery either through collisions on computed group elements or on hash values, or through interactions with the signer. Thus its advantage will be bounded by the probability of finding a collision on computed group elements plus the probability of finding a collision on hash values plus the probability of finding informations on the secret by an interaction with the signer. In the latter case, we show that the attacker can only obtain information if it succeeds on a parallel attack or if it can find a zero of a polynomial equation derived from the equality tested to know if a signature is valid, i.e. $c = H(g^z \bar{h}^{-c}, m)$.

# 5    Formalization of an Interactive Generic Algorithm

## 5.1    Formalization

The main difficulty in formalizing interactive generic algorithms is to capture the idea of random hash function. Following the idea of the generic model, we consider a symbolic representation of the interactions with the hash oracle by introducing a type *Val* of random variables that will represent the results of the interactions with the hash oracle. In addition, we define an interpretation function from *Val* to $\mathbb{Z}_q$. In order to fix terminology, we will refer to elements of *Val* as symbolic hash values and to their interpretation as hash results.

An interactive generic algorithm is defined in the figure 2. As explained above, we introduce a type *Val* of symbolic hash results and a type *Sec* of symbolic secrets (see line 1). Then, we model inputs as a non-repeating list of polynomial expressions over secrets (see line 3). We assume that all ciphertexts have the type *SymbM* (see line 2). *SymbH* (see line 4) takes a list of coefficients instead of a computed group element i.e, a formal result for an hash query $i : SymbH$ is of the form $(a, m, c)$, where $m$ is a ciphertext.

Interactive generic algorithms are defined inductively (see line 6) and may consist of an empty step, or a mexstep i.e, a computation of group elements using the function *mex*, or an hashstep i.e, a query to the hash oracle, or a signstep i.e, an interaction with the signer; let us remenber what is an interaction with the signer, the signer picks a random $r$ in $\mathbb{Z}_q$ and sends $g^r$ to the user which sends $c = H(g^r, m)$ and the signer responds $z := r + cx$.

To make a *signstep* (see line 10) i.e, an interaction with the signer, we need to have an hash value $i : SymbH$ and a secret $r : \mathbb{Z}_q$ (it is the secret that the signer picks in $\mathbb{Z}_q$ and sends $g^r$ to the attacker); and we take an $i : SymbH := (a, m, c)$ to send to the signer $c = H(a, m)$.

Interactive generic algorithms have three kinds of outputs:

– The symbolic hash outputs (see line 12) are just the list of *SymbH* and we can obtain the list of concrete hash outputs (see line 20) by applying

```
 1 Parameter Sec Val:Set.
 2 Parameter SymbM:Set.
 3 Parameter input:list $\mathbb{Z}_q[Sec]$.
 4 Definition SymbH:=(list $\mathbb{Z}_q$) *SymbM*Val.
 5
 6 Inductive IGA : Type :=
 7    erun: IGA
 8  | mexstep: IGA $\to$ list $\mathbb{Z}_q$ $\to$  IGA
 9  | hashstep: IGA $\to$ SymbH $\to$  IGA
10  | signstep: IGA $\to$ SymbH $\to$ Sec$\to$  IGA .
11
12 Fixpoint SymbHOut ($\mathcal{A}$ : IGA) : list SymbH:=
13 match $\mathcal{A}$ with
14    erun $\Rightarrow$ nil
15  | mexstep $\mathcal{A}$' e $\Rightarrow$ SymbHOut $\mathcal{A}$'
16  | hashstep $\mathcal{A}$' (a,m,c) $\Rightarrow$(a,m,c)::(SymbHOut $\mathcal{A}$')
17  | signstep $\mathcal{A}$' _ _$\Rightarrow$ SymbHOut $\mathcal{A}$'
18  end.
19
20 Definition ConcrHashOutput(r:IGA)($\tau$:Val$\to\mathbb{Z}_q$):(list $\mathbb{Z}_q$):=
21 map $\tau$ (map $\lambda$(x,y,z).z (SymbHOut $\mathcal{A}$)).
22
23 Fixpoint SymbMexOutput($\mathcal{A}$:IGA): list $\mathbb{Z}_q[Sec]$:=
24    match $\mathcal{A}$ with
25    | erun $\Rightarrow$nil
26    | mexstep $\mathcal{A}$' e $\Rightarrow$ (mex e input)::(SymbMexOutput $\mathcal{A}$')
27    | hashstep $\mathcal{A}$' _ $\Rightarrow$ SymbMexOutput $\mathcal{A}$'
28    | decstep $\mathcal{A}$' _ $\Rightarrow$ SymbMexOutput $\mathcal{A}$'
29 end.
30
31 Definition ConcrmexOutput($\mathcal{A}$: IGA)($\sigma$:Sec$\to\mathbb{Z}_q$):(list $\mathbb{Z}_q$):=
32 map $\lambda$x.$[\![x]\!]_\sigma$ (SymbMexOutput $\mathcal{A}$).
33
34 Definition mk_z($\tau$:Val$\to\mathbb{Z}_q$) (r:$\mathbb{Z}_q$) (c:Val) (x:$\mathbb{Z}_q$) $\mathbb{Z}_q$:=
35 ($\tau$ c)+ r*x.
36
37 Fixpoint IdealSign($\mathcal{A}$:IGA)($\tau$:Va $\to\mathbb{Z}_q$) ($\sigma$:Sec$\to\mathbb{Z}_q$): listT $\mathbb{Z}_q$:=
38  match $\mathcal{A}$ with
39    erun $\Rightarrow$ nil
40  | mexstep $\mathcal{A}$' e $\Rightarrow$ IdealSign $\mathcal{A}$' $\tau$ $\sigma$
41  | hashstep $\mathcal{A}$' _ $\Rightarrow$ IdealSign $\mathcal{A}$' $\tau$ $\sigma$
42  | signstep $\mathcal{A}$' (a,m,c) r $\Rightarrow$ (mk_z $\tau$ ($\sigma$ r) c
43    (Eval (head (tail input))))::(IdealSign $\mathcal{A}$' $\tau$ $\sigma$)
44  end.
45
46 Definition $\mathcal{CO}_H$($\mathcal{A}$: IGA)($\tau$:Val$\to\mathbb{Z}_q$):Prop:=
47 $\forall$ e e':Val, e $\in$ (map $\lambda$(x,y,z).z (SymbHOut $\mathcal{A}$)) $\wedge$
48       e' $\in$ (map $\lambda$(x,y,z).z (SymbHOut $\mathcal{A}$)) $\wedge$ e - e'$\neq$0 $\wedge$
    ($\tau$ e)-($\tau$ e')=0 .
```

**Fig. 2.** Formalizatiom of interactive algorithm for parallel attack

an evaluation function *rom* in the last element of the list of symbolic hash outputs.

− Symbolic group outputs (see line 23) are polynomials constructed as linear combinations of inputs in the same way of non-interactive generic algorithms. Concrete group outputs (see line 31) are obtained from the symbolic group outputs by using the extension of an interpretation function $\sigma$ from polynomial expressions to elements in $\mathbb{Z}_q$. mk_z (see line 34) returns the $z := c + rx$ computed by the signer by evaluating the hash result $c$ with an interpretation function *rom*.

− The outputs of the signer (see line 37) are the computed elements $z$.

We can find a non-trivial collisions among hash outputs (see line 46) if we can find two polynomials $e$ $e' : Val$ non identically equal in the hash outputs such that the interpretation of $e - e'$ under *rom* is 0.

Interactive generic algorithm can succeed on a one-more signature forgery if it can find a collision on computed group elements or on hash values or if the interpretation under the function $\sigma$ of the derived polynomial (3) is 0 (knowing that the equality (4.1) does not hold) or if it succeed on a parallel attack.

## 5.2   Security of Blind Signatures Against Interactive Attacks

The way to obtain a one more valid signature is given in the figure 3.

A one-more signature forgery can only succeed in either of four cases:

1. $\mathcal{A}$ find among the $\tau$ equations $H(f_k, m_i) = -a_{k,0} + \sum_{j=1}^{l} a_{k,j} c_j$ (4.1) a solvable subsystem of $l+1$ equations, let us notice that we see the equation (4.1) as the polynomial $\sum_{j=1}^{l} a_{k,j} c_j - a_{k,0} - H(f_k, m_i)$ in $\mathbb{Z}_q[c_1, \ldots, c_l]$. We must apply the ROS-problem to find a bound of the probability of finding a solvable subsystem of $l+1$ equations. To formalize the ROS-problem, we do not take a function $F : \mathbb{Z}_q^l \to \mathbb{Z}_q$ but a function $F : (list \ \mathbb{Z}_q) \to \mathbb{Z}_q$ with a list of length $l$. The variables $c_1, \ldots, c_l$ are of the type $Val$ so we see each equation (4.1) like a polynomials in $\mathbb{Z}_q[Val]$. And we compose the function $F : (list \ \mathbb{Z}_q) \to \mathbb{Z}_q$ like $G \circ F' + coeff$ where $F' : Val \to \mathbb{Z}_q$ is an interpretation function that maps formal variables to actual values, $G : (list \ \mathbb{Z}_q) \to Val$ and $coeff$ is an element of $\mathbb{Z}_q$. Finally, be given the coefficients $a_{k,j} \in \mathbb{Z}_q$ for $j = 1, \ldots, l$ and $k = 1, \ldots, \tau$ (*list_a_k*), the list of coefficients $coeff \in \mathbb{Z}_q$ (*list_coeff*) and a function $G : (list \ \mathbb{Z}_q) \to Val$, we have a list of $\tau$ polynomials of the form $a_{k,1} c_1 + \ldots + a_{k,l} c_l - coeff - F'(G(a_{k,1}, \ldots, a_{k,l})$ and the ROS-problem is to find a sublist of $l+1$ polynomials having a common solution. If we let *ROS_pb* be this condition, *ROS_pb* is an event in $Val \to \mathbb{Z}_q$.

   For the moment, we have a paper proof of the ROS-problem but for this proof, we need to formalize the determinant of a matrix in Coq and we did not ever do it, so for the moment it is an axiom.

**Proposition 2.** $Pr(ROS\_pb \ list\_a_k \ list\_coeff \ G) \leq \frac{\binom{\tau}{l+1}}{q}$

```
 1 Definition list_ak(A:IGA):(list (list ℤ_q)):=
 2 map λ(x,y,z).x (SymbHOut  A)).
 3
 4 Definition list_coeff(A:IGA):(list ℤ_q):=
 5 map λ(x,y,z).x (map λ(x,y,z).x (SymbHOut  A))).
 6
 7 Definition mk_G(l:listSymbH)(a:list ℤ_q):Val:=
 8 if ((h::a),m,c) ∈ l then c
 9                     else ?.
10
11 Definition G(r:IGA):(list ℤ_q)→Val:=
12 mk_G (SymbHOut r).
13
14 Definition Pol_H_neq(g:listT Val)(τ:Val→ℤ_q)(h:SymbH):Prop=
15 let h:=(f_k,m,c) in
16 let ∑_{j=1}^{l} a_{k,j}c_j:=sum (tail (tail (Ft h))) (map τ g) in
17 let a_{i,0}:=(head (Ft h)) in
18 let c_i:=(τ (Td h)) in
19 a_{i,0} - ∑_{j=1}^{l} a_{k,j}c_j +c_i≢0.
20
21 Definition Pol_H_Pred(r:IGA) (τ:Val→ℤ_q) :=
22 nb_P_true (Pol_H_neq (map λ(x,y,z).z(SymbHOut r))τ)(IdealOutput r)≤1+1.
23
24 Definition Sign(r:IGA)(τ:Val→ℤ_q)(h:SymbH)(r_i:Sec):ℤ_q[Sec]=
25 let h:=(f_k,m,c) in
26 let log_g f_k :=(mk_pol (Ft h) (inp r)) in
27 let c_i:=(τ (Td h)) in
28 let x:=(mk_pol (head (tail input))) in
29 let z_i:=(mk_pol r_i)+ci*x in
30 log_g f_k +c_i*x-z_i.
31
32 Fixpoint list_Sign(r:IGA)(τ:Val→ℤ_q):list ℤ_q[Sec]:=
33 match r with erun ⇒ nil
34              | mexstep r' _ ⇒ list_Sign r τ
35              | hashstep r' _ ⇒list_Sign r τ
36              | signstep r' h r_i ⇒(Sign r' τ h z)::(list_Sign r' τ)
37    end.
38
39 Fixpoint Signer(A:IGA)(σ:Sec→ℤ_q)(τ:Val→ℤ_q){struct A}:Prop:=
40 ∀ p:ℤ_q[Sec], p ∈ (list_Sign r τ) ∧ [[p]]_σ ≡ 0.
```

**Fig. 3.** Make a valid signature

To apply the ROS-problem i.e, to have the list of the $\tau$ polynomials $\sum_{j=1}^{l} a_{k,j}c_j - a_{k,0} - H(f_k, m_i)$, we must have the list of coefficients $a_{k,j} \in \mathbb{Z}_q$ for $j = 1,\ldots,l$ and $k = 1,\ldots,\tau$ (see line 1 of the figure 3), the list of coefficients $coeff := a_{k,0}$ for $k = 1,\ldots,\tau$ (see line 4) and a function

$G : (list\ \mathbb{Z}_q) \rightarrow Val$ (see line 11). As `SymbH:=(list Zq)*SymbM*Val`, we define the function G by:

```
Fixpoint mk_G(l:list SymbH)(a:list Zq):Val:=
match l with      nil    ⇒  ?
             | (h,a',c)::tl⇒ if a=a' then c
                             else (mk_G tl a)
end.
```

`(Ros_pb` $\tau$`(list_ak r) (list_coeff r) (G r))` is the condition to find $l + 1$ polynomials having a common solution $c_1, \ldots, c_l$. Then we send the solution $c_1, \ldots, c_l$ to the signer that responds $z_1, \ldots z_l$. We obtain one-more signature by the setting:

$$c_i' = -a_{k,0} + \sum_{j=1}^{l} a_{k,j} c_j \quad and \quad z_i' = a_{k,-1} + \sum_{j=1}^{l} a_{k,j} z_j$$

2. For some $i$, $1 \leq i \leq l+1$ equation (4.1) does not hold (see line 21) but equation (3) holds i.e, there exists at least a polynomial p $\in$`(list_Sign r` $\tau$`)` such that its interpretation under the function $\sigma$ is 0, each interaction with the signer provides a polynomial $a_{i,0} - \sum_{j=1}^{l} a_{k,j} c_j + c_i'$ (2), thus after $l$ interactions with the signer, we obtain a list of $l$ polynomials (2) (see line 32). This corresponds to the second case to obtain a valid signature $z_i'$. We let $Sign(\mathcal{A})$ be this condition for an attacker $\mathcal{A}$.
3. There is a collision of group elements.
4. There is a collision of hash values $H(f_i, m_i) = H(f_j, m_j)$, where $m_i = m_j$, $f_i \neq f_j$ and $a_{i,k} = a_{j,k}$ for $k = 0, \ldots, l$.

## 5.3   Properties of Interactive Generic Algorithms

In this section, we let a interactive generic algorithm $\mathcal{A}$ be given the generator $g$, the public key $h$, and oracles for the hash function $H$ and for signature oracle. Let $\mathcal{A}$ performs $t$ generic steps including $t''$ mex-steps, $\tau$ queries to the hash oracle and $l$ interactions $(r_1, c_1, z_1), \ldots, (r_l, c_l, z_l)$ with the signer. We assume the input $l_1, \ldots, l_{t'}$ to be polynomial expressions over secrets . Further, we let $d$ be the maximal degree of the polynomials $l_j$ for $1 \leq j \leq t'$ where $t'$ is the number of input.

**Proposition 3.** $\forall \mathcal{A}$ :IGA, $Pr(\mathcal{CO}(\mathcal{A})) \leq \dfrac{\binom{t'}{2} d}{q - \binom{t'}{2} d}$

*Proof.* All outputs are of the form $f_i = \sum_{1 \leq j \leq t'} a_j^i\ l_j(s_1, \ldots, s_k)$, where $p_i = \sum_{1 \leq j \leq t'} a_j^i\ l_j(x_1, \ldots, x_k)$ is a polynomial of degree $d$. Hence there exists a collision $f_i = f_{i'}$ iff $(s_1, \ldots, s_k)$ is a root of $p_i - p_{i'}$. There are $\binom{t''}{2}$ equalities of the form $f_i = f_{i'}$ to test, hence $\binom{t''}{2}$ polynomials of the form $p_i - p_{i'}$, each of which is not identical to 0 (as there are non-trivial collisions), and has degree $\leq d$. So we can use an extension of the Schwartz lemma [5] to deduce the expected result.

**Proposition 4.** $\forall \mathcal{A}$ :IGA, $Pr(\mathcal{CO}_H(\mathcal{A})) \leq \frac{\binom{\tau}{2}d}{q-\binom{\tau}{2}d}$

*Proof.* In the same way of proposition 3.

**Proposition 5.** $\forall \mathcal{A}$ :IGA, $Pr(Sign(\mathcal{A})) \leq \frac{(d+1)l}{q}$

*Proof.* The proof is by induction of the interactive generic algorithm $\mathcal{A}$. The only interesting case is when the algorithm interacts with the signer. In this case, we can find information on the secret iff $\sigma$ is a solution of the extracted polynomial corresponding to the equation (3) which is of degree $d$.

**Proposition 6.** $\forall \mathcal{A}$ :IGA, $Pr(ParAttack(\mathcal{A})) \leq \frac{\binom{\tau}{l+1}}{q}$

*Proof.* $ProbPar\_Attack(\mathcal{A}) \leq Pr(ROS\_pb \ (list\_ak \ \mathcal{A}) \ (list\_coeff \ \mathcal{A}) \ (G \ \mathcal{A}))$
In our formalization, we have an hash function of type $(list \ \mathbb{Z}_q) \times M \rightarrow Val$, where $M$ is the set of all ciphertexts.

More precisely, we have a type $SymbH := (list \ \mathbb{Z}_q) \times M \times Val$, i.e, instead of having $c = H(f, m)$, where $f = g^{a_{-1}+a_0+a_1 x + \sum_{j=1}^l a_j r_j}$, we have $((a_{-1}, \ldots, a_l),$ $m, c) : SymbH$ where $c = H(g^{a_{-1}+a_0+a_1 x + \sum_{j=1}^l a_j r_j}, m)$. Moreover, in our formalization on the ROS-problem, we do not take a function $F : \mathbb{Z}_q^l \rightarrow \mathbb{Z}_q$ but a function $F : (list \ \mathbb{Z}_q) \rightarrow \mathbb{Z}_q$ with a list of length $l$. So to have a function in $(list \ \mathbb{Z}_q) \rightarrow \mathbb{Z}_q$, we define a function $G : Run \rightarrow (list \ Zq) \rightarrow Val$ (see line 11). Having an interactive generic algorithm $\mathcal{A}$, we have the function $rom(G(\mathcal{A})) : (list \ \mathbb{Z}_q) \rightarrow \mathbb{Z}_q$. So we can apply the ROS-problem.

In the interactive setting, we consider that the advantage of the attacker is bounded the probability of finding non-trivial collisions on computed group elements or hash values plus the probability of finding a zero of a polynomial resulting on an interaction with the signer plus the probability of succeeding on a parallel attack.

**Proposition 7.** $\forall \mathcal{A}$ :IGA, $Advantage(\mathcal{A}) \leq Pr(\mathcal{CO}(\mathcal{A})) + Pr(\mathcal{CO}_H(\mathcal{A})) + Pr(Sign(\mathcal{A})) + Pr(ROS\_pb \ (list\_ak \ \mathcal{A}) \ (list\_coeff \ \mathcal{A}) \ (G \ \mathcal{A}))$.

# 6   Conclusion

We have extended our previous machine-checked account of the GM and ROM to establish security bounds for interactive algorithms, and in particular to show the security of signature schemes against forgery attacks. Our results generalize existing results to the case of an arbitrary generic algorithm, and provide more rigorous bounds than those present in the literature.

Machine-checked proofs of provable cryptography has barely been scratched. Much work remains to be done in the context of the GM and ROM: in particular, we intend to provide a machine-checked treatment of ROS, and to exploit our formalizations to prove the security of realistic protocols, following e.g. [7,23]. An even more far-fetched goal would be to give a machine-checked account of a formalism that integrates the computational view of cryptography, and provable cryptography.

*Acknowledgments.* I am grateful to Gilles Barthe, for his constructive and detailed advices and to the anonymous referees for their useful comments.

# References

1. M. Abadi and R. M. Needham. Prudent engineering practice for cryptographic protocols. *Transactions on Software Engineering*, 22(1):6–15, January 1996.
2. Martín Abadi and Phillip Rogaway. Reconciling two views of cryptography (the computational soundness of formal encryption). In *IFIP International Conference on Theoretical Computer Science (IFIP TCS2000)*, Sendai, Japan, 2000. Springer-Verlag, Berlin Germany.
3. M. Backes, B. Pfitzmann, and M. Waidner. A universally composable cryptographic library, 2003.
4. H. Barendregt and H. Geuvers. Proof assistants using dependent type systems. In A. Robinson and A. Voronkov, editors, *Handbook of Automated Reasoning*, volume II, chapter 18, pages 1149–1238. Elsevier Publishing, 2001.
5. G. Barthe, J. Cederquist, and S. Tarento. A Machine-Checked Formalization of the Generic Model and the Random Oracle Model. In D. Basin and M. Rusinowitch, editors, *Proceedings of IJCAR'04*, volume 3097 of *Lecture Notes in Computer Science*, pages 385–399, 2004.
6. M. Bellare and P. Rogaway. Random oracles are practical: A paradigm for designing efficient protocols. In *Proceedings of the 1st ACM Conference on Computer and Communications Security*, pages 62–73. ACM Press, November 1993.
7. D. Brown. Generic Groups, Collision Resistance, and ECDSA, 2002. Available from http://eprint.iacr.org/2002/026/.
8. Coq Development Team. *The Coq Proof Assistant User's Guide. Version 8.0*, January 2004.
9. Whitfield Diffie and Martin E. Hellman. New directions in cryptography. *IEEE Transactions on Information Theory*, IT-22(6):644–654, 1976.
10. A. Fiat and A. Shamir. How to Prove Yourself: Practical Solutions to Identification and Signature Problems. In *Proc. CRYPTO'86*, volume 286 of *Lecture Notes in Computer Science*, pages 186–194. Springer-Verlag, 1986.
11. formalization of probability
. http://www-sop.inria.fr/everest/personnel/Sabrina.Tarento/useful_files.html.
12. R. Impagliazzo and B. Kapron. Logics for reasoning about cryptographic constructions, 2003.
13. S. Lang. *Algebra*. Addison Wesley, 1983.
14. P. Lincoln, J. Mitchell, M. Mitchell, and A. Scedrov. Probabilistic polynomial-time equivalence and security analysis. In J. M. Wing, J. Woodcock, and J. Davies, editors, *Proceedings of FM'99—Volume I*, volume 1708 of *Lecture Notes in Computer Science*, pages 776–793. Springer-Verlag, 1999.
15. C. Meadows. Open issues in formal methods for cryptographic protocol analysis. In V.I. Gorodetski, V.A. Skormin, and L.J. Popyack, editors, *Proceedings of MMMACNS*, volume 2052 of *Lecture Notes in Computer Science*. Springer-Verlag, 2001.
16. J. Mitchell, A. Ramanathan, A. Scedrov, and V. Teague. A probabilistic polynomial-time calculus for analysis of cryptographic protocols (preliminary report). In S. Brookes and M. Mislove, editors, *17-th Annual Conference on the Mathematical Foundations of Programming Semantics*, number 45, Aarhus, Denmark, 2001.

17. John C. Mitchell, Mark Mitchell, and Andre Scedrov. A linguistic characterization of bounded oracle computation and probabilistic polynomial time. In *IEEE Symposium on Foundations of Computer Science*, pages 725–733, 1998.
18. V. I. Nechaev. Complexity of a determinate algorithm for the discrete logarithm. *Mathematical Notes*, 55(2):165–172, 1994.
19. B. Pfitzmann and M. Waidner. A model for asynchronous reactive systems and its application to secure message transmission. In *Proceedings of SOSP'01*, pages 184–201. IEEE Press, 2001.
20. C.-P. Schnorr. Security of Blind Discrete Log Signatures against Interactive Attacks. In S. Qing, T. Okamoto, and J. Zhou, editors, *Proceedings of ICICS'01*, volume 2229 of *Lecture Notes in Computer Science*, pages 1–12. Springer-Verlag, 2001.
21. C.-P. Schnorr and M. Jakobsson. Security of Signed ElGamal Encryption. In T. Okamoto, editor, *Proceedings of ASIACRYPT'00*, volume 1976 of *Lecture Notes in Computer Science*, pages 73–89. Springer-Verlag, 2000.
22. V. Shoup. Lower bounds for discrete logarithms and related problems. In W. Fumy, editor, *Proceedings of EUROCRYPT'97*, volume 1233 of *Lecture Notes in Computer Science*, pages 256–266. Springer-Verlag, 1997.
23. N. Smart. The Exact Security of ECIES in the Generic Group Model. In B. Honary, editor, *Cryptography and Coding*, pages 73–84. Springer-Verlag, 2001.
24. J. Stern. Why provable security matters? In E. Biham, editor, *Proceedings of EUROCRYPT'03*, volume 2656 of *Lecture Notes in Computer Science*, pages 449–461. Springer-Verlag, 2003.

# Sanitizable Signatures

Giuseppe Ateniese[1], Daniel H. Chou[1], Breno de Medeiros[2], and Gene Tsudik[3]

[1] Johns Hopkins Univ., Dept. of Comp. Sci., 3400 N. Charles Street,
Baltimore, MD 21218, USA
{ateniese, dchou}@cs.jhu.edu

[2] Florida State Univ., Dept. of Comp. Sci., Tallahassee, FL 32306, USA
breno@cs.fsu.edu

[3] Univ. of California, D. Bren Sch. of Inform. and Comp. Sci.,
Dept. of Comp. Sci., Irvine, CA 92697, USA
gts@ics.uci.edu

**Abstract.** We introduce the notion of *sanitizable signatures* that offer many attractive security features for certain current and emerging applications. A sanitizable signature allows authorized semi-trusted censors to modify – in a limited and controlled fashion – parts of a signed message without interacting with the original signer. We present constructions for this new primitive, based on standard signature schemes and secure under common cryptographic assumptions. We also provide experimental measurements for the implementation of a sanitizable signature scheme and demonstrate its practicality.

## 1  Introduction and Motivation

In government, military and corporate environments, information is often compartmentalized in a way that one's role or security clearance determines access rights with respect to a resource, such as a database or a document. Thus, two subjects with different security clearances can "see" the same information with varying granularity of detail. For example, the United States Government sometimes releases certain previously classified documents in "sanitized" form, often as a result of a request made through the Freedom of Information Act (FOIA). A document thus released is usually sprinkled with blacked-out sections which, for various reasons, remain confidential. More specifically, individual words, sentences, paragraphs and even entire sections of a document can be either deleted or substituted with dummy data prior to being released.

Now, suppose that someone needs to refer to, or cite from, a sanitized document. In this case, to avoid liability, it is necessary to ascertain the source and the integrity of the document. Plain digital signatures (e.g., RSA or DSA) provide the means to achieve both source authentication and data integrity. More exotic constructs, such as *Redactable Signatures* [23], allow anyone to obtain a valid signature of the redacted document without any help from the original signer. However, there are situations where a duly authorized third party (censor) may need to *modify* the document in some controlled and limited fashion. In doing so, the authorized censor needs to somehow come up with a valid signature for

S. De Capitani di Vimercati et al. (Eds.): ESORICS 2005, LNCS 3679, pp. 159–177, 2005.

the updated document, without contacting the original signer. There could be many possible reasons for not asking the original signer to re-sign, including: (1) the signer's key has expired, (2) the original signature was securely time-stamped via, e.g., [18], (3) the signer may not be reachable/available, (4) each new signature would cost too much, either in terms of real expense or in terms of computation. In this paper, we introduce the notion of *sanitizable signatures* precisely in order to address these needs.

Informally, a *Sanitizable Signature Scheme* allows a semi-trusted censor to modify *designated* portions of the document and produce a valid signature on the legitimately modified document without any help from the original signer. These designated portions of the document are blocks or segments explicitly indicated as mutable under prior agreement between the signer and the censor. The censor can produce a valid signature only if it modifies these portions and no other parts of the message.

To illustrate the utility of sanitizable signatures, the rest of this section discusses several potential application scenarios.

## 1.1 Multicast and Database Applications

Sanitizable signatures are quite well-suited for customizing authenticated multicast transmissions. For example, in a subscription-based internet multimedia database, sponsors may wish to insert personalized commercials into messages at various points of the broadcast. It is desirable to authenticate these messages to allow the subscribers to distinguish legitimate contents from spam. Since real-time authentication may be too costly, one solution is for each vendor to sign the commercial once and allow the database administrator to customize the individual commercials by replacing the generic identity field with the actual subscriber's identity, at various points of the commercial. This way, the subscriber can verify that the commercial comes from a legitimate source (i.e., it is not spam) and the sponsors do not have to sign each customized broadcast. Furthermore, the database administrator is not forced to divulge personal information of its subscribers without their consent.

A related application of sanitized signatures is editing movie content. Depending on the age of the subscriber, the administrator can replace offensive language with watered-down substitutes rather than blip out the words. Again, sanitized signatures provides the desired benefits.

In the same vein, sanitizable signatures can be used in outsourced database applications. Database outsourcing [19] is a recent and important industry trend whereby a Database Service Provider offers adequate resources to host its clients' databases as well as mechanisms to efficiently manipulate and access outsourced data. Database outsourcing poses numerous security challenges since it involves a client storing its data at an external – and often untrusted – provider site. To this end, it is essential to protect the integrity and authenticity of that data from both malicious outsider attacks and the Database Service Provider itself. This is usually achieved by having the client sign each database record before outsourcing [21]. Later, when a user queries a database owned by a client of the Database Service Provider but physically stored at the latter, the provider acts as an authorized re-distributor of outsourced data. In this role, it needs to ensure that users – who obtain portions of the database (as replies to queries) – cannot redistribute the results and themselves become unauthorized "de facto" distributors. With the aid of sanitizable signatures, a query reply (i.e., a set of database records) can be manipulated by the provider in a way that each returned record is signed by its original owner (client), but personalized for the specific user who posed the query.

More generally, sanitizable signatures can be viewed as a valuable tool for combatting certain types of software piracy and unauthorized content distribution. If the actual content owner is off-line and an authorized on-line distributor is used to sell or supply content to users, the benefit of sanitizable signatures is the ability of the distributor to easily personalize signed (i.e., authentic) content for each user or each transaction. While this would clearly not put a stop to piracy (since multiple corrupt users can always trade ill-begotten content among themselves), it would preclude honest users from being duped by unauthorized or fraudulent re-sellers/re-distributors of valuable content.

## 1.2   Medical Applications

The additional functionalities and flexibility of sanitizable signatures may also help protect the privacy of medical records. Under the Health Insurance Portability and Accountability Act of 1996 (HIPAA), covered entities are required to comply with the Standards for Privacy of Individually Identifiable Health Information (the Privacy Rule) [38]. The Privacy Rule specifies the criteria for creating both de-identified and limited data sets from protected health information (PHI) for research purposes. In particular, covered entities must remove direct identifiers of the individual or of relatives, employers, or household members of the individuals before PHI can be legally released for research purposes.

Compare the scenarios of a cancer study and an epidemic study. The two studies require different temporal resolution when creating limited data sets from PHI. In a cancer study, the exact dates when treatments are administered to the patient may not be necessary to the study. It is important, however, to note the length of time between treatments. On the other hand, in an epidemic study, it may be necessary to include exact treatment dates so the limited data set could reveal trends and patterns necessary for creating an epidemiological model.

Sanitizable signatures can be used to ensure the integrity, authenticity, and anonymity of PHI in both cases. In general, sanitizable signatures can accommodate different level of data de-identification, supporting the "minimum necessary" disclosure standard of HIPAA Privacy Rule. This provides flexibility not available in redactable signatures.

## 1.3   Secure Routing

A crucial aspect of security in modern routing protocols is the protection of exchanges of connectivity information between routers. An important feature of a major class of routing protocols – called *distance vector* – is the direct exchange of routing tables among neighboring routers. *Distance vector* protocols require each router to maintain tables where each entry contains a destination and a route metric (cost) to that destination. More advanced *path vector* protocols, in addition, require each router to maintain – for each routing table entry, i.e., for each destination – an actual shortest route/path to that destination. The best-known path vector protocol is the Border Gateway Protocol (BGP) [33] widely used in the Internet.

There have been several proposals for supporting authentication of origin and data integrity in routing protocols, typically via digital signatures (see, for example, [27] and [24]). Indeed, routing message authentication is imperative for resistance against powerful – especially, Byzantine – adversaries. While mounting Byzantine attacks against routing algorithms is generally difficult, the transitivity of trust implied by the very essence of distance and path vector algorithms compounds the impact of any successful attack. Protecting *link state* protocols against Byzantine attacks, as in [27], is simpler than the same task for distance or path vector protocols such as [24]. A general architecture for link state protocols with Byzantine robustness has been developed rather early on, in [31], whereas, no equivalent architecture for path vector protocols has been proposed.

The main challenge in authenticating path vector routing messages is that – unless we assume complete transitivity of trust – for each path vector, a separate signature by each hop in the route is required. The combined cost of verifying multiple per-hop signatures becomes a serious burden on intermediate routers. This can be mitigated by using *transitive signatures* [26,6,37], which allow anyone to use the public keys of routers to combine several edge signatures (where edges are a pair of adjacent routers along the route) into a single path signature (from the source or any intermediate router to the destination or a subsequent intermediate router).

Sanitized signatures provide an alternative mechanism. The main difference between using transitive and sanitized signatures is that the latter delegate the ability to aggregate signatures to specific routers, while transitive signatures allow any router to aggregate. The explicit delegation model afforded by sanitized signatures is more flexible, as it permits the implementation of arbitrary trust infrastructures with respect to route aggregation.

Finally, we observe that similar techniques are applicable in on-demand MANET routing protocols [10], such as Dynamic Source Routing (DSR) [22]. DSR uses flooding to discover a shortest path to a destination. A route is collected incrementally, during flooding propagation, with each router adding itself to the route as it processes a route request message. It is easy to see that sanitized signatures are also appropriate in this setting and offer the same benefits as in path vector protocols.

## 2   Related Work

Several concepts are related to sanitizable signatures, including incremental cryptography and homomorphic signatures, which encompass transitive, redactable and context-extraction signatures.

*Incremental cryptography* seeks to construct cryptographic primitives with an efficient update property. Namely, if an incremental cryptographic algorithm produces a value when applied to a document, then the value may be very efficiently re-computed on a variant of the document obtained by applying a pre-defined transformation rule – in particular, more efficiently than recomputing the algorithm from scratch with the new document. Incremental cryptography was defined in Bellare et al [3,4], including applications to incremental hashing and signing. A separate construction of an incremental signature scheme with certain privacy properties has been provided by Bellare and Micciancio [5].

Incremental and sanitizable signatures are similar in that they support signature re-computation through a process different than initial signature generation; however, they differ in that the latter supports delegation of the ability to perform updates to another party, while the former provides a mechanism for the original signer to perform updates more efficiently than through re-signing an entire document.

*Homomorphic signatures:* In a series of talks, Rivest [34] proposed the design of signature schemes that allow "forgeries" of pre-determined types. More specifically, a signer would need his/her private key to generate a signature on a document, but arbitrary parties could use simply the knowledge of the public key to modify the document in locations and fashion pre-selected by the signer, and obtain a new signature on the transformed document without interaction with the original signer. This concept was then formalized as *homomorphic signature schemes* in [23]. A particular construction made possible through the use of homomorphic signature schemes is a redactable signature (also [23]). When a document is redacted, each redacted bit position is replaced with the same special symbol to represent the location of the deletions. Explicitly marking the locations of the redactions is necessary to thwart semantic attacks. A sanitized document can be view as a redacted document that allows arbitrary bit substitution in the location of the deletions. However, there are other fundamental differences between sanitizable signatures and redactable signatures. As with other homomorphic constructions, redactable signature schemes allow anyone with the knowledge of the public key to generate a valid signature on the redacted document. This property is not always desirable in a digital signature scheme. In contrast, only the censor would be able to generate a valid signature on a modified (sanitized) document. Moreover, in our basic construction, the signer can incontestably prove that the censor sanitized the document. Thus, sanitizable signatures provide (and require) greater accountability. Furthermore, once a signature is redacted, it is impossible to undo the redaction and recover the signature on the original message. On the other hand, the censor can undo the changes to the mutable portions of the message and produce a "sanitized" signature that corresponds to the original message.

A related concept to redactable signature is that of content-extraction signatures [36]. These are essentially redactable XML signatures, where the redaction operation efficiently removes XML nodes – permitting customization of publishable information to comply with privacy and confidentiality demands of dynamic distributed applications.

*Transitive signatures* are essentially homomorphic signatures, where the operation in question is path concatenation on (undirected or directed) graphs. Optimized constructions for transitive signatures, more efficient than general homomorphic techniques, have been proposed [26,6,37]. The interest in transitive signatures stem from their potential applicability to secure routing in computer networks [12], by enabling route-path signature aggregation. Namely, if a secure routing protocol is implemented via router signatures on each hop, the computational load on routers does not scale well, as increasingly long chains of signatures need to be verified. Transitive signatures permit any intermediate routers to collapse routes to a single signed source-current router pair (or to contract the route in any other intended fashion), thus achieving better efficiency as well as security: In some cases it may not be in the interest of routers (specially edge routers) to disclose the topology of the (internal) network they protect.

We remark that sanitizable (as well as redactable) signatures can be employed to achieve the route-path reduction efficiently – but under different trust models. Transitive and redactable signatures require intermediate routers to know only the public key of previous routers in the path in order to remove their signature to the authenticated path. On the other hand, sanitizable signatures would permit routers to delegate the ability to remove their signature to specific trusted routers. We believe that this trust model is more flexible and more representative of practical security architectures, where only some entities are entrusted with security policies for a network, and allowed to "edit" or sanitize network-security related information on behalf of other entities, as discussed in section §1.3.

*Automatic Sanitization of Internet Traffic:* There exists an entire area of research on sanitizing raw Internet packet traces for sharing and research purposes. Most of this work studies different ways of anonymizing TCP/IP packet header fields, for instance see [32,39]. The seminal work of Pang and Paxson [30] focuses on sanitizing also packet payloads and has been extended and generalized by Bishop et al. [8].

That line of research seeks to develop methods of expressing privacy policies and then to create tools that can interpret such policies to automatically sanitize Internet traffic [30,8]. While not directly related to this paper (since they do not deal with cryptographic primitives, such as signatures), we believe that the techniques developed in [30,8] could be combined with ours for mutual advantage.

## 3   Sanitizable Signatures

We define a sanitizable signature scheme as a secure digital signature scheme that allows a semi-trusted censor to modify certain *designated* portions of the message and produce a valid signature of the resulting (legitimately modified) message with no interaction with the original signer. More concretely, a sanitizable signature scheme must have the following properties:

1. *Immutability.* The censor should not be able to modify any part of the message that is not specifically designated as sanitizable by the original signer.
2. *Privacy.* Given a sanitized signed message with a valid signature, it is impossible for anyone (except the signer and the censor) to derive any information about the portions of the message that were sanitized by the censor. In other words, all sanitized information is unrecoverable.[1]
3. *Accountability.* In case of a dispute, the signer can prove to a trusted third party (e.g., court) that a certain message was sanitized by the censor.
4. *Transparency.* Given a signed message with a valid signature, no party – except the censor and the signer – should be able to correctly guess whether the message has been sanitized.

We further distinguish among two flavors of transparency: *weak* and *strong*. Weak transparency means that the verifier knows exactly which parts of the message are potentially sanitizable and, consequently, which parts are immutable.

In contrast, strong transparency guarantees that the verifier does not know which parts of the message are immutable and thus does not know which parts of a signed message could potentially be sanitizable.

Either transparency flavor can be beneficial depending on the specific application. We stress that strong transparency is not always better. In certain circumstances, *weak transparency* is actually preferable. For example, if a document originally signed by some government official is later released by a certain government agency – acting as a censor – under the Freedom of Information Act, the general public would likely prefer knowing which parts of the document could have been sanitized.

Our construction only provides for weak transparency. Accordingly, we only provide a formal security model for weak transparency, in terms of an indistinguishability property.

## 3.1   Model

In this section, a formal definition of a sanitizable signature is given in terms of the algorithms that constitute the scheme and their security properties.

A sanitizable signature scheme is a set of four efficient algorithms (as usual, efficiency is defined in terms of a security parameter):

**Key generation:** For simplicity, we assume that each party could potentially be a censor. Principal $P_i$ uses this probabilistic algorithm to compute two public-private key pairs:

$$(pk^i_{sign}, sk^i_{sign}), (pk^i_{sanit}, sk^i_{sanit}) \xleftarrow{R} 1^k,$$

where $k$ is a security parameter. The first set of keys is for a standard digital signature algorithm, while the second is useful to perform sanitization steps.

---

[1] Unless of course the original message is stored by the signer and/or the censor.

**Sign:** Takes as input a message $m$, a private signing key $sk^i_{sign}$, a public sanitization key $pk^j_{sanit}$, random coins $r$, and produces a signature

$$\sigma \leftarrow SIGN\left(m, r; sk^i_{sign}, pk^j_{sanit}\right).$$

**Verify:** A deterministic algorithm that, on input a message $m$, a possibly valid signature $\sigma$ on $m$, a public signing key $pk^i_{sign}$ and a sanitization key $pk^j_{sanit}$, outputs TRUE or FALSE:

$$VERIFY\left(m, \sigma; pk^i_{sign}, pk^j_{sanit}\right) \rightarrow \{TRUE, FALSE\}.$$

**Sanitize:** An algorithm that, on input a message $m$, a signature $\sigma$ on $m$ under public signing key $pk^i_{sign}$, a private sanitizing key $sk^j_{sanit}$, and a new message $m'$, produces a new signature $\sigma'$ on $m'$.

$$\sigma' \leftarrow SANIT(m, \sigma, m'; pk^i_{sign}, sk^j_{sanit}).$$

We now discuss security requirements of this definition.

**Security Requirements of Sanitizable Signatures:** A sanitizable signature as above should satisfy the following criteria:

**Correctness:** A signature produced by the SIGN algorithm should be accepted by the VERIFY algorithm:

$$\forall \quad \sigma = SIGN(m, r; sk^i_{sign}, pk^j_{sanit});$$
$$VERIFY(m, \sigma; pk^i_{sign}, pk^j_{sanit}) = TRUE$$

**Unforgeability:** Without the knowledge of the private signing key it is difficult to produce a valid signature on a message that verifies against the associated public key, *except by resorting to the sanitization process.* The exact formulation of this concept can be provided within an adversarial-game framework, detailed in 3.1.

**Indistinguishability:** It is the property that, for any pair of messages $m_1, m_2$, and any choices of private signing key $sk^i_{sign}$, and public sanitizing key $pk^j_{sanit}$, the following distributions $S_1$ and $S_2$ are computationally indistinguishable:

$$S_1 = \{\sigma; \sigma = SIGN(m_1, r; sk^i_{sign}, pk^j_{sanit})\}$$

and

$$S_2 = \{\sigma; \sigma = SIGN(m_2, r; sk^i_{sign}, pk^j_{sanit})\},$$

where $r$ is chosen uniformly at random in the coin space of the SIGN algorithm.

**Identical Distribution:** Values produced by the SANIT algorithm are distributed identically to those produced by the SIGN algorithm. In particular, if a signature $\sigma$ on message $m$ (with random coins $r$) is sanitized to signature $\sigma'$ on message $m'$, then there exist coins $r'$ for which $\sigma'$ is an original signature on $m'$:

$$SANIT(m, \sigma, m'; pk_{sign}^i, sk_{sanit}^j) = \sigma' = SIGN(m', r'; sk_{sign}^i, pk_{sanit}^j).$$

The above formulation of a sanitizable signature is not the only reasonable one. For instance, the requirement that the sanitization algorithm produces the exact outputs as the sign algorithm is not necessary as long as its outputs are 1) accepted by the verification algorithm, and 2) indistinguishable from the outputs of the sign algorithm. We adopt the stricter formulation instead as it is still general enough to capture the constructions we propose; because it has the benefit of being easier to formulate and understand; and because of closer parallel with related research literature – see, for instance, the formulation of transitive signatures in [6].

Referring back to the more informal requirements at the beginning of this section, we point out that the indistinguishability requirement provides for privacy, while the identical distribution implies the weak transparency property.

The unforgeability requirement (typical of signature schemes) involves some subtleties in the case of sanitizable signatures, as the sanitization process is a bona-fide forgery algorithm. In order to formulate this concept more precisely it is necessary to consider a stateful signer, since one must keep track of all previously issued signatures and queries to the sanitize algorithm in order to decide which signatures should be infeasible to compute without the private signing key.

Note that the unforgeability requirement implies that only the censor is able to change the message while maintaining the signing value constant. Therefore, a signer can prove to a judge the involvement of the censor in producing a sanitized message, by showing both the sanitized and the original messages and their common signing value. This implies that *accountability* follows from the unforgeability requirement.

We now proceed to define unforgeability via an adversarial game framework.

**Unforgeability as an Adversarial Game:** Let $\mathcal{A}$ be an algorithm that seeks to forge signatures. We assume that $\mathcal{A}$ has oracle access to the SIGN as well as to the SANITIZE algorithms.

The sign oracle $\mathcal{O}^{sk_{sign}}$ is initialized with a positive integer $q_a$ which indicates the number of queries it will accept during the period of the experiment. Similarly, the sanitize oracle $\mathcal{O}^{sk_{sanit}}$ is initialized with integer $q_b$, the maximum number of queries it will answer. Either oracle, if its quota of queries has been exhausted, answers all further queries with the special symbol $\perp$.

A sanitizable signature scheme is *unforgeable* if every efficient adversary has negligible probability of success in the following 2-phase experiment. Given a security parameter, and a pair of signing and sanitizing public keys, the adversary can interact with the associated SIGN and SANITIZE oracles. At the end of the first phase the adversary outputs a state (representing the knowledge acquired during the first phase) and a message $m$ of its choice. In the second phase, the adversary again interacts with the oracles SIGN and SANITIZE, and its output is a candidate signature $\sigma$. The adversary wins if $m$ was not queried to either the SIGN or SANITIZE oracles during either phase of the experiment, and if $\sigma$ is a valid sanitizable signature on $m$. The advantage of the adversary is computed as its success probability over all instances of size $k$ and random choices made by the adversary.

We say that a sanitizable signature is $(\epsilon, k, q_a, q_b, t)$-*unforgeable* if for all probabilistic algorithms running in at most $t$ steps, making no more than $q_a$ queries to the SIGN algorithm and no more than $q_b$ queries to the SANITIZE algorithm has probability of success smaller than $\epsilon$ on problem instances of size $k$.

# 4   Construction Based on Chameleon Hashes

In this section we provide a construction of sanitizable signatures based on chameleon hashes presented in [1]. We follow the well-established encode-and-sign paradigm and construct a generalized signature scheme compatible with standard signature schemes (e.g. RSA or DSS). As with any digital signature scheme, a sanitizable signature scheme needs to bind the signer to the message signed, thus providing non-repudiation. Our sanitizable signature schemes are practical and efficient.

Chameleon signatures were introduced by Krawczyk and Rabin [25], and in turn are related to the notion of undeniable signatures [9,13,14].

## 4.1   Setup

The parties involved are: A signer $S$ with public and private keys $(pk_{sign}, sk_{sign})$ associated with the signature scheme, a (semi-trusted) censor $C$ with public and private keys $(pk_{sanit}, sk_{sanit})$ associated with a chameleon hashing scheme, a verifier $V$, and a judge $J$ (trusted third party).

Our construction consists of the following components:

- A secure digital signature scheme with signature, $s(\cdot)$, and verification, $v(\cdot)$, operations. We employ any standard signature scheme with any hash-and-encode mechanisms, such as RSA-EMSA-PSS [7,35]. Note that we use SIGN for the sanitizable signature and $s(\cdot)$ for the underlying signature algorithm to avoid confusion, and similarly for VERIFY and $v(\cdot)$. The notation $s_{sk}(m, r)$ stand for the output of the basic signature algorithm applied to the value of an hash-and-encode function with input $m$; if the signature scheme is probabilistic, the optional value $r$ indicates the auxiliary random coins $r$.
- A chameleon hashing scheme [25,1]. A chameleon hash computed over a message $m$ with randomness $r$, and under public key $pk$ will be denoted by $CH_{pk}(m, r)$. A chameleon hash (or *trapdoor commitment*) has the same properties of any cryptographic hash function and, in particular, it provides collision resistance. However, the owner of the private key $sk$ corresponding to the public key $pk$ can find collisions, i.e., messages $m'$ such

that $CH_{pk}(m,r) = CH_{pk}(m',r')$. By definition, chameleon hashes are always probabilistic algorithms, and to verify the correctness of a computed chameleon hash value $C$ it is necessary to provide both the original message $m$ and the randomness $r$ used.

## 4.2   Sanitizable Signing

Suppose we wish to sign a document $m = (m_1, ..., m_t)$ that is partitioned into $t$ blocks, for some constant $t$. First, the signer selects a random unique document identifier $ID_m$ and decides which portions, say $m_{i_1}, ..., m_{i_k}$, of the document can be modified by the censor with public key $pk_{sanit}$. This allows the signer to compute a chameleon hash, denoted by $CH_{pk_{sanit}}(\cdot)$, under the censor's public key, on those portions of the message:

$$\sigma = SIGN(m, r; sk_{sign}, pk_{sanit}) := \mathrm{s}_{sk_{sign}}(ID_m||t||pk_{sanit}||\bar{m}_1||\dots||\bar{m}_t),$$

where $\bar{m}_i = CH_{pk_{sanit}}(ID_m||i||m_i, r_i)$ for $i \in \{i_1, i_2, \dots, i_k\}$, otherwise $\bar{m}_i = m_i||i$. The value $r$ should be interpreted as the concatenation of all the random coins $r_{i_k}, i = 1, \dots, k$. In order to verify the above signature, one needs $\sigma$, $m$, $r$, and *auxiliary information to allow for segmentation of $m$ into blocks.*

The length of the sanitizable signature is proportional to the number of *mutable* message blocks only (that is, the number of chameleon hashes in the input), because the verification of each chameleon hash requires an auxiliary randomness parameter. We stress that the underlying signature scheme is computed on a single, fixed-length (e.g., 160-bit) value, the hash-encoding of the concatenated input.

Because only the censor knows the private key corresponding to $pk_{sanit}$, it only can find collisions of the chameleon hash with arbitrary message blocks substituting for the original message block values. In particular, the censor can produce triples $(ID_m, i, m_i')$ such that:

$$CH_{pk_{sanit}}(ID_m||i||m_i, r_i) = CH_{pk_{sanit}}(ID_m||i||m_i', r_i').$$

Notice that the signer can prove that it did not generate a signature on a sanitized message by revealing the original message to a trusted third party (the judge). The fact that a collision of the chameleon hash exists implies that the censor has sanitized the document (only the censor can compute collisions). Note the use of the document identifier $ID_m$, and a block index. These are needed to prevent re-use of mutable blocks within a message or across messages that would enable changing of documents without censor intervention by re-use of sanitized blocks.

## 4.3   Chameleon Hash

It is important to remark that not all the chameleon hashes are suitable for our construction. For instance, the chameleon hash defined in [25] on a pair $(m,r)$ is of the form $CH_y(m,r) = y^m g^r$, where $y = g^x$ and $g$ is the generator of a prime order cyclic group and $x$ is the private key. If the original message is sanitized and transformed into $(m', r')$ then the signer can recover the private key $x$. Indeed, from $g^m y^r = g^{m'} y^{r'}$, $x$ can be computed as $x = \frac{m'-m}{r-r'}$.

This *key exposure* problem was first addressed in [2], where a partial solution via identity-based constructions is proposed, and fully explored in [16,1]. In particular, in [1] a *strongly unforgeable*[2] chameleon signature scheme is provided, with the property that no trapdoors are ever revealed through collisions. This is in contrast with other constructions in [2,16,1], where at least an ephemeral trapdoor is compromised with each forgery.

Since our sanitizable signature construction requires strongly unforgeable chameleon hashes, it must use the scheme introduced in [1], which is related to a twin Nyberg-Rueppel signature [29,28]. The scheme specifies a prime [3] $p$ of bitlength $\kappa$, i.e., $p = uq + 1$, where $q$ is also prime, and a generator $g$ of the subgroup of squares of order $q$. The private key $x$ is selected at random in $[1, q-1]$, and the public key is $(g, y = g^x)$. Let $\mathcal{H}$ be a (traditional) collision-resistant hash function, mapping arbitrary-length bitstrings to strings of fixed length $\tau$: $\mathcal{H} : \{0,1\}^* \to \{0,1\}^\tau$.

To commit to a message $m$, it is sufficient to choose randomness $r = (\rho, \delta) \in \mathbf{Z}_q \times \mathbf{Z}_q$, and compute (cf. [1]):

$$e = \mathcal{H}(m, \rho); \text{ and } CH_y(m, \rho, \delta) = \rho - (y^e g^\delta \mod p) \mod q.$$

While the commitment can be computed by any party, the computation of a collision requires knowledge of the private key $x$, as follows. Let $C$ denote the output of the chameleon hash on input $(m, r) = (m, \rho, \delta)$. First, a random value $k' \in [1, q-1]$ is generated and then the other values are computed as: $\rho' = C + (g^{k'} \mod p) \mod q$, $e' = \mathcal{H}(m', \rho')$, and $\delta' = k' - e'x \mod q$. Notice that indeed:

$$\rho' - (y^{e'} g^{\delta'} \mod p) \mod q = C + (g^{k'} \mod p) - (g^{xe'} g^{\delta'} \mod p) \mod q = C.$$

Therefore, $(m', r') = (m', \rho', \delta')$ is the sought collision.

### 4.4   Security Requirements

*Correctness:* It is clearly achieved, since the SIGN and VERIFY algorithms are modifications of a basic signature scheme, wherein mutable message blocks have been substituted by chameleon hashes.

*Indistinguishability:* In [1], it is shown that the chameleon hash based on the twin Nyberg-Rueppel signature provides *semantic security*, i.e., it is impossible to distinguish the distributions

$$S_1^y = \{(m_1, r, C); \ C = CH_y(m_1, r)\} \text{ and } S_2^y = \{(m_2, r, C); \ C = CH_y(m_2, r)\}.$$

---

[2]  This terminology is not used in [1], but we adopt it here as it is related to the strong unforgeability of signature schemes.

[3]  For conciseness of description, we discuss the Nyberg-Rueppel signature in the classical setting $\mathbf{Z}_p^*$. However, the same scheme can be defined over elliptic curves and would have better performance at comparable security settings.

This is exactly the same requirement for indistinguishability of sanitizable signatures. It is straightforward to verify that this semantic security furthermore implies privacy.

*Identical distribution of sanitized and original signatures:* The sanitization algorithm invokes the trapdoor collision-finding algorithm of the chameleon hash, in effect obtaining an alternative set of inputs to the sign algorithm that evaluate to the same signing value. Moreover, the outputs of the chameleon hash are statistically independent of the input message – again, see [1], and the proof for the semantic security property. The output distributions for SIGN and SANIT are therefore identical, and from that it follows that changes to the mutable parts of the message are undetectable (weak transparency).

*Unforgeability:* Our proof works by contradiction. Assuming the existence of an efficient adversary that defeats our chameleon-hash based sanitizable signature construction we show how to construct either an efficient algorithm to break the underlying signature scheme, or an efficient algorithm to compute chameleon hash collisions. The proof is straightforward but lengthy so we have postponed it to appendix §A.

# 5   Extensions and Other Constructions

One natural extension is to allow for multiple censors, each able to modify different portions of the document. To achieve this, one may simply list all the public keys in the argument to the signature (and use each public key for the chameleon hash of the corresponding message block):

$$SIGN(m, r; sk_{sign}, pk^1_{sanit}, \dots, pk^t_{sanit}) :=$$
$$S_{sk_{sign}}(ID_m||t||pk^1_{sanit}|| \cdots ||pk^t_{sanit}||\bar{m}_1|| \dots ||\bar{m}_t).$$

A different extension is to allow for distributed, threshold-trust censors. This can be easily achieved by using a threshold version of the chameleon hashing scheme.

A more interesting extension is to support *strong transparency*. One way to accomplish this would be for the signer to use the multiple-censor extension described above, declare every block of the message mutable, but assign public keys of non-existing (dummy) censors to the blocks the signer wish to remain unmodified. Unfortunately, in practice it may be difficult to hide the information about which censors are fictitious, since probably there will be only a few well-known censors and any other public key would give rise to suspicion of non-existence.

## 5.1   Hybrid Scheme

The construction described below is an extension of the redactable signature schemes, discussed in [23], based on the Gennaro-Halevi-Rabin signature [17].

It can be seen as an *improved* redactable signature of constant size which combines the advantages of both redactable and sanitizable signatures. In particular, the signature allows message blocks to be redacted by anyone while unredacted blocks can be sanitized by a censor.

The signature in [17] requires an RSA-type modulus $n$ which is the product of two *safe* primes, $p$ and $q$, that is, such that $(p-1)/2$ and $(q-1)/2$ are also primes. The public key is $(v, n)$ for a randomly selected $v \in \mathbf{Z}_n^*$. To sign a message $m$, first compute the hash of it $\mathcal{H}(m)$ and then release $y$ such that $y^{\mathcal{H}(m)} = v$ mod $n$.[4]

In [23], the following method is described to compute redactable signatures on a document $x = (x_1, \ldots, x_k)$: First generate a document identifier $ID_x$ and then release the signature $(ID_x || y)$ where $y = v^{1/(\mathcal{H}(ID_x || 1 || x_1) \times \cdots \times \mathcal{H}(ID_x || k || x_k))}$ mod $n$. As reported in [23], to redact the message block $x_i$ it is sufficient to release the new signature $(ID_x || y')$ where $y' = y^{\mathcal{H}(ID_x || i || x_i)}$.

To make the redactable signature above sanitizable, we simply replace each triple $\mathcal{H}(ID_x, i, x_i)$ that can be sanitized with $\mathcal{H}(ID_x || i || \mathrm{CH}_y(ID_x || i || x_i))$, that is each message block $x_i$ is replaced with a chameleon hash of it computed under the public key of the censor. Now the censor will be able to modify the $i^{\text{th}}$ block and produce a valid sanitized signature. Note that the proof of security in [23] still holds because the outer hash $\mathcal{H}(\cdot)$ remains unchanged.

## 5.2    Attribute Tags

Certain applications may require the censor to modify mutable parts of the message so that the new parts satisfy prescribed semantics or policies. For instance, the censor could replace an address only with a generic geographic location, an exact date only with a time period, an integer only with another integer in a specific range, or a certain age with "senior" or "minor," and so on.

A simple solution is to prepend an immutable attribute tag to a mutable section of the message and expect the verifier to check that the data type of the mutable portion matches the specifications of the prepended attribute tag. The original signer could, for instance, prepend to a mutable part the phrase "Address (or area):" and make it immutable. In this way the verifier of the signature will expect after that phrase either an address or a geographic location. Clearly, with this method, the original signer can specify the type of the mutable part and which conditions it should satisfy. For instance, the immutable phrase "Value (integer in $[0, 100]$):" indicates that the next mutable value must be an integer and in the range from 0 to 100.

## 6    Implementation

We implemented our basic sanitizable signature construction with the Nyberg-Rueppel-based chameleon hash, and performed a series of experiments to demonstrate the efficiency of sanitizable signatures.

---

[4] Note that $\gcd(\mathcal{H}(m), \phi(n)) = 1$ with overwhelming probability.

## 6.1   Experiment Setup

Our implementation incorporates OpenSSL 0.9.7e Library routines. The code is compiled with gcc 3.4.2 (Red Hat). All tests are run under Fedora Core 3 with Linux 2.6.9 kernel on Pentium-4 2.6-GHz PC with 512 MB of RAM.

The 1024-bit keys used for RSA signatures are generated using OpenSSL's command-line RSA key generation routine. We used OpenSSL Diffie-Hellman library routines to generate our 1024-bit Nyberg-Rueppel key using 5 as the generator (OpenSSL is optimized for 2 or 5 as the generator). Unfortunately, one cannot store the key as Diffie-Hellman parameters because OpenSSL does not write DH keys to file. So we store the Nyberg-Rueppel keys in DSA format.

In our implementation we chose hash-and-sign RSA as the generic signature algorithm and SHA-1 as the generic hash algorithm. Notice that hash-and-sign RSA is not secure but we are using it just as a lower-bound for our performance measurements. In a real scenario, a secure hash-and-encode scheme should be used, such as EMSA-PSS [7,35].

We applied our implementation on two 1 KB random message blocks. The first block is the modifiable portion of the document; the second block is the fixed portion. To generate a sanitizable signature, we apply the Nyberg-Rueppel-based chameleon hash to the first block, concatenate the result to the second message block, and finally apply hash-and-sign RSA signature. We used 128-bit labels to serve as message block IDs. Signing and verifying both use OpenSSL RSA signature routines.

## 6.2   Results

We applied each specific operation 1000 times. The average performance results from our experiments, where the amount of time specified is for a single operation, are summarized in Table 1. These results show that the execution time for each operation we tested is of the order of 10 milliseconds. Hence the Nyberg-Rueppel-based sanitizable signature scheme is practical and efficient. Furthermore, sanitizable signing costs about four times the signing time of RSA signature with SHA-1, while providing significant subsequent advantages in a setting where sanitization is required.

While sanitizable Nyberg-Rueppel verification is faster than signing, its relative performance vis-a-vis RSA-SHA-1 verification is worse. This results from verification being approximately 10 times faster than signing for RSA signatures, while only about 1.3 times faster for sanitizable Nyberg-Rueppel.

We note that the OpenSSL library, while implementing several optimizations for the RSA cryptosystem, does not include optimized code for discrete logarithm

**Table 1.** Performance of OpenSSL primitives and Nyberg-Rueppel sanitizable signature algorithms

| SHA-1 | $RSA_{sign}$ | $RSA_{verify}$ | $CH_{NR}$ | $CH_{NR}$ (Collision) | $SIGN$ | $VERIFY$ |
|---|---|---|---|---|---|---|
| 0.027 ms | 10.653 ms | 0.609 ms | 33.863 ms | 28.196 ms | 44.518 ms | 34.497 ms |

constructions. In particular, it does not support optimizations for simultaneous multiple exponentiation, as described in [20], and its performance is an order of magnitude slower than libraries such as Crypto++ [11].

# 7  Conclusions

Sanitizable signatures allow a semi-trusted censor to modify designated portions of a document and then produce a valid signature of the legitimately modified document without help from the signer. Moreover, a verifier cannot determine whether a received signature has been sanitized by the censor. We have implemented the scheme and the performance results obtained demonstrate that the scheme is practical and efficient.

*Acknowledgments.* We are grateful to Aniello Del Sorbo for helping with configuration issues of OpenSSL. We thank the anonymous referees of ESORICS 2005 for their insightful comments. This work was partially supported by NSF.

# References

1. G. Ateniese and B. de Medeiros. On the key-exposure problem in chameleon hashes. *Proceedings of the Fourth Conference on Security in Communication Networks (SCN'04)*, Lect. Notes Comp. Sci., vol. 3352. Springer-Verlag, 2005. Full version: Cryptology ePrint Archive, Report 2004/243, http://eprint.iacr.org/2004/243

2. G. Ateniese and B. de Medeiros. Identity-Based Chameleon Hash and Applications. In Ari Juels, ed., *Proc. of Financial Cryptography (FC 2004)*, Lect. Notes Comp. Sci., vol. 3110, pp. 164–180. Springer-Verlag, 2004

3. M. Bellare, O. Goldreich, and S. Goldwasser. Incremental cryptography: the case of hashing and signing. In Y. Desmedt, ed., *Advances in Cryptology–CRYPTO '94*, Lect. Notes Comp. Sci., vol. 839, pp. 216-233. Springer-Verlag, 1994.

4. M. Bellare, O. Goldreich, and S. Goldwasser. Incremental cryptography with application to virus protection. In *Proc. of the Twenty-Seventh Annual ACM Symposium on Theory of Computing (FOCS'95)*, pp. 45–56. ACM Press, 1995.

5. M. Bellare and D. Micciancio. A new paradigm for collision-free hashing: Incrementality at reduced cost. In *Advances in Cryptology–Eurocrypt'97*, Lect. Notes Comp. Sci., vol. 1233. Springer-Verlag, 1997.

6. M. Bellare and G. Neven. Transitive signatures based on factoring and RSA. In Y. Zheng, ed.,*Advances in Cryptology–ASIACRYPT'02*, Lect. Notes Comp. Sci., vol. 2501, pp. 397–414. Springer-Verlag, 2003.

7. M. Bellare, P. Rogaway. PSS: Provably secure encoding method for digital signature. IEEE P1363a: Provably secure signatures. http://grouper.ieee.org/-groups/1363/p1363a/pssigs.html (1998)

8. M. Bishop, B. Bhumiratana, R. Crawford, and K. Levitt. How to Sanitize Data. Proceedings of the 13th IEEE International Workshops on Enabling Technologies: Infrastructures for Collaborative Enterprises (WETICE-2004). Pp. 217-222. June 2004, Modena, Italy.

9. J. Boyar, D. Chaum, I. B. Damgård, T. P. Pedersen. Convertible undeniable signatures. In *Advances in Cryptology–CRYPTO'90*, Lect. Notes Comp. Sci., vol. 537, pp. 189–205. Springer-Verlag, 1990.

10. M. Burmester and T. van Le. Secure communications in Ad-hoc networks. In *Proc. of the 5th IEEE Information Assurance Workshop (IAW'05)*, pp. 234–241. 2004.

11. Crypto++ Library 5.2.1. http://www.eskimo.com/ weidai/cryptlib.html

12. S. Chari, T. Rabin, and R. Rivest. An efficient signature scheme for route aggregation. Unpublished manuscript, 2002. http://theory.lcs.mit.edu/ rivest/-publications.html

13. D. Chaum. Zero-knowledge undeniable signature. In *Advances in Cryptology–EUROCRYPT'90*, Lect. Notes Comp. Sci., vol. 473, pp. 458–464. Springer-Verlag, 1990.

14. D. Chaum and H. Antwerpen. Undeniable signatures. In *Advances in Cryptology - CRYPTO'89*. Lect. Notes Comp. Sci., vol. 435, pp. 212–216. Springer-Verlag, 1991.

15. D. Chaum, E. van Heijst, B. Pfitzmann. Cryptographically strong undeniable signatures, unconditionally secure for the signer. In *Advances in Cryptology–CRYPTO'91*, Lect. Notes Comp. Sci., vol. 576, pp. 470-ff. Springer-Verlag, 1991.

16. X. Chen, F. Zhang, and K. Kim. Chameleon hashing without key exposure. In *Proc. of the 7th International Information Security Conference (ISC'04)*, Lect. Notes Comp. Sci., vol. 3225, pp. 87–98. Springer-Verlag, 2004.

17. R. Gennaro, S. Halevi, and T. Rabin. Secure hash-and-sign signatures without the random oracle. In *Advances in Cryptology–EUROCRYPT'99*, Lect. Notes Comp. Sci., vol. 1592, pp. 123–139. Springer-Verlag, 1999.

18. S. Haber and W. S. Stornetta. How to Time-Stamp a Digital Document. In *Advances in Cryptology–CRYPTO'90*, Lect. Notes Comp. Sci., vol. 537, pp. 437–455. Springer-Verlag, 1990.

19. Hakan Hacigümus, Balakrishna R. Iyer, and Sharad Mehrotra. Executing SQL over encrypted data in the database-service-provider model. In *Proc. Intern. Conf. Management of Data (ACM SIGMOD 2002)*, pp. 216–227. ACM Press, 2002.

20. A. J. Menezes, P. C. van Oorschot and S. A. Vanstone. *Handbook of Applied Cryptography*. CRC Press, 2001.

21. Einar Mykletun, Maithili Narasimha, and Gene Tsudik. Authentication and Integrity in Outsourced Databases. In *Proc. of the Network and Distributed System Security Symposium (NDSS'04)*, 10 pp. Internet Society (ISOC) Press, 2004. http://www.isoc.org/isoc/conferences/ndss/04/proceedings/Papers/-Mykletun.pdf

22. D. Johnson and D. Maltz. Dynamic Source Routing in Ad Hoc Wireless Networks, Mobile Computing, 1996.

23. R. Johnson, D. Molnar, D. Song, and D. Wagner. Homomorphic signature schemes. In B. Preneel, ed., *Topics in Cryptology–CT-RSA 2002*, Lect. Notes Comp. Sci.., vol. 2771, pp. 244–262. Springer-Verlag, 2002.

24. S. Kent, C. Lynn and K. Seo. Secure Border Gateway Protocol (Secure-BGP), IEEE Journal on Selected Areas in Communications, April 2000.

25. H. Krawczyk and T. Rabin. Chameleon signatures. In *Proceedings of the Network and Distributed Systems Security Symposium (NDSS 2000)*, pp. 143–154.

26. S. Micali and R. Rivest. Transitive signature schemes. In B. Preneel, ed., *Topics in Cryptology–RSA-CT'02*, Lect. Notes Comp. Sci., vol. 2271, pp. 236–243. Springer-Verlag, 2002.

27. S. L. Murphy, M. R. Badger, and B. Wellington. OSPF with digital signatures. Internet Engineering Task Force (IETF) Request for Comments (RFC) 2154, June 1997.

28. D. Naccache, D. Pointcheval, and J. Stern. Twin signatures: An alternative to the hash-and-sign paradigm. In P. Samarati, ed., *Proceedings of the Eighth Annual ACM Conference on Computer and Communications Security*, pp. 20-27. ACM Press, 2001.

29. K. Nyberg and R. A. Rueppel. Message recovery for signature schemes based on the discrete logarithm problem. In *Designs, Codes, and Cryptography*, vol. 7(1–2), pp. 61–81. Kluwer Academic Publishers, 1996.
30. R. Pang and V. Paxson. A High-level Programming Environment for Packet Trace Anonymization and Transformation. In Proc. ACM SIGCOMM 2003.
31. R. Perlman. Network layer protocols with Byzantine robustness. Ph.D. thesis, Dept. of Elect. Eng. and Comp. Sci., Massachusetts Institute of Technology, August 1988.
32. M. Peuhkuri. A method to compress and anonymize packet traces. In Proceedings of the ACM SIGCOMM Internet Measurement Workshop, November 2001.
33. Y. Rekhter and T. Li. Border Gateway Protocol 4 (BGP-4), Internet Engineering Task Force (IETF) Request for Comments (RFC) 1771. March 1995.
34. R. Rivest. Two signature schemes. Slides from talk given at Cambridge University, Oct. 17, 2000. http://theory.lcs.mit.edu/ rivest/publications.html
35. RSA Labs: RSA Cryptography Standard: EMSAPSS – PKCS#1 v2.1. (2002)
36. R. Steinfeld, L. Bull, and Y. Zheng. Content extraction signatures. In K. Kim, ed., *Information Security and Cryptology–ICISC'01*, Lect. Notes Comp. Sci., vol. 2288, pp. 285–304. Springer-Verlag, 2002.
37. S. F. Shahandashti, M. Salmasizadeh, and J. Mohajeri. A provably secure short transitive signature scheme from bilinear group pairs. In C. Blundo and S. Cimato, eds., *Security in Communication Networks–SCN'04*, Lect. Notes Comp. Sci., vol. 3352, pp. 60–76. Springer-Verlag, 2005.
38. United States of America Department of Health and Human Services. Standards for Privacy of Individually Identifiable Health Information: Final Rule, Federal Register: August 14, 2002, vol. 67, no. 157.
39. J. Xu, J. Fan, M. Ammar, and S. B. Moon. On the design and performance of prefix preserving IP traffic trace anonymization. In Proceedings of the ACM SIGCOMM Internet Measurement Workshop, November 2001.

# A    Proof of Unforgeability

Let $\mathcal{A}$ be an $(\epsilon, k, q_a, q_b, t)$-forgery algorithm defeating the security of our sanitizable signature construction (notation as in section §3.1); we show how to use this adversary to either undermine the security of the underlying signature scheme, or to find collisions for the chameleon hash signature scheme, in violation of their proven security properties.

**Theorem 1.** *Let $\mathcal{A}$ be an $(\epsilon, k, q_a, q_b, t)$-forger of a sanitized signature scheme. Then there exist an $(\epsilon', k, q_a, t')$-forger of the underlying signature scheme and an $(\epsilon'', k, q_b, t'')$-forger of the chameleon hash function, where the quantities are related by*

$$\epsilon \le \epsilon' + \epsilon''; \quad t \ge t' - q_b t_{collision}; \quad t \ge t'' - q_a t_{sign},$$

*where $t_{collision}$ and $t_{sign}$ are, respectively, the maximum running times of the hash-collision finding and the signing algorithms on instances of size $k$.*

Denote by $\mu$ the intermediate value such that $\sigma = \mathrm{S}_{sk_{sign}}(\mu)$, i.e., $\mu$ is the value that is signed by the underlying signature algorithm in the process of sanitizable-signing $m$. Consider an instance of the forging experiment in which $\mathcal{A}$ succeeds in computing a signature $\sigma$ on a new message $m$, where $m = \mathrm{S}_{sk_{sign}}(\mu)$. This instance must fall in (at least) one of two cases:

*Case 1:* Every query $m'$ to the oracle $\mathcal{O}^{sk_{sign}}$ during $\mathcal{A}$'s execution resulted in signatures $\sigma' = S_{sk_{sign}}(\mu')$ associated to intermediate values $\mu'$ which are distinct from the value $\mu$ for the successful forgery $\sigma = S_{sk_{sign}}(\mu)$.

*Case 2:* There is a query $m_i$ to the oracle $\mathcal{O}^{sk_{sign}}$ such that the response $\sigma_i$ equals $S_{sk_{sign}}(\mu)$, with $m_i$ different from $m$.

In the first case, proceed as follows to build an adversary $\mathcal{B}$ of the underlying signature algorithm. First, $\mathcal{B}$ generates a pair of public and private keys for the chameleon hash function, $(sk_{sanit}, pk_{sanit})$. It uses $sk_{sanit}$ with the collision-finding algorithm for the chameleon hash function to emulate the oracle $\mathcal{O}^{sk_{sanit}}$, and it gives $pk_{sanit}$ to the adversary $\mathcal{A}$. In order to answer $\mathcal{A}$'s signature queries, $\mathcal{B}$ resorts to its own signing oracle for the underlying signature scheme. When $\mathcal{A}$ finishes computing $\sigma$, $\mathcal{B}$ outputs $\mu$ for its choice of target message; and the whole transcript of $\mathcal{A}$'s execution as its state after the first phase. (Note that $\mu$ is available from $\mathcal{A}$'s transcript otherwise the verification of $\mathcal{A}$'s success cannot be ascertained via the sanitized verification algorithm.)

In its second phase, $\mathcal{B}$ just reads $\sigma$ from the state information from the first phase, and terminates successfully whenever $\mathcal{A}$ succeeds, and the execution is an instance of case (1). $\mathcal{B}$'s execution time equals $t' = t + q_b t_{collision}$, where $t$ is the number of steps used by $\mathcal{A}$, $q_b$ is the number of queries to the sanitization oracle, and $t_{collision}$ is the (maximum) number of steps executed by the hash-collision algorithm on instances of size $k$, which $\mathcal{B}$ must perform to emulate answers to the sanitization oracle.

In the second case, algorithm $\mathcal{A}$ could be used to build an adversary $\mathcal{C}$ of the chameleon hash algorithm. First, $\mathcal{C}$ generates a pair of public and private keys for the underlying signature algorithm $(sk_{sign}, pk_{sign})$. It uses $sk_{sign}$ with the underlying signing algorithm $s(\cdot)$ to emulate the signing oracle $\mathcal{O}^{sk_{sign}}$, and conveys $pk_{sign}$ to the adversary $\mathcal{A}$. To answer $\mathcal{A}$'s sanitization queries, $\mathcal{C}$ resorts to the collision-finding oracle for the strongly unforgeable chameleon hash function.

When $\mathcal{A}$ finishes computing $\sigma$, $\mathcal{C}$ retrieves the value $\mu$ and compares it with the values $\mu_i$ that appear in $\mathcal{A}$'s transcript of queries to the signing oracle. Since we are in case (2), there is at least one queried message $m_i$ that differs from $m$ but such that $\mu_i$ equals $\mu$. Note that $m$ can differ from $m_i$ only if they differ in some mutable block (otherwise $\mu \neq \mu_i$). For simplicity of notation we assume that $m$ and $m_i$ are a single block each. Therefore, we have $C = CH_{pk_{sanit}}(m, \rho, \delta) = CH_{pk_{sanit}}(m_i, \rho_i, \delta_i)$, and $\mathcal{C}$ outputs $C, m_i, \rho_i, \delta_i$ as its chosen value to seek collisions against, and the whole transcript of $\mathcal{A}$'s execution as its state after the first phase of the adversarial game.

In its second phase, $\mathcal{C}$ just reads the values $m, \rho, \delta$ from the transcript of $\mathcal{A}$ and outputs it. Therefore, $\mathcal{C}$ succeeds whenever $\mathcal{A}$ succeeds and $\mathcal{A}$'s execution is of type (2). $\mathcal{C}$'s execution time is $t'' = t + q_a t_{sign}$, where $t$ is the number of steps used by $\mathcal{A}$, $q_a$ is the number of $\mathcal{A}$'s queries to the signing oracle, and $t_{sign}$ is the (maximum) number of steps executed by the underlying signing algorithm on instances of size $k$, which is executed to emulate the signing oracle.     $\square$

# Limits of the Cryptographic Realization
# of Dolev-Yao-Style XOR

Michael Backes and Birgit Pfitzmann

IBM Zurich Research Lab
{mbc, bpf}@zurich.ibm.com

**Abstract.** The abstraction of cryptographic operations by term algebras, called Dolev-Yao models, is essential in almost all tool-supported methods for proving security protocols. Recently significant progress was made in proving that Dolev-Yao models can be sound with respect to actual cryptographic realizations and security definitions. The strongest results show this in the sense of reactive simulatability/UC, a notion that essentially means the preservation of arbitrary security properties under arbitrary active attacks and in arbitrary protocol environments, with only small changes to both Dolev-Yao models and natural implementations.

However, these results are so far restricted to cryptographic systems like encryption and signatures which essentially only have constructors and destructors, but no further algebraic properties. Typical modern tools and complexity results around Dolev-Yao models also allow more algebraic operations. The first such operation considered is typically XOR because of its clear structure and cryptographic usefulness. We show that it is impossible to extend the strong soundness results to XOR, at least not with remotely the same generality and naturalness as for the core cryptographic systems. On the positive side, we show the soundness of a rather general Dolev-Yao model with XOR and its realization under passive attacks.

## 1   Introduction

Tool-supported verification of cryptographic protocols almost always relies on abstractions of cryptographic operations by term algebras, called Dolev-Yao models after the first authors [24]. The core of these term algebras are operations like en- and decryption which ideally have very few algebraic properties. However, if one wants to benefit from such abstractions in protocols that also contain operations with more algebraic properties, those operations have to be given a similar specification. A typical such operation is the exclusive or (XOR), see, e.g., [39,18,19], because it is commutative and associative and has significant uses in cryptology, e.g., as the one-time pad, in modes of operation of block ciphers, and in some protocols.

Recent work has essentially bridged the original and long-standing gap between Dolev-Yao models and real cryptographic definitions: It was shown that an almost normal Dolev-Yao model of several important cryptographic system types can be implemented with real cryptographic systems secure according to standard cryptographic definitions in a way that offers reactive (blackbox) simulatability [8]. This security

S. De Capitani di Vimercati et al. (Eds.): ESORICS 2005, LNCS 3679, pp. 178–196, 2005.

notion means that one system (here the cryptographic realization) can be plugged into arbitrary protocols instead of another (here the Dolev-Yao model) and retains essentially arbitrary security properties; it is also called UC for its universal composition properties. Extensions of this simulatability result to more cryptographic primitives were presented in [9,7] and actual uses in protocol proofs in [6,5]. Earlier results considered passive attacks only [4,3,29]. Later papers [38,32,16] consider to what extent restrictions to weaker security properties and/or less general protocol classes allow simplifications compared with [8]. All these papers have in common that they only consider core cryptographic operations, not operations with additional algebraic properties like XOR.

In this paper we study how the soundness results in the sense of reactive simulatability/UC can be extended when an XOR is added to a Dolev-Yao model and its cryptographic implementation. It turns out that this is impossible in a general way. We are quite surprised by this result, because XOR seems a relatively simple operation compared with systems like digital signatures, and it seems well described by its algebraic properties. Note that the question is not whether an XOR is a good and generally usable encryption system by itself, but only whether algebraic abstractions of it are sound. The only positive result we show is a soundness result under passive attacks; apart from this restriction the result is strong in the sense of using reactive simulatability and allowing a broad range of other operations in the Dolev-Yao model. Although early papers on bridging the gap between Dolev-Yao models and cryptography were also for passive attacks only, typical overall Dolev-Yao attackers are active. We therefore regard our negative results for the active case as the more interesting ones.

We want to show that it is not possible to cryptographically realize a Dolev-Yao model that contains XOR together with other usual cryptographic operations via real systems with actual XORs, in the sense of reactive (blackbox) simulatability. This is a meta-theorem formulation on a very high level: There is no current definition of "a Dolev-Yao model" independent of specific system models (like CSP, $\pi$-calculus, IO automata etc.). Nor is "an actual XOR" really well-defined. We aim at coming as close as possible to this meta-theorem with precise statements, but in the end what we show is a series of concrete impossibility results, and it is a matter of taste whether one considers these results to demonstrate the informal meta-theorem. At a minimum, these concrete impossibility results show that soundness results for Dolev-Yao models with XOR cannot be achieved with remotely the same generality and naturalness as for the core cryptographic systems.

*Related Work.* The XOR operation has accompanied cryptography from its beginnings, from simple ciphers in ancient and medieval times, over the one-time pad and the work of Shannon, to its widespread use in modern cryptography where it constitutes an essential component in many cryptographic protocols, e.g., [28,13,45]. To the best of our knowledge, the XOR operation in the symbolic analysis of cryptographic protocols has first been mentioned by Meadows [34] as a possible extension of the NRL analyzer. Since then it has been incorporated in many formal proof tools, e.g., NRL [35], CAPSL [40], Isabelle [42], and OFMC [10]. Recent papers on XOR in Dolev-Yao models mainly studied the decidability and complexity of the insecurity of cryptographic protocols against a Dolev-Yao attack in the presence of deduction rules for the XOR operator [18,19].

This line of work typically continues with abstractions of more general Abelian groups, e.g., [20,22,2], and the exponentiation function as used in many cryptographic systems based on the discrete-logarithm problem, e.g., [36,27,41,21,17,46,1]. While we have not yet considered these extensions, we are convinced that a general use of such operations on other terms would lead to similar problems as with XOR. In the case of exponentiations, however, it may be more realistic than for XOR to make strong restrictions on the types of terms that can be exponentiated and on the use of the XOR results within larger terms, and such restrictions might help.

The first sound formal abstraction of XOR, but only in connection with pseudorandom permutations, not the typical general encryptions etc. of other Dolev-Yao models, and only for passive attacks, was presented in [30,31]. Another sound formal abstraction of XOR was recently presented in [11], but only if XOR is restricted to terms whose corresponding bitstrings are generated according to a uniform distribution, and only for passive attacks.

The security notion of reactive simulatability, a notion of secure implementation that allows arbitrary composition, was first defined generally in [43], based on simulatability definitions for secure (one-step) function evaluation [25,26,12,37,14]. It was extended in [44,15], called UC (universal composability) in the latter, and has since been used in many ways for proving individual cryptographic systems and general theorems. While the definitions of [44,15] have not been rigorously mapped, for the results in this paper the differences do not matter.

As stated, our results, except for a simple first one, only consider the soundness of Dolev-Yao models in the sense of reactive simulatability/UC. We do not exclude that weaker soundness notions such as integrity-only soundness as first investigated in [38] can be extended. Nor do we exclude that certain restricted protocol classes using XOR can be secure in the sense of reactive simulatability even if the Dolev-Yao model as such is not, a direction of work started (not for XOR yet, of course) in [16]. It will be interesting to investigate the precise limits in the future. Nevertheless, we believe that our results show that one cannot achieve the general secure pluggability of a Dolev-Yao realization for a Dolev-Yao model with XOR that has been achieved for core cryptographic operations.

*Overview of this Paper.* As mentioned above, our major results are negative results that aim at demonstrating the informal claim that it is not possible to realize "true Dolev-Yao models" by "real XORs" in a generally composable way. In the following, we summarize our concrete impossibility results. By payload data we denote the type of non-cryptographic data that most Dolev-Yao models have. It denotes data input by the users of the Dolev-Yao model, e.g., letters to be encrypted and signed, or payment data constructed by a payment protocol using the Dolev-Yao model.

- The standard Dolev-Yao model of XOR used in the literature is insecure with respect to every moderately natural implementation when secrecy is required (not necessarily even reactive simulatability) and general terms (e.g., payload data) can be XORed.
- If payload data are used in their original form in real XORs and signatures are one of the cryptographic operations, then every system that securely abstracts from this situation (in the sense of blackbox simulatability) must be able to compute

signatures from whatever cryptographic realization is used. Thus informally it is not truly Dolev-Yao. More precisely, we present a reduction proof showing that such a system can be used to build a signature oracle with minimal additional operations.
- The same result holds with a more complex counterexample if we no longer assume that arbitrary usage of the Dolev-Yao model is allowed, but only assume that certain useful-looking protocols can be built on top of it.
- The same result holds even if the payload data may be encoded in the real system before being used in XORs, but with low or well-structured redundancy such as type tags. To the best of our knowledge, all current implementations of XOR fall into this class or the previous class.
- Even if payload data may be encoded with arbitrary redundancy, a similar result holds where the system that should be a Dolev-Yao model must at least be able to test signatures. I.e., we now make a reduction proof yielding a test oracle, a notion that we first have to define because it is not usual in cryptography.

The basic underlying problem in all these cases is when an honest participant receives an XOR from an active adversary and, after some local operations, tries to convert the result into another type, in particular into payload data, thinking, e.g., that the result is a recovered plaintext. There is no general consistent way for the cryptographic realization and the Dolev-Yao abstraction to know whether such a type conversion should work, and thus to make exactly the required output when the result is really a plaintext, but not when it is not a plaintext and may thus have some cryptographic structure in the real system.

Positively we show reactive simulatability of an extension of the Dolev-Yao-style system from [8] by an XOR with a certain tolerable imperfection (needed to overcome our first negative result) with respect to a natural realization, and under the condition that users are restricted to correct type conversions, a fact that can be verified formally for protocols.

## 2  A Solvable Secrecy Imperfection of XOR

Before going into real impossibility results, we present one imperfection of XOR that would make a sound XOR abstraction different from the XOR abstractions in the literature. However, this imperfection alone could be taken care of by giving the Dolev-Yao adversary additional capabilities, without leaving natural Dolev-Yao models and natural XOR implementations. Thus it is similar, e.g., to the fact that cryptographic encryption cannot keep the length of arbitrary terms secret, which led to the introduction of abstract lengths into the Dolev-Yao-style model of [8].

As far as we know, all Dolev-Yao models with XOR allow participants to XOR arbitrary terms and to convert (typically implicitly) a result that is a term of another type back to that type. For instance, a recipient who receives a one-time pad ciphertext $c = d \oplus k$, where $d$ is a plaintext and $k$ a key, may ask to have $c$ XORed with $k$ and to obtain the plaintext $d$ as output. The adversary has no additional capabilities in these models. In particular, if he receives an XOR of two terms that he both doesn't know, and that both did not occur in other XORs, he cannot retrieve these terms. For instance, an adversary not knowing $k$ and $d$ in the example above cannot retrieve $k$ or $d$.

Now assume that an honest participant XORs two plaintexts written in English and sends the result to the adversary. The result can be cryptanalyzed if the texts are long enough, i.e., a real adversary can retrieve the two plaintexts, e.g., see the section on running-key ciphers in [23]. Hence we must model that an XOR leaks the underlying terms to the adversary unless we know that at least one of these terms is sufficiently random. In this sense, prior Dolev-Yao models of XOR are overly optimistic. Even some data types of significant entropy, like secret or public keys of public-key systems, cannot be used in XORs to hide plaintext data or other cryptographic elements. The reason is that they are not sufficiently uniformly distributed given only the standard cryptographic definitions, i.e., besides the entropy they may contain significant redundancy.

One can deal with this imperfection—and we will do so in the positive result for passive attacks—by introducing a set of random types into the Dolev-Yao model. Elements of a random type are deemed sufficiently random (often pseudo-random in reality) to restrict the adversary to standard algebraic operations on XORs. In the absence of unknown random elements in an XOR, the Dolev-Yao adversary is given the capability to parse the XOR.

## 3    Assumptions for Our Impossibility Results

As explained in the introduction, we want to show that it is not possible to implement *any* Dolev-Yao abstraction by *any* natural realization of XOR in a way that retains arbitrary security properties in arbitrary protocol environments. In order to turn this informal meta-theorem into concrete statements that can be verified or falsified, we need assumptions on what characterizes a Dolev-Yao model, a model of XOR in it, and a real implementation of such a model.

### 3.1    Reactive Simulatability

We start by surveying the notion of reactive simulatability/UC that we use for comparing a Dolev-Yao model and a cryptographic realization with respect to security. As we aim at general impossibility results, we try to avoid model-specific notation and to stay as general as possible.

Reactive simulatability is a general notion for comparing two systems, typically called real and ideal system. It relies on the notion of honest users (potential protocols) that interact with one of these systems and an adversary that mounts attacks against the system and its users. Essentially reactive simulatability states that for all attacks on the real system there exists an equivalent attack on the ideal system. More precisely, blackbox simulatability states that there exists a simulator that can use an arbitrary real adversary as a blackbox, such that arbitrary honest users cannot distinguish whether they interact with the real system and the real adversary, or with the ideal system and the simulator with its blackbox. This is illustrated in Figure 1. Here the machines $M_1$ and $M_2$ jointly denote the real system, TH (trusted host) denotes the ideal system, H the entirety of the honest users, A the real adversary, and Sim the simulator. The combination of Sim and A is the adversary on the ideal system. The reader may regard the individual boxes as IO automata, Turing machines, CSP or $\pi$-calculus processes etc., whatever he or she is most familiar with. The only requirement on the underlying system model is

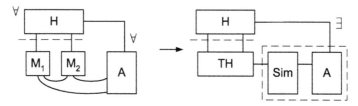

**Fig. 1.** Overview of blackbox simulatability. A real system is shown on the left; an ideal system plus simulator on the right. The views of H must be indistinguishable.

that the notion of an execution of a system when run together with an honest user and an adversary is well-defined. The rigorous notion of equivalence of the attacks is that the honest users' views in such executions are computationally indistinguishable; this is a well-known cryptographic notion from [47].

### 3.2 Interface Behavior of a Dolev-Yao Model with XOR

In this section we describe the functionality that we assume a Dolev-Yao system with XOR offers. This is quite natural, but recall that there is no general definition of this in the literature yet.

As we want to compare the Dolev-Yao model and its cryptographic realization in the sense of reactive simulatability/UC we can assume that they offer the same syntactic user interfaces, i.e., in- and output formats. In terms of Figure 1, this is the interface from TH or $M_1$ and $M_2$, respectively, to the entirety of users H. Similar concepts exist in all variants, in particular [43,44,15] and when extending the observational equivalence from [33] by simulators, e.g., the input and output formats of the ideal and real functionality in [15] and the free channel types in [33]. Syntactically different user interfaces would either simply prevent the same users from using the real and ideal systems or lead to trivial distinguishability.

We make the following assumptions:

- The honest users can ask for standard cryptographic terms to be constructed and sent to other users. In particular this includes nonces, XORs, encryptions, and signatures. We sometimes describe the commands used for this by writing down the desired result term in a quasi-algebraic notation.
- When an honest user receives a term, it gets notified by the system, and can then perform at least some cryptographic operations on this term. We sometimes designate an opaque term $t$ in such a context by the handle notation $t^{\mathsf{hnd}}$.
- The XOR operation, when considered with respect to the user inputs, fulfills the typical algebraic equations such as $(t_1 \oplus t_2) \oplus t_1 = t_2$ for all terms $t_1, t_2$. Note that we can require this independently of how the Dolev-Yao model internally represents terms and how the real system encodes strings (e.g., with type tags or error-correcting codes).
- The users can input payload data and have them output again. They can use payload data as leaves in typical cryptographic terms (e.g., as a message to be encrypted; the examples will show where exactly we assume that payload data can be used).
- The Dolev-Yao model offers some secrecy. At a minimum, we require that it does not leak information about the payload in an encryption to the ideal adversary,

except at most its term structure with types and lengths. Similarly, we require that an XOR with a fresh nonce of sufficient length does not leak information about the other XORed components to the ideal adversary, except at most their term structure and length.

Beyond these minimum assumptions, we will make more assumptions in our first examples, to get easy and natural cases, but we will relax those other assumptions later.

As discussed above, reactive simulatability/UC requires a common representation of terms at the user interface, i.e., some kind of names that designate either abstract terms or real bitstrings when a protocol uses either the ideal or the real cryptographic system. We call these names "handles" following [8]. Note, however, that we do not assume any specific implementation of these handles, in particular not that they are local names represented by successive natural numbers as in [8]. They could even be terms (with a notion of holes where the term cannot be parsed for this user) or cryptographic objects, although for many readers the latter choice would immediately disqualify the ideal system from counting as a Dolev-Yao model.

### 3.3    Characteristics of Dolev-Yao Models and Real Systems

Our next assumptions concern what constitutes an ideal, Dolev-Yao-style system, and what constitutes a real, cryptographic system. We obviously need such assumptions: The notion of reactive simulatability is reflexive. Thus, if an arbitrary Dolev-Yao model with XOR would also count as real, we would trivially have a secure realization of the system by itself. The same would hold if an arbitrary real cryptographic system with XOR would also count as ideal. But this is not what we want.

As we aim for impossibility results for large classes of Dolev-Yao models and realizations, we try to make only minimum requirements on ideality and reality. Note, however, that also a theorem that one particular ideal system, such as from the literature, cannot be realized, would be of some interest, and similarly for statements that specific cryptographic libraries with XOR cannot be idealized.

*Dolev-Yao Models.* The seemingly essential feature of Dolev-Yao models is that they work on term algebras, and not on real cryptographic bitstrings. However, this is not easy to formalize. For instance, given only a list or pairing operation, one can in principle construct terms that correspond to strings, and it may be possible to implement real cryptography on them as very complex term operations. Hence one cannot simply define the presence of terms and the absence of bitstrings as the characteristics of a Dolev-Yao model. Some other properties are easier to define, but not sufficient for our results. For instance, a Dolev-Yao model is expected to be deterministic and independent from concrete underlying cryptographic systems as long as they fulfill certain definitions. However, these properties do not help much to construct counterexamples because the simulator could give random values and algorithms to the ideal system during their first interaction. Another property, which we will use but which is not sufficient for the proofs, is the secrecy of local operations. This means that during a term construction or the parsing of a received term and the potential output of some of its components to the honest user, no intermediate results are exchanged with the ideal adversary. All existing Dolev-Yao models fulfill this property since they treat the parsing of terms and the construction of response terms as monolithic transitions that do not grant the adversary access to the term structure or even the subterms.

We overcome this lack of a clear characterization of Dolev-Yao models by resorting to reduction proofs. We show essentially that every system (in particular a potential Dolev-Yao model) that can faithfully abstract from cryptography and XOR in certain situations, can be used to compute actual cryptographic operations. The reduction consists only of very few and simple operations. This intuitively means that the main work in computing the actual cryptographic operations must be done inside the system that is supposed to be a Dolev-Yao model. This leads us to conclude (again informally) that the system is not actually in Dolev-Yao style.

*Real Systems.* A general characteristics of real systems is that they are distributed. This means that each participant has its own machine, and that the machines are only connected by channels that offer a real adversary well-defined possibilities for observations and manipulation. Specifically for a cryptographic realization of a Dolev-Yao model, we require that the machines only exchange messages according to the user interface commands, i.e., when a term is exchanged between participants according to the protocol. Specifically for XOR we usually assume that the real system contains a real XOR on bitstrings. More precisely, we assume that message elements like signatures or keys have a representation that is fixed for their type, and a real XOR of such message elements is an actual bitstring XOR. In particular, payload data (see Section 3.2) may have an internal representation different from the external one, e.g., with a type tag, but then this fixed representation is used in all XORs. Whether the payload data are used in the XORs in their original form or in a redundant encoding is an important distinction. The first case leads to easier counterexamples and is quite natural, e.g., when one considers XORs in modes of operation like CBC, but we also consider the more complicated case.

# 4    Impossibility Results and Their Consequences

This section contains our major results that aim at demonstrating the informal claim that it is not possible to realize true Dolev-Yao models by real XORs in a generally composable way. We first present counterexamples for simple cases, e.g., for non-redundant representations of payload data and arbitrary users. Then we move to more involved cases, e.g., to data of high redundancy and restricted protocol classes, that require more sophisticated reasoning to establish the unsoundness of Dolev-Yao-style XOR.

## 4.1    Counterexample for Non-redundant Data and Arbitrary Users

Our first example is made under the additional assumption that payload data are non-redundant in XORs, and that there is no restriction on the users H. The example is shown in Figure 2. The real situation is shown on the left, the attempt at a simulation on the right. The real adversary sends a random string $y$ to the machine $M_v$ of an honest participant $v$. The user $v$ gets a notification that a string (or term in the ideal case) was received. The user $v$ then asks to have this received string or term XORed with his or her signature on payload data $d$, and to have the result output as payload data. As there is no

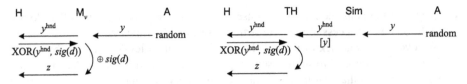

**Fig. 2.** Example for non-redundant data and arbitrary users

redundancy in payload data under the assumptions of this case, the machine $M_v$ cannot recognize that the result is not payload data. Clearly, the user H and the adversary A together can validate in the real system that the bitstring $y \oplus z$ is a valid signature on $d$, assuming the public key $pks$ for this signature is known. (Note that H and A are allowed to interact in the definitions of reactive simulatability, e.g., to model chosen-message attacks and plaintexts becoming public. Actually, in blackbox simulatability, one can simply join H and A.) Hence in the simulation TH must also output a bitstring $z$ with this property. However, this intuitively means that TH can compute a cryptographic signature.

*Reduction proof.* More precisely, we show as a reduction proof that if this situation is simulated correctly, then TH can be used to compute signatures. Thus we construct a signature oracle Sig with TH as a blackbox, and where Sig only performs very few and simple operations itself in the signature computation phase. For its setup, Sig runs honest users and the simulator for the generation of a signature key pair and the publication of the public key $pks$. It publishes the same key. It further generates a random string $y$ and the arrival indication that Sim would give to TH for such a message; this is denoted by $y^{hnd}$ in Figure 2. It waits for TH to notify the user; in slight abuse of notation we again denote this with $y^{hnd}$ because typically both these values are just some handles. Now Sig, when asked to sign a payload $d$, asks TH (as H would do) to XOR the term denoted by $y^{hnd}$ with a signature on $d$, and to output the resulting payload data. It waits for the output $z$ from TH and outputs $s := z \oplus y$. By the arguments above, this is indeed a signature on $d$ valid with respect to $pks$. Note that in the signing phase, the only operations that Sig performs itself are the final XOR and the earlier user inputs requesting the computation of a signature and an XOR and the output of payload data.

This proof seems a clear indication that this TH can compute a signature on an arbitrary message.

### 4.2 Counterexamples for Non-redundant Data and Protocol Restrictions

If every permitted user H consists of a protocol *prot* from a restricted class *Prots* and a user H' of *prot*, then the example from Section 4.1 only still works if a permitted protocol subtracts a signature from a received string and converts the result into payload data. The simplest protocol that does this is written as follows in typical high-level notation, and where $d$ and $sks$ are secrets known to $u$ and $v$.

$$u \to v : \ d' \oplus sig(sks, d);$$
$$v : \ \text{Output } d'.$$

This protocol may or may not belong to the class *Prots* of typical Dolev-Yao models extended by XOR. For instance, the models might not allow joint secret payload data

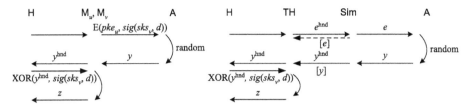

**Fig. 3.** Example for non-redundant data and protocol restrictions

and a joint secret key. If this simple protocol is in the class, then Figure 2 remains a counterexample, even if we know that this protocol is the only use made of the ideal or real cryptographic system: In the real system, $M_v$ cannot know whether $M_u$ started this protocol. Hence whenever it gets a message $y$ supposedly from $M_u$, it applies its protocol step and thus acts as in Figure 2.

Otherwise, the following protocol is more likely to be permitted for arbitrary Dolev-Yao models.

$$v \to u : \ E(pke_u, sig(sks_v, d));$$
$$u \to v : \ d' \oplus sig(sks_v, d);$$
$$v : \ \text{Output } d'.$$

Here $pke_u$ denotes the public encryption key of user $u$ and $sks_v$ the secret signing key of user $v$. By our assumptions on the secrecy offered by Dolev-Yao models, the first term does not leak the encrypted plaintext to the ideal adversary, in particular neither $d$ nor the signature. I.e., as long as TH and Sim are independent of the protocols run on top, TH only outputs an opaque handle $e^{hnd}$ to the ideal adversary to indicate the first term sent, see Figure 3. Then when $M_v$ receives the second message $y$ while $M_u$ did not really send it, the situation is essentially as in Section 4.1: $M_v$ does not know whether $M_u$ sent the second term, so it reacts on any $y$ supposedly from $M_u$. It always outputs a result $z$. This result is passed through to the protocol user H′. So even H′ and A alone (without observing the inner workings of the protocol *prot*) can obtain $y \oplus z$, which should be a valid signature on $d$, which they also know.

### 4.3   Counterexample for Data with Low Redundancy

The situations studied so far no longer serve as counterexamples for implementability of a Dolev-Yao XOR if we restrict the domain of payload data. Then $M_v$ might usually output an error $\downarrow$ instead of $z$. For this, the real system must contain an explicit conversion between input data $d$ and their redundant representation within the realization of terms. We sometimes omit this conversion, but sometimes write it out as data2string (with input pure payloads, and output the redundant encoding) and string2data. We write the domain of string2data as $Datastrings$ and its restriction to strings of length $l$ as $Datastrings_l$.

A common case is that a realization implements a type system by tagging, i.e., by representing all data as pairs of a type tag and the original data, and that the original payload data can be an arbitrary string from an exponentially large domain. If the type

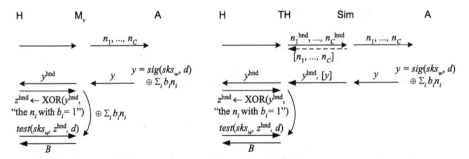

**Fig. 4.** Example for potentially highly redundant data

tag in such a realization is short, the counterexample from Figure 2 still works. More generally, we assume that the family of sets $Datastrings_l$ is not negligible within the family of sets of all strings of length $l$. The string $z$ in the example is uniformly random (a fresh one-time pad $y$ XORed with a fixed string) and thus with not negligible probability we are in the situation as above, which cannot be simulated.

In some real implementations of type systems on strings, in particular XML, the overall part of a string that is fixed by a type is of considerable length, so that the use of a random $y$ no longer works. However, a similar attack works for many realistic cases: Assume that a subset $Fixbits_{data,l}$ of the bits of $Datastrings_l$ is fixed (e.g., opening and closing XML tags), and similarly $Fixbits_{sig,l}$ for signatures. We can increase the latter set by only considering signatures made with one known algorithm and with respect to the known public key $pks_v$. Now if $Fixbits_{sig,l} \supseteq Fixbits_{data,l}$, the adversary can predetermine the necessary bits of $z$ in $y$ by XORing them with the corresponding fixed bits of a signature.

### 4.4 Counterexample for Highly Redundant Data and Arbitrary Users

Before delving into slightly exotic reduction proofs, let us consider one relatively normal case although it does not correspond to a specific underlying assumption: If the redundancy is of a complex form such that Sim cannot parse bitstrings with the structure $y = d' \oplus sig(d)$ where both $d'$ and $d$ are new, and if TH only expects from the ideal adversary and thus from Sim an opaque indication that an XOR has been received (in particular not the string $y$), and if the user later subtracts $d'$ and requests a signature test on the result, then TH can obviously not react correctly, and it is too late to contact Sim because of the secrecy of local operations.

Now we return to the case without additional assumptions, i.e., Sim is arbitrary and may pass arbitrary strings to TH. We use the example from Figure 4. Participant $v$ and the adversary share a large number $C$ of nonces $n_1, \ldots, n_C$ of a certain length $l$ suitable for hiding signatures. Here $C$ is chosen such that the nonces span the whole space $GF(2)^l$. This can be tested on the fly by A, and $C$ be adapted accordingly. Now the adversary chooses a random vector $b \xleftarrow{\mathcal{R}} GF(2)^C$ and computes the linear combination $N := \sum_{i=1}^{C} b_i n_i$ of the nonces; this is as good as a fresh nonce. The adversary also computes a signature $s$ on data $d$ with a secret key $sks_w$ where the public key $pks_w$ was published, and sends $s$ hidden by the new nonce as a message $y = s \oplus N$

to participant $v$. Outside the system, A shares $d$ and $b$ with user $v$, represented in the entirety of users H, corresponding to a chosen-message attack. Then user $v$ gives the commands to subtract the appropriate nonces from $y$ and asks whether the result $z$ is a correct signature on $d$. Alternatively, the adversary does the same with an incorrect signature $s'$. The real machine $M_v$ will always decide this correctly. We now assume that we have an ideal system TH and a simulator Sim that correctly simulates the same situation. Intuitively, we want to show that TH must be able to test cryptographic signatures for this. Formally, we derive a test oracle Test from TH that only performs very simple, algorithm-independent operations outside its subroutine TH during the signature test phase. Intuitively, this shows that after a set-up phase, TH has learned the test algorithm.

While signature oracles are usual in the literature, test oracles are not. When trying to define one, we need to decide on an input distribution for the potential signatures. For instance, if we input random values, the oracle may be correct with overwhelming probability by always outputting false. Or, if we input either a correct signature or a random value, there may be so much trivial redundancy in the real signatures that a very simple oracle can make the distinction. We deal with this problem as follows: We allow a second, arbitrary oracle Fake that tries to fake signatures. It must always output wrong signatures. Intuitively a good oracle Fake makes its fakes as plausible as possible. For instance, for RSA signatures with additional tags, random elements, and fields for the public key and the signed data, it might set all these fields correctly, and choose the rest randomly from the correct mathematical group. We require a test oracle Test to be able to distinguish *every* fake oracle from a correct signature oracle.

Now we perform our reduction proof, i.e., we construct a test oracle Test from the given TH and Sim. We call the fake or sign oracle O. In the setup phase, Test obtains a public signature key $pks_w$ and runs the actions of Sim on this key together with TH. This key and the corresponding $pks_w$ are also in O. It then runs A and Sim choosing $C$ nonces together with TH. Further, Test chooses a random string $y$ and runs Sim upon receipt of $y$ as a message from the adversary for participant $v$. This finishes the set-up phase.

Now, given input data $d$, it calls $s \leftarrow O(d)$ and thus obtains a correct or faked (wrong but possibly plausible-looking) signature $s$. It computes the one-time pad $N$ that makes $s$ fit the previously chosen $y$ by setting $N := s \oplus y$. It solves the equation $N = \sum_{i=1}^{C} b_i n_i$ for a vector $b$ (parts of this can be precomputed). It then makes the user inputs for $b$ to TH, i.e., for all $i$ with $b_i = 1$, it asks TH to XOR the $i$-th nonce to the string. In this situation $M_v$ would have the result $z = s$. Thus, when Test finally inputs the signature test command for $z^{\mathsf{hnd}}$, then $M_v$ would output $B = \text{true}$ if $O = \text{Sig}$ and $B = \text{false}$ if $O = \text{Fake}$. Hence TH almost always does the same. This proves that TH can be used as a test oracle for arbitrary machines Fake. Intuitively, this shows that TH must have the specific cryptographic test algorithm used in the current realization implemented after the set-up phase.

## 4.5   Counterexamples for Highly Redundant Data and Protocol Restrictions

Similar to Section 4.2, we may ask whether reasonable protocol restrictions allow us to exclude the situation from Section 4.4. First, if $M_v$'s action is part of a protocol, we need that participant $v$ is willing to execute the protocol with a corrupted participant $w$. This corresponds to the fact that the adversary may corrupt at least one participant, and that the other participants do not know about this. All Dolev-Yao models we know of allow this trust setting. Secondly, the protocols might not use payload data $d$ and bit vectors $b$ on both sides that were not exchanged using the Dolev-Yao model. For the data, we can assume a signature system with message recovery and let the user retrieve $d$, or we can send $d$ explicitly with the signature, hidden by $N$. It is trivial to adapt the reduction proof to this.

For the bits, we may assume that they are sent as payload data, and that the protocol class is large enough that Sim has no reason to interpret these payload data in relation to specific messages. To go further towards a reasonable protocol with such behavior, assume that we are doing some group communication where every group member adds a nonce to a message, and the recipient subtracts all these nonces. In our situation, a large number of group members is dishonest, so that all these nonces are shared with the adversary. Further, the groups can vary and the current group membership is indicated by the vector $b$ (suitably augmented by a bit for $v$, and bits for the possible other honest group members).

# 5   A Passively Sound Dolev-Yao-Style Model for XOR

The main special case of Dolev-Yao-style XOR that we prove to be sound corresponds to passive attacks only, together with a type-consistency requirement on the protocol above the Dolev-Yao model. In other respects the result is strong: We show reactive simulatability and need no restrictions on the other operations in the Dolev-Yao model; this distinguishes our result from those in [30,11]. Roughly, the benefit of the restriction to passive adversaries is that all XORs are constructed bottom-up. Thus the simulator never receives bitstrings that claim to be XORs but where it does not know how to partition them. The necessity of the type-consistency requirement is shown in Section 5.1. We then sketch our Dolev-Yao version of XOR, in particular the extensions compared with current models in the literature that we need to overcome the secrecy problem from Section 2. Afterwards, we sketch the cryptographic realization of this XOR and the security statement that combines reactive simulatability with passive attacks and the type-consistency requirement. The details of the Dolev-Yao version, the realization, and the simulator are available in a long version; they require significant introduction of notation from the underlying reactively simulatable Dolev-Yao-style model from [8].

## 5.1   The Necessity of Correct Type Conversions

The largest difficulty with XOR even in the passive case is typing. XORs can yield arbitrary bitstrings, while otherwise it seems necessary for achieving reactive simulatability that a Dolev-Yao model is strongly typed. The reason is that the Dolev-Yao model must make a decision what happens if a destructor is applied to a term that is not properly constructed, e.g., if decryption is applied to a term that is not encrypted at all or with a different key. The only result that seems consistently realizable with real cryptosystems is to prescribe that the result is an error. In other words, the terms are considered typed, and many operations (in particular destructors) yield errors when applied to wrong types. In the cryptographic implementation, this must be realized by explicit type tags.

For an XOR, however, the algebraic equations like commutativity and associativity are considered essential, and they apply to pure bitstrings, not to bitstrings with type tags. The real problem with this typing, however, occurs when converting an XOR back into the original element type. This is a standard situation when XOR is used for explicit or implicit encryption: At some time, the subterms in an XOR cancel out except for one; typically random strings cancel out and one term of another type remains, e.g., payload data. This subterm must be usable by its recipient according to its original type. This is easy to realize in the Dolev-Yao model because one can retain the knowledge of the original type of the subterm. However, in a real, distributed cryptographic system, this is not possible: When two terms are XORed, we cannot reliably decide whether the result is of an underlying type. This is obvious if we remove all type tags before XORing (which is one possibility, and comes closest to typical message formats in XORs). It is also true if we XOR base types with their type tags, e.g., data for payloads and sig for a signature, because these tags can occur by chance when XORing arbitrary strings. Then a participant in the cryptographic realization would get a result (e.g., a payload message) which is totally unpredictable in the Dolev-Yao model; this destroys reactive simulatability. One natural solution to circumvent this problem is to forbid wrong typecasts on the user layer. This may sound like a strong restriction, but actually XOR is an operation that a cryptographic library should not offer to end users (e.g., a mail program), but only to cryptographic protocols. For protocols it is usually clear what types are expected at what times, and when one expects to be able to extract some payload from an XOR. Correct behavior in this sense can be verified on the protocol layer if we only allow passive attacks.

## 5.2   The Dolev-Yao-Style XOR

The main new operation for honest users is the XOR itself, called XOR. In our Dolev-Yao model it is implemented with immediate normalization, i.e., if terms $m_1, \ldots, m_j$ are XORed, all those that are XORs themselves are replaced by their parameter lists. The resulting overall parameter list is sorted and duplicates are canceled, i.e., parameters occurring an even number of times disappear and those occurring an odd number of times only occur once.

Honest users can also ask to have an XOR converted back to a different type $x$ by a command conv_xor_to_$x$. This only works if the XOR term (which is normalized) has only one parameter of the correct type.

Finally, honest users can generate nonces of variable length. These are like normal nonce terms with an additional leaf for the length; they are useful for hiding arbitrary other terms in XORs. (The notion of abstract lengths of the underlying library [8] enables protocols to choose the correct lengths.)

The most interesting part is to correctly implement the adversary capability of parsing certain XOR terms; in the underlying model this becomes part of the general command adv_parse available to the adversary. As in other Dolev-Yao models of XOR, this capability depends on previously obtained XORs because a corresponding real adversary may perform linear algebra on the different XORs, which correspond to different linear combinations of the base terms. In addition, we allow the ideal adversary to parse XORs of non-random types as explained in Section 2. Finally, we have to consider that nonces can only hide other terms if they are long enough.

For the linear algebra needed for these goals, we define matrices over $GF(2)$ representing released XORs. Each column of a matrix corresponds to a released XOR and the rows to the existing terms. A coefficient 1 indicates that the term is a top-level parameter in the XOR. We also make a column for each released individual random value. Matrix $A$ indicates the non-random components in each XOR, while $R^{(l)}$ for each $l \in \mathbb{N}$ indicates the random components of length at least $l$, and $\bar{R}^{(l)}$ those of length less than $l$.

We now sketch the algorithm for parsing an XOR term $m$; the corresponding algorithms for nonces are a much simpler version of this.

- Let $(x_1, \ldots, x_h)$ be the arguments of the given term $m$. Let $l$ be the maximum length of a term $x_i$ that is neither random nor yet known to the adversary, i.e., a term to be protected.
- Let $a$, $r^{(l)}$, and $\bar{r}^{(l)}$ denote the vectors that this newly parsed XOR will add to the matrices $A$, $R^{(l)}$, and $\bar{R}^{(l)}$, respectively. Try to solve the equation $R^{(l)}b = r^{(l)}$.
- If no such $b$ exists, the adversary does not learn any new information from this XOR.
- Otherwise let $d := Ab \oplus a$ and $r' := \bar{R}^{(l)}b \oplus \bar{r}^{(l)}$. These are the linear combination of XORs, including the new one, for which we just saw that the random components of at least length $l$ cancel out. Hence we let the ideal adversary learn the non-random terms designated by the vector $d$ and the short random terms designated by the vector $r'$.

### 5.3  Concrete Realization of the Dolev-Yao-Style XOR

In the cryptographic realization, individual machines $M_u$ of individual users operate on real cryptographic bitstrings. As discussed in Section 5.1, these bitstrings are typed in [8], and this is simply done by initial type tags. Whenever several typed bitstrings are XORed, we first remove their type tags, bring all remaining bitstrings to equal length by prepending zeroes, XOR these equal-length bitstrings, and finally prepend a tag xor to the resulting bitstring.

### 5.4  Soundness of the Abstraction

Our security claim is that the cryptographic realization from [8] extended with XOR as sketched in Section 5.3 is as secure as the Dolev-Yao-style model from [8] extended by XOR as sketched in Section 5.2 in the sense of blackbox simulatability, provided that the adversary is restricted to passive attacks and that the surrounding protocol ensures that XORs are only converted if they consist of a single element and the conversion matches the type of this element. We call the latter property of a configuration *correct XOR conversion*, or short CorrXOR.

The rigorous presentation of this property would again need a lot of additional notation from [8], but the essence is simple: For a given trace of the Dolev-Yao style system (i.e., a sequence of inputs, outputs, and states), we say that CorrXOR holds iff for all inputs of the command conv_xor_to_x made by honest users the preconditions of this command described in Section 5.2 are fulfilled. In other words, the honest users only ask for type conversions that the Dolev-Yao model can actually make. We now say that a user machine H fulfills CorrXOR if all traces of the Dolev-Yao model running in interaction with H, independent of the adversary, fulfill CorrXOR. Reactive simulatability with correct XOR conversion means that the comparison of the Dolev-Yao model and the cryptographic realization (see Figure 1) is only made for these users.

Passive attacks in the underlying model can be defined as follows. First, no machines of the cryptographic realization are corrupted. Secondly, all channels are authentic; this is a well-defined notion in the underlying model. The proof of soundness still works if we relax the authenticity restriction by allowing message re-ordering, re-routing, and duplication, i.e., by solely requiring that the adversary only sends messages that it previously received from an honest participant.

For proving reactive simulatability for the original Dolev-Yao-style model and realization without XOR, a simulator Sim has been defined in [8]. We sketch in the long version how we extend the simulator and the proof of correct simulation to deal with XOR.

# 6    Conclusion and Outlook

We have shown that Dolev-Yao models augmented by XOR, the simplest operation with algebraic equations in many formal methods and automated tools for cryptographic protocol proofs, cannot be realized by actual cryptographic libraries in a way that is at the same time natural, secure, and usable without restrictions. Our first result shows that *typical* Dolev-Yao models with XOR are not sound with respect to any secrecy definition; here we only assume that the Dolev-Yao model contains at least a payload data type and allows XORs on it.

The intuitive goal of our more complex results is to show that *no* Dolev-Yao model with usual cryptographic operations and XOR can be securely implemented in the sense of reactive simulatability/UC, i.e., in the sense that the realization can be safely plugged in for the abstraction in arbitrary environments and for arbitrary goals. As there is no formal definition of what is and isn't a Dolev-Yao model, and as the result would certainly not hold if we also called cryptographic realizations Dolev-Yao models, we have approached this intuitive goal by a series of results that make certain precise assumptions about Dolev-Yao models as well as real XORs, and then show impossibility.

On the positive side, we have presented a Dolev-Yao-style model with XOR that has a cryptographic realization secure against passive attacks if the surrounding protocol additionally guarantees that no incorrect conversions of XORs back into other types are attempted.

As future work, we expect that there are possibilities for positive results also under active attacks by strong restrictions on the protocol class or the security properties required, i.e., by no longer requiring reactive simulatability between the Dolev-Yao model as such and its realization. However, we believe that our impossibility results pose severe limits on the applicability of formal methods for XOR and cryptography when ultimately a cryptographically sound implementation is desired. The results certainly also prove that one cannot simply add operations with algebraic properties to a Dolev-Yao model if one aims at general secure realizations, even if the operation on its own seems simple and well characterized by its algebraic properties, as XOR is. We actually believe that the difficulties we had with XOR are not an exception, but the norm. However, this remains future work, except that the results trivially generalize to the Abelian groups $\mathbb{Z}_{2^l}$, into which bitstrings can be bijectively mapped.

## References

1. M. Abadi, B. Blanchet, and C. Fournet. Just fast keying in the pi calculus. In *Proc. 13th European Symposium on Programming (ESOP)*, volume 2986 of *Lecture Notes in Computer Science*, pages 340–354. Springer, 2004.
2. M. Abadi and V. Cortier. Deciding knowledge in security protocols under equational theories. In *Proc. 31st International Colloquium on Automata, Languages and Programming (ICALP)*, volume 3124 of *Lecture Notes in Computer Science*, pages 46–58. Springer, 2004.
3. M. Abadi and J. Jürjens. Formal eavesdropping and its computational interpretation. In *Proc. 4th International Symposium on Theoretical Aspects of Computer Software (TACS)*, pages 82–94, 2001.
4. M. Abadi and P. Rogaway. Reconciling two views of cryptography: The computational soundness of formal encryption. In *Proc. 1st IFIP International Conference on Theoretical Computer Science*, volume 1872 of *Lecture Notes in Computer Science*, pages 3–22. Springer, 2000.
5. M. Backes. A cryptographically sound Dolev-Yao style security proof of the Otway-Rees protocol. In *Proc. 10th European Symposium on Research in Computer Security (ESORICS)*, volume 3193 of *Lecture Notes in Computer Science*, pages 89–108. Springer, 2004.
6. M. Backes and B. Pfitzmann. A cryptographically sound security proof of the Needham-Schroeder-Lowe public-key protocol. *IEEE Journal on Selected Areas in Communications*, 22(10):2075–2086, 2004.
7. M. Backes and B. Pfitzmann. Symmetric encryption in a simulatable Dolev-Yao style cryptographic library. In *Proc. 17th IEEE Computer Security Foundations Workshop (CSFW)*, 2004. Full version in IACR Cryptology ePrint Archive 2004/059, Feb. 2004, http://eprint.iacr.org/.
8. M. Backes, B. Pfitzmann, and M. Waidner. A composable cryptographic library with nested operations (extended abstract). In *Proc. 10th ACM Conference on Computer and Communications Security*, pages 220–230, 2003. Full version in IACR Cryptology ePrint Archive 2003/015, Jan. 2003, http://eprint.iacr.org/.
9. M. Backes, B. Pfitzmann, and M. Waidner. Symmetric authentication within a simulatable cryptographic library. In *Proc. 9th European Symposium on Research in Computer Security (ESORICS)*, volume 2808 of *Lecture Notes in Computer Science*, pages 271–290. Springer, 2003. Extended version in IACR Cryptology ePrint Archive 2003/145, Jul. 2003, http://eprint.iacr.org/.
10. D. Basin, S. Mödersheim, and L. Viganò. OFMC: A symbolic model checker for security protocols. *International Journal of Information Security*, 2004.
11. M. Baudet, V. Cortier, and S. Kremer. Computationally sound implementations of equational theories against passive adversaries. In *Proc. 32nd International Colloquium on Automata, Languages and Programming (ICALP)*, volume 3580 of *Lecture Notes in Computer Science*, pages 652–663. Springer, 2005.
12. D. Beaver. Secure multiparty protocols and zero knowledge proof systems tolerating a faulty minority. *Journal of Cryptology*, 4(2):75–122, 1991.
13. M. Bellare, R. Guérin, and P. Rogaway. XOR MACs: New methods for message authentication using finite pseudorandom functions. In *Advances in Cryptology: CRYPTO '95*, volume 963 of *Lecture Notes in Computer Science*, pages 15–28. Springer, 1995.

14. R. Canetti. Security and composition of multiparty cryptographic protocols. *Journal of Cryptology*, 3(1):143–202, 2000.
15. R. Canetti. Universally composable security: A new paradigm for cryptographic protocols. In *Proc. 42nd IEEE Symposium on Foundations of Computer Science (FOCS)*, pages 136–145, 2001. Extended version in Cryptology ePrint Archive, Report 2000/67, http://eprint.iacr.org/.
16. R. Canetti and J. Herzog. Universally composable symbolic analysis of cryptographic protocols (the case of encryption-based mutual authentication and key exchange). Cryptology ePrint Archive, Report 2004/334, 2004. http://eprint.iacr.org/.
17. Y. Chevalier, R. Küsters, M. Rusinowitch, and M. Turuani. Deciding the security of protocols with Diffie-Hellman exponentiation and products in exponents. In *Proc. 23rd Conference on Foundations of Software Technology and Theoretical Computer Science (FSTTCS)*, pages 124–135, 2003.
18. Y. Chevalier, R. Küsters, M. Rusinowitch, and M. Turuani. An NP decision procedure for protocol insecurity with XOR. In *Proc. 18th Annual IEEE Symposium on Logic in Computer Science (LICS)*, pages 261–270, 2003.
19. H. Comon-Lundh and V. Shmatikov. Intruder deductions, constraint solving and insecurity decision in presence of exclusive or. In *Proc. 18th Annual IEEE Symposium on Logic in Computer Science (LICS)*, pages 271–280, 2003.
20. H. Comon-Lundh and R. Treinen. Easy intruder deductions. Research Report LSV-03-8, Laboratoire Spécification et Vérification, ENS Cachan, France, Apr. 2003.
21. A. Datta, A. Derek, J. C. Mitchell, and D. Pavlovic. A derivation system for security protocols and its logical formalization. In *Proc. 16th IEEE Computer Security Foundations Workshop (CSFW)*, pages 109–125, 2003.
22. S. Delaune and F. Jacquemard. Narrowing-based constraint solving for the verification of security protocols. Research Report LSV-04-8, Laboratoire Spécification et Vérification, ENS Cachan, France, Apr. 2004.
23. D. Denning. *Cryptography and Data Security*. Addison-Wesley, 1982.
24. D. Dolev and A. C. Yao. On the security of public key protocols. *IEEE Transactions on Information Theory*, 29(2):198–208, 1983.
25. O. Goldreich, S. Micali, and A. Wigderson. How to play any mental game – or – a completeness theorem for protocols with honest majority. In *Proc. 19th Annual ACM Symposium on Theory of Computing (STOC)*, pages 218–229, 1987.
26. S. Goldwasser and L. Levin. Fair computation of general functions in presence of immoral majority. In *Advances in Cryptology: CRYPTO '90*, volume 537 of *Lecture Notes in Computer Science*, pages 77–93. Springer, 1990.
27. D. Kapur, P. Narendran, and L. Wang. An e-unification algorithm for analyzing protocols that use modular exponentiation. In *Proc. 14th International Conference on Rewriting Techniques and Applications (RTA)*, pages 165–179, 2003.
28. H. Krawczyk. LFSR-based hashing and authentication. In *Advances in Crptology: CRYPTO '94*, volume 839 of *Lecture Notes in Computer Science*, pages 129–139. Springer, 1994.
29. P. Laud. Semantics and program analysis of computationally secure information flow. In *Proc. 10th European Symposium on Programming (ESOP)*, pages 77–91, 2001.
30. P. Laud. *Computationally Secure Information Flow*. PhD thesis, Universität des Saarlandes, 2002. http://www.cs.ut.ee/~peeter_l/research/csif/lqpp.ps.gz.
31. P. Laud. Pseudorandom permutations and equivalence of formal expressions (abstract). In *14th Nordic Workshop on Programming Theory*, pages 63–65, 2002.
32. P. Laud. Symmetric encryption in automatic analyses for confidentiality against active adversaries. In *Proc. 25th IEEE Symposium on Security & Privacy*, pages 71–85, 2004.

33. P. Lincoln, J. Mitchell, M. Mitchell, and A. Scedrov. A probabilistic poly-time framework for protocol analysis. In *Proc. 5th ACM Conference on Computer and Communications Security*, pages 112–121, 1998.

34. C. Meadows. Using narrowing in the analysis of key management protocols. In *Proc. 10th IEEE Symposium on Security & Privacy*, pages 138–147, 1989.

35. C. Meadows. A model of computation for the NRL protocol analyzer. In *Proc. 7th IEEE Computer Security Foundations Workshop (CSFW)*, pages 84–89, 1994.

36. C. Meadows and P. Narendran. A unification algorithm for the group Diffie-Hellman protocol. In *Proc. WITS*, 2002.

37. S. Micali and P. Rogaway. Secure computation. In *Advances in Cryptology: CRYPTO '91*, volume 576 of *Lecture Notes in Computer Science*, pages 392–404. Springer, 1991.

38. D. Micciancio and B. Warinschi. Soundness of formal encryption in the presence of active adversaries. In *Proc. 1st Theory of Cryptography Conference (TCC)*, volume 2951 of *Lecture Notes in Computer Science*, pages 133–151. Springer, 2004.

39. J. Millen. The Interrogator model. In *Proc. 16th IEEE Symposium on Security & Privacy*, pages 251–260, 1995.

40. J. Millen. CAPSL: Common Authentication Protocol Specification Language. Technical Report MP 97B48, The MITRE Corporation, 1997.

41. J. Millen and V. Shmatikov. Symbolic protocol analysis with products and Diffie-Hellman exponentiation. In *Proc. 16th IEEE Computer Security Foundations Workshop (CSFW)*, pages 47–61, 2003.

42. L. Paulson. The inductive approach to verifying cryptographic protocols. *Journal of Cryptology*, 6(1):85–128, 1998.

43. B. Pfitzmann and M. Waidner. Composition and integrity preservation of secure reactive systems. In *Proc. 7th ACM Conference on Computer and Communications Security*, pages 245–254, 2000. Extended version (with Matthias Schunter) IBM Research Report RZ 3206, May 2000, http://www.semper.org/sirene/publ/PfSW1_00ReactSimulIBM.ps.gz.

44. B. Pfitzmann and M. Waidner. A model for asynchronous reactive systems and its application to secure message transmission. In *Proc. 22nd IEEE Symposium on Security & Privacy*, pages 184–200, 2001. Extended version of the model (with Michael Backes) IACR Cryptology ePrint Archive 2004/082, http://eprint.iacr.org/.

45. A. T. Sherman and D. A. McGrew. Key establishment in large dynamic groups using one-way function trees. *IEEE Transactions on Software Engineering*, 29(5):444–458, 2003.

46. V. Shmatikov. Decidable analysis of cryptographic protocols with products and modular exponentiation. In *Proc. 13th European Symposium on Programming (ESOP)*, volume 2986 of *Lecture Notes in Computer Science*, pages 355–369. Springer, 2004.

47. A. C. Yao. Theory and applications of trapdoor functions. In *Proc. 23rd IEEE Symposium on Foundations of Computer Science (FOCS)*, pages 80–91, 1982.

# Security-Typed Languages for Implementation of Cryptographic Protocols: A Case Study

Aslan Askarov and Andrei Sabelfeld

Dept. of Computer Science, Chalmers University of Technology, 41296 Göteborg, Sweden
{aaskarov, andrei}@cs.chalmers.se

**Abstract.** Security protocols are critical for protecting modern communication infrastructures and are therefore subject to thorough analysis. However practical implementations of these protocols lack the same level of attention and thus may be more exposed to attacks. This paper discusses security assurance provided by security-typed languages when implementing cryptographic protocols. Our results are based on a case study using Jif, a Java-based security-typed language, for implementing a non-trivial cryptographic protocol that allows playing online poker without a trusted third party. The case study deploys the largest program written in a security-typed language to date and identifies insights ranging from security guarantees to useful patterns of secure programming.

## 1 Introduction

Networked commerce, health, and military applications critically depend on underlying security protocols. Malicious attacks on these systems target vulnerabilities of two basic kinds—vulnerabilities of protocols and vulnerabilities of protocol implementations. Although the first kind of vulnerabilities is dangerous, the descriptions of security protocols are often open to public and are subject to thorough analysis by security experts. As a result, discovering and exploiting protocol-level weaknesses is significantly more daunting than attacking flaws in protocol implementations (cf. the need for a paradigm shift in cryptology [4]). This is also confirmed by CERT® incident reports where most of exploited flaws come from inadequate implementations. In the context of protocols, recent discoveries of multiple vulnerabilities in different implementations of the well studied SSL/TLS protocols [1] uncover insecure implementations that can be exploited to allow a remote attacker to execute arbitrary code.

To defend against implementation-level attacks, modern security technology relies on common principles for building secure software [47], including prudent techniques for deploying cryptographic software [23]. Moreover, since the paradigm shift in cryptology, much work has been done on timing, cache, power-consumption, and other implementation-level attacks. Nevertheless, the resulting principles and techniques are somewhat ad-hoc; they provide no end-to-end guarantees that systems preserve the confidentiality of secret data. For example, these principles and techniques provide little help in preventing an accidental leak of a secret key to a public field, or revealing a secret bid in an online auction before all participants have committed their bids. These are examples of undesired information flows that compromise confidentiality.

S. De Capitani di Vimercati et al. (Eds.): ESORICS 2005, LNCS 3679, pp. 197–221, 2005.

Security-typed languages have emerged over the past decade as an attractive approach to preventing insecure information flows (see [39] for a survey). These languages allow labeling sensitive data with security levels (naturally extending conventional types to *security types*). Security type systems regulate flows between data at different security levels, providing tight control over information flow.

Recent developments [33, 5, 37] raise hope for the possibility of regulating the propagation of sensitive information by security type systems in realistic languages. Furthermore, compilers for these languages such as Jif [36] (based on Java) and Flow-Caml [45] (based on Caml) have been developed. Nevertheless, "despite this large body of literature and considerable, ongoing attention from the research community, information-flow based enforcement mechanisms have not been widely (or even narrowly!) used" [48].

The challenge is whether security-typed languages scale up to real systems. In particular:

- *How helpful are security types for identifying potential insecurities in security-critical code?*
- *How laborious is the process of security typing? Does it force unnecessary restrictions on code?*
- *Is the security assurance provided by security types transparent enough?*
- *What is the general balance of benefits and drawbacks when using security-typed languages?*

Addressing these challenges seems impossible without practical experience in deploying security-typed languages. Motivated by this, we have performed an in-depth case study of securing an implementation of a non-trivial cryptographic protocol in the security-typed language Jif. To the best of our knowledge, this implementation is the largest program written in a security-typed language so far.

The focus of the case study is a protocol for online poker without a trusted third party (also known as *mental poker* [44]). This protocol has direct application in e-gambling, but it is also generally interesting because its security goals are similar to those of many other protocols. These goals include confidentiality in an environment of mutual distrust (in the absence of a trusted third party), auditability, fairness, and detection of cheating with high probability. This gives us a range of security properties that are useful in security-critical applications. For example, in online voting, it is important that every vote remains confidential yet the result (such as the number of votes for each candidate) becomes known to the public after the election is over. Besides confidentiality, a form of auditability is a desired security property here—it should be possible to recount the results. Another example with similar goals is an online auction protocol with mutual distrust. Participants reveal their secret bids only when the bidding phase has been completed. That the participants cannot alter their bids in the verification phase is also a form of auditability.

It is worth mentioning that the threat model adopted in this paper does not include covert channels that are due to probabilistic, timing, power-consumption, and cache behavior. Neither integrity nor availability issues are treated in our setting. While these restrictions are inherited from Jif's threat model, they are not fundamental to security-typed languages. Indeed, there are such languages capable of treating various covert channels [3, 41], as well as integrity [25, 49] and availability [51].

The case study has been conducted in three steps. First, we have implemented a baseline implementation in a conventional programming language (Java). Second, we have lifted this implementation to Jif. Finally, we have distributed the Jif implementation in order to simulate a realistic scenario where players run their parts of the protocol on their respective machines.

The case study has resulted in a range of insights into the challenges above (whose summary we defer to the conclusion). Further, the case study has suggested the need for richer mechanisms of information release (currently lacking not only in Jif but in most available information flow analyses). Additionally, we have developed patterns for secure programming that help streamline the process of security typing. Furthermore, we have uncovered some vulnerabilities and problems in Jif that lead to interesting directions for improvements.

The rest of the paper is organized as follows. Section 2 provides some background about the protocol for mental poker and the Jif language. Section 3 discusses the three different implementations. The lessons learned from the case study are reported in Section 4. Section 5 presents some programming patterns that have emerged from our experience in security-typed programming. Section 6 comments on related work. Section 7 concludes the paper.

## 2   Background

This section contains necessary background on protocols for mental poker and an introduction to security-typed languages and Jif.

### 2.1   Protocols for Mental Poker

**Mental poker.** In the popular card game of poker players with fully or partially concealed cards make wagers into a central pot. After several rounds of betting the pot is awarded to the remaining player or players with the best combination of cards. Mental poker is a well-known problem in cryptography on how to "play a fair game of poker [. . . ] over the phone" [44] or how to play poker without a trusted third party (TTP). This problem continues to attract researchers and many solutions have been proposed [22, 12, 13, 29, 28, 43, 8, 6].

Crépeau has outlined some objectives for mental poker [12], summarized as follows:

1. Uniqueness of cards: every card must appear exactly once—either in the deck or in the hand of one player. This property can only be broken as a result of detectable cheating.
2. Uniform distribution of cards: the hand of each player must be possible with equal probability and must depend on decisions made by every player.
3. Absence of TTP: players trust neither each other nor any third party.
4. Cheating detection with high probability: the probability that a player may cheat without being detected must decrease fast (exponentially) with respect to some

security parameter that the players must agree on before the game. Also, the amount of work to accomplish the protocol should increase reasonably (polynomially) with respect to this parameter.

5. Complete confidentiality of cards: no information about any card from the deck may be obtained without the approval of every opponent. Also, no information may be obtained from a player's hand without his or her approval.

6. Minimal effect of coalitions: when more than two players are involved, some players could establish secret communication and exchange all their knowledge about the game. Nonetheless they should not be able to learn more than what they can deduce from the cards in their coalition.

7. Confidentiality of strategy: losing players may keep their cards secret at the end of a game.

Although protocols that claim to achieve all these properties have been proposed [13, 29, 28], they are demanding to computation time and are unacceptable in practice [18, 24]. For our case study, we have adopted a protocol by Castellà-Roca et al. [8] that achieves these properties (with the exception of the last one) and is practical in terms of computational requirements.

**Castellà-Roca et al. TTP-free protocol.** In this protocol all players cooperate in shuffling, so that no player coalition can force a particular outcome. Every player generates a random permutation of the card deck and keeps it secret; the player then commits this permutation using a bit commitment protocol. The shuffled deck is formed by the composition of all players' permutations.

Turning a physical card face down corresponds to encryption. Shuffling a card corresponds to a mathematical operation over the card's representation. The protocol uses an additive and multiplicative homomorphic cryptosystem, such as [17], to shuffle a deck of cards and maintain the privacy of the cards. The outcome of permuting an encrypted card and decrypting it is the same as if the card had been permuted without prior encryption.

When the game is over, the players reveal their encryption keys and permutations for validation. Requiring the disclosure of players' strategies after the game is a limitation of this protocol. On the other hand, it raises an interesting security goal of preventing hand revelation earlier in the game.

### 2.2   Security-Typed Languages and Jif

**Secure information flow.** Information flow from object $x$ to object $y$ occurs whenever the value of $y$ is affected by the value of $x$. *Explicit flows* are results of assignment statements (e.g., y=x), I/O statements, and value returns by functions. The flow in these cases is caused by the operation explicitly; whether the operation is reached during execution does not necessarily depend on the value of $x$. By contrast, *implicit flows* [16] occur whenever $x$ affects $y$ through control flow, i.e., the execution of a statement that updates $y$ depends on $x$. For example, in the fragment y = 1; if (x == 0) y = 0, the if statement causes an implicit flow from variable $x$ to $y$.

The problem of information flow is relevant for security if, for instance, $x$ stores sensitive information and $y$ is a public system output. In this case, the control of how sensitive information propagates in the program is crucial for protecting confidentiality. Generally, program data can be associated with *security levels*, which constitute a *security lattice* [15]. The higher the security level is located in the lattice the more sensitive information is associated with this level. Figure 1 presents two

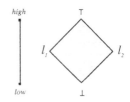

**Fig. 1.** Examples of lattices

examples of lattices: a two-element lattice with *high* and *low* levels corresponding to secret and public information; and a four-element lattice with a public element $\bot$, a top secret element $\top$, and two mutually incomparable intermediate elements $\ell_1$ and $\ell_2$. Information flow is considered *secure* if the level of the flow target is higher than (or the same as) the level of the flow origin.

**Decentralized label model.** The decentralized label model (DLM) [34] is a security model in which *principals* express their privacy concerns via *labels*. Principals in DLM (e.g., users, groups, and roles) may own, update, and release information. Labels are used to guarantee confidentiality. Every label consists of a set of *policies* that express privacy requirements. A privacy policy has two parts: an owner and a set of readers; and is written in the form *owner:readers*. By definition, an owner is implicitly contained in its readers set. A principal is allowed to read data if and only if it is contained in the reader sets of all policies of the label attached to the data.

**Jif.** Jif [33, 36] is an extension of the Java language with DLM labels. In Jif, methods can be granted *authority* to act for some set of principals. Authority regulates the ability of a method to *declassify* (or downgrade) the data: weaken or remove a policy in a label. This is possible if a policy is owned by a principal that is a part of the process authority.

An example of a label written in Jif syntax is {Alice:Bob,Carol;}. This label contains a single policy in which Alice is the owner; and Alice, Bob, and Carol are the readers. The label {Bob:Alice;Alice:Carol;} contains two policies. In this label Alice is the only principal present among readers of both policies. Hence, only Alice can read the data.

Variable types in Jif are composed of two parts: a regular Java type, such as boolean, and a security label, indicating how the value stored in this variable may propagate. For instance, the type boolean{Alice:Bob} represents a boolean that Alice owns and Alice and Bob can read. The bottom security level corresponding to public data has label {} (with the empty list of policies).

In security-typed languages implicit flows are often controlled by the *program-counter label (pc)*. This label tracks dependencies of the program counter. Recall an example given earlier (displayed in Listing 1) with some variable definitions. Here, the pc in the branch of the if

```
int {Alice:} x;
int {} y = 1;
...
if (x == 0) y = 0;
```

**Listing 1.** Implicit flow

statement captures the dependency on $x$ and, thus, has label {Alice:}. The assignment statement is rejected by the compiler because the variable $y$ is less secure than the pc.

*Method declarations and constraints.* Method declarations in Jif may be annotated with two optional labels, called *begin-label* and *end-label*. Begin-label is a lower bound on the side effects of a method. That is, Jif prevents calling a method if pc at the invocation point is higher than the begin-label of the method being invoked. By default, if no begin-label is specified, it is assumed that the method has no side effects and can be called regardless of pc of the caller (i.e., from any context). A method's end-label carries information about how much can be learned by observing if the method terminates normally or raises an exception. After the method invocation, pc of the caller is affected by the end-label of the method that has been called.

Arguments and return values can also be labeled with their security levels. An example of a method declaration is:

```
public boolean{Alice:Bob} validate{Alice:}(String{} s, int{} hash):{Alice:}
```

In this example, the function `validate` takes two arguments both of which are of the bottom security level. The return value has label `{Alice:Bob}`. Both the begin- and end-labels are `{Alice:}`.

Jif methods may contain a list of *constraints* prefixed by the keyword `where`. Two kinds of constraints are useful for our purposes: (i) `authority($p_1,\ldots,p_n$)`, listing principals that this method is authorized to act for, and (ii) `caller($p_1,\ldots,p_n$)`, listing principals whose authority the caller of the method is required to possess in order to run this method. We return to some security implications of these constraints in Section 5.4.

*Exceptions.* In contrast to Java, Jif disallows unchecked runtime exceptions. Consider the program (which is rejected by the Jif compiler) in Listing 2. If variable `secret` is zero, `ArithemeticException` is thrown by the method `div`. Observing whether this exception takes place would expose some information about the value of `secret`.

```
public class IntegerLeak {
    private int {Alice:} secret;
    public int{Alice:} div(int{} a) {
        return a/secret;
    }
}
```

**Listing 2.** Flow via exception

*Parameterized classes.* Jif classes and interfaces can be parameterized over labels and principals. This is useful for building reusable data structures. For instance, instead of writing two separate `Player` classes for Alice and Bob, which would only differentiate in the labels of the corresponding variables, one can write a single class `Player[P]` parameterized over principal variable P. Later in the instantiation, this parameter is replaced by the actual principal (e.g., Alice or Bob).

```
class X[label L] {
    private int {L} p;
    public int{L} getP() {return this.p;}
    public void setP{L} (int {L} n) {
        this.p = n;
    }
}
```

**Listing 3.** Parameterized class

Listing 3 displays an example of a Jif class parameterized over label L. This label is used in the declaration of class fields, such as p, and methods, such as `getP()` and `setP()`. An example of how this class can be instantiated with label `{Alice:}` is `X[{Alice:}]{Alice:} x = new X[{Alice:}]()`. Note the two labels that appear in the declaration of the variable x. The first one is a parameter of the class, while the second is the label of the referring variable.

*Array labels.* Being mutable data containers, arrays have two labels: one for the elements of an array, and the other for the array itself and its length. A single label for arrays would allow *laundering attacks* (i.e., code that exploits a vulnerability in a protection mechanism in order to leak more information than intended). Assume that arrays only had a single label. A variable `indeck` of type `int[]{}` with a single label `{}` could be assigned to a variable `hand` typed `int[]{Alice:}`. Then it would be safe to assign a variable `cardvalue` labeled `{Alice:}` to an element of array hand. However, this value would become visible through the variable `indeck`. This provides an illustration of a laundering attack.

An example array declaration is `int{Alice:}[]{}` hand. This array denotes Alice's hand of cards. The length of the array has the bottom label (`{}`); indeed, it is publicly known *how many* cards a player has. In contrast, the *values* of the actual cards are secret for others. Therefore, the elements of the array are labeled as `{Alice:}`.

*Declassification.* Many secrets have their lifetimes, after which they are not secrets anymore. Controlled information release or *declassification* is an important aspect of security-typed languages. It is safe to move data to a higher position in the security lattice. However, declassification relabels program variables so that the resulting label can be *less* restrictive than the original. Declassification in Jif is expressed via `declassify` statements. The process is required to have sufficient authority to declassify data. For example, to declassify a variable x of type `int{Alice:}` to `int{}` a process is required to have the authority of Alice. An example of a declassification statement is `y = declassify(x,{})`. Here, the `declassify` statement returns the value of $x$ relabeled to `{}`, which is assigned to $y$.

# 3    Implementation

This section discusses the three different implementations we have developed [2]. The baseline implementation is in Java, the two remaining ones are in Jif. For both Jif implementations we assume the presence of two principals Alice and Bob (without loss of generality we assume two players).

## 3.1    Java Baseline Implementation

One motivation for an implementation in Java is to set a baseline implementation that would have been produced by ordinary Java programmers. Another reason is that debugging Jif programs often becomes burdensome. The baseline implementation follows Castellà-Roca et al.'s protocol for two players (Alice and Bob). It can be straightforwardly extended to multiple players. In this implementation, we have developed the main functional part of the program. A player is represented by a class `Player`. This class contains the player's data (such as the name, the hand of cards, cryptographic keys, and the game log) and methods that implement initialization, card drawing, and ending protocols. These methods are called by the game coordination routines.

## 3.2  Jif Implementation

The second implementation lifts the Java version to Jif (as realized by the current distribution Jif 1.1.1). Following the security objectives, we have adopted the security lattice in Figure 2. The sensitive information of the players carries the labels {Alice:} and {Bob:}. The data passed between the players is downgraded to the bottom level ({}).

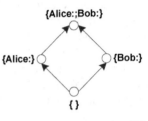

**Fig. 2.** Security lattice for Jif implementation

Lifting Java programs to Jif involves the following steps: (i) writing signatures for necessary Java API classes, (ii) changing some of the classes to Jif analogues, (iii) parameterizing classes over labels and principals, (iv) assigning labels to class fields, (v) assigning begin- and end-labels to functions and arguments, (vi) handling runtime exceptions, and (vii) writing helper functions for declassification of large data structures. Note that, there is no linear dependency in performing these steps—the process of lifting may (and is likely to) consist of a number of iterations and repetitive refactoring. Below we discuss these steps in detail.

*Writing signatures.* To compile against existing Java API classes, the Jif implementation needs Jif signatures for these classes. Although writing signatures is a relatively simple task compared to Jif programs, this should be done with care. It is possible to misuse this feature (see Section 4.4 on problems and vulnerabilities related to signatures).

*Changing to Jif analogues.* Writing class signatures for Java classes can be avoided if there is a Jif analogue providing the same functionality. For example, the Jif implementation uses jif.util.ArrayList instead of java.util.Vector. The former is written completely in Jif, which makes its usage both safer and more convenient.

*Parameterizing classes.* Class parameterization is heavily used by the Jif implementation. Most of the classes are parameterized over an invariant label L, which stands for the security level of the information stored in instances of these classes. The main class of the implementation Player[principal P, label L] is parameterized over the player principal P, and the label of the output channel L. Therefore, in this class the label {P:;L} corresponds to the high label and {L} to the low one.

*Assigning labels to class fields.* It is important to identify which variables contain sensitive information and how restrictive their labels should be. It is sometimes convenient to use high labels for low data, for example, when a low variable is only used in a high context.

*Assigning labels to functions and arguments.* Recall that begin- and end-labels in method declarations are related to side effects in the program: in this implementation we identify side effects in Jif programs by the following events: (i) assignment to a non-final member variable, (ii) assignment to a mutable data structure such as an array or a class, and (iii) calling a method with side effects.

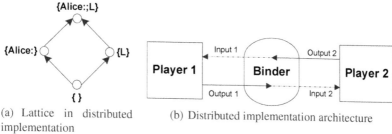

(a) Lattice in distributed implementation

(b) Distributed implementation architecture

**Fig. 3.** Distributed implementation

*Catching/throwing runtime exceptions.* Because unchecked exceptions may lead to information leaks, Jif requires runtime exceptions to be handled. Our Jif implementation uses the following disciplines:

- Declare and throw: an exception is declared in the method header and the responsibility to handle it is passed to the caller. However, this exception still has to be handled by the caller; moreover, its origin becomes obscured for the caller since it may be thrown at different points in the method.
- Avoiding exceptions: Jif compiler has a simple, yet useful, dataflow analysis that may detect if a local variable is null at a particular program point.
- Catch and ignore: there are two scenarios when a programmer might want to ignore an exception:
  - there are sufficient guarantees in the code that the exception may not be thrown, and
  - the programmer deliberately hides the presence of the exception.
- Catch and handle: exception may be handled, and a custom application exception is thrown by the method that contains information about the error.

The ArgCheck pattern (Section 5.1) describes how `NullPointerExceptions` caused by method arguments can be handled.

*Modularizing declassification.* See the Declassifier pattern in Section 5.2.

### 3.3 Distributed Jif Implementation

The third implementation has been developed to provide a "real-world" application of Jif. In this implementation players run as different processes and standard input/output is used as a communication medium.

Figure 3(a) displays the security lattice for one of the players (Alice). Here L is the label of the run-time environment. Sensitive variables in the program are labeled by {Alice:;L}. System outputs have the label {L}. The lattice for the other player's process is similar.

Figure 3(b) illustrates how the distribution works: two player processes communicate through a binding process so that I/O pipes of both processes are connected to that process.

The introduction of distribution to the Jif implementation involves these steps: (i) changing the logic of the coordinating process to take care of the distribution, (ii) writing helper classes for serialization of objects into strings and visa versa (strings can be easily exchanged by the processes), and (iii) writing a synchronization program that interconnects two processes via pipes.

## 4   Evaluation

This section reports on lessons we have learned from this case study. We compare the three implementations, evaluate security assurance provided by the security-typed implementations, discuss the role of declassification, and report some problems we have uncovered in Jif.

### 4.1   Comparison of the Three Implementations

**Java vs. Jif implementation.** Lifting Java programs to Jif is not straightforward. Section 5 presents useful programming patterns we have developed over the process of lifting. The Jif implementation is a result of successive refactoring iterations over the initial Java version. The main impact is caused by the security label annotations of program variables. These labels propagate further into the begin- and end-labels of the methods. Following this propagation, we have rewritten Java methods in such a way that the Jif version either repairs a discovered flow or declares it explicitly either via a declassification statement or via a method header. This technique increases assurance that the program protects the confidentiality of sensitive variables.

Explicit declassification helps specifying exactly which data is downgraded, who authorizes downgrading, and where in code it is downgraded. Thanks to declassification statements, intended leaks in the program are reduced to declassification points in the code. A detailed discussion of the declassification points in our implementation is presented later in this section.

Jif has helped uncover some insecurities in the Java implementation. Although it is not obvious how these particular insecurities can be exploited, they still represent potential vulnerabilities. One of the interesting insecurities we have discovered in the Java implementation is due to exceptions occurring at high security levels. Listing 4 illustrates this insecurity:

```
public class ExceptionLeak[label L] {
    private int{} readInput{}() { ... }
    public void exceptionLeak{}()  throws Exception{
        while (true) {
            int{} x = readInput();
            highMethod(x);
        }
    }
    private int{L} highDenominator;
    private int{L} highCounter;
    private int{L}[]{L} highArray;
    private void highMethod{}(int{} x)
    throws ArithmeticException, NullPointerException, ArrayIndexOutOfBoundsException {
        highArray[highCounter++] = x/highDenominator;
    }
}
```

**Listing 4.** Example of leaks via exceptions

Here, any of exceptions `ArrayIndexOutOfBoundsException`, `ArithmeticException`, or `NullPointerException` can be thrown in a high context reflecting problems in the high variables `highDenominator`, `highArray`, and `highCounter`. Therefore, the caller of `highMethod` on line 6 obtains information not only about the successful termination of the method but also details on what kind of exception has occurred and, in more complicated scenarios, the stack trace back to the origin of the exception! The SuccessFlag pattern (Section 5.5) describes how one can prevent such leaks.

**Jif vs. distributed Jif implementation.** While the second implementation reveals important security issues, the third one is more interesting from a practical point of view. From this perspective, the second implementation may be considered as an intermediate step toward the final distributed version. The second and third implementations have both been developed in Jif. Most of the code from the second implementation is reused in the third. Thus, the third implementation benefits from the security guarantees that are achieved in the second version and, in addition, is a simple, yet fully functional, example of a distributed program written in a security-typed language.

Because the distributed Jif implementation encompasses the features of the intermediate Jif implementation, the rest of the discussion refers to the distributed Jif implementation as the Jif implementation, unless specified otherwise.

## 4.2 Security Assurance

Recall from Section 2 the security objectives provided by the underlying protocol: (1) uniqueness of cards, (2) uniform distribution of cards, (3) absence of TTP, (4) cheating detection with high probability, (5) complete confidentiality of cards, and (6) minimal effect of coalitions. Although these objectives are addressed by protocol design, our goal is to ensure that the protocol implementation may not violate these objectives. Let us discuss how these objectives are addressed by the Jif implementation.

The first and the second properties rely on the random number generators, supported by Java API. The third property (absence of TTP), which is crucial to the protocol, is not broken by our implementation. Indeed, the implementation does not introduce a TTP as there are only two principals—the players. Cheating detection is supported in our implementation via logging the messages that players exchange. In the verification phase of the game this log is used to check if either of the players has cheated. Note that the sixth objective does not apply to a two-player implementation. For a multi-player extension, control over the propagation of sensitive information (as provided by the security-type system) is essential for minimizing the effect of coalitions.

The most interesting objective is the fifth one (complete confidentiality of cards). It is for this objective that we capitalize on using security types. Tight control of confidentiality is guaranteed by assigning high-security labels to the following program variables:

- instance of the cryptosystem that stores the secret key for homomorphic encryption;
- signature key used for signing messages;
- player's hand: decrypted values of the player's cards; and
- player's secret permutation (for commutative shuffling) and variables related to this permutation.

**Table 1.** Declassification points

| GR | POINT | WHAT | WHO | WHERE | WHEN |
|---|---|---|---|---|---|
| I | 1 | Public key for signature | Anyone | Initialization | Before game start, before seal is open |
| | 2 | Public security param | Player | Initialization | Before game start, before seal is open |
| II | 3 | Message signature | Player | Sending msg | Any time |
| | 4–7 | Protocol init data | Player | Initialization | Before game start, before seal is open |
| | 8–10 | Encrypted permuted card | Player | Card drawing | During game, before seal is open |
| III | 11 | Decryption flag | Player | Card drawing | During game, before seal is open, after player obtains card |
| IV | 12 | Player's secret encryption key | Player | Verification | After game end, after seal is open |
| | 13–14 | Player's secret permutation | Player | Verification | After game end, after seal is open |

Labeling these variables as high restricts the flow of sensitive data to public outputs. Jif's type system prevents unintended flows of sensitive information unless otherwise specified by `declassify` statements. This reduces the manual security analysis of the system down to inspection and justification of `declassify` statements in code. This is the subject of the following section.

### 4.3  Authority and Declassification

Label assignment reduces possibilities for information leaks to the program points where declassifications occur. Declassification is possible if the running process has enough authority to relabel the data. The ability to grant a class or a method authority is useful but also a potentially dangerous feature since this authority may be misused for inappropriate declassification of confidential information. The Jif implementation grants the authority of the player to the following two functions: (i) function that returns the public key of the player and (ii) function that coordinates the game process.

There are 14 declassification points in the main class of the Jif implementation. For each declassification Table 1 states *what* is declassified, *who* declassifies data, *where* in the program, and *when* declassification may occur (the last column uses the notion of seal defined in group IV below). These aspects correspond to dimensions of information release [42]. Accordingly, the declassification points can be naturally grouped as follows.

I Declassification of naturally public data (points 1–2). Functions for generating signature keys return `KeyPair` data structure. It contains both a private and a public component and, as a whole, is labeled as high. In order to return the public key, a separate high copy of the key has to be obtained and declassified. Similarly, the public parameter of the homomorphic cryptosystem is extracted from an instance of the cryptosystem. Again, we obtain a high copy of this parameter and declassify it separately. These declassifications are safe, since they affect neither the sensitive part of the key nor the secret parameter of the cryptosystem.

II Declassification following signatures and encryptions in the underlying protocol (points 3–10). This is the largest group of declassification points. The first such point is related to the digital signature of the messages. Because computation of the signature involves a private key, the result gets tainted by the high label of the private key and becomes high. Here we rely on the cryptographic properties of the calculated signature and assume it is safe to declassify the computed result. The obtained declassified signature is attached to the message.

The rest of the declassifications in this group are applied to encrypted values created in the context with a high pc label. The motivation for these declassifications is similar to the one for signatures. These declassifications are safe as far as we trust the underlying cryptographic protocol.

III Declassification of the success flag in finishCardDraw() (point 11). See the SuccessFlag pattern (Section 5.5) for motivation and details.

IV Declassification of sensitive information for verification (points 12–14): After a game completes, the protocol requires players to exchange their private keys and secret permutations in order to verify the fairness of each other. This is a common scenario for security protocols that rely on bit commitment. It is important that these functions are not used earlier than they are supposed to, i.e., it is important *when* information is downgraded. Jif's declassification mechanism is not powerful enough to support such temporal properties. Therefore, we introduce a so called *seal*, a boolean flag that changes its value at most once after initialization. The seal is initialized in the constructor of the Player class. Its integrity is checked in the methods that implement game protocols. The seal is *opened* once the sensitive information that it protects is released. This is done in the methods that declassify the keys and secret permutation. Next time there is a call to a method that assumes the seal's integrity, a runtime exception is thrown indicating that this call violates the security properties of the protocol. That is, one is not allowed to declassify data prematurely. Implementation details of the seal technique are presented in the section on patterns.

The artifact of four different categories of declassification (with independent reasons for justifying each of them) opens up the question of an adequate treatment of the multifaceted nature of declassification. In particular, there is need for enforcing temporal information release policies. This provides a basis for our future work (cf. Section 7).

## 4.4 Jif's Vulnerabilities and Problems

Many of the insights we have gathered in the case study are not Jif-specific. However, as Jif is the most ambitious security-typed language to date, it is useful to highlight some vulnerabilities and problems discovered in the Jif compiler.

**Signature misuse.** Jif uses existing Java libraries by means of class signatures. A signature is a file with Jif-style method declarations. Jif programs are type-checked against these headers, but pre-compiled Java binaries are used at runtime. An example of where we use Java API with Jif signatures is DSA signature scheme, which has internal random values that need to remain secret.

However, a flow can be easily introduced if labels declared in the method header do not correspond to the code in the library. An example of such a weakness is a signature of `System.arraycopy` function from the current Jif distribution.

```
public static native void arraycopy(Object{dst} src, int{dst} src_position, Object dst,
                                     int{dst} dst_position, int{dst} length)
throws (IndexOutOfBoundsException, ArrayStoreException, NullPointerException);
```

This method has no begin-label, which implies the absence of side effects. However, the copy of an array in the memory is an obvious side effect that should be reflected in the begin-label of the method. Listing 5 is an example of how this weakness can be exploited.

```
public class TestLeak[label L] {
    private int{L}[] secret;
    private int{}[] output;
    public void leak() {
        try { System.arraycopy(secret, 0, output, 0, secret.length);
        } catch (Exception ignored) { }
    }
}
```

**Listing 5.** Leakage via invalid method signature

In this example, function `leak()` calls `System.arraycopy` to copy data from the high array `secret` into the low array `output`. Nevertheless, this code is accepted by the Jif compiler since it trusts the provided method signature.

**Parameterized signatures.** Recall class X from Section 2.2 with label annotations erased to obtain a Java class. Listing 6 is an example of a vulnerable signature that can be written for such class.

```
class X {
    public native int {this} getP();
    public native void setP{this}(int{this}n);
}
```

**Listing 6.** Vulnerable signature for class

Here, `{this}` is a label of the current instance. This signature is exposed to the attack similar to the array-laundering attack from Section 2.2. However, this attack can be prevented by parameterizing the signature as it is shown in Listing 7.

Generally, a class should be parameterized if a variable of that class can be modified after the instantiation. While such flows are captured in pure Jif programs by the type system, they are not

```
class X[label L]{
    public native int {L} getP();
    public native void setP{L}(int{L} n);
}
```

**Listing 7.** Correct signature for class

prevented in class signatures. It is the author of a signature who is responsible for its correctness.

**Relabeling mutable data containers.** Assume there is an array x of type `int{}[]{}` which we want to relabel to type `int{Alice:}[]{Alice:}`. The assignment statement `int{Alice:}[]{Alice:}` y = x is rejected by the Jif type system as it is exposed to the laundering attack similar to the one described in Section 2.2. A possible solution is to create a separate copy of an array, upgrading elements one-by-one.

```
int{Alice:}[]{Alice:} x = new int[y.length];
for (int i = 0; i < y.length, i++) y[i] = x[i];
```

Similar code has to be written if one wants to relabel an instance of some parameterized class. Declassification is another example of relabeling, so the same argument applies when there is need to downgrade an array or a class instance. As a consequence, the programmer is forced to write relabeling (and declassification) code for every complex data structure that is used at different security levels. In our Jif implementation, we resolve this problem with the Declassifier pattern (Section 5.2).

**Missing Java features.** Although Jif includes a large subset of Java, some useful features of Java, such as inner classes and `super` calls, are missing. The lack of inner classes and `super` calls have not proven a substantial obstacle. Most important in the context of this case study is the lack of support for serializability for parameterized classes. As a result, serialization routines used in the distributed implementation need to be written manually for every class.

## 5 Programming Patterns

As discussed in Section 4, enriching Java code with security types is not straightforward. To help streamline this process we have developed patterns for secure programming in Jif. These patterns help resolve insecurities in baseline code in a uniform and transparent fashion. Appendix A presents examples and code listings for each pattern sketched below.

### 5.1 ArgCheck: Checking Arguments in Jif

This pattern suggests raising `IllegalArgumentException` if an argument provided to a method is null. This exception type is more informative than `NullPointerException`. Also, because an exception is raised, Jif's built-in `NullPointerException` analysis ensures that `NullPointerException` no longer needs to be handled for this argument, which results in transparent code for the rest of the method.

### 5.2 Declassifier: Declassification of Large Data Structures

Because arrays and parameterized classes are mutable data containers they cannot be completely declassified with a single `declassify` statement. Each field of such a class or element of an array needs to be relabeled separately. This pattern uses a single class `Declassifier` that contains static declassification and upgrade methods for every data type used in the program. This class is parameterized over a principal P whose authority is used for declassification and a label L to which the data is downgraded. Thus, declassification methods in this class accept arguments of the level {P:;L} and return low copies of them relabeled to {L}. Similarly, upgrade routines return high copies of their arguments relabeled from {L} to {P:;L}.

In this pattern, the class `Declassifier` has no authority, and all declassification methods in the class require the caller to have the authority of P to declassify data. One can also imagine an alternative version of this class which combines encryption and declassification transparently for the caller. Then, the caller of the method receives an encrypted (and declassified) value without having the authority necessary for declassification. We can assume that this kind of declassification is safe as the caller of the method receives an encrypted value. While helpful, this scenario is not used in our implementation since it is the player who owns, encrypts, and declassifies the data.

### 5.3    EffectOrder: Ordering Effects

Some declassifications in a program may be avoided if the code is rearranged so that low operations (such as input) precede operations that affect the pc label.

### 5.4    ReqAuth: Requiring Authority vs. Granting it

Jif's `authority` clause in method declarations can be easily misused. This clause grants the authority of a principal opening up possibilities for declassification by any caller. Often, it is safer to use a `caller` clause. This avoids granting authority and prevents the method from being called when the calling process does not have the required authority.

### 5.5    SuccessFlag: Declassification of a Success Flag

This pattern prevents the propagation of exceptions thrown at a high security level to callers at a lower level. A caller is still notified about the failure; however, no detailed data, such as the call stack, is passed to the caller. Instead, the high code that can generate an exception is enclosed by a `try...catch` block; a boolean flag tracks whether the `try` block has terminated with an exception. This variable is then declassified immediately after the `try...catch` block; a low exception is thrown depending on the flag's value.

### 5.6    Seal: Seal Class

Sealing is used to enforce temporal properties such as preventing secret-key declassification from happening earlier in the game. Unlike the other patterns, this is a combination of conventional programming techniques and security features of Jif.

The class has two parameters: the owning principal P and the label L. This label stands for the lowest security level at which the seal is visible. The value of the seal is stored in the boolean variable `open`, which is only accessible to the owner P. The `caller` constraint in the class constructor requires that the calling process should have the authority of P. Initially, the value of the variable `open` is `false`. It may only change to `true` in the method `unseal()`. Similar to the constructor, this method has the `caller` constraint. This prevents calling `unseal()` from program contexts that do not have the authority of the seal's owner. Note that the actual validation occurs at run-time.

The method `isOpen()` returns the value of the seal. It grants the authority of the owning principal to the process in order to declassify the current value to the visible level L. The method `assertIntegrity()` is similar to `isOpen()` and is a suggested way of checking whether the seal has been opened.

### 5.7    KeySignature: Signature for Key Generation

This pattern shows how the signature of a class that generates encryption keys can be specified to avoid declassifying public keys (declassification group I in Section 4). This signature is parameterized over two labels corresponding to the labels of public and private keys. Then, method headers can be written in such a way that `getPublic()` returns a low value and `getPrivate()` returns a high one. Thus, declassification is avoided. This, however, does not eliminate the flow but makes it invisible to Jif.

## 6    Related Work

Although the theoretical area of information flow security is rather mature [21, 19, 38, 39], there is little evidence for the scalability of information flow controls in practice. Below we discuss some latest progress in this area.

On the security assurance side, this work fits into a recent classification of declassification [42] that, however, considers only information release policies (not declassification mechanisms). Nevertheless, the what, who, where, and when columns of Table 1 correspond to the dimensions of declassification from [42].

A related recent development that investigates the practical use of declassification policies is Li and Zdancewic's work on web scripting languages. With the target of enforcing *relaxed noninterference* [30] they develop a type system for web programming [31]. To what extent this language addresses challenges for practical security has not so far been reported, however.

Giambiagi and Dam have investigated how *admissibility* justifies the security of a simple payment protocol [14]. In subsequent work [20], they separate protocol specification from its implementation such that implementation is guaranteed to reveal no more information than the specification of a protocol. The implementation language, however, is rather distant from a realistic language like Jif. Recently, Chong and Myers have considered temporal release policies in the context of an ML-like language [9, 10]. Their *noninterference "until"* policies are intended to guarantee that secrets are released after a certain statically-enforceable condition becomes true. This approach, however, abstracts away from how the release conditions are enforced. An intriguing direction for future work is exploring the sealing technique further in order to enforce conditional release policies similar to admissibility and noninterference "until."

Heldal et al. [26, 27] show how UML can be integrated with Jif in order to introduce declassification early in the design process. This line of work is promising for modularizing declassification and can lead to a way of combining declassification-free Java code with security-critical Jif code in such a way that declassification statements agree with declassification at the modeling level.

Jif/split [49, 50] performs systematic partitioning of Jif programs into distributed components. Unfortunately, Jif/split does not support parameterized classes (due to compatibility issues with Java's serialization) which would be an obstacle for splitting our Jif implementation of the protocol.

As for the largest implementations in security-typed languages reported so far, we are aware of a battleship game protocol implemented in Jif/split [49, 50] and an evaluation of an earlier version of Jif on a library of cryptographic primitives [46]. However, these implementations are relatively light (500 and 800 lines of code, respectively, vs. 4500 lines in this study).

# 7   Conclusion

As a proof of concept, we have implemented a non-trivial cryptographic protocol in a security-typed language. The implementation has resulted in the largest program written in a security-typed language to date. The case study has given useful evidence on challenges for practical information flow security (cf. Section 1). We discuss insights into these challenges in turn:

- *How helpful are security types for identifying potential insecurities in security-critical code?*
  We have found security types useful for preventing explicit and implicit insecure flows. We have also uncovered insecurities in the baseline implementation due to liberal handling of exceptions and mutable data structures (cf. Section 4.1 and 4.4).
- *How laborious is the process of security typing? Does it force unnecessary restrictions on code?*
  All three implementations have been coded by a graduate student (the first author). The baseline implementation consumed around 60 man-hours of development work. The Jif implementation and distributed Jif implementation consumed 150 and 80 man-hours respectively, excluding the time to learn Jif. The case study indicates that although lifting Java code to Jif takes some experience to master, the security-typed result is not significantly distant from the original code. Furthermore, we have developed patterns for secure programming (cf. Section 5) to make programming with security types clearer and more convenient.
- *Is the security assurance provided by security types transparent enough?*
  This is the territory of the most interesting findings. Jif's mechanism for declassification has proven to be useful for localizing information release to certain well-marked parts of the program (declassify points). The case study, however, suggests that there are various reasons for declassifying at different points. Not only does one need to control *what* information is released, by *whom* and *where* in the system, but also *when* it is safe to release information (cf. Section 4.3). For example, the declassification of the result of encryption (as in the card shuffling phase) and the declassification of the secret key (as in the commitment verification phase) have distinct reasons and hence need to be protected in distinct ways. One disadvantage of Jif (as many other information release mechanisms [20, 40, 35, 32, 30]) is that its treatment of declassification disregards the multifaceted nature of declassification.
- *What is the general balance of benefits and drawbacks when using security-typed languages?*
  Apart from the (dis)advantages we have already discussed, modularity (due to the compositionality of the type system) and selective type annotation (due to security type inference) have proven particularly helpful. On the other hand, debugging tools and extensive documentation currently lack for security-typed languages, which forces programmers to debug code in baseline implementations written in conventional languages. Another unaddressed issue is the connection between high-level

security policies for information release and declassification statements in the code. One can argue that manual inspection of declassification points can, in some cases, be acceptable but, generally, there is need for expressing security policies in high-level languages (perhaps modeling languages) ensuring that these policies are enforced in code. For recent steps in this direction, see [26, 27, 7].

*Future work.* The case study has strongly suggested that existing information release mechanisms need further improvement. A lesson we have learned is that different kinds of declassifications need to be treated differently.

In order to alleviate this problem, we plan to generalize the seal-like data construction to represent declassification that may only happen once a certain condition has been satisfied (as, e.g., the mental poker protocol has reached its verification phase, or all bids are placed in an online auction protocol). This would lead to enforcing stronger (and more intuitive) security guarantees statically.

At the next level of ambition, we intend to connect language-based declassification to security assurance that is provided with respect to information release policies. For example, it remains to be seen how this approach can be connected to conditional release policies such as admissibility [14, 20] and noninterference "until" policies [9, 10]. A long-term goal is to provide a toolbox of declassification mechanisms for each of the *what*, *who*, *where*, and *when* axes of information release [42].

Another strand of worthwhile future work is improving Jif's shortcomings (cf. Section 4.4). We plan to explore automated refactoring techniques for pattern design (e.g., [11]) in order to facilitate program transformations that result in security typed programs. Another interesting problem is connected to relabeling mutable data structures. We believe it can be improved by introducing an operation that would combine declassification and object cloning so that a relabeled separate copy of an object would be created. This would prevent laundering attacks via object aliases. Also, this would make programming in Jif easier because traversing mutable data structures for the sole purpose of declassification would no longer be needed. A structured way of doing this is by defining a Jif interface `Declassifiable` that would allow an operation `declassifyAndClone` to be performed on the classes that implement the interface.

Although the case study is the largest of the kind, it is not large enough to be an example of real production code. In order to investigate additional subtleties that come with such code, we plan to run a student project to extend the case study to a fully fledged application for mobile devices.

*Acknowledgments.* Thanks are due to Michael Hicks, Boniface Hicks, Stephen Chong, and anonymous reviewers for helpful comments.

# References

1. CERT® advisory CA-2003-26: Multiple vulnerabilities in SSL/TLS implementations, October 2003. http://www.cert.org/advisories/CA-2003-26.html.
2. Jif source code for the mental poker protocol, March 2005. http://www.cs.chalmers.se/~aaskarov/jifpoker.

3. J. Agat. Transforming out timing leaks. In *Proc. ACM Symp. on Principles of Programming Languages*, pages 40–53, January 2000.
4. R. Anderson. Why cryptosystems fail. In *ACM Conference on Computer and Communications Security*, pages 215–227, November 1993.
5. A. Banerjee and D. A. Naumann. Secure information flow and pointer confinement in a Java-like language. In *Proc. IEEE Computer Security Foundations Workshop*, pages 253–267, June 2002.
6. A. Barnett and N. P. Smart. Mental poker revisited. In *Proc. Cryptography and Coding IMA International Conference*, volume 2898 of *LNCS*, pages 370–383. Springer-Verlag, December 2003.
7. L. Bauer, J. Ligatti, and D. Walker. Composing security policies with Polymer. In *Proc. ACM Conf. on Programming Language Design and Implementation*, June 2005. To appear.
8. J. Castellà-Roca, J. Domingo-Ferrer, A. Riera, and J. Borrell. Practical mental poker without a TTP based on homomorphic encryption. In *Progress in Cryptology-Indocrypt*, volume 2904 of *LNCS*, pages 280–294. Springer-Verlag, December 2003.
9. S. Chong and A. C. Myers. Security policies for downgrading. In *ACM Conference on Computer and Communications Security*, pages 198–209, October 2004.
10. S. Chong and A. C. Myers. Language-based information erasure. In *Proc. IEEE Computer Security Foundations Workshop*, June 2005. To appear.
11. M. Ó. Cinnéide. Automated refactoring to introduce design patterns. In *Proc. ACM International Conference on Software Engineering*, pages 722–724, 2000.
12. C. Crépeau. A secure poker protocol that minimizes the effect of players coalitions. In *Advances in Cryptology: Crypto'85*, volume 218 of *LNCS*, pages 73–86. Springer-Verlag, 1986.
13. C. Crépeau. A zero-knowledge poker protocol that achieves confidentiality of the players' strategy or how to achieve an electronic poker face. In *Advances in Cryptology: Crypto'86*, volume 263 of *LNCS*, pages 239–247. Springer-Verlag, 1987.
14. M. Dam and P. Giambiagi. Confidentiality for mobile code: The case of a simple payment protocol. In *Proc. IEEE Computer Security Foundations Workshop*, pages 233–244, July 2000.
15. D. E. Denning. A lattice model of secure information flow. *Comm. of the ACM*, 19(5):236–243, May 1976.
16. D. E. Denning and P. J. Denning. Certification of programs for secure information flow. *Comm. of the ACM*, 20(7):504–513, July 1977.
17. J. Domingo-Ferrer. A new privacy homomorphism and applications. *Information Processing Letters*, 60(5):277–282, 1996.
18. J. Edwards. Implementing electronic poker: A practical exercise in zero-knowledge interactive proofs. Master's thesis, Dept. of Computer Science, University of Kentucky, 1994.
19. R. Focardi and R. Gorrieri. Classification of security properties (part I: Information flow). In R. Focardi and R. Gorrieri, editors, *Foundations of Security Analysis and Design*, volume 2171 of *LNCS*, pages 331–396. Springer-Verlag, 2001.
20. P. Giambiagi and M. Dam. On the secure implementation of security protocols. In *Proc. European Symp. on Programming*, volume 2618 of *LNCS*, pages 144–158. Springer-Verlag, April 2003.
21. J. A. Goguen and J. Meseguer. Security policies and security models. In *Proc. IEEE Symp. on Security and Privacy*, pages 11–20, April 1982.
22. S. Goldwasser and S. Micali. Probabilistic encryption and how to play mental poker keeping secret all partial information. In *Proc. ACM Symp. Theory of Computing*, pages 365–377, 1982.
23. P. Gutmann. Lessons learned in implementing and deploying crypto software. In *Proc. USENIX Security Symp.*, pages 315–325, August 2002.

24. R. Hanna, A. Rideout, and D. Ziegler. Secure peer-to-peer texas hold'em. Course project, MIT. http://web.mit.edu/ardonite/6.857/, 2003.
25. N. Heintze and J. G. Riecke. The SLam calculus: programming with secrecy and integrity. In *Proc. ACM Symp. on Principles of Programming Languages*, pages 365–377, January 1998.
26. R. Heldal and F. Hultin. Bridging model-based and language-based security. In *Proc. European Symp. on Research in Computer Security*, volume 2808 of *LNCS*, pages 235–252. Springer-Verlag, October 2003.
27. R. Heldal, S. Schlager, and J. Bende. Supporting confidentiality in UML: A profile for the Decentralized Label Model. In *Proc. International Workshop on Critical Systems Development with UML*, pages 56–70, 2004.
28. K. Kurosawa, K. Katayama, and W. Ogata. Reshufflable and laziness tolerant mental card game protocol. *IEICE Transactions*, E80-A(1):72–78, 1997.
29. K. Kurosawa, Y. Katayama, W. Ogata, and S. Tsujii. General public key residue cryptosystems and mental poker protocols. In *Advances in Cryptology: EuroCrypto'90*, volume 473 of *LNCS*, pages 374–388. Springer-Verlag, 1991.
30. P. Li and S. Zdancewic. Downgrading policies and relaxed noninterference. In *Proc. ACM Symp. on Principles of Programming Languages*, pages 158–170, January 2005.
31. P. Li and S. Zdancewic. Practical information-flow control in web-based information systems. In *Proc. IEEE Computer Security Foundations Workshop*, June 2005. To appear.
32. H. Mantel and D. Sands. Controlled downgrading based on intransitive (non)interference. In *Proc. Asian Symp. on Programming Languages and Systems*, volume 3302 of *LNCS*, pages 129–145. Springer-Verlag, November 2004.
33. A. C. Myers. JFlow: Practical mostly-static information flow control. In *Proc. ACM Symp. on Principles of Programming Languages*, pages 228–241, January 1999.
34. A. C. Myers and B. Liskov. A decentralized model for information flow control. In *Proc. ACM Symp. on Operating System Principles*, pages 129–142, October 1997.
35. A. C. Myers, A. Sabelfeld, and S. Zdancewic. Enforcing robust declassification. In *Proc. IEEE Computer Security Foundations Workshop*, pages 172–186, June 2004.
36. A. C. Myers, L. Zheng, S. Zdancewic, S. Chong, and N. Nystrom. Jif: Java information flow. Software release. Located at http://www.cs.cornell.edu/jif, July 2001–2004.
37. F. Pottier and V. Simonet. Information flow inference for ML. *ACM TOPLAS*, 25(1):117–158, January 2003.
38. P. Ryan. Mathematical models of computer security—tutorial lectures. In R. Focardi and R. Gorrieri, editors, *Foundations of Security Analysis and Design*, volume 2171 of *LNCS*, pages 1–62. Springer-Verlag, 2001.
39. A. Sabelfeld and A. C. Myers. Language-based information-flow security. *IEEE J. Selected Areas in Communications*, 21(1):5–19, January 2003.
40. A. Sabelfeld and A. C. Myers. A model for delimited information release. In *Proc. International Symp. on Software Security (ISSS'03)*, volume 3233 of *LNCS*, pages 174–191. Springer-Verlag, October 2004.
41. A. Sabelfeld and D. Sands. Probabilistic noninterference for multi-threaded programs. In *Proc. IEEE Computer Security Foundations Workshop*, pages 200–214, July 2000.
42. A. Sabelfeld and D. Sands. Dimensions and principles of declassification. In *Proc. IEEE Computer Security Foundations Workshop*, June 2005. To appear.
43. C. Schindelhauer. A toolbox for mental card games, 1998. http://citeseer.ist.psu.edu/schindelhauer98toolbox.html.
44. A. Shamir, R. Rivest, and L. Adleman. Mental poker. *Mathematical Gardner*, pages 37–43, 1981.
45. V. Simonet. The Flow Caml system. Software release. Located at http://cristal.inria.fr/~simonet/soft/flowcaml/, July 2003.

46. S. Tse and G. Washburn. Cryptographic programming in Jif. Course project, 2003. http://www.cis.upenn.edu/~stse/bank/main.pdf.
47. J. Viega and G. McGraw. *Building Secure Software: How to Avoid Security Problems the Right Way.* Addison-Wesley, 2001.
48. S. Zdancewic. Challenges for information-flow security. In *Proc. Programming Language Interference and Dependence (PLID)*, August 2004.
49. S. Zdancewic, L. Zheng, N. Nystrom, and A. C. Myers. Untrusted hosts and confidentiality: Secure program partitioning. In *Proc. ACM Symp. on Operating System Principles*, pages 1–14, October 2001.
50. L. Zheng, S. Chong, A. C. Myers, and S. Zdancewic. Using replication and partitioning to build secure distributed systems. In *Proc. IEEE Symp. on Security and Privacy*, pages 236–250, May 2003.
51. L. Zheng and A. C. Myers. End-to-end availability policies and noninterference. In *Proc. IEEE Computer Security Foundations Workshop*, June 2005. To appear.

# A   Programming Patterns

We describe further details on some programming patterns that one may find useful when programming in Jif, or lifting Java programs to Jif. A brief summary of these patterns appears in Section 5.

### A.1   ArgCheck: Checking Arguments in Jif Functions

The obligation to handle runtime exceptions in Jif can easily make code more clunky than necessary. Consider, for example, a Java function:

```
public boolean validate(byte [] p, Matrix mx) {
    if (!mx.validate(p)) return false;
}
```

If the argument mx is null, NullPointerException is thrown. Straightforward porting of this function may lead to the following Jif code:

```
public boolean validate{L}(byte{L}[]{L}p, Matrix[L]{L} mx):{L} throws NullPointerException{
    if (!mx.validate(p)) return false;
}
```

This code declares the exception in the method header. Listing 8 illustrates how the above function can be modified so that IllegalArgumentException is thrown whenever an argument is null. Due to Jif's NullPointerException analysis it is not necessary to handle NullPointerException for mx.

```
public boolean validate{L}(byte{L}[]{L} p, Matrix[L]{L} mx):{L}
throws IllegalArgumentException {
    if (mx == null) throw new IllegalArgumentException();
    if (!mx.validate(p)) return false;
}
```

**Listing 8.** Checking arguments in Jif functions

This pattern achieves more transparent code as all arguments are checked in advance before they are used; also, the type of a declared exception is more specific to the error.

## A.2   Declassifier: Declassification of Large Data Structures

Consider the class IntPair in Listing 9. Listing 10 is an example
of a method in Declassifier that
downgrades an object of the type
IntPair[{P:;L}]{P:;L} to the type
IntPair[L]{L}. The first declassification on line 2 downgrades the reference
to the object. Line 4 declassifies the

```
public class IntPair[label L] {
    private int x, y;
    public IntPair(int{L} _x, int{L} _y) {
        this.x = _x; this.y = _y;
    }
    public int{L} getX() { return this.x; }
    public int{L} getY() { return this.y; }
}
```

**Listing 9.** IntPair

fields of the object a and constructs a new object at the low security level that has
the same value as a.

```
  public static IntPair[L]{L} declassifyIntPair(IntPair[{P:;L}]{P:;L}a1) where caller(P) {
2     IntPair[{P:;L}] a = declassify(a1, {L});
      if (a == null) return null;
4     return new IntPair[L](declassify(a.getX(),{L}), declassify(a.getY(),L));
  }
```

**Listing 10.** Method

A similar approach needs to be applied for upgrading a mutable object from one
security level to another. A disadvantage of this approach is that it requires the constructors of the relabeled classes to have all class fields as arguments. This is not always
desirable since the values of private variables, (e.g., the internal state of an object) are
not always supposed to be instantiated in constructors.

## A.3   EffectOrder: Ordering Effects

Some program statements in Jif may affect the pc label. If pc is high, low side effects
are not allowed without prior declassification. Sometimes, it is possible to avoid such
a declassification by ordering program statements so that low side effects precede the
statements that taint pc with a higher label. Consider an example where readData and
update functions are defined as follows:

```
public String{L} readData{L}():{L} { ... }
public void update{L;H}(String{L} x):{L;H} throws NullPointerException { ... }
```

Now, consider a code snippet where low input is interleaved with high update calls and
which is rejected by the compiler (unless pc is declassified before the second read).

```
1   String{L} a = readData(); // low side effect
2   update(a);                // high statement, pc becomes high
3   String{L} b = readData(); // low side effect, rejected because pc is high
4   update(b);                //
```

After the call to update function on line 2, pc becomes high, and the call to the function readData on line 3 is rejected. The revision below demonstrates how this can be
repaired by ensuring that the low function calls precede the high ones.

```
String{L} a = readData(); // low side effect
String{L} b = readData(); // low side effect, ok
update(a); // high statement effect, ok
update(b); // high statement effect, ok
```

## A.4   ReqAuth: Requiring Authority vs. Granting it

Consider examples of two functions that reveal the secret permutation of the player, declassifying it to a lower label:

```
public byte{L}[]{L} revealPermutation{L}() where authority (P) { ... }
```

```
public byte{L}[]{L} revealPermutation{L}() where caller (P)    { ... }
```

The first example grants the authority of the player to the method. This implies that the method can be called from any context. Such a declaration is dangerous because secret information can be easily leaked. In contrast, the second example grants no authority but requires the caller to have necessary authority for declassification: calling this method from a context where the calling process does not have the authority of the principal P is rejected by the compiler.

## A.5   SuccessFlag: Declassification of a Success Flag

Listing 4 in Section 4.1 is an example of code that needs to release information about the termination of the method without leaking the details on why the method failed to terminate normally. Listing 11 shows how one can use a boolean flag variable to track the termination path of high methods.

```
1   public void foo{L}():{L} throws Exception where caller(P) {
2       boolean ok = false;
3       try { ... // code that can throw high exception
4           ok = true;
5       } catch (Exception ex) { ... } // handling high exception
6       if (declassify (!ok, {L})) { throw new Exception(); }
7   }
```

**Listing 11.** Declassification of success flag

In this example, the boolean flag ok is initialized on line 2. High code that can generate exceptions is enclosed by a try ... catch statement, so that possible exceptions are caught and handled on line 5. The assignment ok=true on line 4 may generate no exception and is the last one within the try block. Line 6 declassifies the value of this variable and, depending on this value, it may generate a low exception that will propagate to the caller.

## A.6   Seal: Seal Class

Listing 12 presents the structure of the seal class that is described in Section 5.6.

```
1   /* Seal belongs to a principal P, and is visible at the level L */
2   public class Seal[principal P, label L]  authority(P) {
3       private boolean{P:;L} open; /*actual value of the seal */
4       /* require the principal to create this */
5       public Seal{P:;L}() where caller(P) {  this.open = false;    }
6       /* require the principal to unseal it */
7       public void unseal{P:;L}() where caller (P) { this.open = true;  }
8       /* anyone at the level L can check it */
9       public boolean{this;L} isOpen():{L} where authority (P) {
10          return declassify (open, {this;L});
11      }
12      /* similar to previous */
13      public void assertIntegrity():{L} throws SecurityException {
```

```
14          if (this.isOpen()) throw new SecurityException();
15      }
16  }
```

**Listing 12.** Seal class

Listing 13 shows how sealing is used. Line 1 declares a seal that belongs to Alice
and is observable by everyone. It is initialized in the method `init()`. The `work()`
method checks if the seal has been opened before it is called. The seal is opened in
`revealSecret()` method. If `work()` is called after the seal is opened, the exception
`SecurityException` is thrown.

```
1   private Seal[Alice,{}] seal; // declaration
2   public void init() where caller(Alice) { // initialization
      this.seal = new Seal[Alice, {}]();
      ...
    }
    public void work() throws SecurityException, NullPointerException{
      this.seal.assertIntegrity();   // check the integrity in the beginning of the method
      ...
    }
    public void revealSecret() where caller (Alice)  throws NullPointerException{
      this.seal.unseal();
      ... // declassification goes next
    }
```

**Listing 13.** Usage of seal

## A.7   KeySignature: Signature for Key Generation

Listings 14 and 15 are two signatures for
Java's `java.security.KeyPair` class.
The usage of the first one requires an
instance of the `KeyPair` class to be
high, because it contains a sensitive
private key. Declassification is applied
when information about the public key is
needed. This declassification is safe because the released information is naturally public.

The declassification-free version is
parameterized over two labels—for the
private and public keys. In this case, a
parameterized signature avoids declassification by labeling method headers
appropriately. Both of the approaches
are acceptable, providing a trade-off between explicit flow control and ele-
gance.

```
public final class KeyPair{
  public KeyPair(PublicKey{this} publicKey,
              PrivateKey{this} privateKey) {}
  public native PublicKey{this} getPublic();
  public native PrivateKey{this} getPrivate();
}
```

**Listing 14.** Non-parameterized signature for
KeyPair

```
public final class KeyPair[label L, label H]{
  public KeyPair(PublicKey{L} publicKey,
              PrivateKey{L;H} privateKey) {}
  public native PublicKey{L} getPublic();
  public native PrivateKey{L;H} getPrivate();
}
```

**Listing 15.** Parameterized signature for KeyPair

# Augmented Oblivious Polynomial Evaluation Protocol and Its Applications

Huafei Zhu and Feng Bao

Department of Information Security, Institute for Infocomm Research,
A-Star, Singapore 119613
{huafei, baofeng}@i2r.a-star.edu.sg

**Abstract.** In this paper, we first introduce a new notion called augmented oblivious polynomial evaluation (AOPE), a useful notion to deal with the general oblivious polynomial evaluation protocol. And then we propose a novel implementation of our AOPE protocol. Finally we show that our construction is provably secure within our model. The potential areas of application of this protocol are numerous (two-party computation, bidding protocol, keyword search problem, and so on...).

**Keywords:** Augmented oblivious polynomial evaluation, homomorphic commitment scheme, homomorphic public key encryption.

## 1    Introduction

Oblivious polynomial evaluation (OPE) first introduced by Naor and Pinkas [12], is a protocol involving two parties, a sender whose input is a polynomial $f(x) \in F[x]$ of degree $m$ ($m \geq 1$), and a receiver whose input is a value $a \in F$, where $F$ is a finite field. At the end of execution of the protocol the receiver learns $f(a)$ and the sender learns nothing. There are two constructions proposed in [12]. The first construction is based on a conjecture that given a randomly chosen input to the polynomial list reconstruction problem, the value of the polynomial at $x = 0$ is pseudo-random. The second construction is more efficient but based on more stronger security assumption that the value of the polynomial at $x = 0$ is pseudo-random even given some additional hints about the location of the values of the polynomial. Unfortunately, their constructions were shown to be weaker than expected in [2]. Thus it is still an unsolved problem to implement secure and efficient OPE protocol.

### 1.1    This Work

Let $F=Z/rZ$, and $f$ be $f(x) = a_0 + a_1 x + \cdots + a_m x^m \bmod r$. We provide two observations in order to construct the proposed OPE scheme:

- a general OPE protocol for a finite field $F$ where $f$ has general order can be obtained from OPE protocol for prime field where the order of $f$ is one.

S. De Capitani di Vimercati et al. (Eds.): ESORICS 2005, LNCS 3679, pp. 222–230, 2005.

– an OPE protocol for a finite field $F$ where the order of $f$ is one can be obtained from an OPE protocol over an integer ring where the order of $f$ is one. An OPE protocol for an integer ring where the order of $f$ is one can be obtained when a trusted initializer distributes a public key of RSA system.

We now explain the first observation (the main contribution of this paper). Suppose Alice has a polynomial $f$ at hand. She first randomly selects $a_{j0} \in F$, $a_{j1} \in F$ such that $a_{j,0} + a_{j,1} = a_j + r$ (computed over integer domain $Z$), for $j = 1, \cdots, m - 1$. Here, $f(x) = a_0 + a_1 x + \cdots + a_m x^m \bmod r = a_0 + (a_{1,0} + a_{1,1})x + \cdots + (a_{m-1,0} + a_{m-1,1})x^{m-1} + a_m x^m \bmod r$. $f(x)$ can be further written as $a_0 + a_{1,0}x + (a_{1,1} + a_{2,0}x)x + \cdots + (a_{m-1,1} + a_m x)x^{m-1}$. Bob who holds the secret input $\alpha$ perform OPE protocol, obtains $(a_{j,1} + a_{j+1,0}\alpha)$ for all $1 \le j \le m - 1$ together with $(a_0 + a_{1,0}\alpha)$, and thus $f(\alpha)$. Notice that the finite field $F$ must be a prime field, so that $a_{j,1} + a_{j+1,0}\alpha$ can be uniformly distributed among $F$. Throughout the following discussion, we assume that $r$ is a prime number.

We further explain the second observation. Suppose Bob has an integer $0 \neq \alpha < r$, and Alice has $f(x) = ax + b \bmod r$. Bob generates public key and secret keys of Paillier's cryptographic system and sends $E_B(\alpha)$ and public key $E_B$ to Alice. Alice then selects long enough integers $u, v$ satisfying $u = a \bmod r$, and $v = b \bmod r$, and sends $E_B(\alpha)^u E_B(1)^v = E_B(u\alpha + v)$ to Bob. Alice further proves to Bob that all performance are correct against the common reference string – a public key of commitment scheme (RSA modulus) provided by the trusted initializer. Bob performs decryption and obtains $u\alpha + v \bmod r = a\alpha + b$ if the proof is correct.

The security definition of our protocol should be viewed as an enhanced version of Naor and Pinkas' definition [12]. That is, we allow an adversary to corrupt one of participant (either $P$ or $V$ could be malicious within our 2-party client/server model). The proof of security is standard. That is the rewinding of the malicious party is allowed within our model since a malicious party is not allowed to communicate with distinguisher $D$, i.e., the distinguisher $D$ only gets to see the transcript to protocol execution which is significant difference from the argument of the universally composable property [3]. We also remark that the rewinding of a malicious party is strictly forbidden in Canetti's model [3], however, we do not deal with the security of our AOPE protocol in Canetti's model throughout the paper.

In summary, the main contribution of this paper are following. We introduce an interesting yet useful notion called augmented oblivious polynomial function evaluation (AOPE) in this paper. And we also propose an efficient implementation of the AOPE protocol and show that our construction is provably secure in the common reference string model assuming that a static adversary corrupts $P$ or $V$.

## 1.2 Road Map

The rest of paper is organized as follows: in Section 2 building blocks which will be used for constructing of AOPE protocol are sketched; In section 3.1 syntax and

security of AOPE protocol are proposed and in Section 3.2 our implementation
and security proof of the implementation are presented. In Section 4, we provide
a novel application of our AOPE protocol to realize greater gate protocol. And
we conclude our works in Section 5.

## 2  Building Blocks

We briefly review the following building blocks that will be used throughout the
paper.

### 2.1  Paillier's Public Key Encryption Scheme

Paillier investigated a novel computational problem, called Composite Residuosity Class Problem, and its applications to public key cryptography in [14]. Our
construction will heavily rely on this probabilistic encryption scheme which is
sketched below.

The public key is a $k_1$-bit RSA modulus $n = pq$, where $p, q$ are two large safe
primes. The plain-text space is $Z_n$ and the cipher-text space is $Z_{n^2}^*$. To encrypt
$\alpha \in Z_n$, one chooses $r \in Z_n^*$ uniformly at random and computes the cipher-text
as $E_{PK}(a, r) = g^a r^n \bmod n^2$, where $g = (1 + n)$ has order $n$ in $Z_{n^2}^*$. The private
key is $(p, q)$.

The encryption function is homomorphic, i.e., $E_{PK}(a_1, r_1) \times E_{PK}(a_2, r_2)$
$\bmod n^2 = E_{PK}(a_1 + a_2 \bmod n, r_1 \times r_2 \bmod n)$.

Another interesting result of Paillier's public key encryption scheme is that it
can be viewed as a commitment scheme as well since given a cipher-text $c := g^a r^n$
$\bmod n^2$, we first compute $a \in Z_n$ from the following equation $\frac{L(c^\lambda \bmod n^2)}{L((1+n)^\lambda \bmod n^2)} \bmod n$
and then compute $r$ from the equation $r \in Z_n^* = c'^{n^{-1} \bmod \lambda} \bmod n$, where $\lambda =$
$lcm(p - 1, q - 1)$, $n = pq$.

### 2.2  Fujisaki-Okamoto Commitment Scheme

Let $s$ be a security parameter. The public key is a $k_2$-bit RSA modulus, where $\underline{P}$,
$Q$ are two large safe primes. We assume that neither $P$ nor $V$ knows factorization
$\bar{N}$. Let $g_1$ be a generator of $QR_N$ and $g_2$ be an element of large order of the
group generated by $g_1$ such that both discrete logarithm of $g_1$ in base $g_2$ and the
discrete logarithm of $g_2$ in base $g_1$ are unknown by $P$ and $V$.

We denote $C(a, r_a) = g_1^a g_2^{r_a} \bmod N$ a commitment to $x$ in base $(g_1, g_2)$,
where $r_a$ is randomly selected over $\{0, 2^s N\}$. This commitment scheme first
appeared in [10] and reconsidered by Damgård and Fujisaki [7] is statistically
secure commitment scheme, i.e.:

-$P$ is unable to commit itself to two values $a_1, a_2$ such that $a_1 \neq a_2$ in $Z$ by
the same commitment unless $P$ can factor $N$ or solves the discrete logarithm of
$g_1$ in base $g_2$ or the the discrete logarithm of $g_2$ in base $g_1$.

-$C(a, r_a)$ statistically reveals no information to $V$, i.e., there is a simulator
which outputs simulated commitment to $a$ which are statistically indistinguishable from true ones.

Notice that this commitment is homomorphic, i.e, $C(a+b, r_a+r_b) = C(a, r_a) \times C(b, r_b)$. This property is useful when $P$ wants to prove that the committed value $a \in [x, y]$. Also notice that Paillier's encryption scheme is only homomorphic with respect to addition RSA modulus. If we want the output of oblivious polynomial evaluation protocol defined over $Z$ (so that $V$ can verify the correctness of its received messages), then $k_1$ should be chosen large enough compared with the sizes of inputs of participants.

## 2.3   Proof of Knowledge of Encryptions

Given a cipher-text $\text{Enc}(x)$ which is computed from Paillier's encryption scheme, the prover should provide a proof that he knows $x$ and $x$ lies in a given interval $I$ specified in the protocol. There is efficient protocol presented by Damgård and Jurik already in [6]. The basic idea is the following: given $\text{Enc}(x)$, the prover provides a commitment $C(x, r_x)$ which is computed from Fujisaki-Okamoto commitment scheme, proves that the commitment contains the same number as the encryption, and then uses Baudot's protocol [1] to prove that $m \in I$. More precisely,

-Let $T$ be the maximum bit length of $x$. The prover chooses at random $u$, an integer of length $T + 2k$, where $k$ is a security parameter. He sends $a=\text{Enc}(u)$, $b=C(u)$ to the verifier;

-The verifier chooses a $l$-bit challenge $e$;

-The prover opens the encryption $a(\text{Enc}(x)^e) \bmod N^2$ and the commitment $bC(x)^e \bmod N$, to reveal in both cases the number $z = u + ex$. The verifier checks the opening were correct.

The protocol can be made non-interactive in the standard way using a hash function and the Fiat-Shamir paradigm. It is also statistically zero-knowledge in the random oracle mode.

# 3   AOPE Protocol

## 3.1   Syntax and Security Definition

An augmented OPE protocol consists of three participants: system initiator $I$, $P$ and $V$. The auxiliary information of individual participant is first generated as follows:

- on input $k_2$, $I$ outputs an instance of Fujisaki and Okamoto's commitment scheme. The public key $PK_c$ of the commitment scheme is called common reference string which will be used by each participant in the system;
- on input $m$, $r$ and $k_2$, $P$ outputs a polynomial $f(x)$ of degree $m$ defined over $Z/rZ$, together with a commitment $C(f) := ((C(a_0 + r), \cdots, C(a_m + r))$ of $f(x)$; Notice that the commitment of $f(x)$ is defined as $(C(a_0 + r), \cdots, C(a_m + r))$ but not $(C(a_0), \cdots, C(a_m))$;
- on input $k_1$, $V$ outputs an instance of Paillier's encryption scheme for $V$. The public key/ secret key pair is denoted by $(PK_v, SK_v)$;

To define the functionality of AOPE protocol, an imaginary TTP is introduced. And then TTP involves in the following performance:

- $P$ runs with TTP and proves to TTP that a chosen polynomial $f(x)$ is correct; Otherwise, a random $f(x)$ defined over $Z/rZ$ is assigned;
- $V$ runs with TTP and proves to TTP that a chosen value $\alpha$ is correct; otherwise, a random $\alpha$ is assigned by TTP from $Z/rZ$;
- The output of $P$ is a null string while the output of $V$ is $f(\alpha)$;

Definition 1: An AOPE protocol is said secure for a sender $P$ if for any malicious chooser $V$, there exists a simulator $sim_V$ that plays the role of $V$ in the ideal world such that for any polynomial time distinguisher $D$, the view of $V$ in real conversation is computationally indistinguishable from that simulated by $sim_V$.

Definition 2: An AOPE protocol is said secure for a chooser $V$ if for any malicious prover $P$, there exists a simulator $sim_P$ that plays the role of $P$ in the ideal world such that for any polynomial time distinguisher $D$, the view of $P$ in real conversation is computationally indistinguishable from that simulated by $sim_P$.

Definition 3: We say that an AOPE protocol is secure for any static and probabilistic polynomial time (PPT) adversary if it is secure for both the sender and the chooser.

## 3.2   The Construction

The following implementation of AOPE consists of two phases: initializer setup and oblivious polynomial evaluation.

- In initial reprocessing phase: a sender $P$ chooses a polynomial $f(x) = a_0 + a_1x + \cdots + a_mx^m \bmod r$ at hand over a finite field $Z/rZ$, where $r$ is a prime number, $0 \neq a_j \in Z/rZ$. $P$ then commits the chosen polynomial $f(x)$ using the common reference string − the public key $PK_c$ of a specified Fujisaki and Okamoto's commitment scheme ( or its improved version by Damgård and Fujisaki [7]), allowing $P$ or $V$ to commit to an integer $a$ of sufficiently long size and prove efficiently in zero-knowledge that $a$ belongs to some interval using the technique of Baudot [1] (thus, our model is within the common reference string model). At the end of processing phase, $P$ publishes commitments $C(f)$ of the chosen polynomial $f(x)$.
- Inputs of participants: the input of $P$ is the polynomial $f(x)$, and the correspondent commitment $C(f)$: $=(C(a_0 + r), \cdots, C(a_m + r))$ of polynomial $f(x)$. The input of $V$ is the commitment $C(f)$ and a value $x \in Z/rZ$.
- Oblivious polynomial evaluation phase: in this phase, we assume that $V$ has available a homomorphic public key encryption scheme $E$ (e.g., Paillier's public key encryption scheme [14]). Then $P$ and $V$ involve the following steps:
  - $V$ sends the public key $PK_v$ to $P$, and also sends the encryption $E(\alpha)$ together with the proof that $\alpha$ is chosen in a correct interval by means

of Baudot's protocol [1], where $\alpha \in Z/rZ$ is chosen secretly by $V$ which can be viewed as an non-zero value within the interval $\{0,1\}^{\log(r)}$, $E(\alpha)$: $=E_{PK_v}(\alpha)$;

- Upon receiving $E(\alpha)$ and the correspondent proof that $E(\alpha)$ is the encryption of a correct value, $P$ verifies the correctness of proof. If the proof is correct, $P$ proves to $V$ that $P$ knows that the commitment is correct (each $a_j$ lies in a correct interval), the knowledge of de-commitment of $C(f)$;

- $P$ then randomly selects $a_{j,0} \in Z$, $a_{j,1} \in Z$ such that $a_{j,0} + a_{j,1} = a_j + r$, for $j = 1, \cdots, m-1$ (all computations are defined over the integer domain $Z$). $f(x)$ can now be written as $a_0 + a_{1,0}x + (a_{1,1} + a_{2,0}x)x + \cdots + (a_{m-1,1} + a_m x)x^{m-1}$: $=(l_0(x), \cdots, l_{m-1}(x)) \bullet (1, x, \cdots, x^{m-1})$, where $l_0(x)$: $=a_0 + a_{1,0}x$, $l_j(x)$:$= (a_{j,1} + a_{j+1,0}x)$ and $l_{m-1}(x)$: $=(a_{m-1,1} + a_m x)$; Finally, $P$ recommits $f(x)$ as following: $C(l_0) = (C(a_0, r_0), C(a_{1,0}, r_{1,0})$; $C(l_j) = (C(a_{j,1}, r_{j,1}), C(a_{j+1,0}, r_{j+1,0}))$; $C(l_{m-1}) = (C(a_{m-1,1}, r_{m-1,1}), C(a_m, r_m))$.

- $P$ then sends $(C(l_0), \cdots, C(l_{m-1}))$ to Bob, together with a sequence of proof such that $C(a_{j,0}) \times C(a_{j,1}) = C(a_j)$ by means of proof of the equality of two commitments;

- Given $E(\alpha)$ and for each $l_j(x)$, $P$ further computes $\beta_j$: $=E(1)^{a_{j,1}} \times E(\alpha)^{a_{j+1,0}}$, together with a proof that: (1) $P$ knows the decomposition of $\beta_j$ correspondent to the bases of $E(1)$ and $E(\alpha)$; and (2) each exponent equals to correspondent commitment of $C(l_j)$. Notice that the correctness of $E(1)$ can be verified by $V$ since $V$ has the secret key of $E$; That is given the Fujisaki-Okamoto's commitments: $C(a)$ and $C(b)$ and the Paillier encryption $E(x)$ one can directly prove that $E(ax + b) = E(x)^a E(1)^b$, i.e., one combines the proof of knowledge of the values committed to $C(a)$ and $C(b)$, and the proof that one knows $a$ and $b$ such that $E(ax + b) = E(x)^a E(1)^b$. There are tons of examples in the literature where this is done (see for instance, the works already done by Chaum and Pedersen [4], and by Camenisch and Shoup [5]).

- Once $V$ received the correct value of $\beta_j$, it obtains the exact value of $f(x)$ thereafter.

This ends the description of our implementation.

### 3.3   The Proof of Security

In this section, we are able to show the following interesting statements:

Lemma 1: for each malicious $V$, there exists a simulator $sim_V$ that plays the role of $V$ in the ideal process for carrying out the functionality of AOPE protocol such that for any polynomial time distinguisher $D$, the view of $V$ in real conversation is computationally indistinguishable from that simulated by $sim_V$.

Proof: $sim_V$ first generates system parameters – the public key of the underlying commitment scheme and the correspondent secret key. The public key of the commitment scheme is defined as a common reference string while the secret key of commitment scheme will be used as trapdoor information which is known only by $sim_V$. Notice that the action of $V$ in our implementation is to generate an encryption $E(\alpha)$ together with the proof that $\alpha$ is chosen in a correct interval by means of Baudot's protocol [1]; Thus, $sim_V$ simply rewinds the malicious $V$ to obtain the correct $\alpha$ with over-whelming probability; Once $sim_V$ has $\alpha$, it forwards $\alpha$ to TTP. And TTP replies $sim_V$ with $f(\alpha)$. Now $sim_V$ further rewinds the random tape of $V$ so that $sim_V$ obtains the malicious $V's$ private random string that is used in the real implementation and thus simulation of transcripts can be generated as that in the real world protocol.

Lemma 2: for each malicious prover $P$, there exists a simulator $sim_P$ that plays the role of $P$ in the ideal process for carrying out the functionality of AOPE protocol such that for any polynomial time distinguisher $D$, the view of $P$ in real conversation is computationally indistinguishable from that simulated by $sim_P$.

Proof: In this time $sim_P$ first generates system parameters as the real protocol described above. The public key of the underlying commitment scheme is $(N, g_1, g_2)$, the secret key (trapdoor of the commitment scheme) is $(P, Q, w)$, where $N = PQ$, $g_2 = g_1^w$, $g_1 \in QR_N$ is a common reference string. Then by applying the standard rewinding technique, $sim_P$ can extract $a_i$ and $a_{i,0}$ and $a_{i,1}$ such that $a_i = a_{i,0} + a_{i,1} \mod r$ from its proof. Once $a_i$, $a_{i,0}$ and $a_{i,1}$ are all known, $sim_P$ forward these values to TTP. TTP replies $sim_P$ a value $\alpha$. The rest simulation of the protocol is then trivial since $P$ proves no knowledge to $V$ further except for the equation that $\beta = f(\alpha)$. Since there is a simulator $sim_1$ for proving that $\beta_0$ equals $a_0 + a_{1,0}\alpha$, and $sim_j$ for proving that $\beta_j$ equals $a_{j-1,0} + a_{j,1}\alpha$ if the sub-protocols are constructed from the idea used by Chaum and Pedersen [4], and by Camenisch and Shoup [5] already. It follows that $sim_P$ can be defined as the concatenation of $sim_1 \| \cdots \| sim_m$. It is easy to see that the view generated by $sim_P$ is computationally indistinguishable from that generated by $P$ in the real world protocol.

Combining Lemma 1 and Lemma 2, we have the main statement below.

Theorem: The AOPE protocol is provably secure if the underlying Fujisaki-Okamoto's commitment scheme is informational hiding and computational biding as well Paillier's encryption scheme is semantically secure in the common reference string model.

## 4   Applications

There are two main types of applications in which OPE protocol is useful: first when it is required to enable the receiver to obliviously obtain a value from a $m$-wise independent space. The second application is when it is desired to preserve anonymity in cryptographic protocols which require a user to get a value of a polynomial held by the sender without revealing the choice of the sender. Thus our AOPE protocol can be applied to the scenario of keyword search protocol [11] and [8] and the privacy preserving auctions [13] as well as private matching and set intersection [9]. We now further suggest the following implementation of the greater gate protocol by applying our AOPE protocol:

Greater gate protocol can be abstracted as the following problem: on input two commitments $C(a)$ and $C(b)$ (Alice holds $a$ privately while Bob holds $b$ privately). The output of is $>$ or $\leq$. This protocol is useful for real world applications. We now apply our AOPE protocol to deal with this problem as a supportive example to demonstrate the power of our AOPE protocol.

- On input $a$, Alice chooses two non-zero random strings $s_a$, $r_a$ from $\{0,1\}^k$ and provides the commitment $C(a)$ of $a$ and the commitments $C(s_a)$ for $s_a$ and $C(r_a)$ for $r_a$ using Fujisaki-Okamoto's commitment scheme. Similarly, on input $b$, Bob chooses two non-zero random strings $s_b$, $r_b$ from $\{0,1\}^k$ and provides the commitment $C(b)$ of $b$ and the commitments of $s_b$ and $r_b$ using the same Fujisaki-Okamoto's commitment scheme.
- Alice and Bob then involve the processing of the following computation: $\delta$: $=(a-b)(r_a+r_b)$. Notice that $\delta$ can be rewritten as $\delta = (ar_a+s_a) + (ar_b+s_b)$ $-(r_ab + s_a)$ - $(br_b + s_b)$ (in the rest of paper, all computations are defined over the integer domain);
  - Alice computes $\alpha_a$: $=(ar_a + s_a)$ while Bob computes $\alpha_b := (br_b + s_b)$ locally.
  - on input $C(a)$, $C(r_b)$ and $C(s_b)$, Alice and Bob run AOPE protocol together so that Alice obtains $\beta_a$: $=(ar_b + s_b)$ while Bob knows nothing;
  - on input $C(r_a)$, $C(s_a)$ and $C(b)$, Alice and Bob run AOPE protocol together so that Bob obtains $\beta_b := (r_ab + s_a)$ while Alice knows nothing;
- Once given $\beta_a$, Alice can compute $\gamma_a = \alpha_a + \beta_a$; And at the same time Bob can compute $\gamma_b = \alpha_b + \beta_b$;
- Alice sends $\gamma_a$ to Bob while Bob sends $\gamma_b$ to Alice;

The rest work of Alice is to show Bob that $\gamma_a$ is computed from $\alpha_a + \beta_a$ while Bob's task is to show Alice that $\gamma_b$ is computed from $\alpha_b + \beta_b$. To convince Bob $\gamma_a$ is computed from $\alpha_a + \beta_a$, Alice processes the following protocol with Bob. That is,

- Alice computes $E_A(\alpha)$ and proves to Bob that both the encryption $E_A(a)$ and the commitment $C(a)$ hide the same non-zero value, where $E_A$ stands for Alice's encryption scheme (it is specified by an instance of Paillier's encryption with sufficiently long public key $N_A$) by means of Damgård and Jurik approach;
- Bob then sends $E_A(1)$ to Alice; Since Alice has private key correspondent to $E_A$, it follows that the correctness of Bob's encryption can be verified.
- Alice then proves to Bob that $E_A(\alpha_a) = E_A(a)^{r_a} E_A(1)^{s_a}$ by means of the standard technique used already by Chaum and Pedersen [4], and by Camenisch and Shoup [5];
- Since Alice and Bob can run AOPE protocol together so that Alice obtains $E_A(\beta_a)$, thus Alice can compute the encryption of $E_A(\gamma_a)$: $=E_A(\alpha_a) E_A(\beta_a)$. Alice further proves to Bob that $\gamma_a$ and $t_a$ are exact decryption of $E_A(\gamma_a)$, where $t_a$ is a random string used to generate the cipher-text $E_A(\gamma_a)$. Notice

that this is possible since Paillier's encryption can be viewed as alternative commitment scheme (both message and a random string can be extracted from the cipher-text with the help of private key) due to the observation stated in Section 2.

## 5 Conclusion

In this paper, a new notion called augmented oblivious polynomial evaluation is introduced and formalized and then a novel yet efficient implementation of the primitive is proposed which has been proved secure with our model assuming that the underlying Fujisaki-Okamoto commitment scheme is unconditional hiding and computational binding, together with Paillier's encryption is semantic secure. Like its sibling notion, our protocol has numerous applications as well.

## References

1. Fabrice Boudot: Efficient Proofs that a Committed Number Lies in an Interval. Proc. of EUROCRYPT 2000: 431-444, Springer Verlag.
2. Daniel Bleichenbacher1 and Phong Q. Nguyen. Noisy Polynomial Interpolation and Noisy Chinese Remaindering. EUROCRYPT 2000, LNCS 1807, pp. 53-69, 2000.
3. R. Canetti: Universally Composable Security: A New Paradigm for Cryptographic Protocols. FOCS 2001: 136-145
4. David Chaum, Torben P. Pedersen: Wallet Databases with Observers. CRYPTO 1992: 89-105.
5. Jan Camenisch, Victor Shoup: Practical Verifiable Encryption and Decryption of Discrete Logarithms. CRYPTO 2003: 126-144
6. Ivan Damgård, Mads Jurik: Client/Server Tradeoffs for Online Elections. Proc. of Public Key Cryptography 2002: 125-140. Springer Verlag.
7. Ivan Damgård, Eiichiro Fujisaki: A Statistically-Hiding Integer Commitment Scheme Based on Groups with Hidden Order. Proc. of ASIACRYPT 2002: 125-142, Springer Verlag.
8. Michael J. Freedman1, Yuval Ishai, Benny Pinkas, and Omer Reingold. Keyword Search and Oblivious Pseudorandom Functions, 2nd Theory of Cryptography Conference (TCC'05).
9. Michael J. Freedman, Kobbi Nissim, Benny Pinkas: Efficient Private Matching and Set Intersection. EUROCRYPT 2004: 1-19
10. E. Fujisaki, T. Okamoto. Statistically zero knowledge protocols to prove modular polynomial relations. Crypto'97. 16-30, 1997.
11. Wakaha Ogata and Kaoru Kurosawa, Oblivious keyword search. Journal of Complexity, Vol.20, pp.356-371, 2004.
12. Moni Naor, Benny Pinkas: Oblivious Transfer and Polynomial Evaluation. STOC 1999: 245-254
13. Moni Naor, Benny Pinkas, Reuban Sumner: Privacy preserving auctions and mechanism design. ACM Conference on Electronic Commerce 1999: 129-139.
14. Pascal Paillier: Public-Key Cryptosystems Based on Composite Degree Residuosity Classes. Proc. of EUROCRYPT 1999: 223-238, Springer Verlag.

# Using Attack Trees to Identify Malicious Attacks from Authorized Insiders

Indrajit Ray and Nayot Poolsapassit

Colorado State University,
Fort Collins, CO 80523, USA
{indrajit, nayot}@cs.colostate.edu

**Abstract.** A major concern for computer systems security is the threat from malicious insiders who execute perfectly legitimate operations to compromise system security. Unfortunately, most currently available intrusion detection systems (which include anomaly and misuse detection systems) fail to address this problem in a comprehensive manner. In this work we propose a framework that uses an attack tree to identify malicious activities from authorized insiders. We develop algorithms to generate minimal forms of attack tree customized for each user such that it can be used efficiently to monitor the user's activities. If the user's activities progress sufficiently up along the branches of the attack tree towards the goal of system compromise, we generate an alarm. Our system is not intended to replace existing intrusion detection and prevention technology, but rather is intended to complement current and future technology.

## 1  Introduction

Intrusion detection systems are an important tool to system administrators in their fight against malicious attacks on systems. These tools monitor different system activities and report on anything that can be construed as malicious. The system administrator looks at the reports generated by the intrusion detection system and (based on experience to some extent) determines which of the activities are malicious. In this work, we propose a quantitative approach to help system administrators make sound judgements regarding ensuing attacks. Our system is intended to complement existing tools to fight the war against crackers.

Existing intrusion detection systems suffer from two shortcomings. First, not many of them do a good job in handling threats from malicious insiders. These attacks, which are often considered to cause the majority of security breaches, can arise in one of two ways: (i) A user uses perfectly legitimate operations to exploit known system vulnerabilities and launches an attack. (ii) A user uses information and resources that do not fall directly under the category of computer system resources, and launches attack. An example of the former is the buffer overflow attack using the Unix "lpr" command in HP True64 Unix operating system as reported by CERT in CERT-VU #651377 (see http://www.kb.cert.org/vuls/id/IAFY-5DQPFL). We are more interested in addressing these types of attacks. The latter category is considerably more difficult to prevent, detect or deter. Addressing such threats is beyond the scope of the current work.

S. De Capitani di Vimercati et al. (Eds.): ESORICS 2005, LNCS 3679, pp. 231–246, 2005.

A second concern with intrusion detection systems is that they generate alerts only after they are able to see the misuse signatures or some deviations from norm. A malicious activity may result from a sequence of perfectly innocuous activities. Intrusion detection systems do not report on these activities mostly to prevent information overload for the system administrator. Thus the intrusion detection system generates an alarm only after the cause for alarm has occurred. In many situations however, this may already be too late.

These two factors lead us to propose a new approach that can be used to predict attacks arising from an insider's activities. Our work uses the user-intent analysis approach proposed earlier by Upadhyaya et al. [2, 14, 15, 16]. Upadhyaya et al's approach consists of ensuring that during a particular session a user remains reasonably within the scope of a previously declared set of activities. Any digression beyond this reasonable limit constitutes a misuse of system and steps are taken to protect against such digressions. However, this approach fails to account for the fact that a user may remain completely within the scope of a previosuly declared set of activities and still be able to launch attacks. This is where our approach contributes.

We begin by assuming that it is possible to enumerate the different attacks that a user can launch against a given system. This assumption is not unreasonable for known attacks. Almost all network vulnerability scanners provide such information. We then determine all the possible actions by which a user can launch an attack against the system. We map these actions against a user's session scope to identify which sequences of these actions can potentially lead to system compromise. Next we monitor each user's activities to see if and how they match against these sequences. Depending on the match we propose an estimator of attack probability.

Our approach is different from classical intrusion detection systems. It works as an early warning system. We continuously provide the system administrator an estimator of attack probability. Thus we cannot associate a rate of false positives or negatives with our technique. Our objective is to ensure that the system enters an alert mode once the probability of an attack is determined to be sufficiently strong. The notion of "sufficiently strong" is based on perceived risks. In the alert state, the following actions will be undertaken to ensure the survivability of information in case of an actual attack.

1. Allocate additional resources to assist in data collection by logging system wide activities more aggressively, saving system states more frequently and initiating recovery contingency plans by coordinating with other monitors.
2. Re-distribute essential services to other safer portions of the network.
3. Introduce mechanisms to handle possible attacks including ways to contain the attack.

All these activities are continued until either an intrusion is actually signaled by accompanying intrusion detection system or no further signs of attack are identified.

The advantage of our approach is that it is a flexible and resource efficient technique for security management. At the same time it is a guarded approach. If an attack succeeds (which is determined by techniques other than ours), it allows the system to be in a fully prepared mode for subsequent recovery.

The rest of the paper is organized as follows. In section 2 we briefly discuss the work by Upadhyaya et al. which is the starting point of our work. Section 3 discusses our proposed approach. We begin the section with an overview of our approach. In section 3.1 we introduce the notion of augmented attack trees which helps us model system wide vulnerabilities that a user can potentially exploit. We further refine the augmented attack tree in section 3.2 to propose the minimal cut of an attack tree with respect to a given user intent. Finally section 4 concludes the paper.

## 2   Background and Related Work

In [14, 15, 16] the authors propose CIDS, a host-based concurrent intrusion detection scheme. The system is based on *user work profiling* [5]. This technique assumes that if one can encapsulate the intent of a user in a reasonable manner, then it is possible to assess intrusions by monitoring the activities on-line. The system works as follows. Sometime prior to login, a user submits a description of his intended system usage. This forms the user's *session scope*. The system converts the scope to a "SPRINT" (Signature Powered Revised Instruction Table) plan which is a list (may be ordered) of quadruples of the form $< subject, action, object, period >$. Here "subject" represents a user, "action" is an operation performed by the subject (such as login, logout, read etc.), "object" is the target of an action (such as files, programs, messages, printers etc.), and "period" represents the time interval for the duration of the action. Each quadruple represents a *verifiable assertion*, a concept that is a generalization of IDES's [4] specification of user characteristics, and can be monitored on-line. When a user is active, a monitor process (called the "Watchdog") monitors the user's commands and checks them against the user's SPRINT plan. Deviations beyond a certain tolerance limit is considered potential intrusions and CIDS generates alerts for such deviations. The basic CIDS system flow diagram is shown in figure 1.

The basic scheme [16] described above is improved upon by the authors in a later work [14]. In particular, the authors adopt the notion of reasonableness check to address

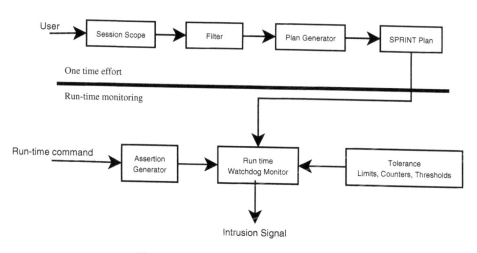

**Fig. 1.** Flow diagram for the CIDS system

issues like "what is a reasonable SPRINT plan" and "what is a reasonable deviation from the SPRINT plan". The authors use risk analysis techniques to estimate, from a given SPRINT plan, what events can possibly occur in the future (including their probabilities of happening) and the costs associated with those events.

One drawback of this work is that the authors do not address the scenario when a user does not deviate in any manner from the SPRINT plan, but still is able to launch an attack. The authors consider deviations from the SPRINT plan to be malicious, which is okay. However, their system fail to generate an alert if the user does not deviate from the SPRINT plan. Our work addresses this particular problem.

## 3    The Attack Prediction System

Our attack prediction system works briefly as follows. We begin by developing a model of network risks. We augment the notion of attack trees [8, 11] for this purpose. We introduce the notion of "attack probability" as labels of nodes in the attack tree. Next we iteratively apply each user's SPRINT plan to the augmented attack tree, to generate a trimmed attack tree for each user. We call such an attack tree the minimal cut of an attack tree with respect to the user intent. Branches of this trimmed attack tree represent, in a concise manner, all the different ways by which a user can use his assigned job privileges to launch an attack on the system. In the event such a trimmed attack tree does not exist for a particular user, we can safely claim that the user's current job description does not pose a threat to the system. This does not necessarily mean, however, that we can cease to monitor this user's activities. If we allow a user to deviate from her/his SPRINT plan as is done in the original work [2] then we should continue monitoring the user as proposed in that work. For this work we will assume that the users we are planning to monitor are the ones who, by virtue of their work definition, are able to launch attacks against the system.

In the following sections we describe each component of our system in details. We begin by describing how we augment the notion of attack trees to model network risks.

### 3.1    Augmented Attack Trees

Attack trees have been previously proposed [3, 8, 11] as a systematic method to specify system security based on varying attacks. They help organize intrusion and/or misuse scenarios by

1. utilizing known vulnerabilities and/or weak spots in the system, and
2. analyzing system dependencies and weak links and representing these dependencies in the form of an And-Or tree.

For every system that needs to be defended there is a different attack tree[1]. The nodes of the tree are used to represent the stages towards an attack. The root node of the tree represents the attacker's ultimate goal, namely, cause damage to the system. The

---

[1] Actually there can be a forest of trees. However, a forest can be always collapsed to a single tree. So we will assume that there is a single tree.

interior nodes, including leaf-nodes, represent possible system states (that is subgoals) during the execution of an attack. System states can include level of compromise by the attacker (such as successful access to a web page or successful acquisition of root privileges), configuration or state changes achieved on specific system components (such as implantation of Trojan Horses) and other sub-goals that will ultimately lead to the final goal (such as sequence of vulnerabilities exploited). Branches represent a change of state caused by one or more action taken by the attacker. Change in state is represented by either AND-branches or OR-branches. Nodes may be decomposed as

1. a sequence of events (attacks) all of which must be achieved for a this sub-goal to succeed; this is represented by the events being combined by AND branches at the node; or
2. a set of events (attacks), any one of which occurring will result in the sub-goal succeeding; this is represented by the events being combined by OR branches at the node.

The notion of attacks trees is related to the notion of attack graphs that have been proposed by other researchers [1, 6, 7, 9, 12, 13] for network vulnerability analysis. The difference is in the representation of states and actions. Attack graphs model systems vulnerabilities in terms of all possible sequence of attack operations. As pointed out by Ritchey and Ammann [10] a major shortcoming of this approach is its scalability. On the other hand, attack trees model system vulnerabilities in terms of cause and effect. Sequential ordering of events does not have to be captured in attack graphs. Thus constructing an attack tree is significantly less complex than attack graphs. An often cited criticism of attack trees (vis-a-vis attack graphs) is that they are not able to model cycles. However, we believe that this criticism is valid only in cases where attack trees are used to represent sequence of operations leading to attacks, not when they are used to represent the dependency of states reached. A second criticism of using attack tree to model attack scenarios is that they tend to get unwieldy. One contribution of this work is that we provide algorithms to minimize the size of the attck tree so that it is usable.

We assume that a technique is available to generate an attack tree corresponding to the network system we are attempting to defend. Figure 2 shows a simple attack tree for a hypothetical system that we are planning to defend.

In the network in figure 2 there is a server that stores and manages sensitive information. It is connected to a network printer. The network allows users to connect to systems either via wired connections or wirelessly. The ultimate objective of an attacker is to acquire root access on the server. To break the system the attacker may attack either via the buffer overflow attack on the lpr command or via the setuid command. These activities are represented as state transitions in the attack tree. Later on in the paper we define these activities as atomic attacks. The first atomic attack can be done without any pre-condition. The latter can be effected only if the attacker gains user privilege on the server machine.

We augment an attack tree by associating a label $< n, m >$ with each node in the attack tree. The augmented attack tree is defined formally as follows:

**Definition 1.** *An* augmented attack tree *is a rooted tree defined as* $AAT = (V, E, \epsilon, L)$, *where*

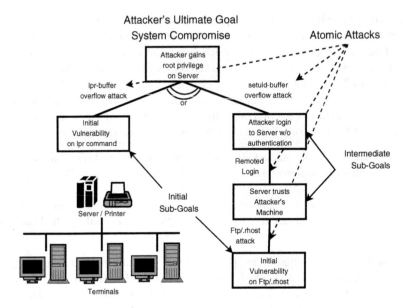

**Fig. 2.** Simple Attack Tree Corresponding to a Hypothetical System

1. *V is the set of nodes in the tree representing the different states of compromise or sub-goals that an attacker need to reach in order to compromise a system. $\mathcal{V} \in V$ is a special node, distinguished from others, that forms the root of the tree. It represents the ultimate goal of the attacker, namely system compromise. The set $V$ can be partitioned into two subsets, $leaf\_nodes$ and $internal\_nodes$, such that*
   (a) *$leaf\_nodes \cup internal\_nodes = V$,*
   (b) *$leaf\_nodes \cap internal\_nodes = \phi$, and*
   (c) *$\mathcal{V} \in internal\_nodes$*
2. *$E \subseteq V \times V$ constitutes the set of edges in the attack tree. An edge $(v_i, v_j) \in E$ represents the state transition (in terms of actions taken) from a child node $v_i \in V$ to a parent node $v_j \in V$ in the tree. The edge $(v_i, v_j)$ is said to be "emergent from" $v_i$ and "incident to" $v_j$. Further if edges $(v_i, v_j)$ and $(v_i, v_k)$ exists in the set of edges, then $v_j$ and $v_k$ represent the same node.*
3. *$\epsilon$ is a set of tuples of the form $< v, decomposition >$ such that*
   (a) *$v \in internal\_nodes$ and*
   (b) *$decomposition \in [AND - decomposition, OR - decomposition]$*
4. *L is a set of attack probability labels. A label $l \in L$ is associated with a node. If $S \in V$ is a node then the attack probability label $l_S$, associated with node S, is given by the tuple $< n, m >$ where m and n are positive integers greater than 0 with $n \leq m$. The value of n for the node S can change over a period of time; however the value of m is fixed for the node S. The item m is termed the least effort to compromise subgoal S while the item n is termed the number of currently compromised subgoals under S.*

   The values $m$ and $n$ in the attack probability label of the root node $\mathcal{V}$ are of particular interest to us. The ratio $\frac{n}{m}$ at any given time provides a measure of how far an attacker has progressed towards the ultimate goal in terms of the least effort along the most advanced attack path that he has been through. Thus this ratio provides the probability of the system getting compromised at that time. The values $m$ and $n$ corresponding to the root node are computed based on the corresponding values for the other nodes. At this time we show how to compute the value of $m$ for any given node. Note that this is a one time effort that is done during system initialization. First, some additional definitions.

**Definition 2.** *Given a node, $v$ in an attack tree such that $v \in internal\_nodes$, the node is an* AND-*decomposition if all edges incident to the node are connected by the* AND *operation.*

**Definition 3.** *Given a node $v$ of an attack tree such that $v \in internal\_nodes$, the node is an* OR-*decomposition if all edges incident to the node are connected by the OR operation.*

An AND-decomposition, $v$, (shown by a single arc among the edges incident to $V$ in figure 2) means that each subgoal of $v$ represented by a child of $v$ needs to be reached in order to reach $v$. An OR-decomposition (shown by a double arc in figure 2) means that the goal $v$ can be reach only if any one of the subgoals is reached. Note that reaching a child goal is only a necessary condition for reaching the parent goal and not a sufficient condition. An instance of an augmented attack tree is shown in figure 3.

Let us assume without loss of generality that the attacker uses one unit of *effort* to perform one atomic attack that furthers his goal. In other words, each hop along

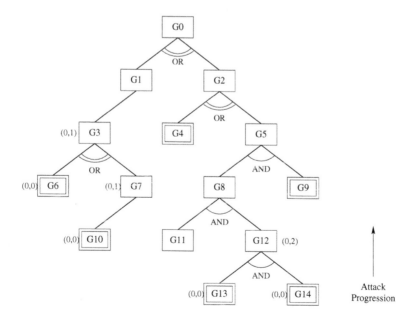

**Fig. 3.** Example of an Augmented Attack Tree

one edge of the attack tree takes one unit of effort to get through. The *least effort to compromise a subgoal* is the minimum effort the attacker needs to compromise the given subgoal. If a given goal $S$ has an OR-decomposition, the least effort is computed as the minimum least efforts of its child nodes plus one unit effort needed to advance to $S$ from the child node. If the goal $S$ has an AND-decomposition then the least effort is the sum of the least efforts of the child nodes plus all additional unit efforts, one for each child node to go to $S$. The following definition captures the steps to compute the least effort for a subgoal $S$.

**Definition 4.** *Given a subgoal* S *and its child subgoals* $S_i$*, the* least effort *to compromise* S*,* $m_s$*, is defined as follows.*

1. *If* S *is a leaf node of the attack tree the least effort is 0.*
2. *If* S *is some interior node and is an AND-decomposition, then* $m_s = Sum(m_{s_i}) + k$ *where* k *is the number of child nodes* $S_i$ *of* S.
3. *If* S *is some interior node and is an OR-decomposition, then* $m_s = Min(m_{s_i}) + 1$.

Henceforth we will use the terms attack tree and augmented attack tree interchangeably to mean the latter.

### 3.2    Minimal Cut of Attack Trees w.r.t. User Intent

An augmented attack tree can be used to model system vulnerabilities in a very effective manner. The attack tree describes all possible ways in which a particular attack can be launched. If there are more than one attacks against a system that we are concerned about, we can generate separate attack trees for each. However, there are a few drawbacks of the attack tree defined as it is now. First, for a complex system the attack tree can become quite deep and spread out. Thus it will become difficult to manage. Second, it is possible that a number of users are executing the same set of operations albeit at different paces. In this case, the cumulative effects of these users' actions will be reflected on the attack tree. If the users are not colluding this does not give the true picture of the state of the attack. For example, let a user have initially launched an attack and have compromised upto subgoal $S_1$ of $S$ in an attack tree. Another user has compromised upto subgoal $S_2$. If the node $S$ is an AND-decompostion of $S_1$ and $S_2$, the model will indicate that subgoal $S$ is compromised. However, if the two users are not co-operating, then this is not the case. Thus, we want to refine the concept of attack tree so that we are able to monitor each individual user's activities. If we believe there is possibility of collusion among attackers we will maintain the system-wide attack tree as generated so far in addition to the per-user attack tree that we are now ready to define.

That a per-user attack tree is relevant is further strengthened by the following observation. For any attack, we may not always need to know all possible ways the attack can be launched, but rather the practical ways. In the case of attacks from insiders, for example, we are interested only in the activities of authorized users in the system. Thus, we want to determine if the operations that a user executes can lead to an attack. This implies that for a particular user, only a portion of an attack tree is relevant. This leads us to propose the notion of a minimal cut of an attack tree with respect to a user intent. We begin with the following definitions.

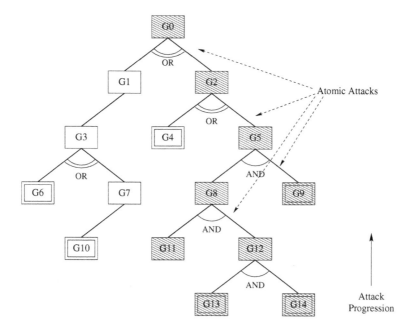

**Fig. 4.** A Possible Attack Scenario

**Definition 5.** *Given an attack tree, AAT, an attack scenario, AS of AAT is defined to be a sub-tree of AAT that is rooted at the root of AAT, and follows one or more branches through the tree to end at one or more leaf nodes of AAT such that*

1. *if the subtree has a node that is an AND-decomposition then the subtree must contain all the children of this node, and*
2. *the sub-tree represents one and only one of the many attacks described by AAT.*

The following figure represents one possible attack-scenario corresponding to the attack graph of figure 3, with the shaded boxes constituting the nodes in the attack scenario.

**Definition 6.** *An edge* $(v_i, v_j)$ *in an attack scenario is called an* atomic attack. *The node* $v_i$ *represents the precondition for the atomic attack and* $v_j$ *is the goal.*

Referring to figure 4 some of the atomic attacks have been shown by dashed arrows. Note that to achieve an atomic attack, the attacker must execute some operations that exploit one or more vulnerabilities in the system. Once a vulnerability has been exploited the attacker executes a set of "attacking operations" that achieve the goal of an atomic attack. Thus,

**Definition 7.** *A suspicious operations set,* $SO^{attk}$, *corresponding to an atomic attack attk, is a set of operations on specific objects that may potentially lead to the culmination of the atomic attack attk.* $SO^{attk}$ *is a set of tuples of the form* $< action, object >$.

We can identify two different types of operations in a suspicious operations set, $SO^{attk}$. The first subset of operations is the set $Vul$ of vulnerable operations. At least one of the operations in the vulnerable set needs to be executed to exploit a vulnerability. An atomic attack can be launched by exploiting one or more vulnerabilities. Similarly each vulnerability can be exploited by executing one or more vulnerable operations. The second subset of operations is the set $Ao$ of attacking operations. All of these needs to be executed to accomplish the atomic attack.

We would like to point out here that we specifically omit the use of the term "sequence" from the definition of suspicious operations set. It is quite possible that only a particular order of execution of the operations will lead to an attack. Since we are interested in estimating the probability of an attack and not just reporting on the attack if and when it is launched, we are interested in all the operations in the set and not just the operations in some particular order.

**Definition 8.** *The set of intended operations of a particular user, IOS, is a projection of the SPRINT plan for the user over attributes action and object.*

We need to be worried about a user's SPRINT plan if some members of the corresponding intended operations set includes a suspicious operations set. We define the intended operations to *abet an attack subgoal* as follows.

**Definition 9.** *Given, an attack subgoal $v_i$ (that is a node in an attack scenario) decomposed as the set $A$ of atomic attacks $attk_i$, the suspicious operations sets corresponding to each atomic attack, $SO_i^{attk}$, and a set of intended operations, $IOS$ for a user, we say that the intended operations abet the attack subgoal if and only if one of the following conditions holds true.*

1. *If $v_i$ is an AND-decomposition with $m$ edges then $\forall i$, $1 \leq i \leq m$, $SO_i^{attk} \subseteq IOS$*
2. *If $v_i$ is an OR-decomposition with $m$ edges then $\exists i$, $1 \leq i \leq m$, $SO_i^{attk} \subseteq IOS$*

*The intended operations abet an attack scenario if the intended operations abet all attack subgoal in that attack scenario.*

Recall that one of our objectives is to determine if a user's activities in a system can lead to an attack on the system. A related objective is to determine the exact way in which an attack can be launched with the user's intended operations. Thus, given an attack scenario, $AS$, consisting of subgoals $(a_1, a_2, \ldots, a_n)$, we need to determine for each user's intended operations, if the intended operations abet every subgoal $a_i \in AS$. If the intended operations do not abet every subgoal $a_i$ in $AS$, it implies that this particular attack scenario cannot arise from the user's activities. However, this does not mean that another attack scenario cannot arise from the same intended operations. What we need to identity, therefore, is the maximal set of attack scenarios that can arise from a given set of intended operations.

**Definition 10.** *The minimal cut, $MC_{IOS}$, of an attack tree, $AAT$ with respect to a particular user intent, $IOS$, is the minimal subtree of $AAT$ which is rooted at the root of $AAT$ and whose leaf nodes are a subset of the leaf nodes of $AAT$, such that the subtree includes the maximal set and only the maximal set of attack scenarios that can arise from $IOS$.*

---

**Algorithm 1** PRUNING ALGORITHM (AAT, r, IOS)

---

{**Description:** This algorithm takes an attack tree and a set of intended operations for a particular user and generates a confined version of the attack tree. The original attack tree is represented as a tree structure in which each node except the leaf nodes, contains an array of adjacency lists. Each element in the array represents an attack subgoal. For each attack subgoal, $V_i$, $Adj[V_i]$ contains a reference to a pre-condition subgoal. Each edge in the set $E$ of edges refer to an atomic attack. The algorithm assumes the existence of a procedure called OPERATIONS that takes an edge $e[u, v]$ corresponding to a state transition in the attack tree and returns the set of operations that result in the state transition. It also assumes a second procedure called PARENT that takes a node $v$ and returns the parent of $v$. The algorithm uses three temporary queues called Explore-List, $E'$ and $V'$ with operation ENQUEUE and DE-QUEUE defined. Finally, the algorithm assumes a procedure DRAW_TREE that builds a tree given a set of nodes and edges}

{**Input:** The attack tree $AAT$, its root, $r$ and the set of intended operations for the user, $IOS$}

{**Output:** The pruned attack tree containing the minimal cut of the attack tree with respect to the user intent.}

ENQUEUE(Explore-List, r)
$E' \leftarrow \phi$
$V' \leftarrow \phi$
**while** Explore-List $\neq \phi$ **do**
  u $\leftarrow$ DEQUEUE(Explore-List)
  ANY_MET $\leftarrow false$
  **for all** $v \in Adj[u]$ **do**
    ENQUEUE(Explore-List,$v$)
    **if** OPERATIONS($[u,v]$) $\subseteq$ IOS **then**
      ENQUEUE($E'$,$[u,v]$)
      ANY_MET $\leftarrow true$
    **end if**
  **end for**
  **if** $(Adj[u] = \phi)$ && $([PARENT(u),u] \in E')$ **then**
    ENQUEUE($V'$,$u$)
  **end if**
  **if** ANY_MET $= true$ **then**
    ENQUEUE($V'$,$u$)
  **end if**
**end while**
DRAW_TREE($V'$,$E'$)

---

We now give two algorithms (algorithms 1 and 2) applying which in sequence gives us a minimal cut of an attack tree with respect to a given user intent. We call the first algorithm the Pruning Algorithm and the second algorithm the Trimming Algorithm. The first algorithm takes an attack tree and generates a subtree rooted at the root of the attack tree such that the subtree contains the desired minimal cut. It removes from the original tree any attack scenarios whose attack subgoals are not abetted by the intended operations. The second algorithm further reduces the subtree produced by the pruning algorithm to produce the minimal cut.

The following theorems hold on the pruning algorithm.

**Theorem 1.** *Let $ATT = (V, E, \epsilon, L)$ be an augmented attack tree and assume that the pruning algorithm is executed on $ATT$ starting with the root node $r \in V$. If the user's actions abet an attack then that attack subgoal will be present in the pruned attack tree generated by the pruning algorithm.*

*Proof.* To prove soundness of the algorithm we need to prove that during its execution the pruning algorithm explores every state $s$ that forms an attack subgoal for the attacker and includes it in the pruned attack tree. To prove completeness, we must prove that if a node $s$ is included in the pruned attack tree it must form an attack subgoal for the attacker.

First let assume that at the termination of the pruning algorithm, an attack subgoal $s \in V$ which can lead to the root of the attack tree exists such that it is not enqueued by the pruning algorithm. The pruning algorithm starts by exploring the root's adjacent nodes and then iteratively explores the adjacent nodes of these. Thus, if there is an unexplored subgoal $s$ left at the termination of the pruning algorithm, it must be the case that that subgoal $s$ is not be reachable from the root. Then according to the definition 1, subgoal $s \notin V$ which contradicts the assumption.

We prove completeness of the algorithm as follows. Let us assume that at the termination of the algorithm there exist a state transition $e[u, v] \in E$ such that $SO_{e[u,v]} \subseteq IOs$ but $e[u, v] \notin E'$. Since all states in an attack tree have been explored, then $e[u, v]$ must have been explored. By definition 9, if user intent IOs abet an atomic attack which corresponds to the state transition $e[u, v]$, it must be explored and included in $E'$. This results in a contradiction.

The pruned attack tree generated by the pruning algorithm may include atomic attacks that however can never materialize from a user's activities. This is because the preconditions to these attacks are never satisfied by the user actions. For example, a user's intent may abet a remote login attack but may not abet the user to perform an ftp/.rhost attack on the target machine. In this case, the attacker cannot perform these atomic attacks at least till such time as they are not permitted to modify their intent. The next algorithm called the trimming algorithm removes these attack scenarios and produces the minimal cut of attack tree.

**Theorem 2.** *If the trimmed attack tree generated from a pruned attack tree by the application of a user's intended operation contains an attack scenario, then the intended operations abet that particular attack scenario.*

*Proof.* Let assume that there exist subgoal $s$ (which its preconditions are met by the user intents) mistakenly removed by the trimming algorithm.

According to the semantic of the trimming algorithm, the *while loop* in the trimming algorithm explores every node in the input pruned tree and the *for loop* trying to discover all possible paths from the leaf nodes to a subgoal currently explored by the *while loop*'s iteration. Then the remove instruction removes a subgoal if and only if the previous *for loop* could not find such a path to the leaf node. We will split subgoal $s$ in 2 cases.

Case 1: If subgoal $s \in V'$ is an initial subgoal, this case could not have happened since the if statement of *line 6* in the procedure detect the leaf node. Then the initial subgoal $s \notin$ Minimal cut if and only if $s \notin V'$ which contradicts the previous assumption.

---

**Algorithm 2** TRIMMING ALGORITHM $(V', E')$

---

{**Description:** This algorithm takes the pruned attack tree generated by the pruninng algorithm, and removes attack goals that the user can never reach.}
{**Input:** The set of nodes from the pruned attack tree, ordered by traversing the tree in breadth first order and stored in an array $V'$, and the corresponding set of edges $E'$}
{**Output:** Minimal cut of an attack tree with respect to user intent}


$i \leftarrow$ SIZEOF(V$'$)
**while** $(i > 0)$ **do**
   $u \leftarrow V'[i]$
   $i \leftarrow i - 1$
   $valid \leftarrow false$
   **if** $Adj[u] = \phi$ **then**
     $valid \leftarrow true$
   **else**
     **for all** $v \in Adj[u]$ **do**
       **if** $v \in V'$ **then**
         $valid \leftarrow true$
       **else**
         remove $(u,v)$ from $E'$
       **end if**
     **end for**
   **end if**
   **if** $\neg valid$ **then**
     remove $u$ from $V'$
   **end if**
**end while**
DRAW_TREE$(V',E')$

---

Case 2: If subgoal $s \in V'$ is an intermediate subgoal, $s$ will be removed by the trimming algorithm if and only if $s$ can not be reached from any initial subgoal. This means the preconditions of an intermediate subgoal $s$ are not met which contradicts the previous assumption.

### 3.3  Computing Probability of Attack by User

We now use the minimal cut of an attack tree with respect to a user intent to determine the probability of an attack originating from that user. Algorithm 3 computes the attack probability label of a subgoal at any given time $t$. By applying this algorithm on the root node of the minimal cut of an attack tree for a user, we get the attack probability label corresponding to the root at time $t$. The ratio n/m at time $t$ gives the probability of the user's attack succeeding at time $t$.

Figure 5 shows an example trace for the algorithm 3. Assume that at time $t$ a malicious user compromises the subgoals shown in the figure. The algorithm computes the $< n, m >$ value for the root of the tree as follows. All leaf-nodes return value (0, 0). Node A.1 and A.3 have the summation equal to (0, 0) since their immediate child nodes

**Algorithm 3** Risk-Analysis(Subgoal A)

{**Description:** This algorithm takes an attack tree subgoal A and returns the attack probability label (n,m) for that goal. Here n refers to the number of nodes that have been compromised on the most advanced attack paths and m refer to the least-effort needed to compromise A on that path.}

{**Input:** A subgoal of an attack tree}

{**Output:** 1. Number of subgoals that have been compromised along the most advanced attack path. 2. Least-effort needed to compromise the subgoal along the most advanced attack path. }

Let n = number of currently compromised subgoal under A on the most advanced attacking path.

Let m = least-effort needed to compromise A on the most advanced path.

**if** A is a leaf node **then**
    return (0,0)
**end if**
**if** A is an AND-Decomposition **then**
    (n,m)← Sum {Risk-Analysis($A_i$) | $\forall A_i Childnodesof A$}
    **if** A is compromised **then**
        return (n+k, m+k)
    **else**
        return (n, m+k)
    **end if**
**else**
    (n, m) ← Max{(n/m) of Risk-Analysis($A_i$) | $\forall A_i Childnodesof A$}
    **if** A is compromised **then**
        return (n+1, m+1)
    **else**
        return (n, m+1)
    **end if**
**end if**

are all leaf nodes. When A.1 is compromised the procedure returns (2, 2). Similarly for A.3 the procedure returns (0, 2). For B.1 and B.3 the values are (1, 1) and (0, 1) respectively. At this point the value of (2, 2) tells us that it takes 2 unit efforts to compromise A.1. The attacker has already compromised A.1 but no damage has been done on A.3. Next we calculate value on A. Eventually, since the root is an AND-decomposition on two branches A and B the least effort is 8 + 2 = 10 and the number of compromised nodes is 3. This yields a probability of attack value of $\frac{3}{10}$ at time $t$.

## 4   Conclusions and Future Work

In this paper, we propose a proactive approach to predicting network attacks that can potentially result from a insider exploiting known system vulnerabilities through the execution of authorized operations. Our system is intended to complement existing intrusion detection systems to help fight unwelcome cracker activities. We develop a quantitative framework. Our approach is proactive in the sense that we want to provide the system administrator an early warning. We want the system to enter an alert mode

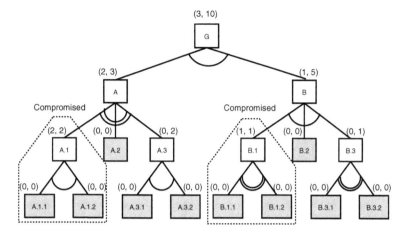

**Fig. 5.** Computing attack probability label for attack subgoal

once the probability of an attack is determined to be sufficiently strong and remain in that state until either an intrusion is actually signaled by an intrusion detection system or no further signs of attack are identified. The advantage of our approach is that it is a flexible and resource efficient technique for security management. At the same time it is a guarded approach. If an attack succeeds, it allows the system to be in a fully prepared mode for subsequent recovery. Moreover, although we develop this framework with insider threats in mind our approach can be easily adapted to predict threats from the outside.

At this stage the model has one shortcoming. The model results in the probability of an ensuing attack to increase continuously or remain static at best. However, in real life, a system administrator may sometimes take certain steps that results in the signs of an attack to subside. In our model this will be reflected by no change in the probability of the attack. We are currently working on this problem. Once that is solved we plan to develop a working prototype and undertake some simulation studies.

## References

[1] P. Ammann, D. Wijesekera, and S. Kaushik. Scalable, graph-based network vulnerability analysis. In *Proceedings of the 9th ACM Conference on Computer and Communications Security, Washington DC.*, pages 217–224, November 2002.

[2] R. Chinchani, S. Upadhyaya, and K. Kwiat. Towards the scalable implementation of a user level anomaly detection system. In *Proceedings of the 2002 IEEE MILCOM Conference, Volume 2*, pages 7 – 10, Anaheim, CA, October 2002.

[3] J. Dawkins, C. Campbell, and J. Hale. Modeling network attacks: Extending the attack tree paradigm. In *Proceedings of the Workshop on Statistical Machine Learning Techniques in Computer Intrusion Detection, Baltimore, MD.* Johns Hopkins University, June 2002.

[4] D. Denning and P. Neumann. Requirements and model for "ides" - "a" real-time intrusion detection expert system. Technical report, Technical Report, Computer Science Laboratory, SRI International, 1985.

[5] The SANS Institute. Intrusion detection faq. Available at http://www.sans.org/resources/idfaq, April 2004.

[6] S. Jha, O. Sheyner, and J. Wing. Minimization and reliability analysis of attack graphs. Technical Report CMU-CS-02-109, School of Computer Science, Carnegie Mellon University, February 2002.

[7] S. Jha, O. Sheyner, and J. Wing. Two formal analyses of attack graphs. In *Proceedings of the 2002 Computer Security Foundations Workshop, Nova Scotia*, pages 45–59, June 2002.

[8] A.P. Moore, R.J. Ellison, and R.C. Linger. Attack modeling for information survivability. Technical Note CMU/SEI-2001-TN-001, Carnegie Melon University / Software Engineering Institute, March 2001.

[9] C. Phillips and L.P. Swiler. A graph-based system for network-vulnerability analysis. In *Proceedings of the 1998 New Security Paradigms Workshop, Chicago, IL*, pages 71–79, January 1998.

[10] R. W. Ritchie and P. Ammann. Using model checking to analyze network. In *Proceedings of the 2000 IEEE Symposium on Security and Privacy*, Oakland, CA, May 2000.

[11] B. Schneier. Attack trees: Modeling security threats. *Dr. Dobb's Journal*, December 1999.

[12] O. Sheyner, J. Haines, S. Jha, R. Lippmann, and J. Wing. Automated generation and analysis of attack graphs. In *Proceedings of the 2002 IEEE Computer Society Symposium on Security and Privacy, Oakland, CA*, May 2002.

[13] L. Swiler, C. Phillips, D. Ellis, and S. Chakerian. Computer-attack graph generation tool. In *Proceedings of DISCEX '0: DARPA Information Survivability Conference and Exposition II*, pages 307–321, June 2001.

[14] S. Upadhyaya, R. Chinchani, and K. Kwiat. An analytical framework for reasoning about instrusions. In *Proceedings of the 2001 IEEE Symposium on Reliable Distributed Systems*, pages 99–108, New Orleans, LA, October 2001.

[15] S. Upadhyaya, R. Chinchani, and K. Kwiat. A comprehensive reasoning framework for information surviability. In *Proceedings of the 2nd Annual IEEE Systems, Man, and Cybernetics Information Assurance Workshop*, pages 148–155, West Point, NY, June 2001.

[16] S. Upadhyaya and K. Kwiat. A distributed concurrent intrusion detection scheme based on assertions. In *Proceedings of the SCS International Symposium on Performance Evaluation of Computer and Telecommunications Systems, Chicago, IL*, pages 369–376, July 1999.

# An Efficient and Unified Approach to Correlating, Hypothesizing, and Predicting Intrusion Alerts*

Lingyu Wang, Anyi Liu, and Sushil Jajodia

Center for Secure Information Systems,
George Mason University,
Fairfax, VA 22030-4444, USA
{lwang3, aliu1, jajodia}@gmu.edu

**Abstract.** To defend against a multi-step network intrusion, its progress needs to be monitored and predicted in real-time. For this purpose, isolated alerts must be correlated into attack scenarios as soon as the alerts arrive. Such efficient correlation of alerts demands an in-memory index to be built on received alerts. However, the finite memory implies that only a limited number of alerts inside a sliding window can be considered for correlation. Knowing this fact, an attacker can prevent two attack steps from both falling into the sliding window by either passively delaying the second step or actively invoking bogus alerts between the two steps. In either case, the correlation effort is defeated.

In this paper, we first address the above issue with a novel *queue graph* (QG) approach. Instead of explicitly correlating a new alert to *all* the old ones that prepare for it, the approach only correlates the new alert to the latest copy of each type of alerts. The correlation with other alerts is kept implicit using the temporal order between alerts. Consequently, the approach has a quadratic (in the number of alert types) memory requirement, and it can correlate two alerts that are arbitrarily far away (namely, an infinitely large sliding window with a quadratic memory requirement). Our second contribution is a unified method based on the QG approach that can correlate received alerts, hypothesize missing alerts, and predict future alerts all at the same time. Empirical results show that our method can fulfill those tasks faster than an IDS can report alerts. The method is thus a promising solution for administrators to monitor and predict the progress of an intrusion, and thus to take appropriate countermeasures in a timely manner.

## 1 Introduction

For most well-administrated networks, a realistic intrusion is usually composed of multiple attacks with earlier ones preparing for later ones. Defending against such *multi-step intrusions* is important but challenging. It is usually impossible to respond to such intrusions based on isolated alerts that correspond to individual attack steps. The reason lies in the well-known impreciseness of Intrusion Detection Systems (IDSs). That is, alerts reported by IDSs are usually filled with false alerts that correspond to either normal traffic or failed attack attempts.

* This work was partially supported by the National Science Foundation under grant CCR-0113515, by Air Force Research Laboratory, Rome under the contract F30602-00-2-0512, and by Army Research Office under the grant DAAD19-03-1-0257.

S. De Capitani di Vimercati et al. (Eds.): ESORICS 2005, LNCS 3679, pp. 247–266, 2005.

The defense of multi-step intrusions will be more effective, if the attack scenarios of such intrusions can be reconstructed from isolated alerts. *Alert correlation* techniques achieve this [1] by exploiting either the similarity in alert attributes or the *a priori* knowledge about alert dependencies (related work will be reviewed in the next section). Alert correlation can also be based on the knowledge about a given network, such as network connectivity and the relationship between vulnerabilities. Regardless of the different knowledge used by correlation methods, the following *nested loop* procedure is usually assumed. That is, for each new alert, a search is performed in previously received alerts to find those who *prepare for* the new one. For off-line applications with a fixed set of alerts, such as computer forensics, this approach is a natural choice with reasonably good performance. For example, by maintaining an in-memory index on alerts, 65k alerts can be processed in less than a second [20].

However, the defense against multi-step intrusions poses a new challenge to existing correlation methods that are based on the nested loop approach. A timely defense requires that each new alert be correlated with older ones as soon as the new alert arrives. This performance requirement demands an in-memory index to be maintained on received alerts. An index on all received alerts would exhaust any finite memory when more and more alerts arrive. Hence, the index can only be maintained for those alerts that are close enough to the new alert, namely, those inside a *sliding window*. Unfortunately, an attacker aware of this fact can prevent any two attack steps from both falling into the sliding window. This can be achieved by either passively delaying the second step or actively invoking bogus alerts between the two steps. In either case, the correlation effort is completely defeated.

In this paper, we first remove the above obstacle towards efficient correlation of intrusion alerts. We propose a novel *queue graph* (QG) data structure for this purpose. The QG only keeps in memory the latest alert matching each of the known exploits (that is, host-bound vulnerabilities). The correlation is explicit only between the new alert and these in-memory alerts, while that between the new alert and other older alerts is kept implicit with the temporal order between alerts. We then study a QG-based correlation method that can not only correlate received alerts, but also hypothesize missing alerts and predict possible future alerts all at the same time. Finally, we evaluate the proposed techniques through implementations and empirical results.

The contribution of this work is two-fold. First, the QG-based alert correlation removes the limitation of a nested loop approach. Our approach has a quadratic memory requirement and a linear time complexity (in the number of known exploits in the given network) that are both independent of the number of received alerts. Hence, the efficiency does not decrease over time. Our approach can correlate alerts that are arbitrarily far away. It thus defeats slowed attacks and injected bogus attacks. Second, the unified approach to alert correlation, hypothesis, and prediction provides a promising solution to the defense of multi-step intrusions. Empirical results indicate that our methods can fulfill the tasks even faster than the IDS can report alerts. Hence, the proposed tech-

---

[1] There are alert correlation techniques used for other purposes, such as correlating multiple victims targeted by the same attacker, but we shall focus on the techniques used for analyzing multi-step intrusions.

niques can help an administrator to monitor and predict the progress of a multi-step intrusion, and thus to take appropriate countermeasures in a timely manner.

The rest of this paper is organized as follows. The next section reviews related work. Section 3 introduces some basic concepts and states our assumptions. Section 4 proposes the QG approach to alert correlation. Section 5 studies a unified method for alert correlation, hypothesis, and prediction. Section 6 evaluates the proposed techniques with implementation and empirical results. Finally, Section 7 concludes the paper and gives future directions.

## 2 Related Work

To reconstruct attack scenarios from isolated alerts, some alert-based correlation techniques employ the a priori knowledge about known attack strategies [6,8,4,9,35] or alert dependencies [3,19,21]. Other techniques do not depend on such knowledge, but cluster alerts through the similarity in their attributes (such as same sources and destinations) [2,5,34,38] or statistical and temporal patterns [16,28]. Hybrid approaches combine different techniques to obtain better results [21,29]. Alert correlation techniques have also been used for other purposes than the analysis of multi-step intrusions, such as to relate alerts to the same attack thread [13]. In real-time applications, the correlation methods based on a nested loop approach either suffer from performance decreases over time or can be easily defeated by slowed attacks and injected bogus attacks. To our best knowledge, this has not been extensively studied. Our work addresses this important issue and provides a solution.

Network vulnerability analyses enumerate potential attack sequences between fixed initial conditions and attack goals [25,30,31,33,15,1,14,24,40,10]. To avoid potential combinatorial explosion in the number of attack sequences, we adopt a notation of attack graphs similar to that of [1,25]. However, we do not assume fixed initial or goal conditions in an attack graph but base the actual start and end of an intrusion on alerts. Efforts in integrating information from different sources include *M2D2*, a formal model of alerts, vulnerabilities, networks, and security tools [18]. By organizing IDS alerts and the reports of vulnerability scanners (or other monitoring tools such as anti-virus software) into a Bayesian network, the alerts corresponding to successful attacks can be distinguished from others with higher confidence [41]. In another recent approach, alert correlation is based on the shortest distance between exploits in an attack graph [23]. We also adopt such a vulnerability-centric approach, because it can effectively filter out bogus alerts that do not match any exploit in the given network. However, the correlation in [23] still assumes a nested loop approach, and hence has the same limitation in real-time applications.

Broken scenarios caused by missing alerts are reassembled through clustering alerts with similar attributes [22], and those caused by incomplete knowledge are pieced together through statistical analyses [29,28]. Instead of repairing a broken scenario afterwards, our method can tolerate and hypothesize missing alerts at the same time of correlation. This unified approach makes our method more appropriate for real-time applications. Real-Time detection of isolated alerts is studied in [17,27]. Some products claim to have the capability of real-time analyses of alerts, such as the Tivoli Risk Manager [12], although their efficiency and resistance to slowed attacks may need further study. The RUSSEL language used in the ASAX system is similar to our QG approach in that the analysis of data only requires one-pass of data processing, although the RUSSEL language is designed for the generic analysis of audit trails [11].

# 3   Preliminaries

This section reviews relevant concepts and states our notations and assumptions about those concepts. First, we discuss *attack graph* in Section 3.1. We then address intrusion alerts and alert correlation in Section 3.2. Finally, we address the *nested loop* approach and its limitations in Section 3.3.

## 3.1   Attack Graph

An *attack graph* represents the *a priori* knowledge about a given network in terms of vulnerabilities and connectivity [1,33]. An attack graph is a directed graph having two type of vertices, *exploits* and *security conditions*. Exploits are host-bound vulnerabilities. More precisely, an exploit is a triple $(vul, src, dest)$ that indicates the following facts. The vulnerability $vul$ exists on the host $dest$, and the two hosts $src$ and $dest$ are connected ($src$ and $dest$ may refer to the same host in a local exploitation, and those exploitations that involve more than two hosts are beyond the scope of this paper). Security conditions refer to the network states that are required or implied by exploits, such as privilege levels or trusts. The interdependencies between exploits and security conditions form the edges of an attack graph. An edge from a security condition to an exploit indicates that the exploit cannot be executed until the security condition has been satisfied; an edge from an exploit to a security condition indicates that executing the exploit will satisfy the security condition.

*Example 1.* Figure 1 depicts part of an attack graph. In the attack graph, security conditions appear as ovals and exploits as rectangles. The edges in the attack graph reflects that the buffer overflow exploit can be executed only if the attacker can access the source host and the vulnerable service exists on the destination host.

We assume attack graphs can be obtained by analyzing the given network with existing tools. For example, the Topological Vulnerability Analysis (TVA) tool reported

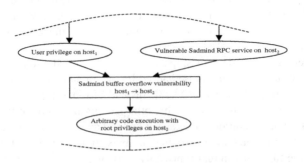

**Fig. 1.** An Example of Attack Graph

in [14] can model 37,000 vulnerabilities taken from 24 information sources including X-Force, Bugtraq, CVE, CERT, Nessus, and Snort. We assume the attack graph is
updated in a timely fashion upon changes in network topology and configuration. We
assume that the attack graph of a given network can be placed in memory. Unlike the
number of alerts which may increase indefinitely over time, the size of an attack graph is
usually relatively stable. The required memory can thus be predetermined and allocated
accordingly. We leave the case when the attack graph does not fit in memory as future
work. Different from the attack graph in [33,30], we do not assume fixed initial or goal
conditions in an attack graph. Instead, the actual start and end of an intrusion are based
on alerts reported by IDSs. We do not assume external host addresses can be trusted
and thus our attack graphs use wildcards for external addresses. This may cause false
correlations when multiple attackers concurrently launch similar attacks while they do
not intend to cooperate with each other.

To simplify our discussion, we introduce some notations to formally denote attack
graphs. Let $E$ be the set of exploits discovered in a subject network, and $C$ be the
set of relevant security conditions. Denote the *require* and *imply* relationship between
exploits and security conditions as two relations $R_r \subseteq C \times E$ and $R_i \subseteq E \times C$,
respectively. Then an attack graph is the directed graph $G(E \cup C, R_r \cup R_i)$. The *prepare-
for* relationship between exploits, as captured by many alert correlation methods [3,19],
is simply the composite relation $R_e = R_i \circ R_r$.

## 3.2 Intrusion Alert

Intrusion alerts are suspicious events reported by IDS sensors placed in the given network. Although the alerts reported by different IDSs may vary in format, they typically contain attributes like the type of events, the address of the source and destination
host, the time stamp, and so on. Our discussion does not depend on specific format
of alerts, and hence we simply regard each alert as a relational tuple of relevant attributes. The schema of the relation will usually be clear from context. For example,
with the schema *(event type, source IP, destination IP, time stamp)*, an alert will have the
form of *(RPC portmap sadmind request UDP, 202.77.162.213, 172.16.115.20, 03/07-
08:50:04.74612)*.

We adopt a vulnerability-centric approach to correlating alerts that is similar to [23].
Roughly speaking, the approach first matches alerts with corresponding exploits and
then correlate alerts based on the knowledge encoded in an attack graph. The matching
has two parts, that is the mapping from the event type attributes of alerts to the vulnerability attributes of exploits, and the comparison between the addresses of the source and
destination hosts. The mapping from event types to vulnerabilities can be established
using domain knowledge, such as the correspondence between Snort identifiers and
Nessus identifiers available in OSSIM [26]. The comparison between host addresses
supports using wildcards in exploits for untrustworthy external addresses. For simplicity, we denote the matching between alerts and exploits as a function $f$ from the set
of alerts $A$ to the set of exploits $E$ (more generally, an event type can match multiple
vulnerabilities, and one way to handle this is to *duplicate* any alert of that even type
such that each copy of the alert matches exactly one exploit).

Using the vulnerability-centric approach can potentially mitigate the negative impact of disruptive alerts. For example, if the attacker blindly launches some Windows-specific attacks on UNIX machines, then the reported alerts will be ignored by the approach. On the other hand, the approach also has limitations in that relevant alerts do not always match exploits. For example, an ICMP PING matches no vulnerability, but it signals the probing preparation for following attacks. Such relevant alerts can be identified based on attack graphs and the knowledge about alert types. We accommodate them by allowing exploits to have alert types in the place of vulnerability attributes. Such special *exploits* are inserted into attack graphs and the function $f$ is extended accordingly.

Our methods critically depend on temporal characteristics of alerts, such as timestamps and the order of arrivals. In practice, those characteristics are expected to exhibit much uncertainty due to various delays in hosts and network, especially when alerts are from multiple sensors placed differently. We address such temporal impreciseness in more details in Section 4.3. We assume the clocks of IDS sensors are loosely synchronized with the correlation engine. This can be achieved in many different ways depending on specific IDS systems. For example, Snort has built-in support of automatic time synchronization through the network time protocol (NTP) [32]. We leave the case where attackers may temper with the clocks as future work.

### 3.3   The Nested Loop Approach and Its Limitations

A natural way to correlate alerts is to search previously received alerts for those who prepare for the new alert. Such a *nested loop* approach is assumed by many correlation methods. Suppose we have a sequence of alerts ascending in time, $a_0, a_1, \ldots, a_n$. For each $i = 1, 2, \ldots, n$, the approach searches $a_0, a_1, \ldots, a_{i-1}$ for those $a_j$'s that satisfy $f(a_j) R_e f(a_i)$. However, this does not imply that $a_i$ must be compared to every $a_j (0 \leq j \leq i-1)$, although it comprises a naive implementation of the search. The search can certainly be optimized with standard indexing schemes. More specifically, an index on $a_0, a_1, \ldots, a_{i-1}$ is employed for searching the alerts that may prepare for $a_i$. After $a_i$ is processed, the index needs to be updated by inserting an entry for $a_i$. By maintaining such an index in memory, the nested loop approach can have a relatively good performance (for example, 65k alerts can be processed in less than one second [20]).

It is not always possible to have enough memory for indexing all the alerts. Hence, a *sliding window* approach comes to the rescue. That is, only the alerts close enough to the new alert are considered for correlation. For the alert $a_i$, the search is only performed on $a_{i-k}, a_{i-k+1}, \ldots, a_{i-1}$, where $k$ is a given window size determined by available memory. Apparently, an unavoidable tradeoff exists between the performance and completeness of correlation. On one hand, performance requires $k$ to be small enough so the index fits in memory. On the other hand, a smaller $k$ means less alerts will be considered for correlation with the new alert, and this may cause incomplete result because two related alerts may actually be separated by more than $k$ others.

The tradeoff between performance and completeness causes a more serious problem for real-time correlation, where performance is critical and alerts accumulate in time. The problem can be exacerbated by those attackers who are aware of the ongoing

detection effort. An attacker can employ the following *slow attack* to defeat alert correlation. More specifically, given an arbitrarily large window size $k$, for any two attacks
that raise the correlated alerts $a_i$ and $a_j$, the attacker can delay the second attack until
at least $k$ other alerts have been raised since $a_i$, so $j - i > k$ meaning $a_i$ and $a_j$ will
not be correlated. Instead of passively awaiting, a smarter attacker can actively launch
bogus attacks between the two real attack steps, so the condition $j - i > k$ can be satisfied in a shorter time. The attacker can even script bogus attack sequences between the
real attack steps, such that a deceived correlation engine will be kept busy in producing
bogus attack scenarios, while the real intrusion will be advanced in peace of mind.

## 4   The Queue Graphs (QG) Approach to Correlating Alerts

This section proposes a novel Queue Graph (QG) data structure to remove the limitation
discussed in the previous section. First, we make a key observation about implicit and
explicit correlation in Section 4.1. We then introduce the QG data structure and discuss
correlating alerts using QG in Section 4.2. Finally, we address the issue of imprecise
temporal characteristics of alerts in Section 4.3.

### 4.1   Implicit Correlation and Explicit Correlation

The key observation is that the correlation between alerts does not always need to be
explicit. In Figure 2, suppose the first three alerts $a_i$, $a_j$, and $a_k$ all match the same
exploit $f(a_k)$ (that is, their event types match the same vulnerability and the same source
and destination hosts are involved); the alert $a_h$ matches another exploit $f(a_h)$; $f(a_k)$
prepares for $f(a_h)$. Hence, $a_i$, $a_j$, and $a_k$ should all be correlated with $a_h$. However,
if the correlation between $a_k$ and $a_h$ is explicitly recorded (shown as a solid line in
the figure), then the correlation between $a_j$ and $a_h$ can be kept implicit (shown as a
dotted-line). More precisely, the facts $f(a_j) = f(a_k)$ and $f(a_k)R_ef(a_h)$ jointly imply
$f(a_j)R_ef(a_h)$, and the facts that $a_j$ is before $a_k$ and $a_k$ is before $a_h$ jointly imply that
$a_j$ must also be before $a_h$. Similar arguments apply to the correlation between $a_i$ and $a_h$.

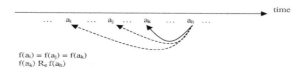

**Fig. 2.** Implicit and Explicit Correlation

To generalize the above observation, a new alert only needs to be explicitly correlated with the *latest* alert matching each exploit. The correlation with other older alerts
matching the same exploit can be kept implicit with the temporal order (for example, $a_j$
is before $a_k$ and $a_k$ is before $a_h$) and the matching from alerts to exploits (for example,
$a_j$ and $a_k$ match the same exploit). In the above case, if $a_k$ is indeed the latest alert
matching $f(a_k)$, then only the correlation between $a_h$ and $a_k$ needs to be explicit [2].

---

[2] This is analogous to a moving-average or smoothing model, although what is concerned here is
not the accumulated effect of one sequence, but the relationship between multiple sequences.

As we shall show shortly, this distinction between implicit and explicit correlation can reduce the complexity and memory requirement of correlation. Intuitively, for each exploit the correlation algorithm only needs to search backward for the first ($a_k$ in the above case) alert matching that exploit. For the nested loop approach, however, the correlation is always explicit. Hence, the approach must unnecessarily search all the previous alerts, as discussed in Section 3.3.

### 4.2    Correlating Alerts Using Queue Graphs

Based on the observation about the implicit and explicit correlation, we design an in-memory data structure, namely, *Queue Graph*. A queue graph is an in-memory materialization of the given attack graph with enhanced features (the purpose of the features will be clear in the following sections). Each exploit is realized as a queue of length one, and each security condition as a variable.

The realization of edges is a little more complicated. Starting from each exploit $e_i$, a breadth-first search (BFS) is performed in the attack graph by following the directed edges. For each edge encountered during the search, a *forward* pointer is created to connect the corresponding queue and variable. Similarly, another search is performed by following the directed edges in their reversed direction, and a *backward* pointer is created for each encountered edge. Later we shall use the backward edges for correlation purposes and use the forward edges for prediction purposes.

The two collections of pointers are then placed at a separate *layer* tailored to the queue that corresponds to the exploit $e_i$. The reason for separating pointers into layers is as follows. A BFS always creates a tree (namely, the BFS tree), and hence later another BFS starting from the same queue can follow only the pointers at that layer. This later BFS will then be performed within a *tree* instead of a *graph*, reducing the complexity from quadratic to linear. We first illustrate the concepts in Example 2.

*Example 2.* In Figure 3, from left to right are a given attack graph, the corresponding queues (shown as buckets) and variables (shown as texts), and the (both forward and backward) pointers at different layers. Notice that the layer one pointers do not include those connecting $v_2$ and $Q_3$, because a BFS in the attack graph starting from $e_1$ will reach $c_2$ only once (either via $e_2$ or via $e_3$, but we assume $e_2$ in this example). The layer one pointers thus form a tree rooted at $Q_1$.

In Section 3.3, we discussed how a nested loop approach correlates alerts that prepare for each other. As a comparison, we now perform the same correlation using a

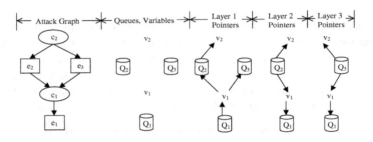

**Fig. 3.** An Example Queue Graph

queue graph (we shall discuss other correlation requirements in Section 5). Intuitively, we let the stream of alerts flow through the queue graph, and at the same time we collect correlation results by searching the queue graph. More specifically, each incoming alert is first matched with an exploit and placed in the corresponding queue. Then, because the length of each queue is one, a non-empty queue must dequeue the current alert before it can enqueue a new alert.

During this process, the results of correlation are collected as a directed graph, namely, the *result graph*. First, each new alert is recorded as a vertex in the result graph. Second, when a new alert forces an old alert to be dequeued, a directed edge between the two alerts is added into the result graph, which records the temporal order between the two alerts and the fact that they both match the same exploit. Third, after each new alert is enqueued, a search starts from the queue and follows two consecutive backward pointers; for each non-empty queue encountered during the search, a directed edge from the alert in that queue to the new alert is added into the result graph. This is illustrated in Example 3.

*Example 3.* Consider correlating the four alerts $a_i$, $a_j$, $a_k$, and $a_h$ in Figure 2 with the queue graph given in Figure 3, and suppose $f(a_h) = e_1$, $f(a_k) = e_2$, and no other alerts match $e_1$ or $e_2$ besides $a_i$, $a_j$, $a_k$, and $a_h$. First, when $a_i$ arrives, it is placed in the empty queue $Q_2$. Then, $a_j$ forces $a_i$ to be dequeued from $Q_2$, and a directed edge $(a_i, a_j)$ in the result graph records the facts that $a_i$ is before $a_j$ and they both match $e_2$. Similarly, $a_k$ replaces $a_j$ in $Q_2$, and a directed edge $(a_j, a_k)$ is recorded. Finally, $a_h$ arrives and occupies $Q_1$, a search starting from $Q_1$ and following two layer one backward pointers will find the alert $a_k$ in $Q_2$. Hence, a directed edge $(a_k, a_h)$ records the only explicit correlation.

**Definition 1.** *Let $G(E \cup C, R_r \cup R_i)$ be an attack graph, where $E = \{e_i \mid 1 \le i \le n\}$, $C = \{c_i \mid 1 \le i \le m\}$, $R_r \subseteq C \times E$, and $R_i \subseteq E \times C$.*

- *For $k = 1, 2, \ldots, n$,*
  - *use $BFSR(k)$ to denote the set of edges visited by a breadth-first search in $G(E \cup C, R_r \cup R_i)$ starting from $e_k$, and*
  - *use $BFS(k)$ for the set of edges visited by a breadth-first search in $G(E \cup C, R_r^{-1} \cup R_i^{-1})$ staring from $e_k$, where $R_r^{-1}$ and $R_i^{-1}$ are the inverse relations.*
- *The queue graph $Q_g$ is a data structure with the following components:*
  - $Q = \{Q_i \mid 1 \le i \le n\}$ *are $n$ queues of length one,*
  - $V = \{v_i \mid 1 \le i \le m\}$ *are $m$ variables,*
  - *for each $k = 1, 2, \ldots, n$,*
    - $P_k = \{< Q_j, v_i > \mid (c_i, e_j) \in BFS(k)\} \cup \{< v_i, Q_j > \mid (e_j, c_i) \in BFS(k)\}$ *are the layer $k$ backward pointers, and*
    - $PR_k = \{< v_i, Q_j > \mid (c_i, e_j) \in BFSR(k)\} \cup \{< Q_j, v_i > \mid (e_j, c_i) \in BFSR(k)\}$ *are the layer $k$ forward pointers.*

Definition 1 formally characterizes the queue graph data structure. To rephrase Example 2 using those notations, the queue graph has three queues $Q = \{Q_1, Q_2, Q_3\}$ and two variables $V = \{v_1, v_2\}$. The layer one backward pointers are $P_1 = \{< Q_1, v_1 >,$

$< v_1, Q_2 >, < Q_2, v_2 >, < v_1, Q_3 >\}^3$, and the layer one forward pointers are $\mathcal{PR}_1 = \phi$. The layer two pointers include $\mathcal{P}_2 = \{< Q_2, v_2 >\}$ and $\mathcal{PR}_2 = \{< Q_2, v_1 >, < v_1, Q_1 >\}$. The layer three pointers include $\mathcal{P}_3 = \{< Q_3, v_2 >\}$ and $\mathcal{PR}_3 = \{< Q_3, v_1 >, < v_1, Q_1 >\}$.

The process for correlating alerts using a queue graph, as illustrated in Example 3, is more precisely stated as the procedure *QG_Alert_Correlation* in Figure 4. The result graph $G_r$ has a set of vertices $V$ and two separate sets of edges $E_r$ and $E_l$. The edges in $E_r$ correspond to the explicit correlations and those in $E_l$ record the temporal order between alerts matching the same exploit. Initially, we set the queues in $\mathcal{Q}$, the sets $V$, $E_r$, and $E_l$ as empty. The first step of the procedure inserts the new alert into the result graph. The second step dequeues a non-empty queue and updates the result graph by adding an edge between the old alert and the new alert. The third step enqueues the new alert into the queue graph. The fourth step does correlation by searching for the alerts that need to be explicitly correlated to the new alert.

**Procedure** *QG_Alert_Correlation*
**Input:** A queue graph $Q_g$ (with $n$ queues and $m$ variables), the initial result graph
$\quad\quad G_r(V, E_r \cup E_l)$, and an alert $a_{new}$ satisfying $f(a_{new}) = e_i$ for some $1 \leq i \leq n$
**Output:** The updated result graph $G_r(V, E_r \cup E_l)$
**Method:**
$\quad$ 1. **Insert** $a_{new}$ into $V$
$\quad$ 2. **If** $Q_i$ contains an alert $a_{old}$
$\quad\quad$ **Insert** edge $(a_{old}, a_{new})$ into $E_l$
$\quad\quad$ **Dequeue** $a_{old}$ from $Q_i$
$\quad$ 3. **Enqueue** $a_{new}$ into $Q_i$
$\quad$ 4. **For each** $Q_j (1 \leq j \leq n)$ satisfying $< Q_i, v_k >\in \mathcal{P}_i$ and $< v_k, Q_j >\in \mathcal{P}_i$, for some $1 \leq k \leq m$
$\quad\quad$ **If** $Q_j$ contains an alert $a_j$
$\quad\quad\quad$ **Insert** $(a_j, a_{new})$ into $E_r$
$\quad$ 5. **Return** $G_r(V, E_r \cup E_l)$

**Fig. 4.** A Procedure for Correlating Alerts with Queue Graphs

*Complexity Analysis.* The procedure *QG_Alert_Correlation* demonstrates the advantages of the QG approach over the nested loop approach (some of the features of a queue graph, such as the variables and the forward pointers, are not used by the procedure and will be needed in the next section). First, the time for processing each new alert with the QG approach is linear in $(m + n)$, that is the number of exploits and security conditions in the attack graph. In Procedure *QG_Alert_Correlation*, the fourth step visits at most $(m + n)$ edges, because it searches in a *tree* (that is, the BFS tree rooted at $Q_i$) by following the layered pointers in $\mathcal{P}_i$; the other steps of the procedure take almost constant time. Hence, the performance of the QG approach does not depend on the number of received alerts, as $n$ and $m$ are relatively stable for a given network. On the other hand, the nested loop approach (without using a sliding window) searches all alerts, and hence the performance keeps decreasing as more and more alerts are received.

Second, the memory usage of the QG approach is roughly $O(n(n + m))$ ($n$ layers, with each layer having maximally $(n + m)$ pointers) [4], and hence does not depend on

---

[3] We use the notation $< a, b >$ for a pointer in a queue graph and $(a, b)$ for an edge in a graph.
[4] The correlation only appends to the result graph but does not read from it, and hence the result graph needs not to be in memory.

the number of received alerts, either. In comparison, the nested loop approach without a sliding window needs memory for indexing on all the received alerts. Third, the QG approach is not vulnerable to slowed attacks, which can easily defeat the nested loop approach using a sliding window as described in Section 3.3. In the procedure *QG_Alert_Correlation*, an alert is dequeued (and no longer considered for correlation) only when a new alert matching the same exploit arrives. Hence, if one alert prepares for another, then no matter how many unrelated alerts are injected, the earlier alert will always sit in the queue graph waiting for the later one [5].

### 4.3   Handling Alerts with Imprecise Temporal Characteristics

The correctness of the QG approach critically depends on the correct order of alerts. However, neither the order suggested by timestamps nor the order of arrivals should be trusted, because the temporal characteristics of alerts are typically imprecise. Instead, we adopt the following conservative approach. First, any two alerts whose timestamps have a difference no greater than a given threshold $t_{con}$ are treated as *concurrent*; the *correct* order of concurrent alerts is always the one that allows the alerts to be correlated. Second, for non-concurrent alerts, the correct order is the one suggested by their timestamps, but alerts are allowed to arrive in a different (and incorrect) order. This conservative approach takes into account varying delays in a network and small differences between the clocks of sensors [6].

The basic QG approach does not work properly if alerts do not arrive in the correct order. To illustrate, consider an alert $a_1$ that prepares for another alert $a_2$ but arrives later then $a_2$. As described in Section 4.2, the procedure *QG_Alert_Correlation* will only look for those alerts that prepare for $a_1$, but not those that $a_1$ prepares for ($a_2$ in this case). Moreover, suppose another concurrent alert $a_2'$ matches the same exploit as $a_2$ does, and it arrives after $a_2$ but before $a_1$. Then, $a_2$ is already dequeued by the time $a_1$ arrives, and hence the correlation between $a_1$ and $a_2$ will not be discovered.

We address this issue through reordering alerts inside a time window before feeding them into the queue graph. More specifically, assume the varying delays are bounded by a threshold $t_{max}$. We postpone the processing of an alert $a_1$ with a timestamp $t_1$ until $t_{max}$ (the larger one between $t_{max}$ and $t_{con}$, when concurrent alerts are also considered) time has passed since the time we receive $a_1$. We reorder the postponed alerts, so they arrive at the correlation engine in the correct order. Then after $t_{max}$ time, any alert $a_2$ will have a timestamp $t_2$ satisfying $t_2 > t_1$ (the worst case is when $a_1$ is not delayed but $a_2$ is delayed $t_{max}$ time, and the fact $a_2$ is received $t_{max}$ later than $a_1$ indicates $t_2 + t_{max} - t_{max} > t_1$, and hence $t_2 > t_1$).

The capability of dealing with concurrent alerts and varying delays comes at a cost. The additional delay introduced for reordering alerts certainly causes an undesired decrease in the timeliness of alert correlation. However, if we choose to report results immediately as each alert arrives, then the imprecise temporal characteristics of alerts may cause incorrect and confusing results. Such results may diminish the value of the

---

[5] In case some temporal constraint states that an alert should not be considered for correlation once it gets *too old*, a timer can be used to periodically dequeue alerts.

[6] We assume the clocks are loosely synchronized, as discussed in Section 3.2.

correlation effort. This reflects the inherent tradeoff between the capability of containing unavoidable uncertainties and the performance of processing alerts.

# 5   A Unified Approach to Alert Correlation, Hypothesis, and Prediction

In this section, we extend the basic QG-based correlation procedure to a unified approach to correlating received alerts, hypothesizing missing alerts, and predicting future alerts. Section 5.1 introduces some key concepts. Sections 5.2 describes the integration of alert correlation with alert hypothesis. Section 5.3 then discusses alert prediction.

## 5.1   Consistent and Inconsistent Alert Sequences

The queue graph approach introduced in Section 4 provides unique opportunities to tolerate and hypothesize alerts missed by IDSs, as well as to predict possible consequences. Intuitively, missing alerts cause *inconsistency* between the knowledge (encoded in attack graphs) and the facts (represented by received alerts). By reasoning about such inconsistency, missing alerts can be plausibly hypothesized. On the other hand, by extending the facts in a consistent way with respect to the knowledge, possible consequences of an intrusion can be predicted. To elaborate on those ideas, we first illustrate consistent and inconsistent sequences of alerts in Example 4 and Example 5.

*Example 4.* The sequence of alerts shown on the left hand side of Figure 5(that is, $a_0, a_3$) is inconsistent with respect to the attack graph, because the security condition $c_3$ is not satisfied before the exploit $e_3$ is executed (as indicated by the alert $a_3$).

*Example 5.* The sequence shown in the middle of Figure 5 (that is, $a_0, a_1, a_3$) is consistent, because executing the exploit $e_1$ (as indicated by the alert $a_1$) satisfies the only security condition $c_3$ that is required by the execution of $e_3$ (as indicated by $a_3$). The sequence shown on the right hand side of Figure 5 is inconsistent, because the security condition $c_4$ is not satisfied before the execution of $e_3$.

To generalize the above examples, we say an exploit is *ready* to be executed if all of its required security conditions are satisfied by previous executions of exploits (or initially satisfied security conditions, such as $c_1$ in Figure 5). We say a sequence of

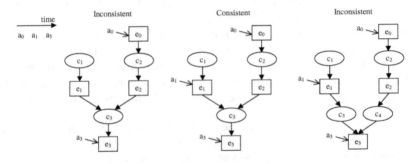

**Fig. 5.** Examples of Consistent and Inconsistent Alert Sequences

alerts is *consistent*, if every alert in the sequence matches an exploit that is ready to be executed by the time the alert is received. Example 4 depicts an inconsistent alert sequence in which the consecutive executions of exploits is broken by missing alerts. Example 5 indicates that the relationship between exploits can be either *disjunctive* (executing $e_1$ or $e_2$ makes $e_3$ ready in the first case) or *conjunctive* (both $e_1$ and $e_2$ must be executed to make $e_3$ ready), and security conditions play an important role in such relationship (the approach in [23] cannot distinguish the two cases in Example 5, because it is based on a simplified version of attack graphs with no security conditions).

## 5.2   Alert Correlation and Hypothesis

In Section 4.2, the correlation algorithm searches for the alerts that prepare for a new alert by following two consecutive pointers. Such an approach only works for consistent alert sequences. For inconsistent sequences, such as those in Example 4 and Example 5, the search will stop at empty queues that correspond to missing alerts and the correlation result will be incomplete. A natural question is, *Can we continue to search and hypothesize missing alerts if necessary?* This question motivates us to propose a unified approach to correlating received alerts and at the same time making hypotheses of missing alerts.

Intuitively, the approach attempts to explain the occurrence of a new alert by including it in a consistent sequence of alerts (alert correlation) and missing alerts (alert hypothesis). More specifically, a search starts from the queue that contains the new alert; it hypothesizes about a missing alert for each encountered empty queue; it stops at each received alert because it knows that this received alert must have already been explained previously. The search expands its frontier in a breadth-first manner [7] after each hypothesis is made, because the hypothesis itself may also need an explanation. Such attempts continue until a satisfactory explanation for the new alert and all the hypothesized ones is obtained. The explanations of all received alerts collectively form the result, that is a graph composed of alerts, hypothesized alerts, and security conditions that are either satisfied or hypothetically satisfied. This is illustrated in Example 6.

*Example 6.* Consider again the three cases, from left to right, in Figure 5 when the alert $a_3$ is received. For the first case, two missing alerts matching $e_1$ and $e_2$ need to be hypothesized and then $a_3$ can be correlated to $a_0$ (through one of the hypothesized alerts). For the second case, no alert needs to be hypothesized because the sequence is already consistent, and $a_3$ needs to be correlated to $a_1$. For the third case, $a_0$ needs to be correlated to $a_1$, and it also needs to be correlated to $a_0$ through a hypothesized alert matching $e_2$.

More precisely, we extend the basic QG approach described in Section 4 by modifying the fourth step of Procedure *QG_Alert_Correlation*. Due to space limitations, we describe how the modified procedure works but leave out more details (a detailed procedure can be found in [39]). Consider a queue graph $Q_g$ with $n$ queues $Q$ and $m$ variables $V$. Each variable in $V$ can now have one of the three values *TRUE*, *FALSE*, and *HYP*,

---

[7] Other approaches, such as a DFS, may work as well, but a queue graph organizes its pointers in layered BFS trees to improve performance, and this makes BFS a preferred choice.

together with a timestamp; those denote a satisfied security condition, an unsatisfied one, a hypothetically satisfied one, and the time of the last update, respectively. Each queue in $\mathcal{Q}$ can contain alerts or hypothesized alerts. The result graph $G_r(V, E_l \cup E_r)$ is similar to that described in Section 4.2. However, the vertex set $V$ now includes not only alerts but also hypothesized alerts and security conditions.

Suppose a new alert $a_{new}$ with the timestamp $t_{new}$ is received and enqueued in the queue $Q_i(1 \leq i \leq n)$. First, we start from $Q_i$ and follow the pointers in $\mathcal{PR}_i$ to set each variable $v_j(1 \leq j \leq m)$ adjacent to $Q_i$ with the value TRUE and the timestamp $t_{new}$. This step records the security conditions satisfied by $a_{new}$. Second, we start from $Q_i$ and make a partial BFS by following the pointers in $\mathcal{P}_i$. The BFS is partial, because it stops upon leaving [8] a variable with the value *TRUE* or the value *HYP* (or a queue that contains a hypothesized alert). This step correlates $a_{new}$ to previously received or hypothesized alerts. The result graph $G_r$ is updated during the above process as follows. First, after we enqueue $a_{new}$ into $Q_i$ and make changes to each $v_j$ adjacent to $Q_i$, we add $a_{new}$ and $v_j$ (that is, the value and timestamp of $v_j$) as vertices, and an edge from $a_{new}$ pointing to $v_j$ into the result graph $G_r$. This step records the fact that the new alert $a_{new}$ satisfies its implied security conditions at time $t_{new}$. Second, during the partial BFS, we record each hypothesis. Whenever we change the value of a variable $v_j$ from *FALSE* to *HYP*, we record this update in $G_r$; similarly, whenever we enqueue a hypothesized alert into an empty queue, we record this hypothesized alert in $G_r$. Third, whenever we leave a variable $v$ and reach a queue $Q$, we insert into $G_r$ a directed edge from each queue $Q$ to $v$; similarly, we insert edges from a queue to its connected variables when we leave the queue.

*Example 7.* Consider the left-hand side case of Figure 5. The first alert $a_0$ will only cause (the variable corresponding to) the security condition $c_2$ to be changed from *FALSE* to *TRUE*. The result graph will be updated with the alert $a_0$ and satisfied security condition $c_2$ and the directed edge connecting them. When $a_3$ is received, a search starts from (the queue corresponding to) $e_3$; it changes $c_3$ from *FALSE* to *HYP*; it inserts a hypothesized alert $a_1$ into $e_1$ and $a_2$ into $e_2$, respectively; it stops at $c_1$ (which is initially set as *TRUE*) and $c_2$ (which has been set as *TRUE* when $a_0$ arrived). The result graph will be updated with the alert $a_3$, the hypothesized alerts $a_1$ and $a_2$, the hypothetically satisfied security condition $c_3$, and the directed edges between them.

*Complexity Analysis.* At first glance, the procedure described above takes quadratic time, because a BFS takes time linear in the number of vertices $(n + m)$ and edges $(n + m)^2$, where $n$ and $m$ is the number of exploits and security conditions in the attack graph, respectively. However, this is not the case. As described in Section 4.2, a queue graph organizes its pointers in separate layers, and each layer is a BFS tree rooted at a queue. Hence, a BFS that starts from a queue and follows the pointers in the corresponding layer will be equivalent to a tree traversal, which takes linear time $(n + m)$. This performance gain seems to be obtained at the price of more memory requirement, because a pointer may appear in more than one layer. However, as described in Sec-

---

[8] Given that a BFS is implemented through manipulating a separate queue as usual, we shall refer to the enqueues as *reaching* and the dequeues as *leaving* to avoid confusions.

tion 4.2, the memory requirement is quadratic (that is, $O(n(n + m))$), which is indeed asymptotically the same as that of the original attack graph.

### 5.3 Attack Prediction

In the previous section, we explain the occurrence of a new alert by searching backwards (that is, in the reversed direction of the edges in attack graphs) for correlated (or hypothesized) alerts. Conversely, we can also predict possible consequences of each new alert by searching forwards. A BFS is also preferred in this case, because the predicted security conditions will be discovered in the order of their (shortest) distances to the new alert. This distance roughly indicates how imminent a predicted attack is, based on the alerts received so far.

The procedure of prediction is similar to that of correlation and hypothesis discussed in the previous section, although they differ in some details. More specifically, after the correlation and hypothesis completes, the prediction starts. It begins at the security conditions satisfied by the new alert and makes a partial BFS in the queue graph by following the pointers in $\mathcal{PR}_i$ (suppose the new alert is enqueued by $Q_i$). The search stops at previously received (or hypothesized) alerts and their (hypothetically) satisfied security conditions to avoid repeating the previous prediction.

The result of the prediction process is a sequence of non-empty sets $Con_1$, $Con_2, \ldots$, with $Con_i (1 \le i \le m)$ containing the security conditions that can possibly be satisfied in $i$ steps from now. Unlike in correlation and hypothesis, the prediction process does not reason about the disjunctive and conjunctive relationship between exploits as discussed in Section 5.1. Instead, a security condition $c$ will appear in the set $Con_i$ as long as there exists a path of length $2i$ (the path consists of both security conditions and exploits) from $c$ to some previously satisfied security condition. Hence, the number $i$ provides a lower bound to the number of exploits that must be executed before $c$ can be satisfied.

## 6  Empirical Results

This section evaluates the proposed correlation, hypothesis, and prediction techniques through implementation and empirical results. The correlation engine is implemented in C++ and tested on a Pentium III 860MHz server with 1G RAM running RedHat Linux. We use Snort-2.3.0 [32] to generate isolated alerts, which are directly pipelined into the correlation engine for analyses. We use Tcpreplay 2.3.2 [37] to replay network traffic from a separate machine to the server running the correlation engine.

We use two data sets for experiments, the Darpa 2000 intrusion detection LLDOS 1.0 by MIT Lincoln Labs [7], and the treasure hunt dataset by the University of California, Santa Barbara [36]. The attack scenario in the Darpa 2000 dataset has been extensively explored before (such as in [19]). Our experiments with the dataset show similar results, validating the correctness of our correlation algorithm. The treasure hunt dataset generates a large amount of alerts (about two million alerts taking about 1.4G of disk space, with most of them being brute force attempts of the same attacks), which may render a nested loop-based correlation method infeasible (we found that even running a simple database query over the data will paralyze the system). In contrast, our correlation engine processes alerts with negligible delays (Snort turns out to be the bot-tleneck).

*Effectiveness.* The objective of the first set of experiments is to justify the effectiveness of the proposed algorithms in alert correlation, hypothesis, and prediction. We use the Darpa 2000 dataset for this purpose, as the attack scenario can be easily referenced in both the included description and previous results, such as [19]. Our correlation algo-rithm produces similar result to that of previous work. However, in contrast to the static result graph seen in those work, our result graph actually *evolves* in time with the con-tinuously arriving alerts. Such a result can more clearly reveal the actual progress of an intrusion (due to space limitations, snapshots of the result graph during real-time corre-lation can be found in [39]). To save space, only the latest alert matching each exploit is shown in the figures in this section.

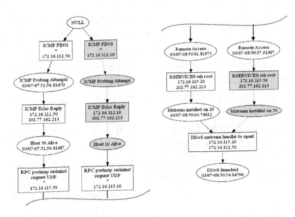

**Fig. 6.** The Hypothesis of Missing Alerts During Correlation

Figure 6 includes two results on hypothesizing missing alerts during the correlation. On the left-side of the figure, two consecutive missing alerts (ICMP PING and ICMP Echo Reply) and the corresponding security conditions are hypothesized (shown as shaded) when an alert (RPC portmap sadmind request UDP) is received but its required security condition (Host 10 Alive) has not been satisfied. The right-hand side of the figure shows a conjunctive relationship between alerts, that is a DDoS mstream traffic between two hosts requires the mstream software to be installed on both hosts. We deliberately deleted the RSERVICES rsh alert on one of the host, which is successfully hypothesized (shown as shaded).

Figure 7 includes a result of alert prediction. In the left figure, some security con-ditions are predicted to be satisfied by possible upcoming alerts. The predicted secu-rity conditions are shown as shaded, and the numbers are placeholders for alerts. The right-hand side figure shows a later snapshot of the result graph, in which some of the predicted security conditions are indeed realized.

*Performance.* The objective of the second set of experiments is to evaluate the real-time performance of the correlation engine. The performance metric includes the resource

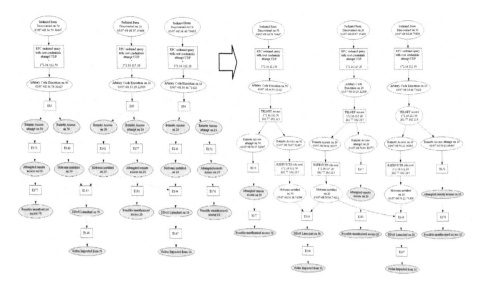

**Fig. 7.** The Prediction of Possible Consequences During Correlation

usage (CPU and memory) and the processing time of each alert. The correlation engine measures its own processing time and treats the delay between receiving two consecutive alerts as Snort's processing time. All the results have 95% confidence intervals within about 5% of the reported values. Figure 8 shows the CPU usage (on the left-hand side) and memory usage (on the right-hand side) over time for the Darpa data set. The correlation engine clearly demands less resources than Snort (on average, the correlation engine's CPU usage and memory usage are both under 10% of Snort's).

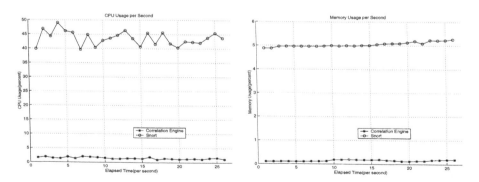

**Fig. 8.** The CPU and Memory Usage

The left chart in Figure 9 shows the processing time per alert (averaged per 22 alerts). Clearly, the correlation engine takes much less time than Snort throughout the processing of the entire data set. The result also proves that the performance of our correlation method does not decrease over time. Instead, the time required for correlating each alert remains fairly steady. Next we examine the scalability of the correlation engine in terms of the number of exploits and security conditions. We use the treasure hunt data set for this purpose. The initial attack graph only has about one hundred exploits. We increase the size of attack graphs by randomly inserting dummy exploits and corresponding security conditions. The inserted exploits increase the complexity of correlation because the correlation engine must search through them. The right chart in Figure 9 shows the average processing time as a function of the attack graph size. The result shows that the average time for correlation scales with the size of attack graph as expected.

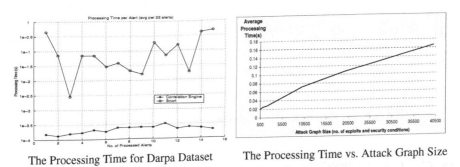

The Processing Time for Darpa Dataset          The Processing Time vs. Attack Graph Size

**Fig. 9.** The Processing Time and Its Relationship with the Size of Attack Graph

We replay network traffic at a high speed (for example, the Darpa data set is replayed in about 26 seconds). Real-world traffic is usually less intensive, and consequently our correlation engine will exhibit a better performance. However, we are aware that real-world traffic may bring up new challenges that are absent in synthesized data sets. We plan to remove such limitations in our future work.

## 7   Conclusion

In this paper, we studied the real-time correlation of intrusion alerts. We identified a limitation in applying the nested loop-based correlation methods and proposed a novel QG approach to remove this limitation. The method has a linear time complexity and a quadratic memory requirement. It can correlate alerts that are arbitrarily far away. Based on the QG method, we proposed a unified method for the correlation, hypothesis, and prediction of alerts. The proposed techniques are implemented and evaluated. Empirical results showed that our correlation engine can process alerts faster than an IDS can report them, making our method a promising solution for an administrator to monitor and predict the progress of multi-step intrusions. Our future work is to integrate the proposed methods in a prototype system and evaluate it with real-world traffic in live networks.

**Acknowledgements.** The authors thank Marc Dacier and the anonymous reviewers for their valuable comments, and Giovanni Vigna for providing the Treasure Hunt dataset.

# References

1. P. Ammann, D. Wijesekera, and S. Kaushik. Scalable, graph-based network vulnerability analysis. In *Proceedings of the 9th ACM Conference on Computer and Communications Security (CCS'02)*, pages 217–224, 2002.
2. F. Cuppens. Managing alerts in a multi-intrusion detection environment. In *Proceedings of the 17th Annual Computer Security Applications Conference (ACSAC'01)*, 2001.
3. F. Cuppens and A. Miege. Alert correlation in a cooperative intrusion detection framework. In *Proceedings of the 2002 IEEE Symposium on Security and Privacy (S&P'02)*, pages 187–200, 2002.
4. F. Cuppens and R. Ortalo. LAMBDA: A language to model a database for detection of attacks. In *Proceedings of the 3rd International Symposium on Recent Advances in Intrusion Detection (RAID'01)*, pages 197–216, 2001.
5. O. Dain and R.K. Cunningham. Building scenarios from a heterogeneous alert system. In *Proceedings of the 2001 IEEE Workshop on Information Assurance and Security*, 2001.
6. O. Dain and R.K. Cunningham. Fusing a heterogeneous alert stream into scenarios. In *Proceedings of the ACM Workshop on Data Mining for Security Applications*, pages 1–13, 2001.
7. 2000 darpa intrusion detection evaluation datasets. http://www.ll.mit.edu/IST/ideval/data/2000/2000_data_index.html, 2000.
8. H. Debar and A. Wespi. Aggregation and correlation of intrusion-detection alerts. In *Proceedings of the 3rd International Symposium on Recent Advances in Intrusion Detection (RAID'01)*, pages 85–103, 2001.
9. S.T. Eckmann, G. Vigna, and R.A. Kemmerer. STATL: An attack language for state-based intrusion detection. *Journal of Computer Security*, 10(1/2):71–104, 2002.
10. D. Farmer and E.H. Spafford. The COPS security checker system. In *USENIX Summer*, pages 165–170, 1990.
11. N. Habra, Charlier B.L., A. Mounji, and I. Mathieu. ASAX: software architechture and rule-based language for universal audit trail analysis. In *Proceedings of the 2nd European Symposium on Research in Computer Security (ESORICS 1992)*, pages 430–450, 2004.
12. IBM. IBM tivoli risk manager. Available at http://www.ibm.com/software/tivoli/products/risk-mgr/.
13. SRI International. Event monitoring enabling responses to anomalous live disturbances (EMERALD). Available at http:// www.sdl.sri.com/projects/emerald/.
14. S. Jajodia, S. Noel, and B. O'Berry. Topological analysis of network attack vulnerability. In V. Kumar, J. Srivastava, and A. Lazarevic, editors, *Managing Cyber Threats: Issues, Approaches and Challenges*. Kluwer Academic Publisher, 2003.
15. S. Jha, O. Sheyner, and J.M. Wing. Two formal analysis of attack graph. In *Proceedings of the 15th Computer Security Foundation Workshop (CSFW'02)*, 2002.
16. Klaus Julisch and Marc Dacier. Mining intrusion detection alarms for actionable knowledge. In *Proceedings of the eighth ACM SIGKDD international conference on Knowledge discovery and data mining*, pages 366–375, 2002.
17. W. Lee, J.B.D. Cabrera, A. Thomas, N. Balwalli, S. Saluja, and Y. Zhang. Performance adaptation in real-time intrusion detection systems. In *Proceedings of The 5th International Symposium on Recent Advances in Intrusion Detection (RAID 2002)*, 2002.
18. B. Morin, L. Mé, H. Debar, and M. Ducassé. M2D2: A formal data model for IDS alert correlation. In *Proceedings of the 5th International Symposium on Recent Advances in Intrusion Detection (RAID'02)*, pages 115–137, 2002.
19. P. Ning, Y. Cui, and D.S. Reeves. Constructing attack scenarios through correlation of intrusion alerts. In *Proceedings of the 9th ACM Conference on Computer and Communications Security (CCS'02)*, pages 245–254, 2002.

20. P. Ning and D. Xu. Adapting query optimization techniques for efficient intrusion alert correlation. Technical report, NCSU, Department of Computer Science, 2002.
21. P. Ning and D. Xu. Learning attack strategies from intrusion alerts. In *Proceedings of the 10th ACM Conference on Computer and Communications Security (CCS'03)*, 2003.
22. P. Ning, D. Xu, C.G. Healey, and R.S. Amant. Building attack scenarios through integration of complementary alert correlation methods. In *Proceedings of the 11th Annual Network and Distributed System Security Symposium (NDSS'04)*, pages 97–111, 2004.
23. S. Noel and S. Jajodia. Correlating intrusion events and building attack scenarios through attack graph distance. In *Proceedings of the 20th Annual Computer Security Applications Conference (ACSAC'04)*, 2004.
24. S. Noel, S. Jajodia, B. O'Berry, and M. Jacobs. Efficient minimum-cost network hardening via exploit dependency grpahs. In *Proceedings of the 19th Annual Computer Security Applications Conference (ACSAC'03)*, 2003.
25. R. Ortalo, Y. Deswarte, and M. Kaaniche. Experimenting with quantitative evaluation tools for monitoring operational security. *IEEE Trans. Software Eng.*, 25(5):633–650, 1999.
26. OSSIM. Open source security information management. Available at http://www.ossim.net.
27. V. Paxson. Bro: A system for detecting network intruders in real-time. *Computer Networks*, 31(23-24):2435–2463, 12 1999.
28. X. Qin and W. Lee. Statistical causality analysis of INFOSEC alert data. In *Proceedings of the 6th International Symposium on Recent Advances in Intrusion Detection (RAID 2003)*, pages 591–627, 2003.
29. X. Qin and W. Lee. Discovering novel attack strategies from INFOSEC alerts. In *Proceedings of the 9th European Symposium on Research in Computer Security (ESORICS 2004)*, pages 439–456, 2004.
30. R. Ritchey and P. Ammann. Using model checking to analyze network vulnerabilities. In *Proceedings of the 2000 IEEE Symposium on Research on Security and Privacy (S&P'00)*, pages 156–165, 2000.
31. R. Ritchey, B. O'Berry, and S. Noel. Representing TCP/IP connectivity for topological analysis of network security. In *Proceedings of the 18th Annual Computer Security Applications Conference (ACSAC'02)*, page 25, 2002.
32. M. Roesch. Snort - lightweight intrusion detection for networks. In *Proceedings of the 1999 USENIX LISA Conference*, pages 229–238, 1999.
33. O. Sheyner, J. Haines, S. Jha, R. Lippmann, and J.M. Wing. Automated generation and analysis of attack graphs. In *Proceedings of the 2002 IEEE Symposium on Security and Privacy (S&P'02)*, pages 273–284, 2002.
34. S. Staniford, J.A. Hoagland, and J.M. McAlerney. Practical automated detection of stealthy portscans. *Journal of Computer Security*, 10(1/2):105–136, 2002.
35. S. Templeton and K. Levitt. A requires/provides model for computer attacks. In *Proceedings of the 2000 New Security Paradigms Workshop (NSPW'00)*, pages 31–38, 2000.
36. Treasure hunt datasets. http://www.cs.ucsb.edu/~vigna/treasurehunt/index.html, 2004.
37. A. Turner. Tcpreplay: Pcap editing and replay tools for *nix. Available at http://tcpreplay.sourceforge.net/.
38. A. Valdes and K. Skinner. Probabilistic alert correlation. In *Proceedings of the 4th International Symposium on Recent Advances in Intrusion Detection*, pages 54–68, 2001.
39. L. Wang, A. Liu, and S. Jajodia. Real-time analyses of intrusion alert streams. Technical report, Center for Secure Information Systems, George Mason University, 2005.
40. D. Zerkle and K. Levitt. Netkuang - a multi-host configuration vulnerability checker. In *Proceedings of the 6th USENIX Unix Security Symposium (USENIX'96)*, 1996.
41. Y. Zhai, P. Ning, P. Iyer, and D. Reeves. Reasoning about complementary intrusion evidence. In *Proceedings of the 20th Annual Computer Security Applications Conference (ACSAC'04)*, pages 39–48, 2004.

# Towards a Theory of Intrusion Detection*

Giovanni Di Crescenzo, Abhrajit Ghosh, and Rajesh Talpade

Telcordia Technologies, Piscataway, NJ, USA
{giovanni, aghosh, rrt}@research.telcordia.com

**Abstract.** We embark into theoretical approaches for the investigation of intrusion detection schemes. Our main motivation is to provide rigorous security requirements for intrusion detection systems that can be used by designers of such systems. Our model captures and generalizes well-known methodologies in the intrusion detection area, such as anomaly-based and signature-based intrusion detection, and formulates security requirements based on both well-known complexity-theoretic notions and well-known notions in cryptography (such as computational indistinguishability).

Under our model, we present two efficient paradigms for intrusion detection systems, one based on nearest neighbor search algorithms, and one based on both the latter and clustering algorithms. Under formally specified assumptions on the representation of network traffic, we can prove that our two systems satisfy our main security requirement for an intrusion detection system. In both cases, while the potential truth of the assumption rests on heuristic properties of the representation of network traffic (which is hard to avoid due to the unpredictable nature of external attacks to a network), the proof that the systems satisfy desirable detection properties is rigorous and of probabilistic and algorithmic nature. Additionally, our framework raises open questions on intrusion detection systems that can be rigorously studied. As an example, we study the problem of arbitrarily and efficiently extending the detection window of any intrusion detection system, which allows the latter to catch attack sequences interleaved with normal traffic packet sequences. We use combinatoric tools such as time and space-efficient covering set systems to present provably correct solutions to this problem.

## 1   Introduction

Informally, an Intrusion Detection system is a system for raising attention towards potential misbehaviors of the system caused by external adversaries. We could think of a 'burglar alarm' in the real world as the physical analogue of an intrusion detection system in the computerized world. (Just as a burglar alarm in the real world, Intrusion Detection only deals with discovering that an intrusion might have happened into a network. A number of additional aspects related to intrusions, such as intrusion avoidance; that is, augmenting systems so to have a lower likelihood of an external attacker that successfully performs an intrusion; or intrusion tolerance; that is, augmenting systems

---

* The research was supported by Telcordia and NSA/ARDA under AFRL Contract F30602-03-C-0239. Any opinions, findings, and conclusions or recommendations expressed in this paper are those of the authors and do not necessarily reflect the views of NSA/ARDA.

S. De Capitani di Vimercati et al. (Eds.): ESORICS 2005, LNCS 3679, pp. 267–286, 2005.
© Springer-Verlag Berlin Heidelberg 2005

so that the intended system behavior does not change even after an intrusion; are the subject of study of different research areas.)

Intrusion Detection is a very active and important research area in the Security literature. We won't attempt to survey or categorize the research in this area, but we note that the origin of the problem is often attributed to [1] and several taxonomies and surveys can be found, for instance, in [3,14,15,16]. Often all techniques in known intrusion detection systems are abstracted as falling under two important principles: *anomaly detection*, according to which traffic significantly different from normal ones can be interpreted as likely to be an attack, and *signature detection*, (also called *misuse detection* or *rule-based detection*), according to which traffic significantly similar to known attack traffic can be interpreted as likely to be the same attack. Both principles offer advantages and disadvantages, and many recent systems combine the two principles, rather than specifically choosing one of them.

Despite the large amount of research in this area, no established common framework exists for the design and analysis of intrusion detection systems. A typical research paper in the area proceeds describing some new ideas for detecting intrusions and justifies their validity by describing a specific implementation experience where both the rate of 'false positives' and the rate of 'false negatives' are low. A notable exception is the seminal paper of [7], which does provide a number of valid and formal guidelines for the design and tools for the analysis of intrusion detection systems. In particular, several papers attribute to [7] the introduction of the anomaly-based detection principle.

OUR MODEL. In this paper we put forward a theoretical framework for a rigorous investigation of intrusion detection systems. Our main motivation is to provide security requirements for intrusion detection systems that can be used to accompany simulation-based approaches in their design and increase the number of properties that can be rigorously proved for such systems. Our framework captures and generalizes the notions of anomaly-based and signature-based intrusion detection. Our security requirements are formulated using cryptographic notions such as computational (in)distinguishability, and analysis tools from probability and complexity theory. Specifically, we define two requirements: sensitivity and detection. The first requirement, "sensitivity", says that a *fixed window* of network traffic entering a system can be alternatively represented so that the output of the representation algorithm behaves quite differently according to whether this traffic comes from normal traffic or from a potentially unknown attack. (We remark that this representation algorithm alone is not sufficient to build an intrusion detection system for a few reasons that we later discuss.) The second requirement, "detection", says that if the representation algorithm satisfies the sensitivity requirement, then a data structure and a classification algorithm should allow to *constructively* detect with high probability any attack among a potentially infinite set of *new attacks* or *variations of known attacks*, and in an *arbitrarily large traffic window*. The difficulty in turning a representation algorithm into data structure and classification algorithms is due to the emphasized text in the previous sentence. According to our model, proving both requirements, possibly under some additional assumption, for a proposed system should give mathematical guarantees that the system is a "satisfactory" Intrusion Detection (ID) system. When coupled with simulation-based investigations on the sensitivity of fixed-window network traffic representations and on the estimation of anomaly-type or signature-type parameters, our framework promises to give a valuable methodology to allow ID designers to increase their claimed properties about their ID systems. Effectively, our model assumes that simulation-based investigations guarantee certain properties about both fixed-window traffic representation and parameter estimation, are satisfied. After this assumption, however, the detection requirement can be formally proved for a given system. We also provide several validations for our model, including the fact that well-known ID systems very often used in practice (most notably, SNORT [22]) can be easily cast into our formalization; and results from a satisfactory implementation experience.

OUR ID SYSTEMS. Under this framework, we obtain two efficient paradigms for intrusion detection systems, one based on nearest neighbor search algorithms, and one based on both the latter and clustering algorithms. Under formally specified assumptions (both stronger than the sensitivity property, one being more applicable than the other), we can prove that our two systems satisfy our detection requirement for an intrusion detection system. (Due to lack of space, we only briefly discuss our second system.)

OPEN QUESTIONS. We believe that our framework raises a number of important open questions on intrusion detection that can be studied using mathematical and/or algorithmic approaches. As an important example, we study the problem of arbitrarily and efficiently extending the detection window of intrusion detection systems, which allows the latter to catch attack sequences interleaved with normal traffic packet sequences (which was not detected in the previously discussed two systems). We present a construction that works for *any* intrusion detection system and is based on particular versions of known combinatorial tools (Covering Set Systems).

ORGANIZATION OF THE PAPER. In Section 2 we present our new framework and all formal definitions. (Validations of the model are in Appendix A.) In Section 3 we present our ID scheme based on Nearest Neighbor Search algorithms and briefly discuss an extension based on Clustering algorithms. In Section 4 we formulate and study the problem of extending the detection window of intrusion detection schemes.

## 2   Model and Formal Definitions

In this section we present our formal model and definitions for intrusion detection schemes. We start by presenting the system and attack model, including the scenario, the mechanics and the algorithms involved in an execution of such systems, and then describe the requirements that we would like an intrusion detection to satisfy. Although we concentrate on *network* intrusion detection, our definitions are applicable to *host* instrusion detection, where the traffic analyzed is entering the particular host.

### 2.1   System and Attack Model

SCENARIO, CONNECTIVITY, ACTION. The scenario we consider is that of a large network, also called *autonomous system* (AS), which may have many points of entry for network traffic, also called the *border gateways* (BG) of the AS. The traffic is generated by external users, and without loss of generality, each user can send traffic to each BG.

We write network traffic as a sequence of atomic *packets*, where each packet can be abstracted as a tuple $p = (sid, time, poe, pl)$, where $sid$ is the identity of the sender, $time$ is a timestamp of the action, $poe$ is the point of entry and $pl$ is the payload. At any time the action in an AS system can be described as a stream of packets entering AS through any of its BG (we will assume for simplicity that all traffic enters through a single BG), where each packet in this stream can trigger an event in the AS.

ATTACK MODEL. Informally, an attack can be any sequence of $c$ packets, for some $c \geq 1$, that successfully alters the state of machines in an AS in order to achieve a specific (malicious) goal. If by $\Phi_t$ we denote the state of the AS at time $t$ (this may include items such as available bandwidth resources and the internal state of all hosts within the AS) we can then define a polynomial time computable predicate $\rho(1^n, t, \Phi_t)$, where $n$ is a security parameter (later we clarify how to choose it). More generally, we can then define an *attack* as an efficiently samplable probability distribution $A$ over all packet sequences $ps = (p_1, \ldots, p_l)$, where $l$ is the length of $A$'s first input, and such that the probability that experiment $E(A)$ is not successful, is negligible, (that is, smaller than $1/p(n)$, for all positive polynomials $p$ and all sufficiently large $n$); and, for any distribution $D$, the probability experiment $E(D)$ is defined as follows.

1. A sequence $p$ of packets is drawn from distribution $D$
2. sequence $p$ is sent into the network
3. AS turns into state $\Phi_t$
4. predicate $\rho(1^n, t, \Phi_t)$ evaluates to bit $b$,

and we say that $E(D)$ is successful if $b = 1$. (Here, an output 0 for $\rho$ is intended to imply that attack $A$ has not been succesfully carried out at time $t$, and 1 otherwise.)

A *class of attacks* $C$ may be simply defined as a set of attacks $\{A_1, A_2, A_3, \ldots\}$.

We also define a *normal traffic distribution* (briefly, normal traffic) as an efficiently samplable probability distribution $N$ over the set of (single) packets, such that the probability that experiment $E(N)$ is successful, is negligible.

ALGORITHMS AND ID MECHANICS. We will define an intrusion detection system as a triple of algorithms:

1. A *representation* algorithm $\mathcal{R}$ (typical actions modeled by this algorithm include data filtering, formatting, plotting, feature selection, etc.)
2. a *data structure* algorithm $\mathcal{S}$, (typical actions modeled by this algorithm include data collection, aggregation, classification; knowledge base creation, etc.)
3. a *classification* algorithm $\mathcal{C}$ (typical actions modeled by this algorithm include: detection in all forms, including pattern-based, rule-based, anomaly-based, etc.; response, refinement, information tracing, visualization, etc.).

The execution of the ID system can be divided into two phases: an *initialization phase* and a *detection phase*. Briefly speaking, algorithm $\mathcal{S}$ is run in the initialization phase and algorithm $\mathcal{C}$ is run in the detection phase; both algorithms $\mathcal{C}$ and $\mathcal{S}$ use algorithm $\mathcal{R}$ as a subroutine. Specifically, in the initialization phase, the data structure algorithm uses the representation algorithm to process a stream of data obtained from normal traffic distribution or known attack distributions; the returned output is some data structure that will help in the detection phase. Here we note that the initialization phase assumes that the traffic generated according to such distributions is not subject to an attack, with the possible exception of simulated known attacks. In the detection phase, the classification algorithm is run on input the data structure and a sequence of traffic packets (possibly subject to a known or new attack), and returns an assessment of whether the input sequence of packets contains an attack (and if so, if this is a new attack or not) or only normal traffic. (We note that this output can be generalized to contain additional information such as an estimate of the probability of either event, etc.) Algorithm $\mathcal{R}$, informally, maps a sequence of data packets entering the AS into a fixed-length tuple, having a more compact form (e.g., a point in a high-dimension space).

## 2.2 Requirements

REQUIREMENTS. Let $n$ be a security parameter; let $N$ be a normal traffic distribution and let $A_1, \ldots, A_t$ be (known) attack distributions such that $N, A_1, \ldots, A_t$ are all efficiently samplable and with pairwise disjoint supports. We define an *intrusion detection system* IDS as a triple of polynomial time algorithms $\mathcal{R}, \mathcal{S}, \mathcal{C}$ with the following syntax.

1. On input $1^n$ and a sequence of $rw$ packets $\boldsymbol{p}$, algorithm $\mathcal{R}$ returns a $d$-tuple $\boldsymbol{r}$.
2. On input $1^n$ and distributions $N, A_1, \ldots, A_t$ algorithm $\mathcal{S}$ returns a data structure $ds$ of size at most $m[int]$.
3. On input $1^n$, a data structure $ds$, a sequence of $m[det]$ packets $\boldsymbol{p}$, a detection window $dw$ and a class of attacks $C$, algorithm $\mathcal{C}$ returns a classification value $out$.

Here, $rw$ is a parameter indicating the window of packets used in a single execution of $\mathcal{R}$ (which we will also call the *representation window* and is normally considered a small value); $m[init]$ is a parameter indicating the length of the stream of packets used in the initialization phase; $m[det]$ is a parameter indicating the length of the stream of packets used in the detection phase, to be classified by $\mathcal{S}$ (which is normally considered an arbitrarily large, but polynomial in $n$ and $rw$, value), and $dw$ is a parameter indicating the maximum distance between the first and last packet of an attack sequence within the stream of packets used in the detection phase. In general, $rw$, $d$, $m[init]$, $m[det]$ and $dw$ are all bounded by a polynomial in $n$; a typical setting would be $rw = O(n)$, $d = O(1)$, $m[init] = n^a$, $m[det] = n^b$, $rw \leq dw \leq m[det]$, for potentially large constants $a, b > 1$. Furthermore, IDS can satisfy the following two requirements of *sensitivity* and *detection*.

**Sensitivity.** Informally, we would like the output tuple of the representation algorithm to capture differences between normal traffic and attack traffic in its small input packet sequence. Capturing these differences is formalized using the notion of computational distinguishability (a particular strong negation of the notion of computational indistinguishability of [12,24], a notion very frequently used in Cryptography), and specifically by requiring distinguishability with respect to a single sample of the distributions.

Formally, we first recall (an adaptation of) the definition of computational distinguishability: Let $t, q$ be positive integers and $\epsilon \in [0,1]$. We say that two distributions $A, B$ are $(t, q, \epsilon)$-*distinguishable* if there exists a probabilistic algorithm $E$ running in time $t$ such that $|p_A - p_B| \geq \epsilon$, where, for $C = A, B$, it holds that $p_C = \{x_1, \ldots, x_q \leftarrow C : E(x_1, \ldots, x_q) = 1\}$.

Now, let $n$ be a security parameter. An asymptotic formulation of this definition can be obtained by considering $t$ and $q$ as functions smaller than some polynomial in $n$.

(By noticeable we mean that it is larger than $1/p(n)$, for some polynomial $p$ and all sufficiently large $n$.) Specifically, assume $A = \{A_n\}$ and $B = \{B_n\}$ are families of distributions; we say that $A$ and $B$ are *computationally distinguishable* if there exists a probabilistic polynomial (in $n$) time algorithm $E$ such that for any polynomial (in $n$) $q$, it holds that $|p_A - p_B| \geq \epsilon(n)$, where $\epsilon(n)$ is noticeable in $n$ and for $C = A, B$, it holds that $p_C = \{x_1, \ldots, x_q \leftarrow C : E(x_1, \ldots, x_q) = 1\}$.

In practice, we recommend running simulation experiments to determine convenient values for $\epsilon(n)$ and therefore for a security parameter $n$ such that the above inequality $|p_A - p_B| \geq \epsilon(n)$ holds.

We recall that an important result, often used in Cryptography, states that two families of distributions are computationally indistinguishable if and only if they are *single-sample* computationally indistinguishable; that is, they satisfy the latter definition for $q(n) = 1$. In our scenarios, the families of distributions will be normal traffic or attack distributions, and therefore, in general, the algorithm $E$ may not have access to an arbitrary number of of samples from these distributions, especially the attack ones (consider the case of an attacker that only tries her attack once). Therefore, our sensitivity definition only considers distinguishability with respect to one sample.

**Definition 1.** Let $A$ be an attack distribution and $N$ be a normal traffic distribution; also, let $t, rw$ be a positive integers and $\sigma \in [0, 1]$. We say that a representation scheme $\mathcal{R}$ is $(t, \sigma, A)$-*sensitive* if distributions $D_N, D_A$ are $(t, 1, \sigma)$-distinguishable, where:

$$D_N = \{p_1, \ldots, p_{rw} \leftarrow N(1^{rw}); r \leftarrow \mathcal{R}(p_1, \ldots, p_{rw}) : r\}$$
$$D_A = \{(a_1, \ldots, a_{rw}) \leftarrow A(1^{rw}); r \leftarrow \mathcal{R}(a_1, \ldots, a_{rw}) : r\}$$

Furthermore, let $C$ be a class of distributions. We say that a representation scheme $\mathcal{R}$ is $(t, \sigma, C)$-*sensitive* if it is $(t, \sigma, A)$-sensitive for all distributions $A$ in class $C$.

In the asymptotic formulation, $n$ is a security parameter, $A$ and $N$ are families of distributions and we say that a representation scheme $\mathcal{R}$ is $C$-*sensitive* if the distributions $D_N$ and $D_A$ are single-sample computationally distinguishable for all $A$ in class $C$, where:

$$D_N = \{p_1, \ldots, p_{rw} \leftarrow N_n(1^{rw}); r \leftarrow \mathcal{R}(1^n, p_1, \ldots, p_{rw}) : r\}$$
$$D_A = \{(a_1, \ldots, a_{rw}) \leftarrow A_n(1^{rw}); r \leftarrow \mathcal{R}(1^n, a_1, \ldots, a_{rw}) : r\}.$$

Finally, we say that an *intrusion detection system* IDS $= (\mathcal{R}, \mathcal{S}, \mathcal{C})$ is $C$-*sensitive* if so is its representation algorithm $\mathcal{R}$.

For $i = 1, \ldots, rw$, let $pos_i$ be the index $ind \in \{1, \ldots, m[det]\}$ such that $q_{ind} = a_i$, where $q_{ind}$ is the $ind$-th packet received during the detection phase. We will also say that IDS has *detection window* $dw$ if it holds that $pos_{rw} - pos_1 \leq dw$.

We remark that if a representation scheme is $(t, \sigma, C)$-sensitive for "good" parameters, this implies both that the representation has not significantly obscured the information necessary to detect attacks in class $C$, and that such information was originally present in the observed packet sequence (an obviously minimal feasibility assumption for intrusion detection). The algorithm $E$ may be viewed as an ideal (perfect) analysis system for detecting attacks in class $C$ using $\mathcal{R}$, as described later. While we will not expect to design such an $E$ for any attack on a given system, we will address the problem of using an estimation for such an algorithm $E$ to detect that a given system is under a certain (known or unknown) attack.

**Detection.** The only property of the representation algorithm is that the *fixed-window* behavior between attack and normal traffic is different on its output, without clarifying anything about the *nature of this difference*, or any *constructive algorithm to distinguish* which of two different outputs is of which type. Instead, we would like the data structure algorithm and the classification algorithm to directly provide "good enough" detection properties on *arbitrarily large* traffic sequences as long as the representation algorithm has "good enough" sensitivity properties on *small* and *fixed* traffic sequences. This conditional detection requirement is captured by the following game. In a first phase, the data structure algorithm is given access to a stream of $m$ packets $p$ and can run the representation algorithm on inputs of length $rw$; furthermore, it is allowed to query both the normal traffic distribution $N$ and several (known) attack distributions $A_1, \ldots, A_t$, for some $t$ polynomial in the security parameter $n$. At the end of this phase, it returns a data structure $ds$. Now, a sequence of $dw$ packets $q$ are somehow generated and the classification algorithm returns an output $out$ saying if $q$ contains a sample from one of the known attacks $A_1, \ldots, A_t$, or a different (unknown) attack $A$ or no attack at all. The intrusion detection system is successful if this classification is correct.

First, we define the probabilistic experiment in the initialization phase: Let $p$ be the sequence of $m$ packets in this phase, let $A_1, \ldots, A_t$ be known attacks and let $N$ denote the normal traffic distribution over single packets; we can define

$$Init(1^m) = \{ds \leftarrow \mathcal{S}^{N, A_1, \ldots, A_t, \mathcal{R}}(p)\},$$

where the notation $\mathcal{S}^{D_1, \ldots, D_k}$ means that algorithm $\mathcal{S}$ can generate several independent samples from distributions $D_1, \ldots, D_k$.

Now we consider the detection phase; let $q$ be the sequence of $dw$ packets generated in this phase, and let $A \equiv A_0$ be a possibly unknown attack different from $A_1, \ldots, A_t$; we say that string $s = (s_0, \ldots, s_t) \in \{0, 1\}^{t+1}$ is *A-correct* if $s_i = 1$ if and only if $q$ contains a tuple of packets in the support of distribution $A_i$, for $i = 0, 1, \ldots, t$. We are now ready to give a formal definition of the detection property.

**Definition 2.** Let $A$ be a (potentially unknown) attack, let $t$ be a positive integer and let $\delta \in [0, 1]$. We say that an intrusion detection system IDS $= (\mathcal{R}, \mathcal{S}, \mathcal{C})$ is a $(t, \delta, A)$-*detector* if for any packet sequence $q$, it holds that $\pi(A, q) \geq \delta$, where we define probability $\pi(A, q)$ as

$$\text{Prob}\left[ds \leftarrow \mathcal{S}^{\mathcal{R}}(1^{m[init]}); out \leftarrow \mathcal{C}^{\mathcal{R}}(1^n, ds, q, A) : out \text{ is } A\text{-correct}\right].$$

Furthermore, let $C$ be a class of distributions. We say that an intrusion detection scheme IDS $= (\mathcal{R}, \mathcal{S}, \mathcal{C})$ is a $(t, \delta, C)$-*detector* if it is $(t, \delta, A)$-detector for all distributions $A$ in class $C$.

In the asymptotic formulation, we let $n$ be a security parameter, and $C$ be a class of families of distributions and we say that an intrusion detection system IDS $= (\mathcal{R}, \mathcal{S}, \mathcal{C})$ is a $C$-*detector* if for $t$ polynomial in $n$, for any $A \in C$ and any $q$, it holds that $\pi(A, q) \geq \delta$, for some $\delta$ noticeable in $n$.

We remark that an intrusion detection scheme can be considered a 'good' detector if it achieves a detection probability $\delta$ 'close enough' to the sensitivity probability $\sigma$ associated with the representation algorithm. In other words, the closest $\delta$ is to $\sigma$, the highest is the detection property of the scheme.

DISCUSSION. We also remark that the sensitivity assumption on the behavior of the representation algorithm $\mathcal{R}$ is a necessary assumption, as otherwise no efficient distinguisher between a normal traffic distributions and an attack distribution exists and therefore no pair of algorithms $\mathcal{S}, \mathcal{C}$ can be a detector. Formally, this implies the following

**Proposition 1.** Let $n$ be a security parameter and $A$ be an attack distribution. Also, let $\mathcal{R}$ be a representation algorithm and assume that $\mathcal{R}$ is not $(t, \sigma, A)$-sensitive for $t$ polynomial in $n$ and $\sigma$ noticeable in $n$. Then, in our model, there exist no algorithms $\mathcal{S}, \mathcal{C}$ such that the ID system $(\mathcal{R}, \mathcal{S}, \mathcal{C})$ is an $(A, \mathcal{R})$-detector.

Model validation arguments can be found in Appendix A. We do note that our approach in formulating model and security requirements has been quite minimalistic and we have made a number of simplifications. Indeed, we believe we have addressed the most basic possible variant of the intrusion detection problem. We do believe that our model will allow in the future a much easier modeling of more elaborated variants, currently studied in the Intrusion Detection literature.

ANALYSIS METHODOLOGY. Given the above definitions of sensitivity and detection, an ideal methodology to analyze an intrusion detection system in our model would prove that a given ID scheme satisfies:

1. the sensitivity requirement (for some appropriate parameter values)
2. the detection requirement (for some appropriate parameter values) under the assumption that it satisfies the sensitivity requirement.

Clearly, 1) and 2) imply that the given ID scheme satisfies the detection requirement. A mathematical proof that an intrusion detection system satisfies the sensitivity requirement seems hard to obtain, even in a formal model, due to the unpredictable nature of a generic unknown attack. Validating the sensitivity of a representation algorithm is therefore left to simulation-based analysis. However, once a heuristic representation algorithm $\mathcal{R}$ is assumed to be $C$-sensitive for a class $C$ of attacks, we consider the major analysis goal in our model to formally prove that a certain classification algorithm $\mathcal{C}$ is a $(C; \mathcal{R})$-detector under this very minimal assumption. In this paper we will get very close to prove this result: specifically, we show that our two schemes are $C$-detectors under slightly stronger (but believable) versions of the sensitivity assumption. We stress that no simulation-based arguments are used in proving this property for our schemes.

## 3   An ID Scheme Based on Nearest Neighbor Search

In this section we present our first intrusion detection scheme, using algorithms for the approximate nearest neighbor search problem. We start by reviewing this problem and the properties that an algorithm for this problem has to satisfy to be applicable to our ID scheme. Then we formulate assumptions on the normal traffic and attack distributions, on the output of the estimation algorithm and on the output returned by a representation algorithm. Finally, we present our ID scheme and observe that it satisfies the detection requirement, as defined in Section 2, under the formulated assumptions. An important property achieved using the nearest neighbor search technique is that of merging and generalizing the anomaly-based and signature-based methodologies into a setting with a well-defined metric. As an example, two traffic flows will be determined to be closer to a signature according to a well-defined distance metric, and we can therefore assign a related confidence on whether each traffic flow is a known attack or not. Analogously, in the anomaly-based case, we can assign a related confidence on whether each traffic flow is an unknown attack or a false positive.

APPROXIMATE NEAREST NEIGHBOR SEARCH. Let $VS$ be a vector space of dimension $d$ and let $\Delta$ be some distance function defined over $VS$. Given a set $S$ of $n$ $d$-component vectors in $VS$, an error parameter $\epsilon$, and a $d$-component vector $q \in VS$, we define the $(1 + \epsilon)$-approximate nearest neighbor of $q$ as the vector $v$ in $S$ such that $\Delta(q, v) \leq (1 + \epsilon) \cdot \Delta(q, w)$, for any $w \in S$. A solution to the approximate nearest neighbor search problem is a pair of algorithms $(Init, Search)$ as follows. First, algorithms $Init$ and $Search$ have the following syntax: on input an $n$-size set $S$ of $d$-length vectors and parameters $\epsilon, \mu$, algorithm $Init$ returns a data structure $ds$; on input data structure $ds$, a vector $v$ and parameter $\epsilon$, algorithm $Search$ returns a vector $w$. Then the problem requires that with probability at least $\mu$ the following holds: 1) $w \in S$, and 2) $w$ is a $(1 + \epsilon)$-approximate nearest neighbor of $v$. We note that we impose efficiency requirements on algorithms for approximate nearest neighbor search that can be of interest for our constructions of ID schemes. In particular, we will require that algorithm $Init$ runs in time polynomial in $n$ and $d$, and that algorithm $Search$ runs in time polynomial in $d$ and $\log n$. (This is because of the fact that algorithm $Init$ will be used in off-line mode in the initialization phase while algorithm $Search$ will be used in on-line mode in the detection phase). We also note that the performance of algorithm $Search$ is required to be significantly faster than $\Theta(dn)$, which is the performance of the naive, brute-force, and exact search algorithm.

Although any efficient solution for the approximate nearest neighbor search problem can be used for the design of our ID scheme, for concreteness, we will use the following result from [13].

**Lemma 1.** [13]   There exists (constructively) a pair of algorithms (Init,Search) that solve the approximate nearest neighbor search problem for $VS = \{0, 1\}^d$ and $\Delta$ equal to the Hamming distance, and has the following efficiency property: $Init$ runs in time $\epsilon^{-2} \cdot poly(dn)$ and $Search$ runs in time $\Theta(\epsilon^{-2} \cdot d \cdot poly(\log(dn)))$.

A SET OF ASSUMPTIONS.   We now describe assumptions on the normal traffic and attack distributions, on the output of the estimation algorithm and on the output returned by the representation algorithm. The assumptions about the normal traffic and attack distributions generalize the usual assumptions underlying the basic principles of anomaly detection (for the normal traffic and unknown attack distributions) and signature detection (for the known attack distributions). The assumption about the estimation algorithm is stating that the estimation of the parameters in the previous assumptions is correct with some (somewhat high) probability. The assumption about the behavior of the representation algorithm is at least as strong as the assumption that the representation algorithm is sensitive, in the sense that if a representation algorithm satisfies this new assumption then it also satisfies the sensitivity definition, as in Section 2 (while it is unclear whether the converse is true). Informally, these assumptions postulate that the representation algorithm returns, given a fixed-length sequence of packets as input, a point in a high-dimensional space, such that any two points belonging to the same distribution, being it normal traffic, a known attack, or a new attack, have 'small' distance, while any two points coming from different distributions have 'large' distance. We now define these assumptions more formally.

**Assumption 1.** Let $N$ be a normal traffic distribution, let $A_1, \ldots, A_t$ be (known) attack distributions and let $A$ be an (unknown) attack distribution.

A representation algorithm is defined as an algorithm that, on input $1^k$ and a sequence of at most $rw$ packets $\boldsymbol{p}$, where $rw$ is polynomial in $k$, returns a $d$-tuple $\boldsymbol{r}$. We say that *distributions* $N, A_1, \ldots, A_t, A$ *are* $(\delta_n, \delta_a, \delta_1, \ldots, \delta_t)$-*oversensitive* if there exists a vector space $VS$ of dimension $d$, a distance function $\Delta$ over $VS$ and a representation algorithm $\mathcal{R}$ such that, for any $\boldsymbol{p}_1, \boldsymbol{p}_2$, denoting as $r_1, r_2 \in VS$ the values such that $\mathcal{R}(\boldsymbol{p}_1) = r_1$ and $\mathcal{R}(\boldsymbol{p}_2) = r_2$, it holds that $\Delta(r_1, r_2)$ is:

1. $\leq \delta_n$ if and only if $\boldsymbol{p}_1, \boldsymbol{p}_2$ were both returned by distribution $N$
2. $\leq \delta_a$ if $\boldsymbol{p}_1, \boldsymbol{p}_2$ were returned by distribution $A$
3. $\leq \delta_i$ if $\boldsymbol{p}_1, \boldsymbol{p}_2$ were returned by distribution $A_i$, for $i = 1, \ldots, t$.

An estimation algorithm is defined as an algorithm returning $(\delta'_n, \delta'_a, \delta'_1, \ldots, \delta'_t)$ when given as input $(1^k, N, A_1, \ldots, A_t, A, VS, \Delta)$. We say that an estimation algorithm $ES$ is $\mu$-correct if it holds that $|\delta_n - \delta'_n| \leq \mu$, $|\delta_a - \delta'_a| \leq \mu$, and $|\delta_i - \delta'_i| \leq \mu$, for $i = 1, \ldots, t$.

We say that a representation scheme $\mathcal{R}$ is $(A, VS, \Delta, \delta'_n, \delta'_a, \delta'_1, \ldots, \delta'_t)$-*oversensitive* if for any $\boldsymbol{p}_1, \boldsymbol{p}_2$, denoting as $r_1, r_2 \in VS$ the values such that $\mathcal{R}(\boldsymbol{p}_1) = r_1$ and $\mathcal{R}(\boldsymbol{p}_2) = r_2$, it holds that $\Delta(r_1, r_2)$ is:

1. $\leq \delta'_n$ if and only if $\boldsymbol{p}_1, \boldsymbol{p}_2$ were both returned by distribution $N$
2. $\leq \delta'_a$ if $\boldsymbol{p}_1, \boldsymbol{p}_2$ were returned by distribution $A$
3. $\leq \delta'_i$ if $\boldsymbol{p}_1, \boldsymbol{p}_2$ were returned by distribution $A_i$, for $i = 1, \ldots, t$.

Finally, the assumption requires that there exists a $\mu$-correct estimation algorithm for the oversensitivity parameters of distributions $N, A_1, \ldots, A_t, A$, and that the representation algorithm $\mathcal{R}$ is $(A, VS, \Delta, \delta'_n, \delta'_a, \delta'_1, \ldots, \delta'_t)$-*oversensitive*, where $\delta'_n, \delta'_a, \delta'_1, \ldots, \delta'_t$ are the parameters returned by the estimation algorithm.

We note that item 1 in the oversensitivity assumptions is an 'if and only if' as we would like that any point generated from an attack distribution, known or unknown, to have distance larger than parameter $\delta_n$ (or $\delta'_n$) from a point generated from a normal traffic distribution.

OUR FIRST ID SCHEME. Let $\delta'_n, \delta'_a, \delta'_1, \ldots, \delta'_t$ be estimations, validated by simulation-based studies, of the parameters $\delta_n, \delta_a, \delta_1, \ldots, \delta_t$ in Assumption 1. Also, let $\mathcal{R}$ be an $(A, VS, \Delta, \delta'_n, \delta'_a, \delta'_1, \ldots, \delta'_t)$-oversensitive representation algorithm with representation window $rw$, where the oversensitivity assumption is also validated by simulation-based studies. (Note that this assumption implies the assumptions that distributions $N, A_1, \ldots, A_t, A$ are $(\delta_n, \delta_a, \delta_1, \ldots, \delta_t)$-oversensitive and therefore we do not need to clearly state the latter assumption below.) Moreover, let (Init,Search) be a pair of algorithms for the NNS problem, satisfying Lemma 1. Specifically, on input a set $S$ of $d$-length vectors and parameter $\epsilon$, algorithm $Init$ returns a data structure $ds$; on input data structure $ds$, a vector $v$ and parameter $\epsilon$, algorithm $Search$ returns (with high probability) a vector $w \in S$ such that $w$ is a $(1 + \epsilon)$-approximate nearest neighbor of $v$. We now describe algorithms $\mathcal{S}$ and $\mathcal{C}$ for our first ID scheme $\text{IDS}_1$ (for simplicity, we assume that the detection window satisfies $dw = rw$).

**Input to Algorithm $\mathcal{S}$:** $1^n$, distributions $N, A_1, \ldots, A_t$, algorithm $\mathcal{R}$, and parameters $\epsilon, \delta_1', \ldots, \delta_t', \delta_n', \delta_a'$.

**Instructions for Algorithm $\mathcal{S}$:**

1. For $i = 1, \ldots, n$,
   for $j = 1, \ldots, rw$,
   uniformly and independently sample $r_{i,j}$ from $D$
   set $x_i = \mathcal{R}(r_{i,1}, \ldots, r_{i,rw})$
2. For $i = 1, \ldots, t$ and $j = 1, \ldots, n$,
   uniformly and independently sample $s_{ij}$ from $A_i$
   set $y_{ij} = \mathcal{R}(s_{ij})$
3. Let $S = \{x_i\}_{i=1}^n \cup \{y_{1j}\}_{j=1}^n \cup \ldots \cup \{y_{tj}\}_{j=1}^n$
4. Let $ds = \text{Init}(S, \epsilon)$ and set $ds = ds \cup S$
5. Return: $ds$.

**Input to Algorithm $\mathcal{C}$:** $1^n, 1^c$, data structure $ds$, algorithm $\mathcal{R}$, packets $p_1, \ldots, p_m$, and parameters $\epsilon, \delta_1', \ldots, \delta_t', \delta_n', \delta_a' > 0$, where $m = m[det] = rw^c$

**Instructions for Algorithm $\mathcal{C}$:**

1. For $\ell = 0, \ldots, m - rw$,
   det $v_\ell = \mathcal{R}(p_{\ell+1}, \ldots, p_{\ell+rw})$
   let $w_\ell = \text{Search}(ds, v_\ell, \epsilon)$
   let $S$ be the set contained in $ds$ such that
   $\quad S = \{x_i\}_{i=1}^n \cup \{y_{1j}\}_{j=1}^n \cup \ldots \cup \{y_{tj}\}_{j=1}^n$
   set $out_h = 0$ for $h = 0, \ldots, t$
   if $w_\ell = y_{ij}$ for some $i \in \{1, \ldots, t\}$ and $j \in \{1, \ldots, n\}$ then
   $\quad$ if $\Delta(w_\ell, y_{ij}) \leq \delta_i'$ then set $out_i = 1$
   $\quad\quad$ else set $out_i = (1, \ell)$
   if $w_\ell = x_j$ for some $j \in \{1, \ldots, n\}$ then
   $\quad$ if $\Delta(w_\ell, x_j) > \delta_n'$ then set $out_0 = (1, \ell)$
2. Return: $(out_0, out_1, \ldots, out_t)$ and halt.

We would like to prove that under the oversensitivity assumption on RS, the system IDS is a successful detector.

By inspection of algorithms $\mathcal{S}, \mathcal{C}$, and by assuming that algorithm $\mathcal{R}$ satisfies Assumption 1, we observe that the successful detection of algorithm $\mathcal{C}$ strictly depends on whether the point $w_\ell$ returned by algorithm Search is the nearest neighbor of $v_\ell$ and whether the estimations $\delta_a', \delta_n', \delta_1', \ldots, \delta_t'$ are sufficiently close to $\delta_a, \delta_n, \delta_1, \ldots, \delta_t$.

Specifically, we observe that if point $w_\ell$ returned by algorithm Search is the *exact* nearest neighbor of $v_\ell$ and it holds that $\delta'_a = \delta_a$, $\delta'_n = \delta_n$ and $\delta'_i = \delta_i$, for $i = 1, \ldots, t$, then then the output $out = (out_0, out_1, \ldots, out_t)$ is $A$-correct. Therefore, the probability that $out$ is not $A$-correct can be bounded, using the union bound, as at most the probability that $w_\ell$ is not the exact nearest neighbor of $v_\ell$ for at least one $\ell \in \{1, \ldots, m\}$, plus the probability that the estimations $\delta'_a, \delta'_n, \delta'_1, \ldots, \delta'_t$ are not correct. We finally note that the former probability is at most $\epsilon$ by Lemma 1 and the latter probability is at most $\mu$ by Assumption 1.

Among all performance metrics of the scheme, we stress the importance of the efficiency of the running time of algorithm $\mathcal{C}$. We then obtain the following

**Theorem 1.** Let $A$ be an attack distribution, and let $\delta_n, \delta_a, \delta_1, \ldots, \delta_t, \epsilon$ be some parameters $> 0$, and let $\delta'_n, \delta'_a, \delta'_1, \ldots, \delta'_t$ be the output of a $\mu$-correct estimation algorithm taking as input $(1^k, N, A_1, \ldots, A_t, VS, \Delta)$.
If $\mathcal{R}$ is an $(A, VS, \Delta, \delta'_n, \delta'_a, \delta'_1, \ldots, \delta'_t)$-oversensitive representation algorithm then the scheme IDS $= (\mathcal{R}, \mathcal{S}, \mathcal{C})$ is a $(\tau, \delta, A)$-detector, where $\delta = 1 - \mu - m \cdot \epsilon$, and for any $\tau =$poly$(n)$. Moreover, scheme IDS is efficient as algorithm $\mathcal{S}$ runs in time poly$(n \cdot rw \cdot \epsilon^{-1})$ and algorithm $\mathcal{C}$ runs in time $O(\epsilon^{-2} \cdot rw \cdot$ polylog$(n \cdot rw))$. Furthermore, IDS has detection window $dw = rw$.

We consider a major open problem in the theory of intrusion detection to design ID schemes with assumptions weaker than Assumption 1. (Due to Proposition 1, the ultimate goal would be that of using the sensitivity requirement as a minimal assumption.)

OUR SECOND ID SCHEME. We only briefly mention that our first ID scheme can be generalized using Clustering algorithms and resulting in a second scheme based on a slightly weaker assumption. The idea we use here is in relaxing the assumption is in allowing several distributions (rather than a single one) for normal traffic. As a consequence, it is not true any more that any two points associated to normal traffic have 'small' distance, but it will hold that any such point has 'close' distance from at least one point generated according to at least one of the normal traffic distributions. Since our second scheme is based on weaker assumptions than our first one, the class of attacks that it can detect is strictly larger than the class of attacks of our first scheme, which points at another interesting capability allowed by our model.

## 4   ID Schemes with Arbitrary-Length Detection Window

In the previous sections we have studied intrusion detection schemes with detection window equal to the representation window. This restriction is, in practice, undesirable as it allows an adversary to perform simple attack strategies that would not be detected by the intrusion detection system. For instance, even for attacks consisting of two packets only, an adversary could send the second packet slightly later than the first packet (precisely, by interleaving between the two packets a number of packets at least as large as the representation window), and the detection window of the system will not contain both packets.

In this section we formally define and study the problem of extending the length of the detection window of an ID scheme. We use combinatorial techniques and apply them to any ID scheme that satisfies the definition in Section 2. Therefore, when applied to our schemes in Section 3, we obtain ID schemes with extended-length detection window under the same assumptions on the representation algorithm.

More formally, a first formulation of this problem could be the following. Given a generic intrusion detection system $\text{IDS}_1=(\mathcal{R}, \mathcal{S}, \mathcal{C})$ with representation window $rw_1$ and detection window $dw_1 = k$, is it possible to construct an intrusion detection system $\text{IDS}_2$ with representation window $rw_2 = rw_1$ and detection window $dw_2 = m$, for any $m =\text{poly}(k)$ ?

We note that the size of the tuple returned by an attack distribution $A$ is defined to be equal to the length of $A$'s first input, which is set, for convenience of parameters, equal to the representation window $rw$. More generally, in our problem formulation we would like to capture the situation of the number of effective attack packets being equal to some $\ell$ such that $1 \leq \ell \leq rw$, which is closer to what expected in practice. Formally, we define an attack distribution $A$ as $\ell$-*effective* if, denoting by $\text{Supp}(A, rw)$ the support of distribution $A$, when run on input $1^{rw}$, the following holds: for each tuple $(a_1, \ldots, a_{rw}) \in \text{Supp}(A, rw)$, there exists an $\ell$-tuple of indices $i_1, \ldots, i_\ell$ such that all $rw$-tuples containing $a_{i_1}, \ldots, a_{i_\ell}$ are in $\text{Supp}(A, rw)$. (Here, such $\ell$-tuple can be considered as the effective attack witness.)

As a consequence, we will study the following problem. Let $C$ be a class of $\ell$-effective attacks. Given a $C$-sensitive intrusion detection system $\text{IDS}_1 = (\mathcal{R}, \mathcal{S}, \mathcal{C})$ with representation window $rw_1$ and detection window $dw_1 = k$, is it possible to construct a $C$-sensitive intrusion detection system $\text{IDS}_2$ with representation window $rw_2 = rw_1$ and detection window $dw_2 = m$, for any $m =\text{poly}(k)$ ?

### 4.1   A Solution Based on Covering Set Systems

We now recall the definition of well-studied combinatorial objects, called covering set systems, and present a generic construction of an intrusion detection system with arbitrary-length detection window from one with a fixed detection window.

**Definition 3.** Let $\ell, k, m$ be positive integers. Let $S$ be a set of size $m$ and let $T = \{T_1, \ldots, T_s\}$ be a set of $k$-size subsets of $S$. We say that $T$ is an $(\ell, k, m)$-*covering set system* for $S$ if for any $\ell$-size $S_i \subseteq S$, there exists a subset $T_j \in T$ such that $S_i \subseteq T_j$. The *space efficiency* of the covering set system $T$ is defined to be the size $s$ of $T$ (and can be a function of $\ell, k, m$). The *time efficiency* of covering set system $T$ is defined to be the running time (as a function of $\ell, k, m$) that an algorithm takes to construct $T$.

As an example, note that the set of all $\ell$-size subsets of $S$ is an $(\ell, k, m)$-covering set system for $S$ having both time and space efficiency $\binom{m}{\ell}$. Covering set systems have been studied in several works (see, e.g., [10,11,9,18,21] and references therein), focusing on somewhat different requirements than ours. We also note that a related and dual notion of set systems (in an area also called Turan Theory) has been applied to other areas in Cryptography, such as secret sharing [19] and secure mixnets [6] (works on this notion typically focus on covering set systems for $k, m$ very close to $\ell$). We are not aware of other applications of covering set systems in the Security area.

**Construction of an IDS with arbitrary detection window.** Let $C$ be a class of $\ell$-effective attacks, and let $\text{IDS}_1=(\mathcal{R}_1, \mathcal{S}_1, \mathcal{C}_1)$ be a $C$-sensitive intrusion detection system with representation window $rw_1$ and detection window $dw_1 = k$. Also, let $T = \{T_1, \ldots, T_m\}$ be a $(\ell, k, m)$-covering set system for set $S = \{1, \ldots, m\}$. We now define an intrusion detection system IDS$_2$=$(\mathcal{R}_2, \mathcal{S}_2, \mathcal{C}_2)$, with representation window $rw_2$ and detection window $dw_2 = m$.

Algorithms $\mathcal{R}_2, \mathcal{S}_2$ are defined as equal to $\mathcal{R}_1, \mathcal{S}_1$, respectively. Algorithm $\mathcal{C}_2$ goes as follows. On input a sequence of $m$ packets $p_1, \ldots, p_m$, it runs $s$ times (using independent randomness) $\mathcal{C}_1$, each time on inputs a sequence of packets $s = p_{j_1}, \ldots, p_{j_k}$, where $T_i = \{j_1, \ldots, j_k\}$; we denote as $(out_{i0}, \ldots, out_{it})$ be the output returned by this execution of $\mathcal{C}_1$. Finally, $\mathcal{C}_2$ returns $(out_0, \ldots, out_t)$, where $out_j = \vee_{i=1}^{m} out_{ij}$, for $j = 1, \ldots, t$.

The sensitivity of $\mathcal{C}_2$ can be proved by using the sensitivity of $\mathcal{C}_1$ and the definition of covering set system. (Very roughly, for each $\ell$-size effective attack sequence $seq$, there exists at least one subset in $T$ that will define a sequence of packets $seq'$ that contains $seq$ and is given as input to $\mathcal{C}_1$ that will detect it). The efficiency of IDS$_2$ depends on the efficiency of the construction for the covering set systems. We note that for $\ell = O(1)$ (which is expected in practice) or for just $s$ polynomial in the security parameter, then algorithm $\mathcal{C}_2$ runs in time polynomial in the security parameter and then so does IDS$_2$.

We obtain the following

**Theorem 2.** Let $C$ be a class of $\ell$-effective attacks. Given a $C$-sensitive intrusion detection system IDS$_1$=$(\mathcal{R}_1, \mathcal{S}_1, \mathcal{C}_1)$ with representation window $rw_1$ and detection window $dw_1 = k$, and given an $(\ell, k, m)$-covering set system for set $S = \{1, \ldots, m\}$ with time efficiency $t$ and space efficiency $s$, it is possible to construct a $C$-sensitive intrusion detection system IDS$_2$ = $(\mathcal{R}_2, \mathcal{S}_2, \mathcal{C}_2)$ with representation window $rw_2 = rw_1$ and detection window $dw_2 = m$, for any $m = \text{poly}(k)$, where algorithm $\mathcal{C}_2$ runs in time $O(t + s \cdot \text{time}(\mathcal{C}_1))$.

We note that in the above theorem the efficiency of algorithm $\mathcal{C}_2$ (and therefore, of IDS$_2$) significantly depends on both time and space efficiency of the covering set system. It is then of interest to obtain covering set systems with satisfactory performance on both parameters and yet working for all choices of $\ell, k, m$. (Specifically, we are willing to sacrifice optimality with respect to space efficiency in order to achieve generality and satisfactory time efficiency.) Furthermore, of additional interest is the practical requirement that the code to generate such systems is simple. Constructions of covering set systems in the combinatorics and theoretical computer science literature mostly focus on achieving space-optimality, even for possibly limited choice of parameters $\ell, k, m$. In the next section we show some constructions that work for all choices of $\ell, k, m$, are simple to generate, and are time and space-efficient for $\ell = O(1)$. Improving these constructions to achieve time and space-efficiency for larger values of $\ell$ is an interesting open problem.

### 4.2   Constructions of Time-Efficient Covering Set Systems

We define $C(\ell, k, m)$ as the minimum, over all $(\ell, k, m)$-covering set systems $T$, of the space efficiency of $T$. We recall that a trivial upper bound of $\binom{n}{\ell}$ on $C(\ell, k, m)$ follows by defining a set $T_i$ as an arbitrary extension of the $i$-th $\ell$-size subset of $S$. Furthermore, we now recall two known lower bounds for $C(\ell, k, m)$. The first bound is simple and follows by observing that each $T_i$ can at most cover $\binom{k}{\ell}$ distinct subsets of size $\ell$ from $S$. The second lower bound is also well-known and due to [20].

**Fact 1.** It holds that
1. $C(\ell, k, m) \geq \frac{\binom{m}{\ell}}{\binom{k}{\ell}}$
2. $C(\ell, k, m) \geq \lceil \frac{m}{k} \cdot C(\ell - 1, k - 1, m - 1) \rceil$

We ideally would like to define general and time-efficient constructions of $T$ also having space efficiency as close as possible to the above lower bounds. Assuming $\ell = O(1)$ and, for simplicity, $k/\ell$ equal to an integer, we now define two constructions that meet these bounds up to a constant.

**Construction 1:**

1. Let $S = \{1, \ldots, m\}$ and $T_1 = \emptyset$.
2. Partition $S$ into $k$-size disjoint subsets $S_1, \ldots, S_{\lceil m/k \rceil}$
3. For $i = 1, \ldots, \lceil m/k \rceil$,
   partition each $S_i$ into disjoint $(k/\ell)$-size subsets $Z_{i,1}, \ldots, Z_{i,\ell}$
4. For each $i_1, \ldots, i_\ell \in \{1, \ldots, \lceil m/k \rceil\}$,
   for each $(a_1, b_1), \ldots, (a_\ell, b_\ell) \in \{(i_j, t) : j, t = 1, \ldots, \ell\}$,
   add $\cup_{i=1}^{\ell} Z_{a_i, b_i}$ to $T_1$,
5. Return: $T_1$.

**Construction 2:**

1. Let $S = \{1, \ldots, m\}$ and $T_2 = \emptyset$.
2. Partition $S$ into $(k/\ell)$-size disjoint subsets $S_1, \ldots, S_{\ell \cdot \lceil m/k \rceil}$
3. For each $i_1, \ldots, i_\ell \in \{1, \ldots, \ell \cdot \lceil m/k \rceil\}$,
   add $\cup_{j=1}^{\ell} S_{i_j}$ to $T_2$,
4. Return: $T_2$.

The above constructions satisfy the following

**Theorem 3.** The above two constructions define $(\ell, k, m)$-covering set systems $T_1, T_2$ for arbitrary positive integers $\ell, k, m$, with time and space efficiency $(t_1, s_1)$ and $(t_2, s_2)$, respectively, where:
1. $s_1 = \binom{\lceil m/k \rceil}{\ell} \cdot \binom{\ell^2}{\ell}$ and $t_1 = \Theta(s_1)$;
2. $s_2 = \binom{\ell \cdot \lceil m/k \rceil}{\ell}$ and $t_2 = \Theta(s_2)$.

# References

1. J. Anderson, *Computer Security Threat Monitoring and Surveillance*, in James P. Anderson Co., Fort Washington, Pa. 1980.
2. S. Axelsson, *The Base-Rate Fallacy and its Implication for the Difficulty of Intrusion Detection*, in Proc. of ACM CCS, 1999.
3. S. Axelsson, *Intrusion Detection Systems: A Survey and Taxonomy*, Technical Report 99-15, Depart. of Computer Engineering, Chalmers University, march 2000.
4. A. Borodin, R. Ostrovsky, and Y. Rabani, *Subquadratic Approximation Algorithms For Clustering Problems in High Dimensional Spaces*, in Proc. of The 31'st ACM Symposium on Theory of Computing (STOC-99)

5. Cisco Flow Collector Overview,
   http://www.cisco.com/univercd/cc/td/doc/product/rtrmgmt/nfc/nfc_3_0/nfc_ug/nfcover.pdf
6. Y. Desmedt and K. Kurosawa, *How to Break a Practical Mix and Design a New One*, in Proc. of Eurocrypt 2000, LNCS vol. 1807, Springer.
7. D. E. Denning, *An Intrusion Detection Model*, in IEEE Transactions on Software Engineering, Vol. SE-13, no. 2, pp. 222-232, 1987.
8. M. Esmaili, R. Safavi Naini, and J. Pieprzyk, *Intrusion Detection: A Survey*, in Proc. of ICCC 1995.
9. D. Gordon, *La Jolla Covering Repository*, web site: http://www.ccrwest.org/cover.html.
10. D. Gordon, G. Kuperberg, and O. Patashnik, *New Constructions for Covering Designs*, Journal of Combinatorial Designs, 3 (1995), pp. 269–284.
11. D. Gordon, G. Kuperberg, O. Patashnik, and J. Spencer, *Asymptotically Optimal Covering Designs*, Journal of Combinatorial Theory A, 75 (1996), pp. 220–240.
12. S. Goldwasser, and S. Micali, *Probabilistic Encryption*, in Journal of Computer and System Sciences, vol. 28, n. 2, 1984, pp. 270–299.
13. E. Kushilevitz, R. Ostrovsky, and Y. Rabani, *Efficient Search for Approximate Nearest Neighbor in High Dimensional Spaces*, in Proc. of the 30's ACM Symposium on Theory of Computing (STOC-98)
14. W. Lee, *A Data Mining Framework for Building Intrusion Detection Models*, in Proc. of IEEE Symposium on Security and Privacy 1999.
15. T. Lunt, *Automated Audit Trail Analysis and Intrusion Detection: A Survey*, in Proc. of 11th National Computer Security Conference, 1988.
16. N. McAuliffe, D. Wolcott, L. Schaefer, N. Kelem, B. Hubbard, and T. Haley, *Is Your Computer Being Misused ? A Survey of Current Intrusion Detection System Technology*, in Proc. of 6th IEEE Computer Security Applications Conference, 1990.
17. Netflow, IETF RFC, ftp://ftp.rfc-editor.org/innotes/rfc3954.txt
18. K. Nurmela and P. Ostergard, *Upper Bounds for Covering Designs by Simulated Annealing*, Congressum Numerantium, 96:93–111, 1993.
19. R. Rees, D. R. Stinson, R. Wei and G. H. J. van Rees, *An application of covering designs: Determining the maximum consistent set of shares in a threshold scheme*, Ars Combinatoria 531 (1999), 225-237.
20. J. Schonheim, *On Coverings*, Pacific Journal of Mathematics, 14:1405-1411, 1964.
21. C. Colbourn and J. Dinitz, THE CRC HANDBOOK OF COMBINATORIAL DESIGNS, CRC Press, Boca Raton, FL 1996 (see D. R. Stinson, Coverings, pp. 260-265)
22. http://www.snort.org
23. Flowtools public-domain software. http://www.splintered.net/sw/flow-tools/
24. A. Yao, *Theory and Application of Trapdoor Functions*, in Proc. of FOCS 85.
25. A. Ghosh, L. Wong, G. Di Crescenzo and R. Talpade, *Infilter: Predictive Ingress Filtering to Detect IP Spoofed Traffic*, in 2nd International Workshop on Security in Distributed Computing Systems (SDCS 2005).

# A    Model Validation

We have gone through a few basic steps towards validation of our model.

WELL-KNOWN PERFORMANCE METRIC OF ID SYSTEMS IN OUR MODEL. All natural performance metrics considered in the ID literature have a rigorous definition according to our model, as we discuss in detail in Appendix A. In particular, we discuss false positive rate, detection probability, detection attempt rate, time and space efficiency, data collection stability, data upgrade rate and performance.

WELL-KNOWN ID SYSTEMS IN OUR MODEL. Well-known ID systems very often used in practice can be easily cast into our formalization. We only discuss the notable case of SNORT [22] and show how its major components can be recast in forms of representation, data structure and classification algorithms. Then we discuss how analysis along the lines of Section 3 can be used to argue a number of interesting facts about one or more SNORT instantiations, even beyond just rigorously proving its detection properties. As an example, our model can be used to rigorously evaluate the tradeoff in two different SNORT instantiations between increased set of rules and efficiency performance of the system. We now proceed in slightly greater detail.

A public domain tool and perhaps the most widely deployed ID systems, SNORT [22] can be abstracted in one-line as a signature-based network intrusion detection system. A little more precisely, SNORT is a rule-based ID system, as it allows the definition and update of rules for traffic classification, and it actually provides somewhat sophisticated detection capabilities, such as information about attack 'origin' and attack 'breach type'. A high level definition of SNORT major components is as follows:

1. *Packet Capture Engine:* this uses a certain library to capture traffic datagrams.
2. *Preprocessor Plug-Ins:* they inspect packet data received from the capture engine and decide whether to analyze it or not, and, if yes, whether to generate an alert of a potential attack. They also perform some data filtering to eliminate traffic that may be malicious to the SNORT application itself.
3. *Detection Engine:* this performs basic tests according to a set of internal rules, each of them typically asking to search for a string/value associated with the rule itself and some particular piece of the packet. As for any signature-based ID system, it contains a preliminary phase of data gathering and main rules definition, and an active phase of online traffic classification.
4. *Output Plug-Ins:* they return high-level information of interest to the ID analyst.

We now show how we can simply fit SNORT into our formalization. Specifically, the representation algorithm $\mathcal{R}$ is composed with both the Packet Capture Engine and the Preprocessor Plug-Ins. The data structure algorithm $\mathcal{S}$ is composed with the rule definition part (both in the preliminary and active phase) and the preliminary phase of the Detection Engine. Finally, the classification algorithm $\mathcal{C}$ is composed with the active phase of the Detection Engine as well as the Output Plug-Ins. Technically, it is more appropriate to talk of SNORT as of an ID system suite, rather than a single ID system, as its detection success may significantly change according to how the above 4 components are instantiated. It is clear then that for each instantiation, one could prove a theorem similar in spirit to Theorem 1. One major difference, however, is that, given that the rules used by any SNORT instantiation fall under the signature detection principle, any SNORT instantiation will only be able to detect attacks $A$ that are among the known attacks $A_1, \ldots, A_t$ (while other schemes including the one given in Section refse-scheme1 combine and generalize the anomaly and signature detection principles.) Still, theorems in our model can be used in order to compare the advantages and disadvantages of different rule sets in different SNORT instantiations. For instances, a very basic question for which our model can provide quantitative answers, is that of evaluating the tradeoff between the convenience of enlarging the set of rules (i.e., using a weaker assumption and obtaining stronger detection results) and the degrade in certain performance metrics (such as running time, detection attempt rate and data upgrade rate).

A similar abstraction can be done for several other well-known signature-based ID systems. We remark that our formalization captures also anomaly-based ID systems (in fact, our system in Section 3 is an hybrid of both approaches: anomaly-based and signature-based).

DESIGN/ANALYSIS PLAN FOR ID SYSTEMS IN OUR MODEL. It is possible to formulate a detailed plan for the design and analysis methodology of ID systems in our model (thus, further elaborating on the discussion at the end of Section 2.2), that automatically integrates simulations and implementation experiences with theoretical analysis. In general, we will consider the following (summarized) step-by-step design and analysis methodology for ID systems:

1. Assumptions about normal traffic distributions and single attacks or attack classes distributions are rigorously formulated in terms of a set $PS$ of parameters.
2. An algorithm $ES$ is defined to produce a set $PS'$ of parameters estimating the parameters in $PS$
3. Algorithms $\mathcal{R}, \mathcal{S}, \mathcal{C}$ are defined using estimations in $PS'$.
4. An assumption is made about the estimation property of algorithm $ES$ and the assumption is validated through simulation-based studies.
5. An assumption is made about the sensitivity property of algorithm $\mathcal{R}$ and the assumption is validated through simulation-based studies.
6. The detection property of algorithms $\mathcal{S}, \mathcal{C}$ for the given attack class is mathematically proved under the assumption that $\mathcal{R}$ satisfies the sensitivity property.

Note that we could have included the estimation algorithm in the formalization above but we decided not to do so not to overburden the formalism (alternatively, estimates could be returned by the algorithm $\mathcal{R}$ itself). We underline the highly desirable modularity of this approach: an ID designer can mix-and-match representation and parameter estimation algorithms validated through simulation studies with data structure and classification algorithms that are mathematically proved correct. In the rest of this paper we will concentrate on the latter part: defining data structure and classification algorithms that are mathematically proved correct under the assumption that the associated representation algorithm is sensitive to a given attack or class of attacks. We stress that this is performed for *any* classification algorithm satisfying the sensitivity property and therefore the reader should not expect a simulation-based analysis, but rather a mathematical correctness proof for the detection property of the classification algorithm.

OUR IMPLEMENTATION EXPERIENCE. One implementation in [25] of an ID system (using the system discussed in Section 3) performs quite satisfactorily on several practical performance metrics (in addition to the desired theoretical properties established here). Specifically, in [25], together with other coauthors, we detail an implementation of a version of our ID system in Section 3, based on Nearest Neighbor Search, as a component of a larger system for the detection of IP spoofed traffic. There we run experiments designed to quantify the ability to detect various kinds of attacks (of both voluminous and stealthy nature), the detection rate, the false positive rate, and the variance with the location of attack sources. Except for pathological cases and very high attack loads, the implementation has a detection rate of about 80 % and a false positive rate of about 2 % in testbed experiments using Internet traffic and real cyberattacks. The implementation is compromised of various system level components deployed at various locations within a target network. NetFlow [17] is enabled on Border Routers (BRs) in large IP backbone networks. Flowtools [23] software modules can be deployed at various host nodes within the target network. NetFlow data is transmitted to the flowtools modules from the BRs. Statistics generated by Flow-tools are then transferred to the analysis software module, which analyzes the data and can provide notification in case abnormal behavior is detected. A full report on some features and results of our implementation can be found in [25].

PERFORMANCE METRICS. We consider several metrics that can help in measuring the performance of an intrusion detection system receiving as input a stream of $m[det]$ packets and formally redefine them in the described model (this is, of course, non necessarily an exhaustive list); finally, we discuss values for these metrics that would imply satisfactory performance of an intrusion detection system.

False Positive Rate. Informally, a *false positive* happens when an alert for an attack is raised in correspondence of a sequence of packets that does not contain any attack. This is one of the most often considered performance metrics, especially in anomaly-based intrusion detection systems, and reducing the rate of false positives in such systems is one of the biggest areas of research for Intrusion Detection. In our formal model, a false positive can be defined as a sequence $q$ of $dw$ packets such that the string $out = (out_0, out_1, \ldots, out_t)$ returned by algorithm $\mathcal{C}$ when run on input $\mathcal{R}, (1^n, ds, q, A)$, satisfies the following: there exists $i \in \{0, \ldots, t\}$ such that $out_i = 1$ and $q$ does not contain a tuple of packets in the support of distribution $A$. Then the *false positive rate* of an intrusion detection system for sequences up to $m[det]$ packets, is equal to the expected value, over all sequences of length $m[det]$, of the ratio of the number of false positives to the number of sequences of $dw$ packets having nonzero probability of occurrence. Here the probability space is over distributions $N, A, A_1, \ldots, A_t$.

Detection Probability. Informally, the detection probability is the probability that the response from the intrusion detection system is correct, and, clearly, this is the ultimately more interesting parameter. In our formal model, the detection probability with respect an attack $A$ and a sequence $q$ of $dw$ packets is denoted as $\pi(A, q)$ and is formally defined in Definition 2.

Detection Attempt Rate. Informally, the detection attempt rate is the frequency with which a detection attempt is being performed. While an ideal system would check in an $m[det]$-packet sequence for every $dw$-packet subsequence where an attack might appear, more realistic efficiency constraints might prevent the system to do that and therefore detection attempts would be performed less frequently. Let $A$ be an attack distribution, $rw$ be the representation window of the intrusion detection system and denote as $s$ an $m[det]$-packet stream entering into the network. We define the set of $(A, rw, m[det])$-*candidate sequences* as the set of $rw$-packet subsequences in $s$ that might contain a tuple in the support of distribution $A$. The *detection attempt rate* is then the expected value of the ratio of the number of subsequences of $(A, rw, m)$-candidate sequences for which the output of algorithm $C$ is $A$-correct, to the number of all $(A, rw, m)$-candidate sequences. Here, again, the probability space is over distributions $N, A, A_1, \ldots, A_t$.

Initialization and Detection Time and Space Efficiency. Informally, the initialization (resp., detection) time and space efficiency are the running time and the space complexity of the intrusion detection system during the initialization phase (resp., the detection phase). In our model, we define the *initialization time efficiency* (resp., *initialization space efficiency*) as the running time (resp., storage complexity) of $S$ as a function of $n, m[init], \sigma, \delta$; we then define the *detection time efficiency* (resp., *detection space efficiency*) as the running time (resp., storage complexity) of $C$ as a function of $n, m[init], dw, m[det], \sigma, \delta$.

Data Collection Stability. Informally, the data collection stability parameter is the amount of storage that is necessary in the initialization phase in order to guarantee the claimed detection properties of an intrusion detection system for an $m[det]$-packet stream in the detection phase. In our model, we denoted this parameter as a free parameter and defined as the length of the output of algorithm $S$; in general, it can be set as a function of other parameters $n, \sigma, \delta, dw, m[det]$.

Data Upgrade Rate. Informally, the data upgrade rate denotes how often the data structure is upgraded; at one extreme, a system could periodically discard the previously collected data and rerun the initialization phase; at the other extreme, a system could use every packet received by the network in order to update the data structure. Formally, this rate can be defined as the expected value of $1 -$ the ratio of the number of packets for which an update of $ds$ has not occurred to the length of the packet stream $m[det]$. Here, again, the expected value is over all $m[det]$-packet sequences and the probability space is over distributions $N, A, A_1, \ldots, A_t$.

Satisfactory Performance. Clearly, one would like an intrusion detection system to optimize all the defined performance metrics. We only remark here on two metrics. In terms of detection, as we observe later, algorithm $C$ cannot find attacks that are not somehow captured by algorithm $R$; therefore, we would require a satisfactory detection probability to be one that minimizes the difference $\delta - \sigma$. In a complexity-theoretic sense, satisfactory time and space efficiency of an intrusion detection system could be required to be equivalent to all algorithms $R, S, C$ running in time polynomial in the security parameter $n$. In a more practical setting, we note that algorithm $S$ is run once and for all in an initialization phase, while algorithms $R, C$ are repeatedly run (in an on-line fashion) in the detection phase. Therefore, we specifically require that algorithms $R, C$ are significantly more efficient; for instance, that they run in time at most polynomial in $\log n$. (We note that both schemes we propose in this paper satisfy this.)

# On Scalability and Modularisation in the Modelling of Network Security Systems

João Porto de Albuquerque[1,2,*], Heiko Krumm[2], and Paulo Lício de Geus[1]

[1] Institute of Computing, State University of Campinas, 13083-970
Campinas/SP Brazil
{jporto, paulo}@ic.unicamp.br
[2] FB Informatik, University of Dortmund, 44221 Dortmund, Germany
{joao.porto, heiko.krumm}@udo.edu

**Abstract.** As the use of computers and data communication technologies spreads, network security systems are becoming increasingly complex, due to the incorporation of a variety of mechanisms necessary to fulfil the protection requirements of the upcoming scenarios. The integrated design and management of different security technologies and mechanisms are thus of great interest. Especially in large-scale environments, the employment of security services and the design of their configurations shall be supported by a structured technique which separates the consideration of the system as a whole from the detailed design of subsystems. To accomplish this goal, this paper presents a scalable approach for the modelling of large security systems, relying on the concepts of policy-based management and model-based management.

## 1 Introduction

The widespread use of computers and data communication technologies, together with an ever-increasing Internet, requires the adoption of protection measures to control the risk of network-based attacks. In consonance with these protection needs, the technology utilised by security systems is growing in complexity. Thus, to the hardening of operating system configurations associated with the use of traditional firewalls [1,2], a series of mechanisms and services are incorporated like Virtual Private Networks (VPNs), end-to-end cryptographic associations (using, for instance, IPSec), authentication services (like Kerberos), authorisation services, and diverse monitoring, logging and auditing, as well as automated intrusion detection systems (IDS).

As those security services and mechanisms are increasingly employed—attaining thereby dazzlingly knotty scenarios—importance and costs of security management escalate. Initially, the management tasks are comprised of the installation and configuration of security services, followed then, during operation, by their monitoring, auditing, adaptation and reconfiguration. Proper abstraction, integration and tool support are thus key factors for easing the management tasks.

---

[*] Scholarship funding by the German Academic Exchange Service (DAAD).

S. De Capitani di Vimercati et al. (Eds.): ESORICS 2005, LNCS 3679, pp. 287–304, 2005.
© Springer-Verlag Berlin Heidelberg 2005

Both policy hierarchies [3] and policy-based management [4] approaches can be profitably used in this context, since they aim at automating management tasks in complex systems. These two approaches work together as follows: management policy hierarchies can be built by initially taking a set of high-level policies and refining them through intermediate levels until reaching mechanically executable policies. Thus, policy-based management uses those relatively low-level policies with distributed management agents that will communicate with each other, interpreting and executing policies specifically assigned to corresponding management roles.

The Model-Based Management approach [5,6,7], in turn, supports the building of those policy hierarchies by means of interactive graphical design. It adopts concepts of object-oriented system design tools and employs a model of the system vertically structured into a set of layers. The objects and associations of a layer represent the system to be managed on a certain abstraction level.

A common problem of these approaches occurs when dealing with larger systems, since the model tends to lose much of its understandability, getting obscure due to the great number of components (as attested in [8]). A canonical way of addressing such problems is to use the principle of *divide and conquer*; i.e. the modularisation of a system into smaller segments would allow us to deal with each of them in detail separately, and to reason about the whole system through a more abstract view of the interaction of those parts.

In this paper, we apply this principle to achieve an approach based on the segmentation of a system into *Abstract Subsystems*. A *Diagram of Abstract Subsystems* constitutes thus a representation of the overall structure of the system in which the details are hidden and dealt with in the internal specification of each subsystem. This abstraction permits a decomposition of the processes of system analysis and design, thereby improving the comprehensibility and scalability of the model. Moreover, this diagram is policy-oriented and provides an interface between a service-oriented view and the depiction of the actual network mechanisms. This modelling technique is also assisted by a software tool, which consists of a graphical editor with additional functions for checking of model-dependent constraints and guiding the policy refinement through the model's hierarchical levels.

As the present work builds upon Model-Based Management, an introduction to the latter is given in the next section. Subsequently, the concept of *Abstract Subsystem* (AS) is presented (Sect. 3), to serve as a basis for the elaboration on the *Diagram of Abstract Subsystems* in Sect. 4 and on the modelling of ASs (Sect. 5). Section 6 discusses results from the application of our modelling technique to a realistic environment, and Sect. 7 presents the automatic model refinement. Lastly, we discuss related work in Sect. 8 and cast conclusions for this paper in Sect. 9.

## 2   Model-Based Management

The concept of Model-Based Management was initially proposed by Lück *et al.* in [5] and later applied to the configuration of several security mechanisms such as packet-filters [6] and VPNs [7]. This approach aims to support the policy-based management by the use of an object-oriented model of the system to be managed. Based upon this model, a policy refinement can be accomplished such that configuration parameters for security mechanisms can be automatically derived.

The structure of the model is shown in Fig. 1 (reproduced from [8]), where three abstraction levels can be distinguished: *Roles & Objects* (RO), *Subjects & Resources* (SR), and *Processes & Hosts* (PH). Each level is a refinement of the superordinated level in the sense of a "policy hierarchy". The uppermost level represents the business-oriented view of the network whereas the lowest level is related to the technical view. The vertical subdivisions differentiate between the model of the actual managed system (with productive and control elements) and the policies that regulate this system. This last category encompasses requirement and permission objects, each of which refers to the model components of the same level and expresses security policies.

The uppermost level (RO) is based on concepts from Role-Based Access Control (RBAC) [9]. The main classes in this level are: *Roles* in which people, who are working in the modelled environment, act; *Objects* of the modelled environment which should be subject to access control; and *AccessModes*; i.e. the ways of accessing objects. The class *AccessPermission* allows the performer of a *Role* to access a particular *Object* in the way defined by *AccessMode*.

The second level (SR in Fig. 1) consists of a more complex set of classes. Objects of these classes represent: (a) people working in the modelled environment (*User*); (b) subjects acting on the user's behalf (*SubjectTypes*); (c) services in the network that are used to access resources (*Services*)—a service has references to all resources it is able to access; (d) the dependency of a service on other services (*ServiceDependency*); and lastly (e) *Resources* in the network. The *ServicePermission* class allows a subject to use a service to access a resource.

The SR level offers a transition from the business-oriented view, represented in RO level, to a more technical perspective, which is service-based. This is accomplished by using a service-oriented management approach to achieve a relatively abstract view of the management system, which is hence defined from the standpoint of the services that the system will provide. As such, the system's internal structure is not expressed in the SR level, but rather in the third level (PH) of the model (Fig. 1).

The lowest level (PH) is responsible for modelling the mechanisms that will be used to implement the security services defined in SR. Therefore, PH will

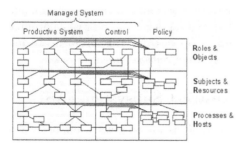

**Fig. 1.** Model Overview

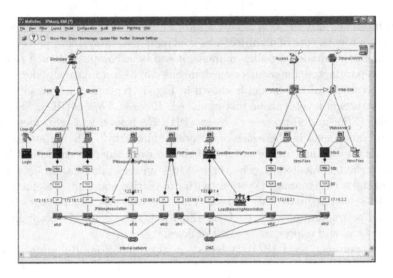

**Fig. 2.** Tool Interface

have even more classes than before, representing for instance the *Hosts*, with
their respective network *Interfaces*, and the *Processes*, that perform commu-
nicative actions relying on *Sockets*. *ProtocolPermissions* allow the transition of
packets between processes. Several other classes are also defined according to the
supported mechanisms. They will not be mentioned here for the sake of brevity.

To support tool-assisted interactive configuration of mechanisms a graphical
tool—whose interface is shown in Fig. 2—is supplied. This tool assists the user
in the modelling of the system by means of a graphical editor with additional
functions for the checking model-dependent constraints.

It can be noted from the previous discussion that the PH level—which shall
depict the entire system, with its processes, hosts, network interfaces etc.—has its
complexity quickly increased as the size of the modelled system grows. This fact
is also illustrated in Fig. 2, which shows the model of a very simple scenario with
only one *AccessPermission* at the uppermost level: the workers of a company
shall be allowed to access the corporate web server. Despite the simplicity of this
RO level, the model unfolds into a considerable number of objects at the lowest
level (bottom of Fig. 2), in order to represent mechanisms like IP-masquerading,
firewalls and load balancers.

Due to the simpleness of this example, the resulting model is still reasonable;
however, it can be noted that models of larger real environments tend to become
quite confusing. In order to overcome this problem we introduce in the next
section the concept of *Abstract Subsystems*.

## 3    Concept of Abstract Subsystem (AS)

An *Abstract Subsystem* (AS) is an abstract view of a system segment; i.e. a
simplified representation of a given group of system components. As such, an AS

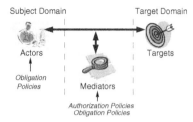

**Fig. 3.** Components of Abstract Subsystems

omits much of the detail that is contained inside of it, presenting instead only the relevant aspects for a global view of the system structure. These aspects are chosen based on a policy-oriented view of the system, which is depicted in Fig. 3.

In this scheme, three types of elements can be distinguished: *actors*, *mediators* and *targets*. The first type (*actors*) stands for groups of individuals in a system which have an *active* behaviour; i.e. they initiate communication and execute mandatory operations according to *obligation policies*.

The second element type encloses *Mediators*, which intermediate communications, receiving requests, inspecting traffic, filtering and/or transforming the data flow according to the *authorisation policies*. They can also perform mandatory operations based on *obligation policies*, such as registering information about data flows. The *Targets*, in turn, are *passive* elements; they contain relevant information, which is accessed by *actors*.

Using this scheme as a foundation, we can now redefine an *Abstract Subsystem* as a non-directed graph whose edges represent potential (bidirectional) communication between its nodes. These nodes can be either of one of the three types mentioned above (*actors*, *mediators* and *targets*) or *connectors*. This last type of component has been added to represent the interfaces of one AS with another; i.e. to allow information to flow from, and to, an AS.

## 4  Diagram of Abstract Subsystems (DAS)

Relying upon the concepts presented in the preceding section, we now introduce a new abstraction level into the modelling of security systems: the *Diagram of Abstract Subsystems* (DAS). This layer is located immediately below the service-oriented view of the system (SR level in Fig. 1) and above the PH layer, which depicts the actual network mechanisms. Its main objective is to describe the *overall structure* of the system to be managed in a modular fashion; i.e. to cast the system into its constituent blocks (ASs) and to indicate the connections between them. Since these blocks consist of a policy-oriented, abstract representation of the actual subsystem components (see Sect. 3), the DAS provides a concise and intelligible view of the system architecture—in a similar sense as the one proposed in [10]. Moreover, this diagram supports the reasoning about the structure of the system *vis-à-vis* the executable security policies, thus making

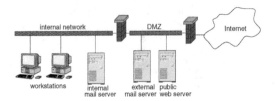

**Fig. 4.** Sample Network Scenario

explicit the distribution of the different participants of these policies over the system.

The DAS is formally a graph, comprised of ASs as nodes and edges which represent the possibility of bidirectional communication between two ASs, as shown at the bottom of Fig. 5. Thus, from a top-down perspective (i.e. from the SR level downwards) this diagram adds four kinds of information to the precedent model: (a) the segmentation of the users, services and resources into subsystems; (b) the structural connections amongst elements and subsystems; and therefore (c) the structural connections amongst the different participants of a policy (actors, mediators and targets); and lastly (d) mediators that are not directly related to SR level services but take part in the communication and filter or transform its data (e.g. firewalls).

In order to make clear the use of the DAS, in the next section we describe the systematic mapping from a service-oriented view of a system to its representation through abstract subsystems, and from this to the modelling of the actual mechanisms. Each step of this mapping is exemplified by means of a test scenario.

## 5    Modelling Abstract Subsystems

The scenario that will be used here relies on a typical network environment, as illustrated in Fig. 4. To this scenario the following network security policies are applied: 1) the users are allowed to browse the WWW from the internal workstations; 2) the users may send e-mails to the Internet from the workstations; 3) mail from the Internet shall be permitted to get to the external mail server, which in turn may forward it to the internal mail server; 4) external users using the Internet may access the company's public web server; and 5) users are allowed to fetch e-mails from the internal mail server to the workstations.

The modelling of these policies according to the principles referred in Sect. 2 produces the first two levels of Fig. 5. The basic objects are: the roles "Employee" and "Anonymous Internet User", and the *Objects* "Internal e-mail", "Website", "Internet e-mail" and "Internet WWW". These objects are associated with *AccesModes* by means of five *AccessPermissions* (at the top, on the right of Fig. 5), each corresponding to one of the above enumerated policies, which will henceforth be referred to as AP1 to AP5. Thus, for instance, the *AccessPermission* "allow Internet surfing" models the policy statement (1), associating the role

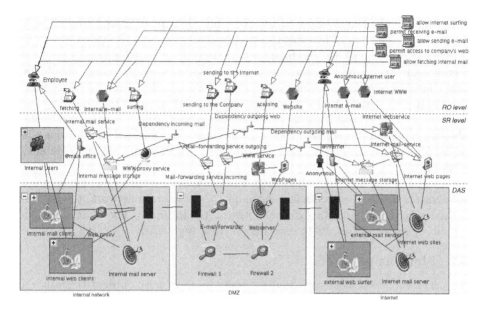

**Fig. 5.** Three-layered Model

"Employee" to "surfing" and "Internet WWW". The other policy statements are analogously modelled by the remaining *AccessPermissions*.

The mapping from the SR level to the *Diagram of Abstract Subsystems* (DAS) is then executed in three steps: (i) the modularisation of the system in conformance with the respective network scenario—i.e. the segmentation into *Abstract Subsystems* (ASs); (ii) the mapping of the elements of the SR level (users, services, resources) to components inside each AS; and (iii) the establishment of structural connections in the DAS, reflecting the associations between elements inside an AS and those between ASs, which are performed by means of *Connector* objects (Sect. 3). Subsequently, each AS can be expanded independently in order to achieve at the PH level a detailed representation of its mechanisms, and thereby enabling the generation of the corresponding configuration files. These steps will be described in turn in the following sections.

### 5.1  Segmentation into ASs

The subdivision of the system into ASs shall be guided by the structural blocks of the analysed environment. The abstract components of a DAS are thus aggregated according to the groups of mechanisms that already exist in the real system, such as departments, workplaces and functions.

An important criterium to be considered is the semantic unity of an AS; i.e. the group of mechanisms enclosed in an AS must have a common property that is clearly distinguishable. As such, this property assures the *cohesion* of the AS, so that it thereby represents a logical grouping identifiable in the real environment (like the ones previously mentioned), instead of only consisting of a mere agglomeration of heterogeneous elements.

On the other hand, the modularisation criterium of *coupling* (also a classical measure in the modularisation techniques of software engineering) should be taken into account in this context as well. The more the elements enclosed in the detailed view of an AS are related exclusively to elements of the same AS (and hence more independent from elements of other ASs), the more concise will be the abstract representation offered by the DAS, since those internal connections will be hidden. In this manner, a lower coupling between ASs improve the scalability of the DAS.

Analysing the scenario illustrated in Fig. 4, the existence of a structural subdivision in three segments is clear, namely: the internal network, the demilitarised zone (DMZ) and the external network (the Internet). Therefore, the DAS for this example has an AS to each one of these segments.

## 5.2   Mapping of Actors

An *actor* will be basically created for each group of hosts/processes (inside a given AS) which originates communication in order to act in conformance with a policy—which at the SR level is called service permission. In this manner, the actor corresponds to the *subject domain* of this permission, or, more precisely, to the part of the domain that is located in a given AS.

Nevertheless, actors can be shared by a number of different service permissions, as long as they have the subject domain comprehended by the actor in common. This contributes to a more compact representation, thus improving the scalability of the model.

In the SR level, the subject domain of service permissions is represented by *User* and *SubjectType* objects; thus each *Actor* will be connected to one or more pairs of these types of objects. In the framework of model-based management, however, service permissions are not directly modelled by the system designer but rather are automatically generated from *AccessPermission* objects located in the uppermost (RO) level. For this reason, the determination of the system's actors must start from an *AccessPermission*; thus taking the *Role* that is associated with it and identifying its corresponding *User* and *SubjectType* objects (in the SR level). Subsequently, one can create an *Actor* object that will contemplate the relevant *AccessPermission* and, consequently, is also related to the service permission that will be generated from it.

Considering our test scenario, an *Actor* object "internal web clients" is created in the AS "internal network" for the first policy—which is modelled by the first *AccessPermission* in Fig. 5, namely "allow Internet surfing" (AP1). Similarly, for the *AccessPermission* AP3 ("allow sending e-mail") the *Actor* "internal mail clients" is created in the same AS, whereas, in the AS "Internet", the actors "external mail sender" and "external web surfer" correspond respectively to the objects "permit receiving e-mail" (AP2) and "permit access to own web" (AP4). The *AccessPermission* "allow fetching e-mail" (AP5) can be covered by the previously created *Actor* "internal mail clients", since its subject domain is the same as that of AP3.

## 5.3 Mapping of Mediators

As regards to *Mediators*, two types can be distinguished. *Mediators* of the first type are a refinement from services which perform the "middleman functions" described in Sect. 3, for instance, proxies and mail forwarders. Therefore, they are achieved by means of a straightforward mapping from those services of the SR level, positioning them in the appropriate AS. Indeed, a service can be covered by a number of *Mediators*, each one residing in a different AS. On the other hand, a given *Mediator* object can map more than one service.

In our sample scenario, the "E-mail-Forwarder" *Mediator*, in the "DMZ" AS, stands for both services of handling incoming and outgoing e-mails. As for the "internal network", the "Web proxy" *Mediator* maps the "WWWProxyService".

The second type of *Mediators* consists of technical mechanisms that are not modelled in the SR level but are required in order to control the communication; i.e. they transform and/or filter it according to authorisation policies (like packet filters, IP-masquerading), or inspect the data according to obligation policies (e.g. IDS, event monitors). In this manner, the system designer shall create this type of mediators whenever these functionalities are required; i.e. a *Mediator* object will then appear wherever a security mechanism like the previously mentioned ones is to be placed in the respective actual network environment.

Examples of the second type of *Mediators* are illustrated in Fig. 5 by the objects "Firewall 1" e "Firewall 2". They have been introduced into the AS "DMZ", precisely in the place where the firewalls are found in the scenario of Fig. 4.

## 5.4 Mapping of Targets

*Targets* are obtained by a quite direct mapping from the pairs of *Service* and *Resource* objects (in the SR level) which encompass a target domain of a service permission, or a part of this domain that is placed in a given AS. In this way, each *Target* object must be connected to at least one pair of *Service* and *Resource* in the SR level, but it can also be shared by different service permissions; in the latter case, relations with other such pairs would be also present—this sharing also contributes to the conciseness of the model. Conversely, each pair of *Service* and *Resource* can be mapped to a number of *Targets*, each one located in different ASs—similar to the case of *Mediators*.

Similar to the actors, the target identification must start by considering the *AccessPermissions* in the RO level. Here, nonetheless, it is the *Object* related to a certain *AccessPermission* that is considered at first in order to establish then the corresponding *Resource* (SR level) and the *Service* which provides access to it. Finally, we create a *Target* to map this pair of objects.

When applying this method to our test scenario, then for the policy AP1 (Sect. 5) the *Target* object "Internet web sites" is created to refine the pair of *Service* and *Resource* of "Internet webservice" and "Internet web pages", since the latter is related to the *Object* "Internet WWW" (at the level RO) of AP1. It is worthwhile to note that, in this case, the *Service* refined from the *AccessMode* "surfing" of AP1 , namely "WWW proxy service", is different from the one previously used as target; this only happens when there is a *ServiceDependency* between these two *Services*. Indeed, the "WWW proxy service" cannot provide access to the *Resource* "Internet web pages" by itself, but relies on the "Internet web service" to do it. This dependency is modelled by the object "Dependency outgoing web" in the SR level (at the centre of Fig. 5).

Proceeding in the same manner, the targets "internal mail server" ("internal network"), "Internet mail server" ("Internet") and "Web server" ("DMZ") map respectively the policies modelled by AP2, AP3 and AP4. As for AP5, the *Target* "internal mail server" can be shared with AP2; as such, there is no need to create another object.

## 5.5  Establishment of Structural Connections

In order to complete the model that has been formed thus far by the application of the procedures of the latter sections, one needs to introduce the associations between objects of the DAS; i.e. formally speaking, to add the edges of the graph. Such associations have a different meaning compared to that of the associations between an element in the SR level and an object of the DAS. While the latter represent abstraction refinements—in the sense of relating levels of a policy hierarchy—the former represent structural connections; i.e. the possibility of communication in the actual system. Despite this, only the connections that are relevant to the abstract view of the system shall be depicted here; these are namely the associations that interconnect the different participants of executable policies: actors, mediators and targets.

Once again, the establishment of these connections starts at an *AccessPermission*. Each of the objects (in the DAS) that correspond to this permission is identified and then associations are created in order to construct paths between the respective actors and targets, traversing the necessary mediators. Whenever one of these paths enters or leaves an AS, *Connector* objects are inserted at this point, representing the communication interfaces of the AS. Thus, the number of *Connectors* in an AS corresponds to the number of available physical interfaces of the actual system. Proceeding in this manner with our test scenario, the *Connector* objects (rectangles) and connection edges (lines) shown in Fig. 5 are obtained.

## 5.6  Expansion of ASs

Starting from the model that has been produced thus far (Fig. 5), the next stage in the model development is to expand each of the ASs separately. This means that, for each AS, the mechanisms inside it shall be modelled according to the usual procedure described in [8], resulting in a detailed representation of these mechanisms; i.e. the PH level. Afterwards, the associations between the PH level components with the objects in the AS have to be drawn, thus establishing a relation of abstraction refinement.

Each *Actor* object of an AS must be then related to its corresponding *Process*- and *UserID*-typed components in the PH level, such that the *Actor* performs the association of these components with *SubjectType* and *User* objects in the

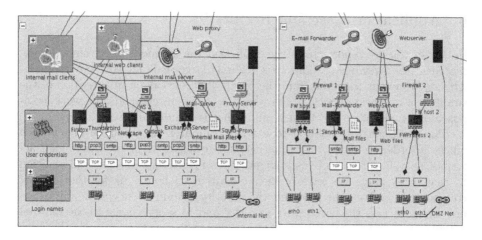

**Fig. 6.** Expanded ASs

SR level. As noted in Sect. 5.2, an *Actor* may be used for more than one pair of *SubjectType* and *User*, thereby corresponding to several service permissions. Hence, to avoid the burden of depicting all of the single associations amongst the objects (of type *User*, *SubjectType*, *UserID* and *Process*) connected to each *Actor*, a table of 4-tuples containing these associations shall be used to store them.

The *Mediator* objects of an AS, in turn, are simply related to one or more *Process*-typed components which implement the corresponding functionalities. With regards to *Targets*, each of them is related to one or more pairs of *Processes* and *Objects* that provide the corresponding services. Therefore, a *Process* in the PH level is related via a *Target* to a *Service* in the SR level, whereas an *Object* is related in a similar fashion to a *Resource*.

Figure 6 presents the PH level model for the ASs "internal network" and "dmz" in our example (see Fig. 5). In Fig. 6, the relation from actors, mediators and targets in the AS (at the top) to objects in the PH level (bottom)—achieved merely by following the principles previously exposed in this section—is graphically indicated by edges. For instance, the *Actors* "internal mail clients" and "internal web clients" in the "internal network" (on the left) are related to PH-level objects that represent the corresponding processes that run in two different workstations, as well the user credentials and login names of the users that may take advantage of these processes. On the other hand, the *Mediator* "E-mail Forwarder" and the *Target* "Webserver" in the AS "DMZ" (on the right) are correspondingly mapped to processes and resources that implement them. These PH objects directly assigned to AS entities are in turn related to a series of other PH objects in order to provide the model with detailed information about the communication, such as the protocol stack and the network interfaces used (see bottom of Fig. 6). In this manner, the correspondence between the abstract view of the system (AS) and its actual mechanisms (PH level) is established.

## 6     Application Case and Results

In this section we report about the application of the modelling technique presented in the previous sections to a realistic large-scale network environment. This environment (inspired from the one in [8]) consists of an extension of the simple test scenario of Sect. 5, in order to address an enterprise network, composed of a main office and branch office, that is connected to the Internet.

The employees are allowed to use the computers in the main and branch offices in order to surf on the Internet and to access their internal e-mail accounts, as well as to send e-mails to internal and external addresses. In addition to that, they may also retrieve their e-mails from home. As for the ongoing communication from the Internet, the security system must enable any external user to access the corporate's web site and to send e-mails to the internal e-mail accounts. Our main goal is then to design the configuration for the security mechanisms that are required to enable and control web-surfing and e-mail facilities for the company's office employees, namely: three firewalls, three VPN gateways, and a web proxy.

Figure 7 presents the DAS obtained for this environment. It is composed by five ASs, representing the logical network segments of the described scenario: "internal network", "dmz", "Internet", "branch office's network" and "remote access point". The *Actors*, *Targets* and *Mediators* of each of these AS and their interconnections through *Connectors* and structural connections are also depicted in Fig. 7. Pictures of the model's overview for the application case and of the detailed PH-level models for the ASs "internal network" and "dmz" are given in the Appendix A.

Analysing the model for this realistic application case, one can clearly perceive the advantages brought forth by the DAS. Altough the detailed information of the PH level encompasses more than 500 objects—representing, for instance, 8 hosts and credentials for 30 users in the internal network, 8 hosts

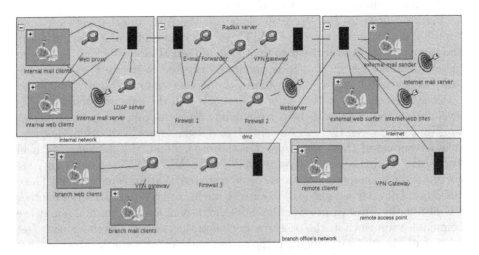

**Fig. 7.** DAS of a complex environment

in the branch office's network and a cluster of 5 web servers in the "dmz" (see Appendix A)—the abstract representation of the DAS (Fig. 7) consists of only 32 objects alltogether. Therefore, it can be noticed that the modelling through abstract subsystems offers concrete advantages in the conciseness and under-standability of the model.

Furthermore, since the environment in this application case is an extension of the test scenario used in Sect. 5, it is possible to compare them, in order to identify the growth behaviour of a DAS. The number of PH objects (which depict the mechanisms of the actual system, and thus reflect the growth of the system itself) increased from 95 in the simple test scenario to 540 in the realistic application case (i.e. a growth of almost 470%). The number of DAS elements, in contrast, rose from 19 (Fig. 5) to 32 (Fig. 7)—i.e. a growth of only less than 69%. We thus conclude that the size of a DAS does not increase in the same pace as the number of elements in the PH level (and thus as the system's mechanisms), but rather the DAS's growth is much slower. This makes clear the scalability gain afforded by the DAS in the support of large models.

Since the number of elements both in the DAS and in the PH levels heav-ily depend on intrinsic characteristics of the environment modelled (such as the entities to be modelled and the possibility of subdividing and grouping them), an unrestricted generalisation of these quantitative results is not possible. Nev-ertheless, in qualitative terms, similar gains can be expected in the modelling of other large-scale networked environments; for they are similar to the typical scenarios presented here.

## 7   Tool Support and Automated Refinement

To support our modelling, a software tool is provided. This tool encloses a dia-gram editor (by means of which Fig. 5, Fig. 6 and Fig. 7 were produced) that allows the inputing of model objects and their relationships, as well as the assign-ment of properties to them. In this manner, each step of the modelling explained in the previous sections is assisted by the tool, which verifies the compliance of the model with structural constraints in the moment particular objects are in-puted. Once the modelling is complete, a series of checks are performed to assure the consistency of the model as a whole.

Though the fully automated derivation of low-level, executable policies from a set of abstract specifications is, in the general case, not practical [11,12], our modelling technique makes possible an automation of the building of a policy hierarchy on the basis of a system's model that is structured in different abstrac-tion levels. Thus, the analysis of the system's objects, relationships and policies of an abstraction level enables the generation of lower level policies, based on the system's model in the lower level and on the relations between the entities of the two layers[1].

---

[1] An extensive elaboration on the policy refinement process and on the consistency checks that are described in this section is beyond the scope of this paper and can be found in [13].

In this process, the support tool firstly derives each one of the given *AccessPermissions* (in the uppermost level RO) into one or more *ServicePermissions* in the SR level (see Sect. 2). Afterwards, a set of *ATPathPermission* (ATPP) objects are generated from the *ServicePermissions*. Each ATPP is a path in the graph (DAS) that represents the permission for an *Actor* to reach a certain *Target* passing through the required *Mediator* and *Connector* objects. The refinement advances with the automatic generation of *ProtocolPermissions* from the ATPPs, using the detailed information contained in the PH level in order to achieve the security policies for this level. Each *ProtocolPermission* is then related to a set of objects, denoting that an initiating process—to which a user credential can be assigned—may communicate, via its co-located protocol entity and a remote protocol, with a serving process in order to access a certain physical resource.

Throughout the above refinement process, a series of conditions are verified against the model, in order to check the consistency of the different abstraction levels and the feasibility of enforcing the high-level policies defined by the administrator. Our experience also shows that, in practice, the modelled network systems are frequently not capable of enforcing the given high-level policies. In this case, the consistency checks cannot be satisfied, and the tool offers indications to the necessary modifications on the system in order to make it congruous to the policies.

Finally, for the last step of model-based security service configuration, a series of back-end modules are executed, where each module corresponds to a special security service product (e.g. Kerberos, FreeS/WAN, Linux IP tables etc.). These back-end functions evaluate the *ProtocolPermissions* and the PH model in order to generate the adequate configuration files for each of the security service products. Further details can be found in [6,7,8].

## 8    Related Work

There are a considerable number of approaches to policy specification both for security management and policy-driven network management purposes (see [11] for a survey). However, regarding the tool-assisted building of policy hierarchies and the automation of the policy refinement process, considerable research remains to be done.

The graphical tool Firmato [14] seems to be the closest available approach to ours, since it supports the interactive policy design by means of policy diagrams and automatically derives the corresponding configuration parameters for mechanisms such as routers, switches, and packet filters. However, since the abstraction levels of graphical policy definitions and configuration parameters are relatively near to each other, its support is restricted to an abstraction level that is close to the system mechanisms. In this respect, the Power prototype [15] has a broader scope, aiming to support the building of policy hierarchies by means of a tool-assisted policy refinement. Nevertheless, Power does not allow a free graphical definition of policies, relying instead on pre-defined templates and wizard engines. Furthermore, neither *Power* nor *Firmato* are concerned with scalability issues; this fact is reflected by the absence of a modular system's representation in these approaches.

## 9   Conclusion

This paper has presented a modelling technique for the management of security systems. The modelling achieves scalability by the segmentation of the system in *Abstract Subsystems*, which enables the processes of model development and analysis to be performed in a modular fashion.

The systematic mapping from a service-oriented system view to a *Diagram of Abstract Subsystems* was covered in detail, encompassing the choice of elements to be represented in the abstract view, as well as the correspondence of these elements to the actual mechanisms of the system. A realistic case study was presented and the results achieved through our modelling were discussed. We have concluded that concrete gains in the understandability and scalability of the modelling of large-scale systems can be expected from the employment of our technique. Furthermore, the tool-assisted modelling and automated policy refinement supported by our prototype tool were also briefly described.

Future work could include improving the representation of policies at the lower levels of the model, in order to ease their handling.

**Acknowledgments.** We would like express gratitude to Helen Mary Murphy Peres Teixeira for reviewing.

## References

1. Cheswick, W.R., Bellovin, S.M., Rubin, A.D.: Firewalls and Internet Security: Repelling the Wily Hacker. 2nd edn. Addison-Wesley (2003)
2. Zwicky, E.D., Cooper, S., Chapman, D.B.: Building Internet Firewalls. 2nd edn. O'Reilly and Associates, Sebastopol, CA (2000)
3. Moffett, J.D., Sloman, M.S.: Policy hierarchies for distributed system management. IEEE JSAC Special Issue on Network Management **11** (1993)
4. Sloman, M.: Policy driven management for distributed systems. Journal of Network and Systems Management **2** (1994) 333–360
5. Lück, I., Schönbach, M., Mester, A., Krumm, H.: Derivation of backup service management applications from service and system models. In R. Stadler, B.S., ed.: Active Technologies for Network and Service Management, Proc. DSOM'99. Number 1700 in Lecture Notes in Computer Science, Heidelberg, Springer Verlag (1999) 243–255
6. Lück, I., Schäfer, C., Krumm, H.: Model-based tool-assistance for packet-filter design. In M. Sloman, J. Lobo, E.L., ed.: Proc. IEEE Workshop Policy 2001: Policies for Distributed Systems and Networks. Number 1995 in Lecture Notes in Computer Science, Heidelberg, Springer Verlag (2001) 120–136
7. Lück, I., Vögel, S., Krumm, H.: Model-based configuration of VPNs. In Stadler, R., Ulema, M., eds.: Proc. 8th IEEE/IFIP Network Operations and Management Symposium NOMS 2002, Florence, Italy, IEEE (2002) 589–602

8. Geist, G.: Model-based management of security services: Integrated enforcement of policies in company networks. Master's thesis, University of Dortmund, Germany (2003) in German.

9. Sandhu, R.S., Coyne, E.J., Feinstein, H.L., Youman, C.E.: Role-based access control models. IEEE Computer **29** (1996) 38–47

10. Porto de Albuquerque, J., de Geus, P.L.: A framework for network security system design. WSEAS Transactions on Systems **2** (2003) 139–144

11. Sloman, M., Lupu, E.C.: Security and management policy specification. IEEE Network, Special Issue on Policy-Based Networking **16** (2002) 10–19

12. Wies, R.: Using a classification of management policies for policy specification and policy transformation. In Sethi, A.S., Raynaud, Y., Fure-Vincent, F., eds.: Integrated Network Management IV. Volume 4., Santa Barbara, CA, Chapman & Hall (1995) 44–56

13. Porto de Albuquerque, J., Krumm, H., de Geus, P.L.: Policy modeling and refinement for network security systems. In: Sixth IEEE International Workshop on Policies for Distributed Systems and Networks, Stockholm, Sweden (2005) 24–33

14. Bartal, Y., Mayer, A.J., Nissim, K., Wool, A.: Firmato: A novel firewall management toolkit. ACM Transactions on Computer Systems **22** (2004) 381–420

15. Mont, M., Baldwin, A., Goh, C.: POWER prototype: Towards integrated policy-based management. In Hong, J., Weihmayer, R., eds.: Proc. IEEE/IFIP Network Operations and Management Symposium (NOMS2000), Hawaii, USA (2000) 789–802

# A    Models of the Application Case

We present here some of the models obtained for the application case analysed in Sect. 6. The growth in the complexity of the PH level is made clear from the comparison of the models of the AS "internal network" in the realistic application case (Fig. 8) with that in the test scenario (left hand of Fig. 6), and similarly for the AS "dmz" (compare Fig. 9 with the right hand of Fig. 6).

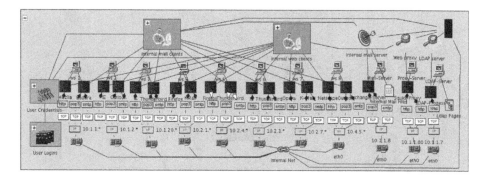

**Fig. 8.** PH-model of the AS "internal network"

In contrast, the superior levels of the modelling show a slower growth behaviour, and hence more scalability. Figure 10 presents the three-layered model for the application case (compare with Fig. 5).

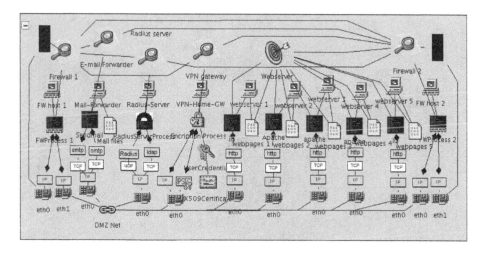

**Fig. 9.** PH-model of the AS "dmz"

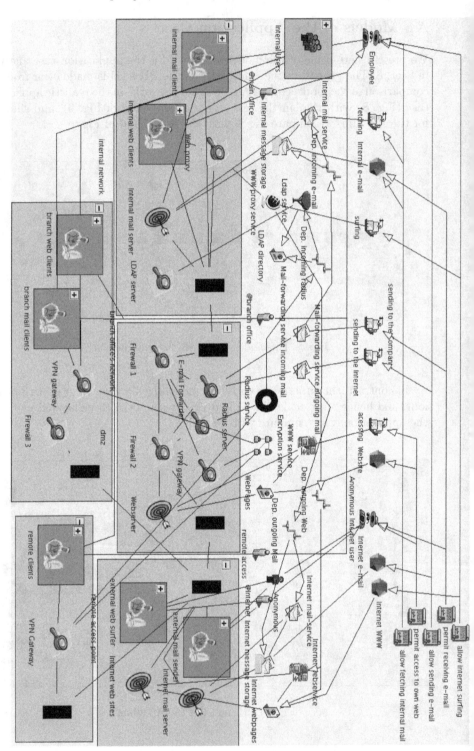

**Fig. 10.** Three-layered model of the Application Case

# Sybil-Resistant DHT Routing

George Danezis[1], Chris Lesniewski-Laas[2],
M. Frans Kaashoek[2], and Ross Anderson[1]

[1] University of Cambridge, Computer Laboratory,
15 J J Thomson Avenue, Cambridge CB3 0FD,
United Kingdom
{George.Danezis, Ross.Anderson}@cl.cam.ac.uk
[2] MIT Computer Science and Artificial Intelligence Laboratory,
The Stata Center, Building 32,
32 Vassar Street, Cambridge, MA 02139, USA
ctl@mit.edu, kaashoek@csail.mit.edu

**Abstract.** Distributed Hash Tables (DHTs) are very efficient distributed systems for routing, but at the same time vulnerable to disruptive nodes. Designers of such systems want them used in open networks, where an adversary can perform a sybil attack by introducing a large number of corrupt nodes in the network, considerably degrading its performance. We introduce a routing strategy that alleviates some of the effects of such an attack by making sure that lookups are performed using a diverse set of nodes. This ensures that at least some of the nodes queried are good, and hence the search makes forward progress. This strategy makes use of latent social information present in the introduction graph of the network.

## 1 Introduction

Distributed Hash Tables (or DHTs) [14,15,12,10] are distributed systems that allow efficient lookup of identifiers and routing to the corresponding nodes. They achieve this by imposing on the routing tables of nodes a rigid structure that guarantees quick convergence to a target.

This rigid structure makes DHTs easy to disrupt by a set of malicious nodes that return useless information instead of helping in the routing. An adversary can create a very large number of bogus nodes and flood the DHT network, in order to disrupt it or degrade its performance. This is called a sybil attack [3].

We present a method that lowers the probability an honest user queries a malicious node. The method takes into account the DHT's introduction graph, which describes which node introduced which to the network. We assume that the adversary is connected to the graph at very few points, but that it can create large numbers of virtual "sybils" behind its attachment points. Following a strategy inspired by Advogato [5], our method turns these few corrupt attachment points into trust bottlenecks. We ensure that queries use a diverse set of nodes, thereby minimising our reliance on a localized set of nodes that might be controlled by the adversary. We also show that trying to minimise the number

S. De Capitani di Vimercati et al. (Eds.): ESORICS 2005, LNCS 3679, pp. 305–318, 2005.

of corrupt nodes in honest nodes' routing tables makes a significant difference to the performance of the DHTs.

The security of DHTs, including routing security which is the main concern of our work, has been the subject of discussion in [13,2]. Trust metrics based on social networks were introduced in Advogato [5]. Advogato uses maximum flow in a network to make trust judgments, but there are other proposals, such as Appleseed [16], which use spreading activation models. Our work uses such social network trust metrics to tackle the sybil attack in structured peer-to-peer systems. Sprout [7] is also making use of social network information, to route messages over trusted nodes. We follow the opposite approach and attempt to eliminate trust bottlenecks, thereby trying not to trust any nodes more than others.

## 2     The Sybil Attack Against DHTs

The basic premise of the *sybil attack* [3] is that an adversary in a peer-to-peer system can easily introduce a very large set of corrupt participants. All of these participants, or *sybils*, are controlled by the adversary; they can be used to compromise security properties of the system or degrade its performance. The latter can be framed in the context of computer security by considering degradation of performance as service denial [9].

A Distributed Hash Table (DHT) is a specialized distributed system that aims to look up identifiers efficiently in order to route messages to and from the corresponding nodes. Our designs will be based on Chord [14], but the principles we will examine (both in terms of understanding the sybil attack and defending against it) are applicable to other systems [15,12,10]. Nodes in Chord arrange themselves into a ring sorted according to their IDs, where each knows its successor. In correct operation, this guarantees that all nodes are reachable. Chord achieves its efficiency by additionally requiring each node to know a small number of other nodes in the network, its *finger table*. Finger nodes are selected to be carefully spaced [4] around the ring address space to ensure that lookups will quickly converge towards a target node.

Lookups can happen in two ways: either recursively or iteratively. In a *recursive* lookup the initiator looks up a particular ID by asking the finger with the closest ID to the target node. The finger node will in turn ask one of its fingers, and this procedure is repeated until the target node is located and the answer propagated back. Iterative routing relies on the initiator of a lookup to query the finger with the closest ID to the target, which in turn returns one of its fingers. The initiating node can then perform further lookups itself, using the additional information until the target node is located. Our sybil resistant lookup strategies will implement a variant of the iterative method, giving the requesting node the most flexibility. Each iteration returns a set of nodes instead of just one.

An adversary can participate in a Chord network by introducing nodes it controls. These malicious nodes take their respective places in the ring structure and populate other nodes' finger tables. The objective of the adversary nodes is to disrupt lookups as much as possible: make them fail if possible or make them very slow otherwise. Two basic strategies malicious nodes can use to sabotage lookups are:

- **Non-cooperation.** Malicious nodes do not provide any information to other nodes. They fail to look up nodes, and just forget about their successors: they return no information. As a result, requests are slower, and the structure of the ring is fractured.
- **Flooding.** Malicious nodes, when prompted for a request, provide another malicious node as the reply. This sends the requesting node in a wild goose chase [13], never successfully finishing its request.

Both non-cooperation and flooding can lead to a standard Chord lookup failing. Using the standard Chord strategy a node looking up a target ID tries to make 'progress': the next hop is chosen from among the nodes discovered between the current hop and the target ID. If all the known nodes in this region are non-cooperating, the lookup will fail. Similarly, flooding nodes will provide a set of corrupt virtual nodes with IDs closer to the target, yet never reaching it. In both cases there will be no answer to the query.

In this paper we will attempt to protect DHTs, and a variant of Chord in particular, against random flooding attacks. Our threat model is based on an adversary that aims to disrupt as many queries as possible through the network, and positions its nodes, at random around the Chord ring. Note that targeted attacks could be more easily accomplished by concentrating the dishonest nodes on particular regions of the ring [13]. Targeted attacks that aim to maximally disrupt queries from or to specific nodes are beyond the scope of our study.

In order to address these attacks, we need to modify the iterative Chord lookup. When choosing a next help, our variant will take into account the sources of information about the previous hops, and strive to avoid relying on a single trust bottleneck.

## 3   The Bootstrap Graph Model

The traditional peer-to-peer model, within which the sybil attack was formulated, views the network as an undifferentiated set of nodes, each with an individual ID. The attacker controls some fraction of these nodes and can cheaply introduce new ones until the network is flooded. Once the fraction of bad nodes exceeds approximately 25%, the system is unable to reliably route queries to the correct ID [2]. So one proposed solution to the sybil attack is to rate limit new nodes joining and to impose a centralized admission control system.

The bootstrap graph adds new elements to the peer-to-peer model that might help tackling the sybil attack without any centralized authority. In most peer-to-peer systems, a new node needs to have a first point of contact with the network in order to join; thus, the nodes in the network must have some previous off-line relationship. We call the set of these relationships the network's introduction graph, or "bootstrap graph". Figure 1 provides an example of such a graph, in which nodes joined in the order of their label numbers.

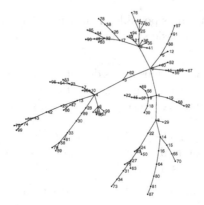

**Fig. 1.** Example of a bootstrap graph

Now, the goal of a secure overlay network is to enable Alice and Bob, nodes in the network, to communicate with each other if there is any path of good nodes between them in the bootstrap graph. In the DHT context, "communicate with each other" means to be able to look up each others' IDs. This is a good security criterion because if there is no such path between Alice and Bob, then they might as well be in separate DHTs: the only nodes common to the two graph components are malicious, so connecting them would require some out-of-band mechanism, i.e. a new bootstrap graph link.

A "flood fill" routing mechanism provides a proof of concept: if Alice flood-fills the bootstrap graph with her query, it will eventually reach every connected good node regardless of the actions of the adversary. However, this is a very inefficient solution, and it is not resiliant to nodes in the path failing. We'd like to solve this problem using less storage and communication cost than flood filling (which is quadratic in the number of nodes).[1]

The methods presented in this paper assume that the bootstrap graph is a tree, which is typical for current DHTs. We analyze the case of an adversary which has managed to convince one honest node to allow it to join the network, perhaps by social engineering. The adversary can then introduce a large number of sybils into the network via this attachment point. The adversary spends much less effort per sybil than it spent obtaining the attachment point. In section 4.3 we examine what happens when a set of sybils are attached to the honest bootstrap graph at more than one points.

In this paper, we only concern ourselves with routing security, i.e. resolving a particular ID to a node. We assume that if we actually reach the target node, we will be able to verify that it owns the target ID, e.g. using self-certifying IDs [1,8]. We won't discuss the security of data stored on nodes, or the mechanics of data block migration as nodes join and leave the network; these must be left to other security layers.

---

[1] Insecure DHTs like Chord achieve polylogarithmic cost; it is an open question whether this is possible for a secure overlay.

### 3.1   Efficient Bootstrap Path Calculation

When the bootstrap graph is a tree, there is an efficient decentralized algorithm for calculating the shortest path between any two nodes. This means that no node is required to know the totality of the bootstrap tree at any time, and the path is constructed as a natural side effect of node lookups.

Each node stores, in addition to IDs and addresses, the path from itself to each node it knows. This includes the node's Chord-ring successor, its predecessor, its finger nodes, and the connections it has in the bootstrap tree. The same is true for all resolutions: the current hop returns not only the ID and address of the next hop, but also the path of bootstrap links from the current hop to the next hop. The path from the querier to the next hop may be computed as the concatenation of the querier-to-current-hop path and the current-hop-to-next-hop path, with any loops removed. In this way, a querier can compute the path from itself to any other node it discovers.

Nodes that first join the network not only have to discover their successor node, predecessor node, and fingers, but also the paths to them. This is done as a side effect of the joining protocol. The new node asks the node it uses to join the network for the IDs of the nodes, and as a result also gets their paths. This allows it to compute its paths to them.

When the bootstrap graph is a tree, nodes can join paths and eliminate all cycles, therefore guaranteeing that they know the shortest path. This is convenient but not necessary for the security properties we will describe next, and extending our algorithms for discovering paths in generic graphs should be possible.

## 4   Reducing the Impact of the Sybil Attack

Our objective is to devise a resolution strategy that will always succeed, and provide better performance than the standard Chord strategy when under a sybil attack. First we shall deal with the issue of failed queries, then we shall assess the efficiency of our approach.

We modify the standard Chord iterative strategy in the following two ways.

1. A node, when queried, returns all nodes that it knows about, and not simply the closest to the target. The node returns its successor, fingers, and connections in the bootstrap tree. Such a modification requires more bandwidth per query, but does not add any latency to standard iterative lookups.
2. Having a set of nodes returned by each query allows the initiator to be in full control of the resolution, and be able to schedule lookups to maximize efficiency and minimize the potential for disruption from corrupt nodes. A number of query strategies can be used to establish which nodes should be queried and in which order.

We will first look at the standard Chord query strategy that selects nodes according to *closeness* in ID space, and then present a radically different query strategy that routes according to trust *diversity*. These two extremes can be combined, as in the *mixed* and *zig-zag* strategies, to provide fast yet robust lookups.

## 4.1    Query Scheduling Strategies

The aim of a node that wants to perform a lookup is to select hops that might provide more information about the address of the target ID, and that are not malicious. The basic Chord strategy, which we will call *closeness routing*, is extremely effective at ensuring the first, but does not take into account the second issue (corrupt nodes): given a set of known nodes, Chord chooses to query the one whose ID is closest to the target. When all nodes are honest, the worst case for performance is that the last hop's successor is the only node closer to the target ID. On the other hand, when some nodes are liars, the ring structure is effectively broken. Thus, looking only at nodes between the initiator and the target of the lookup is not guaranteed to succeed. To address this, we need an alternative resolution strategy.

We have assumed that the set of bad nodes are connected to the rest of the bootstrap network through a single good node. We therefore expect that this single good node, along with the bad node it is directly connected to, will always be in the bootstrap graph path from the quering node to the bad nodes. An intrusion detection approach could be used to detect them — this will not be the strategy we chose to implement since nodes that are not always misbehaving might fool it. Instead we will try to balance the number of requests going to bad nodes by making sure that not too much 'trust' is put on any particular node when answering queries. For the purpose of routing we will consider that a node is trusted if it is on the path of the bootstap graph from the initiator of the request to the queried node. The core of our sybil defense mechanism consists of distributing queries around the network in such a way that no small set of nodes is predominantly present on the paths of the queries.

*Diversity routing* is the purest form of this strategy, and choses nodes to query as following:

1. For each ID lookup the initiator keeps a record of nodes queried. A histogram is computed of the frequency with which each node in the network has been on the path of the queries so far. This can be thought as a 'trust profile' of this particular lookup at any time (Fig 2, step (1)).
2. A node proceeds by answering the follwing question: which node is to be queried next to get more information concerning the node looked up, given the trust profile so far? We associate with each candidate node the 'trust profile' the lookup would have if it was to be used (Fig 2, step (2)).
3. Then the different trust profiles are compared to each other in order to assess which one increases the least the trust put on a single or a small set of nodes. This can be done by sorting the 'trust profile' for each candidate by descending order, and creating a 'trust list' of their values: the first value would be the number of paths the most trusted node was on, and so forth. Then the candidate nodes can be ranked by sorting lexicographically their respective sorted 'trust lists' (Fig 2, step (3)). We then chose the smallest element as the next node to query.

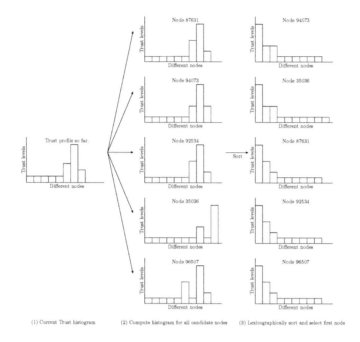

**Fig. 2.** Illustrating a step of the diversity routing node selection

**Table 1.** Number of queries to satisfy 100 lookups in closeness and diversity routing (100 good nodes)

| Number of bad nodes | Closeness | Diversity |
|---|---|---|
| 1 | 373 | 552 |
| 50 | 1400 | 1359 |
| 100 | 3183 | 2610 |
| 200 | 6977 | 4807 |
| 400 | 18434 | 12543 |

Figure 2 illustrates a step of the diversity routing strategy. Strarting with the nodes that are known to the querying node, this strategy is repeated, until the target ID node is found.

The above strategy tries to distribute queries across the network, taking into account bottlenecks that might indicate a sybil attack point. Adversary nodes that introduce a large number of sybils will aquire high values in the trust profile and nodes behind them will not be used until other nodes in the network are queried. Yet the diversity strategy does not make by itself any progress towards the target node. Note that sybil nodes are not excluded but a balance is maintained between queries to sybils and other nodes.

We expect this strategy to be more efficient than pure Chord when there are more sybils than honest nodes. In particular it will always yield the answer to a query, even if it has to ask the whole network. Still this strategy remains terribly inefficient under normal circompstances. Table 1 shows the number of nodes queried to satisfy 100 random ID requests, where there are 1, 50, 100, 200 and 400 sybil nodes flooding 100 honest nodes.

## 4.2   Mixed Strategies

In order to maintain some efficiency we need to introduce some bias to choose nodes that are closer to the target. Two strategies have been assessed.

A first approach is to provide a balance between the closeness and the diversity of nodes, and we call this *mixed routing*. This can easily be implemented: given the rank $c_i$ of a node according to closeness, and the rank $d_i$ of the node according to the strategy that provides diversity, and a balance factor $b \in [0, 1]$, we calculate the new rank $r_i$:

$$r_i = bc_i + (1 - b)d_i \tag{1}$$

Nodes can then be sorted according to $r_i$ in decending order, and the first one chosen to be queried next. Table 2 illustrates the number of queries required to satisfy 100 random lookups in a network of 100 good nodes flooded by 1, 50, 100, 200 and 400 nodes. It is clear that this mixture strategy balances the two key factors, closeness and trust diversity. It provides better results than either of the pure strategies for a lower number of sybils (100 and 200) but does not perform better than the diversity strategy in case there are a lot more sybils than honest nodes.

The best results have been achieved using *zig-zag routing*. Instead of trying to select diverse yet close to the target nodes, as mixed routing attempts to do, the closeness strategies and diversity strategies are alternatively employed. First a node that is close to the target is queried, then a node that is diverse is chosen, and so forth. With each set of diversity routing the pool of known nodes becomes more likely to contain honest nodes, and then the step of closeness routing selects the closest node and queries it for the target.

As table 2 shows zig-zag routing outperforms closeness as the number of malicious nodes grows, as well as mixed routing. Zig-zag routing is also easier to analyze. In the absence of any malicious nodes the lookup will take at most

**Table 2.** Number of queries to satisfy 100 lookups in closeness, mixed and zig-zag routing (100 good nodes)

| Number of bad nodes | Closeness | Mixted (b = 0.2) | Zig-Zag | Good entries in finger table |
|---|---|---|---|---|
| 1 | 373 | 1696 | 510 | 99% |
| 50 | 1400 | 2172 | 1291 | 65% |
| 100 | 3183 | 2358 | 2104 | 46% |
| 200 | 6977 | 4842 | 3606 | 30% |
| 400 | 18434 | 15110 | 7004 | 20% |

double the amount of queries to resolve, than using the standard Chord strategy. This is due to the fact that one in two steps implements the Chord strategy. When there are malicious nodes in the network the diversity step ensures that the pool of known nodes retains its quality: it makes sure mostly honest nodes are queried to populate it. On the other hand the closeness step ensures progress towards the target ID, by choosing out of a the pool of known nodes, the closest to the target.

Simulations were run and the histograms describing how many queries (i.e. steps of the iterative routing strategy) were necessary to satisfy 100 requests are plotted in Figure 3. Note that a significant number of requests are satisfied by few ($< 10$) queries even when a lot of sybils are introduced in the system. Zig-zag routing retains this property as the sybils multiply, while closeness routing becomes increasingly inefficient.

Note that under extreme flooding, the zig-zag strategy (and any strategy based on bootstrap graphs) will be following the bootstrap graph to route between two honest nodes. This makes them fragile against node churn, that could even be the result of malice, and heavy sybil attacks. Providing routing security under such extreme conditions is beyond our scope.

## 4.3   The Effects of Increased Infiltration

In our analysis so far we have assumed that the set of sybils nodes are attached to the honest part of the bootstrap graph at one honest node only. We briefly assess how our most effective defense mechanism, the zig-zag strategy, handles sybils being attached to multiple points of the bootstrap graph, or in other words an adversary that has fooled more honest nodes.

We performed 100 requests in the DHT, made of 100 good nodes, using the zig-zag and the closeness routing strategies, and record how many nodes have been queried to answer them. We repeated the experiment for 100 and 200 additional bad nodes in the network, connected to $1, 10, 20 \ldots 90, 100$ distinct good nodes. The rest of the bad nodes were only introduced by these 'attached' bad nodes. Figure 4 summarises the results.

In the experiment with 100 bad nodes (Figure 4, black lines) we observe that the zig-zag strategy outperforms the standard closeness strategy until more than 80 bad nodes have infiltrated the network. For higher values closeness (represented by the straight line) outperforms the zig-zag strategy, which is due to the overhead it introduces: it only makes progress in one out of two steps.

On the other hand as the overall number of sybils increases, as in our experiment with 200 bad nodes (Figure 4, dotted lines), our zig-zag strategy outperforms the standard closeness strategy even when the adversary has managed to infiltrate and connect to every single one of the 100 honest nodes. It is encouraging that the number of requests 'stabilises' for more than 30 infiltrated nodes, and infiltrating more of them does not seem to degrade the performance of the network further. An adversary that chooses to infiltrate more and more honest nodes will therefore experience diminishing returns.

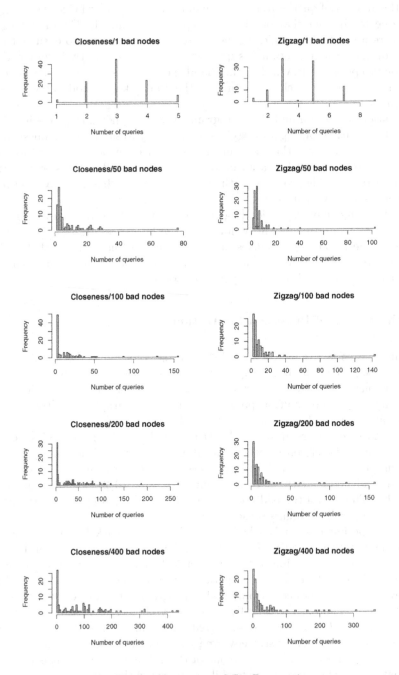

**Fig. 3.** Closeness and Zig-Zag routing

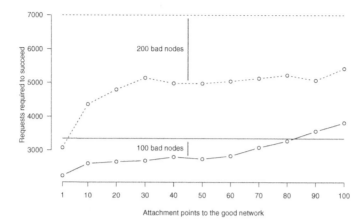

**Fig. 4.** The number of requests required to satisfy a query increase with the number of sybil nodes attached to the honest network. The network used was composed of 100 honest nodes, and 1 to 100 attachment points for 100 and 200 sybils. In each case the horisontal line denotes the standard closeness strategy, while the other set of points denotes the zig-zag strategy under increased infiltration.

These initial simulation results indicate that there is an optimal number or percentage of infiltrated nodes to disrupt the network, after which the adversary does not get much advantage. Still we cannot do away with our initial assumption that the bootstrap graph should contain a connected components with all honest nodes, otherwise an adversary would be able to split the network in many separate ones to better attack it.

### 4.4   Balanced Finger Tables

The diversity based strategy, and the zig-zag strategies, make sure that a fair share of good nodes are selected to answer a query. Yet the quality of the information provided, even by good nodes, decreases as more sybils are introduced in the network. The reason for this is that their finger tables are populated with an increasing number of sybils that will not contribute to answering the queries.

The solution to this is to select fingers according to a strategy that ensure that good nodes are still present. A variant of the strategy based on the ordered 'trust lists' described above in the context of lookups can be used for that purpose.

Chord fingers are distributed around the ring in a manner that maximizes the efficiency of lookups. The original design is very deterministic and requires nodes to pick fingers half way across the ring, a quarter across, an eight, and so forth. The idea behind this distribution is that nodes will know mostly about their immediate successors, but also some far away nodes to make far lookups efficient.

We propose a sybil-resistant finger distribution: A set of 32 fingers are selected with an exponential distribution around the ring. This reflects the Chord

**Table 3.** Number of queries to satisfy 100 lookups in closeness, mixed and zig-zag routing (100 good nodes) with diverse routing tables

| Number of bad nodes | Closeness | Mixed (b = 0.2) | Zig-Zag | Good entries in finger table |
|---|---|---|---|---|
| 1 | 309 | 1634 | 413 | 99% |
| 50 | 809 | 1962 | 725 | 66% |
| 100 | 1519 | 1503 | 1056 | 53% |
| 200 | 3581 | 1801 | 1400 | 37% |
| 400 | 8762 | 5873 | 3627 | 26% |

paradigm, of discovering more about the immediate environment. Out of these fingers the 16 are selected in the following manner: the successor is first used to create a 'trust profile' of the table. Then all the candidate fingers are assessed to find out which would least increase the trust put into a small set of nodes, using the 'trust list' strategy described above. The procedure is repeated with all selected fingers contributing to the 'trust profile', until 16 fingers have been chosen.

Requests routed using these more trust 'balanced' finger tables exhibit a better performance as illustated in table 3. Note that the percentage of corrupt finger entries is lower than in table 2, when the strategy described was not in use. The efficiency results are positively correlated to the degree of finger table corrution.

## 5   Conclusions

Distributed Hash Tables are very efficient distributed systems to lookup identifiers, and in the past it has been demonstrated that they can be made robust against node churn, random failures, and fluctuating network conditions [6,11]. We devise strategies that make DHTs resilient to malicious nodes trying to poison lookups by providing inaccurate information. We achieve this by routing queries, not only to make them converge fast to their destinations, but also in a way that minimizes trust bottle necks. This minimizes the amount of poisoned information that honest nodes receive from hostile sybils controlled by the adversary.

The strategies we present have been validated through extensive testing and simulations, whose results have been presented. It is worthwhile noting that routing is still possible, and more efficient than broadcasting, even when honest nodes are in a small minority (our tables illustrate the ratio of 1 honest node to 4 sybils). We have also validated through simulation that our approach would protect the network, even if a large number of sybil nodes manage to infiltrate the network by fooling many honest nodes into introducing them. Furthermore one could describe our approach as 'value free', in that there is no attempt to classify nodes into good and bad: we simply try to spread the queries across all nodes in the trust graph. Intrusion detection strategies could be devised that correlate the quality of the information provides with nodes, to determine which are the bad nodes. Making such a mechanism strategy proof is a hard problem.

Our algorithms also refrains from making global judgments about nodes: there is no such thing as a good node or a bad node, but only nodes that are connected to the requesting node through different paths. As a result we expect our algorithms to be of use when two mutually hostile groups of nodes decide to form a common DHT. While members of one group might provide poor, or no information, to members of the other group, they would behave properly to each other. Our approach should be able to cope with this model.

Finally we hope that this work contributes to a redefinition of 'identity' when used in a distributed systems security setting, as the position of a party in a social, or other, network, rather than an arbitrary external identifier. The traditional identity based approach requires additional infrastructure to assign identities, such as admission control and public key infrastructures that are expensive and difficult to implement in any network, let alone in a fully decentralized peer-to-peer setting. We have shown that preserving this contextual information can yield simpler and more robust mechanisms for dealing with adversaries.

*Acknowledgments.* George Danezis and Chris Lesniewski-Laas are supported by the Cambridge-MIT Institute (CMI) project on 'Third generation peer-to-peer networks' and part of this work was done while visiting MIT CSAIL.

# References

1. Tuomas Aura, Aarthi Nagarajan, , and Andrei Gurtov. Analysis of the hip base exchange protocol. In *10th Australasian Conference on Information Security and Privacy (ACISP 2005)*, Brisbane, Australia, July 2005.
2. Miguel Castro, Peter Druschel, Ayalvadi Ganesh, Antony Rowstron, and Dan S. Wallach. Secure routing for structured peer-to-peer overlay networks. In *5th Usenix Symposium on Operating Systems Design and Implementation*, Boston, MA, December 2002.
3. John R. Douceur. The sybil attack. In *Proceedings for the 1st International Workshop on Peer-to-Peer Systems (IPTPS 02)*, Cambridge, Massachusetts, March 2002.
4. J. Kleinberg. The small-world phenomenon: An algorithmic perspective. In *32nd ACM Symposium on Theory of Computing*, 2000.
5. Raph Levien. Attack resistant trust metrics. Draft Ph.D. Thesis, at U.C. Berkeley.
6. J Li, J Stribling, TM Gil, R Morris, and F Kaashoek. Comparing the performance of distributed hash tables under churn. In *International Workshop on Peer-to-Peer Systems (IPTPS04)*, 2004.
7. Sergio Marti, Prasanna Ganesan, and Hector Garcia-Molina. SPROUT: P2P routing with social networks. In *First International Workshop on Peer-to-Peer and Databases (P2P&DB 2004)*, March 2004.
8. David Mazires. *Self-certifying file system.* PhD thesis, MIT, May 2000.
9. Roger M. Needham. Denial of service: an example. *Communications of the ACM*, 37(11):42–46, 1994.

10. Sylvia Ratnasamy, Paul Francis, Mark Handley, Richard Karp, and Scott Shenker. A scalable content-addressable network. In *Proc. ACM SIGCOMM 01*, San Diego, California, August 2001.

11. S Rhea, D Geels, T Roscoe, and J Kubiatowicz. Handling churn in a dht. In *USENIX Annual Technical Conference*, June 2004.

12. Antony Rowstron and Peter Druschel. Pastry: Scalable, distributed object location and routing for large-scale peer-to-peer systems. In *Heidelberg, Germany,*, Heidelberg, Germany, 2001.

13. Emil Sit and Robert Morris. Security considerations for peer-to-peer distributed hash tables. In *Proceedings for the 1st International Workshop on Peer-to-Peer Systems (IPTPS 02)*, Cambridge, Massachusetts, March 2002.

14. Ion Stoica, Robert Morris, David Karger, M. Frans Kaashoek, , and Hari Balakrishnan. Chord: A scalable peer-to-peer lookup service for internet applications. In *Proc. ACM SIGCOMM 01*, San Diego, California, August 2001.

15. Ben Y. Zhao, John D. Kubiatowicz, , and Anthony D. Joseph. Tapestry: An infrastructure for fault-resilient wide-area location and routing. Technical Report UCB//CSD-01-1141, U. C. Berkeley, April 2001.

16. Cai-Nicolas Ziegler and Georg Lausen. Spreading activation models for trust propagation. In *IEEE International Conference on e-Technology, e-Commerce, and e-Service (EEE '04)*, Taipei, Taiwan, March 29-31 2004,.

# Botnet Tracking: Exploring a Root-Cause Methodology to Prevent Distributed Denial-of-Service Attacks

Felix C. Freiling, Thorsten Holz\*, and Georg Wicherski

Laboratory for Dependable Distributed Systems, RWTH Aachen University
http://www-i4.informatik.rwth-aachen.de/lufg/

**Abstract.** Denial-of-Service (DoS) attacks pose a significant threat to the Internet today especially if they are distributed, i.e., launched simultaneously at a large number of systems. *Reactive* techniques that try to detect such an attack and throttle down malicious traffic prevail today but usually require an additional infrastructure to be really effective. In this paper we show that *preventive* mechanisms can be as effective with much less effort: We present an approach to (distributed) DoS attack prevention that is based on the observation that coordinated automated activity by many hosts needs a mechanism to remotely control them. To prevent such attacks, it is therefore possible to identify, infiltrate and analyze this remote control mechanism and to stop it in an automated fashion. We show that this method can be realized in the Internet by describing how we infiltrated and tracked IRC-based *botnets* which are the main DoS technology used by attackers today.

## 1   Introduction

An important witness of the increasing professionalism in Internet crime are so called *Denial-of-Service* (DoS) attacks. A DoS attack is an attack on a computer system or network that causes a loss of service to users, typically the loss of network connectivity and services by consuming the bandwidth of the victim network or overloading the computational resources of the victim system [13]. Using available tools [5], it is relatively easy to mount DoS attacks against remote networks. For the (connection-oriented) Internet protocol TCP, the most common technique is called *TCP SYN flooding* [19,4] and consists of creating a large number of "half open" TCP connections on the target machine, thereby exhausting kernel data structures and making it impossible for the machine to accept new connections. For the (connectionless) protocol UDP, the technique of *UDP flooding* consists of overrunning the target machine with a large number of UDP packets thereby exhausting its network bandwidth and other computational resources.

---

\* Thorsten Holz was supported by Deutsche Forschungsgemeinschaft (DFG) as part of the Graduiertenkolleg "Software for mobile communication systems" at RWTH Aachen University.

S. De Capitani di Vimercati et al. (Eds.): ESORICS 2005, LNCS 3679, pp. 319–335, 2005.

Like spam, it is well-known that DoS attacks are extremely hard to prevent because of their "semantic" nature. In the terminology of Schneier [18], semantic attacks target the way we assign meaning to content. For example, it is very hard to distinguish a DoS attack from a peak in the popularity of a large website. Using authentication it is in principle possible to detect and identify the single origin of a DoS attack by looking at the distribution of packets over IP addresses. However, it is almost impossible to detect such an attack if multiple attack hosts act in a coordinated fashion against their victim. Such attacks are called *Distributed Denial-of-Service* (DDoS). DDoS attacks are one of the most dangerous threats in the Internet today since they are not limited to web servers: virtually any service available on the Internet can be the target of such an attack. Higher-level protocols can be used to increase the load even more effectively by using very specific attacks, such as running exhausting search queries on bulletin boards or mounting *web spidering attacks*, i.e., starting from a given website and then recursively requesting all links on that site.

In the past, there are several examples of severe DDoS attacks. In February 2000, an attacker targeted major e-commerce companies and news-sites [9]. The network traffic flooded the available Internet connection so that no users could access these websites for several hours. In recent years, the threat posed by DDoS attacks grew and began to turn into real cybercrime. An example of this professionalism are blackmail attempts against a betting company during the European soccer championship in 2004 [2]. The attacker threatened to take the website of this company offline unless the company payed money. Similar documented cybercrime cases happened during other major sport events. Furthermore, paid DDoS attacks to take competitor's websites down were reported in 2004 [1]. These type of attacks often involve so called *botnets* [11], i.e., networks of compromised machines that are remotely controlled by an attacker. Botnets often consist of several thousand machines and enable an attacker to cause serious damage. Botnets are regularly used for DDoS attacks since their combined bandwidth overwhelms the available bandwidth of most target systems. In addition, several thousand compromised machines can generate so many packets per second that the target is unable to respond to so many requests.

Defensive measures against DDoS can be classified as either preventive or reactive [14]. Currently, reactive techniques dominate the arena of DDoS defense methods (the work by Mirkovic *et al.* [13] gives an excellent survey over academic and commercial systems). The idea of reactive approaches is to detect the attack by using some form of (distributed) anomaly detection on the network traffic and then react to the attack by reducing the malicious network flows to manageable levels [15]. The drawback of these approaches is that they need an increasingly complex and powerful sensing and analysis infrastructure to be effective: the approach is best if large portions of network traffic can be observed for analysis, preferably in real-time.

Preventive methods either eliminate the possibility of a DDoS attack altogether or they help victims to survive an attack better by increasing the resources of the victim in relation to those of the attacker, e.g., by introducing some form of strong authentication before any network interaction can take place (see for example work by Meadows [12]). Although being effective in theory, these survival methods always boil down to an arms race between attacker and victim where the party with more resources wins. In practice, it seems as if the arms race is always won by the attacker, since it is usually easier for him to increase his resources (by compromising more machines) than for the victim, which needs to invest money in equipment and network bandwidth.

Preventive techniques that aim at DDoS attack avoidance (i.e., ensuring that DDoS attacks are stopped before they are even launched) have received close to no attention so far. One reason for this might be the popular folklore that the only effective prevention technique for DDoS means to fix all vulnerabilities in all Internet hosts that can be misused for an attack (see for example Section 5 of [14]). In this paper we show that this folklore is wrong by presenting an effective approach to DDoS prevention that neither implies a resource arms race nor needs any additional (authentication) infrastructure. The approach is based on the observation that coordinated automated activity by many hosts is at the core of DDoS attacks. Hence the attacker needs a mechanism to remotely control a large number of machines. To prevent DDoS attacks, our approach attempts to identify, infiltrate and analyze this remote control mechanism and to stop it in an automated and controlled fashion. Since we attack the problem of DDoS at the root of its emergence, we consider our approach to be a root-cause method to DDoS defense.

It may seem unlikely that it is possible to automatically analyze and infiltrate a malicious remote control method crafted by attackers for evil purposes. However, we provide evidence of the feasibility of our strategy by describing how we successfully tracked and investigated the automated attack activity of botnets in the Internet. The idea of our methods is to "catch" malware using *honeypots*, i.e., network resources (computers, routers, switches, etc.) deployed to be probed, attacked, and compromised. Honeypots run special software which permanently collects data about the system behavior and facilitates automated post-incident forensic analysis. From the automated analysis we derive the important information necessary to observe and combat malicious actions of the botnet maintainers. In a sense, our approach can be characterized as turning the methods of the attackers against themselves.

The paper is structured as follows: Section 2 gives a brief overview over botnets and their usage for DDoS attacks. In Section 3 we introduce a general methodology to prevent DDoS attacks and exemplify a technical realization in Section 4. We present our results in Section 5 and conclude this paper with Section 6.

## 2   Distributed Denial-of-Service Using Botnets

In this section we give a brief overview over botnets and how they can be used to mount DDoS attacks. More technical details can be found in [22]. A botnet is a network of compromised machines running programs (usually referred to as *bot*, *zombie*, or *drone*) under a common *Command and Control* (C&C) infrastructure. Usually, the controller of the botnet compromises a series of systems using various tools and then installs a *bot* to enable remote control of the victim computer via Internet Relay Chat (IRC).

Newer bots can even automatically scan whole network ranges and propagate themselves using vulnerabilities and weak passwords on other machines. After successful invasion, a bot uses Trivial File Transfer Protocol (TFTP), File Transfer Protocol (FTP), HyperText Transfer Protocol (HTTP), or CSend (an IRC extension to send files to other users) to transfer itself to the compromised host. The binary is started and tries to connect to the hard-coded master IRC server on a predefined *port*, often using a *server password* to protect the botnet infrastructure. This server acts as the C&C server to manage the botnet. Often a *dynamic DNS name* is provided rather than a hard coded IP address, so the bot can be easily relocated. Using a *specially crafted nickname*, the bot tries to join the *master's channel*, often using a *channel password*, too. In this channel, the bot can be remotely controlled by the attacker.

Commands can be sent to the bot in two different ways: via sending an ordinary command directly to the bot or via setting a special topic in the channel that all bots interpret. For example, the topic

```
advscan lsass 200 5 0 -b
```

tells the bots to spread further with the help of a known vulnerability (the Windows *lsass* vulnerability). The bots should start 200 concurrent threads that should scan with a delay of 5 seconds for an unlimited time (parameter 0). The scans should target machines within the same Class B network (parameter -b). As another example, the topic

```
http.update http://<server>/rBot.exe c:\msy32awds.exe 1
```

instructs the bots to download a binary from the Internet via HTTP to the local filesystem and execute it (parameter 1).

If the topic does not contain any instructions for the bot, then it does nothing but idling in the channel, awaiting commands. That is fundamental for most current bots: they do not spread if they are not told to spread in their master's channel. Figure 1 depicts the typical communication flow in a botnet.

In order to remotely control the bots, the controller of a botnet has to authenticate himself before issuing commands. This authentication is done with the help of a classical authentication scheme. At first, the controller has to login with his username. Afterwards, he has to authenticate with the correct password to approve his authenticity. The whole authentication process is only allowed from a predefined domain, so that only certain people can start this process. Once an attacker is authenticated, he has complete control over the bots and can execute arbitrary commands.

Today, botnets are most often used to mount DDoS attacks in the Internet. All common bots include several different possibilities to participate in these attacks. Most commonly implemented, and also very often used, are TCP SYN [19,4] and UDP flooding attacks. For example, the command

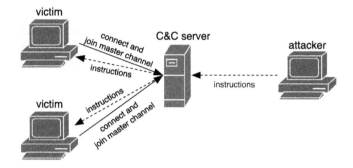

**Fig. 1.** Communication flow in a botnet

```
ddos.syn XXX.XXX.XXX.XXX 80 600
```

instructs the bots within the botnet to start a TCP SYN flooding attack against the specified IP address against TCP port 80 for 600 seconds. Another example is the following command:

```
udp XXX.XXX.XXX.XXX 18000 50000 100
```

It instructs the bots to mount a UDP flooding attack against the specified target with 18,000 packets of a size of 50,000 bytes using a delay of 100 milliseconds between each packet. Note that the C&C IRC server that is used to connect all bots is in most cases also a compromised machine.

## 3   Preventing Distributed Denial-of-Service Attacks

In this section we introduce a general methodology to prevent DDoS attacks. It is based on the following line of reasoning:

1. To mount a successful DDoS attack, a large number of compromised machines are necessary.
2. To coordinate a large number of machines, the attacker needs a remote control mechanism.
3. If the remote control mechanism is disabled, the DoS attack is prevented.

We will substantiate this line of reasoning in the following paragraphs.

### 3.1   A Large Number of Machines Is Necessary

Why does an attacker need a large number of machines to mount a successful DDoS attack? If an attacker controls only few machines, a DDoS attack is successful only if the total resources of the attacker (e.g., available bandwidth or possibility to generate many packets per second) are greater than the resources of the victim. Otherwise the victim is able to cope with the attack. Hence, if this requirement is met, the attacker can efficiently overwhelm the services offered by the victim or cause the loss of network connectivity.

Moreover, if only a small number of attacking machines are involved in an attack, these machines can be identified and counteractive measures can be applied, e.g., shutting down the attacking machines or blocking their traffic. To obfuscate the real address of the attacking machines, *IP spoofing*, i.e., sending IP packets with a counterfeited sender address, is often used. Furthermore, this technique is used to disguise the actual number of attacking machines by seemingly increasing it. However, IP spoofing does not help an attacker to conduct a DDoS attack from an efficiency point of view. It does not increase the available resources, but it even reduces them due to computing efforts for counterfeiting the IP addresses. In addition, several ways to detect and counteract spoofed sender address exist, e.g., ingress filtering [7], packet marking [20], or ICMP traceback [3,17]. The IP distribution of a large number of machines in different networks makes ingress filter construction, maintenance, and deployment much more difficult. Additionally, incident response is hampered by a high number of separate organizations involved.

So control over a large number of machines is necessary for a successful DDoS attack.

## 3.2   A Remote Control Mechanism Is Necessary

The success of a DDoS attack depends on the volume of the malicious traffic as well as the time this traffic is directed against the victim. Therefore, it is vital that the actions of the many hosts which participate in the attack are well-coordinated regarding the type of traffic, the victim's identity, as well as the time of attack.

A cautious attacker may encode all this information directly into the malware which is used to compromise the zombies that form the DDoS network. While this makes him harder to track down, the attacker loses a lot of flexibility since he needs to plan his deeds well in advance. Additionally, this approach makes the DDoS attack also less effective since it is possible to analyze the malware and then reliably predict when and where an attack will take place. Therefore it is desirable to have a channel through which this information can be transferred to the zombies on demand, i.e., a remote control mechanism.

A remote control mechanism has many more advantages:

1. The most effective attacks come by surprise regarding the time, the type and the target of attack. A remote control mechanism allows an attacker to react swiftly to a given situation, e.g., to mount a counterattack or to substantiate blackmail threats.
2. Like any software, malware is usually far from perfect. A remote control mechanism can be used as an automated update facility, e.g., to upgrade malware with new functionality.

In short, a DDoS attack mechanism is only effective if an attacker has some type of remote control over a large number of machines. Then he can issue commands to exhaust the victim's resources at many systems, thus successfully attacking the victim.

### 3.3   Preventing Attacks

Our methodology to mitigate DDoS attacks aims at manipulating the root-cause of the attacks, i.e., influencing the remote control network. Our approach is based on three steps:

1. Infiltrating the remote control network.
2. Analyzing the network in detail.
3. Shutting down the remote control network.

In the first step, we have to find a way to smuggle an *agent* into the control network. In this context, the term agent describes a general procedure to mask as a valid member of the control network. This agent must thus be customized to the type of network we want to plant it in. The level of adaptation to a real member of the network depends on the target we want to infiltrate. For instance, to infiltrate a botnet we would try to simulate a valid bot, maybe even emulating some bot commands.

Once we are able to sneak an agent into the remote control network, it enables us to perform the second step, i.e., to observe the network in detail. So we can start to monitor all activity and analyze all information we have collected.

In the last step, we use the collected information to shut down the remote control network. Once this is done, we have deprived the attacker's control over the other machines and thus efficiently stopped the threat of a DDoS attack with this network. Again, the particular way in which the network is shut down depends on the type of network.

### 3.4   Discussion

The methodology described above can be applied to different kinds of remote control networks and is thus very general. The practical challenge of the methodology is to automate the infiltration and analysis process as much as possible. In all these cases, the zombies need to establish a communication channel between themselves and the attacker. If it is possible to "catch" this malware in a controlled way, it is possible to extract a lot of information out of it in an automated fashion. For example, if contact to the attacker is set up by establishing a regular network connection, the network address of the attacker's computer can be automatically collected.

To many readers, the methodology may sound like coming directly from a James Bond novel and it is legitimate to ask for evidence of its feasibility. In the following section we give exactly this evidence. We show that this method can be realized in the Internet by describing how we infiltrated and tracked IRC-based botnets which are the main DDoS technology used by attackers today.

## 4   An Example: Tracking Botnets

In this section we exemplify a technical realization of the methodology we introduced above. We present an approach to track and observe botnets that is able to prevent DDoS attacks.

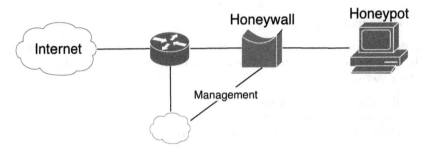

**Fig. 2.** Setup for tracking botnets

As already stated in the last section, tracking botnets is clearly a multi-step operation: First one needs to gather some data about an existing botnet. This can for instance be obtained with the help of botnets or via an analysis of captured malware. With the help of this information it is possible to smuggle a client into the network.

We first introduce two techniques to retrieve the necessary information from a botnet which enables us to infiltrate in it. The necessary information includes:

- DNS/IP-address of IRC server and port number.
- Password to connect to IRC-server (optional).
- Nickname of a bot and `ident` [10] structure.
- Name of IRC channel to join and (optional) channel password.

The first method to retrieve this information is based on *honeypot* technology and is presented in Section 4.1. The second method is more lightweight and presented in Section 4.2. Then we describe the observation and analysis process in which we collected further information (Section 4.3). Finally, in Section 4.4 we give a small overview of possible ways to shut down a botnet.

### 4.1   Collecting Malware with Honeypots

A *honeypot* is a network resource (computers, routers, switches, etc.) deployed to be probed, attacked, and compromised. A *honeynet* is a network of honeypots. Honeypots run special software which permanently collects data about the system behavior and facilitates automatic post-incident forensic analysis. The collected data enables us to determine the necessary information about an existing botnet. A detailed introduction to honeypots can for example be found in [6].

Using a so called *GenII Honeynet* [21] containing some Windows honeypots, we are able to collect all necessary information. We deployed a typical GenII Honeynet with some small modifications as depicted in Figure 4.1.

The Windows honeypot runs an unpatched version of Windows 2000 or Windows XP. This system is thus very vulnerable to attacks. It is located within the internal network of RWTH Aachen University. On average, the expected lifespan of the honeypot is less than ten minutes. After this small amount of time, the honeypot is often successfully exploited by automated malware. The shortest compromise time was only a few seconds: Once we plugged the network cable in, a bot compromised the machine and installed itself on the machine.

As explained in the previous section, a bot tries to connect to the C&C server to obtain further commands once it successfully attacked the honeypot. This is where the *Honeywall* comes into play. The Honeywall is a transparent bridge that enables the two tasks *Data Control* and *Data Capture*. Due to the Data Control facilities, it is possible to control the outgoing traffic. Using available tools for Data Control we can replace all suspicious in- and outgoing messages. A message is suspicious if it contains typical IRC messages for command and control, for example " `TOPIC` ", " `PRIVMSG` ", or " `NOTICE` ". Thus we are able to inhibit the bot from accepting valid commands from the master channel. It can therefore cause no harm to others and therefore we have caught a bot inside our Honeynet. As a side effect, we can also derive all necessary sensitive information for a botnet from the data we have obtained up to that point in time: The Data Capture capability of the Honeywall allows us to determine the DNS/IP-address the bot wants to connect to and also the corresponding port number. In addition, we can derive from the Data Capture logs the nickname, the ident information, the server's password, channel name, and the channel password as well. So we have collected all necessary information and the honeypot can catch further malware. Since we do not care about the captured malware for now, we rebuild the honeypot every 24 hours to have a "clean" system every day. This has proven to be a good time span since after this amount of time the honeypot tends to become unstable due to installed malware.

### 4.2   Collecting Malware with Mwcollect

The approach described in the previous section works, but has several drawbacks:

- A honeypot will crash regularly if the bot fails to exploit the offered service, e.g. due to a wrong offset within the exploit.
- The honeypot itself has to be closely monitored in order to detect changes on the system. Furthermore, these changes have to be analyzed carefully to detect malware.
- The approach does not scale well; observing a large number of IP addresses is difficult.

To overcome these limitations, we developed a program called *mwcollect* to capture malware in non-native environments. This tool simulates several vulnerable services and waits for them to be exploited. It is comparable to a *low-interaction honeypot* like *honeyd* [16]. In contrast to *honeyd* it is tailored to collecting of malware and offers possibilities that *honeyd* cannot offer, e.g. better packet handling and more flexibility.

*mwcollect* is based upon a very flexible and modularized design. The core module – the actual daemon – handles the network interface and coordinates the actions of the other modules. Furthermore, the core module implements a *sniffer mode* which records all traffic to a special log file. This can for example be useful if an unknown exploit is detected that needs to be further analyzed.

Several modules, which register themselves in the core, fulfill the actual tasks. There are basically four types of modules:

- *Vulnerability modules* open some common vulnerable ports (e.g. TCP Port 135 or 2745) and simulate the vulnerabilities according to these ports.
- *Shellcode parsing modules* analyze the shellcode, an assembly language program which executes a shell, received by one of the vulnerability modules. These modules try to extract generic URLs from the shellcode.
- *Fetch modules* simply download the files specified by an URL. These URLs do not necessarily have to be HTTP or FTP URLs, but can also be TFTP or other protocols.
- *Submission modules* handle successfully downloaded files, for example by writing it to disk or submitting it to a database.

*Vulnerability modules* seem to be the most important part of *mwcollect*, but in fact they are not more important than every other module, they all require each other. Moreover, the vulnerable service emulation is not very sophisticated, but functional: Often malware does not require an indistinguishable emulation of a real service but an approximation of it. In most cases it is thus sufficient to provide some minimal information at certain offsets in the network flow. This information is used by the malware to calculate the offsets it can use to exploit the service. Upon successful exploitation, the payload of the malware is passed to another kind of modules.

Currently there is only one *shellcode parsing module* that is capable of analyzing all shellcodes we have found up to now. The module first recursively detects *XOR decoders* in a generic way. An XOR decoder is a common way to encrypt the actual shellcode in order to evade intrusion detection systems. Afterwards the module decodes the code itself according to the computed key and then applies some pattern detection, for example `CreateProcess` and `URLDownloadToFileA` detection patterns. The results are further analyzed and if an URL is detected, it is passed to the fetch modules. A module that parses shellcodes in an even more generic way by emulating a Windows Operating System environment is currently under development.

*Fetch modules* have the simple task of downloading files from the Internet. There are currently three different fetch modules: one for TFTP, one for generic HTTP and FTP URLs and finally one for CSend and similar transfer methods used by different species of bots.

Finally, *submission modules* handle successfully downloaded files. Currently there are three different types of submission modules:

- A module that stores the file in a configurable location on the filesystem and is also capable of changing the ownership.
- A module that submits the file to a central database to enable distributed sensors with central logging interface
- A module that checks the file with the help of different anti-virus scanners for known malware. Optionally this module sends an alert to enable an early warning system. Therefore, *mwcollect* can also be seen as a kind of intrusion detection system.

Two further features of *mwcollect* are important to efficiently collect malware: *virtualized filesystem* and *shell emulation*.

A common technique to infect a host via a shell is to write commands for downloading and executing malware into a temporary file and then execute this file. Therefore a *virtual filesystem* was implemented to enable this type of attacks. Every shell session has its own virtual filesystem so concurrent infection sessions using similar exploits do not conflict. The temporary file is analyzed and the malware is downloaded from the Internet in an automated way.

Some Malware does not spread by download shellcodes but by providing a shell to the attacker. Therefore it is sometimes required to spawn and emulate a Windows shell. *Shell emulation* is centralized in the core module since only one type of shell is emulated. However, modules can register additional commands that extend the possibilities for the malware. *mwcollect* currently simulates a rudimentary shell and implements several commands: `echo`, `ftp.exe` and `tftp.exe`, as well as batch file execution.

The big advantage of using *mwcollect* to collect malware is clearly both stability and scalability: A bot trying to exploit a honeypot running Windows 2000 with payload that targets Windows XP will presumably crash the service. In most cases, the honeypot will be forced to reboot. In contrast to this, *mwcollect* can be successfully exploited by all of those tools and hence catch a lot more binaries this way. Furthermore, *mwcollect* can listen on many IP addresses in parallel. We tested the program with 256 IP addresses and it scaled well.

To derive the sensitive information of the botnet from the collected malware, a further analysis is necessary. A possible way to extract the information from the captured malware is *reverse engineering*, the process of carefully analyzing a program without having its source code. This process is time consuming, but we have developed some techniques that enables us to extract the information within a few minutes. A better approach is an automated analysis with the help of a honeynet. The setup depicted in Figure 4.1 can be used for this purpose. Upon startup, the Windows honeypot downloads a piece of malware from a database located somewhere in the Internet. It executes the file and reboots itself after a few minutes. During this time span, the bot installs itself on the honeypots and connects to the C&C server. With the help of the Honeywall, we are again able to extract all necessary information. In addition, the honeypot resets the hard disk during each reboot so that a clean image is booted each time.

In a third approach, we are currently implementing a virtual machine that implements an environments in which the bot can be executed. This virtualization emulates a Windows environment and enables us to efficiently analyze the malware.

## 4.3   Observing Botnets

Once we have collected all sensitive information of the botnet, we start to infiltrate the botnet as we have all the necessary data. In a first approach, it is possible to setup a normal IRC client and try to connect to the network. If the operators of the botnets do not detect this client, logging of all commands can be enabled. This way, all bot commands and all actions can be observed. If the network is relatively small (i.e., less then 50 clients), there is a chance that the bogus client will be identified since it does not answer to valid commands. In this case, the operators of the botnets tend to either ban and/or DDoS the suspicious client.

But there are many problems with this approach: Some botnets use very strongly stripped down C&C server which is not RFC compliant so that a normal IRC client can not connect to this network. A possible way to circumvent this situation is to find out what the operator has stripped out, and modify the source code of the IRC client to override it. Furthermore, this approach does not scale very well. Tracking more than just a few botnets is not possible since a normal IRC client will be overwhelmed with the amount of logging data and it does not offer a concise overview of what is happening.

Therefore we use an IRC client optimized for botnet tracking called *drone*. This software was developed by two members of the German Honeynet Project and offers several decent techniques for observing botnets:

- Multi-server support to track a large number of botnets in parallel
- Excessive debug-logging interface so that it is possible to get information about RFC non-compliance issues very fast and fix them in the client
- Automated downloading of malware identified within the botnet
- Modular interface to un/load modules at runtime

Furthermore, *drone* is capable of using SOCKS v4 proxies so we do not run into problems if it's presence is noticed by an attacker in a botnet. The SOCKS v4 proxies are on dial-in accounts in different networks so that we can easily change the IP addresses of our infiltrated bot.

When observing more than a couple of networks, we began to check if some of them are linked, and group them if possible. Link-checking is simply realizable: our client just joins a specific channel on all networks and detects if more than one client is there, thus concluding the the networks controlled by several C&C servers are linked. Surprisingly, many networks are linked.

## 4.4   Preventing DDoS Attacks Caused by Botnets

Several ways to prevent DDoS attacks caused by botnets exist that we want to sketch in this section. Since we observe the communication flow within the botnet, we are also able to observe the IP addresses of the bots unless this information is obfuscated, e.g., by modifying the C&C server. Thus one possible way to stop DDoS attacks with this methodology is to contact the owner of the compromised system. This is however a tedious and cumbersome job, since many organizations are involved and these organizations are spread all over the world. In addition, the large number of bots make this approach nearly infeasible, only an automated notification system could help.

Another approach to prevent DDoS attacks caused by botnets aims at stopping the actual infrastructure, in particular the C&C server, since this component is vital for the remote control network. One possible way to stop the C&C

server is described in [8]: Most botnets use a dynamic DNS name instead of a hard-coded IP address for the C&C server. So if the DNS name is changed so that it resolves to an IP address in a private subnet as defined in RFC 1918, the bots are not able to connect to the central server. Thus the remote control network is efficiently shut down. For this approach, the assistance of the DNS provider is needed, though.

In addition, the collected information about botnets enable another way to stop the botnet. We know the IP address of the C&C server and are thus able to locate it. If the operator of the network cooperates, it is possible to shut down this server and thus shutting down the remote control network.

## 5  Results

In this section we present some of the findings we obtained through our observation of botnets. Data is sanitized so that it does not allow one to draw any conclusions about specific attacks against a particular system, and protects the identity and privacy of those involved. The information about specific attacks and compromised systems was forwarded to DFN-CERT (Computer Emergency Response Team) based in Hamburg, Germany.

The results are based on the observations collected with just two sensors. One sensors uses the approach depicted in Section 4.1 and is located within the network of RWTH Aachen University. The other sensor is based on the technique and software introduced in Section 4.2 and is located within a dial-in network of a German ISP.

We start with some statistics about the botnets we have observed in the last five months:

- *Number of botnets*: We were able to track about 180 botnets during the last five months. Some of them went offline (e.g. C&C server went offline or inexperienced attackers) and at the time of writing (March 2005) we are tracking about 60 active botnets.
- *Number of hosts*: During these few months, we saw more than 300,000 unique IP addresses joining at least one of the channels we monitored. Seeing an IP means here that the C&C server was not modified to not send a JOIN message for each joining client. If an IRC server is modified not to show joining clients in a channel, we do not see IPs here. Furthermore some IRC server obfuscate the joining clients IP address and obfuscated IP addresses do not count as seen, too. This shows that the threat posed by botnets is probably worse than originally believed. Even if we are very optimistic and estimate that we track a significant percentage of all botnets and all of our tracked botnet C&C servers are not modified to hide JOINs or obfuscate the joining clients IPs, this would mean that more than one million hosts are compromised and can be controlled by malicious attackers.
- *Typical size of Botnets*: Some botnets consist of only a few hundred bots. In contrast to this, we have also monitored several large botnets with up to 50,000 hosts. The actual size of such a large botnet is hard to estimate.

Often the attackers use heavily modified IRC servers and the bots are spread across several C&C servers which are linked together to form a common remote control network. We use link-checking between IRC servers to detect connections between different botnets that form one large botnet. Thus we are able to approximate the actual size.

As a side note: We know about a home computer which got infected by 16 different bots, so its hard to make an estimation about world bot population here.

- *Dimension of DDoS-attacks*: We are able to make an educated guess about the current dimension of DDoS-attacks caused by botnets. We can observe the commands issued by the controllers and thus see whenever the botnet is used for such attacks. From the beginning of November 2004 until the end of March 2005, we were able to observe 406 DDoS-attacks against 179 unique targets. Often these attacks targeted dial-up lines, but there are also attacks against bigger websites or other IRC server.
- *Spreading of botnets*: Commands issued for further spreading of the bots are the most frequent observed messages. Commonly, Windows systems are exploited and thus we see most traffic on typical Windows ports used for file sharing.
- *"Updates" within botnets*: We also observed updates of botnets quite frequently. Updating in this context means that the bots are instructed to download a piece of software from the Internet and then execute it.

We conclude that our general methodology described in Section 3 is feasible and the automated approach described in Section 4.2 is effective. We collected more than 5500 binaries (about 800 unique ones) with mwcollect in just one week on a single sensor. This sensor has only one IP address and is connected to the Internet via a German DSL dial-in provider with 4 MBit downstream and 2 MBit upstream. About five percent of the unique files were broken due to failures during TFTP transfer. We are currently in the process of analyzing these files. Once we have implemented a virtualization mechanism to efficiently and automatically analyze the collected files, we hope to be able to significantly increase the number of botnets we observe. In addition, this information can be used to prevent DDoS attacks by shutting down the C&C server.

## 6    Conclusion and Further Work

DDoS attacks have become increasingly dangerous in recent years and we are observing a growing professionalism in the type of Internet crime surrounding DDoS. In this paper we have introduced a technique for DDoS attack prevention that neither implies a resource arms race nor needs any additional infrastructure. In contrast to previous work in this area our approach is preventive instead of reactive. Our technique attacks a root-cause of DDoS attacks: in order to be effective, an attacker has to control a large number of machines and thus needs a remote control network. Our methodology aims at shutting down this control network by infiltrating it and analyzing it in detail.

We have exemplified a technical realization of this methodology considering as example the tracking of IRC-based botnets. Such a botnet is a network of compromised machines that can be remotely controlled by an attacker through Internet relay chat technology. Due to their immense size (tens of thousands of systems can be linked together), these botnets pose a severe threat to the Internet community, e.g., since their aggregated resources can be used to overwhelm most targets with a DDoS attack. We have shown that an automation of this approach is possible to a high degree. With the help of honeypots, i.e., network resources deployed to be compromised, we are able to automate the process of collecting sensitive information of the remote control network by automatically "collecting" malware. Via an automated analysis of the captured binaries we are furthermore able to extract the sensitive information that allow to shut down the control network.

With the help of just two sensors we were able to track a significant number of botnets within a few months. In the future we want to analyze how good our approach scales. Therefore we want to deploy more sensors within different networks. In addition, we aim at speeding up the automated analysis process so that it becomes even more effective. This can for example be achieved with the help of a generic shellcode parser or a virtual machine that analyzes and extracts the sensitive information from the captured binaries.

Moreover, the data we captured while observing the botnets show that these control networks are used for more than just DDoS attacks. Possible usages of botnets can be categorized as listed below. And since a botnet is nothing more then a tool, there are most likely other potential uses that we have not listed:

- *Spamming*: Some bots offer the possibility to open a SOCKS v4/v5 proxy – a generic proxy protocol for TCP/IP-based networking applications – on a compromised machine. After having enabled the SOCKS proxy, this machine can then be used for nefarious tasks such as sending bulk email (*spam*) or phishing mails. With the help of a botnet and thousands of bots, an attacker is able to send massive amounts of spam. Some bots also implement a special function to harvest email-addresses from the victims.
- *Attacking IRC Chat Networks*: Botnets are also used for DDoS attacks against Internet Relay Chat (IRC) networks. Popular among attackers is especially the so called *clone attack*: In this kind of attack, the controller orders each bot to connect a large number of clones to the victim IRC network. The victim is overwhelmed by service request from thousands of (cloned) bots.
- *Manipulating online polls/games*: Online polls/games are getting more and more attention and it is rather easy to manipulate them with botnets. Since every bot has a distinct IP address, every vote will have the same credibility as a vote cast by a real person. Online games can be manipulated in a similar way.
- *Sniffing Traffic*: Bots can also use a packet sniffer to watch for interesting clear-text data passing by a compromised machine. The sniffers are mostly used to retrieve sensitive information like usernames and passwords.

- *Keylogging*: If the compromised machine uses encrypted communication channels (e.g. HTTPS or POP3S), then just sniffing the network packets on the victim's computer is useless since the appropriate key to decrypt the packets is missing. But most bots also implement functions to log keystrokes. With the help of a keylogger it is very easy for an attacker to retrieve sensitive information.
- *Harvesting of information*: Sometimes we can also observe the harvesting of information from all compromised machines. With the help of special commands the operator of the botnet is able to request a list of sensitive information from all bots.

With our method we can shut down the root-cause of all of these types of nuisances, and hence our method is not restricted to combat DDoS.

In the future, we hope to develop more advanced honeypots that help us to gather more information about threats such as botnets. Examples include *client-side honeypots* that actively participate in networks (e.g., by crawling the web, idling in IRC channels, or using P2P-networks) or modify honeypots so that they capture malware and send it to anti-virus vendors for further analysis. It is also to be expected that future botnets will use communication facilities other than IRC (like potentially decentralized P2P-communication or covert channels). Our methodology seems valid also for these scenarios, although more research in this area is still needed.

## Acknowledgments

We thank Lucia Draque Penso for reading a previous version of this paper and giving valuable feedback that substantially improved it's presentation. In addition, we would like to thank the authors of *drone*, an IRC client optimized for botnet tracking, for their hard word in writing the program.

## References

1. FBI report on Operation Cyberslam. Internet: `http://www.reverse.net/operationcyberslam.pdf`, Accessed March 2005, February 2004.
2. Hacker threats to bookies probed. Internet: `http://news.bbc.co.uk/1/hi/technology/3513849.stm`, Accessed March 2005, February 2004.
3. S. M. Bellovin. ICMP traceback messages, March 2001. Internet Draft.
4. Computer Emergency Response Team. CERT advisory CA-1996-21 TCP SYN Flooding Attacks. Internet: `http://www.cert.org/advisories/CA-1996-21.html`, 1996.
5. D. Dittrich. Distributed Denial of Service (DDoS) attacks/tools resource page. Internet: `http://staff.washington.edu/dittrich/misc/ddos/`, 2000.
6. M. Dornseif, F. C. Gärtner, and T. Holz. Vulnerability assessment using honepots. *Praxis der Informationsverarbeitung und Kommunikation (PIK)*, 4(27):195–201, 2004.
7. P. Ferguson. Network ingress filtering: Defeating denial of service attacks which employ IP source address spoofing, May 2000. Request for Comments: RFC 2827.

8. T. Fischer. Botnetze. In *Proceedings of 12th DFN-CERT Workshop*, March 2005.
9. L. Garber. Denial-of-service attacks rip the Internet. *Computer*, 33(4):12–17, April 2000.
10. M. S. Johns. Identification protocol, February 1993. Request for Comments: RFC 1413.
11. B. McCarty. Botnets: Big and bigger. *IEEE Security & Privacy*, 1(4):87–90, 2003.
12. C. Meadows. A formal framework and evaluation method for network denial of service. In *Proceedings of the 1999 IEEE Computer Security Foundations Workshop*, pages 4–13. IEEE Computer Society Press, 1998.
13. J. Mirkovic, S. Dietrich, D. Dittrich, and P. Reiher. *Internet Denial of Service: Attack and Defense Mechanisms*. Prentice Hall PTR, 2004.
14. J. Mirkovic and P. Reiher. A taxonomy of DDoS attacks and defense mechanisms. *ACM SIGCOMM Computer Communications Review*, 34(2):39–54, Apr. 2004.
15. J. Mirkovic, M. Robinson, P. Reiher, and G. Kuenning. Alliance formation for DDoS defense. In *Proceedings of the New Security Paradigms Workshop 2003*. ACM SIGSAC, Aug. 2003.
16. N. Provos. A virtual honeypot framework. In *Proceedings of 13th USENIX Security Symposium*, 2004.
17. S. Savage, D. Wetherall, A. R. Karlin, and T. Anderson. Practical network support for IP traceback. In *Proceedings of the 2000 ACM SIGCOMM Conference*, pages 295–306, August 2000.
18. B. Schneier. Inside risks: semantic network attacks. *Communications of the ACM*, 43(12):168–168, Dec. 2000.
19. C. L. Schuba, I. V. Krsul, M. G. Kuhn, E. H. Spafford, A. Sundaram, and D. Zamboni. Analysis of a denial of service attack on TCP. In *Proceedings of the 1997 IEEE Symposium on Security and Privacy*, pages 208–223. IEEE Computer Society, IEEE Computer Society Press, May 1997.
20. D. X. Song and A. Perrig. Advanced and authenticated marking schemes for IP traceback. In *Proceedings of IEEE Infocom 2001*, April 2001.
21. The Honeynet Project. Know Your Enemy: GenII Honeynets, November 2003. http://www.honeynet.org/papers/gen2/.
22. The Honeynet Project. Know your Enemy: Tracking Botnets, March 2005. http://www.honeynet.org/papers/bots.

# Quantifying Probabilistic Information Flow in Computational Reactive Systems

Michael Backes

IBM Zurich Research Laboratory
mbc@zurich.ibm.com

**Abstract.** Information flow and non-interference are well-established techniques for expressing both integrity and privacy properties. Because of the enormous potential to transmit information using probabilistic methods of cryptography, interest has arisen in extending the traditional notions of information flow to fully reactive settings that allow for reasoning about arbitrary interactive systems, and in particular arbitrary cryptographic protocols. We propose definitions for quantifying the amount of information that users are able to transmit to each other in such reactive settings, and we in particular address computational restrictions and error probabilities so that our definitions are suited for complexity-theoretic reasoning about cryptographic systems. We show that our definitions are preserved under simulatability, which constitutes the cryptographic notion of a secure implementation, and we link our definitions to non-interference by showing that a zero or negligible quantity of information flow is equivalent to perfect or computational probabilistic non-interference, respectively.

## 1 Introduction

Information flow and non-interference have become powerful possibilities for expressing both privacy and integrity requirements. The concept of information flow was first investigated for secure operating systems by Lampson [17] and subsequently by Bell and LaPadula [4] and Denning [7]. Initiated by the work on non-interference of Goguen and Meseguer [11,12], various definitions have subsequently been proposed that rigorously specify when information flow is considered to occur for possibilistic and non-deterministic systems [33,24,37,26,30,10,22,23] and for probabilistic systems [13,14,25,35,32]. Whereas these lines of work concentrated on the absence of information flow in various settings, they were accompanied by work that gave quantitative measurements of the information that might flow between certain users, motivated by use cases where some flow of information might be inevitable or acceptable [27,16,20,5,8].

Recently, interest has arisen in generalizing definitions of information flow so that they allow for reasoning about real cryptographic protocols in order to capture the variety of cryptographic techniques that can be used to transmit information in a secret or undetectable way, e.g., encryption or steganographic tech-

S. De Capitani di Vimercati et al. (Eds.): ESORICS 2005, LNCS 3679, pp. 336–354, 2005.
© Springer-Verlag Berlin Heidelberg 2005

niques. The incorporation of cryptographic reasoning into information flow definitions posed major challenges because a faithful analysis of cryptography requires
not only probabilistic behaviors but also error probabilities and polynomial-time
restrictions in terms of computational complexity. Moreover, a suitable definition
has to capture a reactive environment, i.e., continuous interaction between users,
an adversary, and the system. These problems recently led to the notion of computational probabilistic non-interference [1,2], which was the first definition that
allowed for reasoning about information flow in a reactive setting and the presence of cryptography. However, quantitative measurements of information flow
in reactive settings and particularly in the presence of arbitrary cryptographic
protocols have not been addressed yet.

We present the first definitions for quantifying the amount of information
that one user is able to transmit to another user within a reactive setting.
We present definitions for unconditional security that are suitable for reasoning
about informational-theoretically secure or non-cryptographic systems, as well
as computational definitions that comprise complexity-theoretic reasoning such
as polynomially bounded adversaries, allow error probabilities, and are tightly
related to well-established cryptographic notions such as computational indistinguishability. Roughly, our approach to quantify an information flow from a high
user to a low user is to consider different behaviors of the high user that result
in different views of the low users (different probability distributions), to then
measure the distance of these distributions, and to finally maximize the resulting measurement for different behaviors of the high user. Both the unconditional
and the computational definitions comprise malicious or predefined behaviors of
third parties as well as timing aspects.

We show that our definitions are preserved under simulatability, which constitutes the cryptographic notion of a secure implementation, i.e., securely implementing a specification in the sense of simulatability may not increase the transmitted information in the unconditional case, and only by a negligible quantity
in the computational case. This significantly simplifies the determination of the
information flow quantity permitted within a cryptographic system, since simulatability helps to eliminate cryptography-related details such as error probabilities and computational restrictions. Moreover, we show that a zero or negligible
quantity of information flow is equivalent to perfect and computational probabilistic non-interference. With our simulatability preservation theorem, this in
particular allows for a short, alternative proof that non-interference properties
are preserved under simulatability [1].

*Further Related Literature.* The only definitions of information flow that reside
in a reactive scenario and that allow for complexity-theoretic reasoning have
been presented by Backes and Pfitzmann in [1,2] based on the model of reactive
simulatability [29,3]; quantitative aspects of information flow are, however, not
considered there.

The work that comes closest to ours in terms of quantifying information
flow is the one on *approximate non-interference* of Di Pierro et al. [8]. They
defined the notion of $\varepsilon$-confinement that captured that information flow is still

acceptable if the distance of views of specific user deviate only up to probability $\varepsilon$. Although their definition does not address computational aspects as needed for cryptographic purposes, our work is nevertheless inspired by some of their ideas. Lowe [20] measured the amount of information in a non-probabilistic setting by counting the number of different behaviors of the high user that yield different views for the low user. Clark et al. [5] proposed syntax-directed inference rules for computing estimates on information flow in an imperative language. Both works do not aim to deal with computational aspects.

Early ideas of quantitative security based on Shannon's information theory go back to Denning's work [6], which was subsequently used in [27,16] to measure the quantity of covert channels. The investigated settings, however, were simplistic in that the channels were memoryless, there was no input feedback in the channel, and only uncorrelated inputs; moreover, no computational restrictions were taken into account there. This stands in blatant contrast to reactive scenarios that allow for expressing and analyzing arbitrary (cryptographic) primitives and protocols, where inputs and user behaviors are typically highly correlated and protocols are highly stateful. We consider it interesting future work to extend the information-theoretic line of work to our unconditional definitions, and we have some basic ideas on this subject that we intend to pursue.

Recent research has also investigated non-interference properties involving real cryptographic primitives, but without investigating quantitative aspects. Laud [18,19] presented a sequential language for which he expressed real computational secrecy. The definition is non-reactive and specific to encryption as the only cryptographic primitive. Volpano [34] investigated conditions for safely using one-way functions in a programming language, but his underlying definition does not express non-interference, but the secrecy of a specific secret.

*Outline of the Paper.* In Section 2 we briefly review the underlying model of reactive simulatability, which is an asynchronous probabilistic execution model with distributed scheduling, including computational aspects as needed for cryptography. We give our definitions for capturing the quantity of information transmitted between two users in a fully reactive scenario—including the presence of cryptographic techniques—in Section 3. In Section 4 we show that our definitions are preserved under simulatability, and we finally show in Section 5 that a zero or negligible quantity of information flow is equivalent to existing notions of perfect and computational probabilistic non-interference. We conclude with a summary of our results in Section 6.

## 2    The Model of Reactive Simulatability

Our work is based on the model of reactive simulatability [29,3], which is an asynchronous probabilistic execution model with distributed scheduling that provides universal composability properties while including computational aspects as needed for cryptography. The model is automata based, i.e., protocols are executed by interacting machines, and event-based, i.e., machines react on certain inputs. All details of the model that are not necessary for understanding are omitted here; for completeness, we give rigorous definitions of the relevant notions in Appendix A.

## 2.1  General System Model

A *machine* is a probabilistic IO automaton (extended finite-state machine) in a slightly refined model to allow complexity considerations. For these automata Turing-machine realizations are defined, and the complexity thereof is measured in terms of a common security parameter $k$, given as the initial work-tape content of every machine. A *structure* consists of a set $\hat{M}$ of connected machines and a subset $S$ of free *ports*, called *service ports*. Each structure is complemented to a *configuration* by a set of *user* machines $U$ and an *adversary* machine A. The machines in $U$ connect only to ports in $S$, whereas A connects to the remaining free ports $\bar{S}$ of the structure and may interact with the users. We denote the set of configurations of a structure $(\hat{M}, S)$ by $\mathsf{Conf}(\hat{M}, S)$ and the subset of polynomial-time configurations by $\mathsf{Conf}_{\mathsf{poly}}(\hat{M}, S)$.[1]

The general scheduling model in [29,3] gives each connection $c$ (from an output port c! to an input port c?) a buffer, and the machine with the corresponding clock port $c^{\triangleleft}!$ can schedule a message there when it makes a transition. In real cryptographic systems, network connections are typically scheduled by A, which usually serves as a master scheduler, but the model allows for specifying other designated master schedulers as well as local schedulers for specific connections. Scheduling of machines is done sequentially, so there is exactly one active machine M at any time. If this machine has clock-out ports, it can select the next message to be scheduled. If that message exists, it is delivered by the buffer and the unique receiving machine is the next active machine. If M tries to schedule multiple messages, only one is taken, and if it schedules none or the message does not exist, the special master scheduler is scheduled.

This means that a configuration has a well-defined notion of *runs*, also called *traces* or *executions*. Formally a run is essentially a sequence of *steps*, and each step is a tuple of the name of the active machine in this step and its input, output, and old and new local state. As the underlying state-transition functions of the individual machines are probabilistic, one can define a probability space on the possible runs by a canonical construction as for Markov chains, cf. [3] for the precise definition. We call the corresponding random variable $run_{conf,k}$ for a configuration *conf* and the security parameter $k$. One can restrict a run $r$ to a machine M or a set of machines $\hat{M}$ by retaining only the steps of these machines; this is called the *view* of these machines. For a configuration *conf*, the corresponding random variables over the probability space of all possible runs are denoted by $view_{conf,k}(\mathsf{M})$ and $view_{conf,k}(\hat{M})$, respectively.

---

[1] Here and elsewhere we change some notation of [29,3] from so-called systems to structures. These systems contain several possible structures, derived from an intended structure with a trust model. Here we can always work with individual structures.

## 2.2    Partition Configurations for Defining Information Flow

Structures and configurations in their general form impose no restrictions regarding which user can connect to which service ports, e.g., users in different configurations might connect to a different subset of the service ports. For quantifying information flow in a reactive environment, as well as for the mere detection of information flow as defined in [1,2], we need security domains between which we can analyze the flow of information. It is intuitive to regard the possible protocol participants as security domains. However, to be independent of the details of the actual user and the adversary machines, we represent users by the ports they connect to in the considered structure $(\hat{M}, S)$, and the adversary by the remaining free ports of the structure. This means that we consider a partition $\Gamma = \{S_i \mid i \in \mathcal{I}\}$ of the set $S$ of service ports, where $\mathcal{I}$ is an arbitrary finite index set. We can now designate each user $\mathsf{H}_i$ with $i \in \mathcal{I}$ by the subset of service ports $S_i$ it connects to. For a given structure and a partition of its service ports, those configurations where each user only connects to its ports of the partition, and where the adversary connects to the remaining free ports of the structure are called *partition configurations*. A characteristic of partition configurations is that the different user machines and the adversary have no direct connections, because otherwise they could trivially transmit information without relying on the possibilities granted by the structure. Moreover, a specific fair master scheduler $\mathsf{X}$ is added to the configuration because if the adversary were allowed to schedule the connections to and from the users, it could always achieve probabilistic information flow, cf. [1,2] for more details. We denote the set of partition configurations of a structure $(\hat{M}, S)$ and partition $\Gamma$ by $\mathsf{Conf}(\hat{M}, S, \Gamma)$ and the subset of polynomial-time ones by $\mathsf{Conf}_{\mathsf{poly}}(\hat{M}, S, \Gamma)$. Finally, we consider the subset of partition configurations where users are only allowed to perform a certain number of steps. This will allow us to reason about timing aspects of information flow. We call a partition configuration with index set $\mathcal{I}$ a *timed partition configuration for a function* $\varphi\colon \mathcal{I} \to (\mathbb{N} \to \mathbb{N} \cup \{\infty\})$, if the user $\mathsf{H}_i$ in this configuration only makes $\varphi(i)$ outputs (as a function of $k$, the security parameter). We call the set of these configurations $\mathsf{Conf}^{\varphi}(\hat{M}, S, \Gamma)$ and the set of polynomial ones $\mathsf{Conf}^{\varphi}_{\mathsf{poly}}(\hat{M}, S, \Gamma)$.

# 3    Measuring Probabilistic Information Flow in Reactive Settings

We now define the amount of information that one user is able to transmit to another user via a particular structure. Using standard terminology, we call these two users the *high user* and the *low user*. The remaining users are referred to as *third parties*.

Roughly speaking, the idea of quantifying information flow is that we consider different behaviors of the high user that result in different views of the low users, and measure the distance between these different views. Finally, we maximize this distance for all possible behaviors of the high user, which gives the desired measure of the information quantity. The notion hence provides information on how much two behaviors of the high user might differ in the worst case, given only the view of the low user, and it hence resembles the similarity relation of [8].

It remains to decide to what extent the third parties might contribute to the information flow. The most stringent choice is to regard every third party as malicious, i.e., it fully exploits its possibilities to help the high user to transmit information to the low user. Formally, this means that we quantify over the behavior of all third parties to maximize the distance, and we speak of the *worst-case information quantity* in this scenario. This approach is the one commonly taken in the literature, as it gives an upper bound on the amount of information flow under worst-case assumptions. Moreover, it is naturally linked to the notion of non-interference, i.e., absence of information flow, as we will see in Section 5. Based on this core definition, we introduce several variants and extensions, including more benign behaviors of the third parties as well as timing aspects.

**Definition 1.** *(Worst-Case Information Quantity)* Let $(\hat{M}, S)$ be a structure, let $\Gamma = \{S_i \mid i \in \mathcal{I}\}$ be a partition on the set $S$ of service ports for a finite set $\mathcal{I}$, and let $||\cdot, \cdot||$ be a distance of user views, i.e., of probability distributions. Furthermore, let $H, L \in \mathcal{I}$ be given. Then the *worst-case information quantity* $\mathcal{Q}^{||\cdot,\cdot||}_{(\hat{M},S,\Gamma)}(H, L)$ that the high user $\mathsf{H}_H$ is allowed to transmit to $\mathsf{H}_L$ is defined as

$$\mathcal{Q}^{||\cdot,\cdot||}_{(\hat{M},S,\Gamma)}(H, L) := \max_{conf_1, conf_2 \in \mathsf{Conf}(\hat{M},S,\Gamma)} ||view_{conf_1,k}(\mathsf{H}_L), view_{conf_2,k}(\mathsf{H}_L)||,$$

such that $conf_l$ is of the form $conf_l := (\hat{M}, S, U_l, \mathsf{A})$ with $U_l = \{\mathsf{H}_H^{(l)}, \mathsf{H}_L, \mathsf{X}\} \cup \{\mathsf{H}_i \mid i \in \mathcal{I} \setminus \{H, L\}\}$ for an arbitrary adversary $\mathsf{A}$ and arbitrary users $\mathsf{H}_H^{(1)}, \mathsf{H}_H^{(2)}, \mathsf{H}_L$, and $\mathsf{H}_i$ for $i \in \mathcal{I} \setminus \{H, L\}$. The *polynomial-time worst-case information quantity* $\mathcal{Q}_{\mathcal{P}}{}^{||\cdot,\cdot||}_{(\hat{M},S,\Gamma)}(H, L)$ is defined similarly by taking the maximum over $\mathsf{Conf}_{\mathsf{poly}}(\hat{M}, S, \Gamma)$. ◇

Several extensions of this definition are useful. First, it is often more natural to consider fixed behaviors for some of the third parties because in real world examples, e.g., when a spy attempts to transmit information out of a company, it is unlikely that every employee will help the spy to do so. Formally, this means that we consider fixed user behaviors for a subset $\mathcal{J} \subseteq \mathcal{I}$, i.e., we parameterize the information quantity by a set $\mathcal{M} := \{\mathsf{H}_j \mid j \in \mathcal{J}\}$. The remaining users are considered malicious as in the previous definition. We speak of the *generalized information quantity* here because we obtain the worst-case definition as the special case $\mathcal{M} = \emptyset$.

**Definition 2.** *(Generalized Information Quantity)* Consider the preconditions as in Definition 1 and let $\mathcal{M} := \{\mathsf{H}_j \mid j \in \mathcal{J}\}$ be given for fixed machines $\mathsf{H}_j$ and $\mathcal{J} \subseteq \mathcal{I}$. Then the *generalized information quantity* $\mathcal{Q}^{||\cdot,\cdot||,\mathcal{M}}_{(\hat{M},S,\Gamma)}(H, L)$ *with respect to* $\mathcal{M}$ is defined as

$$\mathcal{Q}^{||\cdot,\cdot||,\mathcal{M}}_{(\hat{M},S,\Gamma)}(H, L) := \max_{conf_1, conf_2 \in \mathsf{Conf}(\hat{M},S,\Gamma)} ||view_{conf_1,k}(\mathsf{H}_L), view_{conf_2,k}(\mathsf{H}_L)||,$$

such that $conf_l$ is of the form $conf_l := (\hat{M}, S, U_l, \mathsf{A})$ with $U_l = \{\mathsf{H}_H^{(l)}, \mathsf{H}_L, \mathsf{X}\} \cup \{\mathsf{H}_i \mid i \in \mathcal{I} \setminus \{H, L\}\}$ for an arbitrary adversary $\mathsf{A}$ and arbitrary users $\mathsf{H}_H^{(1)}, \mathsf{H}_H^{(2)}, \mathsf{H}_L$, and $\mathsf{H}_i$ for $i \in \mathcal{I} \setminus (\mathcal{J} \cup \{H, L\})$, i.e., the maximum is only taken over those configurations in which the users $\mathsf{H}_j$ for $j \in \mathcal{J}$ are fixed by the parameter $\mathcal{M}$. The polynomial-time variant $\mathcal{Q}_{\mathcal{P}(\hat{M},S,\Gamma)}^{||\cdot,\cdot||,\mathcal{M}}(H, L)$ is defined as usual. ◇

Timing capabilities of certain users are typically of interest, i.e., to model that a spy should not be allowed to send data all the time, or only has limited access to his machine. We use timed partition configurations for this and speak of the *timed* generalized information quantity.

**Definition 3.** *(Timed Generalized Information Quantity)* Consider the preconditions as in Definition 2 and let in addition a function $\varphi \colon \mathcal{I} \to (\mathbb{N} \to \mathbb{N} \cup \{\infty\})$ be given. Then the *timed generalized information quantity* $\mathcal{Q}_{(\hat{M},S,\Gamma)}^{||\cdot,\cdot||,\mathcal{M},\varphi}(H, L)$ *with respect to* $\mathcal{M}, \varphi$ is defined as in Definition 2 except that the maximum is only taken over $\mathsf{Conf}^\varphi(\hat{M}, S, \Gamma)$. The polynomial-time variant $\mathcal{Q}_{\mathcal{P}(\hat{M},S,\Gamma)}^{||\cdot,\cdot||,\mathcal{M},\varphi}(H, L)$ is defined as usual. ◇

# 4  Preservation of Information Quantities Under Simulatability

We now investigate how the information quantity behaves under simulatability, which is the cryptographic notion of secure implementation. For reactive systems, it means that whatever might happen to users in a real structure $(\hat{M}_1, S)$ can also happen to users in an ideal structure $(\hat{M}_2, S)$ (with the same set of service ports to which the same users can connect). Formally, for every set $U$ of polynomial-time users, and every polynomial-time adversary $\mathsf{A}_1$, there exists a polynomial-time adversary $\mathsf{A}_2$ such that the views of the machines in $U$ are computationally indistinguishable when run either with $(\hat{M}_1, S)$ or with $(\hat{M}_2, S)$. This is illustrated in Figure 1. Indistinguishability is a well-known cryptographic notion from [38].

**Definition 4.** *(Computational Indistinguishability)* Two families $(\mathsf{var}_k)_{k\in\mathbb{N}}$ and $(\mathsf{var}'_k)_{k\in\mathbb{N}}$ of random variables on common domains $D_k$ are *computationally indistinguishable* ("$\approx$") iff for every algorithm $\mathsf{Dis}$ (the distinguisher) that is probabilistic polynomial-time in its first input, we have

$$|P(\mathsf{Dis}(1^k, \mathsf{var}_k) = 1) - P(\mathsf{Dis}(1^k, \mathsf{var}'_k) = 1)| \in \mathit{NEGL},$$

where $\mathit{NEGL}$ denotes the set of all *negligible functions*, i.e., $g \colon \mathbb{N} \to \mathbb{R}_{\geq 0} \in \mathit{NEGL}$ iff for all positive polynomials $Q$, $\exists k_0 \forall k \geq k_0 \colon g(k) \leq 1/Q(k)$. ◇

Intuitively, given the security parameter and an element chosen according to either $\mathsf{var}_k$ or $\mathsf{var}'_k$, $\mathsf{Dis}$ tries to guess which distribution the element came from.

**Definition 5.** *(Reactive Simulatability)* Let structures $(\hat{M}_1, S)$ and $(\hat{M}_2, S)$ be given. We say that $(\hat{M}_1, S)$ is *at least as secure as* $(\hat{M}_2, S)$, written $(\hat{M}_1, S) \geq_{\mathsf{sec}}^{\mathsf{poly}}$

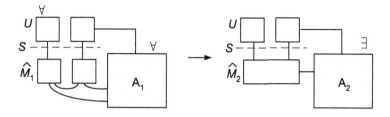

**Fig. 1.** Reactive simulatability: The two views of $U$ must be indistinguishable

$(\hat{M}_2, S)$ if for every configuration $conf_1 = (\hat{M}_1, S, U, \mathsf{A}_1) \in \mathsf{Conf}_{\mathsf{poly}}(\hat{M}_1, S)$, there exists a configuration $conf_2 = (\hat{M}_2, S, U, \mathsf{A}_2) \in \mathsf{Conf}_{\mathsf{poly}}(\hat{M}_2, S)$ such that

$$view_{conf_1}(U) \approx view_{conf_2}(U).$$

We speak of *perfect reactive simulatability*, written $(\hat{M}_1, S) \geq_{\mathsf{sec}}^{\mathsf{perf}} (\hat{M}_2, S)$, if the above formula holds for all (also non-polynomially bounded) configurations of the respective structures, and with indistinguishability replaced by equality. $\diamond$

### 4.1   Preservation of Information Quantities

The following theorem establishes that the information quantity between two users is essentially unchanged under reactive simulatability. More precisely, the theorem states that only a negligible additional quantity of information can be transmitted to the low user when simulatability is applied, provided that the employed distance respects computational indistinguishability in a natural manner, i.e., two ensembles are indistinguishable if and only if their distance constitutes a negligible function. We call such distances *computational distances*. In the case of perfect reactive simulatability, we even show that no additional information can be sent to the low user for any distance. (Note that reactive simulatability is not symmetric, hence we cannot rule out that the user can only transmit *less* information when interacting with a real structure rather than when interacting with the ideal structure.)

These are exactly the properties that already allow modular and cryptographically sound proofs on the abstract level: For instance, an ideal specification that should prohibit the flow of information between two users has information quantity zero because it allows no communication between these two users by construction, e.g., the ideal firewall presented in [1] is of this kind. This is typically much easier to prove than for a cryptographic realization where the restriction on the information flow might be achieved by cryptographic techniques, e.g., digital signatures in the real implementation of the firewall. The theorem hence allows for conveniently analyzing the information flow properties of real cryptographic systems by means of their ideal counterparts, and we can hope that well-established techniques for enforcing the absence respectively measuring the quantity of information flow based on type checking techniques, e.g., [36,9,28,35,31,32,39], can be applied to our setting. Moreover, a negligible amount of information is the best we can hope for in the presence of asymmetric cryptography because a negligible probability of error there always remains.

**Theorem 1.** *(Preservation of Information Quantity)* Let two structures $(\hat{M}_i, S)$ for $i = 1, 2$ be given, let $\Gamma := \{S_i \mid i \in \mathcal{I}\}$ be a partition of $S$ for a finite index set $\mathcal{I}$, and let $H, L \in \mathcal{I}$. Let $\mathcal{M} := \{H_j \mid j \in \mathcal{J}\}$ for some $\mathcal{J} \subseteq \mathcal{I}$ and $\varphi \colon \mathcal{I} \to (\mathbb{N} \to \mathbb{N} \cup \{\infty\})$ arbitrary. Then $(\hat{M}_1, S) \geq^{\mathsf{perf}}_{\mathsf{sec}} (\hat{M}_2, S)$ implies

$$\mathcal{Q}^{||\cdot,\cdot||,\mathcal{M},\varphi}_{(\hat{M}_1, S, \Gamma)}(H, L) \leq \mathcal{Q}^{||\cdot,\cdot||,\mathcal{M},\varphi}_{(\hat{M}_2, S, \Gamma)}(H, L)$$

for every distance $||\cdot, \cdot||$. Moreover, $(\hat{M}_1, S) \geq^{\mathsf{poly}}_{\mathsf{sec}} (\hat{M}_2, S)$ implies

$$\mathcal{Q}_{\mathcal{P}}{}^{||\cdot,\cdot||_c,\mathcal{M},\varphi}_{(\hat{M}_1, S, \Gamma)}(H, L) \leq \mathcal{Q}_{\mathcal{P}}{}^{||\cdot,\cdot||_c,\mathcal{M},\varphi}_{(\hat{M}_2, S, \Gamma)}(H, L) + \epsilon(k)$$

for some $\epsilon \in NEGL$ and every computational distance $||\cdot, \cdot||_c$.     $\square$

*Proof.* Let $conf^1_1 = (\hat{M}_1, S, U_1, \mathsf{A})$ and $conf^1_2 = (\hat{M}_1, S, U_2, \mathsf{A})$ be two (polynomial-time) partition configurations in $\mathsf{Conf}^\varphi(\hat{M}_1, S, \Gamma)$ with $U_l := \{\mathsf{H}^{(l)}_H, \mathsf{H}_L, \mathsf{X}\} \cup \{\mathsf{H}_i \mid i \in \mathcal{I} \setminus \{H, L\}\}$ (for arbitrary machines $\mathsf{H}_i$ for $i \in \mathcal{I} \setminus (\mathcal{J} \cup \{H, L\})$) such that $||(view_{conf^1_1,k}(\mathsf{H}_L), view_{conf^1_2,k}(\mathsf{H}_L))||$ is equal to $\mathcal{Q}^{||\cdot,\cdot||,\mathcal{M},\varphi}_{(\hat{M}_1, S, \Gamma)}(H, L)$ or to $\mathcal{Q}_{\mathcal{P}}{}^{||\cdot,\cdot||_c,\mathcal{M},\varphi}_{(\hat{M}_1, S, \Gamma)}(H, L)$, respectively, in the polynomial case. Owing to $(\hat{M}_1, S) \geq_{\mathsf{sec}} (\hat{M}_2, S)$, (polynomial-time) configurations $conf^2_1$, $conf^2_2 \in \mathsf{Conf}^\varphi(\hat{M}_2, S)$ exist such that $view_{conf^1_1,k}(U_1) \approx view_{conf^2_1,k}(U_1)$ and $view_{conf^1_2,k}(U_2) \approx view_{conf^2_2,k}(U_2)$. Moreover, we obviously have $conf^2_1$, $conf^2_2 \in \mathsf{Conf}^{\varphi'}(\hat{M}_2, S, \Gamma)$ because the users and the set of service ports are unchanged under simulatability, and $\varphi = \varphi'$ as the users' view could otherwise be trivially distinguished in both configurations (the distinguisher waits until one user stops in one configuration but continues to send messages in the other configuration).

We now restrict the views of $U_1$ and $U_2$ to the user $\mathsf{H}_L$ in all configurations. This is the function on the view of both $U_1$ and $U_2$, i.e., a polynomial-time computable function applied to indistinguishable views, hence we obtain $view_{conf^1_1,k}(\mathsf{H}_L) \approx view_{conf^2_1,k}(\mathsf{H}_L)$ and $view_{conf^1_2,k}(\mathsf{H}_L) \approx view_{conf^2_2,k}(\mathsf{H}_L)$. In the following, we abbreviate $view_{conf^i_j,k}(\mathsf{H}_L)$ by $v^{i,j}_k$ for the sake of readability. We obtain $||v^{1,1}_k, v^{1,2}_k|| \leq ||v^{1,1}_k, v^{2,1}_k|| + ||v^{1,2}_k, v^{2,2}_k|| + ||v^{2,1}_k, v^{2,2}_k||$ by the triangle inequality. In the case of perfect reactive simulatability, we have $v^{1,1}_k = v^{2,1}_k$ and $v^{1,2}_k = v^{2,2}_k$ for all $k$, hence $||v^{1,1}_k, v^{1,2}_k|| \leq ||v^{2,1}_k, v^{2,2}_k||$. As $conf^2_1$, $conf^2_2 \in \mathsf{Conf}^\varphi(\hat{M}_2, S, \Gamma)$, Definition 3 implies $||v^{2,1}_k, v^{2,2}_k|| \leq \mathcal{Q}^{||\cdot,\cdot||,\mathcal{M},\varphi}_{(\hat{M}_2, S, \Gamma)}(H, L)$ for all distances $||\cdot, \cdot||$, which completes the proof of the perfect case. In the computational case of reactive simulatability, we have $||v^{1,1}_k, v^{2,1}_k||_c \in NEGL$ and $||v^{1,2}_k, v^{2,2}_k||_c \in NEGL$ for every computational distance $||\cdot, \cdot||_c$. As the class of negligible functions is closed under addition, $\epsilon(k) := ||v^{1,1}_k, v^{2,1}_k||_c + ||v^{1,2}_k, v^{2,2}_k||_c$ is a negligible function again. Now $conf^2_1$, $conf^2_2 \in \mathsf{Conf}^\varphi(\hat{M}_2, S, \Gamma)$ and Definition 3 imply that $||v^{2,1}_k, v^{2,2}_k||_c$ is upper bounded by $\mathcal{Q}_{\mathcal{P}}{}^{||\cdot,\cdot||_c,\mathcal{M},\varphi}_{(\hat{M}_2, S, \Gamma)}(H, L)$ for any computational distance $||\cdot, \cdot||_c$, which completes the proof of the computational case. ∎

# 5    Relationship to Probabilistic Non-interference

In this section, we show that the worst-case information quantity is related in a natural way to the notion of probabilistic non-interference, i.e., to the absence of probabilistic information flow. More precisely, we consider the recently proposed definitions of perfect and computational probabilistic non-interference [1] in reactive systems, and we show that a structure fulfills a non-interference property for particular high and low users if and only if the worst-case information quantity between these users is zero in the case of perfect non-interference or bounded by a negligible function in the case of computational non-interference.

## 5.1    Brief Review of Computational Probabilistic Non-interference

We first review briefly the notions of perfect and computation non-interference in reactive systems. Information flow properties such as non-interference consist of two components: a *flow policy* and a *definition of information flow*. Flow policies specify restrictions on the information flow within a system.

**Definition 6.** *(Flow Policy)* Let a structure $(\hat{M}, S)$ be given, and let $\Gamma = \{S_i \mid i \in \mathcal{I}\}$ denote a partition of $S$ for a finite index set $\mathcal{I}$. A *flow policy* $\mathcal{F}$ of the structure $(\hat{M}, S)$ is a graph $\mathcal{F} = (\Gamma, \rightsquigarrow)$ with $\rightsquigarrow \subseteq \Gamma \times \Gamma$. For $(S_i, S_j) \in \rightsquigarrow$, we write $S_i \rightsquigarrow S_j$, and $S_i \not\rightsquigarrow S_j$ otherwise. Furthermore we demand $S_i \rightsquigarrow S_i$ for all $S_i \in \Gamma$. ◇

Here $S_i \rightsquigarrow S_j$ intuitively means that information may flow from $S_i$ to $S_j$, whereas $S_i \not\rightsquigarrow S_j$ means that it must not. The relation $\not\rightsquigarrow$ is the non-interference relation of $\mathcal{F}$, i.e., $S_H \not\rightsquigarrow S_L$ means that no information must flow from the user connected to the ports $S_H$ to the user connected to the ports $S_L$. To capture this in a way that allows for computational restrictions, error probabilities etc., the notion of probabilistic non-interference from [1] gives the user $\mathsf{H}_H$ (connected to $S_H$) a randomly distributed bit $b$ at the start of the run, and $\mathsf{H}_H$ should try to transmit this bit to $\mathsf{H}_L$ (connected to $S_L$). The user $\mathsf{H}_L$ then outputs a bit $b^*$, which is its guess of the bit $b$. To capture this formally in the model, the specific users have special ports for receiving the initial bit and for outputting their guess, respectively, and special machines $\mathsf{BIT}_H$ and $\mathsf{OUT}_L$ are added that produce the bit $b$ and consume the bit $b^*$. As for partition configurations, the same specific fair master scheduler $\mathsf{X}$ is added to the configuration to prevent from achieving information flow in a trivial manner. The resulting configurations are called *non-interference configurations* for $S_H$ and $S_L$. Then the underlying structure $(\hat{M}, S)$ is defined to fulfill the non-interference requirement defined by flow policy $\mathcal{F}$ in the computational sense (written $(\hat{M}, S) \models^{\mathsf{poly}} \mathcal{F}$) iff for all $H, L$ with $S_H \not\rightsquigarrow S_L$ and all polynomial-time non-interference configurations for $S_H$ and $S_L$, the probability of a correct guess $b = b^*$ is only negligibly greater than pure guessing. A structure fulfills the requirement in the perfect sense (written $(\hat{M}, S) \models^{\mathsf{perf}} \mathcal{F}$) iff the same holds for all (also non-polynomially bounded) configurations and the advantage over pure guessing should be zero. We review the rigorous definitions in Appendix A.

## 5.2   Linking Information Quantity and Non-interference

We now show that a structure fulfills a non-interference requirement if and only if the worst-case information quantity between the respective pairs of users defined by the flow policy is zero or a negligible function in the security parameter $k$, respectively.

The left-to-right direction of this statement is closely related to existing results for previous definitions of non-interference, where it has proved that non-interference implies that the information quantity exchanged between the respective users is zero. In a cryptographic scenario, the notion of a negligibly small information quantity has replaced the total absence of information flow. When considering the converse direction however, an information quantity of zero was not sufficient to establish the non-interference property for many existing definitions of non-interference, which often made these properties too strict for dealing with information flow. For the definition of perfect and computational probabilistic non-interference in the reactive setting, we can establish this converse direction. This might serve as an indication that the reactive definition of non-interference is not overly restrictive and might constitute an important tool for reasoning about absence of information flow in the presence of cryptography.

**Theorem 2.** *(Information Quantity and Non-Interference)* Let a structure $(\hat{M}, S)$, a partition $\Gamma = \{S_i \mid i \in \mathcal{I}\}$ of $S$ for a finite index set $\mathcal{I}$, and a flow policy $\mathcal{F} = (\Gamma, \rightsquigarrow)$ of $(\hat{M}, S)$ be given. Then we have $(\hat{M}, S) \models^{\mathsf{perf}} \mathcal{F}$ (resp. $(\hat{M}, S) \models^{\mathsf{poly}} \mathcal{F}$) iff for all $H, L \in \mathcal{I}$ with $S_H \not\rightsquigarrow S_L$ we have $\mathcal{Q}^{||\cdot,\cdot||}_{(\hat{M},S,\Gamma)}(H, L) = 0$ for all distances $||\cdot, \cdot||$ (resp. $\mathcal{Q}\mathcal{P}^{||\cdot,\cdot||_{\mathsf{c}}}_{(\hat{M},S,\Gamma)}(H, L) \in NEGL$ for all computational distances $||\cdot, \cdot||_{\mathsf{c}}$). □

*Proof.* We only prove the more complicated computational case here; the perfect case can be easily derived from that. We start with the left-to-right direction. Assume for contradiction that $\mathcal{Q}\mathcal{P}^{||\cdot,\cdot||_{\mathsf{c}}}_{(\hat{M},S,\Gamma)}(H, L) \notin NEGL$ for some $H, L$ with $S_H \not\rightsquigarrow S_L$ and some computational distance $||\cdot, \cdot||_{\mathsf{c}}$. This means that there exist two partition configurations $conf_1 = (\hat{M}, S, U_1, \mathsf{A})$ and $conf_2 = (\hat{M}, S, U_2, \mathsf{A})$ from $\mathsf{Conf}_{\mathsf{poly}}(\hat{M}, S, \Gamma)$ with $U_l := \{\mathsf{H}_H^{(l)}, \mathsf{H}_L, \mathsf{X}\} \cup \{\mathsf{H}_i \mid i \in \mathcal{I} \setminus \{H, L\}\}$ such that $||view_{conf_1,k}(\mathsf{H}_L), view_{conf_2,k}(\mathsf{H}_L)||_{\mathsf{c}} = \mathcal{Q}\mathcal{P}^{||\cdot,\cdot||_{\mathsf{c}}}_{(\hat{M},S,\Gamma)}(H, L)$. This implies $view_{conf_1,k}(\mathsf{H}_L) \not\approx view_{conf_2,k}(\mathsf{H}_L)$, i.e., there exists a probabilistic polynomial-time distinguisher Dis such that $|P(\mathsf{Dis}(1^k, view_{conf_1,k}(\mathsf{H}_L)) = 1) - P(\mathsf{Dis}(1^k, view_{conf_2,k}(\mathsf{H}_L)) = 1)| = n(k)$ for a non-negligible function $n$. We now define a non-interference configuration $conf$ that contradicts $(\hat{M}, S) \models^{\mathsf{poly}} \mathcal{F}$. If the high user of $conf$ receives $b = 0$, it acts as $\mathsf{H}_H^{(1)}$, and as $\mathsf{H}_H^{(2)}$ otherwise. The low user of $conf$ act as $\mathsf{H}_L$ but when $\mathsf{H}_L$ would enter final state, the low user uses Dis as a blackbox submachine, runs it on $\mathsf{H}_L$'s view, and outputs the bit that Dis outputs. The low user is polynomial-time because both $\mathsf{H}_L$ and Dis are polynomial-time. The remaining users of $conf$ act as in configuration $conf_1$ and $conf_2$. By the construction of $conf$, the probability of a correct guess

$b = b^*$ of the low user in *conf* is equal to $n(k)$, which yields a contradiction to $(\hat{M}, S) \models^{\mathsf{poly}} \mathcal{F}$.

We now prove the right-to-left direction. Assume for contradiction that $(\hat{M}, S) \not\models^{\mathsf{poly}} \mathcal{F}$. Then there exist $H, L$ with $S_H \not\rightsquigarrow S_L$ and a non-interference configuration *conf* for $S_H, S_L$ such that the probability of a correct guess of the low user in *conf* is equal to $\frac{1}{2} + n(k)$ for some non-negligible function $n$. We now define two partition configurations $conf_1$, $conf_2$ as follows. The user $\mathsf{H}_H^{(1)}$ in $conf_1$ acts as $\mathsf{H}_H$ would if it received $b = 0$, and $\mathsf{H}_H^{(2)}$ in $conf_2$ acts as $\mathsf{H}_H$ would if it received $b = 1$. The user $\mathsf{H}_L$ in $conf_1$ and $conf_2$ acts as the low user in *conf* but instead of outputting the bit $b^*$ to the now non-existing machine $\mathsf{OUT}_L$, it simply stores $b^*$ (to keep it part of its view). The remaining users act as in *conf*. Now, as $n$ is a non-negligible function, we immediately obtain $view_{conf_1, k}(\mathsf{H}_L) \not\approx view_{conf_2, k}(\mathsf{H}_L)$ by construction of $conf_1$ and $conf_2$, and hence $\|view_{conf_1, k}(\mathsf{H}_L), view_{conf_2, k}(\mathsf{H}_L)\|_{\mathsf{c}} \notin NEGL$ for every computational distance $\|\cdot, \cdot\|_{\mathsf{c}}$. This yields $\mathcal{Q}_{\mathcal{P}}^{\|\cdot, \cdot\|_{\mathsf{c}}}{}_{(\hat{M}, S, \Gamma)}(H, L) \geq \|view_{conf_1, k}(\mathsf{H}_L), view_{conf_2, k}(\mathsf{H}_L)\|_{\mathsf{c}} \notin NEGL$ and hence the desired contradiction.  ∎

The key property proved about the notions of perfect and computation probabilistic non-interference in [1] is that they are preserved under reactive simulatability, i.e., if $(\hat{M}_2, S)$ fulfills a non-interference requirement and $(\hat{M}_1, S)$ is at least as secure as $(\hat{M}_2, S)$, then $(\hat{M}_1, S)$ also fulfills this non-interference requirement. Using the results of Theorem 2 and Theorem 1, we can give a very short alternative proof.

**Corollary 1.** *(Preservation of Perfect/Computation Probabilistic Non-interference [1], Sketch)* Let structures $(\hat{M}_1, S)$, $(\hat{M}_2, S)$ be given such that $(\hat{M}_1, S) \geq^x_{\mathsf{sec}} (\hat{M}_2, S)$ for $x \in \{\mathsf{poly}, \mathsf{perf}\}$. Then $(\hat{M}_2, S) \models^x \mathcal{F}$ for a flow policy $\mathcal{F}$ implies $(\hat{M}_1, S) \models^x \mathcal{F}$.  □

*Proof.* Theorem 2 and $(\hat{M}_2, S) \models^{\mathsf{poly}} \mathcal{F}$ imply $\mathcal{Q}_{\mathcal{P}}^{\|\cdot, \cdot\|_{\mathsf{c}}}{}_{\hat{M}_2, S, \Gamma}(H, L) \in NEGL$ for all $H, L$ with $S_H \not\rightsquigarrow S_L$ and all computational distances $\|\cdot, \cdot\|_{\mathsf{c}}$. Theorem 1 implies $\mathcal{Q}_{\mathcal{P}}^{\|\cdot, \cdot\|_{\mathsf{c}}}{}_{\hat{M}_1, S, \Gamma}(H, L) \leq \mathcal{Q}_{\mathcal{P}}^{\|\cdot, \cdot\|_{\mathsf{c}}}{}_{\hat{M}_2, S, \Gamma}(H, L) + \epsilon(k)$ for some $\epsilon \in NEGL$. Hence $\mathcal{Q}_{\mathcal{P}}^{\|\cdot, \cdot\|_{\mathsf{c}}}{}_{\hat{M}_1, S, \Gamma}(H, L) \in NEGL$ because the class of negligible function is closed under addition. Theorem 2 then yields $(\hat{M}_1, S) \models^{\mathsf{poly}} \mathcal{F}$. The perfect case is proved by replacing $\mathcal{Q}_{\mathcal{P}}$ with $\mathcal{Q}$ and by considering arbitrary distances.  ∎

# 6   Conclusion

We have presented the first definitions for quantifying information flow within a reactive setting. The definitions comprise unconditional as well as complexity-theoretic aspects of security and are hence suited for reasoning about information flow even in the presence of cryptography. We have shown that our definitions are preserved under simulatability which constitutes the cryptographic notion of a secure implementation. This significantly simplifies to determine the information flow quantity for cryptographic system since simulatability helps to eliminate cryptography-related details such as error probabilities and computational restrictions; hence we can hope to exploit existing non-cryptographic techniques for this task. We have linked our definitions to existing non-interference definitions by showing that a zero or negligible quantity of information flow is equivalent to perfect and computational probabilistic non-interference. With our simulatability preservation theorem, this has in particular allowed for a short, alternative proof that non-interference properties are preserved under simulatability.

# References

1. M. Backes and B. Pfitzmann. Computational probabilistic non-interference. In *Proc. 7th European Symposium on Research in Computer Security (ESORICS)*, volume 2502 of *Lecture Notes in Computer Science*, pages 1–23. Springer, 2002.
2. M. Backes and B. Pfitzmann. Intransitive non-interference for cryptographic purposes. In *Proc. 24th IEEE Symposium on Security & Privacy*, pages 140–152, 2003.
3. M. Backes, B. Pfitzmann, and M. Waidner. Secure asynchronous reactive systems. IACR Cryptology ePrint Archive 2004/082, Mar. 2004.
4. D. Bell and L. LaPadula. Secure computer systems: Unified exposition and multics interpretation. Computer Science Technical Report ESD-TR-75-306, The Mitre Corporation, 1976.
5. D. Clark, S. Hunt, and P. Malacaria. Quantitative analysis of the leakage of confidential data. In *Proc. Quantitative Aspects of Programming Languages*, volume 59 of *Electronic Notes in Theoretical Computer Science*. Elsevier, 2002.
6. D. Denning. *Cryptography and Data Security.* Addison-Wesley, 1982.
7. D. E. Denning. A lattice model of secure information flow. *Communications of the ACM*, 19(5):236–243, 1976.
8. A. Di Pierro, C. Hankin, and H. Wiklicky. Approximate non-interference. In *Proc. 15th IEEE Computer Security Foundations Workshop (CSFW)*, pages 1–17, 2002.
9. R. Focardi and R. Gorrieri. The compositional security checker: A tool for the verification of information flow security properties. *IEEE Transactions on Software Engineering*, 23(9):550–571, 1997.
10. R. Focardi and F. Martinelli. A uniform approach to the definition of security properties. In *Proc. 8th Symposium on Formal Methods Europe (FME 1999)*, volume 1708 of *Lecture Notes in Computer Science*, pages 794–813. Springer, 1999.
11. J. A. Goguen and J. Meseguer. Security policies and security models. In *Proc. 3rd IEEE Symposium on Security & Privacy*, pages 11–20, 1982.
12. J. A. Goguen and J. Meseguer. Unwinding and inference control. In *Proc. 5th IEEE Symposium on Security & Privacy*, pages 75–86, 1984.
13. J. W. Gray III. Probabilistic interference. In *Proc. 11th IEEE Symposium on Security & Privacy*, pages 170–179, 1990.
14. J. W. Gray III. Toward a mathematical foundation for information flow security. *Journal of Computer Security*, 1(3):255–295, 1992.
15. C. A. R. Hoare. *Communicating Sequential Processes.* International Series in Computer Science, Prentice Hall, Hemel Hempstead, 1985.
16. M. H. Kang, I. S. Moskowitz, and D. C. Lee. A network version of the pump. In *Proc. 16th IEEE Symposium on Security & Privacy*, pages 144–154, 1995.

17. B. W. Lampson. A note on the confinement problem. *Communications of the ACM*, 16(10):613–615, 1973.
18. P. Laud. Semantics and program analysis of computationally secure information flow. In *Proc. 10th European Symposium on Programming (ESOP)*, pages 77–91, 2001.
19. P. Laud. Symmetric encryption in automatic analyses for confidentiality against active adversaries. In *Proc. 25th IEEE Symposium on Security & Privacy*, pages 71–85, 2004.
20. G. Lowe. Quantifying information flow. In *Proc. 15th IEEE Computer Security Foundations Workshop (CSFW)*, pages 18–31, 2002.
21. N. Lynch. *Distributed Algorithms*. Morgan Kaufmann Publishers, San Francisco, 1996.
22. H. Mantel. Unwinding possibilistic security properties. In *Proc. 6th European Symposium on Research in Computer Security (ESORICS)*, volume 1895 of *Lecture Notes in Computer Science*, pages 238–254. Springer, 2000.
23. H. Mantel and A. Sabelfeld. A generic approach to the security of multi-threaded programs. In *Proc. 14th IEEE Computer Security Foundations Workshop (CSFW)*, pages 200–214, 2001.
24. D. McCullough. Specifications for multi-level security and a hook-up property. In *Proc. 8th IEEE Symposium on Security & Privacy*, pages 161–166, 1987.
25. J. McLean. Security models and information flow. In *Proc. 11th IEEE Symposium on Security & Privacy*, pages 180–187, 1990.
26. J. McLean. Security models. Chapter in *Encyclopedia of Software Engineering*, 1994.
27. J. K. Millen. Covert channel capacity. In *Proc. 8th IEEE Symposium on Security & Privacy*, pages 60–66, 1987.
28. A. Myers and B. Liskov. A decentralized model for information flow control. In *Proc. ACM Symposium on Operating System Principles*, pages 129–142, 1997.
29. B. Pfitzmann and M. Waidner. A model for asynchronous reactive systems and its application to secure message transmission. In *Proc. 22nd IEEE Symposium on Security & Privacy*, pages 184–200, 2001. Extended version of the model (with Michael Backes) IACR Cryptology ePrint Archive 2004/082, http://eprint.iacr.org/.
30. R. G. Riccardo Focardi, Anna Ghelli. Using non-interference for the analysis of security protocols. In *Proc. DIMACS Workshop on Design and Formal Verification of Security Protocols*, 1997.
31. A. Sabelfeld and D. Sands. A per model of secure information flow in sequential programs. In *Proc. European Symposium on Programming (ESOP)*, pages 40–58. Springer, 1999.
32. A. Sabelfeld and D. Sands. Probabilistic noninterference for multi-threaded programs. In *Proc. 13th IEEE Computer Security Foundations Workshop (CSFW)*, pages 200–214, 2000.
33. D. Sutherland. A model of information. In *Proc. 9th National Computer Security Conference*, pages 175–183, 1986.
34. D. Volpano. Secure introduction of one-way functions. In *Proc. 13th IEEE Computer Security Foundations Workshop (CSFW)*, pages 246–254, 2000.
35. D. Volpano and G. Smith. Probabilistic noninterference in a concurrent language. In *Proc. 11th IEEE Computer Security Foundations Workshop (CSFW)*, pages 34–43, 1998.
36. D. Volpano, G. Smith, and C. Irvine. A sound type system for secure flow analysis. *Journal of Computer Security*, 4(3):167–187, 1996.

37. J. T. Wittbold and D. M. Johnson. Information flow in nondeterministic systems. In *Proc. 11th IEEE Symposium on Security & Privacy*, pages 144–161, 1990.
38. A. C. Yao. Theory and applications of trapdoor functions. In *Proc. 23rd IEEE Symposium on Foundations of Computer Science (FOCS)*, pages 80–91, 1982.
39. S. Zdancewic and A. C. Myers. Secure information flow and CPS. In *Proc. 10th European Symposium on Programming (ESOP)*, volume 2028 of *Lecture Notes in Computer Science*, pages 46–61. Springer, 2001.

# A    The Model of Reactive Simulatability

In this section we give a more comprehensive review of the model of reactive simulatability [29,3] for the sake of completeness.

## A.1    General System Model

Communication between different machines is done via ports. Inspired by the CSP-notation [15], we write input and output ports as p? and p!, respectively. The input and output ports in a port set $P$ are written in$(P)$ and out$(P)$, respectively. Connections are defined by naming convention: port p! sends messages to p?. To achieve asynchronous timing, a message is not immediately delivered to its recipient, but is first stored in a special machine $\tilde{p}$ called a buffer, where it waits to be scheduled. This can be done by the machine with the unique clock-out port p$^{\triangleleft}$!. To schedule the $i$-th message of buffer $\tilde{p}$, it outputs $i$ at p$^{\triangleleft}$!, see Figure 2. The buffer then delivers the $i$-th message and removes it from its internal list. Most buffers are scheduled either by a specific master scheduler or by the adversary, i.e., one of those has the clock-out port. Ports p! and p?, in contrast to the other four port types occurring at the buffers, are called *simple*, and a *simple machine* has only simple ports and clock-out ports.

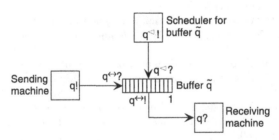

**Fig. 2.** Naming of ports around a buffer. Later one can often abstract from the buffer and simply regard q! and q? as asynchronously connected.

The precise definition of machines is a variant of probabilistic state-transition machines, similar to probabilistic I/O automata as sketched by Lynch [21]. If a machine is switched, it reads an input tuple at its input ports and performs its transition function. This yields a new state and an output tuple. A probabilistic transition function actually describes a finite distribution over the pairs of a new state and an output tuple. Furthermore, each machine has bounds on the length of considered inputs. This allows time bounds independent of the environment.

**Definition 7.** *(Machines)* A *machine* (for an alphabet $\Sigma$) is a tuple

$$\mathsf{M} = (name_\mathsf{M}, Ports_\mathsf{M}, States_\mathsf{M}, \delta_\mathsf{M}, l_\mathsf{M}, Ini_\mathsf{M}, Fin_\mathsf{M})$$

of a machine name $name_\mathsf{M} \in \Sigma^+$, a finite sequence $Ports_\mathsf{M}$ of ports, a set $States_\mathsf{M} \subseteq \Sigma^*$ of states, a probabilistic state-transition function $\delta_\mathsf{M}$, a length function $l_\mathsf{M} : States_\mathsf{M} \to (\mathbb{N} \cup \{\infty\})^{|\mathsf{in}(Ports_\mathsf{M})|}$, and sets $Ini_\mathsf{M}, Fin_\mathsf{M} \subseteq States_\mathsf{M}$ of initial and final states. Its input set is $\mathcal{I}_\mathsf{M} := (\Sigma^*)^{|\mathsf{in}(Ports_\mathsf{M})|}$; the $i$-th element of an input tuple denotes the input at the $i$-th in-port. Its output set is $\mathcal{O}_\mathsf{M} := (\Sigma^*)^{|\mathsf{out}(Ports_\mathsf{M})|}$. The empty word, $\epsilon$, denotes no in- or output at a port. $\delta_\mathsf{M}$ maps each pair $(s, I) \in States_\mathsf{M} \times \mathcal{I}_\mathsf{M}$ to a finite distribution over $States_\mathsf{M} \times \mathcal{O}_\mathsf{M}$.

If $s \in Fin_\mathsf{M}$ or $I = (\epsilon, \ldots, \epsilon)$, then $\delta_\mathsf{M}(s, I) = (s, (\epsilon, \ldots, \epsilon))$ deterministically. Inputs are ignored beyond the length bounds, i.e., $\delta_\mathsf{M}(s, I) = \delta_\mathsf{M}(s, I\lceil_{l_\mathsf{M}(s)})$ for all $I \in \mathcal{I}_\mathsf{M}$, where $(I\lceil_{l_\mathsf{M}(s)})_i := I_i\lceil_{l_\mathsf{M}(s)_i}$ for all $i$.      ◇

In the text, we often write "M" for $name_\mathsf{M}$ as well. In the following, the initial states of all machines are a security parameter $k \in \mathbb{N}$ in unary representation. In order to define the notion of polynomial runtime for these machines, Turing machine realizations of them are defined so that the runtime can be measured in the size of the initial worktape content (typically a security parameter in unary representation).

A *collection* $\hat{C}$ of machines is a finite set of machines with pairwise different machine names and disjoint sets of ports. All machines start with the same security parameter $k$. Let furthermore $\mathsf{ports}(\hat{C})$ denote the set of all ports of all machines in $\hat{C}$. The *completion* $[\hat{C}]$ of a collection $\hat{C}$ consists of all machines of $\hat{C}$ and the buffers needed for all the ports in $\hat{C}$. The *free* ports $\mathsf{free}(\hat{C})$ in a collection are those to which no other port in the collection connects. A collection $\hat{C}$ is *closed* if its completion $[\hat{C}]$ has no free ports except a special master clock-in port $\mathsf{clk}^\triangleleft$?. The machine with this port is the *master scheduler*, to which control returns as a default.

For a closed collection, a probability space of *runs* (sometimes called traces or executions) is defined. The machines switch sequentially, i.e., there is exactly one active machine M at any time, called the *current scheduler*. If this machine has clock-out ports, it can select the next message to be scheduled as explained above. If that message exists, it is delivered by the buffer and the recipient is the next active machine. If M attempts to schedule multiple messages, only one is taken. If it schedules none or the message does not exist, the master scheduler is activated. Formally, runs are sequences of *steps* defined as follows (where the state-transition function of buffers is as explained above).

**Definition 8.** *(Runs)* Given a closed collection $\hat{C}$ with master scheduler X and a security parameter $k$, the probability space of *runs* is defined inductively by the following algorithm. It has variables $r$ for the run under construction and

$M_{CS}$ for the current scheduler, and treats each port as a variable over $\Sigma^*$. Here, $r$ is an initially empty list, $M_{CS}$ a machine name initialized with $X$, and all port variables are initially $\epsilon$ except for $clk^\lhd? := 1$. Probabilistic choices only occur in Phase 1.

1. *Switch current scheduler:* Switch machine $M_{CS}$, i.e., set $(s', O) \leftarrow \delta_{M_{CS}}(s, I)$ for its current state $s$ and in-port values $I$. Then assign $\epsilon$ to all in-ports of $M_{CS}$.
2. *Termination:* If $X$ is in a final state, the run stops.
3. *Buffer new messages:* For each simple out-port q! of $M_{CS}$, switch buffer $\widetilde{q}$ with input $q^{\leftrightarrow}? := q!$, cf. Figure 2. Then assign $\epsilon$ to all these ports q! and $q^{\leftrightarrow}?$.
4. *Clean up scheduling:* If at least one clock out-port of $M_{CS}$ has a value $\neq \epsilon$, let $q^\lhd!$ denote the first such port and assign $\epsilon$ to the others. Otherwise let $clk^\lhd? := 1$ and $M_{CS} := X$ and go back to Phase 1.
5. *Deliver scheduled message:* Switch buffer $\widetilde{q}$ with input $q^\lhd? := q^\lhd!$ (see Figure 2), set $q? := q^{\leftrightarrow}!$ and then assign $\epsilon$ to all ports of $\widetilde{q}$ and to $q^\lhd!$. Let $M_{CS} := M'$ for the unique machine $M'$ with $q? \in \text{ports}(M')$. Go back to Phase 1.

Whenever a machine (this may be a buffer) with name $name_M$ is switched from $(s, I)$ to $(s', O)$, we append a *step* $(name_M, s, I', s', O)$ to the run $r$ for $I' := I\lceil_{I_M(s)}$, except if $s$ is final or $I' = (\epsilon, \dots, \epsilon)$. This gives a family of random variables

$$run_{\hat{C}} = (run_{\hat{C},k})_{k \in \mathbb{N}}.$$

For a number $l \in \mathbb{N}$, the *l-step prefix* of a run $r$ is the list of the first $l$ steps. $\diamond$

Next we define what a machine sees in a run and what events happen at a set of ports, and the probabilities of such views and events.

**Definition 9.** *(Views and Restrictions to Ports)* The *view* of a set of machines $\hat{M}$ in a run $r$ is the subsequence of all steps $(name_M, s, I, s', O)$ where $name_M$ is the name of a machine $M \in \hat{M}$. The *restriction* $r\lceil_S$ of a run to a set $S$ of ports is a sequence derived as follows: First only retain the inputs and outputs, $(I, O)$, from each step, and further restrict $I$ and $O$ to the ports in $S$. Then delete pairs where both $I$ and $O$ have become empty.

The corresponding families of random variables (in the probability space over the runs) are denoted by

$$view_{\hat{C}}(\hat{M}) = (view_{\hat{C},k}(\hat{M}))_{k \in \mathbb{N}} \text{ and}$$

$$run_{\hat{C}}\lceil_S = (run_{\hat{C},k}\lceil_S)_{k \in \mathbb{N}}.$$

With an additional index $l$, we denote the $l(k)$-step prefixes of the views and restrictions. $\diamond$

For a one-element set $\hat{M} = \{H\}$ we write $view_{\hat{C}}(H)$ for $view_{\hat{C}}(\{H\})$.

## A.2  Security-Specific System Model

For security purposes, we have to define how adversaries and honest users connect to specified machines of a collection. First, an adversary may take over parts of the initially intended machines. These machines are then absorbed into the adversary, and the remaining machines form a *structure*. Formally, a structure is a collection of machines in which one additionally distinguishes which free ports honest users can connect to and expect some reasonable service (e.g., message transport in a cryptographic firewall), and which ports are only used by adversaries. The former are the *service ports* in the following definition. Valid honest users should neither try to connect to the remaining free ports of a structure, nor, for unique naming, have ports that already occur inside the structure. This is expressed by *forbidden ports*. The ports connecting to a given port set $P$ are expressed by the complement notation $P^c$, e.g., $\mathsf{q}!^c = \mathsf{q}^{\leftrightarrow}?, \mathsf{q}^{\triangleleft}!^c = \mathsf{q}^{\triangleleft}?, \mathsf{q}^{\leftrightarrow}!^c = \mathsf{q}?$ in Figure 2, and vice versa.

**Definition 10.** *(Structures)* A *structure* is a pair $(\hat{M}, S)$ where $\hat{M}$ is a collection of simple machines called *correct machines*, and $S \subseteq \mathsf{free}([\hat{M}])$ is called *service ports*. If $\hat{M}$ is clear from the context, let $\bar{S} := \mathsf{free}([\hat{M}]) \setminus S$. We call $\mathsf{forb}(\hat{M}, S) := \mathsf{ports}(\hat{M}) \cup \bar{S}^c$ the *forbidden ports*. ◇

A structure is completed to a (multi-party) *configuration* by a set of machines $U$ modeling the honest users, and by a machine A modeling the adversary. As explained above, the machines in $U$ do not have certain ports. A connects to the remaining free ports of the structure.

**Definition 11.** *((Multi-party) Configurations)*

a) A (multi-party) *configuration* of a structure $(\hat{M}, S)$ is a tuple $conf = (\hat{M}, S, U, A)$, where $U$ is a set of simple machines without forbidden ports, i.e., $\mathsf{ports}(U) \cap \mathsf{forb}(\hat{M}, S) = \emptyset$, and $\hat{C} := \hat{M} \cup U \cup \{A\}$ is a closed collection. For simplicity, we often write $run_{conf}$ and $view_{conf}(\hat{M})$ instead of $run_{\hat{C}}$ and $view_{\hat{C}}(\hat{M})$

b) The set of (multi-party) configurations is written $\mathsf{Conf}(\hat{M}, S)$. The subset of configurations with polynomial-time users and a polynomial-time adversary is called $\mathsf{Conf}_{\mathsf{poly}}(\hat{M}, S)$. The index $_{\mathsf{poly}}$ is omitted if it is clear from the context. ◇

Partition and non-interference configurations can now be defined by considering only those users that have a specific set of ports so that they connect exactly to the ports of the structure prescribed by the considered partition. We omit the formal yet lengthy definitions and refer to [1].

## A.3  Definition of Non-interference in the Model

We finally give a precise definition of perfect and computational probabilistic non-interference in the reactive model, i.e., the formal semantics of the

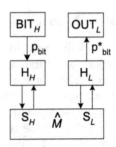

**Fig. 3.** Sketch of the non-interference definition: $H_L$ attempts to guess a bit that $H_H$ is attempting to transfer

$\not\rightsquigarrow$ relation. Usually, expressing this semantics is the most difficult part of an information-flow definition. Given our underlying model, it is somewhat easier because we already have definitions of runs, views, and indistinguishability. Based on these definitions, we can define the probability that the low user correctly guesses the bit that the high user attempts to transmit.

**Definition 12.** *(Guessing Probability)* For a non-interference configuration $conf \in \mathsf{Conf}(\hat{M}, S, \Gamma)$ for $S_H, S_L \in \Gamma$ of a structure $(\hat{M}, S)$, the *guessing probability* $P_{\mathsf{guess}, conf}$ is defined as

$$P_{\mathsf{guess}, conf} := P(b = b^* \mid r \leftarrow run_{conf,k}; b := r\lceil_{\mathsf{p_{bit}}!}; b^* := r\lceil_{\mathsf{p^*_{bit}}?}),$$

with the ports $\mathsf{p_{bit}}!$ and $\mathsf{p^*_{bit}}?$ defined as in Figure 3. This is a function of the security parameter $k$. ◇

Now we are ready to give the non-interference definition, i.e., the definition of the semantics of a flow policy for a reactive setting.

**Definition 13.** *(Non-Interference)* Let a structure $(\hat{M}, S) \in Sys$, and a flow policy $\mathcal{F} = (\Gamma, \rightsquigarrow)$, $\Gamma = \{S_i \mid i \in \mathcal{I}\}$ be given. We say that $(\hat{M}, S)$ *fulfills* the non-interference requirement defined by the flow policy $\mathcal{F}$

a) **perfectly**, written $(\hat{M}, S) \models^{\mathsf{perf}} \mathcal{F}$, iff for every $H, L$ with $S_H \not\rightsquigarrow S_L$ and every non-interference configuration $conf \in \mathsf{Conf}(\hat{M}, S, \Gamma)$ for $S_H$ and $S_L$, we have

$$P_{\mathsf{guess}, conf} \leq \frac{1}{2}.$$

c) **computationally**, written $(\hat{M}, S) \models^{\mathsf{poly}} \mathcal{F}$, iff for every $H, L$ with $S_H \not\rightsquigarrow S_L$ and every polynomial-time non-interference configuration $conf \in \mathsf{Conf}_{\mathsf{poly}}(\hat{M}, S, \Gamma)$ for $S_H$ and $S_L$ there exists a function $\epsilon \in NEGL$ such that

$$P_{\mathsf{guess}, conf} \leq \frac{1}{2} + \epsilon(k).$$

◇

# Enforcing Non-safety Security Policies
# with Program Monitors

Jay Ligatti[1], Lujo Bauer[2], and David Walker[1]

[1] Department of Computer Science, Princeton University
[2] CyLab, Carnegie Mellon University

**Abstract.** We consider the enforcement powers of *program monitors*, which intercept security-sensitive actions of a target application at run time and take remedial steps whenever the target attempts to execute a potentially dangerous action. A common belief in the security community is that program monitors, regardless of the remedial steps available to them when detecting violations, can only enforce safety properties. We formally analyze the properties enforceable by various program monitors and find that although this belief is correct when considering monitors with simple remedial options, it is incorrect for more powerful monitors that can be modeled by *edit automata*. We define an interesting set of properties called *infinite renewal* properties and demonstrate how, when given any reasonable infinite renewal property, to construct an edit automaton that provably enforces that property. We analyze the set of infinite renewal properties and show that it includes every safety property, some liveness properties, and some properties that are neither safety nor liveness.

## 1 Introduction

A ubiquitous technique for enforcing software security is to dynamically monitor the behavior of programs and take remedial action when the programs behave in a way that violates a security policy. Firewalls, virtual machines, and operating systems all act as *program monitors* to enforce security policies in this way. We can even think of any application containing security code that dynamically checks input values, queries network configurations, raises exceptions, warns the user of potential consequences of opening a file, etc., as containing a program monitor *inlined* into the application.

Because program monitors, which react to the potential security violations of *target programs*, enjoy such ubiquity, it is important to understand their capabilities as policy enforcers. Such understanding is essential for developing systems that support program monitoring and for developing sound languages for specifying the security policies that these systems can enforce. In addition, well-defined boundaries on the enforcement powers of security mechanisms allow security architects to determine exactly when certain mechanisms are needed and save the architects from attempting to enforce policies with insufficiently strong mechanisms.

S. De Capitani di Vimercati et al. (Eds.): ESORICS 2005, LNCS 3679, pp. 355–373, 2005.

Schneider defined the first formal models of program monitors and discovered one particularly useful boundary on their power [24]. He defined a class of monitors that respond to potential security violations by halting the target application, and he showed that these monitors can only enforce *safety* properties—security policies that specify that "nothing bad ever happens" in a valid run of the target [18]. When a monitor in this class detects a potential security violation (i.e., "something bad"), it must halt the target.

Although Schneider's result applies only to a particular class of program monitors, other research on formalizing monitors has likewise developed only models that enforce just safety properties. In this paper, we advance the theoretical understanding of practical program monitors by proving that certain types of monitors can enforce non-safety properties. These monitors are modeled by edit automata, which have the power to insert actions on behalf of and suppress actions attempted by the target application. We prove an interesting lower bound on the properties enforceable by such monitors: a lower bound that encompasses strictly more than safety properties.

## 1.1 Related Work

A rich variety of security monitoring systems has been implemented [14,7,9,11,17,4,8,5]. In general, these systems allow arbitrary code to be executed in response to potential security violations, so they cannot be modeled as monitors that simply halt upon detecting a violation. In most cases, the languages provided by these systems for specifying policies can be considered domain-specific aspect-oriented programming languages [15].

Theoretical efforts to describe security monitoring have lagged behind the implementation work, making it difficult to know exactly which sorts of security policies to expect the implemented systems to be able to enforce. After Schneider made substantial progress by showing that safety properties are an upper bound on the set of policies enforceable by simple monitors [24], Viswanathan, Kim, and others tightened this bound by placing explicit computability constraints on the safety properties being enforced [25,16]. Viswanathan also demonstrated that these computable safety properties are equivalent to coRE properties [25]. Fong then formally showed that placing limits on a monitor's state space induces limits on the properties enforceable by the monitor [12]. Recently, Hamlen, Schneider, and Morrisett compared the enforcement power of static analysis, monitoring, and program rewriting [13]. They showed that the set of statically enforceable properties equals the set of recursively decidable properties of programs, that monitors with access to source-program text can enforce strictly more properties than can be enforced through static analysis, and that program rewriters do not correspond to any complexity class in the arithmetic hierarchy.

In earlier theoretical work, we took a first step toward understanding the enforcement power of monitors that have greater abilities than simply to halt the target when detecting a potential security violation [20]. We introduced *edit automata*, a new model that captures the ability of program monitors to insert actions on behalf of the target and to suppress potentially dangerous actions.

Edit automata are semantically similar to deterministic I/O automata [22] but have very different correctness requirements. The primary contribution of our earlier work was to set up a framework for reasoning about program monitors by providing a formal definition of what it even means for a monitor to enforce a property. Although we also proved the enforcement boundaries of several types of monitors, we did so in a model that assumed that all target programs eventually terminate. Hence, from a practical perspective, our model did not accurately capture the capabilities of real systems. From a theoretical perspective, modeling only terminating targets made it impossible to compare the properties enforceable by edit automata to well-established sets of properties such as safety and liveness properties.

## 1.2   Contributions

This paper presents the nontrivial generalization of earlier work on edit automata [20] to potentially nonterminating targets. This generalization allows us to reason about the true enforcement powers of an interesting and realistic class of program monitors, and makes it possible to formally and precisely compare this class to previously studied classes.

More specifically, we extend previous work in the following ways.

- We refine and introduce formal definitions needed to understand exactly what it means for program monitors to enforce policies on potentially nonterminating target applications (Section 2). A new notion of enforcement (called *effective_ enforcement*) enables the derivation of elegant lower bounds on the sets of policies monitors can enforce.
- We show why it is commonly believed that program monitors enforce only computable safety properties (Section 3). We show this by revisiting and extending earlier theorems that describe the enforcement powers of simple monitors. The earlier theorems are extended by considering nonterminating targets and by proving that exactly one computable safety property—that which considers everything a security violation—cannot be enforced by program monitors.
- We define an interesting set of properties called *infinite renewal* properties and demonstrate how, when given any reasonable infinite renewal property, to construct an edit automaton that provably enforces that property (Section 4).
- We prove that program monitors modeled by edit automata can enforce strictly more than safety properties. We demonstrate this by analyzing the set of infinite renewal properties and showing that it includes every safety property, some liveness properties, and some properties that are neither safety nor liveness (Section 5).

## 2   Technical Apparatus

This section provides the formal framework necessary to reason precisely about the scope of policies program monitors can enforce.

## 2.1  Notation

We specify a system at a high level of abstraction as a nonempty, possibly countably infinite set of *program actions* $\mathcal{A}$ (also referred to as program events). An *execution* is simply a finite or infinite sequence of actions. The set of all finite executions on a system with action set $\mathcal{A}$ is notated as $\mathcal{A}^\star$. Similarly, the set of infinite executions is $\mathcal{A}^\omega$, and the set of all executions (finite and infinite) is $\mathcal{A}^\infty$. We let the metavariable $a$ range over actions, $\sigma$ and $\tau$ over executions, and $\Sigma$ over sets of executions (i.e., subsets of $\mathcal{A}^\infty$).

The symbol $\cdot$ denotes the empty sequence, that is, an execution with no actions. We use the notation $\tau; \sigma$ to denote the concatenation of two finite sequences. When $\tau$ is a (finite) prefix of (possibly infinite) $\sigma$, we write $\tau \preceq \sigma$ or, equivalently, $\sigma \succeq \tau$. If $\sigma$ has been previously quantified, we often use $\forall \tau \preceq \sigma$ as an abbreviation for $\forall \tau \in \mathcal{A}^\star : \tau \preceq \sigma$; similarly, if $\tau$ has already been quantified, we abbreviate $\forall \sigma \in \mathcal{A}^\infty : \sigma \succeq \tau$ simply as $\forall \sigma \succeq \tau$.

## 2.2  Policies and Properties

A *security policy* is a predicate $P$ on sets of executions; a set of executions $\Sigma \subseteq \mathcal{A}^\infty$ satisfies a policy $P$ if and only if $P(\Sigma)$. For example, a set of executions satisfies a nontermination policy if and only if every execution in the set is an infinite sequence of actions. A key-uniformity policy might be satisfied only by sets of executions such that the cryptographic keys used in all the executions form a uniform distribution over the universe of key values.

Following Schneider [24], we distinguish between *properties* and more general policies as follows. A security policy $P$ is a *property* if and only if there exists a *characteristic predicate* $\hat{P}$ over $\mathcal{A}^\infty$ such that for all $\Sigma \subseteq \mathcal{A}^\infty$, the following is true.

$$P(\Sigma) \iff \forall \sigma \in \Sigma : \hat{P}(\sigma) \qquad \text{(Property)}$$

Hence, a property is defined exclusively in terms of individual executions and may not specify a relationship between different executions of the program. The nontermination policy mentioned above is therefore a property, while the key-uniformity policy is not. The distinction between properties and policies is an important one to make when reasoning about program monitors because a monitor sees just individual executions and can thus enforce only security properties rather than more general policies.

There is a one-to-one correspondence between a property $P$ and its characteristic predicate $\hat{P}$, so we use the notation $\hat{P}$ unambiguously to refer both to a characteristic predicate and the property it induces. When $\hat{P}(\sigma)$, we say that $\sigma$ *satisfies* or *obeys* the property, or that $\sigma$ is *valid* or *legal*. Likewise, when $\neg\hat{P}(\tau)$, we say that $\tau$ *violates* or *disobeys* the property, or that $\tau$ is *invalid* or *illegal*.

Properties that specify that "nothing bad ever happens" are called *safety properties* [18,3]. No finite prefix of a valid execution can violate a safety property; stated equivalently: once some finite execution violates the property, all extensions of that execution violate the property. Formally, $\hat{P}$ is a safety property on a system with action set $\mathcal{A}$ if and only if the following is true.[1]

$$\forall \sigma \in \mathcal{A}^\infty : (\neg \hat{P}(\sigma) \Rightarrow \exists \sigma' \preceq \sigma : \forall \tau \succeq \sigma' : \neg \hat{P}(\tau)) \qquad \text{(SAFETY)}$$

Many interesting security policies, such as access-control policies, are safety properties, since security violations cannot be "undone" by extending a violating execution.

Dually to safety properties, *liveness properties* [3] state that nothing exceptionally bad can happen in any finite amount of time. Any finite sequence of actions can always be extended so that it satisfies the property. Formally, $\hat{P}$ is a liveness property on a system with action set $\mathcal{A}$ if and only if the following is true.

$$\forall \sigma \in \mathcal{A}^\star : \exists \tau \succeq \sigma : \hat{P}(\tau) \qquad \text{(LIVENESS)}$$

The nontermination policy is a liveness property because any finite execution can be made to satisfy the policy simply by extending it to an infinite execution.

General properties may allow executions to alternate freely between satisfying and violating the property. Such properties are neither safety nor liveness but instead a combination of a single safety and a single liveness property [2]. We show in Section 4 that edit automata effectively enforce an interesting new sort of property that is neither safety nor liveness.

## 2.3   Security Automata

Program monitors operate by *transforming* execution sequences of an untrusted target application at run time to ensure that all observable executions satisfy some property [20]. We model a program monitor formally by a *security automaton* $S$, which is a deterministic finite or countably infinite state machine $(Q, q_0, \delta)$ that is defined with respect to some system with action set $\mathcal{A}$. The set $Q$ specifies the possible automaton states, and $q_0$ is the initial state. Different automata have slightly different sorts of transition functions ($\delta$), which accounts for the variations in their expressive power. The exact specification of a transition function $\delta$ is part of the definition of each kind of security automaton; we only require that $\delta$ be complete, deterministic, and Turing Machine computable. We limit our analysis in this work to automata whose transition functions take the current state and input action (the next action the target wants to execute) and return a new state and at most one action to output (make observable). The current input action may or may not be consumed while making a transition.

We specify the execution of each different kind of security automaton $S$ using a labeled operational semantics. The basic single-step judgment has the

---

[1] Alpern and Schneider [3] model executions as infinite-length sequences of states, where terminating executions contain a final state, infinitely repeated. We can map an execution in their model to one in ours simply by sequencing the events that induce the state transitions (no event induces a repeated final state). With this mapping, it is easy to verify that our definitions of safety and liveness are equivalent to those of Alpern and Schneider.

form $(q, \sigma) \xrightarrow{\tau}_S (q', \sigma')$ where $q$ denotes the current state of the automaton, $\sigma$ denotes the sequence of actions that the target program wants to execute, $q'$ and $\sigma'$ denote the state and action sequence after the automaton takes a single step, and $\tau$ denotes the sequence of at most one action output by the automaton in this step. The input sequence, $\sigma$, is not observable to the outside world whereas the output, $\tau$, is observable.

We generalize the single-step judgment to a multi-step judgment using standard rules of reflexivity and transitivity.

**Definition 1 (Multi-step).** *The multi-step relation* $(\sigma, q) \xRightarrow{\tau}_S (\sigma', q')$ *is inductively defined as follows (where all metavariables are universally quantified).*

1. $(q, \sigma) \xRightarrow{\cdot}_S (q, \sigma)$
2. *If* $(q, \sigma) \xrightarrow{\tau_1}_S (q'', \sigma'')$ *and* $(q'', \sigma'') \xRightarrow{\tau_2}_S (q', \sigma')$ *then* $(q, \sigma) \xRightarrow{\tau_1; \tau_2}_S (q', \sigma')$

In addition, we extend previous work [20] by defining what it means for a program monitor to *transform* a possibly infinite-length input execution into a possibly infinite-length output execution. This definition is essential for understanding the behavior of monitors operating on potentially nonterminating targets.

**Definition 2 (Transforms).** *A security automaton* $S = (Q, q_0, \delta)$ *on a system with action set* $\mathcal{A}$ *transforms the input sequence* $\sigma \in \mathcal{A}^\infty$ *into the output sequence* $\tau \in \mathcal{A}^\infty$, *notated as* $(q_0, \sigma) \Downarrow_S \tau$, *if and only if the following two constraints are met.*

1. $\forall q' \in Q : \forall \sigma' \in \mathcal{A}^\infty : \forall \tau' \in \mathcal{A}^\star : ((q_0, \sigma) \xRightarrow{\tau'}_S (q', \sigma')) \Rightarrow \tau' \preceq \tau$
2. $\forall \tau' \preceq \tau : \exists q' \in Q : \exists \sigma' \in \mathcal{A}^\infty : (q_0, \sigma) \xRightarrow{\tau'}_S (q', \sigma')$

When $(q_0, \sigma) \Downarrow_S \tau$, the first constraint ensures that automaton $S$ on input $\sigma$ outputs *only* prefixes of $\tau$, while the second constraint ensures that $S$ outputs *every* prefix of $\tau$.

## 2.4   Property Enforcement

Several authors have noted the importance of monitors obeying two abstract principles, which we call *soundness* and *transparency* [19,13,8]. A mechanism that purports to enforce a property $\hat{P}$ is *sound* when it ensures that observable outputs always obey $\hat{P}$; it is *transparent* when it preserves the semantics of executions that already obey $\hat{P}$. We call a sound and transparent mechanism an *effective* enforcer. Because effective enforcers are transparent, they may transform valid input sequences only into semantically equivalent output sequences, for some system-specific definition of semantic equivalence. When two executions $\sigma, \tau \in \mathcal{A}^\infty$ are semantically equivalent, we write $\sigma \cong \tau$. We place no restrictions on a relation of semantic equivalence except that it actually be an equivalence relation (i.e., reflexive, symmetric, and transitive), and that properties should not be able to distinguish between semantically equivalent executions.

$$\forall \hat{P} : \forall \sigma, \tau \in \mathcal{A}^\infty : \sigma \cong \tau \Rightarrow (\hat{P}(\sigma) \iff \hat{P}(\tau)) \quad \text{(INDISTINGUISHABILITY)}$$

When acting on a system with semantic equivalence relation $\cong$, we will call an effective enforcer an *effective$_\cong$ enforcer*. The formal definition of effective$_\cong$ enforcement is given below. Together, the first and second constraints in the following definition imply soundness; the first and third constraints imply transparency.

**Definition 3 (Effective$_\cong$ Enforcement).** *An automaton $S$ with starting state $q_0$ effectively$_\cong$ enforces a property $\hat{P}$ on a system with action set $\mathcal{A}$ and semantic equivalence relation $\cong$ if and only if $\forall \sigma \in \mathcal{A}^\infty : \exists \tau \in \mathcal{A}^\infty :$*

1. $(q_0, \sigma) \Downarrow_S \tau$,
2. $\hat{P}(\tau)$, and
3. $\hat{P}(\sigma) \Rightarrow \sigma \cong \tau$

In some situations, the system-specific equivalence relation $\cong$ complicates our theorems and proofs with little benefit. We have found that we can sometimes gain more insight into the enforcement powers of program monitors by limiting our analysis to systems in which the equivalence relation ($\cong$) is just syntactic equality ($=$). We call effective$_\cong$ enforcers operating on such systems *effective$_=$ enforcers*. To obtain a formal notion of effective$_=$ enforcement, we first need to define the "syntactic equality" of executions. Intuitively, $\sigma = \tau$ for any finite or infinite sequences $\sigma$ and $\tau$ when every prefix of $\sigma$ is a prefix of $\tau$, and vice versa.

$$\forall \sigma, \tau \in \mathcal{A}^\infty : \sigma = \tau \iff (\forall \sigma' \preceq \sigma : \sigma' \preceq \tau \ \wedge \ \forall \tau' \preceq \tau : \tau' \preceq \sigma) \qquad \text{(EQUALITY)}$$

An effective$_=$ enforcer is simply an effective$_\cong$ enforcer where the system-specific equivalence relation ($\cong$) is the system-unspecific equality relation ($=$).

**Definition 4 (Effective$_=$ Enforcement).** *An automaton $S$ with starting state $q_0$ effectively$_=$ enforces a property $\hat{P}$ on a system with action set $\mathcal{A}$ if and only if $\forall \sigma \in \mathcal{A}^\infty : \exists \tau \in \mathcal{A}^\infty :$*

1. $(q_0, \sigma) \Downarrow_S \tau$,
2. $\hat{P}(\tau)$, and
3. $\hat{P}(\sigma) \Rightarrow \sigma = \tau$

Because any two executions that are syntactically equal must be semantically equivalent, any property effectively$_=$ enforceable by some security automaton is also effectively$_\cong$ enforceable by that same automaton. Hence, an analysis of the set of properties effectively$_=$ enforceable by a particular kind of automaton is conservative; the set of properties effectively$_\cong$ enforceable by that same sort of automaton must be a superset of the effectively$_=$ enforceable properties.

Past research has considered alternative definitions of enforcement [20]. *Conservative* enforcement allows monitors to disobey the transparency requirement, while *precise* enforcement forces effective monitors to obey an additional timing constraint (monitors must accept actions in lockstep with their production by the target). Because these definitions do not directly match the intuitive soundness and transparency requirements of program monitors, we do not study them in this paper.

# 3    Truncation Automata

This section demonstrates why it is often believed that program monitors enforce only safety properties: this belief is provably correct when considering a common but very limited type of monitor that we model by *truncation automata*. A truncation automaton has only two options when it intercepts an action from the target program: it may accept the action and make it observable, or it may halt (i.e., truncate the action sequence of) the target program altogether. This model is the focus of most of the theoretical work on program monitoring [24,25,16]. Truncation-based monitors have been used successfully to enforce a rich set of interesting safety policies including access control [11], stack inspection [10,1], software fault isolation [26,9], Chinese Wall [6,8,12], and one-out-of-$k$ authorization [12] policies.[2]

Truncation automata have been widely studied, but revisiting them here serves several purposes. It allows us to extend to potentially nonterminating targets previous proofs of their capabilities as effective enforcers [20], to uncover the single computable safety property unenforceable by any sound program monitor, and to provide a precise comparison between the enforcement powers of truncation and edit automata (defined in Section 4).

## 3.1    Definition

A truncation automaton $T$ is a finite or countably infinite state machine $(Q, q_0, \delta)$ that is defined with respect to some system with action set $\mathcal{A}$. As usual, $Q$ specifies the possible automaton states, and $q_0$ is the initial state. The complete function $\delta : Q \times \mathcal{A} \to Q \cup \{halt\}$ specifies the transition function for the automaton and indicates either that the automaton should accept the current input action and move to a new state (when the return value is a new state), or that the automaton should halt the target program (when the return value is *halt*). For the sake of determinacy, we require that $halt \notin Q$. The operational semantics of truncation automata are formally specified by the following rules.

$$\boxed{(q, \sigma) \stackrel{\tau}{\longrightarrow}_T (q', \sigma')}$$

$$(q, \sigma) \stackrel{a}{\longrightarrow}_T (q', \sigma') \hspace{3cm} \text{(T-Step)}$$

    if $\sigma = a; \sigma'$
    and $\delta(q, a) = q'$

$$(q, \sigma) \stackrel{\cdot}{\longrightarrow}_T (q, \cdot) \hspace{3cm} \text{(T-Stop)}$$

    if $\sigma = a; \sigma'$
    and $\delta(q, a) = halt$

As described in Section 2.3, we extend the single-step relation to a multi-step relation using standard reflexivity and transitivity rules.

---

[2] Although some of the cited work considers monitors with powers beyond truncation, it also specifically studies many policies that can be enforced by monitors that only have the power to truncate.

## 3.2   Enforceable Properties

Let us consider a lower bound on the effective$_\cong$ enforcement powers of truncation automata. Any property that is effectively$_=$ enforceable by a truncation automaton is also effectively$_\cong$ enforceable by that same automaton, so we can develop a lower bound on properties effectively$_\cong$ enforceable by examining which properties are effectively$_=$ enforceable.

When given as input some $\sigma \in \mathcal{A}^\infty$ such that $\hat{P}(\sigma)$, a truncation automaton that effectively$_=$ enforces $\hat{P}$ must output $\sigma$. However, the automaton must also truncate every invalid input sequence into a valid output. Any truncation of an invalid input prevents the automaton from accepting all the actions in a valid extension of that input. Therefore, truncation automata cannot effectively$_=$ enforce any property in which an invalid execution can be a prefix of a valid execution. This is exactly the definition of safety properties, so it is intuitively clear that truncation automata effectively$_=$ enforce only safety properties.

Past research has presented results equating the enforcement power of truncation automata with the set of computable safety properties [25,16,20]. We improve the precision of previous work by showing that there is exactly one computable safety property unenforceable by any sound security automaton: the unsatisfiable safety property, $\forall \sigma \in \mathcal{A}^\infty : \neg\hat{P}(\sigma)$. A monitor could never enforce such a property because there is no valid output sequence that could be produced in response to an invalid input sequence. To prevent this case and to ensure that truncation automata can behave correctly on targets that generate no actions, we require that the empty sequence satisfies any property we are interested in enforcing. We often use the term *reasonable* to describe computable properties $\hat{P}$ such that $\hat{P}(\cdot)$. Previous work simply assumed $\hat{P}(\cdot)$ for all $\hat{P}$ [20]; we now show this to be a necessary assumption. The following theorem states that truncation automata effectively$_=$ enforce exactly the set of reasonable safety properties.

**Theorem 1 (Effective$_=$ $T^\infty$-Enforcement).** *A property $\hat{P}$ on a system with action set $\mathcal{A}$ can be effectively$_=$ enforced by some truncation automaton $T$ if and only if the following constraints are met.*

1. $\forall \sigma \in \mathcal{A}^\infty : \neg\hat{P}(\sigma) \Rightarrow \exists \sigma' \preceq \sigma : \forall \tau \succeq \sigma' : \neg\hat{P}(\tau)$        (SAFETY)
2. $\hat{P}(\cdot)$
3. $\forall \sigma \in \mathcal{A}^\star : \hat{P}(\sigma)$ *is decidable*

*Proof.* Please see our companion technical report [21] for the proofs of all the theorems presented in this paper.

We next delineate the properties effectively$_\cong$ enforceable by truncation automata. As mentioned above, the set of properties truncation automata effectively$_=$ enforce provides a lower bound for the set of effectively$_\cong$ enforceable properties; a candidate upper bound is the set of properties $\hat{P}$ that satisfy the following extended safety constraint.

$$\forall \sigma \in \mathcal{A}^\infty : \neg\hat{P}(\sigma) \Rightarrow \exists \sigma' \preceq \sigma : \forall \tau \succeq \sigma' : (\neg\hat{P}(\tau) \vee \tau \cong \sigma') \qquad (\text{T-SAFETY})$$

This is an upper bound because a truncation automaton $T$ that effectively$_\cong$ enforces $\hat{P}$ must halt at some finite point (having output $\sigma'$) when its input ($\sigma$) violates $\hat{P}$; otherwise, $T$ would accept every action of the invalid input. When $T$ halts, all extensions ($\tau$) of its output must either violate $\hat{P}$ or be equivalent to its output; otherwise, there is a valid input sequence for which $T$ fails to output an equivalent sequence.

Actually, as the following theorem shows, this upper bound is almost tight. We simply have to add computability restrictions on the property to ensure that a truncation automaton can decide when to halt the target.

**Theorem 2 (Effective$_\cong$ $T^\infty$-Enforcement).** *A property $\hat{P}$ on a system with action set $\mathcal{A}$ can be effectively$_\cong$ enforced by some truncation automaton $T$ if and only if there exists a decidable predicate $D$ over $\mathcal{A}^\star$ such that the following constraints are met.*

1. $\forall \sigma \in \mathcal{A}^\infty : \neg\hat{P}(\sigma) \Rightarrow \exists \sigma' \preceq \sigma : D(\sigma')$
2. $\forall (\sigma'; a) \in \mathcal{A}^\star : D(\sigma'; a) \Rightarrow (\hat{P}(\sigma') \wedge \forall \tau \succeq (\sigma'; a) : \hat{P}(\tau) \Rightarrow \tau \cong \sigma')$
3. $\neg D(\cdot)$

On practical systems, it is likely uncommon that the property requiring enforcement and the system's relation of semantic equivalence are so broadly defined that some invalid execution has a prefix that not only can be extended to a valid execution, but that is also equivalent to *all* valid extensions of the prefix. We therefore consider the set of properties detailed in the theorem of Effective$_=$ $T^\infty$-Enforcement (i.e., reasonable safety properties) more indicative of the true enforcement power of truncation automata.

## 4   Edit Automata

We now consider the enforcement capabilities of a stronger sort of security automaton called the *edit automaton* [20]. We refine previous work by presenting a more concise formal definition of edit automata. More importantly, we analyze the enforcement powers of edit automata on possibly infinite sequences, which allows us to prove that edit automata can effectively$_=$ enforce an interesting, new class of properties that we call *infinite renewal* properties.

### 4.1   Definition

An *edit automaton* $E$ is a triple $(Q, q_0, \delta)$ defined with respect to some system with action set $\mathcal{A}$. As with truncation automata, $Q$ is the possibly countably infinite set of states, and $q_0$ is the initial state. In contrast to truncation automata, the complete transition function $\delta$ of an edit automaton has the form $\delta : Q \times \mathcal{A} \to Q \times (\mathcal{A} \cup \{\cdot\})$. The transition function specifies, when given a current state and input action, a new state to enter and either an action to *insert* into the output stream (without consuming the input action) or the empty sequence to indicate that the input action should be *suppressed* (i.e., consumed from the input without being made observable). We previously defined edit automata that could also perform the following transformations in a single step: insert a finite sequence of actions, accept the current input action, or halt the target [20]. However, all of these transformations can be expressed in terms of suppressing and inserting single actions. For example, an edit automaton can halt a target by suppressing all future actions of the target; an edit automaton accepts an action by inserting and then suppressing that action (first making the action observable and then consuming it from the input). Although in practice these transformations would each be performed in a single step, we have found the minimal operational semantics containing only the two rules shown below more amenable to formal reasoning. Explicitly including the additional rules in the model would not invalidate any of our results.

$$\boxed{(q, \sigma) \xrightarrow{\tau}_E (q', \sigma')}$$

$$(q, \sigma) \xrightarrow{a'}_E (q', \sigma) \qquad \text{(E-INS)}$$

if $\sigma = a; \sigma'$
and $\delta(q, a) = (q', a')$

$$(q, \sigma) \xrightarrow{\cdot}_E (q', \sigma') \qquad \text{(E-SUP)}$$

if $\sigma = a; \sigma'$
and $\delta(q, a) = (q', \cdot)$

As with truncation automata, we extend the single-step semantics of edit automata to a multi-step semantics with the rules for reflexivity and transitivity.

## 4.2    Enforceable Properties

Edit automata are powerful property enforcers because they can suppress a sequence of potentially illegal actions and later, if the sequence is determined to be legal, just re-insert it. Essentially, the monitor feigns to the target that its requests are being accepted, although none actually are, until the monitor can confirm that the sequence of feigned actions is valid. At that point, the monitor inserts all of the actions it previously feigned accepting. This is the same idea implemented by intentions files in database transactions [23]. Monitoring systems like virtual machines can also be used in this way, feigning execution of a sequence of the target's actions and only making the sequence observable when it is known to be valid.

As we did for truncation automata, we develop a lower bound on the set of properties that edit automata effectively$_\cong$ enforce by considering the properties they effectively$_=$ enforce. Using the above-described technique of suppressing invalid inputs until the monitor determines that the suppressed input obeys a property, edit automata can effectively$_=$ enforce any reasonable *infinite renewal* (or simply *renewal*) property. A renewal property is one in which every valid infinite-length sequence has infinitely many valid prefixes, and conversely, every invalid infinite-length sequence has only finitely many valid prefixes. For example, a property $\hat{P}$ may be satisfied only by executions that contain the action $a$.

This is a renewal property because valid infinite-length executions contain an infinite number of valid prefixes (in which $a$ appears) while invalid infinite-length executions contain only a finite number of valid prefixes (in fact, zero). This $\hat{P}$ is also a liveness property because any invalid finite execution can be made valid simply by appending the action $a$. Although edit automata cannot enforce this $\hat{P}$ because $\neg \hat{P}(\cdot)$, in Section 5.2 we will recast this example as a reasonable "eventually audits" policy and show several more detailed examples of renewal properties enforceable by edit automata.

We formally deem a property $\hat{P}$ an infinite renewal property on a system with action set $\mathcal{A}$ if and only if the following is true.

$$\forall \sigma \in \mathcal{A}^\omega : \hat{P}(\sigma) \iff \{\sigma' \preceq \sigma \mid \hat{P}(\sigma')\} \text{ is an infinite set} \qquad (\text{RENEWAL}_1)$$

It will often be easier to reason about renewal properties without relying on infinite set cardinality. We make use of the following equivalent definition in formal analyses.

$$\forall \sigma \in \mathcal{A}^\omega : \hat{P}(\sigma) \iff (\forall \sigma' \preceq \sigma : \exists \tau \preceq \sigma : \sigma' \preceq \tau \wedge \hat{P}(\tau)) \qquad (\text{RENEWAL}_2)$$

If we are given a reasonable renewal property $\hat{P}$, we can construct an edit automaton that effectively$_=$ enforces $\hat{P}$ using the technique of feigning acceptance (i.e., suppressing actions) until the automaton has seen some legal prefix of the input (at which point the suppressed actions can be made observable). This technique ensures that the automaton eventually outputs every valid prefix, and only valid prefixes, of any input execution. Because $\hat{P}$ is a renewal property, the automaton therefore outputs all prefixes, and only prefixes, of a valid input while outputting only the longest valid prefix of an invalid input. Hence, the automaton correctly effectively$_=$ enforces $\hat{P}$. The following theorem formally states this result.

**Theorem 3 (Lower Bound Effective$_=$ $E^\infty$-Enforcement).** *A property $\hat{P}$ on a system with action set $\mathcal{A}$ can be effectively$_=$ enforced by some edit automaton $E$ if the following constraints are met.*

1. $\forall \sigma \in \mathcal{A}^\omega : \hat{P}(\sigma) \iff (\forall \sigma' \preceq \sigma : \exists \tau \preceq \sigma : \sigma' \preceq \tau \wedge \hat{P}(\tau)) \qquad (\text{RENEWAL}_2)$
2. $\hat{P}(\cdot)$
3. $\forall \sigma \in \mathcal{A}^\star : \hat{P}(\sigma)$ *is decidable*

It would be reasonable to expect that the set of renewal properties also represents an upper bound on the properties effectively$_=$ enforceable by edit automata. After all, an effective$_=$ automaton cannot output an infinite number of valid prefixes of an invalid infinite-length input $\sigma$ without outputting $\sigma$ itself. In addition, on a valid infinite-length input $\tau$, an effective$_=$ automaton must output infinitely many prefixes of $\tau$, and whenever it finishes processing an input action, its output must be a *valid* prefix of $\tau$ because there may be no more input (i.e., the target may not generate more actions).

However, there is a corner case in which an edit automaton can effectively$_=$ enforce a valid infinite-length execution $\tau$ that has only finitely many valid prefixes. If, after processing a prefix of $\tau$, the automaton can decide that $\tau$ is the only valid extension of this prefix, then the automaton can cease processing input and enter an infinite loop to insert the remaining actions of $\tau$. While in this infinite loop, the automaton need not output infinitely many valid prefixes, since it is certain to be able to extend the current (possibly invalid) output into a valid one.

The following theorem presents the tight boundary for effective= enforcement of properties by edit automata, including the corner case described above. Because we believe that the corner case adds relatively little to the enforcement capabilities of edit automata, we only sketch the proof in the companion technical report [21].

**Theorem 4 (Effective= $E^\infty$-Enforcement).** *A property $\hat{P}$ on a system with action set $\mathcal{A}$ can be effectively= enforced by some edit automaton $E$ if and only if the following constraints are met.*

$$
1.\ \forall \sigma \in \mathcal{A}^\omega : \hat{P}(\sigma) \iff \left(
\begin{array}{l}
\forall \sigma' \preceq \sigma : \exists \tau \preceq \sigma : \sigma' \preceq \tau \wedge \hat{P}(\tau) \\
\vee\ \hat{P}(\sigma)\ \wedge \\
\exists \sigma' \preceq \sigma : \forall \tau \succeq \sigma' : \hat{P}(\tau) \Rightarrow \tau = \sigma\ \wedge \\
\text{the existence and actions of } \sigma \\
\text{are computable from } \sigma'
\end{array}
\right)
$$

*2. $\hat{P}(\cdot)$*
*3. $\forall \sigma \in \mathcal{A}^\star : \hat{P}(\sigma)$ is decidable*

We have found it difficult to precisely characterize the properties that are effectively≅ enforceable by edit automata. Unfortunately, the simplest way to specify this set appears to be to encode the semantics of edit automata into recursive functions that operate over streams of actions. Then, we can reason about the relationship between input and output sequences of such functions just as the definition of effective≅ enforcement requires us to reason about the relationship between input and output sequences of automata. Our final theorem takes this approach; we present it for completeness.

**Theorem 5 (Effective≅ $E^\infty$-Enforcement).** *Let $D$ be a decidable function $D : \mathcal{A}^\star \times \mathcal{A}^\star \to \mathcal{A} \cup \{\cdot\}$. Then $R_D^\star$ is a decidable function $R_D^\star : \mathcal{A}^\star \times \mathcal{A}^\star \times \mathcal{A}^\star \to \mathcal{A}^\star$ parameterized by $D$ and inductively defined as follows, where all metavariables are universally quantified.*

- $R_D^\star(\cdot, \sigma, \tau) = \tau$
- $(D(\sigma; a, \tau) = \cdot) \Rightarrow R_D^\star(a; \sigma', \sigma, \tau') = R_D^\star(\sigma', \sigma; a, \tau')$
- $(D(\sigma; a, \tau) = a') \Rightarrow R_D^\star(a; \sigma', \sigma, \tau') = R_D^\star(a; \sigma', \sigma, \tau'; a')$

*A property $\hat{P}$ on a system with action set $\mathcal{A}$ can be effectively≅ enforced by some edit automaton $E$ if and only if there exists a decidable $D$ function (as described above) such that for all (input sequences) $\sigma \in \mathcal{A}^\infty$ there exists (output sequence) $\tau \in \mathcal{A}^\infty$ such that the following constraints are met.*

*1. $\forall \sigma' \preceq \sigma : \forall \tau' \in \mathcal{A}^\star : (R_D^\star(\sigma', \cdot, \cdot) = \tau') \Rightarrow \tau' \preceq \tau$*
*2. $\forall \tau' \preceq \tau : \exists \sigma' \preceq \sigma : R_D^\star(\sigma', \cdot, \cdot) = \tau'$*

*3.* $\hat{P}(\tau)$
*4.* $\hat{P}(\sigma) \Rightarrow \sigma \cong \tau$

As with truncation automata, we believe that the theorems related to edit automata acting as effective$_=$ enforcers more naturally capture their inherent power than does the theorem of effective$_\cong$ enforcement. Effective$_=$ enforcement provides an elegant lower bound for what can be effectively$_\cong$ enforced in practice.

*Limitations.* In addition to standard assumptions of program monitors, such as that a target cannot circumvent or corrupt a monitor, our theoretical model makes assumptions particularly relevant to edit automata that are sometimes violated in practice. Most importantly, our model assumes that security automata have the same computational capabilities as the system that observes the monitor's output. If an action violates this assumption by requiring an outside system in order to be executed, it cannot be "feigned" (i.e., suppressed) by the monitor. For example, it would be impossible for a monitor to feign sending email, wait for the target to receive a response to the email, test whether the target does something invalid with the response, and then decide to "undo" sending email in the first place. Here, the action for sending email has to be made observable to systems outside of the monitor's control in order to be executed, so this is an unsuppressible action. A similar limitation arises with time-dependent actions, where an action cannot be feigned (i.e., suppressed) because it may behave differently if made observable later. In addition to these sorts of unsuppressible actions, a system may contain actions uninsertable by monitors because, for example, the monitors lack access to secret keys that must be passed as parameters to the actions. In the future, we plan to explore the usefulness of including sets of unsuppressible and uninsertable actions in the specification of systems. We might be able to harness earlier work [20], which defined security automata limited to inserting (insertion automata) or suppressing (suppression automata) actions, toward this goal.

## 5    Infinite Renewal Properties

In this section, we examine some interesting aspects of the class of infinite renewal properties. We compare renewal properties to safety and liveness properties and provide several examples of useful renewal properties that are neither safety nor liveness properties.

### 5.1    Renewal, Safety, and Liveness

The most obvious way in which safety and infinite renewal properties differ is that safety properties place restrictions on finite executions (invalid finite executions must have some prefix after which all extensions are invalid), while renewal properties place no restrictions on finite executions. The primary result of the current work, that edit automata can enforce any reasonable renewal property, agrees with the finding in earlier work that edit automata can enforce *every* reasonable property on systems that only exhibit finite executions [20]. Without infinite-length executions, every property is a renewal property.

Moreover, an infinite-length renewal execution can be valid even if it has infinitely many invalid prefixes (as long as it also has infinitely many valid prefixes), but a valid safety execution can contain no invalid prefixes. Similarly, although invalid infinite-length renewal executions can have prefixes that alternate a finite number of times between being valid and invalid, invalid safety executions must contain some finite prefix before which all prefixes are valid and after which all prefixes are invalid. Hence, every safety property is a renewal property. Given any system with action set $\mathcal{A}$, it is easy to construct a non-safety renewal property $\hat{P}$ by choosing an element $a$ in $\mathcal{A}$ and letting $\hat{P}(\cdot)$, $\hat{P}(a; a)$, but $\neg \hat{P}(a)$.

There are renewal properties that are not liveness properties (e.g., the property that is only satisfied by the empty sequence), and there are liveness properties that are not renewal properties (e.g., the nontermination property only satisfied by infinite executions). Some renewal properties, such as the one only satisfied by the empty sequence and the sequence $a; a$, are neither safety nor liveness. Although Alpern and Schneider [3] showed that exactly one property is both safety and liveness (the property satisfied by every execution), some interesting liveness properties are also renewal properties. We examine examples of such renewal properties in the following subsection.

## 5.2   Example Properties

We next present several examples of renewal properties that are not safety properties, as well as some examples of non-renewal properties. By the theorems in Sections 3.2 and 4.2, the non-safety renewal properties are effectively$_=$ enforceable by edit automata but not by truncation automata. Moreover, the proof of Theorem 3 in our companion technical report [21] shows how to construct an edit automaton to enforce any of the renewal properties described in this subsection.

*Renewal properties.* Suppose we wish to constrain a user's interaction with a computer system. A user may first obtain credentials (e.g., a Kerberos ticket) and then log in. If he has obtained no credentials then executing a log-in action causes him to be logged in as a guest. At no time, however, can the user log in as "root." The process of logging in to the system may repeat indefinitely, so we might write the requisite property $\hat{P}$ more specifically as $(a_1{}^\star; a_2)^\infty$, where $a_1$ ranges over all actions for obtaining credentials, $a_2$ over actions for logging in, and $a_3$ over actions for logging in as root.[3] This $\hat{P}$ is not a safety property because a finite sequence of only $a_1$ events disobeys $\hat{P}$ but can be extended (by appending $a_2$) to obey $\hat{P}$. Our $\hat{P}$ is also not a liveness property because there are finite executions that cannot be extended to satisfy $\hat{P}$, such as the sequence containing only $a_3$. However, this non-safety, non-liveness property is a renewal property because infinite-length executions are valid if and only if they contain infinitely many (valid) prefixes of the form $(a_1{}^\star; a_2)^\star$.

---

[3] As noted by Alpern and Schneider [3], this sort of $\hat{P}$ might be expressed with the (strong) *until* operator in temporal logic; event $a_1$ occurs *until* event $a_2$.

Interestingly, if we enforce the policy described above on a system that only has actions $a_1$ and $a_2$, we remove the safety aspect of the property to obtain a liveness property that is also a renewal property. On the system $\{a_1, a_2\}$, the property satisfied by any execution matching $(a_1{}^\star; a_2)^\infty$ is a liveness property because any illegal finite execution can be made legal by appending $a_2$. The property is still a renewal property because an infinite execution is invalid if and only if it contains a finite number of valid prefixes after which $a_2$ never appears.

There are other interesting properties that are both liveness and renewal. For example, consider a property $\hat{P}$ specifying that an execution that does anything must *eventually* perform an audit by executing some action $a$. This is similar to the example renewal property given in Section 4.2. Because we can extend any invalid finite execution with the audit action to make it valid, $\hat{P}$ is a liveness property. It is also a renewal property because an infinite-length valid execution must have infinitely many prefixes in which $a$ appears, and an infinite-length invalid execution has no valid prefix (except the empty sequence) because $a$ never appears. Note that for this "eventually audits" renewal property to be enforceable by an edit automaton, we have to consider the empty sequence valid.

As briefly mentioned in Section 4.2, edit automata derive their power from being able to operate in a way similar to intentions files in database transactions. At a high-level, any transaction-based property is a renewal property. Let $\tau$ range over finite sequences of single, valid transactions. A transaction based policy could then be written as $\tau^\infty$; a valid execution is one containing any number of valid transactions. Such transactional properties can be non-safety because executions may be invalid within a transaction but become valid at the conclusion of that transaction. Transactional properties can also be non-liveness when there exists a way to irremediably corrupt a transaction (e.g., every transaction beginning with *start;self-destruct* is illegal). Nonetheless, transactional properties are renewal properties because infinite-length executions are valid if and only if they contain an infinite number of prefixes that are valid sequences of transactions. The renewal properties described above as matching sequences of the form $(a_1{}^\star; a_2)^\infty$ can also be viewed as transactional; each transaction must match $a_1{}^\star; a_2$.

*Non-renewal properties.* An example of an interesting liveness property that is not a renewal property is general availability. Suppose that we have a system with actions $o_i$ for opening (or acquiring) and $c_i$ for closing (or releasing) some resource $i$. Our policy $\hat{P}$ is that for all resources $i$, if $i$ is opened, it must eventually be closed. This is a liveness property because any invalid finite sequence can be made valid simply by appending actions to close every open resource. However, $\hat{P}$ is not a renewal property because there are valid infinite sequences, such as $o_1; o_2; c_1; o_3; c_2; o_4; c_3; ...$, that do not have an infinite number of valid prefixes. An edit automaton can only enforce this sort of availability property when the number of resources is limited to one (in this case, the property is transactional: valid transactions begin with $o_1$ and end with $c_1$). Even on a system with two resources, infinite sequences like $o_1; o_2; c_1; o_1; c_2; o_2; c_1; o_1; ...$ prevent this resource-availability property from being a renewal property.

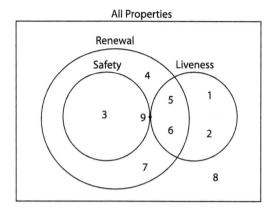

**Fig. 1.** Relationships between safety, liveness, and renewal properties

Of course, there are many non-renewal, non-liveness properties as well. We can arrive at such properties by combining a safety property with any property that is a liveness but not a renewal property. For example, termination is not a renewal property because invalid infinite sequences have an infinite number of valid prefixes. Termination is however a liveness property because any finite execution is valid. When we combine this liveness, non-renewal property with a safety property, such as that no accesses are made to private files, we arrive at the non-liveness, non-renewal property in which executions are valid if and only if they terminate and never access private files. The requirement of termination prevents this from being a renewal property; moreover, this property is outside the upper bound of what is effectively= enforceable by edit automata.

Figure 1 summarizes the results of the preceding discussion and that of Section 5.1. The Trivial property considers all executions legal and is the only property in the intersection of safety and liveness properties.

# 6   Conclusions

When considering the space of security properties enforceable by monitoring potentially nonterminating targets, we have found that a simple variety of monitor enforces exactly the set of computable and satisfiable safety properties while a more powerful variety can enforce any computable infinite renewal property that is satisfied by the empty sequence. Because our model permits infinite sequences of actions, it is compatible with previous research on safety and liveness properties.

Awareness of formally proven bounds on the power of security mechanisms facilitates our understanding of policies themselves and the mechanisms we need to enforce them. For example, observing that a stack-inspection policy is really just an access-control property (where access is granted or denied based on the history of function calls and returns), which in turn is clearly a safety property, makes it immediately obvious that simple monitors modeled by truncation automata are sufficient for enforcing stack-inspection policies. Similarly, if we can observe that infinite executions in a property specifying how users log in are valid if and only if they contain infinitely many valid prefixes, then we immediately know that monitors based on edit automata can enforce this renewal property. We hope that with continued research into the formal enforcement bounds of various security mechanisms, security architects will be able to pull from their enforcement "toolbox" exactly the right sorts of mechanisms needed to enforce the policies at hand.

## Acknowledgments

We wish to thank Ed Felten for pointing out the operational similarity between edit automata and database intentions files. In addition, Kevin Hamlen, Fred Schneider, Greg Morrisett, and the anonymous reviewers provided insightful comments on an earlier version of this paper. ARDA grant NBCHC030106, DARPA award F30602-99-1-0519, and NSF grants CCR-0238328 and CCR-0306313 have provided support for this research.

## References

1. M. Abadi and C. Fournet. Access control based on execution history. In *Proceedings of the 10th Annual Network and Distributed System Symposium*, Feb. 2003.
2. B. Alpern and F. Schneider. Recognizing safety and liveness. *Distributed Computing*, 2:117–126, 1987.
3. B. Alpern and F. B. Schneider. Defining liveness. *Information Processing Letters*, 21(4):181–185, Oct. 1985.
4. L. Bauer, J. Ligatti, and D. Walker. Types and effects for non-interfering program monitors. In M. Okada, B. Pierce, A. Scedrov, H. Tokuda, and A. Yonezawa, editors, *Software Security—Theories and Systems. Mext-NSF-JSPS International Symposium, ISSS 2002, Tokyo, Japan, November 8-10, 2002, Revised Papers*, volume 2609 of *Lecture Notes in Computer Science*. Springer, 2003.
5. L. Bauer, J. Ligatti, and D. Walker. Composing security policies with polymer. In *Proceedings of the ACM SIGPLAN 2005 Conference on Programming Language Design and Implementation*, Chicago, June 2005.
6. D. F. C. Brewer and M. J. Nash. The chinese wall security policy. In *Proceedings of the IEEE Symposium on Security and Privacy*, pages 206–214, 1989.
7. G. Edjlali, A. Acharya, and V. Chaudhary. History-based access control for mobile code. In *ACM Conference on Computer and Communications Security*, pages 38–48, 1998.
8. Ú. Erlingsson. *The Inlined Reference Monitor Approach to Security Policy Enforcement*. PhD thesis, Cornell University, Jan. 2004.
9. Ú. Erlingsson and F. B. Schneider. SASI enforcement of security policies: A retrospective. In *Proceedings of the New Security Paradigms Workshop*, pages 87–95, Caledon Hills, Canada, Sept. 1999.
10. Ú. Erlingsson and F. B. Schneider. IRM enforcement of Java stack inspection. In *Proceedings of the IEEE Symposium on Security and Privacy*, pages 246–255, Oakland, California, May 2000.

11. D. Evans and A. Twyman. Flexible policy-directed code safety. In *Proceedings of the IEEE Symposium on Security and Privacy*, Oakland, CA, May 1999.

12. P. W. L. Fong. Access control by tracking shallow execution history. In *Proceedings of the IEEE Symposium on Security and Privacy*, Oakland, California, USA, May 2004.

13. K. Hamlen, G. Morrisett, and F. Schneider. Computability classes for enforcement mechanisms. Technical Report TR2003-1908, Cornell University, Aug. 2003.

14. C. Jeffery, W. Zhou, K. Templer, and M. Brazell. A lightweight architecture for program execution monitoring. In *PASTE '98: Proceedings of the 1998 ACM SIGPLAN-SIGSOFT workshop on Program analysis for software tools and engineering*, pages 67–74. ACM Press, 1998.

15. G. Kiczales, J. Irwin, J. Lamping, J.-M. Loingtier, C. V. Lopes, C. Maeda, and A. Mendhekar. Aspect-oriented programming. *ACM Comput. Surv.*, 28(4es):154, 1996.

16. M. Kim, S. Kannan, I. Lee, O. Sokolsky, and M. Viswantathan. Computational analysis of run-time monitoring—fundamentals of Java-MaC. In *Run-time Verification*, June 2002.

17. M. Kim, M. Viswanathan, H. Ben-Abdallah, S. Kannan, I. Lee, and O. Sokolsky. Formally specified monitoring of temporal properties. In *European Conference on Real-time Systems*, York, UK, June 1999.

18. L. Lamport. Proving the correctness of multiprocess programs. *IEEE Transactions of Software Engineering*, 3(2):125–143, 1977.

19. J. Ligatti, L. Bauer, and D. Walker. Edit automata: Enforcement mechanisms for run-time security policies. Technical Report TR-681-03, Princeton University, May 2003.

20. J. Ligatti, L. Bauer, and D. Walker. Edit automata: Enforcement mechanisms for run-time security policies. *International Journal of Information Security*, 4(1–2):2–16, Feb. 2005.

21. J. Ligatti, L. Bauer, and D. Walker. Enforcing non-safety security policies with program monitors. Technical Report TR-720-05, Princeton University, Jan. 2005.

22. N. A. Lynch and M. R. Tuttle. Hierarchical correctness proofs for distributed algorithms. In *Proceedings of the 6th annual ACM Symposium on Principles of distributed computing*, pages 137–151. ACM Press, 1987.

23. W. H. Paxton. A client-based transaction system to maintain data integrity. In *Proceedings of the 7th ACM symposium on Operating systems principles*, pages 18–23. ACM Press, 1979.

24. F. B. Schneider. Enforceable security policies. *ACM Transactions on Information and Systems Security*, 3(1):30–50, Feb. 2000.

25. M. Viswanathan. *Foundations for the Run-time Analysis of Software Systems*. PhD thesis, University of Pennsylvania, 2000.

26. R. Wahbe, S. Lucco, T. Anderson, and S. Graham. Efficient software-based fault isolation. In *Proceedings of the 14th Symposium on Operating Systems Principles*, pages 203–216, Asheville, Dec. 1993.

# Soundness of Formal Encryption in the Presence of Key-Cycles

Pedro Adão[1,*], Gergei Bana[2,**], Jonathan Herzog[3], and Andre Scedrov[2,* * *]

[1] Center for Logic and Computation, IST, Lisboa, Portugal
[2] Department of Mathematics, University of Pennsylvania, Philadelphia, USA
[3] The MITRE Corporation
pad@math.ist.utl.pt, {bana, scedrov}@math.upenn.edu,
jherzog@mitre.org

**Abstract.** Both the formal and the computational models of cryptography contain the notion of message *equivalence* or *indistinguishability*. An encryption scheme provides *soundness* for indistinguishability if, when mapping formal messages into the computational model, equivalent formal messages are mapped to indistinguishable computational distributions. Previous soundness results are limited in that they do not apply when *key-cycles* are present. We demonstrate that an encryption scheme provides soundness in the presence of key-cycles if it satisfies the recently-introduced notion of *key-dependent message* (KDM) security. We also show that soundness in the presence of key-cycles (and KDM security) neither implies nor is implied by security against chosen ciphertext attack (CCA-2). Therefore, soundness for key-cycles is possible using a new notion of computational security, not possible using previous such notions, and the relationship between the formal and computational models extends beyond chosen-ciphertext security.

## 1 Introduction

'Security' is the Rorschach blob of theoretical computer science: every model of computation has attempted to define it in its own way. In the area of cryptographic protocols, two models are noteworthy for their natural definitions and rigorous proofs. The first of these models, the *computational model*, is derived from complexity theory. Its definitions are phrased in terms of the asymptotic behavior of Turing machines, and its main

---

* Partially supported by FCT grant SFRH/BD/8148/2002. Additional support from FEDER/FCT project Fiblog POCTI/2001/MAT/37239 and FEDER/FCT project QuantLog POCI/MAT/55796/2004.

** Partially supported by OSD/ONR CIP/SW URI 'Software Quality and Infrastructure Protection for Diffuse Computing" through ONR Grant N00014-01-1-0795. Additional support from NSF Grant CNS-0429689.

* * * Partially supported by OSD/ONR CIP/SW URI "Software Quality and Infrastructure Protection for Diffuse Computing" through ONR Grant N00014-01-1-0795 and OSD/ONR CIP/SW URI "Trustworthy Infrastructure, Mechanisms, and Experimentation for Diffuse Computing" through ONR Grant N00014-04-1-0725. Additional support from NSF Grants CCR-0098096 and CNS-0429689.

S. De Capitani di Vimercati et al. (Eds.): ESORICS 2005, LNCS 3679, pp. 374–396, 2005.
© Springer-Verlag Berlin Heidelberg 2005

proof technique is the reduction. The other of these two models, the *formal model (or, Dolev-Yao model)*, is so-named because of its genesis in the field of formal methods. Its definitions are phrased in terms of process algebras and state machines (particularly non-deterministic ones) and it uses many different proof methods (including automated ones).

In this work, we consider the relationship between these two models; more precisely, the relationship between a simplified formal model following the technique of Abadi and Rogaway, and the computational implementation of this model. There are two key differences between them: their representations of messages and the powers they give to the adversary.

- In the *computational model*, messages are families of probability distributions over bit-strings (indexed by the security parameter). The adversary is modeled as an algorithm of realistic computational power: probabilistic polynomial-time.
- The *formal model* imposes a great deal more structure. Messages are expressions, built according to a particular grammar. The atomic messages are symbols representing keys, random values, texts, and so on. More complex messages can be built from simpler ones via the two operations of pairing and encryption. The adversary is given only limited power to manipulate these expressions, such as separating a concatenation or decrypting an encryption (if it knows the needed key).

Despite these differences, certain intuitions can be translated between the two models in the expected way. In particular, under carefully chosen conditions, *indistinguishability of messages* can be mapped directly from one model to the other. In the formal model of Abadi and Rogaway, two expressions are thought to be indistinguishable to the adversary, also called *formally equivalent*, if their only differences lie in encryption terms that cannot be decrypted by the formal adversary. In the computational model, on the other hand, messages are families of probability distributions on bit-strings. Indistinguishability of computational messages is captured by the standard notion of computational indistinguishability (i.e., indistinguishability by an efficient algorithm).

*Relating the two models.* Once a computational encryption scheme is fixed, an intuitive function establishes the relationship between the two models. This function (called *interpretation*), maps each formal expression to an ensemble (indexed by the security parameter) of probability distributions over bit-strings. Given an encryption scheme, and hence a particular interpretation function, one can then ask whether all pairs of equivalent formal messages map to indistinguishable probability distribution ensembles. If so, we say that *soundness* holds[1] and it implies that the formal model is a faithful abstraction of the computational model in the sense that security of the formal model implies security in the computational.

The first soundness result of this type is due to Abadi and Rogaway in the symmetric-key encryption setting [2]. They demonstrated that soundness holds when the security level of the computational encryption algorithm is 'type-0,' a property of their own

---

[1] This particular kind of soundness is but one piece of a much larger definition, but as a convenient shorthand we will use 'soundness' in this paper to mean soundness of message indistinguishability.

devising. This result was later translated to the public-key setting (which is also the setting we will consider in this paper) by Micciancio and Warinschi [41]. They found that soundness in this setting is guaranteed by encryption schemes that satisfy the standard definition of chosen-ciphertext security (CCA-2 in the notation of [13]). This power of chosen-ciphertext security has been confirmed by subsequent extensions [29,19]. However, both the original result of Abadi and Rogaway and the later extensions (including those that use CCA-2 security) share a common limitation: they do not necessarily apply in the presence of key-cycles.

*A persistent question.* A formal message $M$ contains a *key-cycle* if it contains encryption terms $\{M_1\}_{K_1}, \{M_2\}_{K_2}, \ldots, \{M_n\}_{K_n}$ (where $\{M_i\}_{K_i}$ denotes the encryption of the message $M_i$ with the public key $K_i$) such that $M_i$ contains the key necessary to decrypt $\{M_{i+1}\}_{K_{i+1}}$ and $M_n$ contains the key necessary to decrypt $\{M_1\}_{K_1}$. The simplest key-cycle is the message $\{K^{-1}\}_K$, where $K^{-1}$ denotes the (private) decryption key associated with the encryption key $K$, but more complex key-cycles are possible (e.g., $\{K_2^{-1}\}_{K_1} \{K_1^{-1}\}_{K_2}$).

The formal model makes no distinction between those messages that posses key-cycles and those that do not. Further, the presence of a key-cycle will not prevent a formal expression from being interpreted as a computational distribution ensemble in the natural way. However, neither the soundness result of Abadi and Rogaway nor subsequent soundness demonstrations (described in Section 2) are known to hold for such messages. (In fact, the stronger of these results [10,19] assume that no private or symmetric keys are encrypted at all!)

Thus, the question of key-cycles is both interesting in its own right and has implications in a larger context. The standard security definitions for computational encryption, such as CCA-2 security, do not obviously imply security in the presence of key-cycles [38]. The formal model, on the other hand, assumes that key-cycles do not weaken encryption in any way. Therefore, the issue of key-cycles may represent a 'gap' between the formal and computational models, and thus might shed light on their general relationship.

*Gaps between the two models.* The majority of the results relating the two models show the formal model to be sound with respect to standard definitions of the computational model—with some notable exceptions. Some aspects of the formal model have been shown to be overly strong relative to the computational model. For example, the original soundness results of Abadi and Rogaway assumed that formal encryption concealed all aspects of the plaintext. In particular, their result requires that symmetric encryption hides (among other things)the length of the plaintext. Unfortunately, this cannot be achieved for many contexts. Soundness in these other contexts is considered by Micciancio and Warinschi [41], Laud [34], Bana [11], Micciancio and Panjwani [39] and Adão, Bana and Scedrov [3], who require a weaker notion of formal equivalence. (In keeping with this, we will use the more complex formal model that addresses these weaknesses.)

On the other hand, other aspects of the formal model have been shown to be overly weak compared to the computational one. Canetti and Herzog [19] and Backes and Pfitzmann [9], for example, have demonstrated that the formal definition of secrecy (in the context of key-exchange protocols) is strictly weaker than the computational definition. That is, some protocols may satisfy the formal notion of security but not the computational one. Having demonstrated this gap, the authors close it by providing a strictly stronger formal definition that abstracts the computational definition in a demonstrably faithful way.

Thus, at least two 'gaps' between the formal and computational models have been uncovered. In both cases, their resolution forced changes onto the formal model. Should the resolution of the problem of key-cicles again cause changes to the formal model, or could it this time be more naturally resolved through modifications to the computational model?

*An alternate approach.* Laud [33] has proposed a solution to the problem of key-cycles which takes the first approach. That is, Laud's solution provides soundness in the presence of key-cycles, but does so by weakening the notion of formal equivalence. It is assumed that key-cycles somehow always 'break' the encryption and the formal adversary is strengthened so as to be always able to 'see' inside the encryptions of a key-cycle.

Soundness in the presence of key-cycles naturally holds under this assumption, but we feel that the price paid is too high. Formal equivalence should reflect the ability of the formal adversary to distinguish messages, which should in turn reflect the actual extent to which the computational adversary can distinguish messages. It is often unreasonable from a cryptographer's point of view to *a priori* assume that the computational adversary can break all key-cycles. We therefore propose, in this work, to demonstrate soundness in the presence of key-cycles not by weakening encryption in the formal model but by strengthening it in the computational one.

*Our work.* In this paper, we resolve the issue of soundness in the presence of key-cycles by using the notion of *key-dependent message* (KDM) security for asymmetric encryption. This definition was recently introduced simultaneously both by Black, Rogaway and Shrimpton [14], who consider it in their own right, and by Camenisch and Lysyanskaya [16], who use it for an anonymous credential system.

We, however, will use it to demonstrate two points:

1. As expected, and predicted by Black *et al.*, this new definition is strong enough to provide soundness in the presence of keys cycles. That is, a KDM-secure encryption scheme provides soundness for the existing and unweakened formal model.

2. Also, soundness *requires* new computational definitions of security. That is, we demonstrate that soundness and KDM security neither imply nor are implied by chosen-ciphertext (CCA-2) security, the strongest known definition of security in the (standard) computational model.[2]

Thus, the problem of key-cycles was a genuine gap between the formal and computational models at the time of the original Abadi-Rogaway result, but with recent advances in the computational model it can be repaired. Also, soundness in the presence of key-cycles demonstrates that there is more to the relationship between the formal and

---

[2] A stronger notion of security, plaintext-awareness, is known, but it is defined (generally) only in the random-oracle model and so is regarded as non-standard. See Herzog, Liskov and Micali [30] for fuller discussion and an alternate definition.

computational models (in the case of asymmetric encryption) than chosen-ciphertext security.

*Limitations.* We note that our results contain a few limitations of their own. Firstly, we consider a passive adversary only. Secondly, KDM security has only been actually implemented in the random oracle model, a non-standard variation of the computational model. Lastly, we use a weakened version of the formal model in which encryptions reveal the length of the plaintext and the key used to encrypt. (Rephrased in the language of Abadi and Rogaway [2], we consider 'type-3' encryption and not 'type-0.')

However, it should also be noted that these limitations are smaller than they may first seem. We consider a passive adversary solely for simplicity. We expect that our results can be extended to consider active adversaries (as was the original Abadi-Rogaway result) and regard our work as a 'first step' towards that extension. Secondly, we do not use the random oracle in this work. We use only the *definition* of KDM security, which is well-founded in the standard computational model and does not rely upon the random oracle. Lastly, the issue of type-3 vs. type-0 encryption is orthogonal to our work. We express our definitions and results in the style of type-3 encryption for two reasons: to be in keeping with recent extensions, and because only type-3 security is guaranteed by the standard computational definitions. (That is, definitions such as chosen-ciphertext security do not *a priori* conceal the encryption key or the length of the plaintext.) However, our results will map directly to their type-0 analogies provided that the computational encryption scheme is length- and key-concealing as well as being KDM-secure.

*Overview of the paper.* We begin with a discussion of some previous work (Section 2). We then present (Section 3) modified versions of Abadi and Rogaway's soundness definition and result. As mentioned above, we consider encryption schemes that reveal the key used to encrypt and the length of the plaintext.

We then show that (adaptive) chosen-ciphertext security alone cannot ensure soundness in the presence of key-cycles (Section 4). Thus, soundness for key-cycles could not have been demonstrated with the computational definitions available to Abadi and Rogaway, and new definitions were necessary.

We then present the notion of KDM security (Section 5.1) and show that it is strong enough to imply soundness in the presence of key-cycles (Section 5.2). We also show (Section 5.3) that KDM-security is in fact a new notion: it neither implies nor is implied by CCA-2 security. To finish our discussion on the relationships between the different security notions, we also show that soundness does not imply semantic security (IND-CPA security, in the notation of [13]).

We conclude (Section 6) with the discussion of some future work.

*Acknowledgements.* This work was done while the first author was a visiting student at the University of Pennsylvania. We want to thank J. Black, A. Gordon, S. Hohenberger, A. Lysyanskaya, T. Shrimpton, and D. Unruh for their valuable comments and informative discussions. Some of our joint work was done during the Protocol eXchange meetings. We thank S. Pinsky, E. Zieglar, and G. Dinolt for organizing the meetings and providing a conducive and encouraging atmosphere. Lastly, we also thank the anonymous referees for their extensive comments and suggestions.

## 2  Previous Work

Work intended to bridge the gap between the cryptographic and the formal models started with several independent approaches, including Lincoln, Mitchell, Mitchell, and Scedrov [36], Canetti [18], Pfitzmann, Schunter and Waidner [43,44], and Abadi and Rogaway [2]. In [2], formal terms with nested operations are considered specifically for symmetric encryption, the adversary is restricted to passive eavesdropping, and the security goals are formulated as indistinguishability of terms. This was extended in [1] from terms to more general programs, but the restriction to passive adversaries remained. We discuss other extensions of [2] further below. Several papers consider specific models or specific properties, *e.g.,* Guttman, Thayer, and Zuck [26] specifically consider strand spaces and information-theoretically secure authentication.

A process calculus for analyzing security protocols in which protocol adversaries may be arbitrary probabilistic polynomial-time processes is introduced in [36]. In this framework, which provides a formal treatment of the computational model, security properties are formulated as observational equivalences. Mitchell, Ramanathan, Scedrov, and Teague [42] use this framework to develop a form of process bisimulation that justifies an equational proof system for protocol security.

The approach by Pfitzmann, Schunter and Waidner [43,44] starts with a general reactive system model, a general definition of cryptographically secure implementation by simulatability, and a composition theorem for this notion of secure implementation. This work is based on definitions of secure *function* evaluation, *i.e.,* the computation of one set of outputs from one set of inputs [27,37,15,17]. The approach was extended from synchronous to asynchronous systems in [45,18], which are now known as the *reactive simulatability framework* [45,8] and the *universal composability framework* [18]. A detailed comparison of the two approaches may be found in [23].

The first soundness result of a formal model under active attacks has been achieved by Backes, Pfitzmann and Waidner [10] within the reactive simulatability framework. Their result comprises arbitrary active attacks and holds in the context of arbitrary surrounding interactive protocols and independently of the goals that one wants to prove about the surrounding protocols; in particular, property preservation theorems for the simulatability have been proved, *e.g.,* for integrity and secrecy [4,9]. While the original result in [10] considered public-key encryption and digital signatures, the soundness result was extended to symmetric authentication and to symmetric encryption in [7] and [6], respectively.

Concurrently with [10], an extension to asymmetric encryption, but still under passive attacks, is in [30]. Asymmetric encryption under active attacks is considered in [28] in the random oracle model. Laud [34] has subsequently presented a cryptographic underpinning for a formal model of symmetric encryption under active attacks. His work enjoys a direct connection with a formal proof tool, but it is specific to certain confidentiality properties and restricts the surrounding protocols to straight-line programs in a specific language. Herzog *et al.* [30] and Micciancio and Warinschi [41] also give a cryptographic underpinning under active attacks. Their results are narrower than that in [10] since they are specific for public-key encryption, but consider simpler real implementations. Moreover, [30] relies on a stronger assumption, which was subsequently weakened by Herzog [29]. The approach in [41] restricts the classes of protocols and protocol properties that can be analyzed. The work of [41] was subsequently extended by Micciancio and Panjwani [39] to prove soundness of a group-key distribution protocol in the presence of a CPA-secure scheme. Cortier and Warinschi [21] use automated tools for proving that symbolic integrity and specific secrecy proofs are sound with respect to the computational model in the case of protocols that use nonces, signatures and asymmetric encryption (see below for the relationship between symbolic and cryptographic secrecy). Bana [11] and Adão, Bana, and Scedrov [3] extend the original Abadi-Rogaway result to weaker encryption schemes. Laud and Corin [35] consider extensions to composite keys, while Baudet, Cortier, and Kremer [12] consider extensions to equational theories and to static equivalence.

Impagliazzo and Kapron [32] suggest a formal logic for reasoning about probabilistic polynomial-time indistinguishability. Datta, Derek, Mitchell, Shmatikov, and Turuani [24] describe a cryptographically sound formal logic for proving protocol security properties without explicitly reasoning about probability, complexity, or the actions of a malicious attacker.

Recently, there has been concurrent and independent work on linking symbolic and cryptographic secrecy properties. Cortier and Warinschi [21] have shown that symbolically secret nonces are also computationally secret, *i.e.*, indistinguishable from a fresh random value given the view of a cryptographic adversary. Backes and Pfitzmann [9] and Canetti and Herzog [19] have established new symbolic criteria that suffice to show that a key is cryptographically secret. Backes and Pfitzmann formulate this as a property preservation theorem from the formal model to a concrete implementation while Canetti and Herzog link their criteria to ideal functionalities for mutual authentication and key exchange protocols. Backes and Pfitzmann have additionally provided a new definition of secrecy of payloads, *i.e.*, application data, in a reactive framework, and they pointed out a sufficient symbolic criteria to derive if a payload is cryptographically secret.

The first cryptographically sound security proofs of the Needham-Schroeder-Lowe protocol have been presented concurrently and independently in [5] and [47]. While the first paper conducts the proof within a deterministic, symbolic framework, the proof in the second paper is done from scratch in the cryptographic approach; on the other hand, the second paper proves stronger properties and further shows that chosen-plaintext-secure encryption is insufficient for the security of the protocol.

The relation between these two models is not one-way, that is, there is also research regarding the other direction, *completeness*. (That is, an interpretation enforces completeness if two formal messages must be equivalent whenever their interpretations are indistinguishable.) Micciancio and Warinschi [40] show that a sufficiently strong encryption scheme enforces completeness for indistinguishability properties, and later Horvitz and Gligor [31] strengthened this result by giving an exact characterization of the computational requirements on the encryption scheme under which completeness holds. Later, it was shown by Bana [11] and Adão, Bana, and Scedrov [3] that completeness also holds for a more general class of (weaker) encryption systems. We only briefly mention that the simulatability-based results of [10,7,6] have shown completeness implicitly to establish the notion of simulatability. We do not discuss completeness any further in this work.

Finally, we stress that none of the aforementioned results hold in the presence of key-cycles. As we mentioned in the introduction, this problem was addressed by Laud [33] in a different way from the one that we will address in this paper.

# 3 Computational Soundness for Indistinguishability

We start presenting the formal model, and then describe the computational model in a fairly standard way. Then, we introduce the notion of soundness we consider in this paper: that equivalent formal expressions represent indistinguishable computational distribution-ensembles.

In general, this is almost entirely identical to the treatment of Abadi and Rogaway [2], with three exceptions: we deal with asymmetric encryption, formal encryptions reveal the keys used to encrypt, and formal expressions have an associated 'length.'

## 3.1 The Formal Model

In this model, messages (or *expressions*) are defined at a very high level of abstraction. The simplest expressions are symbols for atomic keys and bit-strings. More complex expressions are created from simpler ones via encryption and concatenation, which are defined as abstract, 'black-box' constructors.

**Definition 1 (Expressions).** *Let* **Keys** $= \{K_1, K_2, K_3, ...\}$ *be an infinite discrete set of symbols, called the set of encryption keys, and* **Keys**$^{-1} = \{K_1^{-1}, K_2^{-1}, K_3^{-1}, ...\}$ *the corresponding set of decryption keys. Let* **Blocks** *be a finite subset of* $\{0, 1\}^*$. *We define the* set of expressions, **Exp**, *by the grammar:*

$$\textbf{Exp} ::= \textbf{Keys} \mid \textbf{Keys}^{-1} \mid \textbf{Blocks} \mid (\textbf{Exp}, \textbf{Exp}) \mid \{\textbf{Exp}\}_{\textbf{Keys}}$$

*We will denote by* $Keys(M)$ *the set of all encryption keys occurring in* $M$ *and by* $Keys^{-1}(M)$ *the set of decryption keys in* $M$. *Expressions of the form* $\{N\}_K$ *are called* encryption terms.

Expressions may represent either a single message sent during an execution of the protocol, or the entire knowledge available to the adversary. In this second case, the expression contains not only the messages sent so far, but also any additional knowledge in the adversary's possession (such as the public keys and compromised private keys).

We wish to define when two formal expressions are indistinguishable to the adversary. Intuitively, this occurs when the only differences between the two messages lie within encryption terms that the adversary cannot decrypt. In order to rigorously define this notion, we first need to formalize when an encryption term is 'undecryptable' by the adversary, which in turn requires us to define the set of keys that the adversary can learn from an expression.

An expression might contain keys in the clear. The adversary will learn these keys, and can then use them to decrypt encryption terms of the expression—which might reveal yet more keys. By repeating this process, the adversary can learn the set of *recoverable decryption keys*:

**Definition 2 (Visible Subterms, Recoverable Decryption Keys).** *Let vis* $(M) \subseteq$ ***Exp****, the visible subterms of* $M$*, be the smallest set of expressions containing* $M$ *such that:*

1. $(N_1, N_2) \in vis\,(M) \implies N_1 \in vis\,(M)$ *and* $N_2 \in vis\,(M)$*, and*
2. $\{N\}_K \in vis\,(M)$ *and* $K^{-1} \in vis\,(M) \implies N \in vis\,(M)$.

*Let R-Keys*$(M)$*, the set of recoverable decryption keys in* $M$*, be vis* $(M) \cap$ ***Keys***$^{-1}$.

This allows us to identify those encryption terms of an expression that will be 'opaque' to the adversary: those protected by at least one non-recoverable decryption key. Thus, we wish to say that two expressions are equivalent if they differ only in the contents of their 'opaque' encryption terms.

However, computational realities force us to add two ways in which an opaque encryption may leak information: they now reveal the key used to encrypt, and they now reveal the 'length' of the plaintext. This second condition requires that the notion of length be added to the formal model [40,29,11]:

**Definition 3 (Formal Length).** *We introduce a function symbol with fresh letter* $\ell$ *with the following identities:*

- *For all blocks* $B_1$ *and* $B_2$*,* $\ell(B_1) = \ell(B_2)$ *iff* $|B_1| = |B_2|$,
- $\forall i, j \in \mathbb{N},\ \ell(K_i) = \ell(K_j)$ *and* $\ell(K_i^{-1}) = \ell(K_j^{-1})$,
- *If* $\ell(M_1) = \ell(N_1)$, $\ell(M_2) = \ell(N_2)$ *then* $\ell((M_1, M_2)) = \ell((N_1, N_2))$*, and*
- *If* $\ell(M) = \ell(N)$*, then for all* $K_i$*,* $\ell(\{M\}_{K_i}) = \ell(\{N\}_{K_i})$.

We introduce this function in order to be able to express that the encryption operation may leak information about the length. We note that when **Blocks** is just $\{0, 1\}$, then equality of $\ell(M)$ and $\ell(N)$ implies that $M$ and $N$ have identical type trees.

*Remark 1.* The addition of lengths to the formal model is fairly recent, and is not necessary for soundness if computational encryption can hide the length of the plaintext.

Recall that our goal is to define formal equivalence of messages. This requires us to define what is 'observable' for an adversary in an expression. In order to express that, we define the so-called *pattern* of an expression, and two expressions will be considered equivalent when their patterns are (roughly speaking) identical:

**Definition 4 (Pattern).** *We define the* set *of patterns,* ***Pat****, by the grammar:*

$$\textbf{Pat} ::= \textbf{Keys} \mid \textbf{Keys}^{-1} \mid \textbf{Blocks} \mid (\textbf{Pat}, \textbf{Pat}) \mid \{\textbf{Pat}\}_{\textbf{Keys}} \mid \Box_{\textbf{Keys}, \ell(Exp)}$$

*The pattern of an expression* $M$*, denoted by pattern*$(M)$*, is derived from* $M$ *by replacing each encryption term* $\{M'\}_K \in vis\,(M)$ *(where* $K^{-1} \notin$ *R-Keys*$(M)$*) by* $\Box_{K, \ell(M')}$.
*For two patterns* $P$ *and* $Q$*,* $P = Q$ *is defined the following way:*

- *If* $P \in$ ***Blocks*** $\cup$ ***Keys*** $\cup$ ***Keys***$^{-1}$*, then* $P = Q$ *iff* $P$ *and* $Q$ *are identical.*
- *If* $P$ *is of the form* $\Box_{K, \ell(M')}$*, then* $P = Q$ *iff* $Q$ *is of the form* $\Box_{K, \ell(N')}$*, and* $\ell(M') = \ell(N')$ *in the sense of Definition 3.*
- *If* $P$ *is of the form* $(P_1, P_2)$*, then* $P = Q$ *iff* $Q$ *is of the form* $(Q_1, Q_2)$ *where* $P_1 = P_2$ *and* $Q_1 = Q_2$.
- *If* $P$ *is of the form* $\{P'\}_K$*, then* $P = Q$ *iff* $Q$ *is of the form* $\{Q'\}_K$ *where* $P' = Q'$.

The symbol $\Box_{K,\ell(M')}$ in a pattern reveals that some expression was encrypted with the key $K$ and its length is $\ell(M')$. (Abadi and Rogaway replace these undecryptable terms by $\Box$.)

One last complication remains before we can define formal equivalence. Consider two formal expressions that differ only in the names of the keys in them, but such that if there are identical keys in one of them, there are corresponding identical keys in the other in the same place. On the other hand, two keys, say, $K_1$ and $K_2$, have the same meaning: a randomly drawn key, using the same key-generation algorithm. It does not matter if we replace one of them with the other. The appearance of a new key in an expression just means a freshly generated key, it does not matter what name we give it. What matters is only where the identical keys are in an expression, and where are the differing ones. We wish to formalize the notion of equivalence in such a way that renaming the keys yields in equivalent expression. Therefore, two formal expressions should be equivalent if their patterns differ only in the names of their keys.

**Definition 5 (Key-Renaming Function).** *A bijection* $\sigma : \textbf{Keys} \to \textbf{Keys}$ *is called a key-renaming function. For any expression (or pattern)* $M$, $M\sigma$ *denotes the expression (or pattern) obtained from* $M$ *by replacing all occurrences of keys* $K$ *in* $M$ *by* $\sigma(K)$ *(including those occurrences as indices of* $\Box$*) and all occurrences of keys* $K^{-1}$ *in* $M$ *by* $(\sigma(K))^{-1}$.

We are finally able to formalize the symbolic notion of equivalence:

**Definition 6 (Equivalence of Expressions).** *We say that two expressions* $M$ *and* $N$ *are* equivalent, *denoted by* $M \cong N$, *if there exists a key-renaming function* $\sigma$ *such that* $pattern(M) = pattern(N\sigma)$.

Our main focus in this paper is on key-cycles:

**Definition 7 (Key-Cycles).** *A formal message* $M$ *contains a key-cycle if it contains encryption terms* $\{M_1\}_{K_1}, \{M_2\}_{K_2}, \ldots, \{M_n\}_{K_n}$ *(where* $\{M_i\}_{K_i}$ *denotes the encryption of the message* $M_i$ *with the public key* $K_i$*) such that* $M_i$ *contains the key necessary to decrypt* $\{M_{i+1}\}_{K_{i+1}}$ *and* $M_n$ *contains the key necessary to decrypt* $\{M_1\}_{K_1}$. *In this case we say that we have a key-cycle of length* $n$.

## 3.2   The Computational Model

The fundamental objects of the computational world are strings, strings $= \{0,1\}^*$, and families of probability distributions over strings. These families are indexed by a *security parameter* $\eta \in$ parameters $= \mathbb{N}$ (which can be roughly understood as key-lengths). Two distribution families $\{D_\eta\}_{\eta \in \mathbb{N}}$ and $\{D'_\eta\}_{\eta \in \mathbb{N}}$ are *indistinguishable* if no efficient algorithm can determine from which distribution a value was sampled:

**Definition 8 (Negligible Function).** *A function* $f : \mathbb{N} \to \mathbb{R}$ *is said to be* negligible, *written* $f(n) \leq \text{neg}(n)$, *if for any* $c > 0$ *there is an* $n_c \in \mathbb{N}$ *such that* $f(n) \leq n^{-c}$ *whenever* $n \geq n_c$.

**Definition 9 (Indistinguishability).** *Two families* $\{D_\eta\}_{\eta \in \mathbb{N}}$ *and* $\{D'_\eta\}_{\eta \in \mathbb{N}}$, *are* indistinguishable, *written* $D_\eta \approx D'_\eta$, *if for all PPT adversaries* A,

$$\left| \Pr\left[ d \longleftarrow D_\eta; \mathsf{A}(1^\eta, d) = 1 \right] - \Pr\left[ d \longleftarrow D'_\eta; \mathsf{A}(1^\eta, d) = 1 \right] \right| \leq \text{neg}(\eta)$$

In this model, pairing is an injective *pairing function* $[\cdot, \cdot]$ : strings × strings → strings such that the length of the result only depends on the length of the paired strings. An encryption scheme is a triple of algorithms $(\mathcal{K}, \mathcal{E}, \mathcal{D})$ with key generation $\mathcal{K}$, encryption $\mathcal{E}$ and decryption $\mathcal{D}$. Let plaintexts, ciphertexts, publickey and secretkey be nonempty subsets of strings. The set coins is some probability field that stands for coin-tossing, *i.e.*, randomness.

**Definition 10 (Encryption Scheme).** *A computational asymmetric encryption scheme is a triple* $\Pi = (\mathcal{K}, \mathcal{E}, \mathcal{D})$ *where:*

- $\mathcal{K}$ : parameters × coins → publickey × secretkey *is a key-generation algorithm with security parameter* $\eta$,
- $\mathcal{E}$ : publickey × plaintexts × coins → ciphertexts *is an encryption function, and*
- $\mathcal{D}$ : secretkey × strings → plaintexts *is such that for all* $(e, d) \in$ publickey × secretkey *and* $\omega \in$ coins

$$\mathcal{D}(d, \mathcal{E}(e, m, \omega)) = m \text{ for all } m \in \text{plaintexts}.$$

*All these algorithms must be computable in polynomial time in the size of the input not counting the* coins. *(For this reason, the set* parameters *is usually represented as* $1^*$.*) We insist that* $|\mathcal{E}(e, m, w)| = |\mathcal{E}(e, m, w')|$ *for all* $e \in$ publickey, $m \in$ plaintexts *and* $w, w' \in$ coins, *where* $|x|$ *stands for the binary length of x. We also insist that* $0^* \subseteq$ plaintexts. *We lastly insist that for all e and x, all elements in the support of* $\mathcal{E}(e, x)$ *are of the same length and that this length depends only on* $|x|$ *and* $\eta$ *(when* $(e, d) \longleftarrow \mathcal{K}(1^\eta)$).

## 3.3  Relating the Two Models

In order to prove any relationship between the formal and computational worlds, we need to define the *interpretation* of expressions and patterns. Once an encryption scheme is picked, we can define the interpretation function $\Phi$, which assigns to each expression or pattern $M$ a family of random variables $\{\Phi_\eta(M)\}_{\eta \in \mathbb{N}}$ such that each $\Phi_\eta(M)$ takes values in strings. As in Abadi and Rogaway [2], this interpretation is defined in an algorithmic way. The full formalism is given in Appendix B, but we present an informal overview here. For expressions:

- Blocks are interpreted as strings,
- Each key is interpreted by running the key generation algorithm,
- Pairs are translated into computational pairs,
- Formal encryptions terms are interpreted by running the encryption algorithm.

We will denote by $[\![M]\!]_{\Phi_\eta}$ the distribution of $\Phi_\eta(M)$ and by $[\![M]\!]_\Phi$ the ensemble of $\{[\![M]\!]_{\Phi_\eta}\}_{\eta \in \mathbb{N}}$. For the interpretation of patterns, everything is the same as for the interpretation of expressions, but we also have:

- The interpretation of a pattern $\square_{K, \ell(M)}$ for a given security parameter $\eta$ is given by $\Phi_\eta(\{0^{|\Phi_\eta(M)|}\}_K)$ where $|\Phi_\eta(M)|$ is the binary length of $\Phi_\eta(M)$, which must be the same for all samples (due to our assumptions about encryption schemes). We can call the sequence $\{|\Phi_\eta(M)|\}_{\eta \in \mathbb{N}}$ the *interpretation* of $\ell(M)$.

For any pattern $M$, let $\Phi(M) = \{\Phi_\eta(M)\}_{\eta \in \mathbb{N}}$ be the family of random variables given by the interpretation, $[\![M]\!]_{\Phi_\eta}$ the distribution of $\Phi_\eta(M)$ and $[\![M]\!]_\Phi$ the ensemble of distributions $\{[\![M]\!]_{\Phi_\eta}\}_{\eta \in \mathbb{N}}$.

We can now define the notion of soundness.

**Definition 11 (Soundness).** *We say that an interpretation is* sound, *or that an encryption scheme* provides soundness, *if the interpretation $\Phi$ (resulting from the encryption scheme) is such that*

$$M \cong N \Rightarrow [\![M]\!]_\Phi \approx [\![N]\!]_\Phi$$

*for any expressions $M$ and $N$.*

The primary result of Abadi and Rogaway given in [2] is that, in the symmetric case, soundness is guaranteed by sufficiently strong cryptography (called 'type-0') if the expressions $M$ and $N$ have no key-cycles. Subsequent work [41] translates this result to the setting of asymmetric encryption, and derives that a similar soundness property (in the absence of key-cycles) is guaranteed by chosen-ciphertext security. Subsequent work [29,19] confirms that chosen-ciphertext security suffices for several extensions, so long as key-cycles are prohibited. In the next section, we show that this prohibition was necessary: in the presence of key-cycles, chosen-ciphertext does not necessarily guarantee soundness.

## 4 Chosen-Ciphertext Security Is Not Enough

In this section we show that these notions of security, which were standard when the results of Abadi and Rogaway were published, are not strong enough to ensure soundness in the case of key-cycles. That is, it is possible to construct encryption schemes that satisfy the standard notions of security (in particular, CCA-2 in the notation of [13]) but fail to provide soundness in the presence of key-cycles.

**Definition 12 (IND-CCA2—Adaptive Chosen Ciphertext Security).** *A computational public-key encryption scheme $\Pi = (\mathcal{K}, \mathcal{E}, \mathcal{D})$ provides* indistinguishability under the adaptive chosen-ciphertext attack *if for all PPT adversaries A and for all sufficiently large security parameters $\eta$:*

$$\Pr[\ (e, d) \longleftarrow \mathcal{K}(1^\eta);$$
$$m_0, m_1 \longleftarrow A^{\mathcal{D}_1(\cdot)}(1^\eta, e);$$
$$i \longleftarrow \{0, 1\};$$
$$c \longleftarrow \mathcal{E}(e, m_i);$$
$$g \longleftarrow A^{\mathcal{D}_2(\cdot)}(1^\eta, e, c):$$
$$b = g \qquad\qquad\qquad ] \le \tfrac{1}{2} + \mathrm{neg}\,(\eta)$$

*The oracle $\mathcal{D}_1(x)$ returns $\mathcal{D}(d, x)$, and $\mathcal{D}_2(x)$ returns $\mathcal{D}(d, x)$ if $x \ne c$ and returns $\perp$ otherwise. The adversary is assumed to keep state between the two invocations. It is required that $m_0$ and $m_1$ be of the same length.*

That is, an adversary should not be able to learn from a ciphertext whether it contains the plaintext $m_0$ or the plaintext $m_1$, even if:

- the adversary knows the public key used to encrypt,
- the adversary can choose the messages $m_0$ and $m_1$ itself, so long as the messages have the same length, and
- the adversary can request and receive the decryption of any *other* ciphertext.

This definition has been shown to be strictly stronger than almost all other definitions, including semantic security [13]. It does not, however, guarantee soundness: A does not have (obviously) access to the private keys, and therefore the messages submitted to the oracles $\mathcal{D}_1$ and $\mathcal{D}_2$ cannot depend on those private keys. Therefore key-dependent messages are not considered and not captured:

**Theorem 1.** *CCA-2 security does not imply soundness. That is, if there exists an encryption scheme secure against the chosen-ciphertext attack, then there exists another encryption scheme which is secure against the chosen-ciphertext attack but does not provide soundness.*

We motivate the proof with a simple example: one-time pads. Although this is a form of symmetric encryption and the rest of this paper discusses asymmetric encryption, the main ideas translate:

*Example 1 (One-Time Pad).* Consider a key-cycle of length 1, such as the expression $M = \{K\}_K$. When interpreted using one-time pads, $[\![M]\!]_\Phi$ will become a sequence of elements from $0^*$. However, we note that $M$ is equivalent to the expression $N = \{K'\}_K$, yet the interpretation of $N$ will be a family of uniformly random distributions. Thus, two equivalent expressions yield easily distinguished distribution families.

A similar argument, using CCA-2 encryption schemes instead of one-time pads, will suffice to prove Theorem 1. Given a CCA-2 secure encryption scheme, another CCA-2 encryption scheme is constructed which will provide distinguishable interpretations for expressions $M$ and $N$ above.

*Proof.* Let $\Pi = (\mathcal{K}, \mathcal{E}, \mathcal{D})$ be a CCA-2 secure encryption scheme. We construct a second CCA-2 secure encryption scheme $\Pi' = (\mathcal{K}', \mathcal{E}', \mathcal{D}')$ such that $\mathcal{K}' = \mathcal{K}, \mathcal{D}' = \mathcal{D}$, and $\mathcal{E}'$ is as follows:

- Receive input $(e, m)$, an encryption key and a message;
- Test whether $m$ is the decryption key associated with $e$. For many encryption schemes, key-pairs are recognizable as such via number-theoretic properties. Even when this is not the case, this test can be conducted via the sub-algorithm:
  - Select a random plaintext $r$;
  - Let $c \longleftarrow \mathcal{E}(e, r)$;
  - Let $p \longleftarrow \mathcal{D}(m, c)$;
  - Test whether $p = r$.
- If $m$ is the decryption key associated with $e$, output $m$;
- Otherwise, compute $c' \longleftarrow \mathcal{E}(e, m)$ and output $c'$.

Since $\Pi'$ acts exactly like $\Pi$ when plaintexts and encryption keys are unrelated, $\Pi'$ must be also CCA-2 secure. However, $\Pi'$ cannot be KDM-secure. Let $M$ be the formal expression $\{K^{-1}\}_K$, and let $N$ be the expression $\{K'^{-1}\}_K$. These two expressions are equivalent, but $[\![M]\!]_\Phi$ can be easily distinguished from $[\![N]\!]_\Phi$: the first distribution family will output a decryption key while the second outputs a ciphertext.    $\square$

*Remark 2.* We note that in both the example and the proof, the expression $M$ contains a key-cycle of length 1. What if all key-cycles are of length 2 or more? The one-time pad still fails to provide soundness: the interpretation of $(\{K_1\}_{K_2}, \{K_2\}_{K_1})$ is a pair of completely correlated distributions, while the interpretation of $(\{K_1\}_{K_2}, \{K_3\}_{K_1})$ is a pair of independent distributions. The same question in the public-key setting, however, remains open. That is, there is no known CCA-2 secure encryption scheme which fails to provide soundness for key-cycles that are of length two or more.

Since CCA-2 security implies a number of other definitions [13] (see the figure in Appendix A) we can easily conclude that these other definitions also do not imply soundness:

**Corollary 1.** *Soundness is not implied by any of: NM-CCA-1 security, IND-CCA-1 security, NM-CPA security, or IND-CPA (semantic) security.*

Therefore, soundness with key-cycles could not have been demonstrated with the standardcomputational notions of security available at the time. In the next section, we show that this soundness property can, however, be met with new computational definitions.

## 5 KDM Security and Soundness for Key-Cycles

### 5.1 KDM-Security

In the last section, we showed that the standard notions of security are not strong enough to enforce soundness in the presence of key-cycles. However, *key-dependent message* (KDM) security, which was introduced by Black *et al.* [14] (and in a weaker form by Camenisch and Lysyanskaya [16]), is strong enough to enforce soundness even in this case. (We note that Camenisch and Lysyanskaya also provided a natural application of KDM security, a credential system with interesting revocation properties, and so KDM security is of independent interest as well.)

KDM security strengthens IND-CPA (semantic) security, a weaker form of Definition 12 in which the adversary does not have access to the decryption oracles. However, semantic security still allows the adversary to submit two messages to be encrypted. KDM strengthens this by allowing more general submissions. In particular, in KDM security the adversary can submit not only fixed messages, but also *functions* of the decryption keys.

More precisely, KDM security is defined in terms of oracles $\mathsf{Real}_\mathbf{d}$ and $\mathsf{Fake}_\mathbf{d}$, which work as follows:

– Suppose that for a fixed security parameter $\eta \in \mathbb{N}$, a family of keys is given: $\{(e_i, d_i) \longleftarrow \mathcal{K}(1^\eta)\}_{i \in \mathbb{N}}$. The adversary can now query the oracles providing them with a pair $(j, g)$, where $j \in \mathbb{N}$ and $g : \mathsf{secretkey}^\infty \to \{0,1\}^*$ is a constant length, deterministic function and $\mathbf{d}$ is defined as the sequence $\langle d_1, d_2, \ldots \rangle$:
   • The oracle $\mathsf{Real}_\mathbf{d}$ when receiving this input returns $c \longleftarrow \mathcal{E}(e_j, g(\mathbf{d}))$;
   • The oracle $\mathsf{Fake}_\mathbf{d}$ when receiving this same input returns $c \longleftarrow \mathcal{E}(e_j, 0^{|g(\mathbf{d})|})$.

The challenge facing the adversary is to decide whether he has interacted with oracle $\mathsf{Real}_\mathbf{d}$ or oracle $\mathsf{Fake}_\mathbf{d}$. Formally:

**Definition 13 (KDM Security).** *Let* $\Pi = (\mathcal{K}, \mathcal{E}, \mathcal{D})$ *be an asymmetric encryption scheme. Let the two oracles* Real$_d$ *and* Fake$_d$ *be as defined above. We say that the encryption scheme is* KDM-secure *if for all PPT adversaries* A *and for all sufficiently large security parameters* $\eta$:

$$\left| \Pr\left[(\mathbf{e}, \mathbf{d}) \longleftarrow \mathcal{K}(1^\eta) : \mathsf{A}^{\mathsf{Real}_d}(1^\eta, \mathbf{e}) = 1\right] - \right.$$
$$\left. \Pr\left[(\mathbf{e}, \mathbf{d}) \longleftarrow \mathcal{K}(1^\eta) : \mathsf{A}^{\mathsf{Fake}_d}(1^\eta, \mathbf{e}) = 1\right] \right| \leq \mathrm{neg}(\eta)$$

*Remark 3.* We note that although all known implementations of KDM-security are in the random-oracle model, this definition is well-founded even in the standard model. We also note that this definition is phrased in terms of indistinguishability. One could also imagine analogous definitions phrased in terms of non-malleability, but an exploration of those are beyond the scope of the paper.

## 5.2   Soundness for Key-Cycles

Below, we present our main soundness result: if an encryption scheme is KDM secure, it also satisfies soundness.

**Theorem 2 (KDM Security Implies Soundness).** *Let* $\Pi = (\mathcal{K}, \mathcal{E}, \mathcal{D})$ *be a computational encryption scheme. If* $\Pi$ *is KDM-secure, then* $\Pi$ *provides soundness.*

This theorem holds even when the expressions have encryption-cycles. The proof in this case is a somewhat reduced hybrid argument. In a standard hybrid argument, like the one Abadi and Rogaway used to prove their soundness result, several patterns are put between $M$ and $N$; then, using security, it is proven that soundness holds between each two consecutive patterns, and therefore soundness holds for $M$ and $N$. In our case, we first directly prove that $[\![M]\!]_\Phi$ is indistinguishable from $[\![pattern(M)]\!]_\Phi$. Then, since that holds for $N$ too, and since $pattern(M)$ differs from $pattern(N)$ only in the name of keys, $[\![pattern(M)]\!]_\Phi$ is indistinguishable from $[\![pattern(N)]\!]_\Phi$, therefore the result follows. KDM security is used when we show that $[\![M]\!]_\Phi$ and $[\![pattern(M)]\!]_\Phi$ are indistinguishable.

*Proof.* For an arbitrary key $K$, let $\iota(K)$ denote the index of $K$. For an expression $M$, a set of formal decryption keys $S$, and a function $\tau$ defined on $(\mathbf{Keys} \cup \mathbf{Keys}^{-1}) \setminus S$ such that $\tau|_{\mathbf{Keys}}$ takes values in publickey and $\tau|_{\mathbf{Keys}^{-1}}$ takes values in secretkey, we define a function $f_{M,S,\tau} : \mathsf{coins}^{e(M)} \times \mathsf{secretkey}^\infty \to \mathsf{strings}$ (where $e(M)$ is the number of encryptions in $M$) inductively the following way:

- For $B \in \mathbf{Blocks}$, let $f_{B,S,\tau} : \mathsf{secretkey}^\infty \to \mathsf{strings}$, $f_{B,S,\tau}(\mathbf{d}) = B$;
- For $K \in \mathbf{Keys}$, let $f_{K,S,\tau} : \mathsf{secretkey}^\infty \to \mathsf{strings}$, $f_{K,S,\tau}(\mathbf{d}) = \tau(K)$;
- For $K^{-1} \in \mathbf{Keys}^{-1}$, if $K^{-1} \notin S$, then $f_{K^{-1},S,\tau} : \mathsf{secretkey}^\infty \to \mathsf{strings}$, $f_{K^{-1},S,\tau}(\mathbf{d}) = \tau(K^{-1})$;
- For $K^{-1} \in \mathbf{Keys}^{-1}$, if $K^{-1} \in S$, then $f_{K^{-1},S,\tau} : \mathsf{secretkey}^\infty \to \mathsf{strings}$, $f_{K^{-1},S,\tau}(\mathbf{d}) = d_{\iota(K)}$;
- Let $f_{(M,N),S,\tau} : \mathsf{coins}^{e(M)} \times \mathsf{coins}^{e(N)} \times \mathsf{secretkey}^\infty \to \mathsf{strings}$. Then, $f_{(M,N),S,\tau}$ is defined as
$$f_{(M,N),S,\tau}(\omega_M, \omega_N, \mathbf{d}) = [f_{M,S,\tau}(\omega_M, \mathbf{d}), f_{N,S,\tau}(\omega_N, \mathbf{d})];$$

- Let $f_{\{M\}_K,S,\tau} :$ coins $\times$ coins$^{e(M)} \times$ secretkey$^\infty \to$ strings. Then, $f_{\{M\}_K,S,\tau}$ is defined as

$$f_{\{M\}_K,S,\tau}(\omega, \omega_M, \mathbf{d}) = \mathcal{E}(\tau(K), f_{M,S,\tau}(\omega_M, \mathbf{d}), \omega).$$

We first prove that $[\![M]\!]_\Phi \approx [\![pattern(M)]\!]_\Phi$. Suppose that $[\![M]\!]_\Phi \not\approx [\![pattern(M)]\!]_\Phi$, which means that there is an adversary A that distinguishes the two distributions, that is

$$\Pr(x \longleftarrow [\![M]\!]_{\Phi_\eta} : \mathsf{A}(1^\eta, x) = 1) - \Pr(x \longleftarrow [\![pattern(M)]\!]_{\Phi_\eta} : \mathsf{A}(1^\eta, x) = 1)$$

is a non-negligible function of $\eta$. We will show that this contradicts the fact that the system is KDM-secure. To this end, we construct an adversary that can distinguish between the oracles $\mathsf{Real}_d$ and $\mathsf{Fake}_d$. Let $\mathcal{F}$ denote either of these oracles. Let $\mathbf{e} \in$ publickey$^\infty$ be the array of public keys that $\mathcal{F}$ outputs. From now on, let $S = \mathbf{Keys}^{-1} \setminus$ R-Keys$(M)$, and if $K^{-1} \in S$, let then $\tau(K) = e_{\iota(K)}$. Consider now the following algorithm:

> **algorithm** $B_\eta^{\mathcal{F}}(\mathbf{e}, M)$
>     For $K^{-1} \in$ R-Keys$(M)$, do $(\tau(K), \tau(K^{-1})) \longleftarrow \mathcal{K}(1^\eta)$
>     $y \longleftarrow$ CONVERT2$_\mathbf{e}(M, M)$
>     $b \longleftarrow \mathsf{A}(1^\eta, y)$
>     **return** $b$

> **algorithm** CONVERT2$_\mathbf{e}(M', M)$ with $M' \sqsubseteq M$
>     **if** $M' = K$ where $K \in \mathbf{Keys}$ **then**
>         **return** $\tau(K)$
>     **if** $M' = K^{-1}$ where $K^{-1} \in$ R-Keys$(M)$ **then**
>         **return** $\tau(K^{-1})$
>     **if** $M = B$ where $B \in \mathbf{Blocks}$ **then**
>         **return** $B$
>     **if** $M' = (M_1, M_2)$ **then**
>         $x \longleftarrow$ CONVERT2$_\mathbf{e}(M_1, M)$
>         $y \longleftarrow$ CONVERT2$_\mathbf{e}(M_2, M)$
>         **return** $[x, y]$
>     **if** $M' = \{M''\}_K$ with $K^{-1} \in$ R-Keys$(M)$ **then**
>         $x \longleftarrow$ CONVERT2$_\mathbf{e}(M'', M)$
>         $y \longleftarrow \mathcal{E}(\tau(K), x)$
>         **return** $y$
>     **if** $M' = \{M''\}_K$ with $K^{-1} \notin$ R-Keys$(M)$ **then**
>         $\omega \longleftarrow$ coins$^{e(M'')}$
>         $y \longleftarrow \mathcal{F}(\iota(K), f_{M'',S,\tau}(\omega, .))$
>         **return** $y$

This algorithm applies the distinguisher $\mathsf{A}(1^\eta, \cdot)$ on the distribution $[\![M]\!]_\Phi$ when $\mathcal{F}$ is $\mathsf{Real}_d$, and the distribution of $[\![pattern(M)]\!]_\Phi$ when $\mathcal{F}$ is $\mathsf{Fake}_d$. So, if $\mathsf{A}(1^\eta, \cdot)$ can distinguish $[\![M]\!]_\Phi$ and $[\![pattern(M)]\!]_\Phi$, then $B_\eta^{\mathcal{F}}(\mathbf{e}, M)$ can distinguish $\mathsf{Real}_d$ and $\mathsf{Fake}_d$. But we assumed that $\mathsf{Real}_d$ and $\mathsf{Fake}_d$ cannot be distinguished, so $[\![M]\!]_\Phi \approx [\![pattern(M)]\!]_\Phi$.

In a similar manner, we can show that $[\![N]\!]_\Phi \approx [\![pattern(N)]\!]_\Phi$. It is easy to see that $[\![pattern(M)]\!]_\Phi = [\![pattern(N)]\!]_\Phi$, because the two patterns differ only by key-renaming. Hence $[\![M]\!]_\Phi \approx [\![N]\!]_\Phi$. □

This one result has many powerful implications. Many extensions of the Abadi and Rogaway result simply rely on soundness as a 'black-box' assumption, and are not themselves hindered by key-cycles. By removing the key-cycle restriction from the Abadi-Rogaway result, it is removed from these extensions as well.

Consider, for example, the non-malleability results of Herzog [29]. In this setting, the adversary does not wish to distinguish two expressions but to transform one expression $M$ into another expression $M'$. The formal adversary has only a limited power to do this, and can only produce formal messages in a set called the *closure* of $M$ (denoted $C[M]$). Soundness for this non-malleability property is that no computational adversary, given the interpretation of $M$, can produce the interpretation of an expression outside $C[M]$. As Herzog shows, this soundness for this non-malleability property is directly implied by soundness for indistinguishability of messages (Definition 11). Because we show the KDM security soundness for message indistinguishability, this result of Herzog shows that it also provides soundness for non-malleability properties as well.

### 5.3  A Strictly New Notion

We now provide brief propositions about what Black *et al.* claimed informally: the notion of KDM security is 'orthogonal' to the previous definitions of security. In particular, we claim that KDM security neither implies nor is implied by chosen-ciphertext security (CCA-2). The former is proved directly, Theorem 3, while the latter is a corollary to previous theorems:

**Corollary 2.** *CCA-2 security does not imply KDM-security. If there exists an encryption scheme secure against the chosen-ciphertext attack, there exists an encryption scheme which is secure against the chosen-ciphertext attack but not KDM-secure.*

**Theorem 3.** *KDM security does not imply NM-CPA security. That is, there is an encryption scheme that is KDM-secure, but not NM-CPA secure.*

*Proof.* This is easily seen by inspecting the KDM-secure encryption scheme given by Black *et al.* in the random oracle model [14]. Let $\mathcal{F}$ be a trapdoor permutation generator. Then:

- $\mathcal{K} = \mathcal{F}$ produces pairs $(f, f^{-1})$ where $f$ encodes a trapdoor permutation and $f^{-1}$ encodes its inverse,
- The encryption algorithm $\mathcal{E}$, on input $(f, M)$, selects a random bit-string $r$ and returns the pair $(f(r), RO(r) \oplus M)$ (where $RO$ is the random oracle),
- $\mathcal{D}$, on input $(f^{-1}, C = (c_1, c_2))$, returns $RO(f^{-1}(c_1)) \oplus c_2$.

This scheme is not NM-CPA secure: it is simple to change the ciphertext associated with a message $M$ into the ciphertext of a related message. Note that an encryption of $M$ provides confidentiality by essentially applying a random $r$ as a one-time pad. Thus, changing a single bit of the (second component of a) ciphertext changes the same bit of the plaintext. That is, if $C = (f(r), RO(r) \oplus M)$ is an encryption of $M$, one can easily create $C' = (f(r), RO(r) \oplus \overline{M})$ (where $\overline{M}$ is the bit-wise complement of $M$). $C'$ decrypts to $\overline{M}$. Thus, this KDM-secure encryption scheme does not provide non-malleability of ciphertexts.                                                           □

Due to the various relations among the security notions (see Appendix A) we have the following corollary:

**Corollary 3.** *KDM security implies neither NM-CCA1 security nor CCA2 security.*

We conclude our discussion on the relationships between different notions of security by showing that soundness does not imply IND-CPA:

**Theorem 4.** *Soundness does not imply IND-CPA. That is, if there exists an encryption scheme with provides soundness, there exists a scheme which provides soundness but is not IND-CPA.*

*Proof.* Let $\Pi = (\mathcal{K}, \mathcal{E}, \mathcal{D})$ be a sound encryption scheme. Let $\Pi' = (\mathcal{K}', \mathcal{E}', \mathcal{D}')$ be the following. Let $\mathcal{K}' = \mathcal{K}$. Let $\mathcal{E}'$ do the same on an input of a pair of a public key and a plaintext $(k, x)$ as $\mathcal{E}$ for all plaintext, except when $x$ is the security parameter given by $k$, in which case $\mathcal{E}'$ outputs a fixed bit-string $\sigma$ of the same length as $\mathcal{E}(k, x)$. $\mathcal{D}'$ is the corresponding modified decryption algorithm.

This encryption scheme is still sound, because the interpretation of any expression with respect to $\mathcal{E}$ is indistinguishable from the interpretation of this same expression with respect to $\mathcal{E}'$. The reason for this is the following: For each security parameter, there is only one string that is encrypted differently by $\mathcal{E}$ and $\mathcal{E}'$. Let $\Phi$ and $\Phi'$ denote the respective interpretations. For any $K$ public or private key, $[\![K]\!]_\Phi = [\![K]\!]_{\Phi'}$ trivially, and also $[\![B]\!]_\Phi = [\![B]\!]_{\Phi'}$ for any block $B$. Moreover these interpretations hit the security parameter with negligible probability. Now, for any expression $M$, if $[\![M]\!]_\Phi \approx [\![M]\!]_{\Phi'}$ and $[\![M]\!]_{\Phi'}$ hits the security parameter with negligible probability, then $[\![\{M\}_K]\!]_\Phi \approx [\![\{M\}_K]\!]_{\Phi'}$, and $[\![\{M\}_K]\!]_{\Phi'}$ hits the security parameter with negligible probability. Similarly for pairing. Therefore, by induction, the two interpretations of a given expression are indistinguishable.

On the other hand, it is easy to see, that $\Pi'$ is not IND-CPA secure, because an adversary who submits as candidate messages the security parameter and $0^\eta$ (that is, outputs $m_0 = 0^\eta$, $m_1 = 1^\eta$) will certainly be able to determine which of the two messages was encrypted.

These statements are summarized in a figure in Appendix A.

## 6    Conclusions

We have considered computational soundness of formal encryption. This property states that formal equivalence of symbolic expressions implies computational indistinguishability when the symbolic expressions are interpreted using a given computational encryption scheme. Computational soundness was proved in Abadi and Rogaway [2] under the assumption that there are no key-cycles and that a computational encryption scheme satisfies a strong version of semantic security (so-called type-0 in the sense of Abadi and Rogaway [2]). We have considered a modification of their logic in the case of which-key revealing and message-length revealing, asymmetric encryption schemes (which corresponds to so-called type-3 in the sense of Abadi and Rogaway [2]). In the presence of key-cycles, we have proved that the computational soundness property follows from the key-dependent message (KDM) security proposed by Black *et al.* [14]. As far as we know, this is the first time that in order to achieve soundness, the computational model is strengthened and not the formal model weakened. We have also shown that the computational soundness property neither implies nor is it implied by security against chosen ciphertext attack, CCA-2. This is in contrast to many previous results where forms of soundness are implied by CCA-2 security.

Our work presents several directions for future research. Firstly, several questions about KDM security (independently of any soundness considerations) remain unanswered. An implementation of KDM security in the standard model remains to be found, although there are several natural candidates (for instance Cramer-Shoup [22]). Conversely, there remains to be found a natural (*i.e.*, non-constructed) example of an encryption scheme which is secure in the sense of CCA-2 but is not KDM-secure. Further, the constructed examples of such encryption schemes only fail to provide KDM security when presented with key-cycles of length 1. It may be possible that CCA-2 security implies KDM security when all key-cycles are of length 2 or more. Lastly, similar questions can also be posed in the setting of symmetric-key encryption—a course of investigation we are currently investigating.

With regard to soundness, on the other hand, it seems desirable to extend our results from the passive-adversary setting to that of the active adversary. Also, we show that the relationship between the formal and computational models requires more than chosen-ciphertext security. While it demonstrates that KDM security is also necessary, it does not show it to be sufficient—even when conjoined with CCA-2 security. That is, this investigation is not complete; it is more than likely additional properties will be revealed as necessary as soundness is more fully explored.

# References

1. M. Abadi and J. Jürjens. Formal eavesdropping and its computational interpretation. In *Proc. 4-th International Symp. on Theor. Aspects of Comp. Software (TACS)*, Springer LNCS Vol. 2215, pp. 82–94, 2001.
2. M. Abadi and P. Rogaway. Reconciling two views of cryptography (the computational soundness of formal encryption). *J. Cryptology*, 15(2):103–127, 2002. Prelim. version in IFIP TCS'00.
3. P. Adão, G. Bana, and A. Scedrov. Computational and information-theoretic soundness and completeness of formal encryption. In *Proc. 18-th IEEE Computer Security Foundations Workshop (CSFW)*, pp. 170–184, IEEE Comp. Soc. Press, 2005.
4. M. Backes and C. Jacobi. Cryptographically sound and machine-assisted verification of security protocols. In *Proc. 20-th Annual Symp. on Theor. Aspects of Comp. Sci. (STACS)*, Springer LNCS Vol. 2607, pp. 675–686, 2003.
5. M. Backes and B. Pfitzmann. A cryptographically sound security proof of the Needham-Schröeder-Lowe public-key protocol. *IEEE J. Selected Areas in Communications*, 22(10):2075–2086, 2004. Prelim. version in FSTTCS'03.

6. M. Backes and B. Pfitzmann. Symmetric encryption in a simulatable Dolev-Yao style cryptographic library. In *Proc. 17-th IEEE Computer Security Foundations Workshop (CSFW)*, 2004. Full version on ePrint 2004/059.
7. M. Backes, B. Pfitzmann, and M. Waidner. Symmetric authentication within a simulatable cryptographic library. In *Proc. 8-th European Symp. on Research in Comp. Security (ESORICS)*, Springer LNCS Vol. 2808, pp. 271–290, 2003. Extended version on ePrint 2003/145.
8. M. Backes, B. Pfitzmann, and M. Waidner. Secure asynchronous reactive systems. ePrint 2004/082.
9. M. Backes and B. Pfitzmann. Relating symbolic and cryptographic secrecy. *IEEE Trans. on Dependable and Secure Computing*, 2(2):109–123, 2005. Full version on ePrint 2004/300.
10. M. Backes, B. Pfitzmann, and M. Waidner. A composable cryptographic library with nested operations. In *Proc. 10-th ACM Conf. on Computer and Communications Security (CCS)*, pp. 220–230, ACM Press, 2003. Full version on ePrint 2003/015.
11. G. Bana. *Soundness and Completeness of Formal Logics of Symmetric Encryption*. PhD thesis, University of Pennsylvania, 2004. Available on ePrint 2005/101.
12. M. Baudet, V. Cortier, and S. Kremer. Computationally sound implementations of equational theories against passive adversaries. In: ICALP'05, Springer LNCS Vol. 3580, pp. 652–663, to appear.
13. M. Bellare, A. Desai, D. Pointcheval, and P. Rogaway. Relations among notions of security for public-key encryption schemes. In CRYPTO '98, Springer LNCS Vol. 1462, pp. 26–45, 1998. Full version available at http://www.cs.ucsd.edu/users/mihir/papers/relations.html.
14. J. Black, P. Rogaway, and T. Shrimpton. Encryption-scheme security in the presence of key-dependent messages. In *Proc. 9-th Annual International Workshop on Selected Areas in Cryptography (SAC)*, Springer LNCS Vol. 2595, pp. 62–75, 2002.
15. D. Beaver. Secure multiparty protocols and zero knowledge proof systems tolerating a faulty minority. *J. Cryptology*, 4(2):75–122, 1991.
16. J. Camenisch and A. Lysyanskaya. An efficient system for non-transferable anonymous credentials with optional anonymity revocation. In *EUROCRYPT 2001*, Springer LNCS Vol. 2045, pp. 98–118, 2001.
17. R. Canetti. Security and composition of multiparty cryptographic protocols. *J. Cryptology*, 3(1):143–202, 2000.
18. R. Canetti. Universally composable security: A new paradigm for cryptographic protocols. In *42-nd IEEE Symp. on Foundations of Comp. Sci. (FOCS)*, pp. 136–145, IEEE Comp. Soc. Press, 2001. Full version on ePrint 2000/067.
19. R. Canetti and J. Herzog. Universally composable symbolic analysis of cryptographic protocols (the case of encryption-based mutual authentication and key exchange). ePrint 2004/334.
20. R. Canetti, O. Goldreich, and S. Halevi. The random oracle methodology, revisited. In *Proc. 30-th Annual ACM Symp. on Theory of Computing (STOC)*, pp. 209–218, ACM Press, 1998.
21. V. Cortier and B. Warinschi. Computationally sound, automated proofs for security protocols. In *Proc. 14-th European Symp. on Programming (ESOP)*, Springer LNCS Vol. 3444, pp. 157–171, 2005.
22. R. Cramer and V. Shoup. A practical public key cryptosystem provably secure against adaptive chosen ciphertext attack. In *CRYPTO '98*, Springer LNCS Vol. 1462, pp. 13–25, 1998.
23. A. Datta, R. Küsters, J. C. Mitchell, and A. Ramanathan. On the relationships between notions of simulation-based security. In *2-nd Theory of Cryptography Conference, TCC 2005*, Springer LNCS Vol. 3378, pp. 476–494, 2005.
24. A. Datta, A. Derek, J. C. Mitchell, V. Shmatikov, and M. Turuani. Probabilistic polynomial-time semantics for a protocol security logic. In ICALP'05, Springer LNCS Vol. 3580, to appear.

25. D. Dolev and A. C. Yao. On the security of public-key protocols. *IEEE Trans. on Information Theory*, 29(2):198–208, 1983. Prelim. version in FOCS'81.

26. J. D. Guttman, F. J. Thayer, and L. D. Zuck. The faithfulness of abstract protocol analysis: Message authentication. In *Proc. 8-th ACM Conf. on Computer and Communications Security (CCS)*, pp. 186–195, ACM Press, 2001.

27. S. Goldwasser and L. Levin. Fair computation of general functions in presence of immoral majority. In *CRYPTO '90*, Springer LNCS Vol. 537, pp. 77–93, 1990.

28. J. Herzog. *Computational Soundness of Formal Adversaries*. Master thesis, MIT, 2002.

29. J. Herzog. *Computational Soundness for Standard Assumptions of Formal Cryptography*. PhD thesis, MIT, 2004. Available at http://theory.lcs.mit.edu/~jherzog/papers/herzog-phd.pdf.

30. J. Herzog, M. Liskov, and S. Micali. Plaintext awareness via key registration. In *CRYPTO 2003*, Springer LNCS Vol. 2729, pp. 548–564, 2003.

31. O. Horvitz and V. Gligor. Weak key authenticity and the computational completeness of formal encryption. In *CRYPTO 2003*, Springer LNCS Vol. 2729, pp. 530–547, Sant 2003.

32. R. Impagliazzo and B. M. Kapron. Logics for reasoning about cryptographic constructions. In *Proc. 44-th IEEE Symp. on Foundations of Comp. Sci. (FOCS)*, pp. 372–381, IEEE Comp. Soc. Press, 2003.

33. P. Laud. Encryption cycles and two views of cryptography. In *Proc. 7-th Nordic Workshop on Secure IT Systems (NORDSEC)*, Karlstad Univ. Studies No. 31, pp. 85–100, 2002.

34. P. Laud. Symmetric encryption in automatic analyses for confidentiality against active adversaries. In *Proc. 2004 IEEE Symp. on Security and Privacy*, pp. 71–85, IEEE Comp. Soc. Press, 2004.

35. P. Laud and R. Corin. Sound computational interpretation of formal encryption with composed keys. In *Proc. 6-th International Conf. on Information Security and Cryptology (ICISC)*, Springer LNCS Vol. 2971, pp. 55–66, 2003.

36. P. Lincoln, J. C. Mitchell, M. Mitchell, and A. Scedrov. A probabilistic polynomial-time framework for protocol analysis. In *Proc. 5-th ACM Conf. on Computer and Communications Security (CCS)*, pp. 112–121, ACM Press, 1998.

37. S. Micali and P. Rogaway. Secure computation. In *CRYPTO '91*, Springer LNCS Vol. 576, pp. 392–404, 1991.

38. S. Micali, C. Rackoff, and B. Sloan. The notion of security for probabilistic cryptosystems. *SIAM J. Computing*, 17(2):412–426, 1998.

39. D. Micciancio and S. Panjwani. Adaptive security of symbolic encryption. In *Proc. 2-nd Theory of Cryptography Conference (TCC 2005)*, Springer LNCS Vol. 3378, pp. 169–187, 2005.

40. D. Micciancio and B. Warinschi. Completeness theorems for the Abadi-Rogaway logic of encrypted expressions. *J. Computer Security*, 12(1):99–130, 2004. Prelim. version in WITS'02.

41. D. Micciancio and B. Warinschi. Soundness of formal encryption in the presence of active adversaries. In *Proc. 1-st Theory of Cryptography Conference (TCC 2004)*, Springer LNCS Vol. 2951, pp. 133–151, 2004.

42. J. C. Mitchell, A. Ramanathan, A. Scedrov, and V. Teague. A probabilistic polynomial-time calculus for the analysis of cryptographic protocols. Full, revised version available on http://theory.stanford.edu/people/jcm/publications.htm. Prelim. report in FOSSACS'04, Springer LNCS Vol. 2987.

43. B. Pfitzmann, M. Schunter, and M. Waidner. Cryptographic security of reactive systems. *DERA/RHUL Workshop on Secure Architectures and Information Flow*, 1999, ENTCS, 2000. http://www.elsevier.nl/cas/tree/store/tcs/free/noncas/pc/menu.htm.

44. B. Pfitzmann and M. Waidner. Composition and integrity preservation of secure reactive systems. In *Proc. 7-th ACM Conf. on Computer and Communications Security*, pp. 245–254, ACM Press, 2000. Extended version (with M. Schunter) IBM Research Report RZ 3206, 2000, http://www.zurich.ibm.com/security/models.

45. B. Pfitzmann and M. Waidner. A model for asynchronous reactive systems and its application to secure message transmission. In *Proc. 2001 IEEE Symp. on Security and Privacy*, pp. 184–200, IEEE Comp. Soc. Press, 2001.

46. A. Sahai. Non-malleable non-interactive zero knowledge and adaptive chosen-ciphertext security. In *40-th IEEE Symp. on Foundations of Comp. Sci. (FOCS)*, pp. 543–553, IEEE Comp. Soc. Press, 1999.

47. B. Warinschi. A computational analysis of the Needham-Schröeder-(Lowe) protocol. In *Proc. 16-th IEEE Computer Security Foundations Workshop (CSFW)*, pp. 248–262, IEEE Comp. Soc. Press, 2003.

# A    Computational Definitions of Security for Asymmetric Encryption Schemes

We present the standard computational notions of security for asymmetric encryption schemes. See Figure 1 for their relationships.

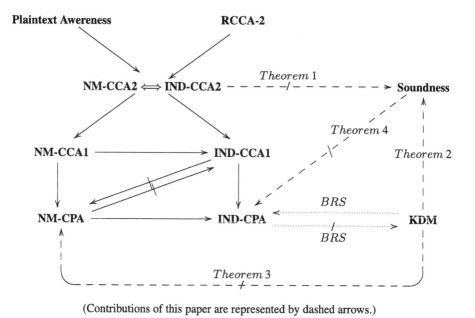

(Contributions of this paper are represented by dashed arrows.)

**Fig. 1.** Relation Among Different Security Notions

## B   Interpretation Algorithm

For a pattern $M$ we define the interpretation as

> **algorithm** $INITIALIZE_\eta(M)$
>   **for** $K \in Keys(M)$ **do** $(\tau(K), \tau(K^{-1})) \longleftarrow \mathcal{K}(1^\eta)$

> **algorithm** $\text{CONVERT}_\eta(M)$
>   **if** $M = K$ where $K \in$ **Keys then**
>     **return** $\tau(K)$
>   **if** $M = K^{-1}$ where $K \in$ **Keys**$^{-1}$ **then**
>     **return** $\tau(K^{-1})$
>   **if** $M = B$ where $B \in$ **Blocks then**
>     **return** $B$
>   **if** $M = (M_1, M_2)$ **then**
>     $x \longleftarrow \text{CONVET}_\eta(M_1)$
>     $y \longleftarrow \text{CONVERT}_\eta(M_2)$
>     **return** $[x, y]$
>   **if** $M = \{M_1\}_K$ **then**
>     $x \longleftarrow \text{CONVERT}_\eta(M_1)$
>     $y \longleftarrow \mathcal{E}(\tau(K), x)$
>     **return** $y$
>   **if** $M = \square_{K,\ell(M')}$, **then**
>     $y \longleftarrow \mathcal{E}(\tau(K), 0^{|\Phi_\eta(M')|})$
>     **return** $y$

We note that expressions are simply patterns in which symbols of the form $\square_{K,\ell(M')}$ do not appear, and thus can be interpreted by this same algorithm.

# Privacy Preserving Clustering

Somesh Jha[1], Luis Kruger[1], and Patrick McDaniel[2]

[1] Computer Sciences Department, University of Wisconsin, Madison, WI, USA
{jha, lpkruger}@cs.wisc.edu
[2] Computer Science and Engineering, Pennsylvania State University, University Park, PA, USA
mcdaniel@cse.psu.edu

**Abstract.** The freedom and transparency of information flow on the Internet has heightened concerns of privacy. Given a set of data items, clustering algorithms group similar items together. Clustering has many applications, such as customer-behavior analysis, targeted marketing, forensics, and bioinformatics. In this paper, we present the design and analysis of a privacy-preserving $k$-means clustering algorithm, where only the cluster means at the various steps of the algorithm are revealed to the participating parties. The crucial step in our privacy-preserving $k$-means is privacy-preserving computation of cluster means. We present two protocols (one based on oblivious polynomial evaluation and the second based on homomorphic encryption) for privacy-preserving computation of cluster means. We have a JAVA implementation of our algorithm. Using our implementation, we have performed a thorough evaluation of our privacy-preserving clustering algorithm on three data sets. Our evaluation demonstrates that privacy-preserving clustering is feasible, i.e., our homomorphic-encryption based algorithm finished clustering a large data set in approximately 66 seconds.

## 1 Introduction

The ease and transparency of information flow on the Internet has heightened concerns of personal privacy [9,49]. Web surfing, email, and other services constantly leak information about who we are and what we care about. Many have accepted that some privacy will be lost in exchange for the benefits of digital services [48]. However, in other domains privacy is so important that its protection is federally mandated [1]. Technologies for protecting privacy are emerging in response to these growing concerns [8,18,45]. Recently, more emphasis has been placed on preserving the privacy of user-data aggregations, e.g., databases of personal information. Access to these collections is, however, enormously useful. It is from this balance between privacy and utility that the area of *privacy preserving data-mining* emerged [3,33].

Unsupervised learning deals with designing classifiers from a set of unlabeled samples. A common approach for unsupervised learning is to first cluster or group unlabeled samples into sets of samples that are "similar" to each other. Once the clusters have been constructed, we can design classifiers for each cluster using standard techniques (such as decision-tree learning [38,44]). Moreover, clusters can also be used to identify features that will be useful for classification. There is significant research on privacy-preserving algorithms for designing classifiers [3,33]. This paper addresses the problem of privacy-preserving algorithms for clustering.

S. De Capitani di Vimercati et al. (Eds.): ESORICS 2005, LNCS 3679, pp. 397–417, 2005.

Assume that Alice $A$ and Bob $B$ have two unlabeled samples $D_A$ and $D_B$. We assume that each sample in $D_A$ and $D_B$ has all the attributes, or the data sets are horizontally partitioned between $A$ and $B$. Alice and Bob want to cluster the joint data set $D_A \cup D_B$ without revealing the individual items of their data sets (of course Alice only obtains the clusters corresponding to her data set $D_A$). In this paper, we assume that clustering the joint data set $D_A \cup D_B$ provides better results than individually clustering $D_A$ and $D_B$. Using a large data set from the networking domain we also demonstrate that clustering the joint data set results in significantly different clusters than individually clustering the data sets (see end of section 5 for details). We present a privacy-preserving version of the $k$-means algorithm where only the cluster means at the various steps of the algorithm are revealed to Alice and Bob.

There are several applications of clustering [14]. Any application of clustering where there are privacy concerns is a possible candidate for our privacy-preserving clustering algorithm. For example, suppose network traffic is collected at two ISPs, and the two ISPs want to cluster the joint network traffic without revealing their individual traffic data. Our algorithm can be used to obtain joint clusters while respecting the privacy of the network traffic at the two ISPs. An application of clustering to network intrusion detection is presented by Marchette [36]. Clustering has been used for forensics [43] and root-cause analysis for alarms [29]. Clustering has also been used in bioinformatics. For example, Dhillon *et al.* [11] have used clustering to predict gene function. We believe that privacy-preserving clustering can be used in bioinformatics where the data sets are owned by separate organizations, who do not want to reveal their individual data sets.

This paper makes the following contributions:

- We present the design and analysis of privacy-preserving $k$-means clustering algorithm for horizontally partitioned data (see Section 3). The crucial step in our algorithm is privacy-preserving of cluster means. We present two protocols for privacy-preserving computation of cluster means. The first protocol is based on oblivious polynomial evaluation and the second one on homomorphic encryption. These protocols are described in detail in Section 4.
- We have also have a JAVA implementation of our algorithm. We believe that modular design of our implementation will enable other researchers to use our implementation. Our clustering tool is available by request. We evaluated the two privacy-preserving clustering algorithms on real data sets. Our first conclusion is that privacy-preserving clustering is feasible. For example, for a large data set (5,687 samples and 12 features) from the speech recognition domain our homomorphic-encryption-based algorithm took approximately 66 seconds. We also observed that both in bandwidth efficiency and execution overhead algorithms based on homomorphic encryption performed better than the one based on oblivious polynomial evaluation. A detailed discussion of our evaluation is given in Section 5.

## 2   Related Work

Privacy issues in statistical databases have been thoroughly investigated [2,10]. Recently privacy-preserving data mining has been a very active area of research. Initial focus in this area was on construction of decision trees from distributed data sets [3,33]. There is also a significant body of research on privacy-preserving mining of association rules [15,46,50]. We will focus on existing work on privacy-preserving clustering.

In general, there are two approaches for designing privacy-preserving machine learning algorithms. The first approach is to use transformations to perturb the data set before the algorithm is applied. This approach for designing privacy-preserving clustering algorithms is taken by several researchers [31,37,41]. A second approach to designing privacy preserving algorithms is to use algorithms from the secure-multiparty computation literature. The advantage of this approach over the perturbation approach is that formal guarantees of privacy can be given for these algorithms. This paper takes the latter approach. Vaidya and Clifton's [51] work is closest to the one presented in this paper. Vaidya and Clifton present a privacy-preserving $k$-means algorithm for vertically-partitioned data sets. As already pointed out in the introduction, our paper considers clustering for horizontally-partitioned data. Vaidya and Clifton's algorithm is based on the secure-permutation algorithm of Du and Atallah [13]. However, Vaidya and Clifton's algorithm has to execute Du and Atallah's protocol for every item in the data set. Therefore, their algorithm is not practical for large data sets. Moreover, Vaidya and Clifton did not perform an experimental evaluation of their algorithm. By contrast, the complexity of our algorithm only depends on the number of steps taken by the $k$-means algorithm and the dimension of the data items. There are distributed clustering algorithms where the goal is to reduce communication costs [12,30]. These distributed clustering algorithms do not consider privacy. However, it will be interesting to investigate whether these algorithms can be made privacy preserving.

In our implementation, we approximate real numbers using intervals (see appendix C). Finite-precision approximation to functions may leak information. Feigenbaum *et al.* [16] show that approximations to functions can be made private by adding noise.

## 3   The $k$-Means Clustering Algorithm

The $k$-means algorithm [14,34] is shown in Figure 1. Assume that we are given $n$ samples $x_1, \cdots, x_n$, where each sample is a $m$-dimensional vector of real numbers. The number of clusters is $c$. The algorithm maintains $c$ means $\mu_1, \cdots, \mu_c$. Initially, assume that the means are assigned arbitrary values. A sample $x_i$ is deemed to be in the cluster $j$ if it is closest to the mean $\mu_j$, where mean of a cluster $\{x'_1, \cdots, x'_r\}$ is $\frac{x'_1 + \cdots + x'_r}{r}$. Distance between two $m$-dimensional vectors $x$ and $y$ is given by $\sum_{j=1}^{m}(x[j] - y[j])^2$, where $x[j]$ is the $j$-th element of the vector $x$. Other distance metrics [14, Chapter 10], such as scatter metrics, can be used instead of the distance metric mentioned above. Each iteration of the $k$-means algorithms recomputes the means and reclassifies the samples. The algorithm terminates when it detects "no change" in the means. The precise definition of "no change" depends on the specific metric being used. We also assume that the initial cluster means are chosen randomly. There is some research on picking the initial cluster means [4]. Various techniques for picking initial cluster means can be easily incorporated into our algorithm. This issue will not be discussed further in the paper.

```
Algorithm (k-means clustering)
  begin initialize n, c, μ₁, · · · , μ_c
    do classify n samples according to nearest μ_i, and
       recompute μ_i
    until no change in μ_i's
    return μ₁, μ₂, · · · , μ_c
  end
```

**Fig. 1.** The $k$-means clustering algorithm

## 3.1 Distributed $k$-Means

Assume that Alice $A$ (party 1) has $z$ samples $\{x_1, \cdots, x_{n_A}\}$, and Bob $B$ (party 2) has $n - n_A$ samples $\{x_{n_A+1}, \cdots, x_n\}$. Each party wants to jointly cluster their samples without revealing any private information. We are assuming that clustering the union of samples from the two parties is more desirable than clustering the two samples individually.

Assume that there is a trusted third party $TTP$. $A$ and $B$ perform iterations locally. However, at each iteration the new cluster means $\mu_i$s are computed by communicating with the $TTP$. Let $C_i^A$ and $C_i^B$ be the cluster corresponding to mean $\mu_i$ for $A$ and $B$, respectively. $A$ sends $c$-pairs $\langle (a_1, b_1), \cdots, (a_c, b_c) \rangle$ to $TTP$, where $a_i = \sum_{x_j \in C_i^A} x_j$ and $b_i = | C_i^A |$ ($a_i$ is the sum of samples in cluster $C_i^A$ and $b_i$ is the number of samples in the cluster $C_i^A$). Analogously, $B$ sends $c$-pairs $\langle (d_1, e_1), \cdots, (d_c, e_c) \rangle$ to the $TTP$, where $d_i = \sum_{x_j \in C_i^B} x_j$ and $e_i = | C_i^B |$. The $TTP$ computes the $c$ means $\langle \mu_1, \cdots, \mu_c \rangle$ and sends them to $A$ and $B$, where $\mu_i = \frac{a_i + d_i}{b_i + e_i}$. We call this algorithm *distributed k-means* or $D_{k\text{-means}}$.

## 3.2 Assumptions

Our goal is to design a privacy-preserving $k$-means that does not use a TTP. Before we present such an algorithm, we state assumptions made in the design of our privacy-preserving algorithm.

*Number of parties.* In this paper we only present the two party case.

*The adversary model.* We assume a semi-honest adversary (also called honest but curious adversary model) [20]. There are standard constructions that transform a protocol that is secure in the semi-honest model and produce a protocol that is secure in a more general malicious model (these constructions are called "semi-honest to malicious" compilers, and details of these constructions can be found in [23]).

*Information disclosure.* Our privacy-preserving algorithm discloses the cluster means at the various steps to the two parties. Therefore, the computation of classifying samples according to the nearest cluster means can be performed locally. Therefore, the complexity of our privacy-preserving algorithm depends only on the number of steps taken by the $k$-means algorithm and the number of features, but not on the size of the data. This is a desirable property because usually the data sets to be clustered can be very large.

### 3.3   Privacy-Preserving $k$-Means

In order, to create a privacy-preserving version of $k$-means that does not use a TTP we have to devise a privacy-preserving protocol to compute the cluster means. Consider the computation of a single cluster mean $\mu_i$. Recall that in distributed $k$-means each party sends $(a_i, b_i)$ and $(d_i, e_i)$ to the TTP, which computes $\frac{a_i + d_i}{b_i + e_i}$; this is precisely the function for which we have to devise a privacy-preserving protocol. This problem can be formally defined as follows:

**Definition 1.** The *weighted average problem (WAP)* is defined as follows: party 1 has a pair $(x, n)$, where $x$ is a real number and $n$ is a positive integer. Similarly, party 2 has pair $(y, m)$. They want to jointly compute $\frac{x+y}{n+m}$. In other words, we need a privacy-preserving protocol for the following functionality:

$$((x, n), (y, m)) \longmapsto (\frac{x+y}{n+m}, \frac{x+y}{n+m})$$

The notation shown above means that the first and second party provide inputs $(x, n)$ and $(y, m)$ to the protocol and both parties receive output $\frac{x+y}{n+m}$. Notice that WAP is different than the classical problem of computing the averages, where $n$ parties have a number and they jointly want to compute the average without revealing their individual numbers. In the classical problem, the number of parties $n$ is known to all the parties. In WAP, the number of points $n$ and $m$ needs to be kept secret.

Let $\mathcal{P}_{WAP}$ be a privacy-preserving protocol for solving WAP. Two protocols for WAP are presented in Section 4. In the privacy-preserving $k$-means algorithm (denoted as $PP_{k\text{-means}}$) $A$ and $B$ use $\mathcal{P}_{WAP}$ instead of the trusted third party $TTP$ to compute the cluster means $\mu_i$s. The algorithm is shown in Fig 2. We only show the part of the algorithm executing at Alice's (party 1) side. Bob (party 2) will execute a similar algorithm at his side.

**Note:** Suppose that the initial clusters are picked randomly. For the privacy-preserving algorithm we need a protocol for two parties to jointly pick a common random vector. Such a protocol is called *coin-tossing into the well* and is based on commitment schemes (see [20, Section 7.4.3.1]).

### 3.4   Proof of Privacy

In this section we provide a proof of privacy for the protocol shown in Figure 2. The proof uses a semi-honest adversary model. Notice that in the distributed $k$-means algorithm $\mathcal{D}_{k\text{-means}}$ both parties only know their input and output. Definition of privacy is based on the intuition that parties should learn nothing more from the messages used in privacy-preserving protocol, i.e., the messages received by a party during an execution of a privacy-preserving protocol can be "effectively computed" by only knowing its input and output. This idea is formalized below:

**Definition 2.** Let $x$ and $y$ be inputs of the two parties and $\langle f_1(x, y), f_2(x, y) \rangle$ be the desired functionality, i.e., the first party wants to compute $f_1(x, y)$ and the second

402 S. Jha, L. Kruger, and P. McDaniel

Algorithm $PP_{k\text{-means}}$ (privacy-preserving $k$-means clustering)
**begin** initialize $n_A, c, \mu_1, \cdots, \mu_c$
   **do** classify $n_A$ samples according to nearest $\mu_i$
     **for** $i := 1$ **to** $c$ **step** 1 **do**
       Let $C_i^A$ be the $i$-th cluster
       Compute $a_i = \sum_{x_j \in C_i^A} x_j$ and $b_i = \mid C_i^A \mid$
       recompute $\mu_i$ by invoking the protocol $\mathcal{P}_{WAP}$
     **od**
     **until** no change in $\mu_i$
     **return** $\mu_1, \mu_2, \cdots, \mu_c$
  **end**

**Fig. 2.** The privacy-preserving $k$-means clustering algorithm

wants to compute $f_2(x, y)$. Let $\Pi$ be a two-party protocol to compute $f$. The view of the first party after having participated in protocol $\Pi$ (denoted by $\text{VIEW}_1^\Pi(x, y)$) is $(x, r, m_1, \cdots m_t)$, where $r$ are the random bits generated by party 1 and $m_1, \cdots, m_t$ is the sequence of messages received by party 1, while participating in protocol $\Pi$. The view $\text{VIEW}_2^\Pi(x, y)$ for the second party is defined in an analogous manner.

We say that $\Pi$ *privately computes* $f$ if there exists probabilistic polynomial-time algorithms (PPTA), denoted by $S_1$ and $S_2$ such that

$$\{S_1(x, f_1(x, y))\}_{x,y} \equiv^s \{\text{VIEW}_1^\Pi(x, y)\}_{x,y}$$
$$\{S_2(x, f_2(x, y))\}_{x,y} \equiv^s \{\text{VIEW}_2^\Pi(x, y)\}_{x,y}$$

In the equation given above, $\equiv^s$ denotes *statistically indistinguishable*. Two probability ensembles $X = \{X_w\}_{w \in S}$ and $Y = \{Y_w\}_{w \in S}$ indexed by $S$ are statistically indistinguishable if for some negligible function $\mu : \aleph \mapsto [0, 1]$ and all $w \in S$,

$$\sum_\alpha \mid Pr(X_w = \alpha) - Pr(Y_w = \alpha) \mid < \mu(\mid w \mid)$$

A function $\mu : \aleph \mapsto [0, 1]$ is called *negligible* if for every positive polynomial $p$, and all sufficiently large $n$'s, $\mu(n) < \frac{1}{p(n)}$. There is a weaker notion of indistinguishability called *computationally indistinguishable*. We will use statistical indistinguishability throughout the paper, but all the results hold even if the weaker notion of indistinguishability is used. Detailed definitions of these concepts can be found in [19,20].

The privacy-preserving $k$-means algorithm uses the privacy-preserving protocol $\mathcal{P}_{WAP}$ for the WAP. Assume that the two parties invoke the protocol $\mathcal{P}_{WAP}$ as an oracle, i.e., both parties write their respective inputs (in this case $(x, n)$ and $(y, m)$) and invoke the oracle which returns the result (in this case $\frac{x+y}{n+m}$). Recall that in the distributed $k$-means algorithms both parties learn the cluster means at various steps. If we use oracle calls to compute the cluster means, then the two parties also learn only the cluster means. So the views in the two cases are *identical*. Hence, the conditions of definition 2 are trivially satisfied. However, there are additional messages exchanged in the protocol $\mathcal{P}_{WAP}$ used to compute the cluster means. We need to ensure that nothing can be learned from these messages. The privacy of protocol shown in Figure 2 follows from the composition theorem [7] stated below ($g$ is the algorithm shown in Figure 2 and $f$ is the protocol $P_{WAP}$ to solve WAP described in Section 4):

**Theorem 1.** (Composition Theorem for the semi-honest model): *Suppose that $g$ is privately reducible to $f$ and that there exists a protocol for privately computing $f$. Then there exists a protocol for privately computing $g$.*

## 4  Privacy-Preserving Protocol for the Weighted Average Problem

In the weighted average problem (WAP) we want to find a privacy-preserving protocol for the following functionality:

$$((x, n), (y, m)) \longmapsto (\frac{x+y}{n+m}, \frac{x+y}{n+m})$$

Recall that a protocol for WAP was used in the privacy-preserving $k$-means algorithm (see Figure 2).

A simple strategy to address this problem is to first approximate the function $\frac{x+y}{n+m}$ by a circuit $C$, and then use standard constructions [21,22,52] to construct a privacy-preserving protocol. Protocols constructed using this strategy have a very high computational overhead. Malkhi *et al.* considered the cost of implementing these protocols in their work in the Fairplay system [35]. They found that the protocol was feasible for small circuits, e.g., a single $\wedge$-gate could be implemented in 410 milliseconds, and more complex integer numerical functions could be implemented on the order of seconds. They further showed the runtimes of these protocols grow quickly with the size of the input and complexity of the implemented function. The most complex function discussed by the authors computed a median of two ten-element integer input sets. This function took over 7 seconds to execute in a LAN environment, and over 16 seconds in an WAN environment. The circuit for computing $\frac{x+y}{n+m}$ is significantly more complex. Hence, with a non-trivial data set, a single computation of cluster means may take several minutes to compute. Note that the underlying costs of Fairplay are not artifacts of the design, but simply the cost of implementing the standard protocols; the reported costs were almost completely dominated with circuit setup and the necessary oblivious transfers.

In this section, we present two privacy-preserving protocols for WAP that are more efficient than the standard protocols. The first protocol is based on oblivious polynomial evaluation and the second on homomorphic encryption. Similarity of WAP with a problem that occurs in protocols for generation of shared RSA keys [6,17] is discussed in appendix B.

### 4.1  Protocol Based on Oblivious Polynomial Evaluation

We will first give a privacy-preserving protocol for a general problem, and then at the end of the subsection demonstrate how we can construct a privacy-preserving protocol for WAP. Consider the following problem.

**Definition 3.** Let $\mathcal{F}$ be a finite field. Party 1 has two polynomials $P$ and $Q$ with coefficients in $\mathcal{F}$. Party 2 has two points $\alpha$ and $\beta$ in $\mathcal{F}$. Both parties want to compute $\frac{P(\alpha)}{Q(\beta)}$. In other words, we want to privately compute the following functionality:

$$((P, Q), (\alpha, \beta)) \longmapsto (\frac{P(\alpha)}{Q(\beta)}, \frac{P(\alpha)}{Q(\beta)})$$

We call this problem *private rational polynomial evaluation (PRPE)*.

The protocol $\mathcal{P}_{PRPE}$ uses a protocol for oblivious polynomial evaluation, which is defined below.

**Definition 4.** Let $\mathcal{F}$ be a finite field. The *oblivious polynomial evaluation* or *OPE* problem can be defined as follows: Alice $A$ has a polynomial $P$ over the finite field $\mathcal{F}$, and Bob $B$ has an element $x \in \mathcal{F}$. After executing the protocol implementing OPE $B$ should *only know* $P(x)$ and $A$ should know nothing.

A protocol to solve the OPE was given by Naor and Pinkas [40]. Let $\mathcal{P}_{OPE}(P, \alpha)$ denote the privacy-preserving protocol for OPE. We provide a protocol $\mathcal{P}_{PRPE}((P, Q), (\alpha, \beta))$ for PRPE, which uses $\mathcal{P}_{OPE}(P, \alpha)$ as an oracle. The protocol is shown in Figure 3.

---

**(Step 1)** Party 1 picks a random element $z \in \mathcal{F}$ and computes two new polynomials $zP$ and $zQ$. In other words, party 1 "blinds" the polynomials $P$ and $Q$.

**(Step 2)** Party 2 computes $zP(\alpha)$ and $zQ(\alpha)$ by invoking the protocol for OPE twice, i.e., invokes the protocol $\mathcal{P}_{OPE}(zP, \alpha)$ and $\mathcal{P}_{OPE}(zQ, \beta)$.

**(Step 3)** Party 2 computes $\frac{P(\alpha)}{Q(\beta)}$ by computing $\frac{zP(\alpha)}{zQ(\beta)}$ and sends it to party 1.

---

**Fig. 3.** Protocol for PRPE

**Theorem 2.** Protocol $\mathcal{P}_{PRPE}((P, Q)(\alpha, \beta)$ shown in Figure 3 is privacy-preserving protocol for PRPE.

**Proof:** The views of the two parties are

$$\text{VIEW}_1^{\mathcal{P}_{PRPE}}(P, Q) = (P, Q, \frac{P(\alpha)}{Q(\beta)})$$

$$\text{VIEW}_2^{\mathcal{P}_{PRPE}}(\alpha, \beta) = (\alpha, \beta, zP(\alpha), zQ(\beta))$$

The view of party 1 consists of its input $(P, Q)$ and output $\frac{P(\alpha)}{Q(\beta)}$. Therefore, there is nothing to prove (see definition 2, we can use $S_1$ as the identity function). The input and output of party 2 are $(\alpha, \beta)$ and $\frac{P(\alpha)}{Q(\beta)}$ respectively. We have to show a PPTA $S_2$ such that $S_2(\alpha, \beta, \frac{P(\alpha)}{Q(\beta)})$ and $\text{VIEW}_2^{\mathcal{P}_{PRPE}}(\alpha, \beta)$ are statistically indistinguishable. Let $z'$ be a random element of $\mathcal{F}$ and $S_2(\alpha, \beta, \frac{P(\alpha)}{Q(\beta)})$ be defined as follows:

$$(\alpha, \beta, z'\frac{P(\alpha)}{Q(\beta)}, z')$$

It is easy to see that the following two ensembles are statistically indistinguishable:

$$(\alpha, \beta, z' \frac{P(\alpha)}{Q(\beta)}, z')$$
$$(\alpha, \beta, zP(\alpha), zQ(\beta))$$

The reason is that if $z$ is a random element of $\mathcal{F}$ then $zQ(\beta)$ is a random element of $\mathcal{F}$ as well. Moreover, the ratio of the third and fourth elements in the view of party 2 is $\frac{P(\alpha)}{Q(\beta)}$, i.e., the output and the third element of the view determine the fourth element of the view.

Recall that $\mathcal{P}_{PRPE}$ uses the protocol $\mathcal{P}_{OPE}$. Using the composition theorem we conclude that $\mathcal{P}_{PRPE}$ is privacy preserving. □

*Protocol for WAP.* First, we show that a protocol $\mathcal{P}_{PRPE}$ for PRPE can be used to solve WAP. Recall that in WAP party 1 and party 2 have inputs $(x, n)$ and $(y, m)$ respectively. In the invocation of $\mathcal{P}_{PRPE}$, party 1 constructs two polynomials $P(w) = w + x$ and $Q(w) = w + n$, and party 2 sets $\alpha = y$ and $\beta = m$. The output both parties receive is equal to $\frac{x+y}{n+m}$, which is the desired output. The proof of privacy for this protocol follows from Theorem 2 and the composition theorem.

### 4.2 Protocol Based on Homomorphic Encryption

Let $(G, E, D, M)$ be a encryption scheme (where $G$ is the function to generate public parameters, $E$ and $D$ are the encryption and decryption functions, and $M$ is the message space respectively) with the following properties:

- The encryption scheme $(G, E, D)$ is *semantically secure* [24]. Essentially, an encryption scheme is semantically secure if an adversary gains no extra information by inspecting the ciphertext. This is formally defined in the appendix (see definition 5).
- For all $m \in M$ and $\alpha \in M$, $m_1 \in E(m)$ implies that $m_1^\alpha \in E(m\alpha)$. Encrypting the same message twice in a probabilistic encryption function can yield a different ciphertext, so $E(m)$ denotes the set of ciphertexts that can be obtained by encrypting $m$.[1]
- There is a computable function $f$ such that for all messages $m_1$ and $m_2$ the following property holds:

$$f(E(m_1), E(m_2)) = E(m_1 + m_2)$$

There are several encryption scheme that have the three properties mentioned above [5,39,42]. In our implementation, we used the *dense probabilistic encryption (DPE)* scheme of Benaloh [5]. The semantic security of the scheme provided by Benaloh is based on the intractability of deciding prime residuosity.

Party 1 and 2 have a pair of messages $(x, n)$ and $(y, m)$. The two parties want to jointly compute $\frac{x+y}{n+m}$ in a privacy-preserving way. Assume that party 1 sets up a

---

[1] Of course, to successfully decrypt two different messages $m$ and $m'$ sets $E(m)$ and $E(m')$ should be disjoint.

probabilistic encryption scheme $(G, E, D, M)$, and publishes the public parameters $G$. We also assume that the probabilistic encryption scheme $(G, E, D, M)$ satisfies the three properties given at the beginning of the section. The protocol $\mathcal{P}_H$ for WAP is shown in Figure 4.

---

- **(Step 1)** Party 1 encrypts $x$ and $n$ and sends the encrypted values $x_1 \in E(x)$ and $n_1 \in E(n)$ to party 2.
- **(Step 2)** Party 2 computes a random message $z \in M$, and encrypts $z \cdot y$ and $z \cdot m$ to obtain $z_1 \in E(z \cdot y)$ and $z_2 \in E(z \cdot m)$. Party 2 computes the following two messages and sends it to party 1:

$$m_1 = f(x_1^z, z_1)$$
$$m_2 = f(n_1^z, z_2)$$

**Note:** In our implementation we use the homomorphic-encryption scheme by [5] where $f$ is multiplication.

- **(Step 3)** Using the two properties of the probabilistic encryption scheme $(G, E, D)$, we have the following:

$$m_1 = E(z \cdot x + z \cdot y)$$
$$m_2 = E(z \cdot n + z \cdot m)$$

Therefore, party 1 can compute $z(x + y)$ and $z(n + m)$, and hence can compute $\frac{x+y}{n+m}$. Party 1 sends $\frac{x+y}{n+m}$ to party 2.

---

**Fig. 4.** Protocol for WAP based on homomorphic encryption

**Theorem 3.** Assume that the probabilistic encryption scheme $(G, E, D)$ has three properties mentioned at the beginning of this sub-section. $\mathcal{P}_H((x, n), (y, m))$ is a privacy-preserving protocol to compute $\frac{x+y}{n+m}$.

The proof of this theorem is straightforward and is given in appendix A. The basic intuition is that party 2 cannot tell the difference between $E(x)$ and $E(n)$ and encryption of two arbitrary messages.

The complexity of encryption and decryption operations of a scheme $(G, E, D, M)$ depends on size of the message space $M$. Therefore, in order to keep the complexity low it is important that the size of the message space be small. However, in order to achieve adequate precision the message space should be large. Chinese remainder theorem (CRT) allows us to perform computation over smaller spaces and then reconstruct the result for a larger message space. Let $p_1, \cdots, p_m$ be $m$ small primes. The two parties execute the protocol described above for $Z_{p_1}, \cdots, Z_{p_m}$. Party 1 receives $z(x + y)$ and $z(n + m)$ modulo $p_i$ (for $1 \leq i \leq m$). CRT allows party 1 to reconstruct $z(x + y)$ and $z(n + m)$ modulo $N = \prod_{i=1}^{m} p_i$. This technique is also used by Gilboa [17].

# 5    Experimental Evaluation

This section looks at the feasibility of our solution by evaluating the cost of the protocol on real data-sets. The goal of this study is to establish the cost of our privacy-preserving clustering algorithms on real applications. We principally seek to understand the performance and privacy tradeoffs inherent to the operation of the protocols.

We evaluated three clustering algorithms. The *simple* scheme is used throughout as a baseline for our experiments. This protocol implements the $k$-means clustering algorithm as described in section 3. This algorithm does not use any privacy-preserving protocols. This represents the nominal cost of clustering, and will be present in any $k$-means clustering approach, independent of if and how privacy is implemented. Throughout this section *features* refer to the dimension of the vectors being clustered and each iteration of the $k$-means algorithm is referred to as *round*. Our first privacy-preserving protocol (referred to as *OPE*) uses oblivious polynomial evaluation. This protocol is described in detail in Section 4.1. For oblivious polynomial evaluation we use the protocol presented by Naor and Pinkas [40]. The next privacy-preserving protocol (referred to as *DPE*) uses homomorphic encryption scheme of Benaloh [5]. This protocol is described in detail in Section 4.2.

*Implementation.* Our system consists of approximately 3000 lines of Java code, split up into a number of self-contained modules. The $k$-means algorithm module implements actual clustering computations as described in Section 3. During each iteration, this module calls the protocol module to compute the cluster means for each dimension of the cluster. The protocol module sets up the framework of communication, and calls the specific protocol handlers with a common interface, depending on which protocol is selected. In the *simple* handler, Alice sends $(x, n)$ to Bob, who computes the cluster mean $\frac{x+y}{n+m}$ and sends it to Alice. The OPE and DPE protocol handlers implement the protocols described in Sections 4.1 and 4.2.

The central results uncovered by this investigation include:

1. Clustering using DPE is two orders of magnitude more bandwidth efficient than OPE, and executes in 4.5 to 5 times less time. This is largely due to bandwidth and computational costs associated with the oblivious transfers used by OPE.
2. Our protocols clustering with perfect fidelity; that is, the clusters resulting from our algorithms are identical to those reported by a $k$-means algorithm with no privacy for reasonable parameter choices.
3. Small, medium, and large data-sets can be clustered efficiently.
4. Costs scale linearly with feature and rounds. The number of samples affects runtime only inasmuch as it increases the number of rounds toward convergence.
5. Protocol parameters affect bandwidth usage by constant factor. Moreover, exponential increases in security or supported message space result in linear increases in execution run-times.

We begin in the following section by exploring several real data-sets representative of expected environments.

## 5.1   Experimental Data

The validity of our experimental approach is partially dependent on the realism of our test data. For this reason, we have obtained a collection of externally provided data-sets representing diverse applications. All experiments described in this section use the *synthetic, river, robot,* and *speech* data-sets detailed below.

We selected the elements of our *synthetic* data-set to enable testing and measure startup costs. This data set includes 4 points uniformly distributed within a 6 dimensional space. By design, the data clusters quickly into 4 "natural" clusters within 2 rounds under the $k$-means algorithm in all experiments.

Originally used in the Computation Intelligence and Learning (COIL) competition, the *river* data-set describes measurements of river chemical concentrations and algae densities [27]. The river data was used to ascertain the summer algae growth of river water in temperate climates. The clustered data is used to inform the relationship between the presence and concentrations of various chemicals in public waterways and algae growth. The river contains 184 samples with 15 features per sample.

The *robot* data-set [26] contains continuous senor readings from the Pioneer-1 mobile robot used for testing computer learning and conceptual development approaches. Each of the 697 samples contains 36 features from sensor arrays of the Pioneer-1 mobile robot. The samples were taken every 100ms and reflect the movements and changing environment in which the robot was tested. The data has been clustered in prior use to recognize experiences with common outcomes.

The *speech* data-set [28] documents the measured voice characteristics of spoken Japanese vowels. Nine male speakers uttered two Japanese vowels /ae/ repeatedly. Sampled at 10kHz, the 640 utterances resulted in 12 features of 5,687 samples. This large data-set is used in the context of our experiments to evaluate the degree to which the proposed protocols scale with the size of the input data. Similar data-sets are clustered frequently to help guide speech recognition software [32].

Each of the data-sets represents a singular corpus. In contrast, our protocols are targeted for applications of clustering with two parties. We model the two party case by randomly subdividing the samples into equal sized subsets and assigning them to each party. In real environments the size of the sets may be vastly different. Our approximation approach ensures that this kind of asymmetry will be transparent to both parties both in execution and performance. That is, the performance of the algorithm is largely independent of the number of samples. However, as we shall see below, the number of features has tremendous effect on the cost of clustering.

The last data set (called the *ping* data-set) was collected by us. The purpose of collecting this data was two fold:

- Test our clustering algorithm on a large data set.
- Construct a data set that can be naturally partitioned to demonstrate that jointly clustering two data sets can produce significantly different results than individually clustering them.

We setup two hosts (referred to as $A$ and $B$) to measure ICMP ping round-trip times. There were 4 ping targets located around the world (one of the ping targets was on the same subnet as host $B$). On each host and for each ping target the pings were grouped in blocks of 200. For each block, a 3-tuple consisting of the following three values was generated: the average time to live (TTL), the average round-trip time (RTT), and fraction of lost packets (%drop). We collected data over a period of 24 hours and generated a data set consisting of 23872 data points, which were evenly divided between host $A$ and $B$. We ran our clustering algorithm on the joint data set, and data sets corresponding to hosts $A$ and $B$.

## 5.2 Experimental Setup

We use the architecture and code described earlier for the experiments described throughout. All experiments are executed on a pair of 3Ghz machines with 2 gigabyte physical memory. The experimental application is running on the Sun Microsystems Java Virtual Machine version 1.5 [47] on the Tao Linux version 1.0 operating system [25]. The protocols are executed on a 100Mbps unloaded LAN with a measured round-trip time of 0.2 milliseconds.

The experiments profile the additional cost of providing privacy in clustering sensitive data. To this end, we focus on three metrics of cost and utility; *communication overhead*, *delay*, and *precision*. Communication overhead records the amount of additional network bandwidth used by the privacy schemes over the simple schemes. Delay measures the additional time required to complete the clustering.

Precision is used to measure the degree to which the approximated clustering diverge from those reported by a simple $k$-means algorithm, and is calculated as follows. Let $X = \{x_1, \ldots, x_n\}$ be the sample data set to be clustered. $C_1 \subseteq 2^X$ is the clustering of $X$ by the simple algorithm, and $C_2 \subseteq 2^X$ is the clustering returned by the OPE algorithm (the DPE metric is defined similarly in the obvious manner). For each pair $(x_i, x_j)$ such that $1 \leq i < j \leq n$ an error occurs if

1. $x_i$ and $x_j$ are in the same cluster in $C_1$, but in $C_2$ they are in different clusters.
2. $x_i$ and $x_j$ in the same cluster in $C_2$, but in $C_1$ they are in different clusters.

The total number of errors is denoted $E$. The maximum number of errors is $N = n(n-1)/2$. The precision $P$ is given by $(N - E)/N$.

Both OPE and DPE have unique parameters which dictate the performance and security of each protocol. The performance of DPE is most effected by the size of the primes used to select the homomorphic encryption keys. Small primes can be cryptanalyzed, and large ones can unnecessarily increase bandwidth use and computational costs. Like RSA, linear increases in the size of the primes should result in exponential security improvements.

We use interval arithmetic to approximate real numbers (see appendix C). The size of the message space in DPE and the finite-field in OPE are chosen to achieve the desired precision. In Benaloh's encryption scheme $r$ denotes the size of the message space. For efficiency reasons we choose $r = 3^k$ (see [5] for details). Two crucial parameters in the oblivious polynomial evaluation protocol of Naor and Pinkas are $D$, the degree of the masking polynomial and $M$, the total number of points used (details of this algorithm can be found in [40]). The sender's masking polynomial $D$ has degree $k.d$, where $d$ is the degree of the polynomial $P$ being evaluated and $k$ is the security parameter. Since in our algorithm the polynomial being evaluated is always linear, the security

**Table 1.** Experimental Results - resource and precision results from experiments over the three data sets. The feature/round statistics show the costs of per feature clustering in a single round of the k-means algorithm, e.g., a single execution of the privacy preserving WAP protocol.

| Test | Rounds | Communications Overhead | | | Delay | | |
|------|--------|-------|------|------|------|------|------|
| | | bytes | bytes feature/rnd | percent increase | milliseconds | milliseconds feature/rnd | percent increase |
| *Synthetic (4 samples, 6 features)* | | | | | | | |
| Simple | 2 | 5959 | 0 | 0% | 168 | 0 | 0% |
| OPE | 2 | 1497823 | 124322 | 25035.48% | 10147 | 831.58 | 5939.88% |
| DPE | 2 | 13580 | 635.08 | 127.89% | 2135 | 163.9166667 | 1170.83% |
| *River (184 samples, 15 features)* | | | | | | | |
| Simple | 16 | 74574 | 0 | 0% | 772 | 0 | 0% |
| OPE | 16 | 29916457 | 124241.17 | 40116.47% | 176133 | 730.67 | 22715.16% |
| DPE | 16 | 234422 | 566.03 | 314.35% | 38721 | 158.12 | 4915.67% |
| *Robot (697 samples, 36 features)* | | | | | | | |
| Simple | 8 | 94005 | 0 | 0% | 1348 | 0 | 0% |
| OPE | 8 | 36569040 | 126649.42 | 38801.16% | 212776 | 734.125 | 15684.57% |
| DPE | 8 | 269698 | 610.04 | 186.90% | 47662 | 160.8125 | 3435.76% |
| *Speech (5,687 samples, 12 features)* | | | | | | | |
| Simple | 33 | 143479 | 0 | 0% | 4198 | 0 | 0% |
| OPE | 33 | 49359739 | 124183.48 | 34402.07% | 294694 | 733.57 | 6919.87% |
| DPE | 33 | 384644 | 509.00 | 268.08% | 66101 | 156.3207071 | 1474.58% |
| *Ping (28,392 samples, 3 features)* | | | | | | | |
| Simple | 9 | 11644 | 0 | 0% | 2765 | 0 | 0% |
| OPE | 9 | 3429688 | 126594.2 | 29354.55% | 23767 | 777.8519 | 759.566% |
| DPE | 9 | 30633 | 703.29 | 163.07% | 9694 | 256.63 | 250.59% |

parameter is simply $D$. Increasing $D$ strengthens the sender's security. Only $D + 1$ points are needed to interpolate, but the receiver sends $(D+1).M$ pairs of values to the sender. Out of each set of $M$ pairs, one of them is related to $\alpha$ (the point the polynomial is being evaluated on), and the other $M - 1$ values are random. The 1-out-of$M$ oblivious transfer protocol (denoted as $OT_1^M$) is repeated $D + 1$ times to learn the required value. So, increasing $M$ strengthens the receiver's security. Unless otherwise specified, we selected $D = 7$ and $M = 6$. For brevity, we do not consider $D$ or $M$ further.

## 5.3   Results

Our first battery of tests broadly profile the performance of OPE and DPE. Shown in Table 1, the most striking characteristic of these experiments is that they demonstrate that OPE protocols consume two orders of magnitude more network resources than the DPE protocols. These costs can be directly attributed to the oblivious transfer algorithms whose primitive cryptographic operations require the transfer of many polynomials between hosts. The total bandwidth costs scaled linearly for both OPE and DPE. That is, the bandwidth costs per feature/round are relatively constant for the given data sets, where we observed 0.03% variance in scaled bandwidth usage in OPE and 9.36%

in DPE. Note that the bandwidth is ultimately of limited interest; the worst case experiment only consumes 47 megabytes of bandwidth over two and a half minutes. Hence, our protocols would have visible impact only the slowest or busiest networks.

A chief feature illustrated by the timing measurements is that DPE is much more time and bandwidth efficient than OPE. Surprisingly, DPE is 4.5 to 5 times faster on all the data-sets for the selected parameters. The reasons for this is that the underlying oblivious transfers incur large message exchanges between the two parties. Hence, in all experiments the limiting factors are bandwidth and computation.[2] The efficiency of DPE with respect to OPE further shows fixed costs (startup) are likewise dominated by the underlying privacy preservation operations. Further, like the bandwidth costs, the execution of each algorithm scale linearly with the number of features and rounds, where each feature round requires 730 and 160 milliseconds for OPE and DPE to complete, respectively.

The cost of privacy-preservation in large data-set clustering is noticeable. For example, a large data-set containing 5687 samples and 12 features takes DPE just 66 seconds to cluster, as opposed to the 4.19 seconds required by its simple $k$-means counterpart. Hence for this experiment, DPE algorithm incurs slowdown of a factor of 15 and the more expensive OPE a factor of 70. These results are, for most applications, clearly within the bounds of acceptable performance. This is particularly encouraging in the face of past attempts; circuit implementations of vastly simpler operations (averaging very small collections of data points) took tens of seconds to complete [35].

*Fairplay.* We compared our protocols for WAP with a simple strategy of approximating the function $\frac{x+y}{n+m}$ by a circuit $C$ and then using standard constructions [21,22,52]. We used Fairplay [35] to securely evaluate the circuit $C$. Fairplay does not support division, so we implemented a circuit for division (our implementation for division uses the standard "long division" method). As expected the privacy-preserving clustering algorithm that uses Fairplay to be very slow. Experimental results confirmed this intuition. For example, for the *ping* data set clustering with Fairplay took $805,416$ milliseconds (recall that clustering with DPE took only $9,694$ milliseconds).

For the parameters we selected the precision of our privacy-preserving algorithms (DPE and OPE) was 100%. The reasons for this are two-fold. The parameter choices for DPE resulted in a message space of $3^{40}$ values, which allowed us to map cluster means to 4 decimal places. Moreover, the data range was small in all our data-sets. Hence, the error rounding caused by using interval arithmetic was inconsequential. Note that in other environments, where the message space is required to be smaller (likely for performance reasons) or the range of data values is large, precision errors may be introduced.

The costs of OPE grow slightly with increases in $D$ and $M$. We experimented with varied parameters of $D$ and $M$ equal 5, 10, 15 on all the non-synthetic data-sets (for a total of 27 experiments) . In all cases increased cost was nominal; the parameter sets slowed the performance of the algorithm down between 60% and 190% over a baseline experiment, i.e., $M = D = 5$. Again, these costs are a direct reflection of the costs of

---

[2] Early implementations of our protocols were limited by the latency caused by many individual round-trips in the protocol. We optimized these these by parallelizing exchanges, where possible. This vastly improved protocol performance, and as a direct result, bandwidth and and computation have since emerged as the limiting factors.

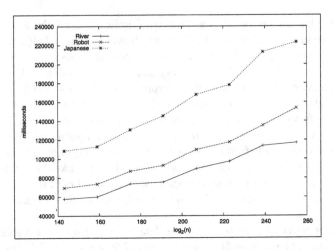

**Fig. 5.** DPE runtime costs by message space - in *milliseconds*, the time to cluster the sample data-sets with various widths of $n$ message spaces

| | Cluster centers |
|---|---|
| $A$ | $(241.76, 32.69, 0.18), (48.00, 75.87, 0.58), (243.00, 59.81, 0.15), (64.00, 0.19, 0.00)$ |
| $B$ | $(47.00, 88.60, 0.74), (251.92, 4.73, 0.19), (242.00, 48.01, 2.70), (133.67, 485.77, 13.78)$ |
| Joint | $(245.26, 28.73, 0.60), (47.51, 82.13, 0.66), (133.67, 485.77, 13.78), (64.00, 0.186, 0.00)$ |

**Fig. 6.** (TTL,RTT,%drop) centers for the four clusters

the underlying oblivious transfer. Not shown, the bandwidth costs in DPE scale by a constant factor proportional to $D$ and $M$.

As illustrated in Figure 5, increases the size $n$ (which is a product of two primes) in DPE has modest affect on the performance of the protocols. Exponential increases in $n$ result in linear increases in message size. Because the network is a limiting factor, such increases are, as shown, reflected in linear slowdowns. Hence, very large intervals or high precision clustering can be supported by small increases in bandwidth consumption. As in OPE, bandwidth costs in DPE scale by a constant factor in these experiments, where each protocol exchange increases directly in proportion to the size of the primes.

For the ping data set our clustering algorithm generated 4 clusters, which correspond to the four target hosts. The centers for the four clusters are shown in Figure 6. As can be clearly seen from the results, clusters found by the algorithm using the joint data set are significantly different than the clusters found in the individual data sets. Therefore, if the goal is to estimate RTT, TTL, and %drop for the target hosts to be used in networking applications (such as routing), then clustering on the joint data set is desirable.

## 6   Conclusion

We presented two privacy-preserving $k$-means algorithms. We also implemented these algorithm and performed a thorough evaluations of our algorithms. There are several avenues for further research. We want to perform further optimizations to our tool to reduce the execution and bandwidth overheads. We want to explore privacy-preserving versions of other clustering algorithms. We are particularly interested in hierarchical clustering algorithms.

## Acknowledgments

We thank Dan Boneh for pointing out the connection between the weighted average problem and generation of shared RSA keys.

## References

1. 104th Congress. *Public Law 104-191: Health Insurance Portability and Accountability Act of 1996*, August 1996.
2. N.R. Adam and J.C. Wortmann. Security-control methods for statistical databases: A comparative study. *ACM Computing Surveys*, 21, 1989.
3. R. Agrawal and R. Srikant. Privacy-preserving data mining. In *Proceedings of the 2000 ACM SIGMOD Conference on Management of Data*, pages 439–450, Dallas, TX, May 2000.
4. P.S. Bardley and U.M. Fayyad. Refining initial points for k-means clustering. In *Proceedings of 15th International Conference on Machine Learning (ICML)*, pages 91–99, 1998.
5. J. Benaloh. Dense probabilistic encryption. In *Workshop on Selected Areas of Cryptography*, pages 120–128, May 1994.
6. D. Boneh and M. K. Franklin. Efficient generation of shared RSA keys. *Journal of the ACM (JACM)*, 48(4):702–722, 2001.
7. R. Canetti. Security and composition of multi-party cryptographic protocols. *Journal of Cryptology*, 13(1):143–202, 2000.
8. Lorrie Cranor, Marc Langheinrich, Massimo Marchiori, Martin Presler-Marshall, and Joseph Reagle. *The Platform for Privacy Preferences 1.0 (P3P1.0) Specification*. W3C Recommendation, 16 April 2002.
9. Lorrie Faith Cranor. Internet privacy. *Communications of the ACM*, 42(2):28–38, 1999.
10. D.E. Denning. A security model for the statistical database problem. *ACM Transactions on Database Systems (TODS)*, 5, 1980.
11. I.S. Dhillon, E.M. Marcotte, and U. Roshan. Diametrical clustering for identifying anti-correlated gene clusters. *Bioinformatics*, 19(13):1612–1619, 2003.
12. I.S. Dhillon and D.S. Modha. A data-clustering algorithm on distributed memory multi-processors. In *Proceedings of Large-scale Parallel KDD Systems Workshop (ACM SIGKDD)*, August 15-18 1999.
13. W. Du and M. J. Atallah. Privacy-preserving cooperative statistical analysis. In *Annual Computer Security Applications Conference ACSAC)*, pages 102–110, New Orleans, Louisiana, USA, December 10-14 2001.
14. R.O. Duda, P.E. Hart, and D.G. Stork. *Pattern Classification*. John Wiley & Sons, 2001.
15. A. Evfimievski, R. Srikant, R. Agrawal, and J. Gehrke. Privacy preserving mining of association rules. In *Eighth ACM SIGKDD International Conference on Knowledge Discovery and Data Mining*, pages 217–228, Edmonton, Alberta, Canada, July 23–26 2002.
16. J. Feigenbaum, Y. Ishai, T. Malkin, K. Nissim, M. Strauss, and R. N. Wright. Secure multiparty computation of approximations. In *28th International Colloquium Automata, Languages and Programming (ICALP 2001)*, Crete, Greece, July 8-12 2001.

17. Niv Gilboa. Two party rsa key generation. In *Advances in Cryptology (CRYPTO '99)*, Santa Barbara, California, USA, August 15-19 1999.

18. Ian Goldberg, David Wagner, and Eric Brewer. Privacy-enhancing technologies for the internet. In *Proc. of 42nd IEEE Spring COMPCON*. IEEE Computer Society Press, February 1997.

19. O. Goldreich. *Foundations of Cryptography: Volume 1, Basic Tools*. Cambridge University Press, May 2001.

20. O. Goldreich. *Foundations of Cryptography: Volume 2, Basic Applications*. Cambridge University Press, 2004.

21. O. Goldreich, S. Micali, and A. Wigderson. How to play any mental game - a completeness theorem for protocols with honest majority. In *19th Symposium on Theory of Computer Science*, pages 218–229, 1987.

22. O. Goldreich, S. Micali, and A. Wigderson. Proofs that yield nothing but their validity or all languages in NP have zero-knowledge proof systems. *Journal of the ACM*, 38(1):691–729, 1991.

23. O. Goldreich and E. Petrank. Quantifying knowledge complexity. In *Computational Complexity*, volume 8, pages 50–98, 1999.

24. S. Goldwasser and S. Micali. Probabilistic encryption. *Journal of Computer and Systems Science*, 28:270–299, 1984.

25. Tao Linux User Group. Tao Linux, version 1.0. http://taolinux.org/, November 2004.

26. Information and Computer Science. *Pioneer-1 Mobile Robot Data*. University of California Irvine, November 1998. http://kdd.ics.uci.edu/databases/pioneer/pioneer.html.

27. Information and Computer Science. *COIL 1999 Competition Data, The UCI KDD Archive*. University of California Irvine, October 1999. http://kdd.ics.uci.edu/databases/coil/coil.html.

28. Information and Computer Science. *Japanese Vowels*. University of California Irvine, June 2000. http://kdd.ics.uci.edu/databases/JapaneseVowels/JapaneseVowels.html.

29. K. Julisch. Clustering intrusion detection alarms to support root cause analysis. *ACM Transactions on Information and System Security (TISSEC)*, 6(4):443–471, November 2003.

30. H. Kargupta, W. Huang, K. Sivakumar, and E. Johnson. Distributed clustering using collective principal component analysis. *Knowledge and Information Systems*, 3(4):405–421, November 2001.

31. M. Klusch, S. Lodi, and Gianluca Moro. Distributed clustering based on sampling local density estimates. In *Proceedings of the Eighteenth International Joint Conference on Artificial Intelligence (IJCAI 2003)*, pages 485–490, 2003.

32. M. Kudo, J. Toyama, and M. Shimbo. Multidimensional Curve Classification Using Passing-Through Regions. *Pattern Recognition Letters*, (11–13):1103–1111, 1999.

33. Y. Lindell and B. Pinkas. Privacy preserving data mining. In *Advances in Cryptology (Crypto 2000)*, pages 36–54, August 2000.

34. S.P. Llyod. Least squares quantization in pcm. *IEEE Transactions on Information Theory*, IT-2:129–137, 1982.

35. Dahlia Malkhi, Noam Nisan, Benny Pinkas, and Yaron Sella. Fairplay – A Secure Two-Party Computation System. In *Proceedings of 13th USENIX Security Symposium*, pages 287–302. USENIX, September 2004. San Diego, CA.

36. D. Marchette. A statistical method for profiling network traffic. In *Workshop on Intrusion Detection and Network Monitoring*, pages 119–128, 1999.

37. S. Merugu and J. Ghosh. Privacy-preserving distributed clustering using generative models. In *Proceedings of the 3rd IEEE International Conference on Data Mining (ICDM 2003)*, pages 211–218, 2003.

38. T.M. Mitchell. *Machine Learning*. McGraw-Hill, 1997.

39. D. Naccache and J. Stern. A new public key cryptosystem based on higher residues. In *Proceedings of the 5th ACM Conference on Computer and Communications Security (CCS)*, San Francisco, California, 1998.

40. M. Naor and B. Pinkas. Oblivious transfer and polynomial evaluation. In *31st Symposium on Theory of Computer Science*, pages 245–254, Atlanta, GA, May 1-4 1999.

41. S. Oliveira and O. R. Zaiane. Privacy preserving clustering by data transformation. In *XVIII Simpósio Brasileiro de Bancos de Dados, 6-8 de Outubro (SBBD 2003)*, pages 304–318, 2003.

42. P. Paillier. Public-key cryptosystems based on composite degree residuosity classes. In *Proceedings of Advances in Cryptology (EUROCRYPT'99)*, 1999.

43. F. Pouget and M. Dacier. Honeypot-based forensics. In *Proceedings Of AusCERT Asia Pacific Information technology Security Conference 2004(AusCERT2004)*, Brisbane, Australia, May 2004.

44. J.R. Quinlan. Induction of decision trees. *Machine Learning*, 1(1):81–106, 1986.

45. D. M. Rind, I. S. Kohane, P. Szolovits, C. Safran, H. C. Chueh, and G. O. Barnett. Maintaining the confidentiality of medical records shared over the internet and the world wide web. *Annals of Internal Medicine*, 127(2), July 1997.

46. S.J. Rizvi and J.R. Harista. Maintaining data privacy in association rule mining. In *Proceedings of 28th International Conference on Very Large Data Bases (VLDB)*, Hong Kong, August 20-23 2002.

47. Sun Microsystems. Sun Java Virutal Machine, version 1.5. http://java.sun.com/, November 2004.

48. Humphrey Taylor. Most people are "privacy pragmatists" who, while concerned about privacy, will sometimes trade it off for other benefits. *The Harris Poll*, (17), March 19 2003.

49. Joseph Turow. Americans and online privacy: The system is broken. Technical report, Annenberg Public Policy Center, June 2003.

50. J. Vaidya and C. Clifton. Privacy preserving association rule mining in vertically partitioned data. In *Eighth ACM SIGKDD International Conference on Knowledge Discovery and Data Mining*, pages 217–228, Edmonton, Alberta, Canada, July 23–26 2002.

51. J. Vaidya and C. Clifton. Privacy-preserving $k$-means clustering over vertically partitioned data. In *Proceedings of the Ninth ACM SIGKDD International Conference on Knowledge Discovery and Data Mining*, pages 206–215, 2003.

52. A.C. Yao. How to generate and exchange secrets. In *27th IEEE Symposium on Foundations of Computer Science*, pages 162–167, 1986.

# A    Definitions and Proofs

**Definition 5.** Assume that the message space $M$ can be sampled in polynomial time, i.e., there exists a probabilistic polynomial time algorithm $A_M$ such that it takes input $1^k$ and generates a message $m \in M$. Let $h : M \rightarrow R$ be a function, which can be thought of as some information about the message, e.g., $h(m) = 1$ iff message has a substring "Bob" in it. Consider the following two games:

- **(Game 1):** Adversary is informed that I am about to choose a message $m$ using the sampling algorithm $A_M$. The adversary is asked to guess $h(m)$.
- **(Game 2):** In addition to the information given in game 1, he is also told the encryption $\alpha \in E(m)$ of the message. The adversary is again asked to guess $h(m)$.

An encryption function $E$ is called *semantically secure* if the difference between the probabilities of the adversary succeeding in the two games is negligible. The probability is computed over the message space.

**Proof of Theorem 3:** The view of the two parties is shown below:

$$\text{VIEW}_1^{\mathcal{P}_H}(x, n) = (x, n, z(x + y), z(n + m))$$
$$\text{VIEW}_2^{\mathcal{P}_H}(y, m) = (y, m, x_1, n_1, \frac{x + y}{n + m})$$

Let $z'$ be a message uniformly chosen from $M$. Define $S_1(x, n, \frac{x+y}{n+m})$ as follows:

$$(x, n, z' \frac{x + y}{n + m}, z')$$

It is easy to see that $S_1(x, n, \frac{x+y}{n+m})$ and $\text{VIEW}_1^{\mathcal{P}_H}(x, n)$ are statistically indistinguishable (this proof is very similar to the proof of Theorem 2 given in Section 4.1).

Recall that $x_1 \in E(x)$ and $n_1 \in E(n)$. Since $(G, E, D)$ is semantically secure, party 2 cannot gain extra information from the encrypted values $x_1$ and $n_1$. In other words. Let $x_1' \in E(x')$ and $n_1' \in E(n')$, where $x'$ and $n'$ are randomly chosen messages. An adversary cannot distinguish between $\text{VIEW}_2^{\mathcal{P}_H}(y, m)$ and $(y, m, x_1', n_1', \frac{x+y}{n+m})$ with more than negligible probability. Therefore, privacy of party 1 with respect to party 2 follows.                                                                □

# B    Generation of Shared RSA Keys and WAP

We assume that all elements are drawn from a finite field $\mathcal{F}$. Suppose that party 1 and 2 have a pair of numbers $(a, b)$ and $(c, d)$ and they want to privately compute $(a+c)(b+d)$. In other words, they want to privately compute the following functionality:

$$((a, b), (c, d)) \longmapsto (a + c)(b + d)$$

This problem is one of the crucial steps in the protocol for sharing RSA keys. Let $\mathcal{P}_{sk}$ be the protocol for solving this problem. We will show that $\mathcal{P}_{sk}$ can be used to design a protocol $\mathcal{P}_{WAP}$ for solving WAP (see Section 4 for a description of this problem). Protocol $\mathcal{P}_{WAP}$ works as follows:

- Party 1 and party 2 generate two random elements $z_1$ and $z_2$ chosen uniformly from $\mathcal{F}$.
- Two parties invoke the protocol $\mathcal{P}_{sk}$ with inputs $(x, z_1)$ and $(y, z_2)$. Each party obtains $r_1 = (x + y)(z_1 + z_2)$.
- Two parties invoke the protocol $\mathcal{P}_{sk}$ with inputs $(n, z_1)$ and $(m, z_2)$. Each party obtains $r_2 = (n + m)(z_1 + z_2)$.
- The two parties obtain $\frac{x+y}{n+m}$ by computing $\frac{r_1}{r_2}$.

Next we argue that $\mathcal{P}_{WAP}$ is privacy preserving. The views of the two parties in this protocol are:

$$\text{VIEW}_1(x, n) = (x, n, (x + y)(z_1 + z_2), (n + m)(z_1 + z_2))$$
$$\text{VIEW}_2(y, m) = (y, m, (x + y)(z_1 + z_2), (n + m)(z_1 + z_2))$$

Let $z'$ be a random element of $\mathcal{F}$ and $S_1(x, n, \frac{x+y}{n+m})$ be defined as follows:

$$\left(x, n, z'\frac{x + y}{n + m}, z'\right)$$

If we fix $x$, $y$, and $z_1$ and pick $z_2$ uniformly from $\mathcal{F}$, then $(x + y)(z_1 + z_2)$ is a random element distributed uniformly over $\mathcal{F}$. Therefore, $\text{VIEW}_1(x, n)$ and $S_1(x, n, \frac{x+y}{n+m}))$ are statistically indistinguishable. Let $z'$ be a random element of $\mathcal{F}$ and $S_2(y, m, \frac{x+y}{n+m}))$ be defined as follows:

$$\left(y, m, z'\frac{x + y}{n + m}, z'\right)$$

It is easy to see that $\text{VIEW}_2(y, m)$ and $S_2(y, m, \frac{x+y}{n+m}))$ are statistically indistinguishable. Using the composition theorem the privacy of $\mathcal{P}_{WAP}$ follows.

## C  Approximating Reals

Assume that real numbers occur in the interval $[M, -M)$. We divide the interval $[M, -M)$ into $2MN$ sub-intervals of size $\frac{1}{N}$. The $i$-th sub-interval (where $0 \leq i < 2MN$) is given by

$$\left[-M + \frac{i}{N}, -M + \frac{i+1}{N}\right)$$

We denote by $I(x)$ as the sub-interval the real number $x$ lies in, i.e. $x \in [-M + \frac{I(x)}{N}, -M + \frac{I(x)+1}{N})$. If $x$ and $y$ are two real numbers that lie in the sub-interval $I(x)$ and $I(y)$, then $x + y$ lies in the sub-interval $[-2M + \frac{I(x)+I(y)}{N}, -2M + \frac{I(x)+I(y)+2}{N})$.

For the rest of the sub-section we will approximate real numbers with the the interval they lie in. In our protocol, a party obtains $z(I(x) + I(y))$ and $z(n + m)$, where $z$ is the random number. Using some simple arithmetic we can deduce that $\frac{z(I(x)+I(y))}{z(n+m)}$ lies in the interval $[-M + \frac{Q}{N}, -M + \frac{Q+1}{N})$, where $Q$ is the quotient of $q_1$ divided by $q_2$. Integers $q_1$ and $q_2$ are shown below:

$$q_1 = MN(z(n + m) - 2) + z(n + m) \cdot z(I(x) + I(y))$$
$$q_2 = z(n + m)$$

In all our algorithms, we have to use a large enough space so that all the operations used to calculate $q_1$ and $q_2$ are exact, i.e., there is no "wrap around". If all the integers used in $q_1$ and $q_2$ are bounded by $2^k$, then the size of the field should be greater than or equal to $2^{4k+5}$.

# Abstractions Preserving Parameter Confidentiality*

Sigrid Gürgens, Peter Ochsenschläger, and Carsten Rudolph

Fraunhofer-Institute for Secure Information Technology SIT, Germany
{guergens, ochsenschlaeger, rudolphc}@sit.fraunhofer.de

**Abstract.** Confidentiality of certain parameters is an essential security requirement for many security sensitive applications. In this paper, conditions for abstractions are formulated in terms of formal language theory to be able to prove parameter confidentiality in an abstract view of a system and then conclude that an *adequate representation* of the property is satisfied in the refined system as well. These conditions essentially depend on an agent's view as well as on an agent's initial knowledge of the system behaviour, which explicitely formalizes assumptions about the system.

## 1 Introduction

Typically, the well-known concepts of non-interference or information flow control address confidentiality of actions: the occurrence or non-occurrence of certain actions of an agent shall not be deducible for another agent based on what it observes. In the literature there is a variety of formalizations of this concept, Mantel [11] gives a good insight into this topic. The subtle differences between these definitions show the spectrum of this kind of confidentiality.

However, non-interference is not suitable for the specification of security requirements in distributed open systems. Here, it can be assumed that all actions concerned with communication might indeed be visible to malicious agents. Nevertheless, confidentiality is required for data transmitted using these actions. An adequate notion of confidentiality therefore has to provide the flexibility to define confidentiality for arbitrary parameters of the actions. The notion of *parameter-confidentiality* presented in [6] provides this flexibility. Parameter confidentiality formalizes the following property: An agent $R$ that monitors a sequence of actions $\omega$ of a system $S$ cannot determine the value of a certain parameter (a certain part of the message, the agent performing the action, etc.) of a specific action or set of actions of the sequence, even if it knows the set of possible parameter values.

It is well known that security of a system is not an add on but must be considered during the whole design process from abstract requirement specifications to a concrete realization of the system. To efficiently employ the notion of parameter confidentiality it is therefore necessary to be able to prove satisfaction of

---

* Part of the work described in this paper was developed within the project SicAri being funded by the German Ministry of Education and Research.

S. De Capitani di Vimercati et al. (Eds.): ESORICS 2005, LNCS 3679, pp. 418–437, 2005.

this property in an abstract view of a system and then conclude that an *adequate representation* of the property is satisfied in the refined system as well. Using our formal framework for security properties [7] in terms of formal languages and language homomorphisms, this paper gives sufficient conditions for such a top down design and explains by a characteristic example its functionality.

Only a few papers discuss confidentiality in combination with refinement. [9] considers degrees of confidentiality and shows that degrees of functionality and confidentiality are inversely related w.r.t. refinement. [12] shows how refinement can be modified to preserve flow properties. [10] gives conditions for certain refinement operators on stream functions to preserve a kind of explicit confidentiality which does not capture implicit information flow. [8] identifies confidentiality preserving refinements in a probabilistic setting.

Another aspect to be taken into consideration is that security properties can only be satisfied relative to particular sets of underlying system assumptions. Examples include assumptions on cryptographic algorithms, secure storage, trust in the correct behaviour of agents or reliable data transfer. Relatively small changes in these assumptions can result in huge differences concerning satisfaction of security properties. Every model for secure systems must address these issues. However, most existing models rely on a fixed set of underlying assumptions (see for example [3] and [13]). These assumptions are often implicitly given by particular properties of the model framework. Thus, it is very hard to verify whether a particular implementation actually satisfies all of these assumptions. Further, imprecise security assumptions might result in correct but useless security proofs and finally in insecure implementations. Therefore, a model for secure systems needs to provide the means to accurately specify underlying system assumptions in a flexible way.

In order to provide the required flexibility, we extend the system specification by two components: *agents' knowledge* about the global system behaviour and *agents' view*. The knowledge about the system consists of all traces that an agent initially considers possible, i.e. all traces that do not violate any of its assumptions about the system, and the view of an agent specifies which parts of the system behaviour the agent can actually see.

The main result of this paper shows that preserving parameter confidentiality under refinement essentially depends on agents' view as well as on agents' knowledge. The effect of agents' view is also considered in [9] and in [8] whereas agents' knowledge is ignored by all papers mentioned above.

In Section 2 the formalization background is introduced. Section 3 recapitulates the definition of parameter confidentiality from [6]. Sufficient conditions for abstractions preserving parameter confidentiality are given in Section 4 and are discussed by examples in Sections 5 and 6.

## 2   System Behaviour and Abstractions

In this section we first give a short summary of the necessary concepts of formal languages to describe system behaviour and abstractions.

The behaviour $S$ of a discrete system can be formally described by the set of its possible sequences of actions (traces). Therefore $S \subseteq \Sigma^*$ holds where $\Sigma$ is the set of all actions of the system, and $\Sigma^*$ is the set of all finite sequences of elements of $\Sigma$, including the empty sequence denoted by $\varepsilon$. This terminology originates from the theory of formal languages [5], where $\Sigma$ is called the alphabet (not necessarily finite), the elements of $\Sigma$ are called letters, the elements of $\Sigma^*$ are referred to as words and the subsets of $\Sigma^*$ as formal languages. Words can be composed: if $u$ and $v$ are words, then $uv$ is also a word. This operation is called *concatenation*; especially $\varepsilon u = u\varepsilon = u$. A word $u$ is called a *prefix* of a word $v$ if there is a word $x$ such that $v = ux$. The set of all prefixes of a word $u$ is denoted by $\mathrm{pre}(u)$; $\varepsilon \in \mathrm{pre}(u)$ holds for every word $u$.

Formal languages which describe system behaviour have the characteristic that $\mathrm{pre}(u) \subseteq S$ holds for every word $u \in S$. Such languages are called *prefix closed*. System behaviour is thus described by prefix closed formal languages. Labeled transition systems are uniquely determined by their sets of labeled paths, which are prefix closed languages. So our method will apply to specifications with an interleaving semantics based on labeled transition systems, as for example any kind of communicating automata.

Different formal models of the same application/system are partially ordered with respect to different levels of abstraction. Formally, abstractions are described by so called alphabetic language homomorphisms. These are mappings $h^* : \Sigma^* \longrightarrow \Sigma'^*$ with $h^*(xy) = h^*(x)h^*(y)$ , $h^*(\varepsilon) = \varepsilon$ and $h^*(\Sigma) \subseteq \Sigma' \cup \{\varepsilon\}$ which implies $h^*(S) \subseteq (\Sigma')^*$. So they are uniquely defined by corresponding mappings $h : \Sigma \longrightarrow \Sigma' \cup \{\varepsilon\}$. In the following we denote both the mapping $h$ and the homomorphism $h^*$ by $h$.

*The Example.* In order to illustrate our approach using an example as simple as possible, in the following we introduce an artificial price offer–order example (which is not supposed to represent appropriate security requirements for any realistic application). In the project CASENET [2,4] funded by the European Commission our approach was successfully applied to real life e-government and e-business applications.

The scenario for the example system consists of a set of two users $\boldsymbol{\mathcal{U}} = \{U, V\}$ and a set of two service providers $\boldsymbol{S} = \{S, T\}$. The following actions can occur in the example system: a service provider sends a price offer for a certain service to a particular user, which is then received by the user. Subsequently, the user can place an order which is in turn received by the service provider. The price is assumed to be the critical parameter to remain confidential. For simplicity, we assume that only two prices are possible. Therefore, the set of prices is $\boldsymbol{M} = \{cheap, exp\}$. For user $USER \in \boldsymbol{\mathcal{U}}$, service provider $SP \in \boldsymbol{S}$ and $price \in \boldsymbol{M}$, the actions of the system are *send-offer(SP,USER,price)*, *rec-offer(USER,SP,price)*, *send-order(USER,SP,price)* and *rec-order(SP,USER,price)*. The first parameter denotes the agent executing the particular action, the second parameter the agent the action is associated with. Note that throughout the paper we denote sets, homomorphisms etc. that belong to our example by expressions in bold face. Thus $\Sigma$ denotes the set of all possible actions of the example, while $\Sigma$ indicates an arbitrary alphabet.

We will now define an abstraction of this system. Here we consider the same sets of agents and prices, but a reduced set of possible actions.

$$\Sigma' = \bigcup_{\substack{USER \in \mathcal{U} \\ SP \in \mathcal{S}, price \in M}} \{send\text{-}offer(SP, USER, price), rec\text{-}offer(USER, SP, price)\}$$

The language homomorphism $h : \Sigma^* \longrightarrow \Sigma'^*$ simply removes all actions for sending and receiving orders:

Let $\Sigma'$ and $\Sigma$ be as defined above. Then we define a homomorphism $h : \Sigma^* \longrightarrow \Sigma'^*$ by

$$h(a) = \begin{cases} a \text{ if } a \in \Sigma' \\ \varepsilon \text{ else} \end{cases}$$

Figure 1 illustrates the effect of applying $h$ to one particular sequence in $\Sigma^*$.

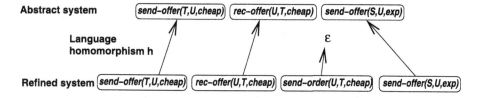

**Fig. 1.** Application of $h$ to a specific sequence in $\Sigma^*$

In the remaining sections of the paper we will formally define confidentiality of the price in the abstract system and then show that this property is satisfied in the abstract system and that $h$ preserves this property. Thus, we are able to conclude that confidentiality of the price is satisfied in the more complex (refined) system as well.

## 3    Parameter Confidentiality

This section gives a brief introduction to parameter confidentiality as introduced in [6].

### 3.1    Agents' View and Knowledge About the Global System Behaviour

We will now explain in more detail our approach to specify agents' view and knowledge about the system and their relations. The specification of the desired system behaviour generally does not include behaviour of malicious agents which has to be taken into account in open systems. An approach which is frequently used for the security analysis of cryptographic protocols is to extend the system specification by explicit specification of malicious behaviour. However, in general malicious behaviour is not previously known and one may not be able to adequately specify all possible actions of dishonest agents. In our approach, the explicit specification of agents' knowledge about system and environment allows to discard explicit specification of malicious behaviour. Every behaviour which is not explicitly excluded by some $W_P$ is allowed.

We consider all agents' knowledge sets to be part of the system specification. As explained in the introduction, agent $P$'s knowledge $W_P \subseteq \Sigma^*$ about the global system behaviour contains all traces that $P$ assumes to be possible. We may assume for example that a message that was received must have been sent before. Thus an agent's $W_P$ will contain only those sequences of actions in which a message is first sent and then received.

Care must be taken when specifying the sets $W_P$ for all agents $P$ in order not to specify properties that are not guaranteed by verified system assumptions. In a setting for example where we assume one time passwords are used, if $P$ trusts $Q$, $W_P$ contains only those sequences of actions in which $Q$ sends a certain password only once. However, if $Q$ cannot be trusted, $W_P$ will also contain sequences of actions in which $Q$ sends a password more than once.

Denoting a system containing malicious behaviour by $S$ and the correct system behaviour by $S_C$, we assume $S_C \subseteq S \subseteq \Sigma^*$. We further assume $S \subseteq W_P$, i.e. every agent considers the system behaviour to be possible. Security properties can now be defined relative to $W_P$.

The set $W_P$ describes what $P$ knows initially. However, in a running system $P$ can learn from actions that have occurred. Satisfaction of security properties obviously also depends on what agents are able to learn. After a sequence of actions $\omega \in S$ has happened, every agent can use its *local view* of $\omega$ to determine the sequences of actions it considers to be possible. In order to determine what is the local view of an agent, we first assign every action to exactly one agent. Thus $\Sigma = \dot{\bigcup}_{P \in \mathbb{P}} \Sigma_{/P}$ (where $\mathbb{P}$ denotes the set of all agents, $\Sigma_{/P}$ denotes all actions performed by agent $P$, and $\dot{\bigcup}$ denotes the disjoint union). The homomorphism $\pi_P : \Sigma^* \to \Sigma^*_{/P}$ defined by $\pi_P(x) = x$ if $x \in \Sigma_{/P}$ and $\pi_P(x) = \varepsilon$ if $x \in \Sigma \setminus \Sigma_{/P}$ formalizes the assignment of actions to agents and is called the *projection* on $P$.

The projection $\pi_P$ is the correct representation of $P$'s view of the system if all information about an action $x \in \Sigma_{/P}$ is available for agent $P$ and $P$ can only see its own actions. In this case $P$'s local view of the sequence of actions *send-offer(P,Q,price) rec-offer(Q,P,price)* for example is *send-offer(P,Q,price)*. However, $P$'s view may be finer. For example it may additionally note other agents' actions without seeing the messages sent and received, respectively. In this case, $P$'s local view of $\omega$ will be equal to *send-offer(P,Q,price) rec-offer(Q)*. $P$'s local view may also be coarser than $\pi_P$. In a system the actions of which are represented by a triple (*global state, transition label, global successor state*), although seeing its own actions, $P$ will not be able to see the other agents' state. Thus, we generally denote the local view of an agent $P$ on $\Sigma$ by $\lambda_P$.

For a sequence of actions $\omega \in S$ and agent $P \in \mathbb{P}$, $\lambda_P^{-1}(\lambda_P(\omega)) \subseteq \Sigma^*$ is the set of all sequences that look exactly the same from $P$'s local view after

$\omega$ has happened. Depending on its knowledge about the system $S$, underlying security mechanisms and system assumptions, $P$ does not consider all sequences in $\lambda_P^{-1}(\lambda_P(\omega))$ possible. Thus it can use its knowledge to reduce this set: $\lambda_P^{-1}(\lambda_P(\omega)) \cap W_P$ describes all sequences of actions $P$ considers to be possible when $\omega$ has happened. As this set is frequently used in this paper, we introduce the following abbreviation: $\Lambda_P(\omega, W_P) = \lambda_P^{-1}(\lambda_P(\omega)) \cap W_P$.

The set $\Lambda_P(\omega, W_P)$ is similar to the possible worlds semantics that have been defined for authentication logics in the context of cryptographic protocols [1,14]. Our notion is more general because for authentication logics $\lambda_P$ and $W_P$ are fixed for all systems, whereas in our approach they can be defined differently for different systems.

Our approach to define agents' local view and system knowledge is the basis for the framework of security requirements introduced in [7].

*Our Example.* We now define local view and knowledge about the system for agents of the abstract version of the example system introduced in Section 2. We assume that each user and service provider can only see its own actions.

For every agent $P \in \mathcal{U} \cup \mathcal{S}$ we define a homomorphism $\lambda'_P : \Sigma'^* \longrightarrow \Sigma'^*$ by

$$\lambda'_P(a) = \begin{cases} a \text{ if } a \in \Sigma'/P \\ \varepsilon \text{ else} \end{cases}$$

We further assume that the knowledge sets $W'_P$ of the agents $P \in \mathcal{U} \cup \mathcal{S}$ in the abstract system are only restricted by an assumption about the communication: No agent considers a sequence of actions possible in which an offer is received without having been sent. Thus, we have the following knowledge sets for $P \in \mathcal{U} \cup \mathcal{S}$:

$$W'_P = \Sigma'^* \backslash$$
$$\bigcup_{\substack{USER \in \mathcal{U}, SP \in \mathcal{S} \\ price \in M}} (\Sigma' \backslash \{send\text{-}offer(SP, USER, price)\})^* \{rec\text{-}offer(USER, SP, price)\} \Sigma'^*$$

$W'_P$ does not contain sequences of actions that start with a sequence without an action $send\text{-}offer(SP, USER, price)$, continues with action $rec\text{-}offer(USER, SP, price)$, and finally ends with any sequence of actions in $\Sigma^*$.

Based on these knowledge sets, the system behaviour of the abstract system can now be defined as $S' = \bigcap_{P \in \mathcal{U} \cup \mathcal{S}} W'_P = W'_P$ for all $P \in \mathcal{U} \cup \mathcal{S}$.

In the remainder of the paper, primed notation denotes expressions associated with the abstract system. Corresponding expressions for the refined system appear unprimed.

## 3.2    Formalizing Parameter Confidentiality

For the example system, we want to specify the property that the price offered to U is confidential from V's perspective. Various aspects are included in our definition. First, we have to consider an agent's local view and its knowledge about the system, as explained in Section 3.1. Then we need to identify the actions in which the price shall be confidential. In our example, only the actions where a price is sent to and received by $U$ are of interest. Thus, we disregard all other actions, i.e. we map them with a suitably chosen homomorphism $\mu$ onto the empty word. From those actions not mapped onto $\varepsilon$, $\mu$ extracts the parameter to be confidential that occurs in the action and associates it with the "type" of the action. The type consists of the name of the action and all parameters that are not required to be confidential.

Hence $\mu(\Lambda_R(\omega, W_R))$ is a set of sequences of types of those actions that are of interest with respect to parameter confidentiality, paired with the respective parameter values being possible from $R$'s local view.

If $\Sigma_t$ denotes a set of types of parameter occurrences and $M$ denotes a set of parameter values then homomorphism $\mu_{\Sigma_t, M} : \Sigma^* \to (\Sigma_t \times M)^*$ can be used to identify the parameters that shall be confidential. For simplicity we write $\mu$ if the related parameter set and the types are obvious.

*Our Example.* For $SP \in \boldsymbol{S}$ and $price \in \boldsymbol{M}$, the homomorphism $\boldsymbol{\mu'}$ for the abstract example system can be defined as follows:

$$\boldsymbol{\mu'}(\textit{send-offer}(SP, V, price)) = \varepsilon$$
$$\boldsymbol{\mu'}(\textit{rec-offer}(V, SP, price)) = \varepsilon$$
$$\boldsymbol{\mu'}(\textit{send-offer}(SP, U, price)) = (\textit{send-offer}(SP, U), price)$$
$$\boldsymbol{\mu'}(\textit{rec-offer}(U, SP, price)) = (\textit{rec-offer}(U, SP), price)$$

This homomorphism $\boldsymbol{\mu'}$ extracts the parameter *price* from all *send-offer* actions for and *rec-offer* actions by user $U$, respectively. Consequently, the type set for the example is given as $\boldsymbol{\Sigma_t} = \{\textit{send-offer}(SP, U), \textit{rec-offer}(U, SP)\}$.

Our aim is now to formalize that $\boldsymbol{\mu'}(\Lambda'_V(\omega, W'_V))$ contains *all possible parameter values*. What are the possible combinations of parameters is the last aspect that needs to be specified. In general it is obviously sufficient if all combinations of parameters are possible. However, in many cases interdependencies between different actions are publicly known and consequently, such a strong requirement would be impossible to be satisfied. In these cases it is reasonable to restrict the combinations of parameters. In our example we assume reliable transmission of messages and therefore $\textit{rec-offer}(USER, SP, price)$ can only occur if $\textit{send-offer}(SP, USER, price)$ has happened before.

The following language $\boldsymbol{K} \subseteq (\boldsymbol{\Sigma_t} \times \boldsymbol{M})^*$ expresses the different combinations of parameter values regarding offers sent to and received by $U$ which are possible in the example system.

$$\boldsymbol{K} = (\boldsymbol{\Sigma_t} \times \boldsymbol{M})^* \setminus$$
$$\bigcup_{\substack{SP \in \boldsymbol{S} \\ price \in \boldsymbol{M}}} \left[ (((\boldsymbol{\Sigma_t} \times \boldsymbol{M}) \setminus \{(\textit{send-offer}(SP, U), price)\})^* \right.$$
$$\left. \{(\textit{rec-offer}(U, SP), price)\}(\boldsymbol{\Sigma_t} \times \boldsymbol{M})^* \right]$$

Using the homomorphism $p_t : (\Sigma_t \times M)^* \to \Sigma_t^*$ that denotes the projection on the types, the following definition expresses parameter confidentiality with respect to a particular $\mu$ and $K$.

**Definition 1.** *[6] Let $M$ be a parameter set, $\Sigma$ a set of actions, $\Sigma_t$ a set of types, $\mu : \Sigma^* \to (\Sigma_t \times M)^*$ a homomorphism, and $K \subseteq (\Sigma_t \times M)^*$ with $K \supseteq \mu(W_R)$.*

*Then M is parameter confidential for agent $R \in \mathbb{P}$ with respect to $\mu$ and $K$ if for each $\omega \in S$*

$$\mu(\Lambda_R(\omega, W_R)) = p_t^{-1}(p_t(\mu(\Lambda_R(\omega, W_R)))) \cap K$$

The left hand side of the above equation consists of the $\mu$-image of the set of sequences of actions agent $R$ considers possible after having monitored $\omega$, while the right hand side contains all possible combinations of parameters by applying $p_t$ and then $p_t^{-1}$. Again, the intersection with $K$ removes all sequences of actions from this set $R$ is not required to consider possible because of information on the system it is allowed to know.

In order to provide a reasonable confidentiality property, the occurrence of parameters in $K$ cannot be too restricted. In most cases it is reasonable to require that apart from interdependencies between actions that are allowed to be known by all agents, all parameter values are possible for each action. This property of $K$ is expressed by the so-called *(L,M)-completeness* of $K$ as described in [6] and obviously holds for the above defined $\boldsymbol{K}$.

We can now show that in our abstract example system, agent V does not know more than it is allowed to know about occurrences of parameters in $M$ when monitoring sequences of actions.

**Proposition 1.** *The set $\boldsymbol{M}$ is parameter confidential for V with respect to $\boldsymbol{\mu}'$ and $\boldsymbol{K}$.*

**Proof:** We show by contradiction that for all $\omega \in \boldsymbol{S}'$ holds
$$\mu'(\Lambda'_V(\omega, W'_V)) \supseteq p_t^{-1}(p_t(\mu'(\Lambda'_V(\omega, W'_V)))) \cap \boldsymbol{K}:$$
Assume we have $\omega \in \boldsymbol{S}$ such that there exists $x \in p_t^{-1}(p_t(\mu'(\Lambda'_V(\omega, W'_V)))) \cap \boldsymbol{K}$ with $x \notin \mu'(\Lambda'_V(\omega, W'_V))$. Then there exists $\omega_1 \in \Lambda'_V(\omega, W'_V)$ with $p_t(\mu'(\omega_1)) = p_t(x)$ but $\mu'(\omega_1) \neq x$.

Further there exists $\omega_2 \notin \Lambda'_V(\omega, W'_V)$ with $\mu'\omega_2 \in K$, $\mu'(\omega_2) = x$ and $\omega_2 \in \mu'^{-1}_{ID}(\mu'_{ID}(\omega_1))$, where the mapping $\boldsymbol{\mu}'_{ID} : \Sigma'^* \longrightarrow (\Sigma' \cup \Sigma_t)^*$ is defined by

$$\boldsymbol{\mu}'_{ID}(a) = \begin{cases} a & \text{if } \boldsymbol{\mu}'(a) = \varepsilon \\ p_1(\boldsymbol{\mu}'(a)) & \text{else} \end{cases}$$

Sequence $\omega_2$ equals $\omega_1$ except for those parameter values that are extracted by $\boldsymbol{\mu}'$. Such an $\omega_2$ exists, because according to the assumption there have to be combinations of parameter values that do not occur in $\Lambda'_V(\omega, W'_V)$.

For all $\delta \in \boldsymbol{\Sigma}'^*$ holds $\mu'(\lambda'_V(\delta)) = \varepsilon$, i.e. every action that can be seen by V is mapped to $\varepsilon$ by $\boldsymbol{\mu}'$. Therefore, with $\omega_2 \in \boldsymbol{\mu}'_{ID}^{-1}(\boldsymbol{\mu}'_I D(\omega_1))$ and $\omega_1 \in (\lambda'_V)^{-1}(\lambda'_V(\omega))$ follows $\omega_2 \in (\lambda'_V)^{-1}(\lambda'_V(\omega))$. As $\omega_2 \notin \Lambda'_V(\omega, W'_V)$ it follows that $\omega_2 \notin \boldsymbol{W}'_V$. This means that in $\omega_2$ there exists a *rec-offer* action by user $U$ without a preceeding *send-offer*. This is in contradiction to $\boldsymbol{\mu}'(\omega_2) \in \boldsymbol{K}$.    □

# 4    Preserving Parameter Confidentiality

This section explains how we conclude from the proof of parameter confidentiality of an abstract view of a system that an *adequate representation* of the property is satisfied in the refined system as well, and constitutes the main contribution of this paper.

For simplicity, we assume that for a system $S \subseteq \Sigma^*$ and homomorphism $\mu'$ on $\Sigma'^* \supseteq h(S)$, the property for the concrete system is defined using the homomorphism $\mu = \mu' \circ h$ (where $f \circ g$ denotes the composition of functions $f$ and $g$). Then the same language $K$ can be used on both levels of abstraction to express the combinations of action types and parameter values. Definition 2 below can be easily transferred to the more general case with different type sets and different homomorphisms. However, the extended definition is more technical while the simplified version is suitable for many realistic scenarios.

Preservation of parameter confidentiality by a homomorphism $h$ is concerned with the parameter values considered possible on the different levels of abstraction. It therefore depends on the local views $\lambda_R$ and $\lambda'_R$ as well as on the relation between the knowledge sets $W_R$ and $W'_R$. These relations between the different levels of abstraction are shown in Figure 2.

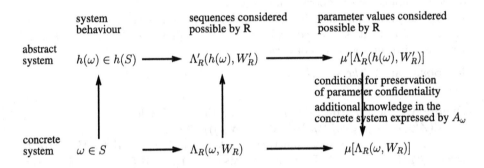

**Fig. 2.** Preserving parameter confidentiality

Definition 2 formulates a condition on language homomorphisms. We will show that homomorphisms satisfying this condition preserve parameter confidentiality, i.e. that if parameter confidentiality is satisfied in the homomorphic image of a system it is satisfied in the system as well.

**Definition 2.** *Let* $h : \Sigma^* \longrightarrow \Sigma'^*$ *and* $\mu : \Sigma^* \to (\Sigma_t \times M)^*$ *be language homomorphisms,* $S \subseteq \Sigma^*$, $R \in \mathbb{P}$, *and* $\lambda'_R$ *the local view of agent* $R$ *in* $\Sigma'^*$. *Then we call the homomorphism* $h$ *parameter confidential for* $R$ *with respect to* $\mu$ *if for all* $\omega \in S$ *there exists* $A_\omega \subseteq \Sigma_t^*$ *such that the following holds:*

$$\mu[\Lambda_R(\omega, W_R)] = \mu'[\Lambda'_R(h(\omega), h(W_R))] \cap p_t^{-1}(A_\omega)$$

So a parameter confidential homomorphism guarantees that the sequences of actions R considers possible after having monitored $\omega$ in $S$ correspond to those R considers possible after having monitored $h(\omega)$ in $S'$. The definition takes into account that usually agents will be allowed to learn additional information in the refined system about the type of actions that have occurred. This additional knowledge is expressed by the set $A_\omega \subseteq \Sigma_t^*$. Applying $p_t^{-1}$ adds all parameter values in M. Therefore, intersection with $p_t^{-1}(A_\omega)$ expresses that agents cannot gain any additional information on *parameter values*. In the case that agents do not learn any new information about action types, we simply have $A_\omega = \Sigma_t^*$ which leads to the much simpler condition $\mu[\Lambda_R(\omega, W_R)] = \mu'[\Lambda_R'(h(\omega), h(W_R))]$.

The next lemma states that if $X \subseteq (\Sigma_t \times M)^*$ is parameter confidential, then the intersection with a set in $(\Sigma_t \times M)^*$ containing all possible parameter values is also parameter confidential.

**Lemma 1.** *Let* $X, K \subseteq (\Sigma_t \times M)^*$ *and* $A \subseteq \Sigma_t^*$. *Then* $X = p_t^{-1}(p_t(X)) \cap K$ *implies* $X \cap p_t^{-1}(A) = p_t^{-1}(p_t[X \cap p_t^{-1}(A)]) \cap K$.

**Proof:** With Lemma A.1, $p_t^{-1}(p_t[X \cap p_t^{-1}(A)]) \cap K = p_t^{-1}(p_t(X) \cap A) \cap K$. According to the remark to Lemma A.1, this is equal to $p_t^{-1}(p_t(X)) \cap p_t^{-1}(A) \cap K$, which by assumption is equal to $X \cap p_t^{-1}(A)$. □

In Theorem 1 we now show that parameter confidential homomorphisms indeed preserve parameter confidentiality as defined in Definition 1.

**Theorem 1.** *Let* $S' \subseteq \Sigma'^*$ *be parameter confidential for agent* $R \in \mathbb{P}$ *with respect to some* $\mu'$ *and* $K$. *Let furthermore* $S \subseteq \Sigma^*$ *and homomorphism* $h : \Sigma^* \longrightarrow \Sigma'^*$ *such that* $h(S) \subseteq S'$ *and* $h(W_R) = W_R'$. *If* $h$ *is parameter confidential with respect to* $R$, *then* $S$ *is parameter confidential for* $R$ *with respect to* $\mu = \mu' \circ h$ *and* $K$.

**Proof:** $S'$ being parameter confidential with $h(S) \subseteq S'$ and $h(W_R) = W_R'$ implies that $\mu'[\Lambda_R(h(\omega), h(W_R))] = p_t^{-1}(p_t \,[\Lambda_R(h(\omega), h(W_R))]) \cap K$. From applying Lemma 1 with $X = \mu'[\Lambda_R(h(\omega), h(W_R))]$ we conclude $\mu'[\Lambda_R(h(\omega), h(W_R))] \cap p_t^{-1}(A_\omega) = p_t^{-1}(p_t\{\mu'[\Lambda_R'(h(\omega), h(W_R))] \cap p_t^{-1}(A_\omega)\}) \cap K$ which is equal to $p_t^{-1}(p_t(\mu[\Lambda_R(\omega, W_R)])) \cap K$, because according to the assumption $h$ is parameter confidential. □

We now introduce a property that is sufficient for a homomorphism to be parameter confidential. In contrast to Definition 2 here we directly compare the image under homomorphism $h$ of what $R$ can learn from $\omega$ in the refined system $S$ with what $R$ can learn from the image of $\omega$ in the abstract system $S'$ (again taking into account what $R$ is allowed to learn). This can result in easier proofs in some cases.

**Theorem 2.** *Let* $h : \Sigma^* \longrightarrow \Sigma'^*$ *be a language homomorphism,* $S \subseteq \Sigma^*$, $R \in \mathbb{P}$, *and let* $\psi' = p_t \circ \mu'$. $h$ *is parameter confidential for* $R$ *with respect to* $\mu$ *if for all* $\omega \in S$ *there exists* $A_\omega \subseteq \Sigma_t^*$ *such that*

$$h[\Lambda_R(\omega, W_R)] = [\Lambda_R'(h(\omega), h(W_R)] \cap \psi'^{-1}(A_\omega).$$

**Proof:** Since $\mu = \mu' \circ h$, we have $\mu[\Lambda_R(\omega, W_R)] = \mu'[h(\Lambda_R(\omega, W_R))]$. By assumption, this is equal to $\mu'[\Lambda_R'(h(\omega), h(W_R)) \cap \psi'^{-1}(A_\omega)]$. This in turn is equal to $\mu'[\Lambda_R'(h(\omega), h(W_R)) \cap \mu'^{-1}(p_t^{-1}(A_\omega))]$ because $\psi' = p_t \circ \mu'$, and with Lemma A.1 follows equality with $\mu'[\Lambda_R'(h(\omega), h(W_R))] \cap p_t^{-1}(A_\omega)$. □

Note that in the case where agents do not learn additional information in the refined system, the sufficient condition of Theorem 2 for homomorphism $h$ for being parameter confidential reduces to

$$h[\Lambda_R(\omega, W_R)] = [\Lambda'_R(h(\omega), h(W_R)],$$

i.e. $A_\omega$ is equal to $\Sigma_t^*$.

For designing a system using various steps of refinement a natural requirement is that the composition of parameter confidential homomorphisms is again parameter confidential.

**Theorem 3.** *Let $h : \Sigma^* \longrightarrow \Sigma'^*$ and $g : \Sigma'^* \longrightarrow \Sigma'''^*$ be homomorphisms parameter confidential for $R \in \mathbb{P}$ with respect to $\mu$ and $\mu'$, respectively, and let $\mu'' = \mu' \circ g$. Then $g \circ h$ is also parameter confidential for $R$ with respect to $\mu$.*

**Proof:** Let $\lambda_R$, $\lambda'_R$, and $\lambda''_R$ be the local views of agent $R$ in $\Sigma$, $\Sigma'$, and $\Sigma''$, respectively. Since $h$ is parameter confidential, $\mu[\Lambda_R(\omega, W_R)] = \mu'[\Lambda'_R(h(\omega), h(W_R))] \cap p_t^{-1}(A_\omega)$. This is equal to $\mu''[\Lambda''_R(g(h(\omega)), g(h(W_R)))] \cap p_t^{-1}(A'_{h(\omega)}) \cap p_t^{-1}(A_\omega)$ because of parameter confidentiality of $g$. Equality to $\mu''[\Lambda''_R(g(h(\omega)), g(h(W_R)))] \cap p_t^{-1}(A'_{h(\omega)} \cap A_\omega)$ follows with the remark to Lemma A.1).    □

We can now introduce a theorem which is the key for proving parameter confidentiality of a refined system based on parameter confidentiality of an abstraction. The theorem uses a couple of conditions that, though very technical, address quite natural conditions on compatibility of homomorphism and local views in the refined and the abstract system. The theorem refers to the case where an agent does not learn additional information about actions in the refined system (see note of Theorem 2). It essentially states that in this case the homomorphism is parameter confidential if the initial knowledge $W_R$ of agent R in the refined system is just the inverse of what R knows in the abstract system.

**Theorem 4.** *Let $h : \Sigma^* \to \Sigma'^*$ be an alphabetic language homomorphism, $h$ surjective, and for $R \in \mathbb{P}$ let $\lambda_R$ and $\lambda'_R$ be the homomorphisms describing the local views of $R$ on $\Sigma$ and $\Sigma'$, respectively. Let furthermore $h'_R : \lambda_R(S) \to \lambda'_R(S')$ a mapping on $S$ with $\lambda'_R \circ h = h'_R \circ \lambda_R$. Let additionally the following conditions hold:*

1. *For all $t' \in \Sigma'$ with $\lambda'_R(t') = \varepsilon$ there exists $t \in \Sigma$ with $\lambda_R(t) = \varepsilon$ and $h(t) = t'$.*
2. *For all $a \in \Sigma$ with $\lambda'_R(h(a)) \neq \varepsilon$ and for all $t' \in \Sigma'$ with $\lambda'_R(t') = \lambda'_R(h(a))$ there exists $t \in \Sigma$ with $\lambda_R(t) = \lambda_R(a)$ and $h(t) = t'$.*
3. *For all $a \in \Sigma$ with $h(a) \neq \varepsilon$ and $\lambda'_R(h(a)) = \varepsilon$ holds $\lambda_R(a) = \varepsilon$.*

*Then $h[\Lambda_R(\omega, h^{-1}(W'_R))] = \Lambda'_R(h(\omega), W'_R)$.*

For the (very technical) proof of this theorem we refer the reader to the appendix.

# 5   Parameter Confidentiality of the Refined Example System

We now consider the refined system as defined in Section 2, which contains an additional set of actions for sending and receiving orders. In Section 3 we have shown that parameter confidentiality of the price offered to U is satisfied in the abstract system. We will now show that this property is preserved by homomorphism $h$ and is therefore satisfied in the refined system as well.

The knowledge sets $W_P$ of the agents $P \in \mathbb{P}$ in the refined system are analogous to those in the abstract system: No agent considers a sequence of actions possible in which an offer and an order, respectively, is received without having been sent before. However, the particular user $V$ knows more about the system. It knows that user $U$ only orders the cheap price, and that he orders only after having received an offer. This additional knowledge is formalized in $W_V^2$ below.

The knowledge sets for agents $P \in \{U, S, T\}$ for the refined system $S$ are defined as follows:

$W_P = h^{-1}(W_P') \cap W_P^1$

where

$$W_P^1 = \Sigma^* \setminus$$
$$\bigcup_{\substack{USER \in \mathcal{U}, SP \in S \\ price \in M}} (\Sigma \setminus \{send\text{-}order\,(USER, SP, price)\})^* \{rec\text{-}order\,(SP, USER, price)\} \Sigma^*$$

The knowledge set for agent $V$ for the refined system $S$ with its additional restrictions is defined as follows: $W_V = h^{-1}(W_V') \cap W_V^1 \cap W_V^2$

where $W_V^1 = W_P^1$ and

$$W_V^2 = (\Sigma \setminus \bigcup_{SP \in S} \{send\text{-}order\,(U, SP, exp)\})^* \setminus$$
$$\bigcup_{SP \in S} (\Sigma \setminus \{rec\text{-}offer\,(U, SP, cheap)\})^* \{send\text{-}order\,(U, SP, cheap)\} \Sigma^*$$

The refined system $S \subseteq \Sigma$ in our example is given as the intersection of all knowledge sets:

$$S = \bigcap_{P \in \mathbb{P}} W_P(\Sigma)$$

We will show that, although $V$ knows more about the concrete system than it knows about the abstract one, with respect to the homomorphism $h$ the two sets are identical. This allows us to make use of Theorem 4.

For specifying parameter confidentiality in $S$, we need to define the local view of $V$ and the type of action(s) we are interested in. The local views of the refined system are analogous to those of the abstract system, i.e. each agent sees its own actions and does not see any (part of) actions of other agents.

The local view $\lambda_V : \Sigma \longrightarrow \Sigma_V$ of agent $V$ is defined as follows:

$$\lambda_V(a) = \begin{cases} a \text{ if } a \in \Sigma_{/V} \\ \varepsilon \text{ else} \end{cases}$$

In the refined system we are again interested in the confidentiality of the price offered to user $U$, i.e. on both abstraction levels we focus on the same type of actions with respect to parameter confidentiality:

The function $\mu$ that extracts action type and parameter is given by $\mu = \mu' \circ h$, i.e.

$$
\begin{aligned}
\mu(\text{send-offer}(SP, V, price)) &= \varepsilon \\
\mu(\text{send-offer}(SP, U, price)) &= (\text{send-offer}(SP, U), price) \\
\mu(\text{rec-offer}(V, SP, price)) &= \varepsilon \\
\mu(\text{rec-offer}(U, SP, price)) &= (\text{rec-offer}(U, SP), price) \\
\mu(\text{send-order}(USER, SP, price)) &= \varepsilon \\
\mu(\text{rec-order}(SP, USER, price)) &= \varepsilon
\end{aligned}
$$

**Proposition 2.** $M$ *is parameter confidential for* $V$ *with respect to* $\mu$ *and* $K$.

**Proof:**

We will show that Proposition 2 holds by applying Theorem 1. Thus we have to show that all conditions of Theorem 1 hold, i.e. that

(i) $h(S) \subseteq S'$ (i.e. $S'$ is indeed an abstract view of $S$),
(ii) $h(W_V) = W'_V$ (i.e. knowledge sets in the refined and the abstract system are consistent),
(iii) and homomorphism $h : \Sigma \longrightarrow \Sigma'^*$ is parameter confidential for $V$ with respect to $\mu$.

**Lemma 2.** $h(S) \subseteq S'$, *i.e for all* $\omega \in S$ *holds* $h(\omega) \in S'$.

**Proof:** We show the lemma by induction over the length of $\omega \in S$.

Induction basis: Let $\omega = \varepsilon$. Then $h(\omega) = \varepsilon \in S'$.
Induction hypothesis: For $\omega_0 \in S$ holds $h(\omega_0) \in S'$.
Induction step: Let us consider $\omega = \omega_0 a$.

  1. $h(a) = \varepsilon$. Then $h(\omega) = h(\omega_0)h(a) = h(\omega_0) \in S'$.
  2. $h(a) \neq \varepsilon, a = \text{send-offer}(SP, USER, price)$ for $USER \in \mathcal{U}$, $SP \in \mathcal{S}$, and $price \in M$.
     Then $h(\omega_0) \in S'$ implies $h(\omega_0 a) = h(\omega_0)a \in S'$.
  3. $h(a) \neq \varepsilon, a = \text{rec-offer}(USER, SP, price)$ for $USER \in \mathcal{U}$, $SP \in \mathcal{S}$, and $price \in M$.
     Then $\omega_0 a \in S$ implies $\omega_0 \in \Sigma^* \text{send-offer}(USER, SP, price)\Sigma^*$.
     It follows that $h(\omega_0) \in \Sigma'^* \text{send-offer}(USER, SP, price)\Sigma'^*$
     and therefore $h(\omega_0 a) = h(\omega_0)h(a) = h(\omega_0)a \in S'$.     $\square$

For the remaining items (ii) and (iii) we first prove a preliminary consideration concerning the fact that in our particular example the additional restrictions on $V$'s knowledge of the system $S$ have no influence on the image under $h$. This is formulated in the next lemma.

**Lemma 3.** *For all* $u \in h^{-1}(W'_V)$ *there exists* $v \in h^{-1}(W'_V) \cap W^1_V \cap W^2_V$ *such that* $h(u) = h(v)$.

**Proof:** The lemma holds trivially for $u \in h^{-1}(W'_V) \cap W^1_V \cap W^2_V$. Thus let $u \in h^{-1}(W'_V) \setminus (W^1_V \cap W^2_V)$, i.e. $u \in h^{-1}(W'_V) \setminus W^1_V \cup h^{-1}(W'_V) \setminus W^2_V$. Then $u = u_1 \ldots u_l$ contains

1. actions $u_{i_1}, \ldots, u_{i_r}$ with $u_{i_x} \in \{rec\text{-}order(SP, USER, price) \mid SP \in \mathcal{S}, USER \in \mathcal{U}, price \in M\}$ without the respective action $send\text{-}order(USER, SP, price)$ before, or
2. actions $u_{j_1}, \ldots, u_{j_s}$ with $u_{j_y} \in \{send\text{-}order(U, SP, exp) \mid SP \in \mathcal{S}\}$, or
3. actions $u_{k_1}, \ldots, u_{k_t}$ with $u_{k_z} \in \{send\text{-}order(U, SP, cheap) \mid SP \in \mathcal{S}\}$ without the respective action $rec\text{-}offer(U, SP, cheap)$ before.

We define $v := f(u)$ where

$$f(u_i) = \begin{cases} \varepsilon & \text{if } u_i \in \{u_{i_1}, \ldots, u_{i_r}, u_{j_1}, \ldots, u_{j_s}, u_{k_1}, \ldots, u_{k_t}\} \\ u_i & \text{else} \end{cases}$$

Since $f$ maps all actions that can cause $u$ not to be element of $W^1_V \cap W^2_V$ onto $\varepsilon$, $v = f(u) \in W^1_V \cap W^2_V$. Since $u \in h^{-1}(W'_V)$ and $h$ keeps all actions $send\text{-}offer(SP, USER, price)$ and $rec\text{-}offer(USER, SP, price)$, $u$ does not contain actions $rec\text{-}offer(USER, SP, price)$ without the respective action $send\text{-}offer(SP, USER, price)$ before. $f$ keeps in particular all actions $rec\text{-}offer$ and $send\text{-}offer$, thus $v = f(u)$ also contains no actions $rec\text{-}offer$ without the respective $send\text{-}offer$ before, hence is element of $h^{-1}(W'_V)$, and therefore element of $h^{-1}(W'_V) \cap W^1_V \cap W^2_V$. $\square$

**Lemma 4.** $h(W_V) = W'_V$

**Proof:** $h(W_V) = h(h^{-1}(W'_V) \cap W^1_V \cap W^2_V)$. Lemma 3 together with Lemma A.2 yields $h(W_V) = h(h^{-1}(W'_V))$. Surjectivity of $h$ implies $h(h^{-1}(W'_V)) = W'_V$ and therefore, $h(W_V) = W'_V$. $\square$

**Lemma 5.** For all $u \in \lambda_V^{-1}(\lambda_V(\omega))$ there exists $v \in \lambda_V^{-1}(\lambda_V(\omega)) \cap W^1_V \cap W^2_V$ such that $h(u) = h(v)$.

**Proof:** Again, the interesting case to show is $u \in \lambda_V^{-1}(\lambda_V(\omega)) \setminus W^1_V \cap W^2_V$. We use the same function $f$ to define $v = f(u)$. With the same argument as above we can deduce that $v \in W^1_V \cap W^2_V$. It remains to show that $v \in \lambda_V^{-1}(\lambda_V(\omega))$, which follows from $\lambda_V(v) = \lambda_V(\omega)$. Since $u \in \lambda_V^{-1}(\lambda_V(\omega))$, $\lambda_V(u) = \lambda_V(\omega)$. Furthermore, for all actions $a$ that are mapped by $f$ onto $\varepsilon$ holds $\lambda_V(a) = \varepsilon$ (none of these actions is performed by $V$), hence $\lambda_V \circ f = \lambda_V$, thus $\lambda_V(v) = \lambda_V(f(u)) = \lambda_V(u) \in \lambda_V^{-1}(\lambda_V(\omega))$. Again we can conclude $v \in \lambda_V^{-1}(\lambda_V(\omega)) \cap W^1_V \cap W^2_V$. $\square$

Finally we have to show that homomorphism $h$ is parameter confidential for $V$.

**Lemma 6.** $h$ is parameter confidential for $V$ with respect to $\mu$.

**Proof:** According to Theorem 2, the assertion holds if there exists $A_\omega$ such that for all $\omega \in \mathcal{S}$, $h(\Lambda_V(\omega, W_V)) = [\Lambda'_V(h(\omega), h(W_V))] \cap \psi'^{-1}(A_\omega)$. We show that this equation holds for $A_\omega = \Sigma_t^*$, i.e. we show that

$$h(\Lambda_V(\omega, W_V)) = [\Lambda'_V(h(\omega), h(W_V))] \tag{1}$$

Lemma A.2 (see Appendix) states that $f(X \cap Y) = f(X)$ if for all $x \in X$ there exists $y \in X \cap Y$ such that $f(x) = f(y)$. According to Lemma 5, this holds for $X = \lambda_V^{-1}(\lambda_V(\omega))$ and $Y = W_V^1 \cap W_V^2$. Since $W_V = h^{-1}(W_V') \cap W_V^1 \cap W_V^2$, this yields $h(\Lambda_V(\omega, W_V)) = h(\Lambda_V(\omega, h^{-1}(W_V')))$. Together with Lemma 4 we can reduce equation 1 to the case where $V$'s knowledge about the system $S$ is just the inverse image of what it knows from $\Sigma'$. It remains to show

$$h(\Lambda_V(\omega, h^{-1}(W_V'))) = \Lambda'_V(h(\omega), W_V')$$

which holds by Theorem 4. Finally we have to show that our example satisfies the respective properties. We do not provide formal proofs here as the assertions are easy to see.

With $h = h$ and $h_R = h$, obviously $\lambda'_R \circ h = h \circ \lambda_R$. Furthermore, we need to exclude some pathological cases concerning inconsistency between the homomorphism and the agents' local views on both abstraction levels (see Lemma A.5). The homomorphism $h$ just maps part of the refined system $S$ onto $\varepsilon$, the other part of $S$ forms $S'$. Of course this homomorphism is surjective. It is also consistent with the agents' local view, as $\lambda'_R$ is simply $\lambda_R$ restricted to the actions in $\Sigma'$. For the same reason, pathological cases as described by the conditions of Theorem 4 cannot occur. Hence the preconditions of Theorem A.4 are fulfilled and the above equation holds.

Thus $h$ is parameter confidential for $V$ with respect to $\mu$.    □

This concludes the proof that $M$ is parameter confidential for $V$ with respect to $\mu$ and $K$.

This proof seems to be rather complex for this artificial small example. However, the general structure of this proof applies to all examples where conditions for Theorem 4 are satisfied. More complicated systems will only result in more elaborate case differentiations.

## 6    A Different Refined System Not Parameter Confidential

In order to give an impression why the condition in Definition 2 fails to hold for a system not being parameter confidential, let us consider a system based on the same set of actions $\Sigma$, the same set of agents, the same knowledge sets, etc., but which has a slightly different local view of agent $V$. $V$ sees all actions performed by itself and additionally all types of actions performed by some other agent, i.e. it sees who sends to whom which type of message, but it cannot see the actual price used in the message. Although $V$ never sees the price, in this example it can deduce it from the observed behaviour combined with its knowledge about the system. This example shows that often it is not sufficient to protect only the transfer of confidential data. In order to achieve confidentiality the complete system behaviour needs to be considered.

Let $\Sigma$, $W_P$, $S$ etc. be as defined in the previous sections. Then $\tilde{\lambda}_V : \Sigma \longrightarrow \Sigma_t \cup \Sigma_{/V}$ with

$$\tilde{\lambda}_V(a) = \begin{cases} a & \text{if } a \in \Sigma_{/V} \\ \text{send-offer}(SP, U) & \text{if } a = \text{send-offer}(SP, U, price) \\ \text{rec-offer}(U, SP) & \text{if } a = \text{rec-offer}(U, SP, price) \\ \text{send-order}(U, SP) & \text{if } a = \text{send-order}(U, SP, price) \\ \text{rec-order}(SP, U) & \text{if } a = \text{rec-order}(SP, U, price) \end{cases}$$

is the local view of agent $V$ in $S$.

**Proposition 3.** $M$ *is not parameter confidential for $V$ with respect to $\mu$ and $K$ if the local view of $V$ is given by $\tilde{\lambda}_V$.*

**Proof Sketch:** We give a short proof sketch for the proposition. The complete proof can be found in the appendix in Section A.2. In order to show that the condition of Definition 2 does not hold we need to show that there exists $\omega \in S$ containing an action *send-offer(S,U,price)* with *price*$\in \{cheap, exp\}$ where $V$ knows the value of the price. Indeed, such an $\omega$ exists because $V$ knows (through its knowledge set $W_V$) that $U$ only orders the cheap price, and he sees that U receives an offer by $S$ and then orders, thus the price offered by $S$ must be equal to *cheap*.

# 7   Conclusions

In this paper we gave sufficient conditions to prove parameter confidentiality in an abstract view of a system and then conclude that an *adequate representation* of the property is satisfied in the refined system as well. The notion of parameter-confidentiality was introduced in a preceding paper [6] to specify confidentiality of certain parameters relative to an agent's knowledge about the system, especially knowledge about dependencies between parameter values in different actions.

As it was discussed in a typical example, the formulated conditions essentially depend on an agent's view as well as on an agent's initial knowledge of the systems behaviour, which explicitly formalizes assumptions about the system.

The universality of our formal definitions, based on formal languages and language homomorphisms, allows to apply them to any specification language with a semantics based on labeled transition systems.

The conditions introduced in this paper fit in our design method for security sensitive systems, where security properties are specified independently from the abstraction level. Suitable language homomorphisms map from lower to higher levels of abstraction. Our design method was successfully applied in the project CASENET funded by the European Commission (IST-2001-32446), where it was used to develop real life applications with certain security properties.

# References

1. M. Abadi and M.R Tuttle. A Semantics for a Logic of Authentication. In *Tenth Annual ACM Symposium on Principles of Distributed Computing, Montreal, Canada,* pages 201–216, August 1991.

2. I. Agudo, S. Gürgens, and J. Lopez. Casenet: One year later. In *18th IFIP International Information Security Conference 2003*, Athens,Greece, 2003.
3. M. Burrows, M. Abadi, and R. Needham. A Logic of Authentication. *ACM Transactions on Computer Systems*, 8, 1990.
4. CASENET. IST project 2001-32446. http://www.casenet-eu.org/.
5. S. Eilenberg. *Automata, Languages and Machines*. Academic Press, New York, 1974.
6. S. Gürgens, P. Ochsenschläger, and C. Rudolph. Parameter confidentiality. In *Informatik 2003 - Teiltagung Sicherheit*. Gesellschaft für Informatik, 2003.
7. S. Gürgens, P. Ochsenschläger, and C. Rudolph. On a formal framework for security properties. *International Computer Standards & Interface Journal (CSI), Special issue on formal methods, techniques and tools for secure and reliable applications*, 2005.
8. M. Heisel, Pfitzmann A., and Santen T. Confidentiality-preserving refinement. In *Proceedings of the 14th IEEE Computer Security Foundations Workshop*, pages 295–305. IEEE Computer Society Press, 2001.
9. J. Jacob. Basic Theorems About Security. *Journal of Computer Security*, 1(4):385–411, 1992.
10. J. Jürjens. Secrecy-preserving Refinement. In *Formal Methods Europe 2001*, LNCS. SV, 2001.
11. H. Mantel. Possibilistic definitions of security – an assembly kit. In *Proceedings of the IEEE Computer Security Foundations Workshop*, pages 185–199, 2000.
12. H. Mantel. Preserving Information Flow Properties under Refinement. In *IEEE Symposium on Security and Privacy, Oakland*, pages 78–91. IEEE Computer Science, 2001.
13. L. C. Paulson. Proving Properties of Security Protocols by Induction. Technical Report 409, Computer Laboratory, University of Cambridg, 1996.
14. G. Wedel and V. Kessler. Formal Semantics for Authentication Logics. In *Computer Security - Esorics 96*, volume 1146 of *LNCS*, pages 219–241, 1996.

# A  Appendix

## A.1  Several Technical Lemmata and Proof of Theorem 4

For arbitrary sets $X$ and $Y$ and $A, C \subseteq X$, $B, D \subseteq Y$ and a mapping $f : X \longrightarrow Y$ we always have the equality $f^{-1}(B) \cap f^{-1}(D) = f^{-1}(B \cap D)$, but only the inclusion $f(A \cap C) \subseteq f(A) \cap f(C)$. However, for particular intersections we have equality:

**Lemma A.1.** *Let $X, Y$ be arbitrary sets, $f : X \longrightarrow Y$ a mapping, and $A \subseteq X, B \subseteq Y$. Then $f(A \cap f^{-1}(B)) = f(A) \cap B$.*

**Proof:** $a \in f(A \cap f^{-1}(B))$ is equivalent to the existence of $b \in A$ with $f(b) \in B$ and $a = f(b)$, which in turn is equivalent to $a \in f(A)$ and $a \in B$.     □

**Lemma A.2.** *Let $X$, $Y$ and $Z$ be arbitrary sets, and $f : X \longrightarrow Z$ a homomorphism. If for all $x \in X$ there exists $y \in X \cap Y$ such that $f(x) = f(y)$ then $f(X \cap Y) = f(X)$.*

**Proof:** Let $a \in f(X)$. Then there exists $b \in X$ with $f(b) = a$. With the assumption if follows the existence of some $c \in X \cap Y$ with $f(c) = f(b) = a$. Thus $a \in f(X \cap Y)$. On the other hand, if $a \in f(X \cap Y)$, then $a \in f(X) \cap f(Y) \subseteq f(X)$, thus $a \in f(X)$.

$\square$

**Lemma A.3.** *Let $h : \Sigma^* \to \Sigma'^*$ be an alphabetic language homomorphism and for $R \in \mathbb{P}$ let $\lambda_R$ and $\lambda'_R$ be the homomorphisms describing the local views of $R$ on $\Sigma$ a $\Sigma'$, respectively. If there exists a mapping $h'_R : \lambda_R(S) \to \lambda'_R(S')$ with $\lambda'_R \circ h = h'_R \circ \lambda_R$ on $S$, then $h(\Lambda_R(\omega, W_R)) \subseteq \Lambda_R(h(\omega), h(W_R))$*

**Proof:** $x \in h(\Lambda_R(\omega, W_R))$ implies the existence of $y \in W_R$ such that $x = h(y)$ and $\lambda_R(y) = \lambda_R(\omega)$. This in turn implies that there exists $y \in W_R$ with $x = h(y)$ and $h_R(\lambda_R(y)) = h_R(\lambda_R(\omega))$. It follows that there exists $y \in W_R$ with $x = h(y)$ and $\lambda'_R(h(y)) = \lambda'_R(h(\omega))$ which finally implies that $x \in \Lambda_R(h(\omega), h(W_R))$.

**Lemma A.4.** *Let $h, h'_R, \lambda_R$ and $\lambda'_R$ be as defined above. If $h$ is surjective, $h(W_R) = W'_R$, and $\lambda'_R \circ h = h'_R \circ \lambda_R$, then $h[\Lambda_R(\omega, h^{-1}(W'_R))] \subseteq \Lambda'_R(h(\omega), W'_R)$.*

**Proof:** Replacing $W_R$ in $h[\Lambda_R(\omega, W_R)] \subseteq \Lambda_R(h(\omega), h(W_R))$ of Lemma A.3 by $h^{-1}(W'_R)$ yields $h[\Lambda_R(\omega, h^{-1}(W'_R))] \subseteq \Lambda'_R(h(\omega), h(h^{-1}(W'_R)))$. Since the surjectivity of $h$ implies $h(h^{-1}(W'_R)) = W'_R$, it follows the assertion.

**Lemma A.5.** *Let $h, \Sigma, \Sigma^*, \lambda_R$ and $\lambda'_R$ be as defined above. Let furthermore the following conditions hold:*

*(1) For all $t' \in \Sigma'$ with $\lambda'_R(t') = \varepsilon$ there exists $t \in \Sigma$ with $\lambda_R(t) = \varepsilon$ and $h(t) = t'$.*

*(2) For all $a \in \Sigma$ with $\lambda'_R(h(a)) \neq \varepsilon$ and for all $t' \in \Sigma'$ with $\lambda'_R(t') = \lambda'_R(h(a))$ there exists $t \in \Sigma$ with $\lambda_R(t) = \lambda_R(a)$ and $h(t) = t'$.*

*(3) For all $a \in \Sigma$ with $h(a) \neq \varepsilon$ and $\lambda'_R(h(a)) = \varepsilon$ holds $\lambda_R(a) = \varepsilon$.*

*Then for all $\omega \in \Sigma^*$ and $x \in \lambda'^{-1}_R(\lambda'_R(h(\omega)))$ holds $h^{-1}(x) \cap \lambda^{-1}_R(\lambda_R(\omega)) \neq \emptyset$.*

**Proof:** We prove the lemma by induction over the length of $\omega$.

Induction basis: Let $\omega = \varepsilon$. Then $\lambda'_R(x) = \varepsilon$ implies $x \in [\Sigma' \cap \lambda'^{-1}_R(\varepsilon)]^*$. By condition (1) it follows the existence of $y \in \Sigma^* \cap \lambda^{-1}_R(\varepsilon)$ with $h(y) = x$ and further $y \in h^{-1}(x) \cap \lambda^{-1}_R(\lambda_R(\varepsilon))$.

Induction hypothesis: The assertion holds for $\omega \in \Sigma^*$ and $x \in \lambda'^{-1}_R(\lambda'_R(h(\omega)))$.

Induction step: Let $\omega \in \Sigma^*$, $a \in \Sigma$, $\lambda'_R(x) = \lambda'_R(h(\omega)h(a)) = \lambda'_R(h(\omega))\lambda'_R(h(a))$.

    1. $\lambda'_R(h(a)) \neq \varepsilon$

        Then there exists $x = u't'v'$ with $t' \in \Sigma'$, $\lambda'_R(u') = \lambda'_R(h(\omega))$, $\lambda'_R(t') = \lambda'_R(h(a))$ and $\lambda'_R(v') = \varepsilon$. Because of the induction hypothesis there exists $u \in \Sigma^*$ with $h(u) = u'$ and $\lambda_R(u) = \lambda_R(\omega)$. Because of condition (2) there exists $t \in \Sigma$ with $h(t) = t'$ and $\lambda_R(t) = \lambda_R(a)$.

        As for the induction basis, it follows that there exists $v \in \Sigma^*$ with $\lambda_R(v) = \varepsilon$ and $h(v) = v'$. As a consequence we have $h(utv) = u't'v' = x$ and $\lambda_R(utv) = \lambda_R(\omega)\lambda_R(a) = \lambda_R(\omega a)$.

2. $\lambda'_R(h(a)) = \varepsilon$

   (a) $h(a) = \varepsilon$

      Then we have $\lambda'_R(x) = \lambda'_R(h(\omega)h(a)) = \lambda'_R(h(\omega))$. The induction hypothesis implies the existence of $y \in \Sigma^*$ with $h(y) = x$ and $\lambda_R(y) = \lambda_R(\omega)$. It follows $h(ya) = x$ and $\lambda_R(ya) = \lambda_R(\omega a)$.

   (b) $h(a) \neq \varepsilon$ and $\lambda'_R(h(a)) = \varepsilon$.

      As above there exists $y \in \Sigma^*$ with $h(y) = x$ and $\lambda_R(y) = \lambda_R(\omega)$. Condition (3) implies $\lambda_R(y) = \lambda_R(\omega a)$.     □

**Lemma A.6.** *If the preconditions of Lemma A.5 hold, then* $\Lambda'_R(h(\omega), W'_R) \subseteq h[\Lambda_R(\omega, h^{-1}(W'_R))]$.

**Proof:** Let $x \in \Lambda'_R(h(\omega), W'_R)$. By Lemma A.5 there exists $y \in \Sigma^*$ with $h(y) = x$ and $\lambda_R(y) = \lambda_R(\omega)$. Thus it follows $y \in \Lambda_R(\omega, h^{-1}(W'_R))$, hence $x \in h[\Lambda_R(\omega, h^{-1}(W'_R))]$.     □

Now Lemma A.6 and Lemma A.4 prove Theorem 4.

## A.2  Proof of Proposition 3

In order to show that the condition of Definition 2 does not hold we need to show that there exist s $\omega \in S$ such that for all $A_\omega \subseteq \Sigma_t^*$ holds

$$\mu[\tilde{\Lambda}_V(\omega, W_V)] \overset{\subseteq}{\neq} \mu'[\tilde{\Lambda}'_V(h(\omega), W_V)] \cap p_t^{-1}(A_\omega) \tag{2}$$

Consider $\omega = send\text{-}offer(S, U, cheap)rec\text{-}offer(U, S, cheap)send\text{-}order(U, S, cheap)$. $V$'s local view of this particular sequence of actions is

$\tilde{\lambda}_V(\omega) = send\text{-}offer(S, U)rec\text{-}offer(U, S)send\text{-}order(U, S)$

and the set of sequences $V$ considers possible contains only one sequence:

$$\tilde{\Lambda}_V(\omega, W_V) = send\text{-}offer(S, U, cheap)rec\text{-}offer(U, S, cheap)$$
$$send\text{-}order(U, S, cheap) \qquad\qquad = \omega$$

The reason for this is that $V$ knows (through his knowledge set $W_V$) that $U$ only orders the cheap price, and he sees that U receives an offer by $S$ and then orders, thus the price offered by $S$ must be equal to *cheap*.

Thus we have for the left hand side of Equation 2

$$\mu[\tilde{\Lambda}_V(\omega, W_V)] = \mu(\omega) = (send\text{-}offer(S, U), cheap)(rec\text{-}offer(U, S), cheap)$$

For the right hand side of Equation 2 we have

$$h(\omega) = send\text{-}offer(S, U, cheap)rec\text{-}offer(U, S, cheap)$$
$$\text{thus}$$
$$\tilde{\lambda}'_V(h(\omega)) = \varepsilon$$
$$\text{therefore}$$
$$\tilde{\lambda}'^{-1}_V(\tilde{\lambda}'_V(h(\omega))) \cap W'_V = (\Sigma' \setminus \Sigma'_{/V})^* \cap W'_V$$

Thus in order to show that $h$ is parameter confidential we would have to show

$$(send\text{-}offer(S, U), cheap)(rec\text{-}offer(U, S), cheap) =$$
$$\mu'[(\Sigma' \setminus \Sigma'/_V)^* \cap W'_V] \cap p_t^{-1}(A_\omega)$$

for some suitable $A_\omega \subseteq \Sigma_t^*$.

Consequently, the sequence $(send\text{-}offer(S, U), exp)(rec\text{-}offer(U, S), exp)$ may not be element of $p_t^{-1}(A_\omega)$. However, we either have

$$\{(send\text{-}offer(S, U), exp)(rec\text{-}offer(U, S), exp),$$
$$(send\text{-}offer(S, U), cheap)(rec\text{-}offer(U, S), cheap)\} \subseteq$$
$$p_t^{-1}(A_\omega) \cap \mu'[(\Sigma' \setminus \Sigma'/_V)^*]$$

that is

$$\mu[\tilde{\Lambda}_V(\omega, W_V)] \overset{\subseteq}{\neq} p_t^{-1}(A_\omega) \cap \mu'[(\Sigma' \setminus \Sigma'/_V)^*]$$

or we have

$$\{(send\text{-}offer(S, U), exp)(rec\text{-}offer(U, S), exp),$$
$$(send\text{-}offer(S, U), cheap)(rec\text{-}offer(U, S), cheap)\} \cap p_t^{-1}(A_\omega)$$
$$\cap \mu'[(\Sigma' \setminus \Sigma'/_V)^*] = \emptyset$$

that is

$$\mu[\tilde{\Lambda}_V(\omega, W_V)] \nsubseteq p_t^{-1}(A_\omega) \cap \mu'[(\Sigma' \setminus \Sigma'/_V)^*]$$

So there is no $A_\omega \subseteq \Sigma_t^*$ such that the condition in Definition 2 is satisfied.

# Minimal Disclosure in Hierarchical Hippocratic Databases with Delegation*

Fabio Massacci[1], John Mylopoulos[1,2], and Nicola Zannone[1]

[1] Department of Information and Communication Technology,
University of Trento - Italy
{massacci, zannone}@dit.unitn.it
[2] Department of Computer Science,
University of Toronto - Canada
jm@cs.toronto.edu

**Abstract.** Hippocratic Databases have been proposed as a mechanism to guarantee the respect of privacy principles in data management. We argue that three major principles are missing from the proposed mechanism: hierarchies of purposes, delegation of tasks and authorizations (i.e. outsourcing), and the minimal disclosure of private information.

In this paper, we propose a flexible framework for the negotiation of personal information among customers and (possibly virtual) enterprises based on user preferences when enterprises may adopt different processes to provide the same service. We use a goal-oriented approach to analyze the purposes of a Hippocratic system and derive a purpose and delegation hierarchy. Based on this hierarchy, effective algorithms are given to determine the minimum set of authorizations needed for a service. In this way, the minimal authorization table of a global business process can be automatically constructed from the collection of privacy policy tables associated with the collaborating enterprises. By using effective online algorithms, the derivation of such minimal information can also be done on-the-fly by the customer wishing to use the services of a virtual organization.

## 1   Introduction

Since the early works on privacy protection in statistical databases [1], privacy research has gained momentum. Changes in the landscape of legislation around the world, and growing consumer attention to the issue have changed attitudes towards security and privacy concerns for database systems. This matches with a substantial body of research on approaches for managing the negotiation of personal information among customers and enterprises [2,3,18,20].

At the basis of every solution for the exchange between enterprises and customers, there is the principle of transparency. Transparency means that when enterprises store data about customers they should disclose to customers which data is collected and how it is used, i.e., for what *purpose* data is maintained. Starting from the landmark

* This work has been partially funded by the IST programme of the EU Commission, through an FET under the IST-2001-37004 WASP project, by the FIRB programme of MIUR under the RBNE0195K5 and RBAU01P5SS projects, by MOSTRO and SMTPPs projects of PAT.

S. De Capitani di Vimercati et al. (Eds.): ESORICS 2005, LNCS 3679, pp. 438–454, 2005.

proposals for Hippocratic databases [3], most privacy-aware technologies use purpose as a central concept around which privacy protection is built. For the transparency requirement, enterprises should declare in their privacy policies the purpose for which data is collected, who can receive it, the length of time the data can be retained and the authorized users who can access it. Looking at such policies customers would be able to understand how their personal data will be used and, in case they agree, disclose them.

Transparency is not the only principle, and another important notion which goes hand in hand with transparency is the notion of minimal disclosure, as defined in the US Privacy Act of 1974 and the EU Directives on Privacy in 1995. This principle requires enterprises to maintain only the information necessary to fulfill the purpose for which it has been collected. The principle of minimal disclosure seems to be easily satisfiable. A company must simply ask the necessary data and leave other useful but unnecessary fields as optional. We all experience this business practice when filling in a web form.

However, enterprises are able to provide their services in different ways, and each different method could require different data. For example, banks may deliver bank statements by email and by regular post. Depending on the method, customers should provide their shipping address or email to the bank. Asking for both addresses as compulsory would clearly violate the principle of minimal disclosure.

If we consider these decisions, the burden of choice is on the human who must decide what to do on the basis of his/her personal feeling of trust of the enterprises. But this is very difficult for complex tasks, where there are many ways to deliver the service. The situation is worse if we consider dynamic coalitions, such as those that might be soon available with Web Services and Business Processes for Web Services. On the server side, we might not have a single enterprise, but rather a host of partners participating in a business process. Further, companies may outsource a large part of data processing to external supplier which on their own may do a similar process.

In some cases, the client process may even no longer be a human deciding to fill an email field with her business email or a freshly created Yahoo address but rather a software client. A software process needs automatic procedures for making such a judgment on the basis of some general criteria provided by the user.

Classical privacy-aware systems such as Hippocratic Databases do not consider these issues of delegation, minimality and their automatic treatment. In this paper we show how to address them.

## 1.1    The Contribution of This Paper

This paper presents a flexible framework for automatically deriving the minimum set of authorizations needed to achieve a service (i.e., the minimal privacy authorization table) from the enterprise privacy policy (privacy policy table) by determining the minimum set of data needed to fulfill required services based on users preferences and the partners entitled to access the data.

Following goal-oriented security requirements engineering approaches [9], we propose to analyze the purposes behind the design of a Hippocratic system, and organize them in hierarchal manner through AND- and OR-decompositions and delegation. Further, we extend that hierarchy by associating to purposes the data needed to accomplish them. Once customers have given a weight to each piece of data, one can determine the minimum set of data for fulfilling the root purpose with respect to user preferences. Reasoning procedures for the fulfillment of users' requirements by different solutions have been already investigated in goal oriented requirements engineering [10,19]. However, their solution is not adequate for our purposes, as it is tailored to off-line analysis by the system designer and not to on-the-fly selection by the system user.

In order to have more efficient algorithms, we represent purpose and delegation hierarchies with hypergraphs [4,5]. Based on this data structure, we provide algorithms for finding a minimal decomposition path that represents the process that uses the minimum set of information to fulfill a purpose, and for efficiently updating it when users change the cost of data items or choose among the alternatives that an enterprise offers for achieving the required service. Then, this path is used to determine the minimum set of authorizations needed to achieve a service.

The remainder of the paper is structured as follows. Next (§2) we introduce a scenario used as running example throughout the paper. We then provide (§3) a brief description of Hippocratic databases. Then, we introduce purpose DAGs in order to represent purpose hierarchies (§4) and discuss how to build a purpose DAG from a Hippocratic database system (§5). Next (§6) we present algorithms for finding and updating the minimum cost path. Finally, we discuss related works and conclude the paper with some directions for future work (§7).

## 2   A Running Example

Our scenario is a revised version of the case study proposed by Agrawal et al. [3].

Mississippi is an on-line bookseller who needs to obtain certain personal information to perform purchase transactions. This information includes name, shipping address, and credit card number. Mississippi views purchase (the root-level "purpose" for its service) as a three-step process: credit assessment, delivery, and notification. Delivery can be done by direct delivery or by post, while notification can be done by email or by fax. Depending on the method of notification, Mississippi needs either email or fax information.

Mississippi relies on Worldwide Express (WWEx) for shipping books. WWEx is a delivery company that offers a global network of specialized services – transportation, international trade support and supply chain services. WWEx also needs personal information to delivery books for Mississippi. This information includes customer name and shipping address. In turn, WWEx depends on local delivery companies for door-to-door delivery. To this end, WWEx delegates customer information to them. In the remainder of the paper, we call $LDC_1,\ldots,LDC_n$ the local delivery companies responsible to deliver books in the zone where the customer lives.

Furthermore, Mississippi relies on the Credit Card Company (CCC) for credit assessment. CCC needs to obtain some information for providing credit assessment. This information includes customer's name and credit card number, and the transaction between Mississippi and the customer. For making credit decisions, CCC wants a credit rating[1]. For this, CCC depends on the Credit Rating Company (CRC). CRC uses statistics to summarize past experience so that predictive analysis can be used to generate

---

[1] Credit rating is a method for interpreting the content of a credit report.

**Table 1.** Database Schema

| table | attribute |
|-------|-----------|
| customer | purpose, customer-id, name, address, email, fax-number, credit-card-info |
| order | purpose, customer-id, transaction, book-info, status |

**Table 2.** Privacy Metadata Schema

| table | attributes |
|-------|-----------|
| privacy-policies | purpose, table, attribute, { external-recipients }, retention |
| privacy-authorizations | purpose, table, attribute, { authorized-users } |

a rating for the customer. Based on the rating, CCC can decide to accept or not the customer transaction.

## 3   A Primer on Hippocratic Databases

Hippocratic databases [2,3] use *purpose* as a central concept and consider it as a "special" attribute occurring in every tables forming the database and associated with each piece of data stored in the database.

*Example 1.* Table 1 shows the schema of two tables, *customer* and *order*, that store the personal information collected by Mississippi.

Then, for each purpose and for each data item stored in the database, we have:

- *external-recipients*: the actors to whom the data item is disclosed;
- *retention-period*: the period during which the data item should be maintained;
- *authorized-users*: the users entitled to access the data item.

Purpose, external recipients, authorized users, and retention period are stored in the database with respect to the metadata schema defined in Table 2 [3]. Specifically, the above information is split into separate tables: external-recipients and retention period are in *Privacy-Policies* Table (PPT), while authorized-users in *Privacy-Authorizations* Table (PAT). The purpose is stored in both of them. PPT contains the privacy policies of the enterprise, while PAT contains the access controls policies that implement the privacy policy and represents the actual disclosure of information. In particular, PAT is created from PPT by instantiating each external recipient with the corresponding users. Therefore, Hippocratic systems define a PAT for each PPT. These tables are equal for every customer, and so they do not appreciate individual user preferences.

*Example 2.* According the PPT of Mississippi, it can access both email and fax number for notifying the status of the order. WWEx, Post Office, and all LDCs can access customer data for direct delivery, delivery by post and door-to-door delivery, respectively. These authorizations match exactly the policies declared in the corresponding PPTs.

Further examples for the PPT of each partner involved in the business process and the corresponding PATs in our running example can be found in [14].

Before users disclose their information, the *Privacy Constraint Validator* is used to verify whether user preferences match the privacy policy of the enterprise. In this way, Hippocratic DBs implement the consent principle. When queries are submitted to the database, the system answers only queries for which the purpose is equal to that for which data has been stored. Further, Hippocratic DBs do not disclose information for purposes different from those for which the owner of the information have previously give the consent. Thus, Hippocratic DBs implement, respectively, the limited use and disclosure principles. To enforce the retention principle, Hippocratic DBs use the *Data Retention Manager* which deletes data items when their retention period is expired.

The limited collection principle requires that enterprises collect the minimum set of data needed to fulfill the purpose for which data is stored. Hippocratic DBs use three components to implement such principle: *Access Analysis*, that identifies for each purpose which data never occurs in query answers; *Granularity Analysis*, that determines the granularity of the required information; *Minimal Query Generation*, that designs queries that disclose the minimum set of data needed for fulfilling a certain purpose.

## 4 Hierarchy and Delegation of Purposes

Hippocratic systems are an elegant and simple solution but do not allow for dynamic situations that could arise with web services and business process software. In such settings, enterprises may provide services in many different ways and may delegate the execution of parts of the service to third parties. This is indeed the case of a virtual organization based on business process for web service where different partners explicitly integrate their efforts into one process. This affects mainly the creation of the PAT.

Agrawal et al. [3] propose to split a purpose into multiple purposes and then store them in the database. In this way, we lose the relation among a purpose and its sub-purposes. Karjoth et al. [11] use a directory-like notation to represent purpose hierarchies. However, this notation does not distinguish if a sub-purpose is derived by AND or OR decomposition, and consequently cannot be used to reason about the fulfillment of the root purpose. Additionally the same sub-purpose may be part of different purposes. This distinction is important from the perspective of minimality of information. For example, providing *both* an email address and a physical address might be needed to provide the password for access to the tracking service and the actual shipping of goods and those purposes may be both necessary (AND) to obtain a certain higher level goal. However, in other cases only one of them could be necessary (OR). Therefore, requiring both of them would be a violation of the minimality principle.

Our approach is based on traditional goal analysis [15], and consists of decomposing purposes into sub-purposes through an AND/OR refinement. If purpose $p$ is AND-decomposed (respectively, OR-decomposed) into sub-purposes $p_1, \ldots, p_n$, then all (at least one) of the sub-purposes must be satisfied for satisfying $p$. The idea is to represent purpose hierarchies with hypergraphs [4,5], and we will call them *purpose directed acyclic graphs* (or *purpose DAGs*, for short).

**Definition 1.** *A purpose DAG $\mathcal{P}$ is a pair $\langle P, D \rangle$ where $P$ is a set of purposes and $D$ is a set of decomposition arcs. Each decomposition arc is an ordered pair $\langle S, t \rangle$ from an arbitrary nonempty set $S \subseteq P$ (source set) to a single node $t \in P$ (target node).*

**Definition 2.** *Let* $\mathcal{P} = \langle P, D \rangle$ *be a purpose DAG. A purpose DAG* $\mathcal{P}' = \langle P', D' \rangle$ *such that* $P' \subseteq P$ *and* $D' \subseteq D$ *and, for each* $\langle S, t \rangle \in D'$, $S \subseteq P'$, *is called* sub purpose DAG *of* $\mathcal{P}$. *This is denoted by* $\mathcal{P}' \subseteq \mathcal{P}$.

The enterprise-wide privacy policies is derived by looking at the Hippocratic database of each partner involved in the business process and merging them into a single purpose DAG. Therefore, purpose DAGs can be recognized as the outcome of a process of refinements of goals and delegation of tasks in security requirements modeling methodologies [9]. Fig. 1 shows an example of purpose DAG. Each node is composed by two parts: a purpose identifier and the list of data items needed to fulfill the purpose. Broken lines partition the purpose DAG in sub purpose DAG, and each of them represents the policies of a single enterprise, and so purposes on the broken line can be seen as services whose execution is delegated to other suppliers.

**Definition 3.** *Let* $\mathcal{P} = \langle P, D \rangle$ *be a purpose DAG,* $X \subseteq P$ *be a non-empty subset of purposes, and* $y$ *be a purpose in* $P$. *A decomposition path* $\mathcal{D}_{X,y}$ *is a set of decomposition arcs* $D' \subseteq D$ *such that either* $y \in X$ *or there exists a decomposition arcs* $\langle Z, y \rangle \in D'$ *and there are decomposition paths* $\mathcal{D}_{X,z} \in D'$ *for each* $z \in Z$.

Essentially, a decomposition path represents a possible process through which an enterprise can fulfill a root purpose. Our goal is to decide which is the process with the "minimum privacy penalty" to fulfill the root purpose with respect to the user's preferences. This can be performed through a quantitative analysis. In order to support quantitative analysis, we need to introduce the notion of weighted purpose DAG.

**Definition 4.** *A* weighted purpose DAG $\mathcal{P} = \langle P, D \rangle$ *is one where each decomposition arc* $\langle X, y \rangle \in D$ *has associated with it a weight* $\omega_{\langle X, y \rangle}$.

Since decomposition paths have a complex structure, different ways can be used to measure the cost of the same decomposition path. Depending on the weight measure, the problem can be polynomially tractable [8] or NP-hard [6,7,17]. The problem of finding a minimal cost hyperpath in a directed hypergraph is shown to be NP-hard when the cost of a hyperpath is the sum of the weights of its hyperarcs [4,5]. By making the cost function additive, Martelli and Montanari [13] were able to formulate a polynomial time algorithm for AND/OR graphs. For additive cost functions, the cost of one edge is counted as many times as it is traversed. Additive cost functions are also considered in hypergraph approaches that find optimal hyperpaths in polynomial time [4,5].

For our purposes, we use an additive cost function. We believe that additive measures are the ones that capture best the intuitive way in which we might wish to protect our privacy. In a nutshell, if the same datum is disclosed N times, then the cost of these disclosures is N, rather than 1. After all, the more a datum is used, the more it is likely that it might be compromised, or the more it is likely to end up in companies not so privacy-aware. The more our data are tossed back and forth the less happy we are.

**Definition 5.** *Let* $X$ *be a source set,* $y$ *be a purpose node, and* $\mathcal{D}_{X,y}$ *be a decomposition path from* $X$ *to* $y$. *The* disclosure penalty *(or* privacy penalty*) to reach* $y$ *starting from* $X$, $dp(X, y)$, *is inductively defined as follows:*

1. *if $y \in X$, then $dp(X, y) = 0$*
2. *if path $\mathcal{D}_{X,y}$ has root $\langle Z, y \rangle$ with subpath $\mathcal{D}_{X,z_1}, \ldots, \mathcal{D}_{X,z_k}$, then $dp(X, y) =$*
   $\omega_{\langle Z,y \rangle} + \sum_{z_i \in Z} dp(X, z_i)$.

## 5   From Hippocratic DBs to Purpose DAG

We now have the machinery to construct a purpose DAG when orchestrating a business process composed by many different partners (each with its own Hippocratic DB). The construction is sketched below.

- For each supplier PPT, purposes are analyzed through a goal refinement process, and so they are structured with respect to AND/OR decomposition. These purpose DAGs are circumscribed by a broken line and labeled with the supplier's name.
- Once we have a DAG for each supplier, we build the DAG representing the privacy policy of the entire business process by merging them.
- Then each purpose is associated with the data items directly needed to achieve the purpose itself (data items needed to achieves its sub-purposes are linked directly to sub-purposes).

Merging is done by looking at the external-recipients field in every PPT: when the external-recipients field is not empty, we connect that purpose with the corresponding purpose (with the same name) occurring in the DAG associated with the supplier that is an instance of some external recipient. If there is more than one instance for the same external recipient, we create a fictitious node and OR decompose it into a number of nodes equal to the number of possible instances. This is also what happens if we have multiple external suppliers for the same purpose. This approach supports complex enterprise strategies and, at the same time, allows customers to directly choose a certain supplier whenever the choice is possible. To support this process, we assume a common ontology among all the actors involved in the purpose DAG.[2]

The last step takes into account the data items we need to satisfy a purpose and the privacy penalty assigned to each data item by users. The idea is to create a node for each data item and link it to the purposes that directly requires it. So, we add to the purpose DAG $n + 1$ nodes where $n$ is the number of data items. Then, if a purpose node has no incoming decomposition arcs, we link to the purpose the data items needed to fulfill it with decomposition arc $\langle X, t \rangle$ where $X$ is the set of data items and $t$ the purpose node. Otherwise, if node $t$ has already an incoming decomposition arc $\langle X', t \rangle$, this is replaced by the decomposition arc $\langle X \cup X', t \rangle$. We link to each data item nodes the last node, *source node*, with arc $\langle \bot, t \rangle$, where $\bot$ is the source node and $t$ is a data item node.

*Example 3.* Fig. 1 shows the purpose DAG extended within data items corresponding to the running example. Each purpose DAG on a broken line represents the hierarchical

---

[2] This assumption is also necessary in Hippocratic database systems. If external recipients of data could assign a semantics to a purpose that is different from the semantics assigned by the Hippocratic database owner we could as well eliminate the entire tagging process and provide all data with purpose "do-what-you-please".

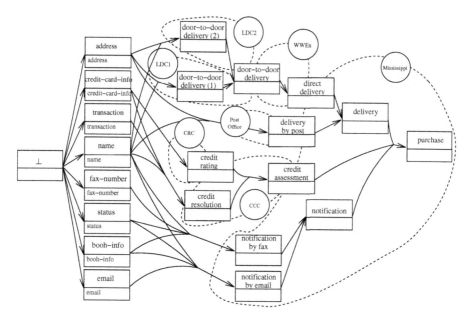

**Fig. 1.** Purpose DAG

model of the privacy policies concerning a partner. In particular, Mississippi AND-decomposes *purchase* into *delivery, credit assessment* whose execution is delegated to CCC, and *notification*. Thus, all sub purposes have to be reached in order to reach the root purpose. Then, the store OR-decomposes *delivery* into *direct delivery* for which it depends on WWEx, and *delivery by post* for which it depends on Post Office. These purposes are the root of the DAGs associated with WWEx and Post Office. Finally, the store achieves *notification* either *by fax* or *by email*. These purposes are not further on decomposed, and so are linked to the data items needed to fulfill them.

Every decomposition arc has disclosure penalty equal to 0, except the decomposition arcs joining source node and data item nodes, and delegation arcs. In the first case, the disclosure penalty corresponds to the cost of perceived disclosure of data. The latter represents the disclosure penalty to delegate information. Both these assignments are given by data owners with respect to their own preferences. In particular, weight on delegation edges from one supplier to the sub-suppliers can be defined by asking the users to specify the level of trust they feel about sub-suppliers.

## 6   Minimum Cost Algorithms

Customers do not want to disclose more data than needed to get the desired service. This corresponds to finding the minimal decomposition path from the source node to the root purpose. This path can be used to build the minimal PAT that represents the minimum set of authorizations for fulfilling the root purpose. A key observation is that such computation cannot in general be done by the company providing the service

**Table 3.** Data Structures

| Data Structure | Type | Description |
|---|---|---|
| $LAST[y]$ | node | Pointer to the last node in the minimal path from source node to simple node $y$. |
| $DISCLOSE[y]$ | integer | Privacy penalty from the source node to node $y$. |
| $NEEDED[y]$ | data item list | Data items needed to fulfill node $y$. |
| $TODO[y]$ | integer | For simple nodes, it says if node $y$ is reachable.<br>For compound nodes, it is the number of simple nodes (that compound $y$) which are not reachable from the source. |

once and for all customers: customers may associate a different privacy penalty to the provision of the same data item. Therefore, they are interested in finding the minimum information cost for fulfilling the root purpose with respect to their own preferences. The computation of minimal preferences is essentially a dynamic on-line process.

In order to design efficient algorithms for dynamic evaluation of privacy preferences, we use *FD-graph* [5] whose definition is given below.

**Definition 6.** *Given a purpose DAG* $\mathcal{P} = \langle P, D \rangle$, *let* $\mathcal{S}$ *be the set of source set, i.e.,* $\mathcal{S} = \{Z|$ *there exists a decomposition arc* $\langle Z, i \rangle \in D$ *and* $|Z| > 1\}$. *The FD-graph of* $\mathcal{P}$ *is a labeled graph* $G(\mathcal{P}) = \langle P_s \cup P_c, A_{or} \cup A_{and} \rangle$, *where:*

1. $P_s \equiv P$ *is a set of* simple nodes;
2. $P_c$ *is the set of* compound nodes *which is in bijective relationship with* $\mathcal{S}$. *If* $Z \in \mathcal{S}$ *is a source set then* $z$ *will denote the corresponding compound node, and any simple node* $z_i$ *in the source set* $Z$ *will be called a* component node *of compound node* $z$;
3. $A_{or} \subseteq (P_c \times P_s) \cup (P_s \times P_s) = \{(z, x)|\langle Z, x \rangle \in D\}$ *is the set of edges referred to as* OR-edges, *in bijective relationship with* $D$;
4. $A_{and} \subseteq P_s \times P_c = \{(z_i, z)|z \in N_c$ *and* $z_i \in Z\}$ *is the set of edges referred to as* AND-edges, *connecting any compound node to its components*

Essentially, a decomposition arc is represented by a compound node with a leaving OR-edge and one or more incoming AND-edges. The OR-edge corresponds to the OR choice of selecting the decomposition arc. Once the decomposition arc is selected, all purposes in its source set must be fulfilled. There is a one-to-one correspondence between the decomposition arcs of a given purpose DAG $\mathcal{P}$ and OR-edges of the corresponding FD-graph $G(\mathcal{P})$. If a decomposition arc of $\mathcal{P}$ has a weight, this is associated to the corresponding OR-edge. FD-graphs can be implemented by maintaining adjacency lists where all OR (AND) edges leaving a node $y$ are organized in $L_{or}(y)$ ($L_{and}(y)$).

When we design a system we can distinguish two phases, namely *Requirements Capture phase* and *Privacy Assessment phase*. Each of these phases involves some operations: the Requirements Capture phase requires an initialization phase and support for deleting arcs, adding arcs, increasing weights and decreasing weights, while the Privacy Assessment phase requires support for deleting arcs and increasing weights.

Next, we present the data structures used in the algorithms. A summary of such data structures is shown in Table 3. In order to retrieve the minimal decomposition path, the idea is to store for each simple node $y$, the incoming decomposition arcs belonging to the minimal decomposition path (*backward pointers* [5]) by using $LAST[y]$. This points to the last node in the minimal decomposition path from source node $\perp$ to simple node $y$, otherwise, if there is no path from $\perp$ to $y$, it is equal to *nil*.

**Table 4.** Algorithms for initializing and updating the minimal decomposition path

| Phase | Name | Input | Description |
|---|---|---|---|
| I | MinimumCost | | Find the minimal decomposition path for a purpose DAG. |
| I | ScanMC | $t$: node $x$: simple-node | Scan OR-edges and update priority queue. Called by MinimumCost. |
| U | WeightIncrease | $\langle X, y \rangle$: decomposition arc $\omega$: weight | Update the minimal decomposition path when arcs are delated or weight is increased. |
| U | ScanWI | $t$: node $x$: simple-node | Scan OR-edges and update priority queue. Called by Insert and WeightIncrease. |

The privacy penalty of the minimal decomposition paths from $\bot$ to any other simple or compound node $y$ is stored in $DISCLOSE[y]$. For every node, the privacy penalty is initialized to infinity ($\infty$). The list of data item needed to fulfill a purpose $y$ is stored in the variable $NEEDED[y]$. At the beginning, for every node $y$, $NEEDED[y] = \emptyset$ except for the nodes associated to a data item where the list contains the data item itself. The symbol $\uplus$ is used to represent concatenation of lists. Finally, the variable $TODO[y]$ is used to store if there is a path from $\bot$ to $y$. A node $y$ is visited if the value of $TODO[y]$ is equal to 0. For any simple node $x$, $TODO[x]$ is initialized to 1, and for any compound node $z$ (with components $z_1, \ldots, z_q$), $TODO[z]$ is initialized to $\sum_{k=1}^{q} TODO[z_k]$.

In the remainder of the section, we present some algorithms for finding and updating the minimum cost decomposition path. A summary of such algorithms is given in Table 4 where I and U are respectively used for initialization and update.

## 6.1   Initialization

Initialization refers to find the minimum cost decomposition path for a new purpose DAG. The following algorithms are based on [5] and are essentially a variant of Dijkstra classical minimum spanning tree algorithm. The algorithms are described in the following, while the pseudocode is given in Fig. 2 and 3.

Algorithm MinimumCost uses a priority[3] queue $PQ$ whose elements have the form $(C_t, I_t, \langle s, t \rangle)$ where $\langle s, t \rangle$ is an OR-edge, and $C_t$ and $I_t$ are, respectively, the privacy penalty and the list of data items associated with the node $t$. The algorithm inserts as a first element in the priority queue the item $(0, \emptyset, \langle \bot, \bot \rangle)$. Then, repeatedly, the algorithm extracts from the queue PQ the node $t$ with minimum priority $C_t$ which is assumed to be the privacy penalty of the minimal decomposition path from $\bot$ to $t$. Thereby, all OR-edges outgoing from $t$ are scanned by procedure ScanMC, all AND-edges $\langle t, z \rangle$ are analyzed. For each compound node $z$, $TODO[z]$ is decreased, and if it is equal to 0 the privacy penalty of the minimal decomposition path from $\bot$ to $z$ is computed. Then, all OR-edges outgoing from $z$ are scanned by procedure ScanMC. Procedure ScanMC aims at analyzing OR-edges $\langle t, x \rangle$: if the ingoing node $x$ is not already visited, the procedure inserts it in the priority queue; otherwise, the penalty of $x$ is updated if and only if edge $\langle t, x \rangle$ improves the old penalty associated with $x$.

---

[3] Lowest data required in, first out.

**Algorithm** MinimumCost
**Output:**
    $DISCLOSE[y]$ : integer;
    $NEEDED[y]$ : data_item_list;
    $TODO[y]$ : integer;
    $LAST[y]$ : node;
**begin**
  make-$PQ$-empty;
  $PQ$-insert(0, $\emptyset$, $\langle \perp, \perp \rangle$);
  $TODO[\perp] := 0$;
  **while** $PQ$-nonempty **do begin**
    $PQ$-extract($C_t, I_t, \langle s, t \rangle$);   {extract from the queue PQ the node $t$ with minimum priority $C_t$}
    $DISCLOSE[t] := C_t$;
    $NEEDED[t] := I_t$;
    $LAST[t] := s$;
    **for each** {OR-edge} $\langle t, x \rangle \in L_{or}(t)$ **do** ScanMC($t, x$);
    **for each** {AND-edge} $\langle t, z \rangle \in L_{and}(t)$ **do begin**
      decrement($TODO[z]$);
      **if** $TODO[z] = 0$     {If node $z$ is reached the privacy penalty of the path from $\perp$ to $z$ is computed}
      **then begin**
          $DISCLOSE[z] := \sum_{z_i \in z} DISCLOSE[z_i]$
          $NEEDED[z] := \uplus_{z_i \in z} NEEDED[z_i]$
          **for each** {OR-edge} $\langle z, x \rangle \in L_{or}(z)$ **do** ScanMC($z, x$);
      **end**
    **end**
  **end**
**end**

**Fig. 2.** Algorithm MinimumCost

**Procedure** ScanMC($t$: node; $x$: simple-node);
**begin**
  $C_{t,x} := \omega_{\langle t,x \rangle} + DISCLOSE[t]$;
  $I_{t,x} := NEEDED[t]$;
  **if** $TODO[t] = 1$         {check if node $t$ has been previously visited}
    **then begin**
      decrement($TODO[t]$);   {if not, node $t$ is marked as reached
      $PQ$-insert($C_{t,x}, I_{t,x}, \langle t, x \rangle$);  and arc $\langle t, x \rangle$ is inserted in PQ}
    **end**
    **else if** $C_{t,x} < C_x$      {otherwise, PQ is update only if arc $\langle t, x \rangle$ improves minimal path}
      **then** $PQ$-decrease($C_{t,x}, I_{t,x}, \langle t, x \rangle$);
**end**

**Fig. 3.** Procedure ScanMC

*Example 4.* Defining default preferences, Mississippi gives a value on data items and delegation steps (Table 5). It prefers to deliver books by using a delivery company because this method is more secure and faster. Further, it prefers to notify by fax. Fig. 4 shows the minimum cost path. Comparing it with Fig. 1, we can see that email does not occur anymore since fax has a lower penalty. Also the DAGs labeled with Post Office and $LDC_2$ are no longer considered since the sum of the penalties associated with WWEx and $LDC_1$ is lower than those associated with Post Office and $LDC_2$.[4]

---
[4] The penalty for delegating data to $LDC_2$ includes the trust level associated with WWEx.

**Table 5.** User Preferences

| Data Item | Cost | Delegation | Cost |
|-----------|------|------------|------|
| name | 1 | CCC | 2 |
| address | 5 | CRC | 4 |
| email | 4 | WWEx | 2 |
| fax-number | 2 | LDC$_1$ | 2 |
| credit-card-info | 10 | LDC$_2$ | 3 |
| transaction | 5 | Post Office | 5 |
| book-info | 2 | | |
| status | 3 | | |

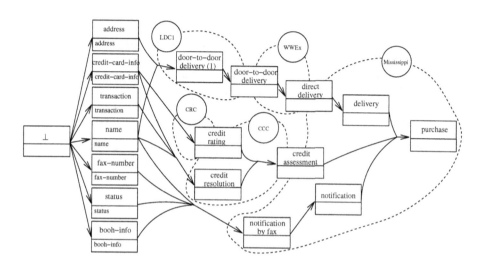

**Fig. 4.** Minimum Decomposition Path

It is possible to prove, as done in [5] that

1. a node $y$ is marked (i.e., $TODO[y] = 0$) if it is reachable from the source node;
2. the algorithm computes correctly the minimal privacy penalty from $\bot$ to any other node in the purpose DAG;
3. the algorithm terminates in linear time in the size of the purpose DAG.

Every purpose can be seen as a business process. Business processes can be combined, and the "new" process can be seen as an atomic process. Atomic processes follow the ACID properties [16] that guarantee that all participants will see the same outcome: in case of success all services make the results of their operation permanent by commitment, otherwise all services undo all operations they have requested and data is not disclosed. Thus, to guarantee consistent and reliable execution, we should check if the minimal path exists. This path is then used to build the PAT where external recipients are instantiated by the corresponding authorized users. This ensures that a user discloses all information needed to fulfill the service only if a path exists and that disclosed information is the minimum cost set of data necessary to fulfill the service.

*Example 5.* Mississippi is authorized to notify the status of the order only by fax, and so it can collect only data related to that purpose for notification. $LDC_1$ can access only data needed for door-to-door delivery, and so WWEx for direct delivery. In turn, Mississippi is entitled to access those data for achieving delivery. Moreover, CRC is authorized to access only data need for credit rating and CCC for credit resolution. Then, CCC can access only those data for performing credit assessment. Finally, Mississippi is entitled to collect data for achieving purchase in accordance with those allowed for its sub purposes. As shown in Fig. 4, Mississippi cannot access customer email.

A comparison among the PATs derived by two approaches is given in [14].

## 6.2   On-the-Fly Update of Customer Privacy Preferences

Both requirements capture and privacy assessment phases require to update the solution when weights are modified. In particular, the privacy assessment phase requires that data structures are maintained and that operations are performed on-line. The idea is to reuse the valid part of the old solution as much as possible.

The problem of dynamically updating the purpose DAG can be essentially divided in two distinct classes depending on the update operations that are possible:

- adding new arcs or decreasing the privacy penalty of an existing arc;
- deleting an existing arc or increasing the privacy penalty of an existing arc.

For sake of generality both possibilities must be considered when devising the theory but we argue that most practical implementations will only have to cope with the second type of updates. Indeed the presence of a decomposition arc corresponds to a business choice done by the enterprise (such as using a supplier). A customer may surely decide *not* to use a particular supplier, without further ado than ticking a checkbox on the web. However, *adding* a supplier or a partner to a business process is a procedure that can be conceived for very dynamic virtual business coalitions, and requires to solve problems (system integration, commercial agreement, legal liabilities etc.) that go well beyond the comparatively simple issue of privacy preferences. So we leave to the technical report [14] the details of the procedure that maintains the minimum cost path when new arcs are inserted or the cost of an existing arc is decreased.

In the case the customer increases the privacy penalty of decomposition arcs, we use algorithm **WeightIncrease** to build the new minimum cost decomposition path. The pseudocode is given in Fig. 5 and 6. The idea is that if the decomposition arc does not belong to the minimum cost decomposition path, this path does not change since we are analyzing only weight increase and arc deletion. If the decomposition arc belongs to the minimal path, we examine the other decomposition arcs having node $t$ as head. To this end, we use the function *backward* $B_{or}$ where, given a node $x$, $B_{or}(x) = \{h \in D | x = head(h)\}$. Essentially, $B_{or}(x)$ is the set of incoming decomposition arcs of $x$. Any time a decomposition arc that does not belong to the minimum cost path is found, it is pruned. The procedure **WeightIncrease** can be simply re-used for the case of arc deletion by defining the weight equal to infinity $(\infty)$.

*Example 6.* Alice, a Mississippi's customer, does not agree with default user preferences given by Mississippi. In particular, she prefers to receive books by post because

```
Procedure WeightIncrease(⟨X, y⟩: decomposition arc, ω: weight);
begin
    if |X| = 1
    then x := the single element of X;
    else x := Compound(X);
    if LAST[y] = x then begin                {arc ⟨x, y⟩ is considered only if it belongs to minimal path}
        DISCLOSE[y] := ω + DISCLOSE[x];
        for each {OR-edge} ⟨s, y⟩ ∈ B_or(y) do ScanWI(s, y);
        while PQ-nonempty do begin
            PQ-extract(C_t, I_t, ⟨s, t⟩);    {extract from the queue PQ the node t with minimum priority C_t}
            DISCLOSE[t] := C_t;
            NEEDED[t] := I_t;
            LAST[t] := s;
            for each {OR-edge} ⟨t, x⟩ ∈ L_or(t) do  ·
                if LAST[x] = t then          {arc ⟨t, x⟩ is considered only if it belongs to minimal path}
                    for each {OR-edge} ⟨s, x⟩ ∈ B_or(x) do ScanWI(s, x);
            for each {AND-edge} ⟨t, z⟩ ∈ L_and(t) do begin
                c := ∑_{z_i ∈ z} DISCLOSE[z_i]
                d := ⊎_{z_i ∈ z} NEEDED[z_i]
                if c < DISCLOSE[z] then begin    {arc ⟨t, z⟩ is considered only if it improves minimal path}
                    DISCLOSE[z] := c
                    NEEDED[z] := d
                    for each {OR-edge} ⟨z, x⟩ ∈ L_or(z) do
                        if LAST[x] = z then      {arc ⟨z, x⟩ is considered only if it belongs to minimal path}
                            for each {OR-edge} ⟨s, x⟩ ∈ B_or(x) do ScanWI(s, x);
                end
            end
        end
end
```

**Fig. 5.** Procedure WeightIncrease

```
Procedure ScanWI(t: node; x : simple-node);
begin
    C_{t,x} := ω_{⟨t,x⟩} + DISCLOSE[t];
    I_{t,x} := NEEDED[t];
    if C_{t,x} < DISCLOSE[x]   {arc ⟨t, x⟩ is considered only if it improves minimal path}
        then if ⟨t, x⟩ ∉ PQ
            then PQ-insert(C_{t,x}, I_{t,x}, ⟨t, x⟩);
            else PQ-decrease(C_{t,x}, I_{t,x}, ⟨t, x⟩);
end
```

**Fig. 6.** Procedure ScanWI

she does not trust to give her address to delivery companies after a bad experience with a local delivery company. To this end, she defines the cost of delegation information to WWEx equal to infinity ($\infty$). Further, she does not have a personal fax and must use her company's fax where faxes are first given to the program manager's secretary for distribution to the staff. Thus, she defines the cost of fax number equal to 20. Fig. 7 shows the minimal path computed with respect to her user preferences. The corresponding PAT [14] shows that Mississippi cannot access her fax number for notification and that WWEx and local delivery companies cannot access any of her data; only Post Office is entitled to access her data for delivering the purchased books.

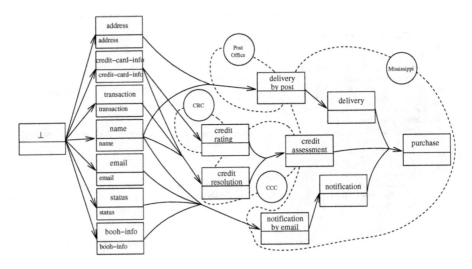

**Fig. 7.** Minimum Decomposition Path

## 7   Related Work and Conclusion

Last years have seen an increasing attention to privacy-protection technologies and the negotiation of private information between customers and companies. Tumer et al. [20] present a framework for Web Services that allows users and enterprises to automatically negotiate personal information. Each data item is defined as *Mandatory* or *Optional* by an enterprise, while users define for each part of their personal information the kind of access, namely *Free*, *Limited*, or *NotGiven*. Then, the framework matches enterprise policies with user preferences. If a mandatory input is not given by a user, enterprises can find alternative strategies in order to reach an agreement with the user.

A policy itself may be sensitive since analyzing the disclosed policies an unauthorized user may infer sensitive information. Therefore, some approaches aim not only to protect personal information, but also policies themselves. LeFevre et al. [12] provide an approach for forcing queries to respect privacy policies stated by an enterprise and users preferences. Their idea is to specify additional conditions to regulate the disclosure of information. Another approach to avoid unauthorized disclosure of sensitive information is Automated Trust Negotiation [18]. It aims to regulate iterative disclosures of credentials and requests between requesters and provider. These approaches are different from ours since we assume that information are committed only after checking that enterprise policies comply with user preferences. We argue that, if policies are not known at priori, users cannot know which data they have to provide. It may be possible that users discover that an enterprise requires more information than they (the users) consider reasonably sufficient to provide the service only when they have already disclosed part of their information.

The main contribution of this paper is a framework for deriving the minimum set of authorizations needed to provide a service by determining the minimum set of information a customer has to give. In particular, our approach provides support to Hippocratic systems for enforcing the limited collection principle when a complex business process is analyzed and user preferences are considered. Indeed Hippocratic systems create a privacy authorization table shared by all customers. This does not allow to distinguish which particular method is used for delivering a service, and so to customize the minimum set of information. Therefore, access analysis is only able to determine which data items are never used for a purpose and, consequently, minimal query generation works on a set of information that is not minimum. Finally, our framework ensures that a user discloses all (and only) the information required by the process that uses the minimum set of information to delivery the service.

There are some issues left as future work. One of these is to introduce an actor hierarchy to model the hierarchical nature of organizations (e.g., company-division-department-individual worker). Further, customers must be assured that they are getting a complete and correct answer to their queries before delegating privacy information. To this end, we are investigating the usage of Merkle Trees to build a global certificate to be provided to the client by composing the individual certificates from the various business partners.

# References

1. N. R. Adam and J. C. Worthmann. Security-control methods for statistical databases: a comparative study. *CSUR*, 21(4):515–556, 1989.
2. R. Agrawal, A. Evfimievski, and R. Srikant. Information sharing across private databases. In *Proc. of the 2003 ACM SIGMOD Int. Conf. on Management of Data*. ACM Press, 2003.
3. R. Agrawal, J. Kiernan, R. Srikant, and Y. Xu. Hippocratic Databases. In *Proc. of VLDB'02*, pp. 143–154. Morgan Kaufmann, 2002.
4. G. Ausiello, P. G. Franciosa, and D. Frigioni. Directed Hypergraphs: Problems, Algorithmic Results, and a Novel Decremental Approach. In *Proc. of ICTCS'01, LNCS 2202*, pp. 312–327. Springer-Verlag, 2001.
5. G. Ausiello, R. Giaccio, G. F. Italiano, and U. Nanni. Optimal Traversal of Directed Hypergraphs. Technical Report TR-92-073, ICSI, September 1992.
6. C. L. Chang and J. R. Slage. An admissible and optimal algorithm for searching AND/OR graphs. *Artif. Intell.*, 2:117–128, 1971.
7. Y. Desmedt and Y. Wang. Maximum flows and critical vertices in and/or graphs. In *Proc. of COCOON'02*, pp. 238–248. Springer-Verlag, 2002.
8. G. Gallo, G. Longo, S. Pallottino, and S. Nguyen. Directed hypergraphs and applications. *Discrete Applied Mathematics*, 42(2-3):177–201, 1993.
9. P. Giorgini, F. Massacci, J. Mylopoulos, and N. Zannone. Requirements Engineering meets Trust Management: Model, Methodology, and Reasoning. In *Proc. of iTrust'04, LNCS 2995*, pp. 176–190. Springer-Verlag, 2004.
10. P. Giorgini, J. Mylopoulos, E. Nicchiarelli, and R. Sebastiani. Reasoning with Goal Models. In *Proc. of ER'02*, pp. 167–181, 2002.
11. G. Karjoth, M. Schunter, and M. Waidner. Platform for Enterprise Privacy Practices: Privacy-enabled Management of Customer Data. In *Proc. of PET'02*. Springer-Verlag, 2002.
12. K. LeFevre, R. Agrawal, V. Ercegovac, R. Ramakrishnan, Y. Xu, and D. J. DeWitt. Limiting Disclosure in Hippocratic Databases. In *Proc. of VLDB'04*, 2004.
13. A. Martelli and U. Montanari. Additive AND/OR Graphs. In *Proc. of IJCAI'73*, pp. 1–11. Morgan Kaufmann Publisher, INC., 1973.

14. F. Massacci, J. Mylopoulos, N. Zannone, Minimal Disclosure in Hierarchical Hippocratic Databases with Delegation, Technical Report DIT-05-051, Univ. di Trento 2005. Available on the web at http://eprints.biblio.unitn.it.
15. N. J. Nilsson. *Problem solving methods in AI*. McGraw-Hill, 1971.
16. M. P. Papazoglou. Web Services and Business Transactions. *World Wide Web: Internet and Web Inform. Sys.*, 6:49–91, 2003.
17. S. Sahni. Computationally related problems. *SIAM J. on Comp.*, 3(4):262–279, 1974.
18. K. Seamons, M. Winslett, and T. Yu. Limiting the Disclosure of Access Control Policies during Automated Trust Negotiation. In *Proc. of NDSS'01*, pp. 109–125. IEEE Press, 2001.
19. R. Sebastiani, P. Giorgini, and J. Mylopoulos. Simple and minimum-cost satisfiability for goal models. In *Proc. of CAiSE'04, LNCS 3084*, pp. 20–35. Springer-Verlag, 2004.
20. A. Tumer, A. Dogac, and H. Toroslu. A Semantic based Privacy Framework for Web Services. In *Proc. of ESSW'03*, 2003.

# Security Notions for Disk Encryption

Kristian Gjøsteen

Department of Telematics,
Norwegian University of Science and Technology, 7491 Trondheim, Norway
`kristian.gjosteen@item.ntnu.no`

**Abstract.** We define security goals and attack models for disk encryption, and prove several results for the resulting security notions, as well as some relationships. We give concrete constructions for every security notion along with security proofs. We briefly discuss the security of some implementations and standards for disk encryption.

## 1 Introduction

It is quite common for confidential and important data to be written to some storage medium (laptop computers, memory sticks, optical or magnetic media, networked storage systems, etc.), but where the physical integrity of the storage medium cannot be guaranteed. The obvious solution is to use cryptography.

While it is possible to include encryption and integrity into application programs, this is often infeasible, either because proper security must be designed into applications, not added as an afterthought, or because the software cannot be modified. The creation of temporary files as well as working copies leave traces on the physical disk, which means that conventional file encryption programs are of little use. Even when such solutions are possible, they will often be difficult to use correctly.

One popular solution is *disk encryption*, where all data is encrypted by the operating system before it is written to the storage medium. This is an attractive solution, because it is potentially very easy to use (being almost transparent to the user), and existing applications can be used unmodified.

We shall consider four different attack scenarios for disk encryption.

**Theft.** The simplest situation is when the storage medium is stolen, where the goal will be confidentiality. The thief should not be able to read the confidential information stored.

**Passive monitoring.** There are situations where the adversary is able to monitor the data being read and written to and from the storage medium, but he is not able to modify the data. One example could be electromagnetic radiation leaking from the cables between the user device and the storage medium. A more plausible example is a storage device connected to a network, where the attacker can read network traffic, but is unable or unwilling to modify traffic. A third example is read-only storage media used for transport.

S. De Capitani di Vimercati et al. (Eds.): ESORICS 2005, LNCS 3679, pp. 455–474, 2005.
© Springer-Verlag Berlin Heidelberg 2005

**Theft with recovery.** A slightly more complicated situation is where the storage medium is first stolen, the theft is discovered, and the medium is subsequently recovered. Obviously, confidentiality remains a goal, but in addition, the storage medium may have been tampered with. We need to be confident in its integrity.

**Active attack.** The most difficult situation is when the adversary has surreptitious read and write access to the storage medium while it is in use (or between sessions). The most extreme example is out-sourced storage accessed via a network, where the adversary either controls the network, or is in complete control of the storage medium (we could say that the adversary is the storage medium).

We define precisely what a disk encryptor is in Sect. 2, and look briefly at two practical implementations of disk encryptors, as well as the work of a standards group. In Sect. 3 we define attack models and security goals (combinations of which form security notions). In Sect. 4 we discuss relationships between various security notions, as well as some general results about what is required to reach various security notions.

In Sect. 5, we give several constructions for disk encryptors, meeting every security notion discussed in Sect. 3. We also discuss the security of the implementations and the standard discussed in Sect. 2. The proofs for the results in Sect. 4 and 5 are somewhat technical, and are included in Appendix A.

## 2 Disk Encryptor

### 2.1 Definitions

We first define what a sector-based storage medium is. Let $S$ be a set of possible sector values (typically $S = \{0,1\}^l$ for some $l$). A *storage medium* for $n$ sectors is an interactive deterministic algorithm. It accepts as input write or read requests, and keeps a list of pairs from $\{0,1,\ldots,n-1\} \times S$. The list is initially empty.

The write request is a pair $(i,s) \in \{0,1,\ldots,n-1\} \times S$ ("store $s$ at index $i$"). The storage medium stores the pair $(i,s)$ in a list, discarding any previously stored pair $(i,s')$, and replies with the special symbol $\top$.

The read request is a number $i \in \{0,1,\ldots,n-1\}$ ("read from index $i$"). If the storage medium has a pair $(i,s)$ in its list, it outputs $s$. Otherwise, it outputs some (fixed) value from $S$.

Let $x = (x_1, x_2, \ldots, x_r) \in S^r$, and let $I$ be a subset of $\{0,1,\ldots,n-1\}$ of cardinality $r$. Order the elements of $I$ and denote the $j$th element by $i_j$. *Reading (writing) $x$ according to $I$* means to read (write) $x_j$ from (to) sector $i_j$.

A *disk encryptor* $\mathcal{D}$ for $N$ plaintext sectors with values in $S$ is an interactive algorithm, accepting input from a user and giving input to a storage medium[1].

The disk encryptor accepts as its first input a key from a set $K$ and possibly a state. As part of its initialization, it may issue read and write requests to the

---

[1] It is possible (and desirable) to allow the disk encryptor and the storage medium to have different sector sizes. To simplify the presentation, we keep sector sizes equal.

storage medium. After initialization, the disk encryptor accepts as input read and write requests.

The disk encryptor may keep a state between read and write requests. We shall assume that this state is publicly known at all times, but that no adversary may modify it. A disk encryptor that does not keep a state is *stateless*.

The write request is a pair $(i, s) \in \{0, 1, \ldots, N - 1\} \times S$. The processing of the write request is probabilistic, and may result in read requests as well as write requests to the storage medium. All the read requests must be completed before any write request occurs. After all the read requests are complete, but before the first write request has been issued, the disk encryptor may stop processing and reply with the special symbol $\perp$ (signifying encryption error). Otherwise, the disk encryptor issues its write requests to the storage medium and replies with the special symbol $\top$ (signifying no error) when processing is complete.

The read request is a number $i \in \{0, 1, \ldots, N - 1\}$. The processing of the read request is deterministic, and will only result in read requests to the storage medium. When the processing is complete, the disk encryptor replies either with a sector value from $S$, or with the special symbol $\perp$, signaling decryption error. The disk encryptor's state should not change as a result of a read request.

We require that the indexes of the read and write requests issued to the storage medium should only depend on the index of the input request, not on the key or the state.

The disk encryptor must guarantee that, in normal operation, if $(i, s)$ was the last write request issued for $i$, then the read request $i$ will return $s$. If no write request $(i, s')$ for any $s'$ has been issued, the disk encryptor may respond arbitrarily to the read request $i$.

To provide secure storage of $N$ sectors with values from $S$, the disk encryptor requires $n \geq N$ sectors of storage medium. The ratio $n/N$ is the *expansion ratio* of the disk encryptor.

We impose one more requirement on a disk encryptor: Any read and write request to the storage medium should result in at most a constant times $\log N$ reads and writes to the storage medium.

The sectors read and written through the user interface of a disk encryptor are the *plaintext sectors*. The sectors on the storage medium are the *ciphertext sectors*.

## 2.2   Existing Implementations and Standards

The following presentation includes three concrete examples of implementations or standards. We shall analyze these systems in Sect. 5.

LoopAES [11] is a disk encryptor for Linux-based computer operating systems. Its stated aim is to provide confidentiality, but not integrity. It encrypts sectors using a block cipher in CBC mode, and has three modes of operation, one using a single key and two different modes using multiple keys.

The documentation is somewhat unclear, but a (possibly deprecated) single key mode seems to use the sector index as initialization vector for CBC mode.

One multiple-key mode apparently uses a pseudo-random function family to derive the initialization vector from the sector index. We discuss these variants in Sect. 5.2. We quote from the purpose of the Security in Storage Working

Group (SISWG) [5]:

> This standard provides a standard architecture for media security and enabling components. Present non-standard, insecure encrypted storage methodologies are augmented, and users will be able to create higher-assurance, standard, interoperable solutions.

They restrict their attention to disk encryptors with expansion rate 1. As we shall see, Theorem 5 will severely limit the security level achievable.

One of their proposed methods for disk sector encryption uses tweakable, sector-wide block ciphers. We discuss this construction in Sect. 5.3.

The disk encryptor called GEOM Based Disk Encryption (GBDE) [7] is part of the computer operating system FreeBSD.

The main idea is that every sector is encrypted using a block cipher in CBC mode. A constant initialization vector is used together with a one-time key. The one-time key is encrypted and written to a different sector using a block cipher in CBC mode. The key for this encryption is derived from a master key, sector index and a salt using a pseudo-random function family.

We discuss scheme in Sect. 5.5, along with other alternatives.

## 3    Security Goals and Attack Models

As usual, we model an attack as a game played between an adversary and a simulator. At the start of the game, the simulator initializes a disk encryptor instance with a randomly chosen key. The adversary is given access to the disk encryptor and the storage medium through the simulator.

In practice, much of the information written to the disk encryptor will either be influenced, known or guessable by the adversary. This means that a chosen ciphertext attack is unrealistic. To simplify modelling, we allow the adversary to write arbitrary data of his choice to the disk encryptor.

The adversary should also have read access to any data written by himself (when relevant). The intuition is that most users would not hesitate in giving the adversary access to data supplied by the adversary.

The simulator must bar read access to any data it has written to the disk encryptor, to keep the adversary from achieving his goals trivially.

The four scenarios in the introduction give us the following attack models[2], which describe the attack conditions.

**Non-adaptive chosen plaintext attack (naCPA).** The adversary gets write access to the disk encryptor. When he is finished writing, he is given read access to the storage medium for the duration of the game. (This corresponds to the theft scenario.)

---

[2] Technically, many more attack models are possible, but we consider only those that seem interesting.

**Chosen plaintext attack (CPA).** The adversary is given read and write access to the disk encryptor. Everything read from and written to the storage medium is simultaneously copied to the adversary. (This corresponds to the passive monitoring scenario.)

**Non-adaptive chosen ciphertext attack (naCCA).** The adversary is given write access to the disk encryptor. When he is finished writing, he is given read and write access to the storage medium. When he is finished with the storage medium, he is given read access to the disk encryptor. (This corresponds to the theft with recovery scenario.)

**Chosen ciphertext attack (CCA).** The adversary is given read and write access to the disk encryptor, and the simulator uses the adversary as storage medium. (This corresponds to the active attack scenario.)

naCPA is the weakest attack. naCCA and CPA are not comparable. CCA is the strongest attack.

We shall now describe a series of security goals for disk encryption. Throughout, we consider a disk encryptor $\mathcal{D}$ providing $N$ plaintext sectors with values from a set $S$.

The classic security goal is confidentiality. Following the standard notion of semantic security, an adversary that has partial information about the plaintext sectors must not be able to deduce anything new by studying the storage medium. We note that this is equivalent to the notion of indistinguishability, where an adversary must distinguish between encryptions of two messages he has chosen.

**Definition 1.** *An adversary $A$ against* semantic security *works as follows: First the adversary specifies a probability space $X$ over $S^r$, an index set $I \subseteq \{0, 1, \ldots, N-1\}$ of cardinality $r$, and a function $f : S^r \to \{0, 1\}$ such that $\Pr[f(x) = 0 \mid x \xleftarrow{r} X] = \Pr[f(x) = 1 \mid x \xleftarrow{r} X] = 1/2$. The simulator samples $x$ from $X$ and writes $x$ to the disk encryptor according to $I$. The adversary then outputs a bit $b \in \{0, 1\}$.*

*Let $E$ be the event that $f(x) = b$. The adversary's advantage is*

$$\mathrm{Adv}_A^{\mathcal{D}, \mathrm{IND}, \cdot} = |\Pr[E] - 1/2|.$$

*Remark 1.* The adversary is assumed to output a description of the probability space $X$ such that the simulator can sample from $X$.

*Remark 2.* For all of the attack games described in this section, we say that an adversary requires time at most $t$ if the described game requires at most time $t$ to complete, counting the work done by the adversary *and* the simulator.

Another important security goal is that of non-malleability, where the adversary should not be able to change the ciphertext sectors to cause any meaningful change in the plaintext sectors.

**Definition 2.** *An adversary A against* non-malleability *works as follows: First the adversary specifies a probability space X over $S^r$, and an index set $I \subseteq \{0, 1, \ldots, N - 1\}$ of cardinality r. The simulator samples $x = (x_1, x_2, \ldots, x_r)$ from X and writes x to the disk encryptor according to I.*

*The simulator will deny any read requests from the sectors in I. The adversary may choose to write to any sector in I. When the ith sector in I is written to, we remove its index from I, decrease r by one, and replace X by the conditional probability space where the ith coordinate is fixed to the value $x_i$.*

*When the adversary terminates, he outputs a relation R on $S^r \times S^r$. The simulator reads $x' = (x'_1, x'_2, \ldots, x'_r)$ from the disk encryptor according to I. Now we replace X with the conditional probability space where the ith coordinate is fixed to the value $x_i$ if $x_i = x'_i$, and sample $x''$ from X.*

*Let $E_0$ be the event that there was no decryption error when reading $x'$, and $x R x'$. Let $E_1$ be the event that there was no decryption error when reading $x'$, and $x'' R x'$. The adversary's success rate is*

$$\mathrm{Succ}_A^{\mathcal{D},\mathrm{NM},\cdot} = |\Pr[E_0] - \Pr[E_1]|.$$

*Remark 3.* The adversary is assumed to output a description of the probability space X such that the simulator can sample from X and the conditional probability spaces.

*Remark 4.* If the adversary cannot change the ciphertext sectors, x will be equal to $x''$, and the adversary has zero sucess rate. Therefore, non-malleability is only relevant for the chosen ciphertext attacks.

In public key cryptography, the adversary is free to construct ciphertexts using the public key. In this way, adversaries can defeat non-malleability without ever tampering with a ciphertext. For private key cryptography, the standard definition [8] allows ciphertexts output by an encryption oracle in the final answer. This mirrors the public key case.

For disk encryption, the equivalent notion would be to allow the adversary to write to the sectors in I without changing the probability space X. We disallow this, thereby separating the goals of indistinguishability and non-malleability.

The following two goals are slightly different. The first (weaker) goal says that the adversary should not be able to cause the encrypted data to change in any way (even randomly). The second (stronger) goal says that any change the adversary makes to the storage medium will result in a decryption error.

**Definition 3.** *An adversary A against* plaintext integrity *works as follows: The simulator keeps a private copy of anything written to the disk encryptor. When data is read from the disk encryptor, it is compared with the private copy.*

*Let E be the event that data successfully read from the disk encryptor is different from the private copy. The adversary's success rate is*

$$\mathrm{Succ}_A^{\mathcal{D},\mathrm{PTXT},\cdot} = \Pr[E].$$

**Definition 4.** *An adversary A against* ciphertext integrity *works as follows: The simulator keeps a private copy of anything the disk encryptor writes to the storage medium. Whenever the disk encryptor reads from the storage medium, it is compared with the private copy.*

*Let E be the event that something the disk encryptor reads from the storage medium is different from the private copy, but the disk encryptor does not signal an error. The adversary's success rate is*

$$\mathrm{Succ}_A^{\mathcal{D},\mathrm{CTXT},\cdot} = \Pr[E].$$

*Remark 5.* We note that an adversary that can replace a sector value with random data has no success rate against non-malleability. Random changes may still represent a problem for certain applications, who will require the stronger notion of plaintext integrity.

# 4   General Results

We follow the concrete security approach of [2]. The main technique is to use an attacker against a notion X to construct an attacker against a notion Y. Since security is the absence of attackers, logic then dictates that security notion Y implies security notion X. To separate notions X and Y, we use one disk encryptor to create a second disk encryption. First we show that the latter does not satisfy notion Y. Second, if the first satisfies notion X, then the second also satisfies notion X. This means that security notion X does not imply security notion Y.

An adversary against non-malleability must be a successful adversary against plaintext integrity. Also, any adversary against plaintext integrity must be an adversary against ciphertext integrity. But the converse is not true: Plaintext integrity does not imply ciphertext integrity, since the ciphertext may contain information that can be changed without affecting the decryption.

**Theorem 1.** *Let $\mathcal{D}$ be a disk encryptor. There exists a disk encryptor $\mathcal{D}'$ and a non-adaptive chosen ciphertext adversary A against ciphertext integrity such that $\mathrm{Succ}_A^{\mathcal{D}',\mathrm{CTXT},\mathrm{naCCA}} = 1$. Further, for any adversary $A'$ against plaintext integrity for $\mathcal{D}'$, there exists an adversary $A''$ against plaintext integrity for $\mathcal{D}$ such that*

$$\mathrm{Succ}_{A''}^{\mathcal{D},\mathrm{PTXT},\cdot} = \mathrm{Succ}_{A'}^{\mathcal{D}',\mathrm{PTXT},\cdot}.$$

*A uses trivial time, and $A''$ requires as much time as $A'$.*

The following theorem says that plaintext integrity does not imply semantic security, because the ciphertext may contain a copy of the plaintext.

**Theorem 2.** *Let $\mathcal{D}$ be a disk encryptor. There exists a disk encryptor $\mathcal{D}'$ and a non-adaptive chosen plaintext adversary A against semantic security for $\mathcal{D}'$ with $\mathrm{Adv}_A^{\mathcal{D}',\mathrm{IND},\mathrm{naCPA}} = 1/2$. Further, for any adversary $A'$ against plaintext integrity for $\mathcal{D}'$, there exists an adversary $A''$ against plaintext integrity for $\mathcal{D}$ such that*

$$\mathrm{Succ}_{A''}^{\mathcal{D},\mathrm{PTXT},\cdot} = \mathrm{Succ}_{A'}^{\mathcal{D}',\mathrm{PTXT},\cdot}.$$

*A uses trivial time, and $A''$ has essentially the same time requirements as $A'$.*

The most interesting result in this section is the following: Semantic security against (non-adaptive) chosen ciphertext attacks follows from semantic security against (non-adaptive) chosen plaintext attacks and ciphertext integrity against (non-adaptive) chosen ciphertext attacks. The idea is that if the adversary changes the ciphertext without causing decryption errors, he is a successful adversary against ciphertext integrity. If not, he reduces to a simple chosen plaintext adversary. (This mirrors results for symmetric cryptosystems in [9].)

**Theorem 3.** *Let $D$ be a disk encryptor, and let $A$ be a (non-adaptive) chosen ciphertext adversary against semantic security. Then there exists a (non-adaptive) chosen ciphertext adversary $A'$ against ciphertext integrity, and a (non-adaptive) chosen plaintext adversary $A''$ against semantic security such that*

$$\text{Adv}_A^{D,\text{IND},(\text{na})\text{CCA}} \leq \text{Succ}_{A'}^{D,\text{CTXT},(\text{na})\text{CCA}} + \text{Adv}_{A''}^{D,\text{IND},(\text{na})\text{CPA}}.$$

*$A'$ and $A''$ has the same time requirements as $A$, except for a trivial amount of processing for every disk encryptor read and write.*

Next, we note that ciphertext integrity and semantic security can be handled independently. This simplifies design and analysis of disk encryptors.

We show this by *composing* disk encryptors. If $D_1$ and $D_2$ are two disk encryptors with keys from $K_1$ and $K_2$, respectively, $D_1 \circ D_2$ is a disk encryptor that works as follows: It takes keys from $K_1 \times K_2$ (the keys are independent). Read and write requests to the composition are forwared to $D_1$. Any storage read and write requests made by $D_1$ are forwarded to $D_2$. If $D_2$ responds with $\bot$ to any request, processing is halted and $\bot$ is output. Otherwise, $D_1$ is allowed to complete its processing, and its result is output.

Since the keys for $D_1$ and $D_2$ are independent, the following theorem holds.

**Theorem 4.** *Let $D_1$ and $D_2$ be two disk encryptors. For any (non-adaptive) chosen plaintext adversary $A_1$ and (non-adaptive) chosen ciphertext adversary $A_2$ against, respectively, semantic security and ciphertext integrity for $D_1 \circ D_2$, there exists a (non-adaptive) chosen plaintext adversary $A_1'$ against $D_1$ such that*

$$\text{Adv}_{A_1'}^{D_1,\text{IND},(\text{na})\text{CPA}} = \text{Adv}_{A_1}^{D_1 \circ D_2,\text{IND},(\text{na})\text{CPA}},$$

*as well as a (non-adaptive) chosen ciphertext adversary $A_2'$ against $D_2$ such that*

$$\text{Succ}_{A_2'}^{D_2,\text{CTXT},(\text{na})\text{CCA}} = \text{Succ}_{A_2}^{D_1 \circ D_2,\text{IND},(\text{na})\text{CCA}}.$$

*$A_1'$ and $A_2'$ have the same time requirements as $A_1$ and $A_2$, respectively.*

If no redundancy is added to the stored data, the best security that can be achieved is semantic security and non-malleability against a non-adaptive chosen ciphertext attack.

**Theorem 5.** *Suppose a disk encryptor $D$ has expansion ratio 1. Then there exists a chosen plaintext adversary against semantic security, a chosen ciphertext adversary against non-malleability, and a non-adaptive chosen ciphertext adversary against plaintext integrity, all with advantage $1/2$ or success rate 1, and trivial time requirements.*

The final result shows that to achieve security against chosen ciphertext attacks, the disk encryptor must keep a state. The attack uses what is commonly known as rollback or replay attacks. These trivially compromise integrity, and also allow attacks on semantic security.

**Theorem 6.** *Let $\mathcal{D}$ be a stateless disk encryptor. Then a chosen ciphertext adversary $A$ against semantic security exists such that*

$$\mathrm{Adv}_A^{\mathcal{D},\mathrm{IND,CCA}} = 1/2.$$

*A has trivial time requirements.*

## 5   Concrete Constructions

We give several constructions for meeting the various security notions described in Sect. 3. The strategy in this section is to show that an adversary against the security would imply an adversary against a building block. If we have faith in the building blocks, faith in the construction follows.

Let $l$ and $m$ be integers larger than zero. Throughout this section, the set of sector values $S$ will be the set of bit strings of length $lm$, $S = \{0,1\}^{lm}$. $N$ will denote the number of plaintext sectors provided by the disk encryptor, and $n$ will be the number of ciphertext sectors required. Let $l_0 = \lceil \log_2 m \rceil$ and $l_1 = \lceil \log_2 N \rceil$.

When convenient, we shall consider integers as bit strings, and vice versa, in the usual manner.

### 5.1   Building Blocks

We are interested in indistinguishable subsets of function families. So let $\bar{F}$ be a function family, and let $F$ be a subset of $\bar{F}$. A *distinguisher $A$ for $F$* plays the following game with a simulator: First, the simulator samples a function either from $F$ or from $\bar{F}$. $A$ is allowed to query the function (and its inverse, if relevant) at up to $q$ points. Then $A$ outputs 0 or 1.

Let $E$ be the event that $A$ outputs 0 when the simulator sampled from $\bar{F}$, or 1 when the simulator sampled from $F$. Then $A$'s distinguishing advantage is

$$\mathrm{Adv}_A^{F,q} = |\Pr[E] - 1/2|.$$

*Pseudo-Random Function Families.* Let $\mathrm{Map}(S, S')$ denote the set of all functions from the set $S$ to the set $S'$. We are interested in finding subsets of $\mathrm{Map}(S, S')$ where the functions are easy to evaluate, but it difficult it is to distinguish random elements of the subset from random elements of $\mathrm{Map}(S, S')$.

**Definition 5.** *Let $S$, $S'$ and $K$ be sets. A* pseudo-random function family (PRF) *$\Phi$ from $S$ to $S'$ indexed by $K$ is a subset $\Phi = \{f_k : S \to S' \mid k \in K\}$ of $\mathrm{Map}(S, S')$, along with a deterministic algorithm that on input of $k \in K$ and $s \in S$ computes $f_k(s)$.*

*We denote an adversary's distinguishing advantage by $\mathrm{Adv}_A^{\mathrm{PRF},\Phi,q}$.*

Typical examples of interesting pseudo-random function families are message authentication codes, such as HMAC [1] and OMAC [6].

*Block Ciphers.* Let $\mathrm{Perm}(S)$ denote the set of all permutations on the set $S$. We are interested in finding subsets of $\mathrm{Perm}(S)$ where the permutations are easy to evaluate, but it is difficult to distinguish random elements of the subset from random elements of $\mathrm{Perm}(S)$.

**Definition 6.** *Let $S$, $K$ be sets. A* pseudo-random permutation family (PRP) *$\Pi$ on $S$ indexed by $K$ is a subset $\Pi = \{f_k \mid k \in K\}$ of $\mathrm{Perm}(S)$, along with two deterministic algorithms that on input of $k \in K$ and $s \in S$ computes $f_k(s)$ and $f_k^{-1}(s)$, respectively.*

*We denote an adversary's distinguishing advantage by $\mathrm{Adv}_A^{\mathrm{PRP},\Pi,q}$.*

Typical examples of pseudo-random permutation families are block ciphers such as AES [3].

We note that any pseudo-random permutation family $\Pi$ on $S$ can be used as a pseudo-random function family from $S$ to $S$, and it is easy to show that for any PRF-distinguisher $A$, there exists a PRP-distinguisher $A'$ such that

$$\mathrm{Adv}_A^{\mathrm{PRF},\Pi,q} \leq \mathrm{Adv}_{A'}^{\mathrm{PRP},\Pi,q} + q^2/|S|.$$

*Tweakable Block Ciphers.* Let $S$ and $T$ be sets. A *tweakable permutation on $S$ tweaked by $T$* is a function $f : T \to \mathrm{Perm}(S)$. When convenient, we abuse notation and denote the action of $f(t)$ on $s$ by $f(t,s)$, considering $f$ as a function $f : T \times S \to S$. Let $\mathrm{Perm}_T(S)$ denote the set of tweakable permutations on $S$.

**Definition 7.** *Let $S, T$ and $K$ be sets. A* tweakable pseudo-random permutation *family $\tilde{\Pi}$ on $S$ indexed by $K$ and tweaked by $T$ is a subset $\tilde{\Pi} = \{f_k \mid k \in K\}$ of $\mathrm{Perm}_T(S)$, along with two deterministic algorithms that on input of $k \in K$, $t \in T$ and $s \in S$ computes $(f_k(t))(s)$ and $(f_k(t)^{-1})(s)$, respectively.*

*We denote an adversary's distinguishing advantage by $\mathrm{Adv}_A^{\mathrm{TPRP},\tilde{\Pi},q}$.*

We refer to [4,10] for further background on tweakable permutations and concrete constructions. We restrict ourselves to noting that there are practical constructions based on block ciphers.

## 5.2 Semantic Security Against Non-adaptive Chosen Plaintext Attack

It is fairly easy to see that a block cipher used in Electronic Code Book (ECB) mode does not provide semantic security against a non-adaptive chosen plaintext attack. We outline two simple constructions that provide semantic security.

Our first construction is also our simplest construction. It is based on the well-known counter mode construction. Let $\Phi$ be a pseudo-random function family from $\{0,1\}^l$ to $\{0,1\}^l$ indexed by $K$.

Define the function $r : \mathrm{Map}(\{0,1\}^l, \{0,1\}^l) \times \{0,1,2,\ldots,N-1\} \to S$ to be function that takes $(f,i)$ to the concatenation of the value of $f(i2^{l_0} + j)$ for $0 \le j < m$, that is,

$$(f,i) \mapsto f(i2^{l_0} + 0)\|f(i2^{l_0} + 1)\|\ldots\|f(i2^{l_0} + m - 1).$$

(Remember that $m \le 2^{l_0}$.)

The disk encryptor $\mathcal{D}_1(\Phi)$ takes keys from $K$, and $n = N$. Suppose the disk encryptor is initialized with the key $k \in K$. Given the write request $(i, s)$, the disk encryptor issues the write request $(i, s \oplus r(f_k, i))$ to the storage medium. Given the read request $i$, the disk encryptor reads $s'$ from the $i$th sector of the storage medium and outputs $s' \oplus r(f_k, i)$.

**Theorem 7.** *Let $\mathcal{D}_1(\Phi)$ be as above, providing $N$ sectors of storage, and let $A$ be a non-adaptive chosen plaintext adversary against semantic security. Then there exists a distinguisher $A'$ for $\Phi$ such that*

$$\mathrm{Adv}_A^{\mathcal{D},\mathrm{IND},\mathrm{naCPA}} = 2\mathrm{Adv}_{A'}^{\mathrm{PRF},\Phi,Nm}.$$

We note that block ciphers are good candidates for efficient pseudo-random function families.

The next construction is based on Cipher Block Chaining mode. CBC mode requires an unpredictable initialization vector, so using the sector index does not provide security. We have two easy options: either use a pseudo-random function family to derive the IV from the sector index (the approach taken by one variant of LoopAES described in Sect. 2.2), or simply run the sector index through the block cipher and use that as an initialization vector.

Let $\Pi$ be a pseudo-random permutation family on $\{0,1\}^l$ indexed by $K$.

The disk encryptor $\mathcal{D}_2(\Pi)$ takes keys from $K$, and $n = N$. Let $\mathcal{D}_2(\Pi)$ be initialized with the key $k \in K$. Given the write request $(i, s)$, the value $s$ is split into blocks $s_1, \ldots, s_m \in \{0,1\}^l$. The IV is derived as $c_0 = f_k(i)$. Then $c_i$ is computed as $f_k(c_{i-1} \oplus s_i)$, and the write request $(i, c_1\|c_2\|\ldots\|c_m)$ is issued to the storage medium.

We leave the read operation and the security proof to the interested reader.

Compared to counter mode above, this scheme is more complicated, requires both the encryption and decryption part of the block cipher, and cannot easily be parallellized. CBC-mode does, however, seem to have wider hardware support, though this will probably change in the future. (Some would say that since counter mode is totally insecure against stronger attacks, and CBC-mode could in practice thwart some stronger attacks, there are security advantages to using CBC-mode. However, if one worries about stronger attacks, one should defend against stronger attacks.)

## 5.3 Non-malleability Against Non-adaptive Chosen Ciphertext Attack

This construction uses a tweakable permutation on the sector level to encrypt the data. Note that the permutation has to be tweakable, otherwise the usual attacks on ECB mode apply.

Let $K$ be a set and $T = \{0, 1, \ldots, N - 1\}$. Let $\tilde{\Pi}$ be a tweakable pseudo-random permutation family on $S$ indexed by $K$ and tweakable by $T$.

The disk encryptor $\mathcal{D}_3(\tilde{\Pi})$ takes keys from $K$, and $n = N$. Let $\mathcal{D}_3(\tilde{\Pi})$ be initialized with the key $k \in K$. Given the write request $(i, s)$, it issues the write request $(i, f_k(i, s))$ to the storage medium. Given the read request $i$, it passes it on to the storage medium and gets a value $s'$. It then returns the value $f_k(i)^{-1}(s)$.

**Theorem 8.** *Let $\mathcal{D}_3(\tilde{\Pi})$ be as above, and let A be a non-adaptive chosen ciphertext adversary against semantic security (non-malleability). Then there exists distinguisher $A'$ and $A''$ for $\tilde{\Pi}$ such that*

$$\mathrm{Adv}_A^{\mathcal{D}_3(\tilde{\Pi}),\mathrm{IND,naCCA}} = 2\mathrm{Adv}_{A'}^{\mathrm{TPRP},\tilde{\Pi},N}$$

*and*

$$\mathrm{Succ}_A^{\mathcal{D}_3(\tilde{\Pi}),\mathrm{NM,naCCA}} \leq 2\mathrm{Adv}_{A''}^{\mathrm{TPRP},\tilde{\Pi},N}.$$

Note that this scheme has expansion rate 1, and by Theorem 5 this is the best we can do with expansion rate 1. Furthermore, this scheme is essentially equivalent to the sector-wide scheme adopted by SISWG (see Sect. 2.2).

## 5.4    Ciphertext Integrity Against Non-adaptive Chosen Ciphertext Attack

The following construction provides ciphertext integrity using a pseudo-random function family.

Let $T = \{0, 1, \ldots, N - 1\}$, and let $\Phi$ be a pseudo-random function family from $T \times S$ to $\{0, 1\}^l$ indexed by $K$.

The disk encryptor $\mathcal{D}_4(\Phi)$ takes keys from $K$, and $n = 2N$. Let $\mathcal{D}_4(\Phi)$ be initialized with the key $k \in K$. Given the write request $(i, s)$, it issues the write requests $(2i, s)$ and $(2i+1, f_k(i, s))$ to the storage medium (the bit string $f_k(i, s)$ is padded with zeros to get a string of length $ml$). Given the read request $i$, it issues the read requests $2i$ and $2i + 1$ to the storage medium, getting values $s'$ and $s''$. If $s'' = f_k(i, s)$ (ignoring zero padding), $s'$ is output, otherwise $\perp$.

**Theorem 9.** *Let $\mathcal{D}_4(\Phi)$ be as above, and let A be a non-adaptive chosen ciphertext adversary against ciphertext integrity. Then there exists a distinguisher $A'$ for $\Phi$ such that*

$$\mathrm{Succ}_A^{\mathcal{D}_4(\Phi),\mathrm{CTXT,naCCA}} \leq \mathrm{Adv}_{A'}^{\mathrm{PRF},\Phi,N} + \frac{N}{2^l}.$$

We note that the zero padding is rather wasteful, but it is required for technical reasons[3]. However, the storage medium can easily arrange to store several checksums in one physical sector, giving an expansion rate of $(m + 1)/m$.

---

[3] If we stored more than one checksum in the same sector, we could change the first checksum, and then read a sector corresponding to an unchanged checksum. The read would return $\top$, but the attacker would win the chosen ciphertext attack game.

We also note that it is easy to construct $\Phi$ using for example HMAC [1] or OMAC [6].

By Theorems 3 and 4, we can compose a scheme from Sect. 5.2 with this scheme to achieve semantic security against non-adaptive chosen ciphertext attacks.

## 5.5   Semantic Security Against Chosen Plaintext Attack

The following construction provides semantic security against a chosen plaintext attack using a pseudo-random function family. It is based on counter mode, but each sector is given its own initialization vector.

Let $\Phi$ be a pseudo-random function family from $\{0,1\}^l$ to $\{0,1\}^l$ indexed by $K$. Let $r : \mathrm{Map}(\{0,1\}^l, \{0,1\}^l) \times \{0,1\}^{l-l_0} \to S$ be the function defined by

$$(f, t) \mapsto f(t2^{l_0} + 0)\|f(t2^{l_0} + 1)\| \ldots \|f(t2^{l_0} + m - 1).$$

(Remember that $m \le 2^{l_0}$.)

The disk encryptor $\mathcal{D}_5(\Phi)$ takes keys from $K$, and $n = 2N$. Let $\mathcal{D}_5(\Phi)$ be initialized with the key $k \in K$. Given the write request $(i, s)$, $\mathcal{D}_5(\Phi)$ samples $j$ from $\{0,1\}^{l-l_0}$, then issues the write requests $(2i, j)$ (where $j$ is padded with zeros) and $(2i + 1, s \oplus r(f_k, j))$.

Given the read request $i$, the disk encryptor issues the read requests $2i$ and $2i + 1$ to the storage medium, getting values $s'$ and $s''$. It then outputs $s'' \oplus r(f_k, s')$ (where the zero padding in $s'$ is ignored).

**Theorem 10.** *Let $\mathcal{D}_5(\Phi)$ be as above, and let $A$ be a chosen plaintext adversary against semantic security that writes at most $q$ sectors to the disk encryptor. Then there exists a distinguisher $A'$ for $\Phi$ such that such that*

$$\mathrm{Adv}_A^{\mathcal{D}_5(\Phi),\mathrm{IND},\mathrm{CPA}} \le \mathrm{Adv}_{A'}^{\mathrm{PRF},\Phi,qm} + q^2/2^{l-l_0}.$$

We note that a similar technique can be used for CBC-mode or with a tweakable block cipher. We also note that the storage medium could arrange to store several initial values in one physical sector, reducing the expansion rate to $(m + 1)/m$.

The above scheme aims to achieve that same goal as FreeBSD's GBDE (see Sect. 2.2). Briefly, GBDE works as follows: it encrypts each data sector using a pseudo-random permutation family $\Pi$ in CBC mode with a fixed IV, but with a random one-time "sector key". The random key is then written to a different sector, encrypted using $\Pi$ and a "key-key" derived from a "master key" and the sector index using a pseudo-random function family $\Phi$.

We sketch a possible proof that GBDE is semantically secure against chosen plaintext attacks: First we replace the pseudo-random function used to derive the "key-keys" with a random function. Then we replace the pseudo-random permutations used to encrypt the "sector keys" with random permutations. If "sector key" is ever reused, the adversary will never learn any information about the "sector keys". Then we replace the pseudo-random permutations used to encrypt the data sectors with random permutations. After the final replacements, the adversary can have no advantage. The resulting bound will be somewhat weaker than that the above theorem.

While we believe $\mathcal{D}_5$ to be a superior construction to GBDE, the latter has the significant advantage of being available for use today.

## 5.6   Ciphertext Integrity Against Chosen Ciphertext Attack

By Theorem 6, a disk encryptor must keep a state to achieve security against chosen ciphertext attack. Our goal is to keep the state as small and simple as possible. The idea is to use an $m$-ary tree of checksums (see Fig. 1). The root of the tree is authenticated using the state, and the state changes with every write.

Let $T$ be the set $\{0, 1, \ldots, 2^l - 1\}$, and let $\varPhi$ be a pseudo-random family of functions from $T \times S$ to $\{0, 1\}^l$ indexed by $K$.

Set $N_1 = N$, and define the sequence $N_j$ by $N_j = \lceil N_{j-1}/m \rceil$. Let $h$ be the smallest integer such that $N_h = 1$. Set $n_1 = N$ and define the sequence $n_j$ by $n_{j-1} + N_{j-1}$. For an integer $i$, we let $i_j = \lfloor i/m^{j-1} \rfloor$.

The disk encryptor $\mathcal{D}_6(\varPhi)$ takes keys from $K$, and $n = n_{h+1} + 1$. Let $\mathcal{D}_6(\varPhi)$ be initialized with the key $k$. It sets the state $\sigma$ to the integer 1.

Denote the value of the sector $n_j + t$, $0 \leq t < N_j$, by $s_t^{(j)}$, and the sector $n_{h+1} = n_h + 1$ by $s^{(h+1)}$. The initialization process first zeros $s_i^{(1)}$ for all $i$. Then it computes the correct checksums $s_{i_j}^{(j)}$ for all $i$ and $1 < j \leq h$ using

$$s_{i_j}^{(j)} = f_k(j2^{l_1} + i_j, s_{mi_j+0}^{(j-1)} \| s_{mi_j+1}^{(j-1)} \| \cdots \| s_{\max\{mi_j+m-1, N_j\}}^{(j-1)}). \qquad (1)$$

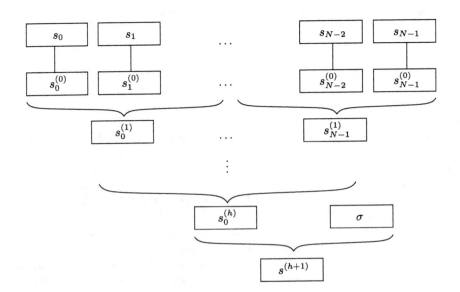

**Fig. 1.** The MAC tree for $\mathcal{D}_6(\varPhi)$

Note that in the concatenation, the zero padding of each $s_t^{(j)}$ is discarded. Finally, it computes $s^{(h+1)}$ using

$$s^{(h+1)} = f_k(\sigma 2^{2l_1}, s_0^{(h)}).\qquad(2)$$

Then the disk encryptor issues the writes $(n_j + i_j, s_{i_j}^{(j)})$ for all $0 \leq i < N$, $1 \leq j \leq h$, and finally the write $(n_{h+1}, s^{(h+1)})$.

Let the write request be $(i, s)$. The disk encryptor reads $s_t^{(j)}$ from the index $n_j + t$, for $i_{j+1}m \leq t < \max\{i_{j+1}m + m - 1, N_j\}$, $1 \leq j \leq h$. Then it reads $s^{(h+1)}$ from the index $n_{h+1}$.

It verifies that any zero padding remains zero, that for all $1 < j \leq h$, (1) holds, and that (2) holds. If any verification fails, $\perp$ is output and processing terminated.

If all of these checks are correct, the disk encryptor changes $s_i^{(1)}$ to be $f_k(i, s)$, updates every $s_{i_j}^{(j)}$ for $1 < j \leq h$ according to (1), increases $\sigma$ by 1, and updates $s^{(h+1)}$ according to (2).

Then it issues the write requests $(i, s)$, $(n_j + i_j, s_{i_j}^{(j)})$ for $1 \leq j \leq h$, and $(n_{h+1}, s^{(h+1)})$, and outputs $\top$.

Given the read request $i$, the disk encryptor reads $s_t^{(j)}$ from index $n_j + t$, for $i_{j+1}m \leq t < \max\{i_{j+1}m + m - 1, N_j\}$, $1 \leq j \leq h$. Then it reads $s_i$ from index $i$ and $s^{(h+1)}$ from index $n_{h+1}$.

Now the disk encryptor verifies that $s_i^{(1)} = f_k(i, s_i)$, that any zero padding remains zero, that the $s_{i_j}^{(j)}$ satisfy (1) for $1 < j \leq h$, and that $s^{(h+1)}$ satisfies (2). If any verification fails, $\perp$ is output, otherwise $s_i$ is output.

**Theorem 11.** *Let $\mathcal{D}_6(\Phi)$ and $h$ be as above, and let $A$ be a chosen ciphertext adversary against ciphertext integrity that writes and reads at most $q$ sectors to the disk encryptor. Then there exists a distinguisher $A'$ for $\Phi$ such that*

$$\mathrm{Succ}_A^{\mathcal{D}_6(\Phi),\mathrm{CTXT,CCA}} \leq \mathrm{Adv}_{A'}^{\mathrm{PRF},\Phi,qmh} + hq^2/2^l + q/2^l.$$

Again, we note that the storage medium can easily arrange to store several checksums in one physical sector, giving an expansion rate of less than 2. This also reduces the number of extra reads to $h + 1$.

If this construction is used in conjunction with one from Sect. 5.5, we get semantic security and non-malleability against chosen ciphertext attacks by Theorems 3 and 4.

We also note that it is easy to replace the state $\sigma$ with something that is easier for a user to remember (or write down), such as a date.

As an example, we compute the numbers for providing one gigabyte of storage ($2^{33}$ bits of storage), using 512 byte sectors ($2^{12}$ bits). Let $l = 7$ and $m = 2^5$. We get that $n_1 = 2^{21}$, $n_2 = 2^{16}$, $n_3 = 2^{11}$, $n_4 = 2^6$, $n_5 = 2$ and $n_6 = 1$. The expansion rate is roughly 1.03. Every read operation requires 8 reads from the storage medium, and every write operations requires 7 reads and 8 writes. Caching can potentially reduce the number of physical reads and writes.

# 6    Concluding Remarks

This paper attempts to define all useful security notions for disk encryption, and determining what is required to achieve those notions.

One common feature of many disk encryption implementations (SISWG's standards work and FreeBSD's GBDE being notable exceptions) is that the documentation says very little about the cryptographic reasoning behind the system, and there is little in the way of useful security analysis. This paper provides a set of formal security notions as well as constructions, which should provide a sound basis for evaluating disk encryption systems.

While the SISWG does an excellent job, providing solutions that are as good as possible under the circumstances, we believe that the restrictions they have imposed on themselves makes it impossible to reach certain worthwhile security notions. Even though the stronger security notions like semantic security and integrity against chosen ciphertext attacks are costly to achieve, it should be up to the users to balance cost against security, not standards.

Also, certain applications require weaker security than some of the solutions considered by SISWG. One example is encryption of swap space. If the disk encryptor is initialized with a random key when the system starts, all that is required to protect the swap space is semantic security against non-adaptive chosen plaintext attacks. Using FreeBSD's GBDE or SISWG's tweakable block ciphers is simply overkill.

# References

1. M. Bellare, R. Canetti, and H. Krawczyk. Keying hash functions for message authentication. In Neal Koblitz, editor, *Proceedings of CRYPTO '96*, volume 1109 of *LNCS*, pages 1–15. Springer-Verlag, 1996.
2. M. Bellare, A. Desai, E. Jokipii, and P. Rogaway. A concrete security treatment of symmetric encryption. In *FOCS 1997*, pages 394–403, 1997.
3. FIPS 197. *Advanced Encryption Standard*. Federal Information Processing Standards Publication. National Technical Information Service, Springfield, Virginia, November 2001.
4. Shai Halevi and Phillip Rogaway. A tweakable enciphering mode. In Dan Boneh, editor, *Proceedings of CRYPTO 2003*, volume 2729 of *LNCS*, pages 482–499. Springer-Verlag, 2003.
5. J. Hughes. Chair of the IEEE security in storage working group, 2004. http://www.siswg.org/.
6. Tetsu Iwata and Kaoru Kurosawa. OMAC: One-key CBC MAC. In Thomas Johansson, editor, *Fast Software Encryption*, volume 2887 of *LNCS*, pages 129–153. Springer-Verlag, 2003.
7. Poul-Henning Kamp. GBDE – GEOM based disk encryption. BSDCON '03, 2003. http://phk.freebsd.dk/pubs/bsdcon-03.gbde.paper.pdf.
8. J. Katz and M. Yung. Complete characterization of security notions for probabilistic private-key encryption. In *Proceedings of the 32nd Annual Symposium on Theory of Computing*, pages 245–254. ACM, 2000.

9. Hugo Krawczyk. The order of encryption and authentication for protecting communications (or: How secure is SSL?). In Joe Kilian, editor, *Proceedings of CRYPTO 2001*, volume 2139 of *LNCS*, pages 310–331. Springer-Verlag, 2001.
10. Moses Liskov, Ronald L. Rivest, and David Wagner. Tweakable block ciphers. In Moti Yung, editor, *Proceedings of CRYPTO 2002*, volume 2442 of *LNCS*, pages 31–46. Springer-Verlag, 2002.
11. Jari Ruusu. LoopAES, 2005. http://loop-aes.sourceforge.net/.

# A    Proofs

## A.1    General Results

*Proof (Theorem 1).* $\mathcal{D}'$ uses one extra sector of storage space. Whenever it receives a write request, it gives the write request to $\mathcal{D}$. If that write returns $\top$, then $\mathcal{D}'$ writes a random value to the extra sector. Whenever it receives a read request, it reads the extra sector, then passes the read request to $\mathcal{D}$.

An adversary that changes the extra sector in an arbitrary fashion and then reads any sector from the disk encryptor will win the ciphertext integrity game.

The extra sector can be simulated by any adversary, so any adversary against plaintext integrity for $\mathcal{D}'$ can be used against $\mathcal{D}$ as well.    □

*Proof (Theorem 2).* If $\mathcal{D}$ provides $N$ plaintext sectors using $n$ ciphertext sectors, $\mathcal{D}'$ will provide $N$ plaintext sectors using $n + N$ ciphertext sectors.

The idea is that $\mathcal{D}'$ keeps an unencrypted copy of the plaintext in the extra $N$ sectors. When reading, this unencrypted copy is ignored. The adversary against semantic security is obvious.

In the game that defines plaintext integrity, the adversary is the only one writing data to the disk encryptor. This means that the extra plaintext copy can easily be simulated, and the theorem follows.    □

*Proof (Theorem 3).* We only consider the chosen ciphertext attack. The adversaries derived from the non-adaptive chosen ciphertext adversary are similar, and we leave them to the reader.

Consider first the chosen ciphertext attack game between the adversary and a simulator. Let $E$ be the event that the bit output by the adversary is correct in this game.

Now we change the game as follows: A copy of anything the disk encryptor writes to the storage medium is kept. If the result of any read request made by the disk encryptor differs from this copy, the disk encryptor's output for the operation is ignored and $\perp$ is returned. Let $E'$ be the event that the bit output by the adversary is correct in this modified game.

We have that

$$\mathrm{Adv}_A^{\mathcal{D},\mathrm{IND},\mathrm{CCA}} = |\Pr[E] - 1/2| \leq |\Pr[E] - \Pr[E']| + |\Pr[E'] - 1/2|.$$

As usual in game hopping, we want to bound $|\Pr[E] - \Pr[E']|$ and $|\Pr[E'] - 1/2|$.

The two games proceed identically until $\perp$ is returned in the modified game, but not in the original game. Let $F$ be the event that this happens. Now we observe that $F$ is the event that leads to success against chosen ciphertext attack.

The adversary $A'$ is then simply $A$, augmented with parts simulating the attack against semantic security. The success rate of $A'$ against ciphertext integrity is $\Pr[F]$, and as usual we have that

$$|\Pr[E] - \Pr[E']| \leq \Pr[F] = \mathrm{Succ}_{A'}^{\mathcal{D},\mathrm{CTXT,CCA}}.$$

The chosen plaintext adversary $A''$ encapsulates $A$. It keeps a copy of the storage medium state. Whenever a read or write request for the storage medium is copied to $A''$, $A''$ fakes a corresponding read or write request for $A$.

When $A$ issues a read or write request to the disk encryptor, $A''$ first issues the read queries for the simulator. (It can do this because the unknown key is not involved in determining these reads.) If $A$'s answers correspond to the copy kept by $A''$, $A$'s request is forwarded to the simulator. Otherwise, $\perp$ is returned.

$A''$ provides $A$ with the same environment as in the modified game. Hence $A$'s success probability in the modified game is equal to the success probability of $A''$. Therefore,

$$|\Pr[E'] - 1/2| = \mathrm{Adv}_{A''}^{\mathcal{D},\mathrm{IND,CPA}}.$$

This concludes the proof.                                                    □

*Proof (Theorem 5).* First, we note that any disk encryptor with expansion ratio 1 must be deterministic, and no matter what the storage medium contains, no read operation will result in a decryption error.

The chosen plaintext adversary against semantic security simply picks two distinct values $x^{(0)}$ and $x^{(1)}$ from $S^N$, and writes $x^{(0)}$ to the disk encryptor. It makes a copy of the storage medium state. Then it outputs the probability space $X$ over $S^N$ such that $\Pr[x = x^{(0)} \mid x \xleftarrow{r} X] = \Pr[x = x^{(1)} \mid x \xleftarrow{r} X] = 1/2$ and $f(x^{(b)}) = b$ for $b \in \{0,1\}$.

After the simulator has written $x^{(b)}$ to the disk encryptor, the adversary compares the contents of the storage medium with its copy. If it matches, 0 is output, otherwise 1 is output. This adversary has advantage $1/2$.

The adversary against non-malleability writes both $x^{(0)}$ and $x^{(1)}$ to the disk encryptor, saving the storage medium states. It then outputs the probability space $X$. When the simulator writes $x^{(b)}$ to the disk encryptor, it replaces the storage medium contents with the one corresponding to $x^{(1-b)}$, and outputs the relation $R = ((x^{(0)}, x^{(1)}), (x^{(1)}, x^{(0)}))$. This adversary has success rate 1.

Finally, the adversary against plaintext integrity writes arbitrary data to the disk encryptor. Then it makes some arbitrary change to the storage medium, and reads back from the disk encryptor. This adversary has success rate 1.   □

*Proof (Theorem 6).* The idea is that since the disk encryptor is stateless, if a state for the storage medium results in a valid read once, that state will always result in a valid read.

The adversary plays the role of the storage medium for the simulator. He chooses (arbitrarily) two different values $x^{(0)}$ and $x^{(1)}$ from $S$, and outputs the probability space $X$ on $S$ satisfying $\Pr[X = x^{(0)}] = \Pr[X = x^{(1)}] = 1/2$, the set $I = \{0\}$, and a function $f : S \to \{0,1\}$ such that $f(x^{(j)}) = j$.

The simulator samples $b$ and writes $x^{(b)}$ to the disk encryptor. At this point, reading from the disk encryptor will return $x^{(b)}$.

The adversary now saves the storage medium state. Then he writes $x^{(0)}$ to the disk encryptor. Since he has written to this sector, the simulator will allow him to read it again. The adversary restores the saved storage medium state, and reads $x^{(b)}$ from the disk encryptor. The adversary now knows $b$.    □

## A.2    Concrete Constructions

*Proof (Theorem 7).* We play two games. In the first game, we sample $f_k$ from $\Phi$ and run the disk encryptor as specified above. Then we simulate a non-adaptive chosen plaintext attack on $\mathcal{D}_1$ for $A$. Let $E$ be the event that the bit output by $A$ is correct.

In the second game, we sample $f$ from $\text{Map}(\{0,1\}^l, \{0,1\}^l)$ and use it instead of $f_k$ in the disk encryptor. Then we simulate a non-adaptive chosen plaintext attack on $\mathcal{D}_1$ for $A$, exactly as in the first game. If $E'$ is the event that the bit output by $A$ is correct, we must have that $\Pr[E'] = 1/2$, since the function values $r(f, i)$ will be independent and uniformly random.

Let $A'$ be the distinguisher that computes the function $r$ by requesting function values for the points $i2^{l_0} + j$, $0 \le j < m$. Then it simulates a non-adaptive chosen plaintext attack on $\mathcal{D}_1$ for $A$. If $A$ guesses correctly, the simulator outputs $0$, otherwise $1$.

If the function $A'$ tries to distinguish was sampled from $\Phi$, everything proceeds as in the first game. The probability that $A'$ correctly answers $0$ is $\Pr[E]$. Otherwise, everything proceeds as in the second game, and the probability that $A'$ correctly answers $1$ is $\Pr[E'] = 1/2$.

We get that

$$\text{Adv}_{A'}^{\text{PRF},\Phi,Nm} = |\Pr[E]/2 + \Pr[E']/2 - 1/2|$$

$$= \frac{1}{2}|\Pr[E] - 1/2| = \frac{1}{2}\text{Adv}_A^{\mathcal{D},\text{IND,naCPA}},$$

which concludes the proof.    □

*Proof (Theorem 8).* We play two games. The first game is the unmodified attack game. In the second game, instead of sampling $f_k$ from $\tilde{\Pi}$, we sample $f$ from $\text{Perm}_T(S)$ and use it instead of $f_k$.

In the second game, two different sectors are encrypted with independent permutations, so every ciphertext sector is independent of the plaintext sector, and any change in the storage medium will induce a random change in the corresponding plaintext sector.

Therefore, the adversary cannot have any advantage against semantic security or success rate against non-malleability in the second game. The theorem follows after a few simple calculations.    □

*Proof (Theorem 9).* Again, we play two games: One where a function is sampled from $\Phi$, and one where it is sampled from $\mathrm{Map}(T \times S, \{0,1\}^l)$.

To succeed in the latter game, the adversary $A$ has to find a value $s$, an index $i$, as well as the function value $f_k(i,s)$. When $f_k$ is replaced by a random function, then for any $s' \in S$ we have that $f(i,s) = s'$ with probability $2^{-l}$. It has at most $N$ chances of getting at least one sector right, giving a success probability of at most $N/2^l$. This concludes the proof.    □

*Proof (Theorem 10).* As usual, we play two games: One where a function is sampled from $\Phi$, and one where it is sampled from $\mathrm{Map}(\{0,1\}^l, \{0,1\}^l)$.

In the latter game, unless the same $j$ is sampled for two different write operations, the adversary has no advantage. The probability that one $j$ is sampled at least twice is at most $q^2/2^{l-l_0}$, which concludes the proof.    □

*Proof (Theorem 11).* As usual, we play two games: One where a function is sampled from $\Phi$, and one where it is sampled from $\mathrm{Map}(T \times S, \{0,1\}^l)$. The first game proceeds exactly as in a real attack.

In the second game, we note that the value of every checksum sector is written using different values from $T$. So all checksums will be independent. Also, the master checksum denoted by $s^{(h+1)}$ will never be written twice using the same value from $T$.

Every time the adversary attempts a read after making a change to the checksum tree such that $s_0^{(h)}$ changes, the probability that the read succeeds is $1/2^l$.

The only way the adversary can change the checksum tree without $s_0^{(h)}$ changing, is by finding a checksum collision. This means that the adversary's success rate in the second game is at most $q^2/2^l + q/2^l$. The theorem follows.    □

# Local View Attack on Anonymous Communication*

Marcin Gogolewski**, Marek Klonowski, and Mirosław Kutyłowski

Institute of Mathematics and Computer Science, Wrocław University of Technology,
ul. Wybrzeże Wyspiańskiego 27, 50-370 Wrocław, Poland
{Marek.Klonowski, Miroslaw.Kutylowski}@pwr.wroc.pl,
marcing@amu.edu.pl

**Abstract.** We consider anonymous communication protocols based on onions: each message is sent in an encrypted form through a path chosen at random by its sender, and the message is re-coded by each server on the path. Recently, it has been shown that if the anonymous paths are long enough, then the protocols provide provable security for some adversary models. However, it was assumed that all users choose intermediate servers uniformly at random from the same set of servers.

We show that if a single user chooses only from a constrained subset of possible intermediate servers, anonymity level may dramatically decrease. A thumb rule is that if Alice is aware of much less than 50% of possible intermediate servers, then the anonymity set for her message becomes surprisingly small with high probability. Moreover, for each location in the anonymity set an adversary may compute probability that it gets a message of Alice. Since there are big differences in these probabilities, in most cases the true destination of the message from Alice is in a small group of locations with the highest probabilities.

Our results contradict some beliefs that the protocols mentioned guarantee anonymity provided that the set of possible intermediate servers for each user is large.

## 1 Introduction

### 1.1 Background

There is a growing need for anonymity in electronic communication. Many anonymity protocols have been proposed – their aim is not only to hide the contents of messages sent, but also who is communicating with whom.

Application area of such protocols is much broader than implementing point-to-point anonymous communication. For instance, they are essential components of various voting schemes [4], some auction protocols [18], anonymous browsing or even they serve as a building block in some secure function evaluation protocols [14].

Existing solutions are generally based on two fundamental ideas - *MIXes* introduced by David Chaum in [3] and *onions* that appeared in a number of papers [19,21,11]. In these protocols the messages are routed through servers called *MIXes* or *MIX-servers*.

---

* Partially supported by the EU within the 6th Framework Programme under contract 001907 (DELIS).

** During work on this paper the first author was on the leave from Adam Mickiewicz University and joined DELIS team at Technical University of Wrocław.

S. De Capitani di Vimercati et al. (Eds.): ESORICS 2005, LNCS 3679, pp. 475–488, 2005.

Generally, there is a common idea behind both solutions – at the beginning we have a batch of ciphertexts submitted by all users. Then a number of steps is executed. During a step each message is appointed to some server, each server recodes the messages obtained and returns them in a random order. In this way, the encoded messages become more and more "mixed".

The problem is that users of many anonymity systems are requested to construct a path of randomly and independently chosen servers for each message, called in this paper *anonymity path*. It concerns all onion-based protocols [19,21,11] and some MIX network architectures. For such protocols, it is assumed that the users have the same knowledge about the servers that can be used as intermediate servers on the path.

In a large and dynamic system it is hard to achieve that all users have the same view of the network. The problem we address in this paper is how secure are anonymous communication protocols, if the users choose the servers for anonymity paths from different sets of servers.

**Related Work.** There are many papers concerning anonymous communication protocols based on MIXes and onions. On the other hand, there are only few papers providing rigorous proofs about immunity of such systems against an adversary. One of the first works in this direction is due to Kesdogan et al. [15]. In this paper cardinality of so-called anonymity set was used as an anonymity measure.

In other papers like [19,5,2,13] sophisticated and very restrictive anonymity measures were used that take into account also correlation between messages. These papers provide rigorous proofs of anonymity in different adversary models: their goal was to show that an anonymity measure reaches appropriate values with high probability for a certain length of an anonymity path.

Still, these proofs use the assumption that all users have exactly the same knowledge of the servers that may be used as intermediate servers on anonymity paths. No attempt has been made to analyze what happens if this assumption is not satisfied. In [9], it has been mentioned that violating this assumption might influence security of the system. A similar suggestion is contained in [6]. However, some people believe that anonymity of a user $A$ is in danger only if the set of potential intermediate servers is small.

**Paper Organization.** In Section 2 we recall basic facts about anonymous communication protocols. In Section 3 we consider dangers that arise when a user is aware of some extra servers and may use them for creating routing paths. Section 4 is devoted to the case when a user is aware of only a constant fraction of servers.

## 2   Anonymity Protocols and Problem Statement

**MIXes.** MIX is a cryptographic primitive introduced in [3]: assume that users $1, 2, \ldots, n$ wish to publish anonymously messages $m_1, m_2, \ldots, m_n$. For this purpose they submit their messages to a *MIX-server* after encrypting them with MIX-server's public key $k$, that is, they submit $E_k(m_1), E_k(m_2), \ldots, E_k(m_n)$. The MIX-server decrypts the ciphertexts obtained with its private key, chooses a permutation $\pi$ uniformly at random, and outputs $m_{\pi(1)}, m_{\pi(2)}, \ldots, m_{\pi(n)}$.

If the MIX-server is honest (i.e. does not reveal permutation $\pi$), then for an external observer the relation between the input and the output of the MIX-server remains hidden. Of course, some additional requirements must be fulfilled. For example, $E$ has to be a probabilistic encryption scheme – otherwise one can establish this relationship by encrypting the output. For further details see [12].

In order to avoid full dependence on a single MIX, systems consisting of many MIX-servers were proposed. A so-called *MIX cascade* was introduced together with MIXes in [3]. In that case a message is encrypted multiple times with public keys of consecutive MIXes. The encrypted messages are processed by the cascade of MIXes – each MIX removes one encryption layer and permutes the results at random.

For better scalability a parallel MIX-cascades can be used: in this case each step is executed by a number of MIXes working in parallel.

There are many mixing strategies (for further details see for instance [20]). This is due to the fact that if a mix is working continuously, then even the best encoding scheme does not automatically guarantee security of the scheme. For the sake of simplicity our analysis cover only the simplest scenario when in each round mix sends all messages from the previous round. However, even in this idealistic scenario we detect severe security threats.

**Onions.** It is a core idea of various theoretical systems as well as working implementations (see e.g. [19,21,11,9]). There are many variants of this protocol. A basic one works as follows:

We assume that a message $m$ has to be sent from a node $A$ to a node $B$. For this purpose node $A$ chooses at random $\lambda$ intermediate nodes, say, $J_1, J_2, \ldots, J_\lambda$ and random strings $r_1, r_2, \ldots, r_{\lambda+1}$. Then an *onion* $O$ is built according to the following recursive formula ($\text{Enc}_X$ means encryption with the public key of $X$):

$$O_\lambda = \text{Enc}_B(m, r_{\lambda+1}),$$
$$O_i = \text{Enc}_{J_i}(J_{i+1}, O_{i+1}, r_{i+1}) \quad \text{for } i < \lambda,$$
$$O = O_1.$$

Then $O$ is sent by $A$ to $J_1$. Node $J_1$ "peels off" the first layer by decryption and receives onion $O_2$, the name of the next server on the path, $J_2$, and a random string. Then $J_2$ becomes $O_2$ and processes it in a similar way. This procedure is repeated until the plaintext $m$ appears after decryption.

Anonymity mechanism of onions is very similar to MIXes. Messages entering the same server at the same time are recoded and permuted at random - just as for a MIX.

For the sake of simplicity of presentation, we assume that a server can send directly a message to any other server in the network. In a real network it might be a better strategy to send messages only to neighbours in each round, since otherwise it is much easier to perform traffic analysis by tapping relatively few lines. Nevertheless, if we consider the model in which a message can be sent only to a neighbor (as considered in [10]), then the same problems arise.

We consider only the idealistic model that is resistant to attacks and traffic analysis: all participants send onions at the same time and all onion paths have the same length. So if the view of the network is the same for all participants, an adversary cannot gain any significant information with high probability if anonymity paths are long enough.

**Adversary Model.** There are many adversary models for anonymity protocols. We consider a passive adversary monitoring traffic of messages in a network. The adversary cannot influence the traffic (for example: insert, duplicate, remove, or modify messages).

The adversary considered in this this paper is global, in the sense that he can eavesdrop at the same time <u>all</u> connections, but can neither corrupt a server nor trace its internal work. The adversary keeps track of all network information (routing, key distribution, etc.), too.

Let us remark that the strongest anonymity results were obtained for the model introduced by Berman et al. in [2], where only a fraction of connection is under adversary's control.

**Definitions of Anonymity.** There are many definitions and measures of anonymity (see e.g. [7] or [16]). The very first definition and the weakest one is based on already mentioned *anonymity set* described in [15]: We consider a single message $A$ from the input of a system. Then we consider the set of all output positions that, from the point of view of the adversary, may contain recoded $A$ with a positive probability. Cardinality of this set divided by number of all messages processed by the system is a measure of anonymity.

The definition based on anonymity set does not take into account that different output positions can be more or less likely to be linked with a particular input. This shortcoming is solved by definition based on entropy introduced in [7]. Unfortunately even this definition is not perfect - it does not take into account dependencies between probability distribution of different messages. The strongest definitions are based on *total variation distance* between distribution of all possible permutations of input messages on output positions and the uniform distribution or a priori distribution [2]. Then all dependencies between different messages are taken into account.

In this paper we use the weak measure based on anonymity set. The reason is simple – we show that in some situations even according to this weak measure only a low anonymity level is achieved.

**Local Versus Global View.** A common assumption in papers dealing with onions as well as MIXes is that the servers on anonymity path are chosen independently uniformly at random over the same set by all users.

It is often believed that even if the users choose from different sets of servers, it does not impact anonymity very much provided that the number of potential servers for each user is sufficiently large. We show that this intuition is wrong – different local views of the network can cause degradation of anonymity in some cases, despite strong results for the case when all local views are the same [2,13,10]. This has important practical implications, since it is extremely difficult to provide the same view of the network in a large dynamic system with servers joining and leaving the network.

## 3   Dangers of Using Extra Servers

In this section we consider a simple scenario, in which anonymity breaks completely down or at least is strongly limited. Our considerations here serve as a kind of warm-up before the next section with a more involved analysis for a more practical setting.

We consider the case with $n$ users, each of them sending a single message. The number of servers in the system that can be used as intermediate nodes is also $n$. However, all users, except Alice, know only $n - k$ of these servers, while Alice is aware of all of them. Let $k$ servers known only to Alice be called *additional* servers. (Our choice of parameters might be different, for instance each server may send more than one message, but we fix the setting for the sake of simplicity.)

The messages are processed as onions. Each sender fixes a random path of length $\lambda$ choosing each server independently and uniformly at random. So Alice may choose additional servers while the other servers cannot use them. We consider here a global passive adversary who wants to detect the destination of the message sent by Alice. We assume that for each single user the adversary knows the set of servers in the system known by the user. So in particular, the adversary knows that if an onion is processed through an additional server, then it must be an encoded message of Alice. If the message of Alice does not go through an additional server, then it remains hidden inside the crowd of other messages. However, even then its location might be limited to a small anonymity set, when the message went recently through an additional server.

By evaluating level of anonymity provided by various systems based on onions, the crucial question is how long must be the random path of each message (see [2], [13]). The main idea is that anonymity improves when the length of the random path increases. However, we shall see that it is false for the scenario considered here.

Let $D$ be a random variable denoting the number of steps between the last moment when the message from Alice hits an additional server and delivery of this message. We call $D$ *effective length* of anonymity path. Since each time a message hits an additional server the adversary knows that it is a message from Alice, for providing anonymity against a global adversary only the *effective length* counts and not $\lambda$. For this reason we analyze behavior of the random variable $D$.

**Claim 1.** *For each $t$, $0 \leq t \leq \lambda$,*

$$\Pr[D > t] = \left(1 - \tfrac{k}{n}\right)^{t+1} .$$

Indeed, treating probability of hitting an additional server as a failure in Bernoulli trails we obtain:

$$\Pr[D > t] = \Pr[D = t + 1] + \Pr[D = t + 2] + \ldots + \Pr[D = \lambda]$$
$$= \left(1 - \tfrac{k}{n}\right)^{t+1} \cdot \tfrac{k}{n} + \left(1 - \tfrac{k}{n}\right)^{t+2} \cdot \tfrac{k}{n} + \ldots + \left(1 - \tfrac{k}{n}\right)^{\lambda-1} \cdot \tfrac{k}{n} + \left(1 - \tfrac{k}{n}\right)^{\lambda}$$
$$= \left(1 - \tfrac{k}{n}\right)^{\lambda} + \left(1 - \tfrac{k}{n}\right)^{t+1} \cdot \left(1 - \left(1 - \tfrac{k}{n}\right)^{\lambda-t-1}\right)$$
$$= \left(1 - \tfrac{k}{n}\right)^{t+1} .$$

Let us note that $\Pr[D > t]$ does not depend on parameter $\lambda$, except for the maximal range of the random variable $D$.

Now we can compute the expected value of $D$:

$$E[D] = \sum_{t=0}^{\lambda-1} \Pr[D > t]$$
$$= \sum_{t=1}^{\lambda} \left(1 - \tfrac{k}{n}\right)^{t} = \left(\tfrac{n}{k} - 1\right) \cdot \left(1 - \left(1 - \tfrac{k}{n}\right)^{\lambda}\right) < \tfrac{n}{k} .$$

Let us discuss these estimations of $D$. First assume that $k/n = \frac{1}{4}$. Then $D > 4$ with probability lower than 0.24. Hence, also anonymity set of the Alice's message is very small with high probability. If $k = \frac{n}{\log n}$ (which is a more realistic scenario), then $E[D] < \log n$. Moreover,

$$\Pr[D > \log n - 1] < \left(1 - \frac{1}{\log n}\right)^{\log n} \approx \frac{1}{e} \; .$$

So, in majority of cases effective length of anonymity path is below $\log n$. On the other hand, for a global adversary model a guaranteed level of anonymity is reached for $\lambda = \Theta(\log^2 n)$ [5] (in fact, after slight changes in the protocol are done). So it may happen that for a given value of $k$ it is impossible to reach a high anonymity level – increasing $\lambda$ in this case does not help at all since the effective length of anonymity path essentially will not increase. Sad but true!

We can provide a similar analysis if the connection graph is not a full graph and connections are dynamic. In such a scenario an adversary can keep track of a particular user by observing some links known only to that user. Onions traversing such links reveal their origins to an adversary (just as the onions hitting an additional server in the analysis above).

## 4   Dangers of a Limited Local View

In this section we consider the case that all users except Alice are choosing intermediate servers from a set $N$, while Alice is aware of only a subset of $N$ of cardinality $c \cdot |N|$, for some $c < 1$. Later in this section we discuss shortly the case that each user has some limited knowledge of the servers from $N$.

We consider a global passive adversary who knows $N$ and the sets of servers known by Alice. The goal of the adversary is to determine the destination of a message sent by Alice based on information gained from observing the traffic.

We shall show that anonymity set of the message of Alice might be surprisingly small and therefore the protocol offers a low level anonymity against a global adversary. A very important point is that increasing the length of anonymity path does not help much: after an initial phase the size of the anonymity set fluctuates around a relatively small value.

These results are quite surprising in view of the results concerning the case when all users choose intermediate servers uniformly at random from the same set $N$. Namely, then increasing the path length improves anonymity level so that finally we get very strong anonymity expressed by a total variation distance between the probability distribution of all permutations of messages and the stationary distribution. There are also results suggesting that the necessary path length is relatively small [19,5] even in the case of presence of global passive adversary. This analysis can be easily extended to a scenario where the connection graph is sparse and Alice is aware only of a subset of available edges.

### 4.1   Process Definition

$N$ denotes the set of all servers that can be used as intermediate servers on anonymity paths. Let $W \subset N$ be the set of servers known to Alice. Let $M$ be the set of messages sent by all users. We assume that $|M| = |N|$ and exactly one message is sent by Alice.

At each step of the protocol the adversary may observe positions of $M$ encoded messages, but the problem is to indicate the position of the message sent by Alice – the messages are recoded at each step in such a way that if two or more of them enter the same server, they cannot be linked to the messages leaving this server after recoding. It is exactly the same mechanism as in the case of a MIX-server [3].

Let a set $N_i$ be the set consisting of all messages $u$ after step $i$ such that it is possible that the message $u$ is the recoded message sent by Alice. More precisely, there exist a (hypothetical) linking between messages entering and leaving each server so that the message sent by Alice at the first step leads to message $u$ after step $i$. In other words, from the adversary point of view, it cannot be excluded that $u$ is a recoded Alice's message and $N_i$ is the anonymity set of the Alice's message after step $i$.

Let $S_i$ be the set of all servers where the messages of $N_i$ occur.

At the very beginning Alice sends exactly one message. So $|N_0| = 1$. Let us consider step $i$ of the protocol. Our goal is to estimate the size of $N_i$ based on the size of $N_{i-1}$. The set $N_i$ consists of two kinds of messages:

**The first kind:** the messages that were in $N_{i-1}$ and are sent at step $i$ to servers within $W$ (let us note that the set $N_{i-1}$ has at least one element, since the message sent by Alice is there).

**The second kind:** the messages that were outside $N_{i-1}$, but went to some servers, where a message of the first kind occurs after step $i$.

At least one message from $N_{i-1}$ that remains within $W$, namely, the encrypted message of Alice. The messages from $N_{i-1}$ that go to servers in the set $N \setminus W$ cannot hold the message from Alice.

In order to estimate the number of messages of the second kind we have to find cardinality of the set $S_i$. The random variable denoting the size of $S_i$ is given by a combination of binomial distribution and so-called bins and balls process. Let $\mathrm{Bin}(v, p)$ be a random variable denoting the number of successes in a Bernoulli process with $v$ trials and success probability $p$ for a single trial. Let $\mathrm{BiBa}(v, u)$ be a random variable denoting the number of non-empty bins (i.e. with at least one ball) after throwing $v$ balls uniformly and independently at random into $u$ bins.

It is easy to see that the number of the messages from $N_{i-1}$ which remain within $W$ at step $i$ is given by the random variable:

$$\mathrm{Bin}(|N_{i-1}| - 1, |W|/|N|) + 1$$

($|N_{i-1}| - 1$ messages are not from Alice, so each of them chooses to stay within $W$ with probability $|W|/|N|$, the term "+1" corresponds to the message of Alice). So finally the size of $S_i$ is a random variable with the same distribution as

$$\mathrm{BiBa}(\mathrm{Bin}(|N_{i-1}| - 1, |W|/|N|) + 1, |W|) \ .$$

A message from the set $M \setminus N_{i-1}$ becomes a member of $N_i$, if at step $i$ it hits one of the servers of $S_i$. So the number of messages of the second kind joining $N_i$ is described by a random variable with binomial distribution

$$\mathrm{Bin}(|M| - |N_{i-1}|, |S_i|/|N|) \ .$$

Finally, we have got the following recursive formulas on random variables:

$$|S_i| = \mathrm{BiBa}(\mathrm{Bin}(|N_{i-1}| - 1, |W|/|N|) + 1, |W|),$$
$$|N_i| = \mathrm{Bin}(|M| - |N_{i-1}|, |S_i|/|N|) + \mathrm{Bin}(|N_{i-1}| - 1, |W|/|N|) + 1,$$
$$|N_0| = |S_1| = 1 .$$

In fact, in the above formulas the sign "=" means that the random variables on the left and right side have the same probability distribution.

Our goal is to estimate the size of $N_\lambda$, which is anonymity set of the message of Alice after $\lambda$ steps of processing the messages.

### 4.2  Analysis

Let us recall that the expected value of a random variable $\mathrm{BiBa}(v, u)$ equals

$$u(1 - (1 - \tfrac{1}{u})^v) \approx u(1 - e^{-\frac{u}{v}}) .$$

The expected value of random variable $\mathrm{Bin}(u, p)$ is $u \cdot p$.

Since we assume that $|N| = |M|$, we simplify the formulas by substituting $|N|$ and $|M|$ by a single symbol $n$. Hence the expected sizes of the sets $S_i$ and $N_i$ are expressed by the following formulas:

$$E[|S_i|] \approx |W| \cdot \left(1 - \left(1 - \frac{1}{|W|}\right)^{\frac{(|N_{i-1}|-1)\cdot|W|}{n}+1}\right)$$

and

$$E[|N_i|] \approx \frac{(|M| - |N_{i-1}|)E[|S_i|] + (|N_{i-1}| - 1)|W|}{n} + 1 .$$

(In the first formula we have written $\approx$ instead of $=$, since we have assumed that the number of messages from $N_{i-1}$ that remain in $W$ equals to the expected number of such messages. Similarly, in the second formula we have replaced $|S_i|$ by $E[|S_i|]$.) After applying the approximation $(1 - \tfrac{1}{a})^b \approx e^{-b/a}$, we get

$$E[|N_i|] \approx \frac{n-|N_{i-1}|}{n} \cdot |W| \cdot \left(1 - e^{-\frac{|N_{i-1}|-1}{n} - \frac{1}{|W|}}\right) + (|N_{i-1}| - 1) \cdot \frac{|W|}{n} + 1 .$$

Let $\Delta(|N_{i-1}|) = E[|N_i| - |N_{i-1}|]$. Hence

$$\Delta(|N_{i-1}|) \approx (n - |N_{i-1}|) \cdot \frac{|W|}{n} \cdot (1 - e^{-\frac{|N_{i-1}|-1}{n} - \frac{1}{|W|}}) \tag{1}$$
$$-|N_{i-1}| \cdot (1 - \frac{|W|}{n}) + (1 - \frac{|W|}{n}).$$

We consider $\Delta(|N_{i-1}|)$ as a function of $|N_{i-1}|$ and we fix the value of $\frac{|W|}{|N|}$. We see that the first term in (1) forces $\Delta$ to be positive and its impact is bigger for small values of $|N_{i-1}|$. The second term in (1) forces $\Delta$ to be negative and its impact grows with the

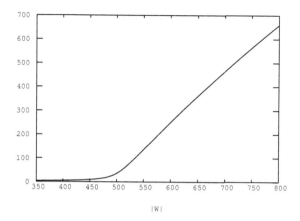

**Fig. 1.** Zero points of Equality 2 as a function of $|W|$ for $n = 1000$

size of $|N_{i-1}|$. So, there is a point where both tendencies have the same strength and so the values of $|N_t|$ oscillate around it. Of course, this equilibrium point depends on $\frac{|W|}{|N|}$.

If we put $\alpha = \frac{|W|}{|N|}$, then we would like to find a value $|N_i|$ such that according to (1), $\Delta(|N_{i-1}|) = 0$. So we have to solve following equation:

$$0 = (n-x)\cdot\alpha\cdot\left(1 - e^{-\frac{x-1}{n} - \frac{1}{\omega_i}}\right) - x\cdot(1-\alpha) + (1-\alpha). \tag{2}$$

We have not found any closed formula for solutions of Equality 2 (as well as some symbolic computation systems). However, one can easily find the solutions numerically. The results for $n = 1000$ and different values of $|W|$ are plotted on Figure 1.

From the numerical results we can learn a somewhat unexpected phenomena. For values of $|W|$ that are significantly lower than $500 = 0.5n$, the equilibrium point has quite small values and the growth rate is quite slow. Around $0.5n$ there is a radical change of the situation: the growth rate increases until the derivative reaches the value close to 0.5. Then, the function is quite well interpolated by a single line. These results suggest that the sizes of anonymity sets $N_i$ remain small for values of $|W|$ that are not too close to $0.5n$. When $|W|$ grows above $0.5n$, then the situation changes abruptly and we should observe that the average size of $N_i$ grows fast with $|W|$.

In the next subsection we compare these results with extensive simulations of the protocol.

## 4.3   Simulation Results

From the previous considerations we can expect that after some number of steps at the beginning of the protocol anonymity set $|N_t|$ should oscillate around a certain value. Since exact formulas describing the stochastic changes of $|N_t|$ or even their fair approximations seem to be very complex, we performed a number of direct simulations to check these tendencies.

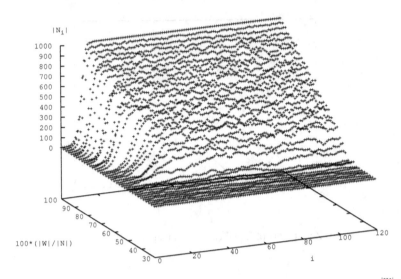

**Fig. 2.** Simulation results - the size of $N_i$ at different steps for different values of $\frac{|W|}{|N|}$.

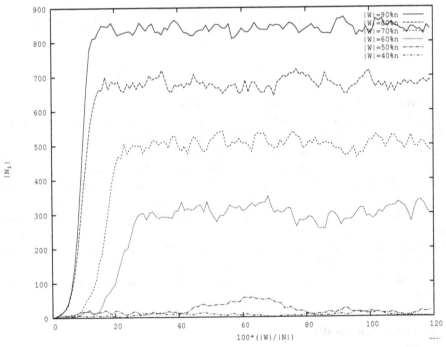

**Fig. 3.** The size of $N_i$ for the same simulations - the results for different values of $\frac{|W|}{|N|}$

We have performed the experiments for different values of $|N|$, but the results hardly depend on $|N|$, except for small values that are not interesting from our point of view. We have performed simulations for different values of $\frac{|W|}{|N|}$.

The next two figures show dependency between $|W|$ and $|N_i|$ in subsequent steps of the protocol. The figures correspond to the cases $|N| = |M| = 1000$ and different values of $|W|$, for $0.3 \cdot |N| \leq |W| \leq |N|$.

Figure 2 is a three dimensional plot. The value plotted is the size of $N_i$ in subsequent steps of the protocol. Different curves correspond to different values of $|W|$ between 30% and 100% of $|N|$ (step 2%).

From Figure 2 one can see that for some values of $\frac{|W|}{|N|}$ anonymity set remains small for all $i$. Then there is a cut-off point for the value of $\frac{|W|}{|N|}$ such that above this point $|N_i|$ grows until it reaches a stable level. This level depends on $\frac{|W|}{|N|}$, just as predicted before (see Figure 1).

Figure 3 presents planar visualization of the same simulation for $|W| = 0.4 \cdot |N|$, $0.5 \cdot |N|$, $0.6 \cdot |N|$, $0.7 \cdot |N|$, $0.8 \cdot |N|$, $0.9 \cdot |N|$. At this point our aim is to convince the reader that there is qualitative gap between anonymity for these values of parameter $|W|$ and relation between sizes of $|W|$ and the average size of $N_i$ is not linear. For $|W| = 0.4 \cdot |N|$, $0.5 \cdot |N|$ the anonymity set has a very small size even if some small deviations occur.

## 4.4  Statistical Analysis

So far we were concerned with the size of $N_i$ only, ignoring probability distribution that for each message from $N_i$ describes the chance that it is the message sent by Alice. It turns out that this probability distribution is highly nonuniform. This property reduces anonymity level offered by the protocol even more.

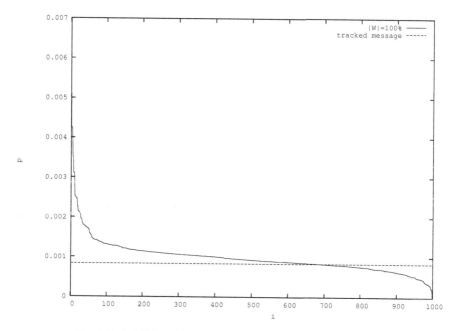

**Fig. 4.** Probabilities after simulation of 20 steps for the case $W = N$

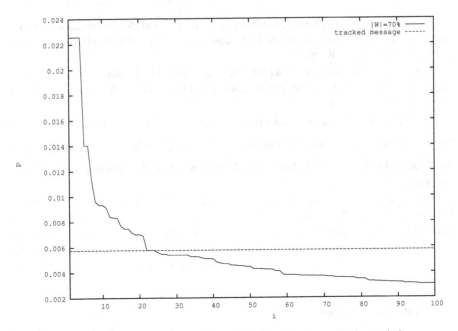

**Fig. 5.** Probabilities after simulation of 20 steps for the case $|W| = 0.7|N|$

We consider the case: $n = 1000$ and the situation after 20 steps. Figure 4 shows the probabilities mentioned for the case when $W = N$, after sorting them. The dashed line shows probability of the message from Alice. As one can expect, the probability distribution is not completely uniform – each probability depends on the number and location of paths leading from Alice to each position after step 20. It is not a big surprise that the message of Alice is in a position that is hard to guess from the probability distribution.

Figure 5 presents an example of simulation results for the same $|N| = 1000$, but this time the size of $W$ is $0.7n$. In this case the anonymity set $N_{20}$ is quite big (near 60% of $N$), so finding $N_{20}$ does not help much. However, experiments show that the actual Alice's message is very likely to be within 3% positions with the highest probabilities.

It is worth to say that such a reduction of the set of suspects for being the message from Alice based on probabilities works when we speed up the computations and determine the probabilities in an incorrect way. Namely, if some message from $N_{i-1}$ leaves $W$, then we do not recompute the probabilities of all members of the anonymity set based on the routes that have occurred in the past, but simply re-scale all probabilities.

### 4.5   Attack Extensions

*Intersection Attack.* Let us assume that Alice sends many messages to the same destination in a row. Then we may apply intersection attack [8,1] and reduce rapidly the anonymity set. The attack has good chances to succeed, since in different rounds the anonymity sets obtained are almost independent, except that the true destination is always the member of the anonymity set. For instance, assume that $|N_\lambda| = |S_\lambda| = 30$,

$N = 1000$, and that during the next execution $|N_\lambda| = 30$. Then the size of intersection of both anonymity sets is given by the random variable $\mathrm{Bin}(29, 30/1000) + 1$ and has expected value about 2. Of course, it does not help Alice, if she sends the messages through different routes.

*Model Extension.* So far we have assumed that all servers except Alice choose the intermediate servers uniformly at random from the whole set $N$. However, one can see that essentially the same attack can be used with high probability if for each user the set of potential intermediate servers is chosen in a way that is stochastically independent from the set of servers known to Alice.

On the other hand, if Alice shares the same set of intermediate servers with other users, then at least it becomes hard to distinguish between them.

## 5   Countermeasures and Conclusions

A common intuition is that in order to achieve a better level of anonymity each user should use as many servers as possible for choosing intermediate servers on anonymity paths. However, in large and dynamic networks this will lead inevitably to a situation that different users will use different sets of servers. Some of them will stay behind and use relatively few servers and some will be fast in changes and use a larger set of servers. As we have shown, <u>both</u> cases are dangerous. The threats do not disappear even if the sizes of the sets used by different users are the same: if a set of servers used by a user is in some sense independent from the sets used by the other users, then the same attack applies.

The problems disappear, if the sets of servers used by different users are the same. However, it is hard to achieve in a dynamic, large scale network without a central control.

Since the hosts are not always honest and there is no authority controlling basic services, anonymous communication becomes a necessary primitive for these dynamic information systems. Therefore the threats discovered are of real importance.

A common strategy in highly dynamic networks is to build an overlay network consisting of a group of servers that are stable and remain in service for a long time. This strategy, used for instance to improve certain features of P2P protocols, is also quite useful for security reasons.

Let us mention yet another solution based on so called-navigators [17]. In this case the anonymity paths are chosen dynamically: a skeleton is established by the user, but subpaths are determined on-the-fly by the servers on the route, so a message sent by Alice may leave the set of servers and our attack breaks down.

## References

1. Agrawal, D., Kesdogan, D., Penz, S.: Probabilistic Treatment of MIXes to Hamper Traffic Analysis. Proceedings of the IEEE Symposium on Security and Privacy, 2003
2. Berman, R., Fiat, A., Ta-Shma, A.: Provable Unlinkability Against Traffic Analysis. Financial Cryptography 2004, Lecture Notes in Computer Science 3110, Springer-Verlag: 266-280

3. Chaum, D.: Untraceable Electronic Mail, Return Addresses, and Digital Pseudonyms. Communication of the ACM 24(2)(1981): 84-88
4. Chaum, D.: Secret-Ballot Receipts and Transparent Integrity. Better and less-costly electronic voting and polling places. Available at http://theory.lcs.mit.edu/~rivest/voting/papers/Chaum-SecretBallotReceiptsTrueVoterVerifiableElections.pdf
5. Czumaj, A., Kanarek, P., Kutyłowski, M., Loryś K.: Distributed Stochastic Processes for Generating Random Permutations. ACM-SIAM Symposium on Discrete Algorithms (SODA) '99, 271-280
6. Danezis, G.: Designing and Attacking Anonymous Communication Systems. CAM-CL-TR-594, University of Cambridge, Computer Laboratory, 2004
7. Danezis, G., Serjantov A.: Towards an Information Theoretic Metric for Anonymity. Privacy Enhancing Technologies 2002, Lecture Notes in Computer Science 2482, Springer-Verlag: 41-53
8. Danezis, G., Serjantov, A.: Statistical Disclosure or Intersection Attacks on Anonymity. Information Hiding '2004, Lecture Notes in Computer Science 3200, Springer-Verlag: 293-308
9. Dingledine, R., Mathewson, N., Syverson P.: Tor: the Second Generation Onion Router. USENIX Security, 2004
10. Gogolewski, M., Kutyłowski, M., Łuczak, T.: Mobile Mixing. International Conference on Information Security and Cryptography 2004, Lecture Notes in Computer Science 3506, Springer-Verlag: 380-3932
11. Gülcü, C., Tsudik, G.: Mixing E-mail with BABEL. ISOC Symposium on Network and Distributed System Security, IEEE 1996: 2-16
12. Goldschlag, D. M., Reed, M. G.,Syverson P.: Private Web Browsing. Journal of Computer Security, Special Issue on Web Security 5(1997): 237-248
13. Gomułkiewicz, M., Klonowski, M., Kutyłowski, M.: Provable Unlinkability Against Traffic Analysis Already After $O(\log(n))$ Steps! Information Security Conference 2004, Lecture Notes in Computer Science 3381, Springer-Verlag: 229-238
14. Jakobsson, M., Juels, A.: Mix and Match: Secure Function Evaluation via Ciphertexts. Advances in Cryptology - Asiacrypt 2000, Lecture Notes in Computer Science 1976, Springer-Verlag: 162–177
15. Kesdogan, D., Egner, J., Büschkes, R.: Stop-and-Go-MIXes Providing Probabilistic Anonymity in an Open System. Information Hiding '1998, Lecture Notes in Computer Science 1525, Springer-Verlag: 83-98
16. Köhntopp, M., Pfitzmann, A.: Anonymity, Unobservability, and Pseudonymity: A Proposal for Terminology. Workshop on Design Issues in Anonymity and Unobservability 2000, Lecture Notes in Computer Science 2009, Springer-Verlag: 1-9
17. Klonowski, M., Kutyłowski, M., Zagórski, F.: Anonymous Communication with On-line and Off-line Onion Encoding. SOFSEM'2005, Lecture Notes in Computer Science 3381, Springer-Verlag: 229-238
18. Kurosawa, K., Ogata, W.: Bit Slice Auction Circuit. ESORICS 2002, Lecture Notes in Computer Science 2502, Springer-Verlag: 24-38
19. Rackoff, C., Simon, D.R.: Cryptographic Defense Against Traffic Analysis. ACM Symposium on Theory of Computing (STOC) '25 (1993): 672-681
20. Serjantov, A., Dingledine, R., Syverson, P.: ¿From a Trickle to a Flood: Active Attacks on Several Mix Types. Information Hiding '2002, Lecture Notes in Computer Science 2578, Springer-Verlag: 36-52
21. Syverson, P., Reed, M. G., Goldschlag, D. M.: Anonymous Connections and Onion Routing. IEEE Journal on Selected Areas in Communication, 1998, 16(4):482-494

# Browser Model for Security Analysis
# of Browser-Based Protocols

Thomas Groß[1], Birgit Pfitzmann[1], and Ahmad-Reza Sadeghi[2]

[1] IBM Zurich Research Lab, Rüschlikon, Switzerland
[2] Ruhr-University Bochum, Bochum, Germany
{tgr, bpf}@zurich.ibm.com
sadeghi@crypto.rub.de

**Abstract.** Currently, many industrial initiatives focus on web applications. In this context an important requirement is often that the user should only rely on a standard web browser. Hence the underlying security services also rely solely on a browser for interaction with the user. Browser-based identity federation is a prominent example of such a service. Very little is still known about the security of browser-based protocols, and they seem at least as error-prone as standard security protocols. In particular, standard web browsers have limited cryptographic capabilities and thus new protocols are used. Furthermore, these protocols require certain care by the user in person, which must be modeled. In addition, browsers, unlike normal protocol principals, cannot be assumed to do nothing but execute the given security protocol.

In this paper, we lay the theoretical basis for the rigorous analysis and security proofs of browser-based protocols. We formally model web browsers, secure browser channels, and the security-relevant browsing behavior of a user as automata. As a first rigorous security proof of a browser-based protocol we prove the security of password-based user authentication in our model. This is not only the most common stand-alone type of browser authentication, but also a fundamental building block for more complex protocols like identity federation.

## 1 Introduction

Browser-based services have received increasing attention in the last years. The idea is simple: users should be able to access the services by only using a standard web browser, which offers a set of basic functionalities. Thus the users send their requests for services as well as receive and view the results by means of the browser. This enables cost-efficient deployment of applications without specific user education. The requirement on such services not to need any special client software is also called *zero-footprint*. Consequently, the underlying security services must also be zero-footprint. Therefore, security services only use a standard browser for user authentication and for retaining a secure channel with the user. They may also request additional security-relevant attributes about the users and third-party confirmation via the browser. We first discuss how non-browser protocols establish such security services and how their methods differ from browser-based protocols. Then we consider research on browser-based protocols in the prominent area of identity federation and point out challenges in establishing rigorous security proofs, before summarizing our contributions.

S. De Capitani di Vimercati et al. (Eds.): ESORICS 2005, LNCS 3679, pp. 489–508, 2005.

*Establishing Secure Channels.* The security services for browser-based protocols mostly focus on establishing mutually authenticated secure channels. The typical approach in other security protocols is to perform a key exchange, based on local master keys, master keys shared with a third party, or public-key certificates, and to subsequently use the exchanged key to secure the communication. A large body of literature on such protocols exists. A seminal work were the Needham-Schroeder protocols [28], although a vulnerability in one protocol was later found by Lowe [20]. Tool-supported proofs were initiated in [25,15,23], based on abstractions of cryptographic primitives introduced in the Dolev-Yao model [6]. Recent tool-supported proofs concentrate on using existing general-purpose model checkers and theorem provers, first in [21,26,4,7,31]. Cryptographic proofs of key-exchange and authentication protocols were initiated by Bellare and Rogaway [1]. Cryptography also added interesting additional properties to pure authentication, e.g., see [17]. Modeling secure channels by a comparison to ideal secure channels, a technique that we will use for the underlying secure channels below, was introduced in [40,35,2]. Analyses specifically for SSL and TLS, and thus close to an underlying mechanism used in browsers, were made in [41,27,32,18].

However, standard browsers simply do not execute most of these protocols. Instead, a browser establishes a server-side authenticated secure channel leveraging a public-key certificate of the server and provides client authentication by other means. The only exception to this method would be SSL or TLS channels with client certificates for 2-party authentication. However, this is not considered truly zero-footprint because the users would have to obtain the certificates. Also, the method would not allow a user to easily use different browsers at different times. Thus it is very rarely used, and not used at all as a basis in larger browser-based security protocols. Hence browser-based protocols are different from all protocols for which prior security proofs exist.

*Identity Federation.* A prominent area of browser-based security protocols is identity federation, which aims at linking a user's (otherwise) distinct identities at several locations. The benefit is that the involved organizations can reduce user management costs, such as the cost of password helpdesks and user registration and deletion. In this area, concrete and complex browser-based security protocols were proposed, e.g., Microsoft's Passport [24], the Security Assertion Markup Language (SAML) standardized by OASIS [29], the Shibboleth project for university identity federation [3], the Liberty Alliance project [19], and WS-Federation [13,14]. Several papers discussed vulnerabilities of such protocols, in particular for Passport [16], the Liberty enabled-client protocol [37], and a SAML profile [10]. Others discussed privacy design principles and details [36,33,34,38]. Basic browser-based authentication without federated identity management is discussed in [9]. As far as the vulnerabilities found were removable security problems (in contrast to fundamental limitations of the browser-based protocol class or matters of taste like privacy), they were removed in the next version of the protocols. However, past experience in protocol design has shown that incorporating countermeasures against known attacks does not guarantee to eliminate all vulnerabilities. Hence it is desirable to devise security proofs.

*Proving Browser-Based Protocols.* It is not trivial to apply previous security proof techniques, both cryptographic techniques and formal-methods techniques, to browser-based protocols. The primary reason is that a browser represents a new party with its own, predefined behavior that impacts the security of the protocols executed across it. In usual security protocols, principals are assumed to execute precisely the security protocol under consideration (unless they are corrupted). A browser, in contrast, reacts on a number of predefined messages, adds information to responses automatically, and stores information such as histories in places that cannot always be assumed secure, e.g., if the browser is in an Internet kiosk. For instance, one of the SAML problems found in [10] is based on the HTTP Referer tag, i.e., a browser feature that is not mentioned at all on the level of the SAML protocol. Another usual issue is that browser-based protocols use a multitude of names for a principal, while other protocols typically assume a one-to-one mapping; for instance, there are URL addresses, identities used in SSL certificates, and identities used in higher protocols. It is easy to forget some name comparisons in protocols and thus to enable man-in-the-middle attacks. All this means that a detailed and rigorous browser model is a prerequisite for convincing security proofs of browser-based protocols, and no such model exists so far. For the resulting model, we currently assume that a real browser does not perform additional actions, because for most security protocols arbitrary additional actions could destroy the security. This could be replaced by more precise assumptions on forbidden additional actions in the future.

Another important special aspect is that due to the limited capabilities of browsers, the user at the browser is an active participant and certain assumptions must be made about the user, e.g., that the user verifies that a secure channel to a trusted server is used before entering an important password.

*Our Contribution.* In this paper, we lay the theoretical basis for research in this area by modeling the major building blocks for browser-based protocols. We present a rigorous and abstract model for a standard web browser as a principal for browser-based protocols. While our model is still extensible – in particular we do not model cookies and scripting but assume a browser with these features turned off – we believe that we have captured the major explicit and implicit browser features that play a role in typical browser-based protocols. In addition, we model the security-relevant browsing behavior of a user, i.e., a machine that implements the explicit constraints on a user that are needed for protocol proofs, but still allows arbitrary behavior apart from that. Furthermore, we model browser channels in order to capture, in particular, the naming issues across multiple protocol layers.

As a first security lemma for a browser-based protocol in our model, we study the security of the initial authentication of the user behind a browser by a password. Initial user authentication is an integral part of all browser-based protocols, and passwords are the standard technique used in the zero-footprint scenario.

A first step in the direction of proofs of browser-based protocols was taken in [11]. There, however, we only modeled exactly those parts of the user and browser behavior that we concretely needed for the protocol, and made assumptions that other things would not happen. These assumptions were made top-down for the needs of the protocol rather than bottom-up from a browser and user model. In this paper, we lay the bottom-up groundwork for such assumptions.

492     T. Groß, B. Pfitzmann, and A.-R. Sadeghi

## 2   Notation

*General Notation.* We use a straight font for constants, including constant Sets and Types, functions, and predicates, where Types are predefined constant sets. We use italics for *variables* and variable *Sets*. Let $\Sigma$ be an alphabet without the symbols $\{$"$\epsilon$", "!", "?", "◁", "[", "]", "//" $\}$. Then $\Sigma^*$ is the set of strings over $\Sigma$ where $\epsilon$ denotes the empty string and $\Sigma^+ = \Sigma^* \setminus \{\epsilon\}$. For a set $S$, $\mathcal{P}(S)$ denotes the powerset of $S$ and $S^*$ the set of finite sequences over $S$. We define $S.\text{add}\,(x)$ as $S := S \cup \{x\}$ and $S.\text{remove}\,(x)$ as $S := S \setminus \{x\}$. Assignment by possibly probabilistic functions is written as $\leftarrow$. Assignment of a value to a tuple of variables means making correspondingly many projections; if one of these fails the entire assignment fails. We denote the set of URL host names, including protocol names such as "https", by URLHost, the set of URL path names by URLHostPath, and the set of URL host and path names by URLHostPath. We write an address $adr \in$ URLHostPath as a pair $(host, path)$ of a host name $host \in$ URLHost and a path. The type ChType := {secure, insecure} contains the channel types available.

*Automata.* We represent our machines such as the browser model as I/O automata, in other words finite-state machines with additional variables. This is a very usual basis for specifying participants in distributed protocols; the first specific use for security is in [22]. Specifically we use the automata model proposed in [35], which has a well-defined realization by probabilistic interactive Turing machines and is therefore linked to more detailed cryptographic considerations where those become necessary in multi-layer proofs. In the following we give a brief overview of this machine model (see also Figure 2). Machines may have multiple fixed connections to other machines organized by means of uni-directional *ports*. We define two types of *simple ports* for message transmission: n? is an input with name $n$ and n! an output port, respectively. The machine model connects simple ports n? and n! with the same name $n$ and opposite direction; these are called *complement* ports. We call ports without such a complement *free* ports. We define a *clock port* $p = (n, ◁, d) \in \Sigma^+ \times \{◁\} \times \{!, ?\}$ as a port that schedules the connection between simple ports n? and n! with same name $n$, or is free itself if this connection does not exist.

A *machine* M is defined as a tuple $\mathsf{M} = (name_{\mathsf{M}}, Ports_{\mathsf{M}}, Vars_{\mathsf{M}}, States_{\mathsf{M}}, \delta_{\mathsf{M}}, Ini_{\mathsf{M}}, Fin_{\mathsf{M}})$ of a name $name_{\mathsf{M}} \in \Sigma^+$, a finite sequence $Ports_{\mathsf{M}}$ of ports, a finite sequence $Vars_{\mathsf{M}}$ of variables, a set $States_{\mathsf{M}} \subseteq \Sigma^*$ of major states, a probabilistic state-transition function $\delta_{\mathsf{M}}$, and sets $Ini_{\mathsf{M}}, Fin_{\mathsf{M}} \subseteq States_{\mathsf{M}}$ of initial and final states. The inputs are tuples $I = (I_i)_{i=1,\ldots,|\text{in}(Ports_{\mathsf{M}})|}$, where $I_i \in \Sigma^*$ is the input for the $i$-th in-port, in($Ports_{\mathsf{M}}$) is the input ports of the machine and $|\text{in}(Ports_{\mathsf{M}})|$ denotes the number of the input ports. Analogously, the outputs are tuples $O = (O_i)_{i=1,\ldots,|\text{out}(Ports_{\mathsf{M}})|}$. The empty word, $\epsilon$, denotes "no in- or output", respectively. The value assignments of variables are tuples $V = (V_i)_{i=1,\ldots,|Vars_{\mathsf{M}}|}$, where $V_i \in \Sigma^*$ is the value for the $i$-th variable in the sequence $Vars_{\mathsf{M}}$. In the following, we usually say "state" for "major state"; however, the state transition function changes the overall state consisting of the major state and the variables.

We define the state transition function $\delta_{\mathsf{M}}$ of a machine M using a notation analogous to UML state diagrams [30], see Figure 1. This is a concise and user-friendly definition method that enables easy graph analysis of the command and information

| Start state | Final success | Final failure | State with name **State1** | Transition |

**Fig. 1.** Key to the state diagrams

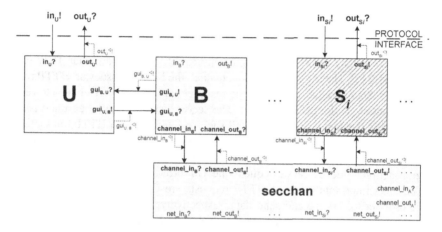

**Fig. 2.** System architecture for browser-based protocols with a browser B, a user U, servers $S_i$, channel abstraction secchan and their ports

flow in security proofs. We define a *transition* in a state diagram as an arrow from a state $s$ to a state $s'$ with label $Event[Guard]//Action$, where $Event$ is a sequence of non-empty inputs to the input ports, $Guard$ is a predicate over $Event$ and the machine's current variable allocation $V$, and $Action$ specifies the computations and outputs of the transition.

*System Overview for Browser-based Protocols.* Figure 2 gives an overview of the automata in our model. We call the generic browser machine B, the user machine that implements the minimum assumptions on secure user behavior U, and the machine that models the behavior of secure channels as implemented within HTTPS (see [39]) by secchan. To analyze and prove browser-based security protocols one complements these general-purpose machines with one or more server machines, here denoted by $S_i$, that jointly execute the browser-based protocol. Furthermore, one configures the user machine U with suitable initial information about trusted parties.

## 3   Ideal Web Browser B

In this section, we describe our model of a web browser. Before the actual definitions, we give an overview of real web browsers.

A web browser acts as the client in transactions of the Hypertext Transfer Protocol (HTTP) [8]. A browser acts on behalf of one single user in a browsing session. However, it may display multiple windows that render different HTTP transactions in parallel. We will model a window by a window identifier *wid* in the communication between U and B; however, the window management of the browser machine is omitted for brevity.

A browser accepts user inputs specifying addresses and retrieves and renders the content associated with these addresses or error messages. It also renders the status of the channel to the server and, if a secure channel is used, the identity of the server. Furthermore, it initiates dialogs with the user to negotiate changes of the channel state, verify a server's authentication or request for user authentication.

HTTP is a client-server protocol in the application layer of the TCP/IP protocol stack. In order to initiate an HTTP transaction, a browser establishes a connection to a server; here it may leverage various transport protocols, in particular TCP/IP, SSL 3.0, or TLS1.0 [5]. Having established a channel, the browser issues an HTTP request to the server. Such a request specifies the resource that the browser intends to retrieve and may contain additional parameters. The server evaluates the request and issues a response using the same channel. We call such an interaction an HTTP transaction. In principle, browsers do not need to hold state beyond such a single transaction. However, real web browser do hold persistent state, e.g., a cache and a browsing history, and they let a transaction influence the subsequent one. Our browser model reflects this behavior.

The most important types of HTTP requests are GET and POST requests, used by the browser to retrieve and send data, respectively. Servers may not only respond with content but also instigate a behavior change in the browser. In particular, HTTP responses with scripted form POST and redirect messages direct the browser to another address of the server's choice. Another HTTP response asks for user authentication by a username-password pair. We model these HTTP messages as abstract formats, i.e., we do not model how the bitstrings are parsed. We focus on the mentioned subset of HTTP messages and their core parameters, because these are the ones that are actively used in browser-based protocols or may have impact on their security.

An important aspect of real web browsers is that they do more than browser-based protocols typically intend. Most prominent is the problem of information flow. On the one hand, this may occur within HTTP requests, e.g., by the HTTP Referer tag. On the other hand, persistent state such as history, cache and password storage provide data flow to the underlying operating system and thus potentially to other parties. Hence the user's log-off from a browser session that removes browser state is also security-relevant. We dedicate Section 3.4 to information-flow aspects.

At present, we do not consider cookies and scripts as many browser-based protocols do not use them directly and it is possible to switch them off.

In Section 3.1 we define the interface of the browser machine B, i.e., its ports and the syntax of permitted in- and output messages. Details of the abstract HTTP messages are treated in Section 3.2. Section 3.3 defines the variables of the browser model. In Section 3.4 we define functions governing the information-flow properties. Finally, Section 3.5 describes the transition function.

### 3.1  Interface of Browser Machine B

The ports of B were already shown in Figure 2. We now discuss the messages exchanged over these ports. We list them all in Table 3 of Appendix A. Here we only explain them as far as it is useful to understand the upcoming state diagram.

The ports gui$_{U,B}$? and gui$_{B,U}$! model the browser's user interface. The input messages enter_address, trigger_address and submit_form issue a request for an address to B. Here enter_address represents an input in the browser's address field, trigger_address models clicking a link and submit_form defines the submission of an HTML form. The output messages established and error inform the user of the channel status. The message channel_change notifies the user of a change of the security level of the channel. The browser uses request_uauth and authenticate in the password-based user authentication dialog. The remaining messages organize a certificate verification dialog with the user. The security of browser-based protocols builds upon the browser machine reliably presenting secure channels and the server identity *sid* to their users. Thus, if an HTTP transaction uses a secure channel, B includes the channel's server identity in each message to U. The user machine U confirms the server identity in each message to B.[1]

The ports channel_out$_B$? and channel_in$_B$! connect the browser to the underlying channel abstraction secchan. We introduce the ports self$_B$! and self$_B$? to reduce the complexity of the state diagrams. Using these ports, we allow the browser to delegate trigger_address and submit_form commands to itself and to treat them on the same command path as the user inputs. The ports in$_B$? and out$_B$! model information flow to the operating system and may be connected to a higher protocol layer or the adversary. We discuss in Section 3.4 how B explicitly leaks information about its state. Loosely speaking, upon an input do_leak at in$_B$? the browser outputs its full persistent state to out$_B$!.

## 3.2  Abstract HTTP Messages

The interface of the secure channel abstraction secchan allows the browser to send very general messages to other machines, but correct browsers only send HTTP messages and only accept messages parsable according to HTTP.

We model an HTTP GET request by an abstract message with format GET(*path*, *query*, *login*, *info_leak*). Here *path* $\in$ URLPath denotes the path of the address to be retrieved and *query* $\in \Sigma^*$ the query string of the URL. The parameter *login* $\in \Sigma^*$ contains the credentials of a password-based user authentication, including the account name. The parameter *info_leak* is a list of name-value pairs from $\Sigma^* \times \Sigma^*$. It models potential additional parameters, e.g., the preceding address in the HTTP Referer tag. We discuss them specifically under the aspect of information flow in Section 3.4. For HTTP POST requests we define POST(*path*, *query*, *login*, *info_leak*) analogously.

We now proceed to describe the HTTP responses. The abstract messages Page(*m*, *close*, *nocache*) and Error(*m*, *close*) model HTTP 200 OK responses and HTTP 40x error responses. Both contain a page $m \in \Sigma^*$ as the payload and a flag *close* $\in$ Bool that directs the browser to close the underlying channel or to keep it alive for further HTTP transactions. This parameter models the token close of the Connection header of HTTP1.1 [8]. The parameter *nocache* $\in$ Bool of Page models the cache-response directive nostore of HTTP1.1, which forces a browser not to store any part of this response and the request that elicited it.

---

[1] We only model that the user sees the server identity, not a channel identifier, because he or she will not notice if a channel is interrupted. Usually, however, a user can distinguish different channels with one partner by different windows.

The abstract message Redirect($adr, path, query, close$) models a redirect (HTTP 302 or 303) to $adr/path?querystring$, where $querystring$ is an encoding of the abstract $query \in \Sigma^*$. Here $adr \in$ URLHost and $path \in$ URLPath. Similarly, POSTForm($adr, path, query, close, nocache$) models a form containing a script that will POST a message whose body encodes the abstract $query$ to the address $adr/path$. The parameters $close$ and $nocache$ are defined as above. In consequence of both messages the browser establishes a channel to the address $adr$ and then sends $path$ and $query$ over that channel. The channel type is implied by the HTTP protocol name "http" or "https" in $adr$.

The abstract message Authenticate() queries the browser for a user authentication.

### 3.3   Variables of Browser Machine B

We now define the browser's variables $Vars_B$. We distinguish *volatile* and *persistent* variables. Volatile variables belong to one HTTP transaction and are deleted in the final state of this transaction, while persistent variables survive individual transactions. We describe the variables in more detail in the full version of this paper [12].

We start by describing the volatile variables. The variable $adr$ contains the address to be retrieved in the given HTTP transaction. It implies the value of $host$ and $ch\_type$. The value of $ch\_type$ specifies the type of the channel the browser establishes to the server with hostname $host$. The variable $method$ contains the HTTP method used in this HTTP transaction, and $source\_uri \in$ Bool states whether the entity issuing the request for $adr$ has a URI of its own. This implies whether a Referer Tag is included in the request. The variable $form$ contains a form compiled from user inputs given by the variable $form\_in$ and a form obtained in the preceding HTTP transaction. The variable $ch \in$ Channel contains the browser's local representation of a channel established to a server, i.e., the data the browser has acquired about the channel. An element of Channel is a tuple $(cid, host, sid, type, free)$ from the domain $\mathbb{N} \times$ URLHost $\times \Sigma^* \times$ ChType $\times$ Bool. Here $cid$ is a channel identifier, $host$ contains the hostname of the server to which the browser channel is connected, and $sid$ names the server's identity in a secure channel and is $\epsilon$ for an insecure channel. The element $type$ represents the channel type (secure or insecure). The element $free$ is used to organize the reuse of existing channels and flags that the channel is currently not associated to a HTTP transaction. The variable $m$ contains the payload of an HTTP response, whereas variable $store$ flags the user's decision whether to store login data in the browser's state. The variable $auto\_req$ determines whether the browser issues the following request automatically to itself.

The first two persistent variables exist for each window: $wid$ is the window identifier, and $prev\_run = (ch\_type, adr, form)$ contains data about the preceding HTTP transaction in this window: the channel type, the address retrieved, and the structure of an HTML form together with hidden value fields already included in the form. The other persistent variables are global for B. The sequence $Channels$ contains representations of type Channel of all channels the browser has established. The set $UAuth$ contains a user's login information the user decided to store in the browser's state, $History$ is a sequence of addresses successfully retrieved by the browser, and $Cache$ models the browser cache as a sequence of pairs of addresses and page contents retrieved from these addresses.

### 3.4   Information Flow Functions

Even correct browsers produce information flow beyond the core parameters of HTTP requests and responses to both communication partners and the underlying operating system. As this information flow may lead to vulnerabilities in browser-based security protocols, we model it explicitly.

We already provided the parameter $info\_leak$ for additional information in abstract HTTP requests. For generating the content of this parameter, we define a function leak2server(). It implicitly works on the current variables of the given window and browser and computes a list of name-value pairs of information to be disclosed. A real browser primarily sends such information in HTTP header tags such as Referer, From or Accept_Language. However, most of these tags do not contain data that we modeled. Hence our default implementation of leak2server only includes the Referer tag, which contains the preceding address if the request was issued by an entity that has a URI of its own: leak2server() = (Referer, $prev\_run.adr$) if $source\_uri$, else $\epsilon$.

Another potential for information flow exists from the persistent variables, which are stored in the underlying operating system. This introduces security and privacy risks especially in kiosk scenarios. We already described that we model leakage of these variables by an input do_leak at port $in_B$?. Upon this input, the browser outputs its entire persistent state as a string $info$ in a message leak($info$) at port $out_B$!. These ports are free by default, so that the adversary can connect to them. Alternatively, they may be made so-called specified ports, which define the interface to a higher protocol. This allows for flexibility in the assumptions about the security of the persistent variables.

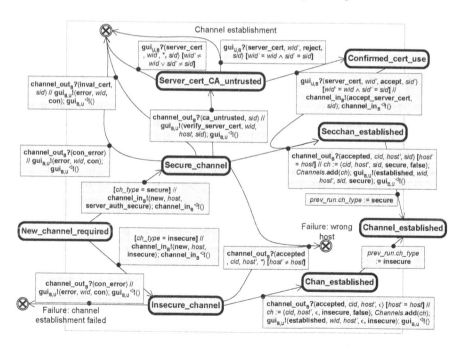

**Fig. 3.** Channel establishment phase of an HTTP transaction

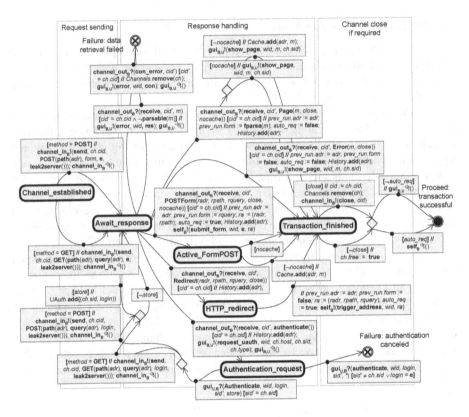

**Fig. 4.** Request handling phase of an HTTP transaction

## 3.5   State-Transition Function

We now define the browser's state transition function $\delta_B$. A browser handles several classes of user actions asynchronously, such as enter_address and log_off. Upon enter_address, trigger_address or submit_form the window with the corresponding window identifier *wid* starts a new HTTP transaction. If there exists an ongoing HTTP transaction, that one's state flow is exited. Upon a log_off command, the browser B exits all state diagrams of HTTP transactions and starts a log-off flow, which closes all channels and deletes the browser state. Figures 3 and 4 contain the main parts of the state diagram of a single HTTP transaction, i.e., an HTTP request-response pair. The start state typically corresponds to the inactive state of the browser window where the user views a page; the transaction is then triggered by the user selecting a link or directly inputting a new URL. The start state can also correspond to a user filling a form or to the middle of a redirect.

The browser begins with a *local negotiation* phase where it notifies its user U about the establishment of a new channel if the desired channel is of a different type than the previous one, e.g., insecure HTTP after secure HTTPS. If the user consents to the channel change, the browser procures a suitable channel. We allow the browser to reuse free channels, i.e., opened but not associated to an ongoing HTTP transaction, with the correct host and security level; this is the *channel reuse* phase. The *channel establishment* phase shown in Figure 3 contains the case that a new channel is needed. It first distinguishes whether the desired channel should be secure or insecure. Establishing an insecure channel is straightforward. Establishing a secure channel involves a certificate test and potential user interaction if the browser is in doubt about a certificate.

Figure 4 starts at State Channel_established from Figure 3 and handles an HTTP request and response. In the *request sending* phase, B issues an HTTP request as a GET or POST according to the *method* of the initial user input and enters State Await_response, where it expects an HTTP response from the server. In the *response handling* phase, B handles different abstract response types: a normal answer Page, an Error, a Redirect, a scripted POST FormPOST, or an authentication request Authenticate. The latter leads to a user interaction in State Authentication_request and finally to the resending of the HTTP request with the login information from the user. The response types Redirect and FormPOST specify an address the browser will send an HTTP request to in the following HTTP transaction. This next HTTP request is treated by the next iteration of the entire state-transition diagram, but to trigger it the browser sends a message to its own port $self_B?$, with the format accepted in the start state.

## 4    Ideal User Browsing Behavior U

In browser-based protocols, the browser's user has an important role because the browser itself only provides rudimentary trust management. The user also controls most of the browser behavior and has the final say about the browser's actions. Thus we consider the user as an active protocol participant and model it by a machine U. In general, U is transparent; however, it enforces the general requirements for browser-based protocols. In particular, it stores data about trust relationships to other parties, performs user authentication including the crucial verification of the server's identity, tests certificates, observes the status of secure channels, and logs off from the browser in error cases.

As shown in Figure 2, the machine U works as a proxy between the browser and the protocol interface. Above the protocol interface, one has to imagine the remaining, protocol- or application-dependent actions of the human user, which we sometimes call the "real user". The machine U forwards normal browser communication from the real user to B and the browser's pages back. In contrast, it handles typical trust tasks solely in interaction with the browser, without involving the real user. With the message compromised, it notifies the real user that the browser behaved against U's expectations and that U aborted the interaction with it.

As in Section 3.3, we distinguish persistent and volatile variables of U. As these variables contain confidential data like passwords, they are also important in an information flow analysis.

The persistent variables of U model its trust relationships. The sequence $T_U$ contains a tuple $(host, sid, login, sec)$ for each server that U has a special relationship with. The tuples have the type Server $=$ URLHost$\times \Sigma^* \times \Sigma^* \times \mathcal{P}($ChType$)$. Here *host* contains the server's hostname, *sid* its identity in a secure channel and *login* the login information for user U. The set *sec* contains the channel types allowed for user authentication with

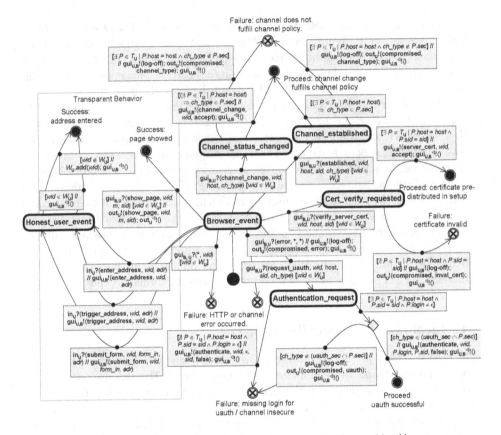

**Fig. 5.** The ideal user browsing behavior represented by machine U

that server. The pairs $(host, sid)$ within this table must be unique. The set $uauth\_sec$ models the general policy of U for allowed channel types for user authentication and contains the channel types that are acceptable.

For the volatile variables, we use similar names as in the browser machine: the address $adr$ and channel type $ch\_type$ refer to the address the browser established a channel to. For secure channels the server identity $sid$ additionally contains the identity according to the server's certificate. The variable $P$ is an instance of the type Server.

We define the state transition function $\delta_U$ by the state diagram in Figure 5. The Start state models the user machine being idle, waiting for an input from the real user with an address $adr$ to retrieve or for a browser event. After having issued an address request to the browser, the machine observes the browser's behavior and reacts to events generated by B. The state machine models *transparent behavior* on the left side (around State Honest_user_event), where it only forwards messages between protocol interface and browser. This transparent part handles the messages enter_address, trigger_address, submit_form, and show_page. The user tracks channel status changes and channels established in the States Channel_status_changed and Channel_established, verifies certificates that B doubts in State Cert_verify_requested, and forwards errors and pages to the protocol interface. The user also handles the user authentication process in State Authentication_request.

## 5  Channel Machine Secchan

Our browser model comes with a channel abstraction secchan for secure and insecure browser channels. For space reasons, we describe this machine only partially here.

As shown in Figure 2, each machine M with network access has two ports channel_in$_M$! and channel_out$_M$? to connect to secchan. The channel machine connects to the adversary by two means. The ports net_out$_M$! and net_in$_M$? are for insecure channels and not needed here. The ports channel_out$_A$! and channel_in$_A$? modeling the imperfections of secure channels. The adversary also controls the network scheduling and decides which messages are delivered.

The machine secchan chooses channel identifiers uniquely and keeps track of channels. To model insecure DNS, it queries the adversary for ports corresponding to hostnames. It has a table $CA$ of tuples $binding = (port, sid, host) \in \Sigma^+ \times \Sigma^* \times$ URLHost linking a certified identity $sid$ and a base hostname $host$ to the port index of a communication partner of secchan. The setup of this table enforces that the identities $sid$ are nonambigously bound to one unique machine M, i.e., if an honest party M controls an identity $sid$ no other machine may act under this identity. We define security domains as tree of URIs covered by a server identity $sid$, for which no other party M* can control a server identity $sid^*$. More formally we define such domains as follows:

**Definition 1 (Channel Security Domain).** *For a binding* (M, $sid_M$, $host_M$), *we call a URIM with* host($URIM$) $\subseteq$ $host_M$ $\subseteq$ $sid_M$ *a* channel security domain *of machine* M *if CA does not contain another entry* (M*, $sid^*$, $host^*$) *with* M* $\neq$ M *and* $host^*$ $\supseteq$ $host$ *for any host* $\subseteq$ host($URIM$). $\diamond$

For handling a concrete channel instance, secchan dispatches the communication to a sub-machine. Such an instance contains the channel identifier $cid$, the port indices of the *initiator* and *responder*, the server's actual address $host$, the server's identity $rid$ and the security level, here server_auth_secure. We depict the most important steps of a secure channel instance in Figure 6 and discuss the establishment of a secure channel in the following.

Clients initiate secure channels to an address $host$ by the command new with the parameter $ch\_type$ = server_auth_secure. Then secchan queries the adversary for the recipient port index R corresponding to $host$, chooses a unique channel identifier $cid$, and dispatches to a sub-machine for a secure channel (Figure 6) with R, $host$, and $cid$ as parameters. The sub-machine contains the channel type $ch\_type$ = server_auth_secure as constant variable. This sub-machine handles further communication. First it notifies the server with the channel identifier $cid$. The server may accept the channel and identify itself under an identity $rid \in$ URLHost. The secure channel instance verifies the server identity in State accept_request: It tests whether it has a tuple $(S, rid, host') \in CA$ such that the current address $host$ lies under the base address $host'$. If yes, it notifies the client that the channel was accepted. From now on, the port indices of client and server are non-ambiguously bound to the channel identifier $cid$. Thus client and server are the fixed *channel partners* of this channel. Both partners may send messages referring to $cid$.

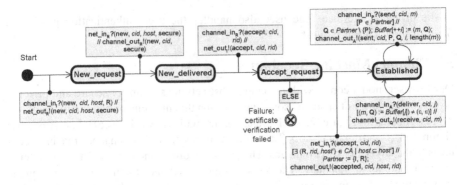

**Fig. 6.** State diagram of a single instance of a secure channel

# 6  Security of User Authentication

In this section, we present the first protocol proof based on a detailed browser model: We show the security of typical password-based user authentication by one server. Such user authentication is an important building block for most other security protocols based on browsers, e.g., in federated identity management.

## 6.1  Authentication Server

The overall system is a special case of the architecture shown in Figure 2. We consider the definition of one server S; of course there can be several such servers and also servers of different types interacting with the same browsers and users. We only rename the free ports of this server from $in_S$? and $out_S$! into $uauth\_in_S$? and $uauth\_out_S$! to indicate that it offers a user authentication service. Further, we specialize the architecture by allowing the adversary full access to the browser's cache and history, i.e., we show that user authentication (in contrast to some other protocols) is not vulnerable to such attacks. This means that the adversary connects to all free ports in Figure 2 that are not defined to belong to the protocol interface.

The inputs at the ports that S does not share with a prior machine and its persistent variables are shown in Tables 1 and 2. We refer to the two parts of an entry $e$ in the user metadata table $MetaU_S$ as $e.id$ and $e.login$. We require that both $id$ and $login$ are unique within the table $MetaU_S$ of a correct server S at all times.

**Table 1.** Protocol in- and outputs of the authentication server S

| Port | Type | Parameters | Description |
|------|------|-----------|-------------|
| $uauth\_in_S$? | | | Input to authentication server S |
| | start | $cid : \Sigma^*$ | Start authentication of channel $cid$ |
| $uauth\_out_S$! | | | Output of authentication server S |
| | done | $cid : \Sigma^*, idu : \Sigma^*$ | Authentication for channel $cid$ finished with identity $idu$, where $\epsilon$ means failure. |

**Table 2.** Persistent variables of the authentication server S

| Name | Domain | Description | Init. |
|---|---|---|---|
| $hosts_S$ | URLHost | Hostname of this server | See setup |
| $sids_S$ | $\Sigma^*$ | Identity of this server for secure channels | See setup |
| $MetaU_S$ | $\mathcal{P}(\Sigma^+ \times \Sigma^*)$ | Pairs of known user identities and login information. | $\emptyset$ |

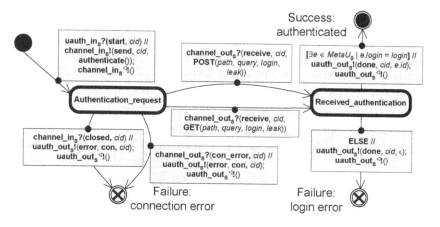

**Fig. 7.** State machine of the user authentication server S

The state machine for one authentication protocol run of server S is shown in Figure 7. The server user (typically a higher protocol) starts authentication for some channel with identifier $cid$. The server sends an authentication request over the channel $cid$. Upon receipt of an authentication message, it looks up whether the included login information is present in its user metadata. If yes, it outputs the corresponding identity as the main part of the authentication result, else $\epsilon$.

## 6.2 Setup Assumptions

As set-up for a particular user machine U and authentication server S, they exchange login information $login_{U,S} \neq \epsilon$ such that U and S are the only parties that obtain information about it. Further, U must know a valid certificate identity of S so that it can verify later that it has a secure channel to S. Formally, the result of the set-up is this:

**Definition 2 (UAuth Setup Assumptions).** *For a user U and an authentication server S we assume:*

a. *The set $T_U$ of U's trusted servers contains an entry $(hostS, sidS, login_{U,S}, \{secure\})$ where $hostS = hosts_S$ and $sidS = sids_S$ for the hostname and identity variables of* S.
b. *The authentication server's user table $MetaU_S$ contains an entry $(id_U, login_{U,S})$, where the user's identity $id_U$ is unique in $MetaU_S$.*
c. *No other variables contain information about $login_{U,S}$.*
d. *The binding table $CA$ of the secure channel abstraction secchan contains a triple $(S, sids_S, hosts_S)$ where $host(URIS) \subseteq hosts_S \subseteq sids_S$ and $URIS$ defines a channel security domain of* S. ◇

### 6.3   Security of User Authentication

We now show that user authentication as defined by the general user machine U and the specific authentication server S is secure. Essentially, security means that when S has performed a successful protocol run of the user authentication protocol, indicated by the output (done, $cid$, $id_U$), then it is indeed connected with the user with identity $id_U$. More precisely, we show in Lemma 1 that such an output implies that S holds a secure channel with channel identifier $cid$ where the communication partner is the browser B of the user U who has this identity $id_U$. We make a relatively strong statement: We have not required that S only makes its requests on secure channels, nor that the user correctly logs out of browser sessions or otherwise protects caches and histories. Extended protocols, e.g., the continued secure use of the channel for which the authentication is made, may need additional assumptions.

**Lemma 1 (User Authentication).** *Let a correct user machine U and authentication server S be given that have performed setup according to Definition 2 at some time with the user identity $id_U$, and let the user's browser B be correct. Then the following statement holds unless an adversary can guess $login_{U,S}$ based on a priori knowledge of its distribution, its length, and the results of previous guessing attempts, which each exclude one potential value: If S outputs* (done, $cid$, $id_U$) *at uauth_outs! then there exists a secure channel instance $SCh_{bs}$ in secchan with*

$$SCh_{bs}.cid = cid \ \wedge \ SCh_{bs}.state = \text{established}$$
$$\wedge \ SCh_{bs}.ch\_type = \text{server\_auth\_secure} \ \wedge \ SCh_{bs}.Partner = \{B, S\}.$$

We present the full proof of Lemma 1 in the long version of this paper [12].     □

## 7   Conclusion

In prior art, browser-based protocols only came with vulnerability analyses and informal security considerations. However, those methods do not guarantee the protocols' security and do not meet the requirements of industry embracing browser-based protocols in complex scenarios. We designed the first model for the rigorous security analysis of browser-based protocols. Our model encompasses generic machines for browsers, user browsing behavior and channel abstraction that allow precise protocol proofs. We have also proven the security of the initial password-based user authentication, a very common protocol on its own and a key ingredient of browser-based protocols. In future work, we will use this model to analyze and prove the security of POST- and artifact-based protocols in the prominent area of identity federation.

### References

1. Mihir Bellare and Phillip Rogaway. Entity authentication and key distribution. In *Advances in Cryptology: CRYPTO '93*, volume 773 of *Lecture Notes in Computer Science*, pages 232–249. Springer, 1994.
2. Ran Canetti and Hugo Krawczyk. Universally composable notions of key exchange and secure channels (extended abstract). In *Advances in Cryptology: EUROCRYPT 2002*, volume 2332 of *Lecture Notes in Computer Science*, pages 337–351. Springer, 2002. Extended version in IACR Cryptology ePrint Archive 2002/059, http://eprint.iacr.org/.

3. Scott Cantor and Marlena Erdos. Shibboleth-architecture draft v05, May 2002. `http://shibboleth.internet2.edu/`.

4. Zhe Dang and Richard Kemmerer. Using the ASTRAL model checker for cryptographic protocol analysis. In *Proc. DIMACS Workshop on Design and Formal Verification of Security Protocols*, 1997. `http://dimacs.rutgers.edu/Workshops/Security/`.

5. Tim Dierks and Christopher Allen. RFC 2246: The TLS protocol, January 1999. Status: Standards Track.

6. Danny Dolev and Andrew C. Yao. On the security of public key protocols. *IEEE Transactions on Information Theory*, 29(2):198–208, 1983.

7. Bruno Dutertre and Steve Schneider. Using a PVS embedding of CSP to verify authentication protocols. In *Proc. International Conference on Theorem Proving in Higher Order Logics (TPHOL)*, volume 1275 of *Lecture Notes in Computer Science*, pages 121–136. Springer, 1997.

8. Roy T. Fielding, Jim Gettys, Jeffrey C. Mogul, Henrik Frystyk, Larry Masinter, Paul Leach, and Tim Berners-Lee. RFC 2616: Hypertext transfer protocol – HTTP/1.1, June 1999. Status: Standards Track.

9. Kevin Fu, Emil Sit, Kendra Smith, and Nick Feamster. Dos and don'ts of client authentication on the web. In *Proceedings of the 10th USENIX Security Symposium*, Washington, D.C., August 2001. USENIX. An extended version is available as MIT-LCS-TR-818.

10. Thomas Groß. Security analysis of the SAML Single Sign-on Browser/Artifact profile. In *Proc. 19th Annual Computer Security Applications Conference*. IEEE, December 2003.

11. Thomas Groß and Birgit Pfitzmann. Proving a WS-Federation Passive Requestor profile. In *2004 ACM Workshop on Secure Web Services (SWS)*, Washington, DC, USA, October 2004. ACM Press.

12. Thomas Groß, Birgit Pfitzmann, and Ahmad-Reza Sadeghi. Browser model for security analysis of browser-based protocols. IACR Cryptology ePrint Archive 2005/127, May 2005. `http://eprint.iacr.org/`.

13. Chris Kaler and Anthony Nadalin (ed.). Web Services Federation Language (WS-Federation), Version 1.0, July 2003. BEA and IBM and Microsoft and RSA Security and VeriSign, `http://www-106.ibm.com/developerworks/webservices/library/ws-fed/`.

14. Chris Kaler and Anthony Nadalin (ed.). WS-Federation: Passive Requestor Profile, Version 1.0, July 2003. BEA and IBM and Microsoft and RSA Security and VeriSign, `http://www-106.ibm.com/developerworks/library/ws-fedpass/`.

15. Richard A. Kemmerer. Using formal verification techniques to analyze encryption protocols. In *Proc. 1987 IEEE Symp. on Security and Privacy*, pages 134–138, Oakland, California, April 1987. IEEE.

16. David P. Kormann and Aviel D. Rubin. Risks of the Passport single signon protocol. *Computer Networks*, 33(1–6):51–58, June 2000.

17. Hugo Krawczyk. SKEME: A versatile secure key exchange mechanism for the Internet. In *Proceedings of the Symposium on Network and Distributed Systems Security (NDSS '96)*, pages 114–127, San Diego, California, February 1996. Internet Society.

18. Hugo Krawczyk. The order of encryption and authentication for protecting communications (or: how secure is SSL?). In *CRYPTO 2001*, volume 2139 of *Lecture Notes in Computer Science*, pages 310–331. International Association for Cryptologic Research, Springer-Verlag, Berlin Germany, 2001.

19. Liberty Alliance Project. Liberty Phase 2 final specifications, November 2003. `http://www.projectliberty.org/`.

20. Gavin Lowe. An attack on the Needham-Schroeder public-key authentication protocol. *Information Processing Letters*, 56(3):131–135, 1995.

21. Gavin Lowe. Breaking and fixing the Needham-Schroeder public-key protocol using FDR. In *Proc. 2nd International Conference on Tools and Algorithms for the Construction and Analysis of Systems (TACAS)*, volume 1055 of *Lecture Notes in Computer Science*, pages 147–166. Springer, 1996.

22. Nancy Lynch. I/O automaton models and proofs for shared-key communication systems. In *Proc. 12th IEEE Computer Security Foundations Workshop (CSFW)*, pages 14–29, 1999.

23. Catherine Meadows. Using narrowing in the analysis of key management protocols. In *Proc. 10th IEEE Symposium on Security & Privacy*, pages 138–147, 1989.

24. Microsoft Corporation. .NET Passport documentation, in particular Technical Overview, and SDK 2.1 Documentation (started 1999), September 2001.

25. Jonathan K. Millen. The interrogator: A tool for cryptographic protocol security. In *Proc. 5th IEEE Symposium on Security & Privacy*, pages 134–141, 1984.

26. J. Mitchell, M. Mitchell, and U. Stern. Automated analysis of cryptographic protocols using murφ. In *Proc. 18th IEEE Symposium on Security & Privacy*, pages 141–151, 1997.

27. John C. Mitchell, Vitaly Shmatikov, and Ulrich Stern. Finite-state analysis of SSL 3.0 and related protocols. In *DIMACS Workshop on Design and Formal Verification of Security Protocols*, September 1997. http://dimacs.rutgers.edu/Workshops/Security/.

28. Roger M. Needham and Michael D. Schroeder. Using encryption for authentication in large networks of computers. *Communications of the ACM*, 21(12):993–999, December 1978.

29. OASIS Standard. Security assertion markup language (SAML) V1.1, November 2002. http://www.oasis-open.org/committees/security/docs/.

30. Object Management Group. Unified modeling language (UML), March 2003. http://www.omg.org/technology/documents/formal/uml.htm

31. Lawrence C. Paulson. The inductive approach to verifying cryptographic protocols. *Journal of Cryptology*, 6(1):85–128, 1998.

32. Lawrence C. Paulson. Inductive analysis of the internet protocol TLS. *ACM Transactions on Information and System Security*, 2(3):332–351, 1999.

33. Birgit Pfitzmann. Privacy in enterprise identity federation - policies for Liberty single signon. In *3rd International Workshop on Privacy Enhancing Technologies (PET 2003)*, volume 2760 of *Lecture Notes in Computer Science*, pages 189–204, Berlin, March 2003. Springer-Verlag, Berlin Germany.

34. Birgit Pfitzmann. Privacy in enterprise identity federation - policies for Liberty 2 single signon. *Elsevier Information Security Technical Report (ISTR)*, 9(1):45–58, 2004. http://www.sciencedirect.com/science/journal/13634127.

35. Birgit Pfitzmann and Michael Waidner. A model for asynchronous reactive systems and its application to secure message transmission. In *Proc. 22nd IEEE Symposium on Security & Privacy*, pages 184–200, 2001. Extended version of the model (with Michael Backes) IACR Cryptology ePrint Archive 2004/082, http://eprint.iacr.org/.

36. Birgit Pfitzmann and Michael Waidner. Privacy in browser-based attribute exchange. In *ACM Workshop on Privacy in the Electronic Society (WPES)*, pages 52–62, Washington, USA, November 2002.

37. Birgit Pfitzmann and Michael Waidner. Analysis of Liberty single-signon with enabled clients. *IEEE Internet Computing*, 7(6):38–44, 2003.

38. Birgit Pfitzmann and Michael Waidner. Federated identity-management protocols — where user authentication protocols may go. In *Security Protocols—11th International Workshop*, Lecture Notes in Computer Science, Cambridge, UK, April 2003. Springer-Verlag, Berlin Germany.

39. Eric Rescorla. Internet RFC 2818: HTTP over TLS, May 2000.

40. Victor Shoup.   On formal models for secure key exchange.   Research Report RZ 3120 (#93166), IBM Research, April 1999.  Version 4, November 1999, available from `http://www.shoup.net/papers/`.
41. David Wagner and Bruce Schneier. Analysis of the SSL 3.0 protocol. In *Proc. 2nd USENIX Workshop on Electronic Commerce*, pages 29–40, 1996.

## A    Details of Browser B

Table 3 contains the interface of B, i.e., its ports and the messages sent or expected there. We now describe the additional functions and predicates used by the state-transition function: The function $\mathsf{ctype}(adr)$ with $\mathsf{ctype} : \mathsf{URLHostPath} \longrightarrow \mathsf{ChType}$ determines the channel type corresponding to the argument $adr$. If the address is HTTPS the channel type is $\mathsf{server\_auth\_secure}$, in other cases insecure. The functions $\mathsf{path}(adr) : \mathsf{URLHostPath} \longrightarrow \mathsf{URLHost}$, $\mathsf{path}(adr) : \mathsf{URLHostPath} \longrightarrow \mathsf{URLPath}$, and $\mathsf{query}(adr) : \mathsf{URLHostPath} \longrightarrow \Sigma^*$ return parts of an URL argument $adr$. We use several predicated for handling of HTML forms: $\mathsf{fparse}(\Sigma^*) : \Sigma^* \longrightarrow \Sigma^*$ extracts a from from a HTML document. The predicate $\mathsf{fmatch}(form, form\_in)$ with $\mathsf{fmatch} : \Sigma^* \times \Sigma^* \longrightarrow \mathsf{Bool}$ checks whether the parameter names of $form$ and the user inputs $form\_in$ match. The function $\mathsf{fmerge}(form, form\_in) : \Sigma^* \times \Sigma^* \longrightarrow \Sigma^*$ merges a given $form$ with the user inputs $form\_in$ to a new form. The predicate $\mathsf{parsable}(m) : \Sigma^* \longrightarrow \mathsf{Bool}$ checks whether message $m$ is parsable according to the HTTP specification for HTTP responses.

**Table 3.** Input and output types of browser machine B

| Port | Type | Parameters | Description |
|---|---|---|---|
| $in_B$? | do_leak | | Leak command from OS |
| $out_B$! | leak | $info : \Sigma^*$ | Info leakage of B to OS |
| $gui_{U,B}$? | | | *Inputs from user* U |
| | enter_address | $wid : \Sigma^*$, $adr$ : URLHostPath | Input in address line |
| | trigger_address | $wid : \Sigma^*$, $adr$ : URLHostPath | Clicking of a link |
| | submit_form | $wid : \Sigma^*$, $m : \Sigma^*$, | |
| | | $adr$ : URLHostPath | Submission of a form |
| | channel_change | $wid : \Sigma^*$, $d$ : {accept, reject} | Consent to sec level |
| | server_cert | $wid : \Sigma^*$, $d$ : {accept, reject}, | Result of cert verify |
| | | $sid : \Sigma^*$ | |
| | authenticate | $wid : \Sigma^*$, $login : \Sigma^*$, | User authentication |
| | | $sid : \Sigma^*$, $store$ : Bool | |
| | log_off | | User logs off from B |
| $gui_{B,U}$! | | | *Outputs to user* U |
| | error | $wid : \Sigma^*$, $type$ : {con, res} | Error notification |
| | established | $wid : \Sigma^*$, $host$ : URLHost, | A channel was established |
| | | $sid : \Sigma^*$, $ch\_type$ : ChType | |
| | channel_change | $wid : \Sigma^*$, $host$ : URLHost, | Channel sec level changed |
| | | $ch\_type$ : ChType | |
| | verify_server_cert | $wid : \Sigma^*$, $host$ : URLHost, | Request to verify cert |
| | | $sid : \Sigma^*$ | |
| | request_uauth | $wid : \Sigma^*$, $host$ : URLHost, | Request for user auth |
| | | $sid : \Sigma^*$, $ch\_type$ : ChType | |
| | show_page | $wid : \Sigma^*$, $m : \Sigma^*$, $sid : \Sigma^*$ | Rendering a payload page |
| $self_B$!, $self_B$? | | | *Selfdelegation of* B |
| | trigger_address | $adr$ : URLHostPath | Triggers a redirect |
| | submit_form | $m : \Sigma^*$, $adr$ : URLHostPath | Scripted form submission |
| $channel\_out_B$? | | | *Inputs from* secchan |
| | accepted | $cid : \Sigma^*$, $host$ : URLHost, | Server accepted channel |
| | | $sid : \Sigma^*$ | |
| | receive | $cid : \Sigma^*$, $m : \Sigma^*$ | Received a message |
| | closed | $cid : \Sigma^*$ | Server closed channel |
| | con_error | $cid : \Sigma^*$ | Connection error notify |
| | ca_untrusted | $sid : \Sigma^*$ | Browser does not trust CA |
| | inval_cert | $sid : \Sigma^*$ | Cert was fully invalid |
| $channel\_in_B$! | | | *Outputs to* secchan |
| | new | $host$ : URLHost, | Establish a new channel |
| | | $type$ : ChType | |
| | send | $cid : \Sigma^*$, $m : \Sigma^*$ | Send message to channel |
| | close | $cid : \Sigma^*$ | Close channel |
| | accept_server_cert | $sid : \Sigma^*$ | User accepted server cert |

# Author Index

# Lecture Notes in Computer Science

For information about Vols. 1–3598

please contact your bookseller or Springer

Vol. 3654: S. Jajodia, D. Wijesekera (Eds.), Data and Applications Security XIX. X, 353 pages. 2005.

Vol. 3653: M. Abadi, L. de Alfaro (Eds.), CONCUR 2005 – Concurrency Theory. XIV, 578 pages. 2005.

Vol. 3652: A. Rauber, S. Christodoulakis, A M. Tjoa (Eds.), Research and Advanced Technology for Digital Libraries. XVIII, 545 pages. 2005.

Vol. 3649: W.M.P. van der Aalst, B. Benatallah, F. Casati, F. Curbera (Eds.), Business Process Management. XII, 472 pages. 2005.

Vol. 3648: J.C. Cunha, P.D. Medeiros (Eds.), Euro-Par 2005 Parallel Processing. XXXVI, 1299 pages. 2005.

Vol. 3646: A. F. Famili, J.N. Kok, J.M. Peña, A. Siebes, A. Feelders (Eds.), Advances in Intelligent Data Analysis VI. XIV, 522 pages. 2005.

Vol. 3645: D.-S. Huang, X.-P. Zhang, G.-B. Huang (Eds.), Advances in Intelligent Computing, Part II. XIII, 1010 pages. 2005.

Vol. 3644: D.-S. Huang, X.-P. Zhang, G.-B. Huang (Eds.), Advances in Intelligent Computing, Part I. XXVII, 1101 pages. 2005.

Vol. 3642: D. Ślezak, J. Yao, J.F. Peters, W. Ziarko, X. Hu (Eds.), Rough Sets, Fuzzy Sets, Data Mining, and Granular Computing, Part II. XXIII, 738 pages. 2005. (Subseries LNAI).

Vol. 3641: D. Ślezak, G. Wang, M. Szczuka, I. Düntsch, Y. Yao (Eds.), Rough Sets, Fuzzy Sets, Data Mining, and Granular Computing, Part I. XXIV, 742 pages. 2005. (Subseries LNAI).

Vol. 3639: P. Godefroid (Ed.), Model Checking Software. XI, 289 pages. 2005.

Vol. 3638: A. Butz, B. Fisher, A. Krüger, P. Olivier (Eds.), Smart Graphics. XI, 269 pages. 2005.

Vol. 3637: J. M. Moreno, J. Madrenas, J. Cosp (Eds.), Evolvable Systems: From Biology to Hardware. XI, 227 pages. 2005.

Vol. 3636: M.J. Blesa, C. Blum, A. Roli, M. Sampels (Eds.), Hybrid Metaheuristics. XII, 155 pages. 2005.

Vol. 3634: L. Ong (Ed.), Computer Science Logic. XI, 567 pages. 2005.

Vol. 3633: C. Bauzer Medeiros, M. Egenhofer, E. Bertino (Eds.), Advances in Spatial and Temporal Databases. XIII, 433 pages. 2005.

Vol. 3632: R. Nieuwenhuis (Ed.), Automated Deduction – CADE-20. XIII, 459 pages. 2005. (Subseries LNAI).

Vol. 3631: J. Eder, H.-M. Haav, A. Kalja, J. Penjam (Eds.), Advances in Databases and Information Systems. XIII, 393 pages. 2005.

Vol. 3630: M.S. Capcarrere, A.A. Freitas, P.J. Bentley, C.G. Johnson, J. Timmis (Eds.), Advances in Artificial Life. XIX, 949 pages. 2005. (Subseries LNAI).

Vol. 3629: J.L. Fiadeiro, N. Harman, M. Roggenbach, J. Rutten (Eds.), Algebra and Coalgebra in Computer Science. XI, 457 pages. 2005.

Vol. 3628: T. Gschwind, U. Aßmann, O. Nierstrasz (Eds.), Software Composition. X, 199 pages. 2005.

Vol. 3627: C. Jacob, M.L. Pilat, P.J. Bentley, J. Timmis (Eds.), Artificial Immune Systems. XII, 500 pages. 2005.

Vol. 3626: B. Ganter, G. Stumme, R. Wille (Eds.), Formal Concept Analysis. X, 349 pages. 2005. (Subseries LNAI).

Vol. 3625: S. Kramer, B. Pfahringer (Eds.), Inductive Logic Programming. XIII, 427 pages. 2005. (Subseries LNAI).

Vol. 3624: C. Chekuri, K. Jansen, J.D.P. Rolim, L. Trevisan (Eds.), Approximation, Randomization and Combinatorial Optimization. XI, 495 pages. 2005.

Vol. 3623: M. Liśkiewicz, R. Reischuk (Eds.), Fundamentals of Computation Theory. XV, 576 pages. 2005.

Vol. 3622: V. Vene, T. Uustalu (Eds.), Advanced Functional Programming. IX, 359 pages. 2005.

Vol. 3621: V. Shoup (Ed.), Advances in Cryptology – CRYPTO 2005. XI, 568 pages. 2005.

Vol. 3620: H. Muñoz-Avila, F. Ricci (Eds.), Case-Based Reasoning Research and Development. XV, 654 pages. 2005. (Subseries LNAI).

Vol. 3619: X. Lu, W. Zhao (Eds.), Networking and Mobile Computing. XXIV, 1299 pages. 2005.

Vol. 3618: J. Jedrzejowicz, A. Szepietowski (Eds.), Mathematical Foundations of Computer Science 2005. XVI, 814 pages. 2005.

Vol. 3617: F. Roli, S. Vitulano (Eds.), Image Analysis and Processing – ICIAP 2005. XXIV, 1219 pages. 2005.

Vol. 3615: B. Ludäscher, L. Raschid (Eds.), Data Integration in the Life Sciences. XII, 344 pages. 2005. (Subseries LNBI).

Vol. 3614: L. Wang, Y. Jin (Eds.), Fuzzy Systems and Knowledge Discovery, Part II. XLI, 1314 pages. 2005. (Subseries LNAI).

Vol. 3613: L. Wang, Y. Jin (Eds.), Fuzzy Systems and Knowledge Discovery, Part I. XLI, 1334 pages. 2005. (Subseries LNAI).

Vol. 3612: L. Wang, K. Chen, Y. S. Ong (Eds.), Advances in Natural Computation, Part III. LXI, 1326 pages. 2005.

Vol. 3611: L. Wang, K. Chen, Y. S. Ong (Eds.), Advances in Natural Computation, Part II. LXI, 1292 pages. 2005.

Vol. 3610: L. Wang, K. Chen, Y. S. Ong (Eds.), Advances in Natural Computation, Part I. LXI, 1302 pages. 2005.

Vol. 3608: F. Dehne, A. López-Ortiz, J.-R. Sack (Eds.), Algorithms and Data Structures. XIV, 446 pages. 2005.

Vol. 3607: J.-D. Zucker, L. Saitta (Eds.), Abstraction, Reformulation and Approximation. XII, 376 pages. 2005. (Subseries LNAI).

Vol. 3606: V. Malyshkin (Ed.), Parallel Computing Technologies. XII, 470 pages. 2005.

Vol. 3605: Z. Wu, M. Guo, C. Chen, J. Bu (Eds.), Embedded Software and Systems. XIX, 610 pages. 2005.

Vol. 3604: R. Martin, H. Bez, M. Sabin (Eds.), Mathematics of Surfaces XI. IX, 473 pages. 2005.

Vol. 3603: J. Hurd, T. Melham (Eds.), Theorem Proving in Higher Order Logics. IX, 409 pages. 2005.

Vol. 3602: R. Eigenmann, Z. Li, S.P. Midkiff (Eds.), Languages and Compilers for High Performance Computing. IX, 486 pages. 2005.

Vol. 3599: U. Aßmann, M. Aksit, A. Rensink (Eds.), Model Driven Architecture. X, 235 pages. 2005.